Post-Traumatic Syndromes in Childhood and Adolescence

Post-Traumatic Syndromes in Childhood and Adolescence

A Handbook of Research and Practice

Edited by Vittoria Ardino

WILEY-BLACKWELL

A John Wiley & Sons, Ltd., Publication

This edition first published 2011
© 2011 John Wiley & Sons Ltd.

Wiley-Blackwell is an imprint of John Wiley & Sons, formed by the merger of Wiley's global Scientific, Technical, and Medical business with Blackwell Publishing.

Registered Office
John Wiley & Sons Ltd, The Atrium, Southern Gate, Chichester, West Sussex, PO19 8SQ, UK

Editorial Offices
The Atrium, Southern Gate, Chichester, West Sussex, PO19 8SQ, UK
9600 Garsington Road, Oxford, OX4 2DQ, UK
350 Main Street, Malden, MA 02148-5020, USA

For details of our global editorial offices, for customer services, and for information about how to apply for permission to reuse the copyright material in this book please see our website at www.wiley.com/wiley-blackwell.

The right of the author to be identified as the author of this work has been asserted in accordance with the UK Copyright, Designs and Patents Act 1988.

Library of Congress Cataloging-in-Publication Data

Post-Traumatic syndromes in childhood and adolescence / edited by Vittoria Ardino.
     p. ; cm.
  Includes bibliographical references and index.
  ISBN 978-0-470-99769-7 (cloth)
1. Post-Traumatic stress disorder in children.   2. Post-Traumatic stress disorder in adolescence.   I. Ardino, Vittoria.
  [DNLM: 1. Stress Disorders, Post-Traumatic.   2. Adolescent.   3. Child.
WM 170 P859 2010]
  RJ506.P55P676 2010
  616.85′21–dc22

                                                                        2010010077

A catalogue record for this book is available from the British Library.

This book is published in the following electronic formats: ePDF [9780470669297]; Wiley Online Library [9780470669280]

Typeset in 10.5/13pt Galliard by Aptara Inc., New Delhi, India.
Printed and bound in Singapore by Fabulous Printers Pte Ltd

1 2011

Contents

About the Editor

Vittoria Ardino is currently Senior Lecturer in Forensic Psychology at the London Metropolitan University (UK) where she teaches psychology of criminal behavior. She is also the President of the Italian Society for the Studies of Traumatic Stress and a board member of the European Society for Trauma and Dissociation and the European Society for Traumatic Stress Studies. Her research interests bridges clinical and forensic psychology with a focus on post-traumatic stress reactions in offender populations. She has presented in various international conferences and published a book and several articles about early trauma and violence. She also delivers consultancy in UK and Italy.

Contributors

Vittoria Ardino School of Psychology, London Metropolitan University, UK

Ron Avi Astor School of Social Work and Education University of Southern California (USC), USA

Thierry Baubet Hôpital Avicenne, Service de Psychopathologie de l'enfant et de l'adolescent, Paris 13 University, Bobigny, France

Naomi Baum Israel Center for the Treatment of Psychotrauma, Herzog Hospital, Jerusalem, Israel

Kathryn A. Becker-Blease Psychology Department, Washington State University Vancouver, USA

Rami Benbenishty The Louis and Gabi Weisfeld School of Social Work, Bar Ilan University, Ramat Gan, Israel

Danny Brom Israel Center for the Treatment of Psychotrauma, Herzog Hospital, Jerusalem, Israel

Elena Camisasca CRIdee, Dipartimento di Psicologia, Universitá Cattolica di Milano, Italy

Don Catherall Feinberg School of Medicine, Northwestern University, Chicago, USA

Scott D. Cicero Rockland Children's Psychiatric Center New York State Office of Mental Health, Orangeburg, and New York University Child Study Center, New York University School of Medicine, USA

Christine A Courtois Christine A Courtois PhD & Associates, Washington DC, USA

Patricia McKinsey Crittenden Family Relations Institute, Florida, USA

Keith R. Cruise Department of Psychology, Fordham University, New York, USA

Anne P. De Prince Psychology Department, University of Colorado at Dever, USA

Paola Di Blasio CRIdee, Dipartmento di Psicologia, Universitá Cattolica di Milano, Italy

B. Heidi Ellis Children's Hospital Boston and Harvard Medical School, Boston, USA

Charles R. Figley School of Social Work and Tulane Traumatology Institute, Tulane University, New Orleans, USA

Kathleen Regan Figley Figley Institute, Tallahassee, USA

Dirk Flower Flower Associates, London, UK

Julian D. Ford Department of Psychiatry, University of Connecticut Health Center, USA

David W. Foy Graduate School of Education and Psychology, Pepperdine University, California, USA

Jennifer J. Freyd Psychology Department, University of Oregon, USA

James Furrow Department of Marriage and Family, Graduate School of Psychology, Fuller Theological Seminary, California, USA

Stefania Grbcic Flower Associates, London, UK

Maggie Kline Marriage and Family Therapist and School Psychologist

Peter Levine Foundation for Human Enrichment, Boulder, Colorado, USA

Giovanni Liotti School of Cognitive Psychotherapy, Rome, Italy

Cheri Lovre Crisis Management Institute, USA

Brigitte Lueger-Schuster Institute of Clinical, biological and differential Psychology, University of Vienna, Austria

Helen Z. MacDonald Natural Center for PTSD, VA Boston Healthcare System, Boston, USA

Shauna McManus Graduate School of Education and Psychology, Pepperdine University, California, USA

Sarah Miragoli CRIdee, Dipartimento di Psicologia, Universitá Cattolica di Milano, Italy

Marie Rose Moro Hôpital Avicenne, Service de Psychopathologie de l'enfant et de l'adolescent, Paris 13 University, Bobigny, France

Kathleen Nader Two Suns, for the Assistance of Traumatized Children and Adolescents, Cedar Park, Texas, USA

Kate B. Nooner Department of Psychology, Montclair State University, and The Nathan S. Kline Institute for Psychiatric Research, Orangeburg, USA

Barbara Oehlberg Education/Child Trauma Consultant, Ohio, USA

Ruth Pat-Horenczyk Israel Center for the Treatment of Psychotrauma, Herzog Hospital, Jerusalem, Israel

Daniele Giovanni Poggioli U.O. Psichiatria e psicoterapia dell'evolutiva, Ospedale Maggiore, Bologna, Italy

Rossella Procaccia CRIdee, Dipartimento di Psicologia, Universitá Cattolica di Milano, Italy

Ann Rasmusson Department of Psychiatry, Boston University School of Medicine, Boston, USA

Dalila Rezzoug Hôpital Avicenne, Service de Psychopathologie de l'enfant et de l'adolescent, Paris 13 University, Bobigny, France

Glenn N. Saxe Children's Hospital Center for Refugee Trauma and Resilience (CHCRTR) and Harvard Medical School, Boston, USA

Miriam Schiff Paul Baerwald School of Social Work and Social Welfare, The Hebrew University of Jerusalem, Israel

Kenneth W. Sewell Department of Psychology, University of North Texas, USA

Raul R. Silva Department of Child and Adolescent Psychiatry, New York University School of Medicine, USA

Eli Somer School of Social Work, University of Haifa, Israel

Jennifer Twiss Children's Hospital Center for Refugee Trauma and Resilience (CHCRTR), Boston, USA

Jennifer J. Vasterling Department of Psychiatry, Boston University School of Medicine, Boston, USA

Barbara Wizansky Senior Clinical Psychologist and EMDR Europe Child Trainer.

Foreword

Christine A. Courtois

Trauma and exposure to trauma are ubiquitous in contemporary society. Available data document a high probability of direct exposure/experience at some time over the course of the lifespan for the average child and adult, as well as increased vulnerability and risk factors for some that make traumatization more likely. *Age is a primary risk factor* for all forms of victimization, whether intrafamilial or within the community (Finkelhor, 2008). Children and adolescents are more likely to be victimized than adults due to a number of vulnerabilities that accompany age; these include personal aspects such as their size, physical and developmental immaturity, dependence, and relative powerlessness; family aspects such as parental availability and ability, and their relative health, mental health, and family structure; and community aspects such as poverty and degree of violence. Additionally, media and instantaneous electronic communication have exponentially increased the possibility of indirect exposure. These make it possible to learn about, share or vicariously experience traumas that were not personally experienced, exposure that occurs in addition to any other that is more personal or direct. If that is not enough, in recent years we have learned that it is possible to be traumatized directly through these same electronic means (cyberbullying, cyberstalking, cyber-sexual predation, exposure to pornography, etc.) and that a high percentage of children and adolescents have already been exposed to victimization of this sort. Taken together, these create a much compounded circumstance of vulnerability and traumatization, one that adults might have trouble processing, much less children.

To date and with some exceptions, children have been almost an afterthought in traumatic stress studies and certainly in the development of diagnostic formulations. The primary focus over the course of the twentieth century has been on combat trauma and its consequences. The current diagnosis of

Post-Traumatic Stress Disorder (PTSD) reflects findings about the consequences of warfare on late adolescent/adult men who had been trained for such exposure. At present, there is no diagnosis of PTSD in children in the *Diagnostic and Statistical Manual of Mental Disorders* (*DSM-IV-TR*) (APA, 2000) although there is mention of how PTSD might manifest differently in children. It is only recently that attention has shifted to childhood trauma and how it might differ from trauma experienced by adults. In particular, as the unique vulnerabilities and risk factors of children (starting within their own families in the form of child abuse and neglect and attachment disturbances) have been recognized, the potential developmental impact of such traumatization has been similarly recognized.

This book is a result of this recognition and is a broad compendium of information about children, their vulnerability to trauma, and the various post-traumatic syndromes that can occur in its wake, including those that co-occur with the criteria of "traditional" PTSD and those that are additional to these (currently identified as complex traumatic stress reactions; Courtois & Ford, 2009) and encompassed within the proposed diagnosis of Developmental Trauma Disorder (van der Kolk, 2005). It surveys the progress that has been achieved in almost three decades of scientific study and focuses on child-centered vs. adult-centered consequences and, in particular, on their developmental impact. This is of critical importance because this is what has not been attended to in the traditional conceptualization of PTSD. The book's focus provides recognition of the different, age- and stage-related ways that children might react to traumatization that are different from those of adults. It also acknowledges that childhood traumatization within a family or other relational context is often repetitive, may be chronic, involves betrayal, and may span developmental epochs. In this way, such ongoing exposure has high potential to impact and even to derail the child's development in a variety of life spheres. The recent findings regarding the biophysiological effects of trauma on children and those of attachment studies have attested to how traumatization truly has a mind–body impact on the developing child. Judy Herman wrote that PTSD enters the child's personality (Herman, 1992) and we now know that it enters the physiology as well.

This book points its readers toward the ecology of the traumatization of children and offers strategies for assessment and treatment from an ecological perspective. It explicitly recognizes that to accurately treat the traumatized child, the trauma needs to be considered (this almost goes without saying but a common finding is that children are routinely diagnosed as ADHD, bipolar, depressed, oppositional-defiant, or conduct-disordered without awareness of or attention to the possibility that their symptoms are, in fact, post-traumatic/dissociative and need direct treatment), and that available protective factors need recognition and boosting. Unrecognized trauma and untreated effects put children at risk for additional distress over the lifespan and makes them vulnerable to revictimization (the latter is especially the case for those who were subjected to incest or other forms of sexual abuse). It is critical that mental health professionals begin to understand much of the material that is included in this text so that they can increase their awareness and expand their range of interventions. The treatment of children is itself preventive: it has the potential of saving the individual from additional post-traumatic distress and victimization; furthermore, it interrupts the intergenerational transmission patterns that have been identified that support what has become known as the cycle of violence, a major step in safeguarding the next generation.

References

American Psychiatric Association (APA) (2000). *Diagnostic and Statistical Manual of Mental Disorders* (4th ed., Text Rev.) (*DSM-IV-TR*). Washington, DC: Author.

Courtois, C. A., & Ford, J. D. (Eds.) (2009). *Treating complex traumatic stress disorders: An evidence-based guide.* New York: Guilford Press.

Finkelhor, D. (2008). *Childhood victimization: Violence, crime, and abuse in the lives of young people.* New York: Oxford University Press.

Herman, J. L. (1992). *Trauma and recovery: The aftermath of violence – from domestic to political terror.* New York: Basic Books.

van der Kolk, B. A. (2005). Developmental trauma disorder. *Psychiatric Annals, 35,* 401–8.

Acknowledgments

This book would not have been possible without the contributions of researchers and clinicians who devoted their professional commitment to the understanding of childhood post-traumatic reactions. I am extremely grateful to all contributors who provided their expertise, experience, and knowledge to this work.

I would also like to acknowledge experts in the trauma field who I have met through ESTSS (European Society for Traumatic Stress Studies). Since I became involved in this society, they have been an incredible source of knowledge, providing a personal challenge to learn and reflect more on trauma and its consequences. Special thanks to Antonia Bifulco, Paola Di Blasio, Miranda Olff, Brigitte Lueger-Schuster who have continuously supported my professional growth.

Among those deserving special credit are the students who contributed ideas, activities, insightful questions to my research on trauma and PTSD in delinquency Special thanks go to my editor Karen Shield at Wiley-Blackwell for her skills and warm support during this process and Maxim Shrestha for his support during the editing process.

Vittoria Ardino
October 2010

Introduction

Vittoria Ardino

Trauma exposure is a significant mental health concern that impacts on children and adolescents in complex ways (Harris, Putnam, & Fairbank, 2006). Younger victims of extreme stress can be seriously affected by the overwhelming challenge of trauma and thus may enter the world with limited cognitive, affective, and behavioral baggage resulting in a spectrum of post-traumatic outcomes. It is commonly understood that youth display a wide range of post-traumatic reactions, including Post-Traumatic Stress Disorder (PTSD) a controversial and yet considerably investigated disorder that may follow a traumatizing experience.

PTSD was formally included in the list of psychiatric disorders in 1980 with the publication of *DSM-III* (American Psychological Association (APA), 1980) and the identification of a triadic cluster of symptoms (reexperiencing, avoidance, and hyperarousal) documented in Vietnam veterans and in rape victims (Perrin, Smith, & Yule, 2000), and later applied to adult civilians.

The first mention of PTSD in children and adolescents had already appeared in the early years of the twentieth century (Saigh & Bremner, 1998); yet decades of studies have demonstrated that children can develop PTSD along with other post-traumatic syndromes. In 1976, Leonore Terr conducted a seminal study on children's reactions to trauma prior to the publication of *DSM-III*. In that year, 26 schoolchildren and their bus driver living in Chowchilla, California, were kidnapped and buried alive in a van for a long period of time before escaping. Terr's important work established that traumatized children exhibited a unique constellation of signs and symptoms in order to master their experience (Terr, 1979). Next, the revised version of *DSM-III* clarified that the diagnosis of PTSD was applicable to children who had "experienced an event outside the range of usual human experience ... that would be markedly distressing to almost anyone" (*DSM-III-R*; APA, 1987).

Post-Traumatic Syndromes in Childhood and Adolescence: A Handbook of Research and Practice, First Edition.
Edited by Vittoria Ardino. © 2011 John Wiley & Sons, Ltd. Published 2011 by John Wiley & Sons, Ltd.

The fourth edition of *DSM* and its revision (APA, 2000) refined consistently the diagnostic criteria for PTSD clarifying Criterion A as follows:

> The person has been exposed to a traumatic event in which both of the following have been present:
>
> 1. The person has experienced, witnessed, or been confronted with an event or events, that involve actual or threatened death or serious injury, or a threat to the physical integrity of oneself or others.
> 2. The person's response involved intense fear, helplessness, or horror. Note: in children, it may be expressed by disorganized or agitated behavior.

This redefinition emphasizes the threatening nature of the traumatic event and the subjective reaction to such an experience, rather than focusing on an event outside any ordinary occurrence as was stipulated in *DSM-III*. Experts also attempted to better clarify diagnostic criteria of PTSD in children and adolescents (i.e. disorganized and agitated behavior in Criterion A.2), noting that repetitive and thematic play, traumatic reenactment, and nightmares focused on both traumatic and nontraumatic content among children's specific reactions. The myriad of studies on child trauma and the revision of diagnostic criteria demonstrate that researchers and clinicians have recognized the importance of identifying specific developmental stress reactions, diagnostic systems, and intervention models. However, PTSD and other trauma-related disorders in children and adolescents have been less extensively studied than in adults leaving the diagnostic systems, and intervention models problematic and the identification of symptoms often developmentally inaccurate and still adult-centered, especially for chronic and complex traumatization (Carrion et al., 2002; Levendosky et al., 2002).

Chronically traumatized children display a conglomeration of trauma-related symptoms that imply pervasive problems of self-regulation and together with attachment relationships, dissociation, depersonalization, and impulse discontrol cannot be considered as "PTSD-only" reactions, but as complex trauma reactions. Complex PTSD (CPTSD) (Herman, 1992; van der Kolk, 1996) is a clinical formulation (which may be included in the proposed *DSM-V* expected out in 2011), which refers to the results of prolonged exposure to trauma and, usually, within a care-giving relationship. Research and intervention in children and adolescents with CPTSD is even more in its infancy and requires further investigation into the necessary multimodal assessment and the use of various psychometric instruments to screen for a variety of issues (Cook et al., 2003; Cook et al., 2005). Likewise, complex trauma interventions that address safety, self-regulation, and the integration of the traumatic experience need to be considered and further investigated (Cook et al., 2005).

Epidemiology of PTSD in childhood

Most epidemiological studies on PTSD have been on older adolescents and adults. Giaconia and colleagues (1995) reported a lifetime prevalence of 6% in a community sample of older adolescents. Kessler and colleagues (1995) reported a lifetime prevalence of 10% using data collected from older adolescents and adults in the US National Comorbidity Survey. An American national representative sample of over 4,000 adolescent boys and girls estimated a percentage of 3.7% for boys and 6.3% for girls (Kilpatrick et al., 2003).

The epidemiological study of the British national survey of mental health of over 10,000 children and young people (Meltzer, Gatward, & Goodman, 2000) reported that 0.4% of children aged 11–15 years were diagnosed with PTSD, with girls showing twice the rate of boys. Below the age of 10 years, PTSD was scarcely registered. In Germany, the prevalence of the disorder in nonclinical samples of adolescents and young adults is reported at 1% for males and 2.2% for females (Perkonigg et al., 2000). Examination of prevalence data among specific subpopulations of youth suggests a much greater problem. For example, in a recent review, Ford and colleagues (2007) documented PTSD rates varying between a low of 3% and a high of 50% among youths in the juvenile justice system. Children from inner-city environments and lower-income families also appear to experience trauma exposure (see Youngstrom, Weist, & Albus, 2003) and PTSD symptoms at much higher rates than expected based on the general epidemiologic literature (Silva et al., 2000). Estimates of the incidence vary enormously as a result of different types of traumatic events. In various studies of the effects of road traffic accidents, rates of 25–30% are reported. A study of 200 young survivors of the sinking of the cruise ship *Jupiter* (Yule et al., 2000) reported an incidence of PTSD of 51%.

Research among clinical samples tends to identify high rates of trauma exposure and co-occurring PTSD. For example, Romero and colleagues (2009) documented that 20.6% of their sample of child and adolescent patients with bipolar disorder reported a lifetime history of physical or sexual abuse. Child patients with a history of abuse were more likely to exhibit chronic and severe patterns of impaired clinical functioning and were over eight times more likely to meet current diagnostic criteria for PTSD in addition to a host of other clinical diagnoses.

Although clearly not an exhaustive review of the prevalence literature, this brief summary reinforces that PTSD is a significant clinical problem that adversely impacts male and female youth, and is found at alarmingly high rates among specific subgroups of children and adolescents. Therefore, considerably increased demands may be made at all levels of primary and secondary child and adolescent mental health services following traumatic events.

Post-Traumatic symptoms in children and adolescents

As stated above, the broad categories of PTSD symptoms (reexperiencing, avoidance/numbing, and increased arousal) are present in children as well as in adults. The requirements of *DSM* criteria for the diagnosis of PTSD in children are that children must exhibit at least one reexperiencing symptom, three avoidance/numbing symptoms, and two increased arousal symptoms. From the age of 8 to 10 years, following traumatic events, children display reactions closely similar to those manifested by adults. Below eight years of age, and in particular below the age of five years, there is less agreement as to the range and severity of the reactions. Scheeringa and colleagues (1995) have suggested an alternative set of criteria for the diagnosis of PTSD in children, placing more emphasis on regressive behavior and new fears, but these have yet to be fully validated.

PTSD symptomatology may be expressed very differently according to the type of traumatic experience, its severity, duration, age of the child, and context of the trauma. Furthermore, children may find unusual ways of expressing their symptoms by comparison to adults. Children and adolescents manifest trauma-related distress according to their psychoaffective maturity (Perrin, Smith, & Yule, 2000). Younger children express their symptoms through play, drawings, and stories and can manifest fears not directly linked to their traumatic experience (e.g., fear of monsters, separation anxiety, irritability) (Yule, 2001). Both children and adolescents may also display aggressive behavior as a result of an acquired difficulty in controlling their impulses, or by poor concentration which, in turn, has a negative impact on their academic achievement. Furthermore, traumatized youths may show emotional detachment and a tendency to isolate themselves from their peers.

Regressive behaviors, such as enuresis, encopresis or thumb sucking, are not unusual (Armsworth & Holaday, 1993). Trauma and PTSD also impact on the ability of children and adolescents to perceive and think about their future, resulting in a sense of a shortened future and skepticism about the possibility of leading a normal life (McNally, 1996).

A wide range of trauma exposures can lead to the development of PTSD symptoms. For example, researchers calculated that approximately 25% of boys and girls interviewed as part of the Great Smokey Mountains Study had experienced one or more extreme lifetime stressors (Costello et al., 2002). Common stressors endorsed in the study included the death of a loved one, witnessing a traumatic event, learning about a traumatic event, and sexual abuse. Similar to the subgroup vulnerability identified above, recent reports from the United States Gulf Coast region continue to confirm that significant trauma effects are found among children and adolescents exposed to natural disasters (Marsee, 2008). Acts of domestic and international terrorism, including the Oklahoma City bombing and the 9/11 destruction of the World Trade Center, have also resulted in notable psychological trauma to children and adolescents (Fairbank, 2008; Gurwitch et al., 2002). In keeping with the literature highlighting that chronic exposure involving multiple traumas often results in greater overall impairment (see Youngstrom et al., 2003), researchers have documented that in addition to "high-dose exposure events," further exposure pre- and post-event is associated with greater impairment and long-term symptom severity. However, trauma sequelae in response to such disasters are not confined to those directly exposed. Otto and colleagues (2007) found that indirect exposure to 9/11 via extensive media coverage resulted in symptom expression among vulnerable children.

In addition to trauma exposure that primarily focuses on event exposure per se, a wide body of literature examines stressors that are inextricably linked to the social network of the child victim. These stressors often involve traumatic event exposure that results in significant disruption in social functioning. Acts of child maltreatment, witnessing and experiencing familial violence, and exposure to community violence are primary examples of such events (Fairbank, 2008). Finkelhor and colleagues recently updated past findings by documenting that a significant proportion of children and adolescents are victims of physical assault, child maltreatment, and sexual victimization. A particularly alarming result from this nationally representative sample of children and adolescents was that the average number of victimizations reported by youth was 3.0 with multiple victimizations often being reported within the same year (Finkelhor et al., 2005). Putnam (2009) summarized findings regarding PTSD symptom development among child sexual abuse survivors. Although there is no uniform outcome associated with sexual abuse victimization, psychological impairment (including PTSD symptoms) varied from 46% to 90% across the reviewed studies. Finally, Wood and colleagues (2002) and Ariga and colleagues (2008) have documented that both adolescent boys and girls involved in delinquent activity report significant exposure to community violence, including witnessing a violent crime, witnessing the murder of someone close to them, and being the victim of a violent crime.

The state-of-the-art of PTSD and other trauma-related disorders in children and adolescents demonstrates that post-traumatic reactions are indeed a major developmental issue and a very complex interplay of a wide spectrum of reactions. This book ventures into this important and still uncharted territory to draw a possible roadmap for researchers and clinicians seeking to critically evaluate what there is left to explore in childhood trauma.

Overview of the book

I had two goals when I designed the book. First, I wanted to identify several critical points in the complex area of child trauma. For this reason, I believed that highlighting the state-of-the-art in assessing and diagnosing PTSD in children and adolescents, in treating them, and in designing new research studies could lead to future developments in the area and to a better effort to help young victims of trauma. Second, I wanted to present the work of some of the major contributors to the field of PTSD in youngsters possibly marking the progress that has been achieved over almost three decades of scientific discoveries and achievements. The book is not intended to be a comprehensive handbook of PTSD in children and adolescents, but rather a tool of reflection and a starting point to envision new areas of exploration after its reading. The structure of the book – presented in the following paragraphs – is shaped according to its goals, with a focus upon central critical areas.

Part I of the book concerns the assessment of PTSD in childhood and adolescence highlighting critical nodes of symptom evaluation in youngsters. In her chapter, Kathleen Nader (Chapter 1) describes and evaluates the main issues in assessing and diagnosing PTSD in youths. The author provides a comprehensive framework of understanding, outlining the need to consider symptoms and disorders, and their variation as an expression of different stages of development. The likelihood of an atypical life trajectory, according to Nader, is increased when, at each phase of development, youths fail to learn to use internal and external resources to adapt to developmental demands. Disruption to emerging skills may undo resilience and create risk and vulnerabilities that have a long-term impact on the child's life. Following on from this, Scott Cicero, Kate Nooner, and Raul Silva (Chapter 2) explain that only a fraction of children exposed to trauma go on to develop PTSD, suggesting the important role played by resilience and vulnerability factors in the development of the disorder. The authors identify risk and protective factors that can serve as a crucial step in establishing early and possibly preventive treatments.

Part II examines specific traumatic events and their role in determining the development of PTSD and specific context-reactions to traumatic events. The first chapter of this part (Chapter 3) is written by Don Catherall and provides a firm grounding for the crucial role played by the family stressors affecting children. The family can be a milieu of major, such as abuse and neglect, and lower magnitude traumatic events. The author focuses on the latter events which potentially do not qualify as Criterion A stressors for PTSD diagnosis but may influence children and adolescents indirectly and have a deleterious impact on their development. Leading on from this, Dalila Rezzoug, Thierry Baubet, and Marie Rose Moro (Chapter 4) describe the trauma of migration within the family adopting a cross-cultural perspective. Large numbers of migrants travel to another country to find a better life. Whatever their previous experience, migrants and their children become vulnerable to trauma resulting from the journey that exposes them to *trans-cultural* risk – as the authors beautifully define the experience of migration – and to traumatic psychopathology. Children and adolescents develop specific vulnerabilities due to the unique experience of "living in two worlds" that are very often not connected: the "inside world," i.e., the world of the family, their mother tongue, and their native culture, and the "outside world," i.e., the host country. From a different angle, in Chapter 5, Elena Camisasca does an excellent job of describing the peculiarities of individual and family responses to the experience of children's medical illness, injury, and medical treatment as referred to the construct of traumatic stress. On the basis of the most recent literature, the chapter explores the predictive role of a series of factors considered to favor or to inhibit the onset of traumatic stress in pediatric illnesses and injuries; these include: sociodemographic variables preceding the traumatic event; the objective nature of the traumatic event and its subjective evaluation; acute distress and physiological arousal reactions; and finally, the parent–child relationship, family functioning, and social support.

Part III explores specific neurobiological and cognitive mechanisms involved in post-traumatic symptomatology in youths. This part contributes to an understanding of the degree of pervasiveness of PTSD and other related post-traumatic reactions on a child's ability to function. The association between trauma and neuroplasticity has been explored lately by several researchers showing a series of brain abnormalities as a result of the trauma and its psychopathology. In their work Helen MacDonald, Jennifer Vasterling, and Ann Rasmusson (Chapter 6) summarize and critically review the literature on neuropsychological functioning in children and adolescents with PTSD, highlighting the specific neuropsychological correlates of PTSD within neurobiological and developmental perspectives shedding light on the multiple interconnected neurobiological systems involved in the activation and deactivation of the stress response and, subsequently, in the development and maintenance of trauma-related psychopathology. The authors also provide a valuable contribution to the discussion of clinical implications and directions for future research. In Chapter 7, Kathryn Becker-Blease, Anne DePrince, and Jennifer Freyd provide a thoughtful account of the debate on if and how victims of child abuse can forget their traumatic experience. Their contribution is an insight into the key interaction between trauma, PTSD, and memory, explaining the logic and mechanisms of amnesia for sexual abuse and providing an overview of the "betrayal trauma theory," a theory proposed by Freyd (1996) to account for the particular motivations that might lead to unawareness following sexual abuse. Leading on from this, Eli Somer (Chapter 8) explores another important feature of cognitive mechanisms involved in post-traumatic reactions, namely dissociation. The author posits that childhood dissociation works as a defensive response during trauma and ensuing dissociative psychopathology. However, Somer claims that dissociation is assumed to be a normal childhood ability that develops as a psychological defense mechanism in the face of extreme or prolonged and inescapable physical, sexual, and emotional trauma. It works as a shield against the conscious experience of overwhelming stress by producing psychological and/or physical analgesia, emotional calming, and a breakdown of the normally integrated experiential components of behavior, affect, sensation, knowledge, and identity.

Part IV is dedicated to the forensic implications of PTSD. The contributions explore children's allegations of abuse and the interconnection between early trauma, PTSD, and antisocial/criminal behavior in youth. Paola Di Blasio, Sarah Miragoli, and Rosella Procaccia (Chapters 9) present an empirical work aimed at investigating the interaction between the quality of children's testimony in court and PTSD symptoms, focusing upon differences in terms of content and structure of allegations provided by victims of child abuse with and without PTSD. Chapters 10 and 11 are complementary and highlight the need to consider the role of early trauma in youth who commit crimes. David Foy, James Furrow, and Shauna McManus (Chapter 10) present a review of studies on the relationship between exposure to violence, post-traumatic symptomatology, and criminal behaviors among male juvenile offenders, with the aim of increasing knowledge, among professionals in mental health or corrections settings, of the linkage between violence exposure in both family and community contexts, post-trauma symptoms, and violent or criminal behavior. Following on from this, Vittoria Ardino (Chapter 11) focuses on information-processing and specific cognitive mechanisms that may favor and maintain the link between PTSD and criminal behavior.

Part V of the book provides a reflective framework of psychosocial and community initiatives available to prevent PTSD in children and adolescents and to help them heal when victims of collective traumas. Barbara Oehlberg (Chapter 12) outlines that trauma is an educational issue in school settings as it interferes with a child's ability to learn and to achieve a good academic standard. The author provides an interesting view of how schools could play a significant role in alleviating the stress of trauma and promoting resilience while performing their mandate to generate the academic achievement of students and prepare them for meaningful citizenship. Leading on from the challenge of community intervention to help youths cope with PTSD, Ruth Pat-Horenczyk, Danny Brom, Naomi Baum, Rami Benbenishty, Miriam Schiff, and Ron Avi Astor (Chapter 13) describe a broad-based school program for providing services for children in the wake of terrorism and war in Israel. They propose a model developed after the escalation of political violence in the Middle East with the outbreak of the Second Intifada in September 2000. Brigitte Lueger-Schuster (Chapter 14) describes her experience of the intervention following the school siege that took place on September 1, 2004 in the town of Beslan, North Ossetia-Alania. The author explains that the aim of the intervention was to provide complementary support to the clinical work, including support for the whole population of Beslan, by establishing a meeting place for direct and indirect victims of the massacre.

In Part VI of the book, several treatment models for working with traumatized children are presented with the aim of reflecting upon how to take into consideration the specificity of children's post-traumatic reactions and their ability to work in a therapeutic relationship differently from an adult. Peter Levine and Maggie Kline (Chapter 15) present the Somatic Experiencing (SE) method, a model used in both the prevention and healing of trauma. Fortunately, professionals, especially those who are able to see children during the first month or so following the incident, are in a position to prevent, or at least mitigate, the damaging effects of overwhelming events. Barbara Wizansky (Chapter 16) discusses the possibility of treating childhood trauma with EMDR (Eye Movement Desensitization Reprocessing) by being aware of the challenge inherent in adapting a focused therapeutic model created for adults to young developing clients. In Chapter 17, Dirk Flower and Stefania Grbcic give an overview of cognitive-behavioral models to treat PTSD cases, providing interesting case studies where CBT has been applied to treat traumatized children. Continuing the cognitive perspective, Kenneth Sewell and Keith Cruise (Chapter 18) present the application of a reformulation of Personal Construct Theory (Kelly, 1955/1991) for understanding and intervening with post-traumatic stress reactions in childhood and adolescence. Chapter 19 is written by Heidi Ellis, Glenn Saxe, and Jennifer Twiss, who propose the model of Trauma Systems Therapy (TST) as an intervention that specifically targets a traumatized child's emotion regulation, the social environment, and the interface between these two elements. There are developing standards for effective social environmental interventions, with the underlying assumption that child traumatic stress is, perhaps more than any other mental health issue, embedded in a social context. In Chapter 20, Patricia McKinsey Crittenden and Daniele Poggioli explore the contribution of attachment theory to the treatment of psychological disorder, in this case PTSD in childhood and adolescence, with a case exemplification of complex PTSD and attachment disturbances along with other symptoms of PTSD.

The penultimate chapter in Part VI is written by Charles Figley, Cheri Lovre, and Kathleen Regan Figley and outlines the perspective of practitioners working with traumatized children who may need help as a result of working with PTSD. In fact, professionals may report symptoms similar to PTSD, called secondary traumatic stress reactions (STS) or compassion fatigue. The authors review compassion fatigue theory and research, and suggest practical ways that child trauma experts can employ to minimize their vulnerability and maximize their resilience.

The final chapter of this book is provided by Julian Ford, who focuses on complex trauma syndromes delineating the future for assessment, diagnosis, and treatment of post-traumatic reactions in youth. In fact, there is a proposed new diagnosis named Developmental Trauma Disorder (DTD; van der Kolk, 2005) that provides a framework for defining the goals of psychotherapy for children with complex traumatic stress disorders, with the aim of better representing the sequelae of chronic exposure. This proposed new diagnosis seems to sustain the hypothesis that future empirical research is needed to test the clinical utility of the spectrum of trauma reactions in children and adolescents, and the problems associated with developmentally adverse experiences. It seems, then, that this area is one that may potentially benefit from conscious efforts by the scientific community to shed light on children who heal trauma.

References

American Psychiatric Association (APA) (1980). *Diagnostic and Statistical Manual of Mental Disorders* (3rd ed.) (*DSM-III*). Washington, DC: Author.

American Psychiatric Association (APA) (1987). *Diagnostic and Statistical Manual of Mental Disorders* (3rd ed., Rev.) (*DSM-III-R*). Washington, DC: Author.

American Psychiatric Association (APA) (2000). *Diagnostic and Statistical Manual of Mental Disorders* (4th ed., Text Rev.) (*DSM-IV-TR*). Washington, DC: Author.

Ariga, M., Uehara, T., Takeuchi, K. et al. (2008). Trauma exposure and post-traumatic stress disorder in female delinquent adolescents. *Journal of Child Psychology and Psychiatry, 49*(1), 79–87.

Armsworth, M. W., & Holaday, M. (1993). The effects of psychological trauma on children and adolescents. *Journal of Counseling and Development, 71*(4), 49–56.

Carrion, V. G., Weems, C. F., Ray, R., & Reiss, A. L. (2002). Toward an empirical definition of pediatric PTSD: The phenomenology of PTSD symptoms in youth. *Journal of the American Academy of Child & Adolescent Psychiatry, 41*(2), 166–73.

Cook, A., Blaustein, M., Spinazzola, J., & Van Der Kolk, B. (2003). *Complex trauma in children and adolescents.* [White paper from the National Child Traumatic Stress Network Complex Trauma Task Force.] Los Angeles, CA: National Center for Child Traumatic Stress.

Cook, A., Spinazzola, J., Ford, J., Lanktree, C. et al. (2005). Complex trauma in children and adolescents. *Psychiatric Annals, 35*(5), 390–8.

Costello, J. G., Erkanli, A., Fairbank, J. A., & Angold, A. (2002). The prevalence of potentially traumatic events in childhood and adolescence. *Journal of Traumatic Stress, 15*(2), 99–112.

Finkelhor, D., Ormroda, R. K., Turner, H. A., & Hambyb, S. L. (2005). Measuring poly-victimization using the juvenile victimization questionnaire. *Child Abuse and Neglect, 29,* 1297–1312.

Ford, J. D., Chapman, J. F., Hawke, J., & Albert, D. (2007). Trauma among youth in the juvenile justice system: Critical issues and new directions. National Center for Mental Health and Juvenile Justice Research Brief. Retrieved January, 2010 from http://www.ncmhjj.com/pdfs/Trauma_and_Youth.pdf or http://www.cwla.org/programs/juvenilejustice/ncmhjjtraumayouth.pdf

Freyd, J. J. (1996). *Betrayal trauma theory: The logic of forgetting childhood abuse.* Cambridge, MA: Harvard University Press.

Giaconia, R. M., Renhertz, H. Z., Silverman, A. B. et al. (1995). Traumas and post-traumatic stress disorder in a community population of older adolescents. *Journal of the Academy of Child and Adolescent Psychiatry, 34,* 1369–80.

Gurwitch, R. H., Sitterle, K. A., Young, B. H., & Pfefferbaum, B. (2002). The aftermath of terrorism. In A. M. La Greca, W. K. Silverman, E. M. Vernberg, & M. Roberts (Eds.), *Helping children cope with disasters and terrorism* (pp. 327–58). Washington, DC: American Psychological Association.

Harris, W. W., Putnam, F. W., & Fairbank, J. A. (2006). Mobilizing trauma resources for children. In A. Lieberman & R. DeMartino (Eds.), *Shaping the future of children's health* (pp. 311–39). Calverton, NY: Johnson & Johnson Pediatric Institute.

Herman, J. L. (1992). Complex PTSD: a syndrome in survivors of prolonged and repeated trauma. *Journal of Traumatic Stress, 5,* 377–91.

Kelly, G. A. (1991). *The psychology of personal constructs: A theory of personality* (Vol. 1). London: Routledge. (Original work published 1955.)

Kessler, R. C., Sonnega, A., Bromet, E. et al. (1995). Post-traumatic stress disorder in the National Comorbidity Survey. *Archives of General Psychiatry*, 52, 1048–60.

Kilpatrick, D. G., Ruggiero, K. J., Acierno, R. E. et al. (2003). Violence and risk of PTSD, major depression, substance abuse/dependence, and comorbidity: Results from the National Survey of Adolescents. *Journal of Consulting and Clinical Psychology*, 71, 692–700.

Levendosky, A. A., Huth-Bocks, A. C., Semel, M. A., & Shapiro, D. (2002). Trauma symptoms in preschool-age children exposed to domestic violence. *Journal of Interpersonal Violence*, 17(2), 150–64.

Marsee, M. (2008). Reactive aggression and post-traumatic stress in adolescents affected by Hurricane Katrina. *Journal of Clinical Child & Adolescent Psychology*, 37(3), 519–29.

McNally, R. J. (1996). Perceptual implicit memory for trauma-related information in Post-Traumatic Stress Disorder. *Cognition & Emotion*, 10(5), 551–6.

Meltzer, H., Gatward, R., & Goodman, R. (2000). *Mental health of children and adolescents in Great Britain*. London: The Stationery Office.

Otto, M. W., Henin, A., Hirshfeld-Becker, D. et al. (2007). Post-Traumatic Stress Disorder symptoms following media exposure to tragic events: Impact of 9/11 on children at risk for anxiety disorders. *Journal of Anxiety Disorders*, 21(7), 888–902.

Perkonigg, A., Kessler, R. C., Stortz, S., & Wittchen, H. U. (2000). Traumatic events and Post-Traumatic Stress Disorder in the community: Prevalence, risk factors, and comorbidity. *Acta Psychiatrica Scandinavica*, 101, 46–59.

Perrin, S., Smith, P., & Yule, W. (2000). Practitioner review: The assessment and treatment of Post-Traumatic Stress Disorder in children and adolescents. *Journal of Child Psychology and Psychiatry*, 41(3), 277–89.

Putnam, S. E. (2009). The monsters in my head: Post-Traumatic Stress Disorder and the child survivor of abuse. *Journal of Counseling and Development*, 87, 80–9.

Romero, S., Birmaher, B., Axelson, D. et al. (2009). Prevalence and correlates of physical and sexual abuse in children and adolescents with bipolar disorder. *Journal of Affective Disorders*, 112(1), 144–50.

Saigh, P. A., & Bremner, J. D. (1998). The history of Post-Traumatic Stress Disorder. In P. A. Saigh & J. D. Bremner (Eds.), *Post-Traumatic Stress Disorder: A comprehensive text* (pp. 1–17). New York: Allyn & Bacon.

Scheeringa, M. S., Zeanah, C. H., & Drell, M. J. (1995). Two approaches to the diagnosis of Post-Traumatic Stress Disorder in infancy and early childhood. *Journal of the American Academy of Child and Adolescent Psychiatry*, 34, 191–200.

Silva, R. R., Alpert, M., Munoz, D. M. et al. (2000). Stress and vulnerability to Post-Traumatic Stress Disorder in children and adolescents. *The American Journal of Psychiatry*, 157, 1229–35.

Terr, L. C. (1979). Children of Chowchilla: A study of psychic trauma. *Psychoanalytic Study of the Child*, 34, 552–623.

van der Kolk, B. A. (2005). Developmental trauma disorder. *Psychiatric Annals*, 35, 401–8.

van der Kolk, B. A., McFarlane, A. C., & Weisaeth, L. (Eds.) (1996). *Traumatic stress: The effects of overwhelming experience on mind, body, and society*. New York: Guilford Press.

Youngstrom, E., Weist, M. D., & Albus, K. E. (2003). Exploring violence exposure, stress, protective factors and behavioral problems among inner-city youth. *American Journal of Community Psychology, 32*(1–2), 115–29.

Yule, W. (2001). Post-Traumatic Stress Disorder in children and adolescents. *International Journal of Psychiatry, 13*, 194–200.

Yule, W., Bolton, D., Udwin, O. et al. (2000). The long-term psychological effects of a disaster experienced in adolescence, I: The incidence and course of PTSD. *Journal of Psychology and Psychiatry, 41*, 503–11.

Wood, J., Foy, D. W., Goguen, C., Pynoos, R., & James, C. B. (2002). Violence exposure and PTSD among delinquent girls. *Journal of Aggression, Maltreatment & Trauma, 16*(1), 109–26.

Part I

Assessment

Chapter One

Evaluation and Diagnosis of PTSD in Children and Adolescents

Kathleen Nader

Introduction

While a more intensely focused attention on youths' traumatic reactions began in the 1970s, debate continues about the exact nature of youths' traumatic stress disorders (Nader, 2008a). Although the literature supports commonalities between disturbances in youths and in adults following traumatic events (House, 2002), reactions vary at different ages and in response to additional factors, such as aspects of the child, the nature and duration of the event, and pre- and post-trauma environments. Nevertheless, many of the scales that assess trauma in youths are based on adult diagnostic criteria and do not include the range of possible effects of trauma. Ideally, research and clinical assessments assist diagnosis and the production of treatment plans that are tailored to the needs of a youth (Cook et al., 2005; Kinniburgh & Spinazzola, 2005; Nader, 2008a). In order to engage in appropriate individualized treatment planning and an accurate understanding of trauma in youth, a greater range of variables must be examined.

Children appear to exhibit a wider range of associated symptoms than adults in their traumatic reactions (House, 2002). Studies have found children with subsyndromal but clinically significant Post-Traumatic Stress Disorder (PTSD) (Carrion et al., 2002; Daviss et al., 2000; Nader, 2008a; Olfson et al., 2001; Vila, Porsche, & Mouren-Simeoni, 1999). Additionally, for children, symptoms may have a number of developmental impacts. Traumatic events may disrupt a youth's brain development, developmental skills, emerging personality traits, and budding skills (Nader, 2008b). For youths, diagnosing traumatic reactions

Post-Traumatic Syndromes in Childhood and Adolescence: A Handbook of Research and Practice, First Edition.
Edited by Vittoria Ardino. © 2011 John Wiley & Sons, Ltd. Published 2011 by John Wiley & Sons, Ltd.

is not as simple as assessing *DSM* PTSD (Nader, 2004, 2008a). Developmental disruptions, functional impairment, and dangerous symptoms such as suicidality may occur from a single or a subset of trauma symptoms (Nader, 2008a; Olfson et al., 2001). For children especially, it is important to distinguish among PTSD, complex traumatic reactions, and traumatic or prolonged grief responses (Cohen et al., 2002; Nader, 1997a, 2008a). Evidence suggests that the treatments that are effective for each of these post-trauma reactions differ (Ford et al., 2005; van der Kolk et al., 2005).

Assessing trauma in youths

Over the last quarter of a century, researchers have perfected scales for assessing and diagnosing *DSM* PTSD in youths. A number of assessment measures for school age youth include PTSD and additional symptoms (Nader, 1997a, 2004, 2008a; Stamm, 1996). Scales are also available to assess PTS in children under the age of six (Nader, Stuber, & Fletcher, 2007; Saylor et al., 1999; Scheeringa & Zeanah, 2005), complicated grief (Dyregrov et al., 2001; Layne et al., 2001; Nader & Prigerson, 2005; Prigerson, Nader, & Maciejewski, 2005), and a variety of related symptoms and variables (Nader, 2008a). Complex trauma measures are undergoing construction (✉measures@twosuns.org). The importance of including multiple sources of information (e.g., youth, parent, teacher, clinician) and methods of assessment (e.g., interview, observation) has been well established.

Symptoms and disorders can be expressed and understood in different ways at varying stages of development (House, 2002), requiring variations in methods, wording, and focus for different age groups (infant, toddler, child and preadolescent, and early and late adolescent; Nader, 2008a). Aspects of normal development must be taken into consideration when assessing symptoms in youth. Certain behaviors, such as fearful inhibition, appear in normal children with particular personality styles and/or at specific developmental phases. Moreover, specific issues, such as self-regulation, may be undermined in particular ways more easily at certain ages.

Although issues such as trust, safety/vulnerability, regression, and self-image can be important for all age groups after their traumatic experiences, these issues have particular significance and differences in their manifestation at specific ages (Table 1.1). Furthermore, after experiencing trauma, youths may exit the normal range of individual behaviors (or behavioral complexes) in either direction. They may become, for example, either extremely inhibited in the expression of emotion or explosive, extremely cautious or excessively risk-taking, and overly defiant or overly compliant. The externalized extremes are more easily observed and may or may not be easier for youths to report for themselves, depending on age, personal fears, or other issues.

Table 1.1 Age, development, and symptoms

Age	Brain Development	Learning, Beliefs, and Behavior	Disruption by Trauma or Complex Trauma
Infants	• Newborns show no activity in the prefrontal cortex and minimal activity in sensori-motor areas of the cortex. Lower centers are active – infants can use all senses to respond to stimuli with emotions • Repeated patterns of emotion, behavior, and interaction build neural connections in the brain • The right brain hemisphere dominates until age 3	• Infants begin to learn cause and effect (their actions lead to consequences) • From attachment relationships, they learn coping, self-soothing, the modulation of affective states, and self-awareness • The natural onset of fear or behavioral inhibition at 9–12 months, for some infants, may work in opposition to earlier rapid approach to novel objects; approach tendencies should be assessed between 4 and 6 months but not between 9 and 12 months	(May show distress in stages as follows.) • Contact seeking (smiling, reaching, gazing and friendly tones) • Protesting (unfriendly utterances or desperate crying) • Persistently fretting, crying excessively, clinging, disturbed eating and sleeping (restless, fitfall) • Resigned behavior (nonaffective silence and withdrawal)
Toddler to preschool	• Shift from right hemisphere dominance (sensing and feeling) to left hemisphere reliance (abstract reasoning, long-range planning, language) • Begin integration of neural communication across hemispheres • With development of orbital prefrontal cortex, separate self from individual others with distinct goals; learning to label emotions; develop emotions such as shame, anxiety, moral anger, empathy, and pride	• Learn to orient to internal and external environments • Develop emotion-regulation through interactions with caregivers • Have egocentric thinking (difficulty taking others' perspectives) but are developing understanding that others can be the center of attention • Believe everything has a consciousness (animism) • Do not understand the permanence of death or the impact of numerous deaths	*toddler* • Signs of anxiety and distress (crying, whining, clinging, disturbed sleep and eating) • Bad dreams • Physical complaints (e.g., pain, discomfort, increased illness) • Distress or dissociation when reminded of event • Periods of listlessness, lethargy • More severe temper tantrums than normal for age

(Continued)

Table 1.1 (*Continued*)

Age	Brain Development	Learning, Beliefs, and Behavior	Disruption by Trauma or Complex Trauma
	• Between ages 3 and 5, the continuing development of the prefrontal cortex underlies developing self-monitoring capacities. The orbitofrontal and ventromedial cortices are responsible for processing and regulating emotion • Growth spurts in brain development with disorganization in the child's brain and behavior occur at ages, 3, 6, 10, prepuberty, and mid-adolescence	• May have difficulty distinguishing fictional and nonfictional events • May recall or dream distressing images • Begin to understand cause and effect • Primarily focus on the present but have a simple understanding of past and future; can develop mental pictures • Develop an understanding of symbolism • Expect everyone to share the same understanding of right and wrong	• Increased negativity • Regressed behavior • Traumatic play or play-like re-enactments • Distress or protest about proximity to places, people, or things that remind of the trauma • Attempts to keep people from talking about what happened or distracts when they do • Increased fearfulness; trauma-specific fears • Changes in relationships (e.g., more distant, avoids some people or seems less willing to go to them; overly compliant) • Seems to feel unsafe • Startles easily *preschooler* • See toddler • May feel like s/he caused the problem • Regression • Aggression • Inhibition • Expects things to go wrong • Under stress, analytic capacities may disintegrate – cognitive, emotional, and behavioral disorganization; tendency to react with extreme helplessness, withdrawal, rage, or confusion. • Impaired cognitive functioning (e.g., language development, IQ)

Middle childhood 6 or 7 to 11 or 12 into adolescence	• Undergo development of *executive functions* (primarily involves prefrontal cortex) • Development of neurochemicals of inhibition as well as growth and complexity of reward systems mark a shift away from impulsiveness and self-protection and toward inhibition and control; learning to balance exploration with self-correction; development of guilt, doubt, envy, vicarious pride or shame	• Egocentrism and animism decline • Develop ability to imagine events outside their own lives • Begin to develop the capacity for abstraction • Only evaluate the logic of statements by comparing them to concrete evidence • Begin to understand the permanence of death • Develop autonomous functioning and genuine engagement in relationships • Develop conscious self-awareness • Gain the ability to assess the direction and meaning of complex emotions • Ability to plan a course of action based on past experience and a frame of reference develops (informed by personal and others' perspectives)	• PTSD • Irrational guilt (feel they may have caused the problem and/or the emotions of others) • Fear • Identification with parent's distress or pain • Internalizing symptoms (crying, poor concentration, intrusive thoughts, low school achievement, withdrawal) • Conflict with others • Emotional and behavioral problems • Hyperactivity • Anxiety • In the absence of responsive care, deficits in self-regulation of affect, behavior, consciousness, self-concept integration, and cognition and difficulties self-soothing • Problems in the ability to label and discriminate among affective states • Difficulties modulating or regulating internal experience and expressing emotions safely • Possible chronic numbing, dissociation, dysphoria, avoidance of affectively laden situations, and/or maladaptive coping strategies • Possible depression and suicidality

(*Continued*)

Table 1.1 (*Continued*)

Age	Brain Development	Learning, Beliefs, and Behavior	Disruption by Trauma or Complex Trauma
			• Overcontrolled (e.g., inflexibility or compulsive behaviors) or undercontrolled behavior (e.g., aggression, oppositional defiance) • Impaired cognitive functioning (e.g., IQ, flexibility, creativity, problem solving, attention, abstract reasoning) • Sense of self as defective, unlovable, helpless, and deficient
Adolescence	• Continue to develop *executive functions*	• See above • Develop hypothetical thinking, deductive reasoning, and establish abstract relationships; can evaluate the logical validity of assertions • Understand the reality of thousands of deaths • To varying degrees, understand the meaning and/or greater impact of an event • Issues of independence, shame and embarrassment, personal vulnerability vs. invulnerability, personal power in relationship to others (dominance vs. submission); and independence vs. dependence become prominent	• PTSD • See above • Resentment or overcompliance with any increased responsibilities because of event • Inhibition of emotions or explosiveness • Excessive independence or dependence • Excessive risk-taking or caution • Over-idealization of an injured or deceased parent and increased conflict toward gaining independence with the other parent • Shame or embarrassment over victimization or injury • Shame over exclusion or separateness from peers

© Nader, 2008. Adapted with permission from Nader (2008b). This table provides general age-specific developmental and other traits and potential reactions. Differences in reactions also occur with certain neurochemical or temperamental tendencies. Children may be more or less fearful, for example.
Sources: Caspi, 1998; Cook et al., 2005; Diareme et al., 2007; Ford, 2009; Nader, 2008a; Piaget & Inhelder, 1969; Siegel, 2003; Stein & Kendall, 2004; Streeck-Fischer & van der Kolk, 2000

Individualized treatment

When an event affects multiple individuals, each individual will have some similar and some different experiences of the event (Nader, 1997a, 2008a). Variations in a person's experience of an event, individual qualities, and personal histories influence perceptions, personal impact, and processing of experiences. In part because of the impact for youths on development and functioning in multiple arenas of life (Nader, 2008a), good treatment requires a good match among method, clinician, and child, as well as flexible adaptation of treatment methods in response to the youth's age/stage of development, personality, skill levels, cultures, family and community environment, personal experience of the trauma, and the nature of the trauma (Cook et al., 2005; Kinniburgh & Spinazzola, 2005; Nader, 2008a).

What we need to know

Researchers/clinicians are in the process of clarifying conceptualizations of simple trauma in children (Nader, 2008a; Scheeringa et al., 2003, 2005), complex trauma, especially as it appears in maltreatment survivors (Cook et al., 2005), and child versus adult complicated grief reactions (Cohen et al., 2002; Nader, 1997b). In order to clearly understand the nature of child and adolescent traumatic reactions, it is essential to (1) obtain detailed information about youths and their lives prior to their exposure to traumatic experiences; (2) recognize differences in normal traits and behaviors for cultures and age groups; (3) delineate traumatic reactions by age group, in response to different types and durations of traumas and/or differences in pre- and peri-traumatic experiences; (4) identify the changing nature of symptoms over time; and (5) identify the aspects of the child (e.g., personality) and other factors (e.g., culture, attachment) that influence traumatic reactions. Examining a limited number of symptoms, based on noncomprehensive conceptualizations or adult findings, may result in a faulty picture of youths' traumatic reactions. In order to understand trauma across age groups, it is essential to assess a wide range of symptoms.

DSM criteria

The current *DSM* PTSD stressor Criterion A did not take into account the greater significance and/or developmental impact of certain events, such as loss of a parent for infants and preschool children (American Psychiatric Association (APA), 2000; Drell et al., 1993; Ford, 2005; Scheeringa & Zeanah, 1995; Scheeringa et al., 2001). Other changes under discussion for PTSD as it applies to children are the following (Nader, 2008a): (1) including additional symptoms in the list of symptoms (Armsworth & Holaday, 1993; Fletcher,

2003); (2) adjusting Criteria C and D lists in the same manner that A and B have been adjusted (Carrion et al., 2002); (3) making childhood PTSD a continuous rather than a dichotomous variable (Fletcher, 2003; Kirmayer, Young, & Hayton, 1995; Putnam, 1998); (4) recognizing the subtypes or subsyndromal forms of PTSD that significantly affect children's lives (Asmundson, Stapleton, & Taylor, 2004; Perry et al., 1995); (5) making adjustments for different age groups; and (6) adding a separate diagnosis for Developmental Disorder or Complex Trauma Disorder for youth (Cook et al., 2005; Ford et al., 2005).

Individual symptoms, such as exaggerated startle response, may predict PTSD or functional impairment, but not necessarily both (Carrion et al., 2002). Years after several classmates were crushed by an elementary school wall that collapsed during a natural disaster, a girl, who had reported only an exaggerated startle response and one or two other arousal symptoms right after the event, began to have panic attacks when under conditions of stress and faced with reminders of the event. Stress and strong winds were enough to engender attacks. Because children with below established *DSM-IV* criteria thresholds may not differ significantly in their impairment and distress (e.g., Criterion F symptoms, Child Behavior Checklist (CBCL) internalizing symptoms, and comorbidity) from children meeting all three criteria (B, C, and D) thresholds (Carrion et al.), some researchers recommend greater focus on the effects of trauma (Angold et al., 1999; La Greca et al., 2002). Variations in the course of youths' symptoms may complicate assessment and comparisons. Youths may alternate periods of reexperiencing with periods of avoidance and numbing (Lubit et al., 2002; Realmuto et al., 1992; Schwarz & Kowalski, 1991). For some children, symptoms or impairment do not appear until months or years after an event (Nader, 2008a; Yule, Udwin, & Bolton, 2002). Future assessments of distress and impairment must encompass multiple manifestations of impairment, variations in timing, and fluctuations in the appearance and evolvement of symptoms.

Perry and colleagues (1995) suggest that, especially for deliberately inflicted traumas, *DSM-IV* does not have adequate descriptive categories for the majority of trauma-related neuropsychiatric syndromes observed in children. In a study of maltreated children (Perry, 1995), only 70% of severely traumatized children with dramatic symptoms of physiological hyperarousal met diagnostic criteria for PTSD. For a sample of 51 Kuwaiti children exposed to severely distressing images of war and death during the Gulf Crisis that ended in 1991 (Nader et al., 1993), an inverse relationship between reexperiencing and arousal symptoms was found within severity levels of traumatic response. Although adolescents in this study had higher levels of difficulty with impulse control, the inverse relationship remained even after partialling out the effects of age. This demonstrates the possibility that the suppression of reexperiencing symptoms may be related to increased levels of arousal. Moreover, the symptoms of hyperarousal alone may disrupt a youth's normal functioning in any or all realms (social, emotional, academic, and other skill development) and drastically upset his/her life trajectory.

Criterion F: Functional impairment

DSM-IV PTSD Criterion F indicates distress or impairment in social, occupational, school, or other important areas of functioning as a part of the diagnosis (APA, 2000). Whether or not PTSD diagnostic criteria are met, functional impairment suggests the need for intervention (Nader, 2008a). In early life, impairment in any aspect of functioning can undermine the normal progression of important developmental skills and resilience factors, such as social and intellectual skills, self-control, self-integration, and self-worth (Deardorff, Gonzales, & Sandler, 2003; Ford, 2009; Haine et al., 2003; Harter, Waters, & Whitesell, 1998). The power of an individual symptom or cluster of symptoms to undermine a youth's ability to function adequately is influenced by many factors. Among the factors are the nature of the child and the event, age at occurrence, length and degree of exposure, support received afterward, and comorbidity (Albano, Chorpita, & Barlow, 2003; Nader, 2001; van der Kolk, 2003; Webb, 2004).

Youths may function adequately, for an extended period of time, despite distress and symptoms because of numbing or because of adult or personal demands. Some of these youths may have delayed or cumulative reactions. A 13-year-old girl, who was molested when gang members broke into her house, was permitted only a few sessions with a therapist. Her father thought she would be fine with the passage of time. The girl managed to function in school and at home, although she remained angry and distant from the father who had been unable to protect her and had removed her from therapeutic intervention. After graduating and leaving home, she had severe problems functioning. Although she minimized the impact of her adolescent experience, she sought therapy in her new location because of her personal and interpersonal problems. She found therapy unrewarding and had difficulties functioning at work, home, and interpersonally even with medication.

Variables that influence reactions and recovery

A number of variables may influence traumatic reactions and recovery (Nader, 2008a). Trauma, for example, may influence resilience factors (for a more detailed overview on risk, protective factors, and resilience, see Chapter 2 by Cicero and colleagues) such as self-esteem or sense of control, which in turn influence outcomes such as mental health status or achievement (Haine et al., 2003; Lindley & Walker, 1993). Levels of variables such as support or resilience may buffer or exacerbate reactions.

In order to avoid missed or cancelled effects when comparing groups of trauma-exposed youths, appropriate subgroups must be identified (DeBellis, Keshaven et al., 1999; Lipschitz, Morgan, & Southwick, 2002; Nader, 2008a). Cultural group is important for categorization as well as to distinguish among pathological and culturally appropriate behaviors (Ahadi, Rothbart, & Ye, 1993; Chen, Rubin, & Li, 1995; Mash & Dozois, 2003). Multiple factors may influence outcomes (e.g., injuries, substance abuse, other disorders, illness, pre- and post-birth conditions, socioeconomic status, culture, heredity, pubertal stage, IQ, age, gender, height, weight, personality, trauma history, comorbidity, time of day of data gathering, time since the event, and assessment method) (De Bellis, Baum et al., 1999; De Bellis, Keshavan et al., 1999; Lipschitz et al., 2002; Nader, 2008a). Two of these are discussed below.

Successful clinical assessment and diagnosis necessitate discovering the preexisting traits (e.g., personality, cultural norms) that mimic or influence the traits and behaviors that are present following a trauma (Keirsey & Bates, 1978; Kirmayer, Young, & Hayton, 1995; Kurcinka, 1998; Myers & Myers, 1980/1995; Nader, 2008a; Phan & Silove, 1997; Westermeyer, 1987, 1990). Traits of negative emotionality and introversion parallel some of the symptoms of trauma, for example. Such traits influence behavior in treatment. For accuracy, parents more easily identify differences in a youth's post- and pre-trauma personality traits before or immediately after the traumatic event.

Personality

"Youths whose trust has been damaged, introverts (Myers & Myers, 1995), or youths with slow-to-warm personality styles (Chess & Thomas, 1991) may need additional time to develop trust. Silence or temporary 'shutdown' may indicate an introvert's need to reflect on thoughts, feelings, and ideas before sharing them; tendency to share thoughts and feelings in bits and pieces … Some youths are particularly attuned to injustice, are sensitive to stimuli and the emotions of others" (Nader, 2008a, p. 157).

Personality traits and styles affect research grouping and treatment needs (Nader, 2008a). Relevant personality subcategories that may influence reactions, treatment methods, and recovery are, for example, (1) *ego-resilients* or *resilients* (well-functioning cognitively, emotionally, and interpersonally); *vulnerable overcontrollers* or *overcontrollers* (few interpersonal skills, shy, inward); and *unsettled undercontrollers* or *undercontrollers* (hostile, disagreeable, show little concern for others) (Block, 1971; Caspi, 1998); (2) *introverted* (inward turning) or *extroverted* (outward turning) (Myers & Myers, 1995) or introverted in combination with an *intuitive* style (focus on abstract realities, symbolic and theoretical ideas) and a *perceiving* style (keep options open rather than readily find closure) (Otis & Louks, 1997); (3) *normal, low reactive* or *high reactive* (Kagan, 1997; Kagan et al., 1995); (4) *easy, difficult* or *slow-to-warm* types (Carey & McDevitt, 1995; Chess & Thomas, 1977, 1991);

and (5) youths who can be characterized by a *Behavioral Activation System* (a neuroanatomical system that is sensitive to cues of reward) or a *Behavioral Inhibition System* (a neuroanatomical system that is sensitive to cues of punishment and nonreward) (Gray, 1972, 1991; Martin & Bridger, 1999; Rothbart & Bates, 1998). Lipschitz et al. (2002) described two biological subtypes of traumatized youths: those with high and those with reduced autonomic responsiveness. The former is anxious, hypervigilant, fearful, and on guard; the latter withdraws, dissociates, and becomes numb and depressed. Failing to separate youths into the appropriate separate personality or other subtypes may result in the canceling of effects in studies and in failure to recognize treatment needs for individuals.

Comorbidity

Significant overlap in symptoms exists among disorders. For *DSM* disorders, when a PTSD diagnosis is possible, it supersedes other diagnoses when symptoms are directly related to a PTSD Criterion A experience and other PTSD criteria algorithms are met (Nader, 2007). Comorbidity is common with PTSD (Kessler, 2000; Nader, 2008a). When studies control for lifetime comorbidities, whether or not adversities meet PTSD Criterion A, their effects include more similarities than differences. Adults with psychiatric disorders significantly more often than others retrospectively report exposure to childhood adversities (Kessler, Davis, & Kendler, 1997). Particular adverse events are not associated with any one class of disorders. Mood and anxiety disorders are often comorbid; mood disorders most often arise after anxiety disorders (de Graaf et al., 2004). The personality traits of neuroticism (Eysenck, 1967), childhood trauma, and parental (especially maternal) psychiatric history have been more strongly associated with comorbidity than with solitary disorders (de Graaf et al., 2004; Kessler et al., 1997). Impairments in functioning have been more strongly associated with comorbid than with single disorders (de Graaf et al., 2004).

For children, comorbidity may indicate a more complicated form of trauma. Youths exposed to traumas that may result in complex reactions have been diagnosed with a number of disorders, including separation anxiety, overanxious, phobic, PTSD, depressive, dissociative, attention deficit hyperactivity, oppositional defiant, eating, sleep, communication, reactive attachment, substance abuse, and conduct disorders (Cook et al., 2005; Streeck-Fischer & van der Kolk, 2000).

Complex reactions

For the sake of effective treatment, it is important to distinguish among the types of reactions youths may have following traumatic events (Ford et al.,

2005; Nader, 2008a; van der Kolk et al., 2005). PTSD and its assessment have been well discussed (Fletcher, 2003, 2008; Nader, 1997a, 2004, 2008a; Wilson & Keane, 1997, 2004). Below is a discussion of complex traumatic reactions in youth.

Complex trauma or developmental disorder

Proposed for *DSM-V,* a disorder variously named Complex or Complicated PTSD, Disorders of Extreme Stress Not Otherwise Specified, or Developmental Trauma Disorder (see also Ford, Chapter 22 in this book for a critical evaluation of trauma-related developmental disorders), refers to a group of symptoms (Table 1.2) most commonly associated with interpersonal, early, extreme, or prolonged stressors (APA, 1994; Herman, 1992; Pearlman, 2001; van der Kolk et al., 2005). Among developmentally adverse interpersonal traumas in early childhood (or *developmental trauma*), Ford (2005, 2009) includes physical, sexual, and emotional abuse, abandonment by caregiver(s), severe and chronic neglect, domestic violence, or death or gruesome injuries as a result of community violence, terrorism, or war.

Evidence suggests that the earlier the onset of trauma and the longer its duration, the greater the likelihood of suffering complex trauma symptoms (Roth et al., 1997; van der Kolk, 2003). Wilson (2004) states that, especially events involving acts of interpersonal assault, violence, abuse or prolonged coercive internment under degrading conditions, "attack the bases of the self and systems of personal meaning" (p. 32) and thus may result in complex trauma. Research evidence also suggests that a percentage of individuals exposed to childhood single nonviolent traumas such as natural disasters experience complicated PTSD as well (van der Kolk et al., 2005). It is possible that aspects of an event (e.g., multiple bloody deaths; specific personal experience) or a child (e.g., attachment disturbances; low resilience) may contribute to the more complicated results of a single traumatic event. A young girl who, during a natural disaster that struck her school killing 10 of her classmates, was thwarted from escaping injury by a close friend, experienced subsequent problems with aggression, relationships, knowing and describing internal states and expressing feelings, loss of belief in God, problems with attention and task completion, and low self-esteem. A boy who, while under gun threat for more than an hour, witnessed mutilations by bullet, the deaths of his best friend, the friend's mother, and multiple others and was himself shot twice, suffered from most of the symptoms of complex trauma (Briere & Spinazzola, 2005; van der Kolk et al., 2005; Table 5.2) for years after his experience (Nader, 2008a).

In the past few years, maltreated children have been the main objects of study in the conceptualization of complex trauma. Attachment is currently a primary focus of this conceptualization. The question has been asked whether instead of a new complex trauma diagnosis, what is needed is a set of *DSM* diagnoses that specifically index ongoing and chronic severe attachment disturbances as

Table 1.2 Conceptualizations of complex trauma domains for individuals traumatized as youths

Herman, 1992, 1997	Cook et al., 2003	van der Kolk et al., 2005	Briere & Spinazzola, 2005	Cook et al., 2005	Ford, 2009 (extracted from paper)
(2) Alterations in affect regulation	(3) Affect regulation	(1) Dysregulation of affect and impulses	(1) Altered self-capacities	(3) Affect regulation	Emotion dysregulation
• Persistent dysphoria	• Difficulty with emotional self-regulation	• Difficulties with affect regulation	• Dysfunctions in affect regulation	• Difficulty with emotional self-regulation	• Neural circuits organized around stress reactivity (automatic rather than autonomous self-regulation)
• Chronic suicidal preoccupation	• Difficulty describing feelings and internal experience	• Excessive risk-taking		• Difficulty labeling and expressing feelings	• Emotions and bodily feelings experienced as signals of danger resulting in
• Self-injury	• Problems knowing and describing internal states	• Difficulties with modulation of anger	(3) Mood disturbances	• Problems knowing and describing internal states	− persistent affective states of anger, anxiety, sadness, and depression
• Explosiveness or extremely inhibited anger (may alternate)	• Difficulty communicating wishes and desires	• Self-destructive behaviors	Affective symptoms or disorders − anxiety, depression, anger, or aggression	• Difficulty communicating wishes and needs	− deficits in basic self-regulation (e.g., in sleep and eating cycles; in self-soothing)
• Compulsive sexual activity or extreme sexual inhibition (may alternate)	(5) Behavioral control	• Suicidal preoccupations	(4) Overdeveloped avoidance reactions	(5) Behavioral control	− behavioral disinhibition (e.g., risk-taking, impulsivity, aggression, addiction)
	• Poor modulation of impulses	• Difficulty modulating sexual involvement	• Substance abuse	• Poor modulation of impulses	
	• Self-destructive behavior		• Tension reduction behaviors such as binging-purging, self-mutilation, suicidality that distract or invoke stress-incompatible affect	• Self-destructive behavior	
	• Aggression against others			• Aggression toward others	
	• Pathological self-soothing behaviors			• Pathological self-soothing behaviors	

(Continued)

Table 1.2 (*Continued*)

Herman, 1992, 1997	Cook et al., 2003	van der Kolk et al., 2005	Briere & Spinazzola, 2005	Cook et al., 2005	Ford, 2009 (extracted from paper)
	• Sleep disturbances • Eating disorders • Substance abuse • Excessive compliance • Oppositional behavior • Difficulty understanding and complying with rules • Reenactment in day-to-day behavior or play (sexual, aggressive, etc.)			• Sleep disturbances • Eating disorders • Substance abuse • Excessive compliance • Oppositional behavior • Difficulty understanding and complying with rules • Reenactment of trauma in behavior or play (e.g., sexual, aggressive)	
(3) Alterations in consciousness • Amnesia or hypermnesia for traumatic events • Transient dissociative episodes • Depersonalization/ derealization • Reliving experiences in the form of PTSD intrusive symptoms or ruminative preoccupation	(4) Dissociation • Distinct alterations in states of consciousness • Amnesia • Depersonalization and derealization • Two or more distinct states of consciousness, with impaired memory for state-based events	(2) Alterations in attention and consciousness • Amnesia • Transient dissociative episodes	(4) Overdeveloped avoidance reactions • Dissociation	(4) Dissociation • Distinct alterations in states of consciousness • Amnesia • Depersonalization and derealization • Two or more distinct states of consciousness • Impaired memory for state-based events	Dissociation • Structural dissociation (loss of self-coherence and integration among aspects of personality and sense of self) • Pathological dissociation

(4) Alterations in self-perception	(5) Alterations in perception of perpetrator	(7) Self-concept	(3) Alterations in self-perception	(4) Distorted perception of the perpetrator	(1) Altered self-capacities	(2) Cognitive disturbances	(7) Self-concept	Self-capacities
• Sense of helplessness or paralysis of initiative • Self-blame, guilt, or shame • Sense of stigma or defilement • Feeling complete differentness (e.g., specialness, utter aloneness, no one can understand, nonhuman	• Preoccupation with relationship with perpetrator (revenge) • Unrealistic attribution of total power to perpetrator (significant power may be accurate) • Paradoxical gratitude or idealization	• Lack of a continuous, predictable sense of self • Poor sense of separateness • Disturbances of body image • Low self-esteem • Shame and guilt	• Guilt/responsibility, shame • Minimizing • Feeling that nobody can understand • Sense of ineffectiveness • Feeling permanently damaged	• Distorted beliefs about the perpetrator • Idealization of the perpetrator • Preoccupation with hurting the perpetrator	• Dysfunctions in identity	• Altered information-processing or schemata associated with, e.g., low self-esteem, self-blame, helplessness, hopelessness	• Lack of a continuous, predictable sense of self • Poor sense of separateness • Disturbances of body image • Low self-esteem • Shame and guilt	• Personality orientation toward *harm avoidance vs. openness to experience* • Deficits in *reflective self-awareness* and integration of information processing required for organized personality and sense of self • Shame

(Continued)

Table 1.2 (*Continued*)

Herman, 1992, 1997	Cook et al., 2003	van der Kolk et al., 2005	Briere & Spinazzola, 2005	Cook et al., 2005	Ford, 2009 (extracted from paper)
• Sense of special or supernatural relationship • Acceptance of perpetrator's beliefs and rationalizations		(4) Distorted perception of the perpetrator • Distorted beliefs about the perpetrator • Idealization of the perpetrator • Preoccupation with hurting the perpetrator			
(6) Alterations in relationships with others • Withdrawal and isolation • Disruptions in intimate relationships • Search for rescuer (may alternate with withdrawal/isolation) • Persistent distrust • Repetitive failures of self-protection	(1) Attachment • Uncertainty about reliability and predictability of the world • Problems with boundaries • Distrust and suspiciousness • Social isolation • Interpersonal difficulties • Difficulty attuning to other people's emotional states • Difficulty with perspective taking • Difficulty enlisting allies	(5) Alterations in relationships with others • Inability to trust • Revictimization • Victimizing others	(1) Altered self-capacities • Dysfunctions in interpersonal relatedness	(1) Attachment • Problems with boundaries • Distrust and suspiciousness • Social isolation • Interpersonal difficulties • Difficulty attuning to other people's emotional states • Difficulty with perspective taking	Attachment/ relationships • Chaotic mix of excessive – help-seeking and dependence – social isolation and disengagement – impulsiveness and inhibition – submissiveness & aggression • Absence of empathy

• Loss of
  sustaining faith
• Sense of
  hopelessness and
  despair

(6) Cognition
• Difficulties in attention
  regulation and executive
  functioning
• Lack of sustained curiosity
• Problems with processing
  novel information
• Problems focusing on and
  completing tasks
• Problems with object
  constancy
• Difficulty planning and
  anticipating
• Problems understanding
  own contribution to what
  happens to them
• Learning difficulties
• Problems with language
  development
• Problems with orientation
  in time and space

---

systems or meaning
• Hopelessness or
  despair
• Loss of
  previously held
  belief systems

(2) Cognitive
disturbances
• Altered information
  processing or
  schemata associated
  with, e.g., pessimistic
  expectations of loss,
  rejection, and danger
  (see also Cognitive
  disturbances in row
  4)

(6) Cognition
• Difficulties in attention
  regulation and
  executive functioning
• Lack of sustained
  curiosity
• Problems with
  processing novel
  information
• Problems focusing on
  and completing tasks
• Problems with object
  constancy
• Difficulty planning and
  anticipating
• Problems
  understanding
  responsibility
• Learning difficulties
• Problems with
  language development
• Problems with
  orientation in time and
  space

Altered brain
development
• Prominence of
  survival brain over
  learning brain –
  warding off harm is
  the primary focus
  rather than healthy
  growth, play,
  exploration,
  rejuvenation,
  learning, and
  developing
  relationships
• Dysregulation in
  core information-
  processing capacities
  (related to cortical
  areas involved in
  synthesizing
  information – new
  learning and
  consolidation in
  memory)

(Continued)

Table 1.2 (*Continued*)

Herman, 1992, 1997	Cook et al., 2003	van der Kolk et al., 2005	Briere & Spinazzola, 2005	Cook et al., 2005	Ford, 2009 (extracted from paper)
	• Acoustic and visual perceptual problems • Impaired comprehension of complex visual-spatial patterns			• Experience-dependent learning (lack of flexible engagement with and response to environment) • Experience expectant learning (relatively automatic, chaotic and fixated thoughts, perceptions, and actions)	
	(2) Biology • Sensori-motor developmental problems • Hypersensitivity to physical contact • Analgesia • Problems with coordination, balance, body tone • Difficulty localizing skin contact • Somatization • Increased medical problems across a wide span (e.g., *Pelvic pain, Asthma, Skin problems, Autoimmune disorders, Pseudoseizures*)	(6) Somatization • Chronic pain • Conversion symptoms • Sexual symptoms • Digestive symptoms • Cardiopulmonary symptoms (e.g., increased resting heart rate)		(2) Biology • Sensori-motor developmental problems • Analgesia • Problems with coordination, balance, body tone • Somatization • Increased medical problems across a wide span (e.g., *Pelvic pain, Asthma, Skin Problems, Autoimmune disorders, Pseudoseizures*)	Somatization • Emotions and bodily feelings experienced as signals of danger resulting in bodily discomfort, preoccupation, pain, and loss of physical function including hysterical symptoms
			(5) PTSD		

© Nader, 2008. Adapted with permission from Nader (2008b). Complex trauma domains of impairment with authors' examples are numbered according to authors' numbering but are aligned against the first place a category appears.
Sources: APA, 1994; Briere & Spinazzola, 2005; Cook et al., 2003, 2005; Ford, 2009; Herman, 1992; van der Kolk & Courtois, 2005; van der Kolk

they appear in older children and adolescents as well as those known for young children (J. Briere, personal communication, March 7, 2008). We may find that complex trauma has a different emphasis or algorithm for youths severely and complexly traumatized by single traumas. In any case, severe traumas and even some individual trauma symptoms may cause developmental disruptions that significantly alter a youth's life (Nader, 2008a).

Attachment

Insecure attachments between caregiver and infant/child may precede any kind of traumatic experience. Insecure attachments are associated with a variety of vulnerabilities, symptoms, and disorders (Nader, 2008a). Among them are vulnerability to increased trauma exposure and traumatic reactions. Insecure attachments (including disorganized attachments), in and of themselves, have been linked to a variety of problems such as aggression, suicidality, low self-esteem, memory problems (Goodman & Quas, 1996), raised cortisol levels in response to stressful or novel situations (Gunnar et al., 1996, Nachmias & Gunnar, 1996), the temperamental dimension of negative emotionality (Rutter, 1997), poor coping skills (Schore, 2003), and, in adolescents, increased hostility, poorer social skills with peers, more nonqualitative romantic relationships, and ongoing problems with parents (Allen & Land, 1999; Hesse et al., 2003; Nader, 2008a). Such attachments have been associated with depressive, anxiety, dissociative, somatic, personality disorder, externalizing, internalizing, and overall psychopathology in young children, children, adolescents, and young adults, as well as in adults maltreated as children (Alexander et al., 1998; Blizard, 2001; Fergusson, Woodward, & Horwood, 2000; Lyons-Ruth, Zeanah, & Benoit, 2003; Nader, 2008a; National Center for Infants, Toddlers, and Families, 1994; West et al., 2001).

Traumas (especially maltreatment) may interfere with attachment relationships (Cook et al., 2005; Nader, 2008a). Disorganized attachments are among the frequently reported insecure attachments that follow abuse. Such attachments revolve around helplessness or coercive control on the part of the child, who may demonstrate alternate clingy, dismissive, and aggressive behaviors (Cook et al., 2005). Significantly disrupted attachments may result in risk of physical disease, psychosocial dysfunction, undermined core biopsychosocial competencies, including increased susceptibility to stress, difficulties regulating emotions, excessive help-seeking and dependency, or social isolation and disengagement. Whether or not traumatic reactions are complex and whether or not insecure attachments are trauma-engendered, insecure attachments suggest the need for appropriate interventions.

Developmental disruptions

For the developing youth, competence in one developmental period provides a foundation for success with subsequent developmental issues (Yates, Egeland,

& Sroufe, 2003). The likelihood of a normative life trajectory is increased when, at each phase of development, youths learn to use internal and external resources to adapt to developmental demands. Youths learn to regulate emotions and to establish desirable peer relationships, for example. Disruptions to emerging skills, such as relationship skills, intelligence, coping and problem-solving, self-regulation, self-esteem, and trust, may undo resilience and send the youth on a trajectory toward problem behaviors or psychopathology. Such disruptions may create risk and vulnerabilities as well as result in increased failure experiences and blocked or reduced opportunities (Nader, 2008a). Although failure to negotiate important developmental tasks does not always precede pathology, it may increase risk. Difficulty returning to a normal developmental progression increases the longer a youth stays on a deviant pathway (Geiger & Crick, 2001; Yates et al., 2003). Major or minor life events that disrupt emotion, physiology, and cognition strain a youth's adaptive capability (Ford, 2010; Ingram & Price, 2001). Although prolonged or repeated traumatic events may be more likely to cause intense developmental disruptions, single traumatic incidents or single symptoms can interfere with normal development, place a youth "out of sync" with his or her peers, interfere with the development of talents and skills, and disrupt a developmental pathway (Nader, 2008a). Single as well as repeated traumas may engender changes in information-processing that greatly affect a youth's life and interactional style. It is important to assess such changes in youths exposed to single or repetitive events.

Traumas may interrupt normal development in a number of important ways (Ford et al., 2005; Nader, 2008a; van der Kolk & Courtois, 2005). Cognitive-processing (i.e., information-processing) may change such that expectations, biases, and compulsions to act (or repetitive, script-like behaviors) contribute to problematic behaviors, negative self-talk, and/or reduced resilience (Nader, 2008a). A youth's natural talents, skills, and intelligence may be undermined; and the ability to attain the states of mind that enhance the success of endeavors may become impossible. Post-Trauma changes, such as an increased sense of helplessness or victimization, pessimism or negative expectations, or lack of impulse control, may repel others. Any of these traumatic results or combinations of them may limit the child's abilities and opportunities for success and desirable relationships. They may contribute to a greatly changed life trajectory. We are only now learning ways to measure these developmental disruptions and changes in traumatized youth (see Nader, 2008a for measures of resilience factors, neurobiology, information-processing, and other post-trauma reactions and variables).

Information-processing

Changes in information-processing may occur as a result of youth's traumatic experiences (Nader, 2008a). Self-talk or automatic emotions related to issues of trust, the intentions of others, the need to self-protect, and other issues may become part of a tendency to automatically react (Ford, 2010). Another result of alterations in information-processing may be any number of *trauma-related roles* or *trauma-engendered scripts* that manifest in a youth's repeated behaviors; thinking about self, others, and the world; and interactions with others (Nader, 1997c, 2008a). A 12-year-old boy endured a mass shooting for more than an hour. He witnessed deaths and mutilations, heard repeated shots followed by screams and moans, suffered personal shooting injuries and the death of friends, and experienced ongoing frightful anticipation of the shooters next shot, along with the need to see what was happening despite the fact that his movement drew the shooter's attention. During the event, his self-talk was sometimes abusive for failure to attack the shooter and sometimes escapist. In his life after the trauma, he moved through several different roles that reflected his strong wishes and desires to act or to be unconscious during what was happening. He became victim, aggressor, rescuer, and addict among other trauma-engendered roles for prolonged periods of time. A number of theories about trauma-engendered roles have emerged in recent years. For example, Thomas (2005) describes altered expectations of protection and Loewenstein (2004) describes attributions of personal badness that may become a part of abused youths' script-like behaviors.

Conclusions

Disparate and similar traumatic experiences with different intensities and differing personal impacts may elicit important variations in children's symptoms, the content of traumatic reexperiencing, and the course and evolution of symptoms and reactions. Although some basic guidelines can assist the formulation of interventions, treatments are best when suited to the clinician and tailored for the traumatized youth. Designing individual assessments requires accurate assessment of a broad range of symptoms, factors, and traits in each child, regardless of the number of traumas endured. Because of trauma's potential to disrupt a number of developmental skills and processes, the symptoms of complex reactions are best assessed for any youth exposed to a traumatic experience. Emotional and behavioral self-regulation, information-processing, and other symptoms that influence them and resilience factors should be assessed. Assessment and diagnosis are most effective when information is gathered from multiple sources and using multiple methods.

References

Ahadi, S. A., Rothbart, M. K., & Ye, R. (1993). Children's temperament in the U.S. and China: Similarities and differences. *European Journal of Personality, 7,* 359–77.

Albano, A. M., Chorpita, B. F., & Barlow, D. H. (2003). Childhood anxiety disorders. In E. J. Mash & R. A. Barkley (Eds.), *Child psychopathology* (1st ed., pp. 279–329). New York: Guilford Press.

Alexander, P. C., Anderson, C. L., Brand, B. et al. (1998). Adult attachment and long-term effects in survivors of incest. *Child Abuse and Neglect, 22*(1), 45–61.

Allen, J. P., & Land, D. (1999). Attachment in adolescence. In J. Cassidy & P. R. Shaver (Eds.), *Handbook of attachment: Theory, research, and clinical applications* (pp. 319–35). New York: Guilford Press.

American Psychiatric Association (APA) (1994). *Diagnostic and Statistical Manual of Mental Disorders* (4th ed.) (*DSM-IV*). Washington, DC: Author.

American Psychiatric Association (APA) (2000). *Diagnostic and Statistical Manual of Mental Disorders* (4th ed., Text Rev.) (*DSM-IV-TR*). Washington, DC: Author.

Angold, A., Costello, E., Farmer, E., Burns, B., & Erkanli, A. (1999). Impaired but undiagnosed. *Journal of the American Academy of Child & Adolescent Psychiatry, 38*(2), 129–37.

Armsworth, M. W., & Holaday, M. (1993). The effects of psychological trauma on children and adolescents. *Journal of Counseling and Development, 72,* 49–56.

Asmundson, G. J. G., Stapleton, J. A., & Taylor, S. (2004). Are avoidance and numbing distinct PTSD symptom clusters? *Journal of Traumatic Stress, 17*(6), 467–75.

Blizard, R. A. (2001). Masochistic and sadistic ego states: Dissociative solutions to the dilemma of attachment to an abusive caretaker. *Journal of Trauma and Dissociation, 2*(4), 37–58.

Block, J. (1971). *Lives through time.* Berkeley, CA: Bancroft Books.

Briere, J., & Spinazzola, J. (2005). Phenomenology and psychological assessment of complex posttraumatic states. *Journal of Traumatic Stress, 18*(5), 401–12.

Carey, W. B., & McDevitt, S. C. (1995). *Coping with children's temperament.* New York: Basic Books.

Carrion, V. G., Weems, C. F., Ray, R. D., & Reiss, A. L. (2002). Toward an empirical definition of pediatric PTSD: The phenomenology of PTSD symptoms in youth. *Journal of the American Academy of Child and Adolescent Psychiatry, 41*(2), 166–73.

Caspi, A. (1998). Personality development across the life course. In W. Damon & N. Eisenberg (Eds.), *Handbook of child psychology, Vol. 3. Social, emotional, and personality development* (5th ed., pp. 311–88). New York: John Wiley & Sons, Inc.

Chen, X., Rubin, K. H., & Li, Z. Y. (1995). Social functioning and adjustment in Chinese children: A longitudinal study. *Developmental Psychology, 31,* 531–9.

Chess, S., & Thomas, A. (1977). Temperamental individuality from childhood to adolescence. *Journal of the American Academy of Child Psychiatry, 16*(2), 218–26.

Chess, S., & Thomas, A. (1991). Temperament. In M. Lewis (Ed.), *Child and adolescent psychiatry: A comprehensive textbook* (pp. 145–59). Baltimore, MD: Williams & Wilkins.

Cohen, J. A., Mannarino, A. P., Greenberg, T., Padlo, S., & Shipley, C. (2002). Childhood traumatic grief: Concepts and controversies. *Trauma, Violence & Abuse, 3*(4), 307–327.

Cook, A., Blaustein, M., Spinazzola, P., & van der Kolk, B. (Eds.) (2003). Complex trauma in children and adolescents. White paper from the National Child Traumatic Stress Network Complex Trauma Task Force. Retrieved from www.NCTSNET.org (accessed December 4, 2008).

Cook, A., Spinazzola, J., Ford, J. D. et al. (2005). Complex trauma in children and adolescents. *Psychiatric Annals, 35,* 390–8.

Daviss, W. B., Mooney, D., Racusin, R. et al. (2000). Predicting posttraumatic stress after hospitalization for pediatric injury. *Journal of American Academy of Child and Adolescent Psychiatry, 59*(5), 576–83.

Deardorff, J., Gonzales, N. A., & Sandler, I. N. (2003). Control beliefs as a mediator of the relation between stress and depressive symptoms among inner-city adolescents. *Journal of Abnormal Child Psychology, 31*(2), 205–17.

De Bellis, M., Baum, A., Birmaher, B. et al. (1999). Developmental traumatology. Part I: Biological stress systems. *Biological Psychiatry, 45,* 1259–70.

De Bellis, M., Keshavan, M., Clark, D. et al. (1999). Developmental traumatology. Part II: Brain development. *Biological Psychiatry, 45,* 1271–84.

de Graaf, R., Bijl, R. V., ten Have, M., Beekman, A. T. F., & Vollebergh, W. A. M. (2004). Rapid onset of comorbidity of common mental disorders: Findings from the Netherlands Mental Health Survey and Incidence Study (NEMESIS). *Acta Psychiatrica Scandinavia, 109,* 55–63.

Diareme, S., Tsiantis, J., Romer, G. et al. (2007). Mental health support for children of parents with somatic illness: A review of the theory and intervention concepts. *Families, Systems, & Health, 25*(1), 98–118.

Drell, M. J., Siegel, C. H., & Gaensbauer, T. (1993). Post-traumatic stress disorder. In C. H. Zeanah, Jr. (Ed.), *Handbook of infant mental health* (pp. 291–304). New York: Guilford Press.

Dyregrov, A., Yule, W., Smith, P. et al. (2001). *Inventory of Complicated Grief for Children.* Copyrighted inventory.

Eysenck, H. J. (1967). *The biological basis of personality.* Springfield, IL: Charles C. Thomas.

Fergusson, D. M., Woodward, L. J., & Horwood, L. J. (2000). Risk factors and life processes associated with the onset of suicidal behaviour during adolescence and early adulthood. *Psychological Medicine, 30*(1), 23–39.

Fletcher, K. E. (2003). Childhood posttraumatic stress disorder. In E. J. Mash & R. A. Barkley (Eds.), *Child psychopathology* (2nd ed., pp. 330–71). New York: Guilford Press.

Fletcher, K. E. (2008). Childhood posttraumatic stress disorder. In E. J. Mash & R. A. Barkley (Eds.), *Child psychopathology* (3rd ed., pp. 398–483). New York: Guilford Press.

Ford, J. D. (2005). Treatment implications of altered neurobiology, affect regulation and information processing following child maltreatment. *Psychiatric Annals, 35,* 410–19.

Ford, J. D. (2009). Neurobiological and developmental research: Developmental implications. In C. Courtois & J. D. Ford (Eds.), *Treating Complex Traumatic Stress Disorders: An Evidence-Based Guide.* New York: Guilford Press.

Ford, J. D., Courtois, C., van der Hart, O., Nijenhuis, E., & Steele, K. (2005). Treatment of complex post-traumatic self-dysregulation. *Journal of Traumatic Stress, 18,* 437–47.

Ford, J. D., Fraleigh, L. A., Albert, D. B., & Connor, D. F. (2010). Child abuse and autonomic nervous system hyporesponsivity among psychiatrically impaired children. *Child Abuse & Neglect, 34*(7), 507–515.

Geiger, T. C., & Crick, N. R. (2001). A developmental psychopathology perspective on vulnerability to personality disorders. In R. E. Ingram & J. M. Price (Eds.), *Vulnerability to psychopathology: Risk across the lifespan* (pp. 57–102). New York: Guilford Press.

Goodman, G. S., & Quas, J. (1996). Trauma and memory: Individual differences in children's recounting of a stressful experience. In N. Stein, P. A. Ornstein, B. Tversky, & C. J. Brainerd (Eds.), *Memory for everyday and emotional events* (pp. 267–94). Hillsdale, NJ: Erlbaum.

Gray, J. (1972). The psychophysiological nature of introversion–extraversion: A modification of Eysenck's theory. In V. D. Nebylisyn & J. A. Gray (Eds.), *Biological bases of individual behavior* (pp. 182–206). New York: Academic Press.

Gray, J. (1991). The neuropsychology of temperament. In J. Strelau & A. Angleitner (Eds.), *Explorations in temperament: International perspectives on theory and measurement* (pp. 105–28). New York: Plenum Press.

Gunnar, M. R., Brodersen, L., Krueger, K., & Rigatuso, J. (1996). Dampening of adrenocortical responses during infancy: Normative changes and individual differences. *Child Development, 67,* 877–89.

Haine, R. A., Ayers, T. S., Sandler, I. N., Wolchik, S. A., & Weyer, J. L. (2003). Locus of control and self-esteem as stress-moderators or stress-mediators in parentally bereaved children. *Death Studies, 27*(7), 619–40.

Harter, S., Waters, P., & Whitesell, N. R. (1998). Relational self-worth: Differences in perceived worth as a person across interpersonal contexts among adolescents. *Child Development, 69*(3), 756–66.

Herman, J. L. (1992, 1997). *Trauma and recovery.* New York: Basic Books.

Hesse, E., Main, M., Abrams, K. Y., & Rifkin, A. (2003). Unresolved states regarding loss or abuse can have "second-generation" effects: Disorganization, role inversion, and frightening ideation in the offspring of traumatized, non-maltreating parents. In M. Solomon & D. J. Siegel (Eds.), *Healing trauma* (pp. 57–106). New York: W. W. Norton & Co.

House, A. E. (2002). *The first session with children and adolescents: Conducting a comprehensive mental health evaluation.* New York: Guilford Press.

Ingram, R. E., & Price, J. M. (2001). The role of vulnerability in understanding psychopathology. In R. E. Ingram & J. M. Price (Eds.), *Vulnerability to psychopathology: Risk across the lifespan* (pp. 3–19). New York: Guilford Press.

Kagan, J. (1997). Temperament and the reactions to unfamiliarity. *Child Development, 68*(1), 139–43.

Kagan, J., Snidman, N., & Arcus, D. (1995). The role of temperament in social development. *Annals of the New York Academy of Sciences, 771,* 485–90.

Keirsey, D., & Bates, M. (1978). *Please understand me.* Del Mar, CA: Prometheus Nemesis.

Kessler, R. C. (2000). Post-Traumatic Stress Disorder: The burden to the individual and to society. *Journal of Clinical Psychiatry, 6*(5), 4–14.

Kessler, R. C., Davis, C. G., & Kendler, K. S. (1997). Childhood adversity and adult psychiatric disorder in the U.S. National Comorbidity Survey. *Psychological Medicine, 27,* 1101–19.

Kinniburgh, K. J., & Spinazzola, J. (2005). Attachment, self-regulation, and competency. *Psychiatric Annals, 35*(5), 424–30.

Kirmayer, L. J., Young, A., & Hayton, B. C. (1995). The cultural context of anxiety disorders. *The Psychiatric Clinics of North America, 18*(3), 503–21.

Kurcinka, M. S. (1998). *Raising your spirited child* (2nd ed.). New York: Harper Perennial.

La Greca, A. M., Silverman, W. K., Vernberg, E. M., & Roberts, M. C. (2002). Introduction. In A. M. La Greca, W. K. Silverman, E. M. Vernberg, & M. C. Roberts (Eds.), *Helping children cope with disasters and terrorism* (pp. 3–33). Washington, DC: APA Press.

Layne, C. M., Savjak, N., Saltzman, W. R., & Pynoos, R. S. (2001). *UCLA/BYU Grief Screening Inventory*. Unpublished instrument. Brigham Young University, Provo, UT.

Lindley, P., & Walker, S. N. (1993). Theoretical and methodological differentiation of moderation and mediation. *Nursing Research, 42*(5), 276–9.

Lipschitz, D. S., Morgan, C. A., & Southwick, S. M. (2002). Neurobiological disturbances in youth with childhood trauma and in youth with conduct disorder. *Journal of Aggression, Maltreatment and Trauma, 6*(1), 149–74.

Loewenstein, R. J. (2004). Commentary on "Cherchez la Femme, Cherchez la Femme: A paradoxical response to trauma." Dissociation of the "bad" parent, preservation of the "good" parent. *Psychiatry, 67*(3), 256–60.

Lubit, R., Hartwell, N., van Gorp, W. G., & Eth, S. (2002). *Forensic evaluation of trauma syndromes in children*. Retrieved March 8, 2005, from www.traumahelp.org/forensic.htm

Lyons-Ruth, K., Zeanah, C. H., & Benoit, D. (2003). Disorder and risk for disorder during infancy and toddlerhood. In E. J. Mash & R. A. Barkley (Eds.), *Child psychopathology* (2nd ed., pp. 589–631). New York: Guilford Press.

Martin, R. P., & Bridger, R. C. (1999). *Temperament assessment battery for children – Revised*. Copyrighted manual and measure.

Mash, E. J., & Dozois, D. (2003). Child psychopathology: A developmental systems perspective. In E. J. Mash & R. A. Barkley (Eds.), *Child psychopathology* (2nd ed., pp. 3–71). New York: Guilford Press.

Myers, I. B., & Myers, P. B. (1980/1995). *Gifts differing*. Palo Alto, CA: Davies Black.

Nachmias, M., & Gunnar, M. (1996). Behavioral inhibition and stress reactivity: The moderating role of attachment security. *Child Development, 67*(2), 508–22.

Nader, K. (1997a). Assessing traumatic experiences in children. In J. Wilson & T. Keane (Eds.), *Assessing psychological trauma & PTSD* (pp. 291–348). New York: Guilford Press.

Nader, K. (1997b). Childhood traumatic loss: The interaction of trauma and grief. In C. R. Figley, B. E. Bride, & N. Mazza (Eds.), *Death and Trauma: The traumatology of grieving* (pp. 17–41). London: Taylor & Francis.

Nader, K. (1997c). Treating traumatic grief in systems. In C. R. Figley, B. E. Bride, & N. Mazza (Eds.), *Death and trauma: The traumatology of grieving* (pp. 159–92). London: Taylor & Francis.

Nader, K. (2001). Treatment methods for childhood trauma. In J. P. Wilson, M. Friedman, & J. Lindy (Eds.), *Treating psychological trauma and PTSD* (pp. 278–334). New York: Guilford Press.

Nader, K. (2004). Assessing traumatic experiences in children and adolescents: Self-reports of *DSM* PTSD Criteria B–D symptoms. In J. Wilson & T. Keane (Eds.),

Assessing psychological trauma and PTSD (2nd ed., pp. 513–37). New York: Guilford Press.

Nader, K. (2007). Assessment of the child following crisis: The challenge of differential diagnosis. In N. B. Webb (Ed.), *Play therapy with children in crisis: Individual, group, and family treatment* (3rd ed., pp. 21–44). New York: Guilford Press.

Nader, K. (2008a). *Understanding and assessing trauma in children and adolescents: Measures, methods, and youth in context.* New York: Routledge.

Nader, K. (2008b). Age, brain development, developmental learning, and traumatic symptoms. Psychological first aid for trauma and traumatic grief. Austin, TX: Two Suns.

Nader, K., & Prigerson, H. (2005). Complicated Grief Assessment (Child Version) – Long Form. A copyrighted scale.

Nader, K., Stuber, M., & Fletcher, K. (2007). *Traumatic play observation scale.* Austin, TX: Two Suns.

Nader, K., Pynoos, R., Fairbanks, L., Al-Ajeel, M., & Al-Asfour, A. (1993). Acute posttraumatic stress reactions among Kuwait children following the Gulf Crisis. *British Journal of Clinical Psychology, 32*, 407–16.

National Center for Infants, Toddlers, and Families (1994). *Diagnostic classification 0–3.* Arlington, VA: Zero to Three.

Olfson, M., Hellman, F., Blanco, C., Guardino, M., & Struening, E. L. (2001). Comorbidity, impairment, and suicidality in subthreshold PTSD. *The American Journal of Psychiatry, 158*, 1467–73.

Otis, G. D., & Louks, J. L. (1997). Rebelliousness and psychological distress in a sample of introverted veterans. *Journal of Psychological Type, 40*, 20–30.

Pearlman, L. A. (2001). Treatment of persons with complex PTSD and other trauma-related disruptions of the self. In J. P. Wilson, M. Friedman, & J. Lindy (Eds.), *Treating psychological trauma and PTSD* (pp. 205–36). New York: Guilford Press.

Perry, B. D. (1995, May). Evolution of symptoms following traumatic events in children. *Proceedings of the 148th Annual Meeting of the American Psychiatric Association*, Miami, FL.

Perry, B. D., Pollard, R., Blakely, T., Baker, W., & Vigilante, D. (1995). Childhood trauma, the neurobiology of adaptation and "use-dependent" development of the brain: How "states" become "traits." *Infant Mental Health Journal, 16*(4), 271–91.

Phan, T., & Silove, D. M. (1997). The influence of culture on psychiatric assessment: The Vietnamese refugee. *Psychiatric Services, 48*(1), 86–90.

Piaget, J., & Inhelder, B. (1969). *The psychology of the child.* New York: Basic Books.

Prigerson, H., Nader, K., & Maciejewski, P. (2005). Complicated Grief Assessment Interview (Child Version) – Short Form.

Putnam, F. W. (1998). Trauma models of the effects of childhood maltreatment. *Journal of Aggression, Maltreatment, & Trauma, 2*, 51–66.

Realmuto, G. M., Masten, A., Carole, L. F. et al. (1992). Adolescent survivors of massive childhood trauma in Cambodia: Life events and current symptoms. *Journal of Traumatic Stress, 5*(4), 589–99.

Roth, S., Newman, E., Pelcovitz, D., van der Kolk, B., & Mandel, F. S. (1997). Complex PTSD in victims exposed to sexual and physical abuse: Results from the

DSM-IV Field Trial for posttraumatic stress disorder. *Journal of Traumatic Stress, 10*(4), 539–55.

Rothbart, M. K., & Bates, J. E. (1998). Temperament. In W. Damon (Series Ed.) & N. Eisenberg (Vol. Ed.), *Handbook of child psychology: Vol. 3. Social, emotional, and personality development* (5th ed., pp. 105–76). New York: John Wiley & Sons, Inc.

Rutter, M. (1997). Clinical implications of attachment concepts: Retrospective and prospective. In L. Atkinson & K. Zucker (Eds.), *Attachment and psychopathology* (pp. 17–46). New York: Guilford Press.

Saylor, C., Swenson, C., Reynolds, S., & Taylor, M. (1999). The Pediatric Emotional Distress Scale: A brief screening measure for young children exposed to traumatic events. *Journal of Clinical Child Psychiatry, 28*(1), 70–81.

Scheeringa, M. S., & Zeanah, C. H. (1995). Symptom expression and trauma variables in children under 48 months of age. *Infant Mental Health Journal, 16,* 259–70.

Scheeringa, M. S., & Zeanah, C. H. (2005). *PTSD Semi-Structured Interview and Observational Record for Infants and Young Children,* Version 1.4. Semi-structured interview.

Scheeringa, M. S., Peebles, C. D., Cook, C. A., & Zeanah, C. H. (2001). Toward establishing procedural, criterion, and discriminant validity for PTSD in early childhood. *Journal of the American Academy of Child & Adolescent Psychiatry, 40*(1), 52–60.

Scheeringa, M. S., Zeanah, C. H., Myers, L., & Putnam, F. (2003). New findings on alternative criteria for PTSD in preschool children. *Journal of the American Academy of Child & Adolescent Psychiatry, 42*(5), 561–70.

Scheeringa, M. S., Zeanah, C. H., Myers, L., & Putnam, F. (2005). Predictive validity in a prospective follow-up of PTSD in preschool children. *Journal of the American Academy of Child & Adolescent Psychiatry, 44*(9), 899–906.

Schore, A. N. (2003). Early relational trauma, disorganized attachment, and the development of a predisposition to violence. In M. Solomon & D. J. Siegel (Eds.), *Healing trauma* (pp. 107–67). New York: W. W. Norton & Co.

Schwarz, E. D., & Kowalski, J. M. (1991). Malignant memories: PTSD in children and adults after a school shooting. *Journal of the American Academy of Child & Adolescent Psychiatry, 30*(6), 936–44.

Siegel, D. J. (2003). An interpersonal neurobiology of psychotherapy: The developing mind and the resolution of trauma. In M. Solomon & D. J. Siegel (Eds.), *Healing trauma* (pp. 1–56). New York: W. W. Norton & Co.

Stamm, B. H. (Ed.) (1996). *Measurement of stress, trauma and adaptation.* Lutherville, MD: Sidran Press.

Stein, P. T., & Kendall, J. (2004). *Psychological trauma and the developing brain: Neurologically based interventions for troubled children.* New York: Haworth Press.

Streeck-Fischer, A., & van der Kolk, B. A. (2000). Down will come baby, cradle and all: Diagnostic and therapeutic implications of chronic trauma on child development. *The Australian and New Zealand Journal of Psychiatry, 34*(6), 903–18.

Thomas, P. M. (2005). Dissociation and internal models of protection: Psychotherapy with child abuse survivors. *Psychotherapy: Theory, Research, Practice, Training, 42*(1), 20–36.

van der Kolk, B. A. (2003). Post-traumatic stress disorder and the nature of trauma. In M. Solomon & D. J. Siegel (Eds.), *Healing trauma* (pp. 168–95). New York: W. W. Norton & Co.

van der Kolk, B. & Courtois, C. (2005). Editorial comments: Complex developmental trauma. *Journal of Traumatic Stress, 18*(5), 385–8.

van der Kolk, B., Roth, S., Pelcovitz, D., Sunday, S., & Spinazzola, J. (2005). Disorders of extreme stress: The empirical foundation for a complex adaptation to trauma. *Journal of Traumatic Stress, 18*(5), 389–99.

Vila, G., Porche, L., & Mouren-Simeoni, M. (1999). An 18-month longitudinal study of posttraumatic disorders in children who were taken hostage in their school. *Psychosomatic Medicine, 61,* 746–54.

Webb, N. B. (Ed.) (2004). *Mass trauma, stress, and loss: Helping children and families cope.* New York: Guilford Press.

West, M., Adam, K., Spreng, S., & Rose, S. (2001). Attachment disorganization and dissociative symptoms in clinically treated adolescents. *Canadian Journal of Psychiatry, 46*(7), 627–31.

Westermeyer, J. (1987). Cultural factors in clinical assessment. *Journal of Consulting and Clinical Psychology, 55*(4), 471–8.

Westermeyer, J. (1990). Working with an interpreter in psychiatric assessment and treatment. *Journal of Nervous and Mental Disease, 178*(12), 745–9.

Wilson, J. P. (2004). PTSD and Complex PTSD. In J. P. Wilson & T. M. Keane (Eds.), *Assessing psychological trauma and PTSD* (2nd ed., pp. 7–44). New York: Guilford Press.

Wilson, J. P., & Keane, T. M. (Eds.) (1997). *Assessing psychological trauma and PTSD.* New York: Guilford Press.

Wilson, J. P., & Keane, T. M. (Eds.) (2004). *Assessing psychological trauma and PTSD* (2nd ed.). New York: Guilford Press.

Yates, T. M., Egeland, B., & Sroufe, A. (2003). Rethinking resilience: A developmental process perspective. In S. S. Luthar (Ed.), *Resilience and vulnerability: Adaptation in the context of childhood adversities* (pp. 243–66). New York: Cambridge University Press.

Yule, W., Udwin, O., & Bolton, D. (2002). Mass transportation disasters. In A. M. La Greca, W. K. Silverman, E. M. Vernberg, & M. C. Roberts (Eds.), *Helping children cope with disasters and terrorism* (pp. 223–39). Washington, DC: APA Press.

Chapter Two

Vulnerability and Resilience in Childhood Trauma and PTSD

Scott D. Cicero, Kate Nooner, and Raul Silva

Introduction

Trauma and its sequelae have been reported since the early twentieth century (for review, see Saigh & Bremner, 1999). The nomenclature of traumatic disturbance has evolved as knowledge has increased regarding the patterns of illness presentation. By 1980, Post-Traumatic Stress Disorder (PTSD) was officially recognized in the *Diagnostic and Statistical Manual of Mental Disorders – Third Edition* (*DSM-III*) (American Psychiatric Association (APA), 1980). Although it was not until the *DSM-III-R* (APA, 1987) that features specific to the developmental differences in children were included in the description of PTSD, early reports described psychological sequelae in children exposed to severe stressors, such as war and maltreatment (Bender & Blau, 1937; Bodman, 1941). Features such as avoidance, hyperarousal, and reexperiencing are chronicled in the reported cases and are very similar to current diagnostic criteria for PTSD.

Children and adolescents in today's society are increasingly exposed to a variety of environmental stressors. Whether domestic or community violence, terrorism, natural disasters or different forms of abuse and neglect, the myriad of stressors provides the substrate for the development of PTSD. *DSM-IV* criteria stipulate a cause-and-effect model or pathway between traumatic event exposure and the development of PTSD. However, only a fraction of children exposed to traumatic events go on to develop the disorder (Spitalny, 2004). This suggests that resilience and vulnerability factors may mediate the development of PTSD. Identifying these risk and protective factors can serve as a crucial step in establishing early and possibly preventive treatments.

Post-Traumatic Syndromes in Childhood and Adolescence: A Handbook of Research and Practice, First Edition.
Edited by Vittoria Ardino. © 2011 John Wiley & Sons, Ltd. Published 2011 by John Wiley & Sons, Ltd.

One approach to understanding resilience and vulnerability factors in the development of PTSD is to cluster them into a classification system by groups. Resilience and vulnerability characteristics in the development of PTSD are multifactorial, requiring an understanding of biological, environmental, psychological/developmental, and social variables. It is also critical to understand how previous experience, stressor-related features, and cognitive attributes contribute to the clinical presentation when working with these individuals.

Biological factors

The role of cognitive ability or intelligence in the development of PTSD has been examined in various studies. As with most topics in the field of mental health, current evidence reflects divergent findings. In a large-scale study by Tiet and colleagues (1998), various stressors were examined for their ability to impact upon functioning. In this study, higher IQs facilitated the adjustment process during stress. Silva and colleagues (2000) also examined the relationship between verbal IQ and the development of PTSD. In their sample, higher verbal IQs represented the most powerful resilience factor. Orr and Pittman (1999) postulated that decreased cognitive capacity may also mediate how individuals process a stressor. Conversely, Saigh (2002) analyzed a cohort of 24 subjects who ranged in age from seven to 17 years and determined that there were higher verbal IQs in those who developed PTSD versus the subjects who did not develop PTSD following serious stressors. The finding persisted even when the comparison was made to a non-clinical control group. There are numerous confounds in interpreting this relation, including issues related to potential brain damage that may occur with certain forms of physical abuse, the effect of early deprivation of some neglected children, and the emotional sequelae of developing PTSD. The importance of having pre-trauma status when studying the interaction between intelligence and stress in an effort to elucidate the mechanism of protection cannot be overstated.

A second biological factor associated with vulnerability to develop PTSD is gender. As in adults, while the rates of exposure to traumatic events are similar for males and females, girls develop PTSD more frequently (Brodsky & Lally, 2004; Elklit, 2002; Kessler et al., 1995; Kilpatrick et al., 2003; Reebye et al., 2000). However, this may not be a consistent finding for all forms of trauma (Breslau et al., 2004). While the likelihood of PTSD development in females is greater than that in males in the face of most forms of assaultive violence (e.g., mugging, shooting, stabbing), the rates associated with trauma such as rape are higher for males (Breslau et al., 2004). It should be noted that rates of PTSD development as a consequence of rape and other forms of sexual assault are greater for both genders than with other forms of trauma. In addition, the rates of rape are lower in males than in females, suggesting that further inquiry is warranted before drawing conclusions about differences in PTSD rates for males and females (Breslau et al., 2004).

For other forms of trauma, investigators such as Breslau and colleagues (2004) found a similar risk of developing PTSD in the two genders. This finding may not be so clear, however, and may be attributed to looking at numbers based on the sole occurrence of PTSD (non-comorbid PTSD). Kilpatrick and colleagues (2003) reported non-comorbid PTSD rates of 1.3% in male adolescents versus 1.5% in their female counterparts. However, when they examined the rates of overall PTSD (i.e., comorbid and non-comorbid), rates in females were nearly twice as high as those in males (6.3% vs. 3.7%, respectively). These findings suggest that in adolescent populations, it is clinically important to consider those cases with comorbid presentations, such as substance abuse, depression, and other pathology – presentations which may be more common than PTSD˜alone.

The gender disparity in developing PTSD has been noted by other authors as well. In a large community sample, Giaconia and colleagues (1995) reported that while 40% of their sample had been exposed to a serious trauma prior to adulthood, rates of developing PTSD were five times higher for females. Some authors (Fehon, Grilo, & Lipschitz, 2001) speculate that there may be a tendency for males to manifest violence in reaction to violent trauma, whereas girls may be more likely to develop internalizing symptoms of PTSD; however, Foy, Furrow, and McManus (Chapter 10) and Ardino (Chapter 11) reflect in this book about how trauma may lead to antisocial behavior across both genders. These gender differences in rates have been noted in settings such as inpatient (Lipschitz et al., 1999) and juvenile correctional (Cauffman et al., 1998). Inpatient female adolescents were twice as likely to develop PTSD as inpatient male adolescents, even when controlling for number and type of trauma; nearly identical findings emerged in the incarcerated adolescent population when female residents were compared to male residents with equivalent trauma histories. Gender differences may be more salient within certain samples, such as inpatients or inmates, than in the general population. The greater the number of studies that examine this observation, the more likely we are to understand its universality.

Environmental factors

Environmental factors can affect the development of PTSD. Theoretically, the development of PTSD requires exposure. The potential environment along with the consequent exposure to the trauma represent a serious risk for the development of this condition. As a result we include exposure within the framework of environmental factors. Exposure to high-index stressors has been noted to increase the risk of developing PTSD in youth (March, 1993). Kilpatrick and colleagues (1998) determined that individuals exposed to more high-index stressors were at greater peril of developing PTSD.

Stress, as it relates to poverty and social adversity, has been noted by investigators to contribute to the development of PTSD. Youth from the inner city who live in high-crime neighborhoods and experience community violence may represent a vulnerable population. Numerous studies have looked at features of stress and PTSD in the inner city. Fitzpatrick and Boldizar (1992) in one inner-city study reported that 70% of African-American youth were exposed to at least one *DSM-III* stressor. Silva and colleagues (2000) reported that 59% of their inner-city clinic sample were exposed to similar stressors. In the report by Fitzpatrick and Boldizar (1992), 27% of those exposed developed the required symptomatology to meet criteria for PTSD, as compared to 22% in the Silva and colleagues sample. The rates of developing PTSD in stress-exposed adolescents across heterogeneous demographic samples in other studies are surprisingly similar (Deykin & Buka, 1997; Giaconia et al., 1995).

Review of the literature has identified an array of stressors that could potentially induce PTSD. In 2000, Silva and colleagues explored how different traumas varied in their ability to produce PTSD in order to ascertain how children respond to different stressors. Full PTSD symptomatology developed at relatively similar rates for cohorts that experienced the three principal types of trauma (sexual abuse, physical abuse, and domestic violence). Since several children experienced multiple types of trauma, multiple regression analysis was used to identify the unique contribution of each of the three primary stressors to the severity of the disorder (defined as the number of PTSD diagnostic features present). Results showed that children who had witnessed domestic violence and those who had been physically abused developed statistically greater symptom severity than those experiencing sexual abuse. This finding is important because when children are exposed to more than one stressor, there may be some traumatic events that are more powerful than others at inducing more severe forms of PTSD. Also, this finding may support the notion that cumulative trauma sensitizes and creates a landscape where the effects of multiple traumatic events undermine resilience factors and increase the vulnerability of individuals to develop PTSD.

The relationship between type of trauma and development of PTSD has been explored by other authors as well. Various authors have reported that different forms of sexual assault, such as rape and sexual abuse, are more likely to yield PTSD when compared to other forms of trauma during adolescence (Breslau et al., 2004; Brodsky & Lally, 2004; Deters et al., 2006; Seedat et al., 2004; Sullivan et al., 2006). Sexual assault was uniformly seen as the most traumatic stressor yielding PTSD. In a study of American Indian adolescents, Deters and colleagues (2006) noted that sexual molestation was the strongest predictor of PTSD. Similarly, Breslau and colleagues (2004) reported that the highest rates of PTSD were for those adolescents who were sexually assaulted or raped, irrespective of gender. Seedat and colleagues (2004) reported double the rates of PTSD onset as a result of sexual abuse when compared to physical assault, witnessing violence, or experiencing a natural disaster. These reports corroborate the findings of Lipschitz and colleagues (1999) that more than 60% of adolescent inpatients who were sexually abused developed PTSD, as compared to 50% of those exposed to family violence and only 28% of those who were physically abused. In that sample, 91% of those who developed PTSD had experienced childhood sexual abuse, as compared to only 32% of those without PTSD.

Evidence continues to emerge that sexual trauma represents a salient pathway toward PTSD. Finkelhor and colleagues (2007a), studying children and adolescents, found that sexual victimization was an independent contributor to trauma symptomatology for those between the ages of 10 and 17. These authors found that adolescents who were sexually traumatized demonstrated an increased risk of revictimization when compared to other adolescents who experienced multiple different traumas. In 1999, Lipschitz and colleagues reported that 62% of adolescents in their sample ranked sexual abuse as their "most stressful" experience. This same sample rated stressors such as witnessing and experiencing community violence as being much less frequently the most stressful trauma they had experienced (13% and 16%, respectively). A conservative estimate would suggest that in at least 30% of adolescents with PTSD, it is related to sexual trauma (Avery, Massat, & Lundy, 2000; Breslau et al., 2004; Walker et al., 2004). These findings highlight the salience of sexual victimization as a pathway toward PTSD in adolescence.

While sexually traumatic events may play a prominent role in the genesis of PTSD, other forms of abuse and neglect also place the adolescent at increased risk. Increased severity of PTSD symptoms has been associated with both physical abuse and neglect (Naar-King et al., 2002; Sullivan et al., 2006; Wolfe et al., 2001). In at least one study the severity of the physical abuse predicted the onset of PTSD symptoms (Naar-King et al., 2002). PTSD is not the only negative outcome in physically abused adolescents as other behavioral and social difficulties may occur more frequently (Pelcovitz et al., 1994). The prevalence of PTSD sequelae in maltreated adolescents highlights the need for proper identification and services for exposed youth.

Psychological/developmental factors

Schnurr and colleagues (1993) studied military subjects using MMPI data collected as college freshmen some years before entering military service. The results demonstrated that some personality factors may contribute to the development of PTSD when compounded by wartime stress. Blanchard and colleagues (1996) examined a similar line of thought to determine if personality disorders and preexisting psychopathology served as risk factors for the development of PTSD. In this study, 132 patients who had been involved in motor vehicle accidents were followed over the ensuing year. Assessments took place within four months of the accidents and then again at six and 12 months afterwards. Initially, about 36% met criteria for PTSD, but it was the existence of Axis II illnesses before the accident that significantly predicted symptom persistence at one year in the patients who developed PTSD. The existence of other psychiatric disorders may also alter the expression of a trauma experience in certain individuals. Silva and colleagues (2000) demonstrated that preexisting anxiety was significantly related to developing PTSD. It seems that antecedent anxiety amplified the expression of PTSD.

Davidson and colleagues (1998) examined interactions between the development of PTSD and familial psychopathology. Two hundred and eighty-five family members of 81 female rape victims were studied. Analysis of the data revealed that family history of major depression predisposed the victim to develop PTSD. This finding supports the notion of familial resilience and vulnerability as risk factors for illness development and expression.

As for academic and behavioral functioning, La Greca and colleagues (1998) conducted a study with 92 children 15 months before Hurricane Andrew. The authors attempted to identify predictors of PTSD. A number of ratings from various sources had been obtained before the hurricane and were available to the authors. Symptoms of PTSD were studied at three and seven months following the event. At the three-month mark, PTSD severity was predicted by baseline ratings of inattention, anxiety, and academic skills. At seven months, only ratings of preexisting anxiety predicted worsening PTSD severity. These findings suggest that premorbid functioning, which in and of itself may be a marker of both resilience and vulnerability, as well as preexisting psychiatric conditions, are mediators of PTSD illness severity.

The finding of preexisting psychiatric illness as a risk factor for developing PTSD was shown in a study by North and colleagues (2002). This study was a three-year follow-up of over 100 subjects who survived a mass shooting. The group was evaluated at three time points for PTSD issues, focusing on details related to remission and delayed identification. Those with preexisting psychiatric illness were at increased risk for the onset of PTSD development.

In contrast to the discussion above, certain psychiatric diagnoses may in fact be less compatible with the development of PTSD symptoms. Silva and colleagues (2000) identified that individuals with externalizing presentations, specifically those with either conduct disorder or oppositional defiant disorder, were less likely to present with subthreshold forms of PTSD. It is possible that these subjects, by virtue of their propensity toward outwardly directed behavior, were less prone to present with the internalizing symptoms associated with PTSD. In trying to reconcile these findings, it is possible to conclude that trauma accentuates features of preexisting psychopathology in some children, and is consistent with the notion that the majority of individuals exposed to a stressor do not go on to develop PTSD.

In addition to personality and preexisting psychopathology, age has been shown to be a factor associated with the development of PTSD. Adolescence is a developmental period of heightened vulnerability to trauma and PTSD (Breslau et al., 2004; Khamis, 2005; Kilpatrick et al., 2003; Schaal & Elbert, 2006). Kilpatrick and colleagues (2003) found that age was the strongest predictor of increased risk for PTSD. Adolescents at the upper end of the age range

(16–17-year-olds) showed greater risk of experiencing trauma and subsequently developing PTSD than those at the lower end of the age range (12–13-year-olds). Breslau and colleagues (2004) reported similar findings in their epidemiologic investigation of trauma exposure and PTSD among urban youth, showing that rates of exposure to traumatic events and PTSD peak at 16–17 years of age, and that such elevated rates in late adolescence are significantly higher than those of early adolescence or early adulthood. The timing of trauma also proved to be important for adolescents, such that trauma occurring within the past year predicted outcomes in adolescence while trauma occurring earlier in childhood did not provide additional predictive power (Finkelhor et al., 2007a).

Adolescence is a highly stressful period of development in which the individual is faced with numerous challenges. The investigations of Kilpatrick and Breslau mirror the finding of van der Kolk (1985) that adolescents were at greater risk than adults for developing PTSD. Adolescence therefore can potentially represent a period of heightened vulnerability during which risk of experiencing trauma is particularly high, as compared to both childhood and adulthood, but the ability to adaptively cope with that trauma is particularly fragile.

Previous experience

The combined impact of stressors may, in and of itself, be a risk factor for the development of PTSD. In particular, long-term factors such as childhood abuse have been studied as possible predictors of the development of PTSD. Carlson and colleagues (2001) examined the role of stressors such as neglect, as well as sexual, physical, and other forms of abuse during childhood, as predictors of adult psychopathology in 178 inpatients. Their findings suggested that retraumatized patients may have an increased likelihood of redeveloping PTSD.

The relationship between cumulative trauma and development of PTSD has been well studied. Studies of adolescents have found a dose–response relationship between trauma history and PTSD severity, in which frequency of traumatic experience correlates with both early onset and increased severity of PTSD symptoms (Boney-McCoy & Finkelhor, 1996; Deters et al., 2006; Dixon, Howie, & Starling, 2005; Horowitz, Weine, & Jekel, 1995; Mghir et al., 1995).

Finkelhor and colleagues found that those adolescents who experienced multiple traumas had more serious victimizations, more non-trauma-related adversities, and higher rates of psychopathology, especially depression, in the year following victimization than other youth (Finkelhor et al., 2007a). Other authors have reported that PTSD and depression are highly comorbid among these youth (Kilpatrick et al., 2003). Finkelhor and colleagues (2007a) demonstrated that multiple episodes of victimization within a one-year period predicted PTSD symptomatology onset when controlling for victimization prior to that year.

Wartime trauma is a potent stressor with expected psychological sequelae. A study conducted by Thabet and Vostanis (1999) investigated the relationship between PTSD and trauma factors related to war in a sample of 239 children from Palestine. The number of traumas each child experienced was the greatest predictor of PTSD symptom severity. This finding highlights the compound and cumulative nature of multiple traumas with regard to the propensity to potentiate greater PTSD morbidity. Once again, previous trauma and multiple traumas must be issues that clinicians incorporate into their assessment, as individuals with these features represent a heightened risk for the development of PTSD.

Recent investigations of adolescents growing up in wartime environments have found a positive relationship between number of traumatic experiences and rates of PTSD (Lavi & Solomon, 2005; Schaal & Elbert, 2006). Related findings were seen in a study of American Indian adolescents, where experiencing six or more traumas was correlated with increased risk of developing PTSD (Deters et al., 2006). In this study, 20% of the overall sample reported experiencing more than six traumas, with nearly 40% of this subgroup meeting full PTSD criteria. In contrast, less than 3% of those experiencing five or fewer traumas met full criteria for PTSD.

That inner-city, predominantly minority youth are exposed to a greater number of traumatic stressors than middle-class youth residing in suburban or rural areas has been well documented (Boney-McCoy & Finkelhor, 1995; Gladstein, Rusonis, & Heald, 1992; Lipschitz et al., 2000; Tolan, Gorman-Smith, & Henry, 2006), with the most frequently named stressor being exposure to community violence. In their review of the literature, Lipschitz and colleagues (2000) reported that over 80% of inner-city adolescents witnessed physical assault, 40% had seen someone shot or stabbed, and almost 25% witnessed homicide. Domestic violence, or violence within the home, has been identified as the second most common traumatic stressor, with levels among inner-city households reported to be approximately six times the national average (Richters & Martinez, 1993). Studies of inner-city adolescent girls have reported domestic violence rates to be from 32% to 50% (Horowitz et al., 1995; Lipschitz et al., 1999; Lipschitz et al., 2000). Inner-city adolescents are much more likely to develop PTSD than their suburban or rural counterparts due to the cumulative effect of multiple traumatic stressors, such as witnessing domestic violence, witnessing community violence (e.g., gang activity), and death or illness of caretakers (e.g., AIDS, asthma) (Davidson & Fairbank, 1993; Kilpatrick et al., 1998). Illustrating this, a study of primarily white, working- and lower middle-class adolescents reported a 43% trauma exposure rate (Giaconia et al., 1995), while four studies of inner-city, predominantly minority youth reported exposure rates of 92% (Lipschitz et al., 2000), 93% (Lipschitz et al., 1999), 98% (Rosenthal, 2000), and 100% (Horowitz et al., 1995).

The experience of multiple traumas may be the norm for a large group of adolescents, particularly those living in the inner city. This finding highlights the need to address ongoing and/or multiple types of trauma, in an effort both to understand the relationship of trauma to possible outcomes and to develop preventive interventions. The increased propensity of inner-city youth to experience trauma puts them in dire need of resources. Interventions which equip the youth with adaptive skills for avoiding or better coping with traumatic incidents may be as important as teaching skills specific to a particular traumatic incident.

Since the connection between current reactions and past experience is not always evident, and because previous traumatic experience has been demonstrated to be a potent risk factor for PTSD, it is critical that a detailed trauma history be taken when working with children exposed to traumatic events. Detailed querying of past traumatic experiences and responses to those experiences is especially important for those children who have experienced a previous pathological response such as PTSD. A previous diagnosis of PTSD may suggest greater vulnerability or decreased resilience, and may place these children at higher risk for development of psychiatric disturbance. Gathering a detailed trauma history also has important clinical implications for treatment and management of symptoms.

Social factors

Both the Carlson group (2001) and Pine and Cohen (2002) emphasized that social support is an important factor to assess when working with children exposed to trauma. Pine and Cohen explain that the role of less than optimal familial and social support cannot be overestimated as a potential vulnerability factor for developing PTSD, highlighting that disruption of social and familial support plays an important role in the development of psychiatric disturbance. It is also important to note that the parental or caregiver response to a traumatic event has significant implications for the child's functioning and outcome after the traumatic exposure. The more distressed and impaired the coping style of the parents, the higher the risk for negative outcomes in children exposed to trauma.

The effect of family and community resources on the development of PTSD has been extensively studied. Intra- and extra-familial resources appear to serve a protective function against the effects of trauma, such that youth with fewer such resources are more likely to develop PTSD symptoms (Bal et al., 2005; Collishaw et al., 2007; Finkelhor, Ormrod & Turner, 2007b; Stewart et al., 2004). Recovery from PTSD has also been empirically shown to benefit from parental or caregiver support and positive attitudes (Breslau et al., 1991), as a result of which parental or caregiver involvement is routinely incorporated into treatment (see Cohen et al., 2000). Social support from parents, peers, and others has been shown to play a protective role both before and after a trauma (Collishaw et al., 2007; Lee et al., 2007; Maschi, 2006; Ozer & Weinstein, 2004), with a possible explanatory mechanism being that the presence of social support decreases the likelihood of exposure to repeated trauma (Finkelhor et al., 2007b). Unfortunately, parental support for many disadvantaged youth is compromised by parental substance abuse, untreated mental health problems, morbidity and early mortality, and inconsistent availability secondary to work-related or relationship-related changes in residence and incarceration (see Horowitz et al., 1995; Lee et al., 2007; Ozer, 2005).

Social support has been shown to increase resilience to adolescent and adult psychopathology (Collishaw et al., 2007). In a longitudinal study of 571 individuals from adolescence into adulthood, resilience in those experiencing physical or sexual abuse was correlated with perceived parental care and positive peer relationships during adolescence. Family support has also served to moderate the relationship between violence exposure and psychological functioning, and more so than other types of support, such as perceived school connection (Ozer, 2005). Whether social support is positive or negative appears to affect outcome: studies show that negative social support, or absence of social support, is consistently correlated with negative outcomes, such as higher rates of adolescent depression (Bal et al., 2005; Lee et al., 2007). Homeless youth, who frequently lack social support, are at greater risk for trauma and PTSD than their counterparts who reside with caregivers (Stewart et al., 2004). In adolescents who are HIV-affected, negative social support was linked to higher rates of depression, lower self-esteem, and conduct problems (Lee et al., 2007). The effect of positive social support, while perhaps less clear, may lie in its ability to build resilience among adolescents who have experienced trauma (Maschi, 2006; Ozer & Weinstein, 2004), and perhaps prevent trauma victims from becoming perpetrators (Maschi, Bradley, & Morgen, 2008).

While social support has been shown to be important in mediating outcome, whether or not a youth receives positive or negative social support may itself depend upon the type of trauma experienced. Youths who are sexually assaulted may be blamed or seen as having "caused" the trauma, producing stigma, shame, and heightened risk for negative outcomes (Charuvastra & Cloitre, 2008). Youths who survive a natural disaster, in contrast, are more likely to be seen as "survivors" and receive positive support, thereby fostering positive self-esteem and possibly reducing the likelihood of negative outcomes (Finkelhor et al., 2007b). Clearly, the impact of positive versus negative social support and the linkage between type of trauma and social support merit further study, particularly if social support is to be targeted in trauma intervention.

Other stressor-related features

Johnson and colleagues (2001) attempted to define which characteristics of a stressor may be related to the development of PTSD in survivors of child sexual abuse. This study consisted of 89 females who were sexually abused as children. Correlational analyses revealed that a number of abuse features were significantly related to the development of PTSD, namely dissociation around the time of the abuse, the subject's feelings that she would be killed, and the victim suffering an injury.

The impact of dissociation as a predisposing factor was also examined by Dancu and colleagues (1996) in another sample of 158 adult females who were criminally assaulted or raped. In this study, the authors employed the Dissociative Experiences Scale as the measure of this construct. The results suggested that those patients who dissociate might be at increased risk for developing PTSD even with different types of stressors. Individuals in their sample who reported being sexually abused during childhood were significantly more likely to dissociate. In another study, Bernat and colleagues (1998) examined the relation between developing post-traumatic stress symptoms and peri-traumatic factors. The sample consisted of 937 undergraduate students, more than 70% of whom were in the first two years of college. In this sample, slightly less than 70% experienced what was deemed a traumatic event. Of this cohort, slightly more than 10% developed complete PTSD criteria. The authors described that negative emotions, dissociation, and the fear that they would be killed all predicted PTSD development.

Following Hurricane Andrew, LaGreca and colleagues (1996) looked at symptoms of PTSD in a large cohort of students. They were reevaluated at 3, 7, and 10 months after the index event. The authors examined numerous variables to predict those who would develop more serious forms of PTSD, including exposure to traumatic events during and after the disaster, demographic characteristics, features related to social support, major life stressors during the ensuing 10 months, and coping styles. The ratings at seven months revealed that children who felt their life was at risk and children with greater levels of disruption had greater PTSD severity.

In each of the reports described, the fear of loss of life constituted a substantial risk factor for the development of PTSD. These findings not only relate to the intrinsic factors associated with the stressor itself but also echo the findings of other studies, where the disruption of social support and the sense of threat to bodily integrity are significant individual risk factors for increased PTSD symptom severity.

In a large-scale study conducted by March and colleagues (1997), data were collected on more than 1,000 children nine months after an industrial fire. The study aimed to investigate the association between PTSD development and certain factors. Children's ages ranged from 10 to 16 years old. A self-report scale was used to assess trauma-related symptomatology. Approximately 12% of this sample met criteria for PTSD. Direct and indirect aspects of degree of exposure were strong predictors of PTSD. This is also consistent with the notion that the greater the dose and duration of traumatic exposure, the higher the risk of developing PTSD. Additionally, subjective lack of self-attributed personal efficacy predicted the development of post-traumatic stress symptoms. Here the issue of self-esteem seems to once again resonate as a resilience feature in the child. Personal efficacy can also relate to the sense of helplessness that can ensue with the threat of personal injury/damage to bodily integrity, as well as to avoidance phenomena.

Saxe and colleagues (2001) studied the impact of morphine administered for acute burns. They studied the course of PTSD six months post-discharge in a sample of 24 children. A meaningful correlation was observed between PTSD ratings and the dose of morphine. Higher doses of the agent were associated with fewer PTSD symptoms, leading the authors to postulate that acute treatment with morphine can secondarily prevent PTSD. At the very least, such research suggests that certain agents administered for physical symptoms might simultaneously attenuate PTSD symptomatology, thus providing a potentially powerful tool to clinicians for diminishing morbidity in those at high risk.

Trauma-related cognitive attributions

Mannarino and Cohen (1996a, 1996b) examined predictors of symptom development in a group of girls who had been sexually abused. Measures were conducted at the time the abuse was disclosed, and 12 months later. The authors utilized the Children's Attributions and Perception Scale, which incorporates items reflecting self-blame and decreased trust. Higher scores predicted more severe presentations at each rating period. The finding of increased self-blame and decreased trust in subjects exposed to trauma suggests a link between stress and increased vulnerability to behavioral illness. The internalization of trauma-related distortions, which is not uncommon in PTSD sufferers, and the persistence of these distortions are also associated with poor outcomes and greater illness severity.

Dougall and colleagues (2001) explored factors related to resilience, including psychosocial variables such as coping through wishful thinking and the sense of loss of control. The sample included individuals injured during motor vehicle accidents. The subjects were assessed at one month, six months, and one year after the accidents. Wishful thinking was a protective factor which correlated with increased resilience and distinguished those that developed PTSD from those that did not. Within the avoidance symptom cluster for PTSD, a foreshortened sense of future and detachment from others are important clinical features that stand contrary to the characteristics of optimism and trust. Lack of trust can also be interpreted as being related to the hypervigilance that is part of the increased arousal criteria. From these studies one can conclude that characteristics such as trust, optimism, and lack of guilt are positive and protective attributes that should be queried as potential indicators of resilience when assessing children who have been exposed to trauma.

Conclusions

Irrespective of the type of trauma, the likelihood that a child in today's society will be exposed to some type of trauma has increased. Certain children may be deeply affected by their trauma, whereas others emerge virtually unscathed.

This chapter has highlighted the resilience and vulnerability factors that may play a role in a child's reaction to trauma.

A child's cognition, gender, and age may exert a significant impact upon his/her experience of traumatic stress, as may the child's prior trauma history, the type and specific characteristics of the trauma itself, and the child's psychological makeup. Importantly, an individual's perception of his/her trauma has a large effect on the development and severity of PTSD symptomatology. Features such as feelings of guilt, helplessness, pessimism, and reduced trust are not highly adaptive, and may increase the likelihood of developing PTSD. When the opportunity for a fight-or-flight response is curtailed, the response of fright may be central to developing PTSD. This is one way of conceptualizing the origins of PTSD. It should be kept in mind that children are more prone than adults to feeling helpless in response to trauma. They are also likely to be more helpless during a traumatic event, both physically and emotionally, due to their limited development and maturity. Ultimately, beyond the individual's perception of the trauma, the manner in which he or she copes during the trauma is important as well.

Dissociation during the trauma may predispose the individual to develop PTSD, and those with prior histories of child abuse may be more likely to demonstrate dissociation as a coping style. Understanding the implication of preexisting psychopathology has proven vital in identifying who may develop PTSD. The presence of certain diagnoses appears to afford increased vulnerability to PTSD while other illnesses may serve as resilience factors. Internalizing disorders such as anxiety and depression may increase the chance of developing PTSD, while externalizing disorders may protect from developing PTSD. One way to conceptualize externalizing and internalizing disorders vis-à-vis PTSD symptoms is to situate these disorders respectively within the schema of fight-or-flight and fright. In this framework, the positive effects of a fight-or-flight reaction, as is consistent with externalizing behaviors, and the negative effects of a fright reaction, consistent with internalizing behaviors, might shed light on individual vulnerabilities and resiliencies as they relate to coping mechanisms. These individual vulnerabilities and resiliencies are, in turn, likely mediated by external factors, such as social supports and the availability of other family and community resources for coping with the traumatic event.

Although we have made significant strides in our understanding of PTSD, additional research is needed in an effort to further elucidate the roles of biological, environmental, psychological/developmental, and social resilience and vulnerability factors, as well as the impact of previous experience, specific stressor-related features, and cognitive attributions, in the development of this illness. The importance of such research cannot be overstated, as increased understanding of the vulnerability factors contributing to PTSD, or the resilience factors protecting from PTSD, may provide additional opportunity for identifying those at risk and then developing early and possibly preventive interventions.

References

American Psychiatric Association (APA) (1980). *Diagnostic and Statistical Manual of Mental Disorders* (3rd ed.) (*DSM-III*). Washington, DC: Author.

American Psychiatric Association (APA) (1987). *Diagnostic and Statistical Manual of Mental Disorders* (3rd ed.-Rev.) (*DSM-III-R*). Washington, DC: Author.

Avery, L., Massat, C. R., & Lundy, M. (2000). Posttraumatic stress and mental health functioning of sexually abused children: *Child and Adolescent Social Work Journal, 17,* 19–34.

Bal, S., De Bourdeaudhuij, I., Crombez, G., & Van Oost, P. (2005). Predictors of trauma symptomatology in sexually abused adolescents: a six-month follow-up study. *Journal of Interpersonal Violence, 20,* 1390–405.

Bender, L., & Blau, A. (1937). The reaction of children to sexual relations with adults. *American Journal of Orthopsychiatry, 7,* 500–18.

Bernat, J. A., Ronfeldt, H. M., Calhoun, K. S., & Arias, I. (1998). Prevalence of traumatic events and peritraumatic predictors of posttraumatic stress symptoms in a nonclinical sample of college students, *Journal of Traumatic Stress, 11*(4), 645–64.

Blanchard, E. B., Hickling, E. J., Barton, K. A. et al. (1996). One-year prospective follow-up of motor vehicle accident victims. *Journal of Behaviour Research and Therapy, 34*(10), 775–86.

Bodman, F. (1941). War conditions and the mental health of the child. *British Medical Journal, 11,* 486–8.

Boney-McCoy, S., & Finkelhor, D. (1995). Prior victimization: a risk factor for child sexual abuse and for PTSD-related symptomatology among sexually abused youth. *Child Abuse & Neglect, 19*(12), 1401–21.

Boney-McCoy, S., & Finkelhor, D. (1996). Is youth victimization related to trauma symptoms and depression after controlling for prior symptoms and family relationships? A longitudinal, prospective study. *Journal of Consulting & Clinical Psychology, 64*(6), 1406–16.

Breslau, N., Davis, G. C., Andreski, P., & Peterson, E. (1991). Traumatic events and posttraumatic stress disorder in an urban population of young adults. *Archives of General Psychiatry, 48,* 216–22.

Breslau, N., Wilcox, H. C., Storr, C. L., Lucia, V. C., & Anthony, J. C. (2004). Trauma exposure and posttraumatic stress disorder: a study of youths in urban America. *Journal of Urban Health, 81,* 530–44.

Brodsky, B. A., & Lally, S. J. (2004). Prevalence of trauma, PTSD, and dissociation in court-referred adolescents. *Journal of Interpersonal Violence, 19*(7), 801–14.

Carlson, E. B., Dalenberg, C., Armstrong, J. et al. (2001). Multivariate prediction of posttraumatic symptoms in psychiatric inpatients. *Journal of Traumatic Stress, 14*(3), 549–67.

Cauffman, E., Feldman, S. S., Waterman, J., & Steiner, H. (1998). Posttraumatic stress disorder among female juvenile offenders. *Journal of the American Academy of Child & Adolescent Psychiatry, 37,* 1209–16.

Charuvastra, A., & Cloitre, M. (2008). Social bonds and posttraumatic stress disorder. *Annual Review of Psychology, 59,* 301–28.

Cohen, J. A., Mannarino, A. P., Berliner, L., & Deblinger, E. (2000). Trauma-focused cognitive behavioral therapy for children and adolescents: an empirical update. *Journal of Interpersonal Violence, 15*, 1202–23.

Collishaw, S., Pickles, A., Messer, J. et al. (2007). Resilience to adult psychopathology following childhood maltreatment: evidence from a community sample. *Child Abuse & Neglect, 31*, 211–29.

Dancu, C. V., Riggs, D. S., Hearst-Ikeda, D., Shoyer, B. G., & Foa, E. B. (1996). Dissociative experiences and posttraumatic stress disorder among female victims of criminal assault and rape. *Journal of Traumatic Stress, 9*(2), 253–67.

Davidson, J. R., Tupler, L. A., Wilson, W. H., & Connor, K. M. (1998). A family study of chronic post-traumatic stress disorder following rape trauma. *Journal of Psychiatric Research, 32*(5), 301–9.

Davidson, J. R. T., & Fairbank, J. A. (1993). The epidemiology of posttraumatic stress disorder. In J. R. T. Davidson & E. Foa (Eds.), *Posttraumatic stress disorder: DSM-IV and beyond* (pp. 147–69). Washington, DC: American Psychiatric Press.

Deters, P. B., Novins, D. K., Fickenscher, A., & Beals, J. (2006). Trauma and posttraumatic stress disorder symptomatology: patterns among American Indian adolescents in substance abuse treatment. *American Journal of Orthopsychiatry, 76*(3), 335–45.

Deykin, E. Y., & Buka, S. L. (1997). Prevalence and risk factors for posttraumatic stress disorder among chemically dependent adolescents. *The American Journal of Psychiatry, 154*(6), 752–7.

Dixon, A., Howie, P., & Starling, J. (2005). Trauma exposure, posttraumatic stress, and psychiatric comorbidity in female juvenile offenders. *Journal of the American Academy of Child & Adolescent Psychiatry, 44*, 798–806.

Dougall, A. L., Ursano, R. J., Posluszny, D. M., Fullerton, C. S., & Baum, A. (2001). Predictors of posttraumatic stress among victims of motor vehicle accidents. *Psychosomatic Medicine, 63*(3), 402–11.

Elklit, A. (2002). Victimization and PTSD in a Danish national youth probability sample. *Journal of the American Academy of Child & Adolescent Psychiatry, 41*, 174–81.

Fehon, D. C., Grilo, C. M., & Lipschitz, D. S. (2001). Correlates of community violence exposure in hospitalized adolescents. *Comprehensive Psychiatry, 42*, 283–90.

Finkelhor, D., Ormrod, R. K., & Turner, H. A. (2007a). Polyvictimization and trauma in a national longitudinal cohort. *Development and Psychopathology, 19*, 149–66.

Finkelhor, D., Ormrod, R. K., & Turner, H. A. (2007b). Re-victimization patterns in a national longitudinal sample of children and youth. *Child Abuse & Neglect, 31*(5), 479–502.

Fitzpatrick, K. M., & Boldizar, J. P. (1992). The prevalence and consequences of exposure to violence among African-American youth. *Journal of the American Academy of Child & Adolescent Psychiatry, 32*(2), 424–30.

Giaconia, R. M., Reinherz, H. Z., Silverman, A. B. et al. (1995). Traumas and posttraumatic stress disorder in a community population of older adolescents. *Journal of the American Academy of Child & Adolescent Psychiatry, 34*(10), 1369–80.

Gladstein, J., Rusonis, E. J. S., & Heald, F. P. (1992). A comparison of inner-city and upper middle-class youths' exposure to violence. *Journal of Adolescent Health, 13*, 275–80.

Horowitz, K., Weine, S., & Jekel J. (1995). PTSD symptoms in urban adolescent girls: compounded community trauma. *Journal of the American Academy of Child & Adolescent Psychiatry, 34,* 1353–61.

Johnson, D. M., Pike, J. L., & Chard, K. M. (2001). Factors predicting PTSD, depression, and dissociative severity in female treatment-seeking childhood sexual abuse survivors. *Child Abuse & Neglect, 25*(1), 179–98.

Kessler, R. C., Sonnega, A., Bromet, E., Hughes, M., & Nelson, C. B. (1995). Post-traumatic stress disorder in the national comorbidity survey. *Archives of General Psychiatry, 52,* 1048–60.

Khamis, V. (2005). Post-traumatic stress disorder among school age Palestinian children. *Child Abuse & Neglect, 29,* 81–95.

Kilpatrick, D.G., Resnick, H. S., Saunders, B. E., & Best, C. L. (1998). Rape, other violence against women and posttraumatic stress disorder: Critical issues in assessing the adversity-stress psychopathology relationship. In B. P. Dohrenwend (Ed.), *Adversity, stress, and psychopathology* (pp. 161–76). New York: Oxford University Press.

Kilpatrick, D. G., Ruggiero, K. J., Acierno, R. et al. (2003). Violence and risk of PTSD, major depression, substance abuse/dependence, and comorbidity: Results from the National Survey of Adolescents. *Journal of Consulting & Clinical Psychology, 71,* 692–700.

La Greca, A., Silverman, W. K., Vernberg, E. M., & Prinstein, M. J. (1996). Symptoms of posttraumatic stress in children after Hurricane Andrew: A prospective study. *Journal of Consulting and Clinical Psychology, 64*(4), 712–23.

La Greca, A. M., Silverman, W. K., & Wasserstein, S. B. (1998). Children's predisaster functioning as a predictor of posttraumatic stress following Hurricane Andrew. *Journal of Consulting and Clinical Psychology, 66*(6), 883–92.

Lavi, T., & Solomon, Z. (2005). Palestinian youth of the intifada: PTSD and future orientation. *Journal of the American Academy of Child & Adolescent Psychiatry, 44,* 1176–83.

Lee, S. J., Detels, R., Rotheram-Borus, M. J., & Duan, N. (2007). The effect of social support on mental and behavioral outcomes among adolescents with parents with HIV/AIDS. *American Journal of Public Health, 97,* 1820–6.

Lipschitz, D. S., Grilo, C. M., Fehon, D., McGlashan, T. M., & Southwick, S. M. (2000). Gender differences in the associations between posttraumatic stress symptoms and problematic substance use in psychiatric inpatient adolescents. *Journal of Nervous & Mental Disease, 188,* 349–56.

Lipschitz, D. S., Winegar, R. K., Hartnick, E., Foote, B., & Southwick, S. M. (1999). Posttraumatic stress disorder in hospitalized adolescents: psychiatric comorbidity and clinical correlates. *Journal of the American Academy of Child & Adolescent Psychiatry, 38,* 385–92.

Mannarino, A. P., & Cohen, J. A. (1996a). Abused related attributions and perceptions, general attributions and locus of control in sexually abused girls. *Journal of Interpersonal Violence, 11,* 162–80.

Mannarino, A. P., & Cohen, J. A. (1996b). A follow-up study of factors which mediate the development of psychological symptomatology in sexually abused girls. *Child Maltreatment, 1*(3), 246–60.

March, J. (1993). What constitutes a stressor? The "Criterion A" issue. In J. Davidson & E. Foa (Eds.), *Posttraumatic stress disorder: DSM-IV and beyond* (pp. 37–54). Washington, DC: American Psychiatric Press.

March, J. S., Amaya-Jackson, L., Terry, R., & Costanzo, P. (1997). Posttraumatic symptomatology in children and adolescents after an industrial fire. *Journal of the American Academy of Child & Adolescent Psychiatry, 36*(8), 1080–8.

Maschi, T. (2006). Trauma and delinquent behavior among males: the moderating role of social support. *Stress, Trauma, and Crisis: An International Journal, 9*(1), 45–72.

Maschi, T., Bradley, C., & Morgen, K. (2008). Unraveling the link between trauma and delinquency: the mediating role of negative affect and delinquent peer exposure. *Youth Violence and Juvenile Justice, 6*(2), 136–57.

Mghir, R., Freed, W., Raskin, A., & Katon, W. (1995). Depression and posttraumatic stress disorder among a community sample of adolescent and young adult Afghan refugees. *Journal of Nervous & Mental Disease, 183*(1), 24–30.

Naar-King, S., Silvern, L., Ryan, V., & Sebring, D. (2002). Type and severity of abuse as predictors of psychiatric symptoms in adolescence. *Journal of Family Violence, 17*, 133–49.

North, C. S., Tivis, L., McMillen, J. C. et al. (2002). Coping, functioning, and adjustment of rescue workers after the Oklahoma City bombing. *Journal of Traumatic Stress, 15*(3), 171–5.

Orr, S. P., & Pitman, R. K. (1999). Neurocognitive risk factors for PTSD. In R. Yehuda (Ed.), *Risk factors for posttraumatic stress disorder* (pp. 125–41). Washington, DC: American Psychiatric Press.

Ozer, E. J. (2005). The impact of violence on urban adolescents: longitudinal effects of perceived school connection and family support. *Journal of Adolescent Research, 20*, 167–92.

Ozer, E. J., & Weinsten, R. S. (2004). Urban adolescents' exposure to community violence: the role of support, school safety, and social constraints in a school-based sample of boys and girls. *Journal of Clinical Child & Adolescent Psychology, 33*, 463–76.

Pelcovitz, D., Kaplan, S., Goldenberg, B. et al. (1994). Posttraumatic stress disorder in physically abused adolescents. *Journal of the American Academy of Child & Adolescent Psychiatry, 33*, 305–12.

Pine, D. S., & Cohen, J. A. (2002). Trauma in children and adolescents: Risk and treatment of psychiatric sequelae. *Biological Psychiatry, 51*(7), 519–31.

Reebye, P., Moretti, M. M., Wiebe, V. J., & Lessard, J. C., (2000). Symptoms of posttraumatic stress disorder in adolescents with conduct disorder: sex differences and onset patterns. *Canadian Journal of Psychiatry, 45*, 746–51.

Richters, J. E., & Martinez, P. (1993). The NIMH community violence project: I. Children as victims of and witnesses to violence. *Psychiatry, 56*, 7–21.

Rosenthal, B. S. (2000). Exposure to community violence in adolescence: trauma symptoms. *Adolescence, 35*, 271–84.

Saigh, P. A. (2000, October). Intellectual functioning of traumatized and non-traumatized inner-city youth. In H. Steiner (Chair), *Current Perspectives on*

Child–Adolescent PTSD Research. Symposium conducted at the 47th Annual Meeting of the American Academy of Child and Adolescent Psychiatry, New York.

Saigh, P. A., & Bremner, D. (1999). The history of posttraumatic stress disorder. In P. A. Saigh & J. D. Bremner (Eds.), *Posttraumatic stress disorder: A comprehensive text* (pp. 1–17). Boston, MA: Allyn & Bacon.

Saxe, G., Stoddard, F., Courtney, D. et al. (2001). Relationship between acute morphine and the course of PTSD in children with burns. *Journal of the American Academy of Child & Adolescent Psychiatry, 40*(8), 915–21.

Schaal, S., & Elbert, T. (2006). Ten years after the genocide: Trauma confrontation and posttraumatic stress in Rwandan adolescents. *Journal of Traumatic Stress, 19*, 95–105.

Schnurr, P. P., Friedman, M. J., & Rosenberg, S. D. (1993). Premilitary MMPI scores as predictors of combat-related PTSD symptoms. *The American Journal of Psychiatry, 150*(3), 479–83.

Seedat, S., Nyamai, C., Njenga, F., Vythilingum, B., & Stein, D. J. (2004). Trauma exposure and post-traumatic stress symptoms in urban African schools. Survey in Cape Town and Nairobi. *The British Journal of Psychiatry, 184*, 169–75.

Silva, R. R., Alpert, M., Munoz, D. M. et al. (2000). Posttraumatic stress disorder: stress and vulnerability in children and adolescents. *The American Journal of Psychiatry, 157*(8), 1229–35.

Spitalny, K. (2004). Clinical findings regarding PTSD in children and adolescents. In R. R. Silva (Ed.), *Posttraumatic stress disorders in children and adolescents* (pp. 141–62). New York: W. W. Norton & Co.

Stewart, S. H., Mitchell, T. L., Wright, K. D., & Loba, P. (2004). The relations of PTSD symptoms to alcohol use and coping drinking in volunteers who responded to the Swissair Flight 111 airline disaster. *Journal of Anxiety Disorders, 18*, 51–68.

Sullivan, T. P., Fehon, D. C., Andres-Hyman, R. C., Lipschitz, D. S., & Grilo, C. M. (2006). Differential relationships of childhood abuse and neglect subtypes to PTSD symptom clusters among adolescent inpatients. *Journal of Traumatic Stress, 19*, 229–39.

Thabet, A. A., & Vostanis, P. (1999). Post-traumatic stress reactions in children of war. *Journal of Child Psychology and Psychiatry and Allied Disciplines, 40*(3), 385–91.

Tiet, Q., Bird, H. R., Davies, M. et al. (1998). Adverse life events and resilience. *Journal of the American Academy of Child & Adolescent Psychiatry, 37*, 1191–200.

Tolan, P., Gorman-Smith, D., & Henry, D. (2006). Family violence. *Annual Review of Psychology, 57*, 557–83.

van der Kolk, B.A. (1985). Adolescent vulnerability to post-traumatic stress disorder. *Psychiatry: Journal for the Study of Interpersonal Processes, 48*, 365–70.

Walker, J. L., Carey, P. D., Mohr, N., Stein, D. J., & Seedat, S. (2004). Gender differences in the prevalence of childhood sexual abuse and in the development of pediatric PTSD. *Archives of Women's Mental Health, 7*, 111–21.

Wolfe, D. A., Scott, K. L., Wekerle, C., & Pittman, A. L. (2001). Child maltreatment: risk of adjustment problems and dating violence in adolescence. *Journal of the American Academy of Child & Adolescent Psychiatry, 40*, 282–89.

Part II

Context-Specific Reactions to Trauma

Chapter Three

The Impact of Lower Magnitude Stressors on Child and Adolescent Development: The Family Context

Don Catherall

Introduction

Child abuse and neglect are the most commonly identified internal family stressors affecting children (see Chapter 2 for a discussion on the impact of other factors). However, many other kinds of internal family stressors can have dire consequences for children. These other events are generally lower magnitude traumatic stressors that do not qualify as Criterion A stressors for the PTSD diagnosis. Additionally, these lower magnitude stressors often manifest their influence indirectly by way of mediating variables that may make the stressors' impact less obvious. This chapter will identify some of the less obvious ways in which lower-magnitude family stressors can have a deleterious impact on the development of children and adolescents.

Small t and large T traumas

The stressors that impact family members can be viewed on a continuum from mild to catastrophic. Within the trauma field, we sometimes refer to these stressors as small t traumas and large T traumas. Large T traumas are major, life-threatening events that satisfy Criterion A of the diagnosis of PTSD. The category of small t traumas refers to events that are also life changing but do not qualify for the stressor criterion of PTSD or acute stress disorder. Included in the small t trauma category are events like divorce, illness, dislocation, and

Post-Traumatic Syndromes in Childhood and Adolescence: A Handbook of Research and Practice, First Edition.
Edited by Vittoria Ardino. © 2011 John Wiley & Sons, Ltd. Published 2011 by John Wiley & Sons, Ltd.

family disruptions such as severe marital problems or cut-offs from extended family. It is important to look at these lower magnitude stressors because they occur so frequently. In a large longitudinal study conducted in North Carolina, about one quarter of children and adolescents had been exposed to a large T stressor in their first 16 years, whereas one third had been exposed to a small t stressor within the previous three months (Costello et al., 2002).

What small t and large T traumas have in common is that they each can severely disrupt the appropriate caretaking of children and adolescents in the family. However, they often differ in the way in which the effects are transmitted among family members, including children.

Secondary traumatization

Small t traumas affect children either (a) directly, in the form of whole family events (e.g., divorce, dislocation) or (b) indirectly, by making parents/caretakers inaccessible (e.g., a grieving or ill parent). In either case, the event is subjectively traumatic for the child because caretaking is disrupted. We generally define the path of influence as indirect when a large T trauma occurs to another family member – the child (or adolescent) is considered to acquire his or her own trauma symptoms as a result of contact with the trauma survivor rather than directly from the trauma. Even though the route is indirect, typical post-traumatic symptoms that reflect the underlying issues of reexperiencing, avoidance, numbing or hyperarousal are likely, though children tend to manifest a variety of other symptoms as well, including developmental regressions.

The concept of *secondary traumatization* refers to the contagion factor – traumatized individuals can infect their loved ones, who become secondarily traumatized (Figley, 1995). The mechanism for transmission of these traumatic effects was at first unclear, but it now appears that children acquire these effects in a different fashion from most adults (Catherall, 2004).

Research conducted in Israel suggests that the primary mechanism of transmission between spouses is living with the traumatized partner's symptoms of anger, paranoia, and hostility (Amir & Lev-Wiesel, 2004). The spouse absorbs the impact of these symptoms more than anyone else in the family (Whiffen & Oliver, 2004). The non-traumatized spouse's symptomatic experience correlates with the extent of the anger, paranoia, and hostility in the traumatized spouse. Living with a hostile partner is bad for one's health.

The mechanism of transmission for children and adolescents appears to be different from that of spouses. Like the spouses, children and adolescents are affected by post-traumatic symptoms in a parent – especially in the mother – and can develop distinct post-traumatic symptoms of their own (Ostrowski, Christopher, & Delahanty, 2007). However, it appears that the mechanism of transmission among children includes processes of identification and learning. Children and adolescents of trauma survivors typically identify with their parents' traumatic experience, which often produces reliving and avoidance symptoms in the children (Rowland-Klein, 2004). Amazingly, this can occur even when the children have never heard their parents' stories about their traumatic experiences. Ten years ago, Anna Baranowsky and her colleagues noted that the children of Holocaust survivors are affected by the parents either obsessively retelling their stories or by an all-consuming silence (Baranowsky et al., 1998).

Additionally, children are exposed to their parents' coping styles and may learn maladaptive coping mechanisms.

The family's job is to protect and nurture

Possibly the most important reason for the evolutionary development of the family as a social unit is to provide a safe, facilitative environment for children and adolescents to develop into adulthood. Any stressor event that obstructs appropriate caretaking and nurturing will interfere with the development of the children and adolescents in the family, effectively disrupting the primary function of the family – to protect and nurture the family members (Catherall, 1997).

There are several kinds of traumatic events that occur both within families and which occur externally and impact families. In most cases, events that traumatize parents or other family members will affect the children and adolescents in the family (Pine & Cohen, 2002; Putnam, 1996; Rojas & Pappagallo, 2004; Stoppelbein & Greening, 2000). One exception was among children affected by Hurricane Andrew: The children's symptoms were not significantly related to the parents' PTSD symptomatology (Vincent, 1998). There is also evidence that there is a greater impact on young children when their mothers are affected than when any other family member is affected (Laor, Wolmer, & Cohen, 2001).

Low magnitude traumatic events, such as mental and physical illness of parents, parental substance abuse (especially alcoholism), poverty, divorce, domestic violence, and excessive parental conflict (even if nonviolent), place children at risk either by making parents unavailable or through destructive acts by parents. In either case, the appropriate caretaking of vulnerable family members is disrupted.

Family stressors

Family stressors can be categorized according to those that originate within the family and those that originate outside of the family. Of course, even this seemingly obvious distinction is not always so clear, since many internal family stressors (e.g., alcoholism) are reactions to earlier external stressors (e.g., trauma). Nevertheless, it is useful to pursue this distinction because it makes a considerable difference to the family members' ability to work together to resolve the impact of the stressor.

External stressors

Stressors that originate outside the family take a variety of forms. They include war, mass disaster, economic misfortune, dislocation, crime, and accident. Stressors involving illness might be viewed as external at times, though mental illness is usually considered to be an internal stressor. The avenue through which external family stressors manifest their impact on the family is largely determined by the family's coping style. This is where the external stressor interacts with internal family variables. Families that cope adaptively and make good use of their resources are at a clear advantage.

The family's capacity to cope effectively starts with the adults' appraisal of the external stressor. Is the stressor controllable? Adults must make this determination and then help children use the appropriate coping style. If the stressor is controllable, then the adults must utilize problem-focused coping to manage the stressor event. But if the stressor is not controllable, then problem-oriented coping only serves to increase the children's anxiety. Instead, adults must help children engage in emotion-focused coping when the stressor is not controllable (Catherall, 2005).

For example, consider the coping required in dealing with a hurricane. Prior to the hurricane's arrival, there are controllable factors, such as boarding windows, storing provisions or even fleeing the vicinity. But once the hurricane has arrived, there is little that can be done except to sit it out in a protected building. At that point, the adults must be able to engage the children and adolescents in emotion-focused coping, such as reading, talking, and playing games. To try to fight the hurricane in some fashion would only make children fearful that they are not safe.

Researchers in Israel studied the impact of uncontrollable stressors on children during the first Gulf War (Weisenberg et al., 1993). At that time, the civilian populace was subject to Scud missile attacks, and there was concern that the missiles might contain poisonous gas. So Israeli families used plastic sheeting and duct tape to seal off a room in their homes where they would go during the attacks. When parents engaged the children in emotion-focused coping, the children tolerated the period in the sealed rooms relatively well. But children who were allowed, or even encouraged, to engage in problem-focused coping – constantly checking the seal to make sure the room was airtight – had higher levels of anxiety.

Another source of anxiety for many children and adolescents in families dealing with external stressors occurs when parents cannot agree on the nature of the stressor – is it controllable or is it uncontrollable? – or on the appropriate coping strategy to deal with the stressor (Catherall, 2005). It is important that the adults in families dealing with external stressors are able to resolve differing appraisals and coping preferences.

Internal stressors

The most difficult stressors for children and adolescents are those that arise within the family. These include domestic violence, incest, physical abuse, addictions (alcoholism and other forms of substance abuse, but also behavioral addictions such as gambling or compulsive spending), mental illness, and severe marital conflict. Any stressor that creates divisions within the family, including external stressors such as economic misfortune, can eventually qualify as an internal stressor. The stressor can be regarded as internal if the family continues to create a stressful atmosphere even in the absence of the external stressor. This is perhaps most clearly seen in marital conflict that starts with an external stressor but continues after the external stressor is resolved.

The most damaging stressor of all for children and adolescents is an internal stressor that is directed at them; i.e., abuse. All forms of abuse – physical, sexual or emotional – place children and adolescents in a terrible dilemma: the person whom they most fear and need to avoid is the same person that they need to rely upon. The betrayal of relational bonds and the abdication of the adult's responsibility for the child's safety and protection play havoc with the child's attachment relationship, often resulting in the chaotic pattern knows as disorganized attachment (Baer & Martinez, 2006), as well as putting the developing child or adolescent at risk in most of the areas discussed in this chapter. The consequences of within-family abuse are the most far-reaching of all stressors encountered by children and adolescents

Stressors and child/adolescent development

Examinations of external traumatic events view the family environment as a major mediating variable influencing children's risk. Studies of internal traumatic events, such as domestic violence or child abuse, typically assume a direct causal link with the development of children's problems. Specific components of the family environment are less often the focus of studies of internal trauma. The goal of this chapter is to offer a framework for categorizing the impact of both kinds of family stressors – external and internal – by focusing on the developmental needs of the children and adolescents in the family. There are five categories of developmental needs that are identified as at risk for disruption by family stressors; some stressors span several of these categories.

Disruption of these developmental needs can produce a variety of negative consequences among developing children and adolescents, not the least of which is that those affected may be at greater risk of developing post-traumatic stress disorders if they are exposed to traumatic events later in life. There is a growing literature suggesting that exposure to traumatic events in early childhood can increase a child's neurobiological vulnerability to developing PTSD later in life (Aspinall, 2004). The developmental areas presented here are primary candidates for the mediating mechanisms that could account for this increased vulnerability.

These categories are important foci for clinicians working with children and adolescents. One way of thinking about these categories is that positive experiences in each may confer greater resilience on the developing child or adolescent.

Categories of developmental needs

Family stressors can disrupt the development of children and adolescents by interfering with: (a) physical safety, (b) healthy attachment, (c) the development of self-esteem, (d) the development of a strong sense of self, and (e) the acquisition of appropriate coping skills.

Stressors can interfere with physical safety

Perhaps the most basic need provided by the family is physical safety. This can be interpreted to include the provision of the physical needs of food, shelter, and clothing, as well as the more obvious aspects of being physically safe. A central need supplied by the families in many urban environments is protection and children whose families provide insufficient protection are exposed to more violence from the surrounding community (Richards et al., 2004). Thus, poverty threatens the family's ability to provide for the physical needs of members – as does dislocation, such as may occur during mass disasters, war/terrorism, and even immigration. But physical safety can also be threatened in families in which the provision of physical needs is not a problem and the threats to physical safety are not direct. Domestic violence makes children feel physically unsafe even when it is not directed at the child (Kimura, 1999), and parental alcohol misuse has been shown to be associated with a much higher risk of traumatic brain injuries in children (Winqvist et al., 2007).

Physical safety is a mental phenomenon as much as a physical one. A child may perceive himself to be unsafe even though he is objectively unhurt. For example, a child who rides in an automobile with an intoxicated driver may perceive himself to be unsafe (which indeed he is). Similarly, a child with a rageful parent may feel unsafe, even though the parent never actually strikes the child. From this point of view, one measure of a child's feeling of safety is his level of physiological arousal. If he constantly anticipates danger and thus lives in a state of heightened arousal, he is not safe. Unfortunately, a common solution to this dilemma is for the child to escape into the decreased arousal state of dissociation.

When we consider the importance of the child's *perception* of his safety, it may help us to understand how a traumatized parent can interfere with the child's experience of physical safety. A parent who is himself constantly aroused and oriented toward impending danger, conveys his or her own perception that safety is lacking. A mentally ill parent who is paranoid can produce a similar experience for the child. Even physical illnesses in the parent may cause some children to feel that they are not safe.

Children's perceptions of safety are also affected by their exposure to a television news focus on dangerous events. There is a growing body of evidence demonstrating a relationship between increased media exposure and post-traumatic difficulties among children (Pfefferbaum et al., 2001; Pfefferbaum et al., 2003).

Stressors can interfere with healthy attachment

In the years since John Bowlby first studied attachment among infants and toddlers separated from their mothers (Bowlby, 1973), our appreciation of its importance in the lives of children has grown rapidly. Today, it is widely accepted that children require a good attachment relationship in order to feel secure. A secure attachment relationship provides a child with a secure base and a safe refuge from a frightening world. There is a variety of ways in which stressor events can interfere with attachment security. The most blatant is loss of the attachment figure. The loss of a parent has traditionally been categorized as a form of abandonment. The child goes through life sensitive to whether others will leave him.

However, an attachment perspective broadens the idea of abandonment to include an emphasis on the context in which the abandonment occurs. Viewed from the child's perspective, insecure attachment can be regarded as "coping with suboptimal childrearing environments" (Bar-On et al., 1998). It is the need for a secure attachment that has been damaged. Thus, the child may not only be sensitive to losing others, but he may have difficulty allowing himself to get attached again. Bowlby showed that the ultimate reaction to an extended separation from the attachment figure is to detach. Children who go through life detached or who have difficulty forming attachments are at increased risk for a variety of problems.

Of course, it is not only loss of attachment figures that contributes to insecure attachment. The research on early attachment suggests that many kinds of parenting failures can result in the development of insecure attachment. Thus, virtually all of the stressor events noted earlier – parental illness (mental or physical), substance abuse problems, parental traumatization, separations, poverty, divorce, domestic conflict, and violence – can interfere with the attachment security of children and adolescents. Some theorists have suggested that disruptions in attachment security may then serve as the underlying mechanism through which traumatic effects are transmitted intergenerationally (Bar-On et al., 1998).

Often, overt stressor events interfere with secure attachment via a relational mediating variable. For example, Mary Main hypothesized that mothers with unresolved traumatic experiences or losses might manifest more frightening behavior with their infants, and that this frightening behavior could be the relational factor that interferes with secure attachment (Main & Hesse, 1990). A study of this phenomenon found support for the hypothesis that mothers who had unresolved losses did manifest more frightening behavior, and the frightening behavior was correlated with increased incidence of disorganized attachment among their infant children (Schuengel et al., 1999).

Protecting the attachment relationship with the parents is of the greatest importance with young children because of their intense dependence on their parents. During adolescence, disruptions in the attachment relationship with a romantic partner are uniquely predictive of depression (more so than the relationship with the parents), although the attachment relationship between adolescent girls and their mothers remains very important (Margolese, Markiewicz, & Doyle, 2006).

Stressors can interfere with the development of self-esteem

The development of good self-esteem is a major contributor to resilience among children and adolescents (Demb, 2006). Among adolescents, low self-esteem has been found to predict poorer mental and physical health, worse economic prospects, and higher levels of criminal behavior during adulthood (Trzesniewski et al., 2006). Among children, self-esteem has been shown to be an important mediating variable in dealing with stressors such as exposure to violence or parent loss (Buckner, Beardslee, & Bassuk, 2004; Haine et al., 2003).

Parents and other adults play the biggest role in influencing the self-esteem of young children. Appropriate mirroring and the provision of optimal frustrations (challenges that children can overcome) help children to build confidence in themselves and their capacity to competently deal with the demands of life. Poor self-esteem contributes to a vicious cycle in which children and adolescents shy away from tackling the kinds of challenges that ultimately help them to build better self-esteem.

The biggest stressor to interfere with the development of good self-esteem is probably just poor parenting practices. Shaming children, disciplining them too harshly, and influencing them through fear rather than love have the effect of making the problem worse instead of better. Many parents resort to attacking the self-esteem of children and adolescents when they cannot influence them through more productive routes (Catherall, 2007). Providing a poor role model is another way that parents can have a negative impact on the child's developing self-esteem. Poor parenting practices are at least partially the result of ignorance and the continuation of maladaptive practices that one learned in childhood. However, stressor events can play a role in causing the poor parenting that leads to problems in self-esteem for children and adolescents.

Parents who have unhealthy parenting tendencies are frequently disturbed themselves. This is often due to either past trauma in their lives or current stressor events which exacerbate the personality traits and maladaptive coping that produce the poor parenting. The traumatized father who lashes out at his loved ones, the alcoholic parent who belittles his child, and the harsh disciplinarian who is still angry at his own childhood parenting experiences are all adults reacting to their own stressors in a manner that interferes with their children's self-esteem.

Stressors can interfere with the development of a strong sense of self

The development of a strong sense of self is a fairly well-accepted need of children and adolescents, but the concept is sometimes used differently by different theorists and overlaps with several other concepts, including internal versus external locus of control, self-efficacy, autonomy, differentiation, separation-individuation, and self-concept. In this chapter, I am using the concept to emphasize the developing child's need for appropriate boundaries. The essential stressor that interferes with the development of a strong sense of self is boundary violation. Among adults, boundaries can be blurred or diminished, as in the oneness experience that accompanies adult intimacy, but the sense of self remains intact (Krass, 1997). Boundary *violations*, however, are very different from the voluntary absence of boundaries that occur during oneness experiences. Among children and adolescents, repeated boundary violations interfere with the development of a strong sense of self (Schetky, 1995).

As in the self-esteem examples, adults may adopt this poor parenting practice (violating children's boundaries) as a result of the impact of stressors in their own lives. The ways in which the boundaries of children and adolescents are violated range from mild to egregious. Probably the most egregious form of boundary violation is childhood sexual abuse. The child is almost always unable to develop a strong, clear sense of self in such a situation and may have to spend many years in treatment later in life building a better sense of self.

But adults interfere with children's boundaries – and the concomitant development of sense of self – in a variety of ways, many of which do not resemble the blatant intrusion of sexual and physical abuse. Often, these are longstanding styles of parenting that have been passed down through families. For example, insisting that children do not feel certain emotions (e.g., "You're not angry at your brother") increases the difficulty for a child to develop his awareness of the range of his feelings, an aspect of his sense of self. Punishing children by denying them their right to privacy, failing to offer them choices or failing to provide them opportunities for decision making are other ways in which parents may unwittingly interfere with a child's self-development.

Lasting damage to the sense of self is reflected in "an unstable self-image based on shame and a core belief that one is permanently damaged, unlovable, and undeserving of love and protection but deserving of maltreatment and abuse" (Courtois, 2005, pp. 96–7), as well as a diminished ability to identify and regulate emotions.

Stressors can interfere with the acquisition of appropriate coping skills

As many of the above examples illustrate, the impact of stressors on children is most often mediated through the parents. If parents can manage the impact of stressors on themselves, then the children are minimally affected. The potential negative impact of major stressors, such as dislocation during time of war, can be minimized if the parents are able to maintain a reasonable semblance of family life. On the other hand, relatively minor stressors, such as the death of a distant relative, can produce significant consequences on children if the parents are themselves unable to manage the event.

A major task of parents is to both provide and teach children and adolescents effective coping mechanisms for managing stressors. Coping mechanisms range from effective to ineffective or even maladaptive, so it is not simply a case of teaching any coping – parents must help children acquire appropriate coping skills. Probably the most maladaptive form of coping passed on in families dealing with major stressors is avoidance, the central coping mechanism in PTSD. The maladaptive nature of avoidance coping has been identified among a variety of situations involving children, including boys dealing with marital conflict between their parents (Nicolotti, El-Sheikh, & Whitson, 2003), children dealing with the experience of living in foster homes (Legualt, Anawati, & Flynn, 2006), asthmatic children dealing with their health issues (Nazarian, Smyth, & Sliwinski, 2006), children adjusting after a residential fire (Jones & Ollenclick, 2005), and children exposed to the 9/11 terrorist attacks dealing with their post-traumatic symptoms (Lengua, Long, & Meltzoff, 2006).

One form of effective coping, known as emotion-focused coping, resembles avoidance but is actually quite different. Effective coping with most major stressors requires a combination of problem-focused and emotion-focused coping skills, as well as an understanding of when to use which kind of skills. Problem-focused coping directs the activity toward dealing with the threat itself, while emotion-focused coping attends to the emotional reaction to the threat. Problem-focused coping is appropriate when there are controllable dimensions to the stressor; emotion-focused coping is best when the stressor cannot be influenced (Gal & Lazarus, 1975; Lazarus & Folkman, 1984). Failure to help children and adolescents know when to use which kind of coping places them at risk. For example, when parents of children with cancer – a largely uncontrollable stressor after the basic treatment regimen is pursued – did not engage the children in sufficient emotion-focused coping, the children were more likely to develop post-traumatic stress symptoms (Fuemmeler et al., 2005).

The role that parents play in helping children to cope with external stressors extends to the importance of controlling media exposure (Pfefferbaum et al., 2001; Pfefferbaum et al., 2003). Parents have to actively monitor children's exposure, as children will often seek greater exposure if they have a personal connection to the external stressor. Children who lost a friend or acquaintance in the Oklahoma City bombing watched significantly more bombing-related television than those who did not lose a friend (Pfefferbaum et al., 2000).

Family dysfunctionality

Clearly, the impact of family stressors on children and adolescents is largely mediated through the parents. In high-functioning families, the parents keep the children physically safe; they promote secure attachment and good self-esteem in the children; they do not intrude excessively on the children's boundaries; and they teach and model effective coping skills. In low-functioning families, the parents fail to pay sufficient attention to these important areas of development.

Irene Stiver (1997) identified three variables that commonly define dysfunctionality in families. These variables reflect the ability of parents to maintain a proper nurturing environment in the midst of demanding stressors. The first variable is the existence of *secrets* in the family. This does not refer to the normal tendency to protect children from the knowledge of certain stressors, such as financial difficulties. When there are significant secrets in a family – generally indicating some forbidden behavior like sexual or substance abuse – it is a sign that the family does not have a healthy flow of communication and some members are engaged in behavior that is counter to the needs of the children.

The second variable is the *emotional availability* of the parents. If parents are themselves closed off, usually as an aspect of how they are dealing with stressors, then the children experience a degree of emotional abandonment. This is likely to create insecure attachment, as well as possible problems with self-esteem and perhaps even feelings of physical safety.

The third variable is the *parentification* of a child. When a child assumes parental duties in the family, he or she is providing caretaking for a parent or sibling. This usually means an adult has abdicated his or her responsibility – thus parentification is almost always accompanied by emotional unavailability of a parent – and the child's needs are not being met. Often, a child will assume this role as a way of creating a niche for him- or herself in the family. But the child's freedom to be carefree and assume that others are taking care of business is inevitably lost when a child is parentified.

Conclusion

This chapter has offered a means of categorizing potential stressors according to five central needs of developing children and adolescents: safety, attachment, esteem, a boundaried sense of self, and appropriate coping skills. Each of these areas of need is of particular importance in dealing with stressors. We have noted three indicators of family dysfunctionality: secrets, emotional inaccessibility of parents, and parentification of children. And we have identified the range of stressor events that can produce these aspects of dysfunctionality and consequently interfere with the needs of children: ranging from small t to large T traumas and including the secondary effects of traumatization of other family members. Stressors may originate externally or internally, but many external stressors eventually result in internal stressors. The most pernicious of all stressor events is abuse of the children and adolescents by an attachment figure.

References

Amir, M., & Lev-Wiesel, R. (2004). The quality of life among survivors' loved ones. In D. R. Catherall (Ed.), *The handbook of stress, trauma, and the family* (pp. 161–77). New York: Brunner-Routledge.

Aspinall, D. L. (2004). The linkage between early childhood trauma, post-traumatic stress disorder, and adolescent substance abuse. *Dissertation Abstracts International: Section B: The Sciences and Engineering, 64*(10-B), 5204.

Baer, J. C., & Martinez, D. C. (2006). Child maltreatment and insecure attachment: A meta-analysis. *Journal of Reproductive and Infant Psychology, 24*, 187–97.

Baranowsky, A. B., Young, M., Johnson-Douglas, S., Williams-Keeler, L., & McCarrey, M. (1998). PTSD transmission: A review of secondary traumatization in Holocaust survivor families. *Canadian Psychology, 39*(4), 247–56.

Bar-On, D., Eland, J., Kleber, R. J. et al. (1998). Multigenerational perspectives on coping with the Holocaust experience: An attachment perspective for understanding the developmental sequelae of trauma across generations. *International Journal of Behavioral Development, 22*(2), 315–38.

Bowlby, J. (1973). *Attachment and loss. Vol. II: Separation: Anxiety and anger.* New York: Basic Books.

Buckner, J. C., Beardslee, W. R., & Bassuk, E. L. (2004). Exposure to violence and low-income children's mental health: Direct, moderated, and mediated relations. *American College of Orthopsychiatry, 74*, 413–23.

Catherall, D. R. (1997). Treating traumatized families. In C.R. Figley (Ed.), *Burnout in families: The systemic costs of caring* (pp. 187–216). Boca Raton, FL: CRC Press.

Catherall, D. R. (2004). Introduction. In D. R. Catherall (Ed.), *The handbook of stress, trauma, and the family* (pp. 1–12). New York: Brunner-Routledge.

Catherall, D. R. (2005). When terrorism threatens family functioning. In D. R. Catherall (Ed.), *Specific stressors: Intervening with couples and families* (pp. 167–87). New York: Brunner-Routledge.

Catherall, D. R. (2007). *Emotional safety: Viewing couples through the lens of affect.* New York: Brunner-Routledge.

Costello, E. J., Erkanli, A., Fairbank, J. A., & Angold, A. (2002). The prevalence of potentially traumatic events in childhood and adolescence. *Journal of Traumatic Stress, 15*(2), 99–112.

Courtois, C. A. (2005). When one partner has been sexually abused as a child. In D. R. Catherall (Ed.), *Family stressors: Interventions for stress and trauma* (pp. 95–113). New York: Brunner-Routledge.

Demb, M. (2006). Resilience in a time of terror: Individual, social, and familial protective factors in Israeli adolescents. *Dissertation Abstracts International: Section B: The Sciences and Engineering, 66*(7-B), 3944.

Figley, C. R. (1995). Compassion fatigue as secondary traumatic stress disorder: An overview. In C. R. Figley (Ed.), *Compassion fatigue: Coping with secondary traumatic stress disorder in those who treat the traumatized* (pp. 1–20). New York: Brunner/Mazel.

Fuemmeler, B. F., Mullins, L. L., van Pelt, J., Carpentier, M. Y., & Parkhurst, J. (2005). Posttraumatic stress symptoms and distress among parents of children with cancer. *Children's Health Care, 34*, 289–303.

Gal, R., & Lazarus, R. S. (1975). The role of activity in anticipating and confronting stressful situations. *Journal of Human Stress, 1*(4), 4–20.

Haine, R. A., Ayers, T. S., Sandler, I. N., Wolchik, S. A., & Weyer, J. L. (2003). Locus of control and self-esteem as stress-moderators or stress-mediators in parentally bereaved children. *Death Studies, 27*, 619–40.

Jones, R. T., & Ollenclick, T. H. (2005). Risk factors for psychological adjustment following residential fire: The role of avoidant coping. In E. Cardena & K. Croyle (Eds.), *Acute reactions to trauma and psychotherapy: A multidisciplinary and international perspective* (pp. 85–99). New York: Haworth Press.

Kimura, M. S. (1999). Mother–child relationships and adjustment of children exposed to marital aggression and violence. *Dissertation Abstracts International: Section B: The Sciences and Engineering, 59*(11-B), 6070.

Krass, M. L. (1997). The river is within us, the sea is all about us: A study of creativity and oneness motivation. *Dissertation Abstracts International: Section B: The Sciences and Engineering, 57*(7-B), 4713.

Laor, N., Wolmer, L., & Cohen, D. J. (2001). Mothers' functioning and children's symptoms 5 years after a SCUD missile attack. *The American Journal of Psychiatry, 158*, 1020–6.

Lazarus, R. S., & Folkman, S. (1984). *Stress, Appraisal and Coping.* New York: Springer.

Legault, L., Anawati, M., & Flynn, R. (2006). Factors favoring psychological resilience among fostered young people. *Children and Youth Services Review, 28*, 1024–38.

Lengua, L. J., Long, A. C., & Meltzoff, A. N. (2006). Pre-attack stress-load, appraisals, and coping in children's responses to the 9/11 terrorist attacks. *Journal of Child Psychology and Psychiatry, 47*, 1219–27.

Main, M., & Hesse, E. (1990). Parents' unresolved traumatic experiences are related to infant disorganized attachment status: Is frightened and/or frightening parental behavior the linking mechanism? In M. T. Greenberg, D. Cicchetti & E. M. Cummings (Eds.), *Attachment in the pre-school years: Theory, research, and intervention* (pp. 161–82). Chicago: University of Chicago Press.

Margolese, S. K., Markiewicz, D., and Doyle, A. B. (2006). Attachment to parents, best friend, and romantic partner: Predicting different pathways to depression in adolescence. *Journal of Youth and Adolescence, 34*, 637–50.

Nazarian, D., Smyth, J. M., & Sliwinski, M. J. (2006). A naturalistic study of ambulatory asthma severity and reported avoidant coping styles. *Chronic Illness, 2*, 51–8.

Nicolotti, L., El-Sheikh, M., & Whitson, M. (2003). Children's coping with marital conflict and their adjustment and physical health: Vulnerability and protective functions. *Journal of Family Psychology, 17*, 315–26.

Ostrowski, S. A., Christopher, N. C., & Delahanty, D. L. (2007). The impact of maternal posttraumatic stress disorder symptoms and child gender on risk for persistent posttraumatic stress disorder symptoms in child trauma victims. *Journal of Pediatric Psychology, 32*(3), 338–42.

Pfefferbaum, B., Gurwitch, R. H., McDonald, N. B. et al. (2000). Posttraumatic stress among young children after the death of a friend or acquaintance in a terrorist bombing, *Psychiatric Services, 51*, 386–88.

Pfefferbaum, B., Nixon, S. J., Tivis, R. D. et al. (2001). Television exposure in children after a terrorist incident. *Psychiatry, 64*(3), 202–11.

Pfefferbaum, B., Seale, T. W., Brandt, E. N. Jr. et al. (2003). Media exposure in children one hundred miles from a terrorist bombing. *Annals of Clinical Psychiatry, 15*, 1–8.

Pine, D. S., & Cohen, J. A. (2002). Trauma in children and adolescents: Risk and treatment of psychiatric sequelae. *Biological Psychiatry, 51*, 519–31.

Putnam, F. W. (1996). Posttraumatic stress disorder in children and adolescents. *American Psychiatric Press Review of Psychiatry, 15*, 447–67.

Richards, M. H., Larson, R., Miller, B. V. et al. (2004). Risky and protective contexts and exposure to violence in urban African American young adolescents. *Journal of Clinical Child & Adolescent Psychology, 33*, 138–48.

Rojas, V.M., & Pappagallo, M. (2004). Risk factors for PTSD in children and adolescents. In R. R. Silva (Ed.), *Posttraumatic stress disorders in children and adolescents: Handbook* (pp. 38–59). New York: W. W. Norton & Co.

Rowland-Klein, D. (2004). The transmission of trauma across generations: Identification with parental trauma in children of Holocaust survivors. In D. R. Catherall (Ed.), *The handbook of stress, trauma, and the family* (pp. 117–36). New York: Brunner-Routledge.

Schetky, D. H. (1995). Boundaries in child and adolescent psychiatry. *Child and Adolescent Psychiatric Clinics of North America, 4*, 769–78.

Schuengel, C., Bakerman-Kranenburg, M. J., & van IJzendoorn, M. H. (1999). Frightening maternal behavior linking unresolved loss and disorganized infant attachment. *Journal of Consulting and Clinical Psychology, 67*, 54–63.

Stiver, I. P. (1997). Chronic disconnections: Three family contexts. In B. S. Mark & J. A. Incorvaia (Eds.), *The handbook of infant, child, and adolescent psychotherapy, Vol. 2: New directions in integrative treatment* (pp. 439–59). Lanham, MD: Jason Aronson.

Stoppelbein, L., & Greening, L. (2000). Posttraumatic stress symptoms in parentally bereaved children and adolescents. *Journal of the American Academy of Child & Adolescent Psychiatry, 39*, 1112–19.

Trzesniewski, K. H., Donnellan, M. B., Moffitt, T. E. et al. (2006). Low self-esteem during adolescence predicts poor health, criminal behaviour, and limited economic prospects during adulthood. *Developmental Psychology, 42*, 381–90.

Vincent, N. R. (1998). Children's reactions to Hurricane Andrew: A forty-four month follow-up study. *Dissertation Abstracts International: Section B: The Sciences and Engineering, 59*(2-B), 0891.

Weisenberg, M., Schwarzwald, J., Waysman, M., Solomon, Z., & Klingman, A. (1993). Coping of school-age children in the sealed room during Scud missile bombardment and postwar stress reactions. *Journal of Consulting and Clinical Psychology, 61*, 462–67.

Whiffen, V. E., & Oliver, L. E. (2004). The relationship between traumatic stress and marital intimacy. In D. R. Catherall (Ed.), *The handbook of stress, trauma, and the family* (pp. 139–59). New York: Brunner-Routledge.

Winqvist, S., Jokelainen, J., Luukinen, H., & Hillbom, M. (2007). Parental alcohol misuse is a powerful predictor for the risk of traumatic brain injury in childhood. *Brain Injury, 21*(10), 1079–85.

Chapter Four

Stories of Children and Adolescents from Other Cultures: The Trauma of Migration

Dalila Rezzoug, Thierry Baubet, and Marie Rose Moro

Introduction

Large numbers of migrants flee from their native countries to Europe seeking asylum after experiencing traumas or looking for economic survival. Regardless of their previous experiences, migrants and their children develop vulnerabilities as a result of their migration, a life experience which has exposed them to *trans-cultural* risk and post-traumatic syndromes. Some faced torture, war, and daily insecurity and had to develop defense mechanisms to survive in terrifying contexts. Others are overwhelmed by migration per se, which requires a difficult adjustment process to a new world.

This chapter focuses on individuals who are most vulnerable to migration trauma, namely children and adolescents. More specifically, the chapter explores how early experiences of asylum children and adolescents may contribute to their later vulnerability to trauma when they migrate to another country. Specific characteristics of these populations will be considered in terms of cultural expression of traumatic symptoms related to migration.

The reflections presented here are derived from the clinical work done in the trans-cultural psychiatry clinic (Moro, 1994, 1998, 2003, 2007; Rezzoug et al., 2007) at the Avicenne Hospital in France and from the humanitarian work with *Médecins sans Frontières* in conflict areas (Lachal, Ouss-Ryngaert, & Moro, 2003; Moro & Lebovici, 1995; Rezzoug et al., 2008).

Post-Traumatic Syndromes in Childhood and Adolescence: A Handbook of Research and Practice, First Edition.
Edited by Vittoria Ardino. © 2011 John Wiley & Sons, Ltd. Published 2011 by John Wiley & Sons, Ltd.

Context before exile

Most of our clients had not chosen to leave their country; they had to. Fleeing meant leaving everything behind: people and belongings. They were forced to sacrifice their familiar cultural cocoon and, often, they faced loss and grief, with the burden of not knowing where their families were, if they were still alive, or where they were buried. In addition, fear of retaliation against those left behind elicited distressing feelings of guilt or despair. Many migrants could no longer count on the support of their families to help them cope; if they had still been in their country of origin they would have been able to find the family, the group, a common framework of cultural rituals, and all the other elements that enable the development of a collective awareness. Once excluded from or unable to access the cultural framework of understanding to cope with death, separation, and grieving, some refugees become distressed, fragile, and vulnerable (Fazel & Stein, 2002; Gonsalves, 1992; Lustig et al., 2004; Papadopoulos, 2001).

The arrival in a new country is a crucial "turning point" in the stories of asylum-seekers and migrants. The country of refuge represents an ambivalent experience which promotes a contrast between an ideal image of a democratic state respecting human rights and bringing protection, and the much harder reality of obtaining social support and a visa as a legal migrant. Migrants, then, experience an acute sense of loneliness often resulting in depression and a sense of shortened future. Thus, in our experience, symptomatic de-compensation occurs most frequently after exile, sometimes several months or years later. Exile-related traumas exacerbate familial and relational challenges within the family (Nathan, 1986, 1987) and undermine the development of good parent–children interactions as a result of serious loss and a complicated intergenerational transmission of cultural beliefs. During resettlement, adults lose their social status, combined with intrinsic difficulties of learning a language, new societal rules, and cultural rituals. Altogether, this experience undermines parenting quality, which may also have been compromised in the country of origin as a consequence of war, insecurity, and poverty.

The concept of trauma in a trans-cultural realm

Exile promotes a traumatic experience that encompasses the individual reaction; indeed, trauma impacts on the whole family and on the societal groups. Displacement, separation, deaths massively affect family abilities to protect the youngsters, who may therefore experience trauma through very distressed adults around them.

In the trans-cultural context, clinicians have to enable the disclosure of the traumatic experience and its related reactions by taking into consideration two key points. On the one hand, PTSD is a western concept which requires a cultural framework of understanding because its classic diagnostic criteria do not fully express all possible manifestations of the impact of trauma as culture-driven representations and expressions of suffering and symptoms. On the other hand, post-traumatic reactions could also be described as stable processes across cultures. Altogether, Baubet and Moro (2003) and Rousseau and Drapeau (1998) described these processes as trans-culturally invariant.

Furthermore, exile is a result of a trauma caused by intentional human acts, such as torture, rape, and ethnic cleansing, that very often lead to a prolonged traumatic exposure and to serious personality shifts of the victims. Judith Lewis Herman has proposed the concept of the "complex post-traumatic stress disorder" to describe the sequelae of prolonged, repeated trauma, in particular among individuals exposed to captivity and coercive control in a context of collective traumas or family traumas such as physical and sexual abuse (Frey, 2001; Herman, 1992; van der Kolk, 1996). The clinical features of Complex PTSD (CPTSD) involve chronic difficulty in emotion regulation and in engagement with sexual activity, which leads to self-harm, suicidal, impulsive, or risk-related behaviors. Furthermore, dissociative disorders and psychosomatic problems are also present along with a disruption of personality accompanied by feelings of guilt or shame in relation to what has been experienced. Finally, individuals with CPTSD also have difficulties in establishing or maintaining relationships because of their lack of trust.

Trauma is the result of a shock that could not be anticipated and that is accompanied by terror. Freud (1963) linked terror to a sudden danger: the self is put *out of action* because its defense mechanisms are unable to protect the mind from the traumatic stimuli (A. Freud, 1965; Freud & Burlingham, 1943).

Lionel Bailly (1999) conceptualized psychological trauma and its consequences as an attack on one's life story defined as a "life theory." A life theory is an individual representation of the world, life, relationships which incorporates taboos and societal rules. When a life theory is undermined, the rapport with the world and others is also undermined. According to Nathan (1990), a traumatic experience has the power to shatter one's perspective of the world and the self, along with the rules that regulate a community.

Various cultures hold a representation of terror; Nathan (1990) emphasizes the role of *breaching* and *extracting* present in all terror-related disorders, and comparable with the psychoanalytical model adopted by the authors of this chapter. For example, in the Maghreb, *khal'a* defines terror as a breaching of (or breaking into) the body; the Arabic word is related to "tearing out" or "away," or to extraction. The breaching part of the trauma may be represented as an entity which manifests itself in the aftermath, on the occasion of another traumatic event, or more precisely, as a *djinn*. Among the Quechua Indians, Le Susto describes a similar dual movement of breaching and extracting: terror creates a wound and the soul leaves the body (Pury-Toumi, 1990). There are other traumatic representations: the notion of *calor* in Salvador, or *ataques de nervios* in Latin America, where somatization is frequent. Somatization can be conveyed through chronic pain causing disability, or acute pain, in particular among torture victims, sometimes leading to an underestimation of their condition and inappropriate treatment with painkillers.

Treating trauma in children and adolescents who have experienced exile

Asylum families are reached out to by social services via different channels. Children may present developmental difficulties, such as language disorders or a learning disability; in this case, schools and mother and childcare services bring the needs of those families to public attention. Children can also be referred by physicians or psychiatrists working in emergency units and by social workers or charities set up for asylum-seekers. The provision of care to such clients requires a multidisciplinary and flexible approach to offer simultaneously psychological treatment and an understanding of the medical, social, and political issues linked to a migrant's situation (Rezzoug et al., 2008). The following case illustrates the impact of trauma on asylum-seeker families and the consequent vulnerability of their children.

The case of Heba

Heba and her mother have frequented our department for several years. When Heba first visited the department she was five years old; she is now 10.

Heba's mother (Ms A) visited the emergency unit several times in a serious state of distress and confusion. She frequently wandered all day and sometimes she took her daughter with her. Her wandering was provoked by hearing voices which told her to go out and look for her husband. She also experienced amnesia and derealization. A clinical interview conducted in Arabic identified Complex Post-Traumatic Disorder in comorbidity with depression and dissociative fugues as a result of extreme war-related trauma.

Ms A had commanded a women's corps in her country of origin (in the Horn of Africa) and she had experienced imprisonment and torture. In her country, the population was not protected from deployment; children in particular witnessed daily extreme violence perpetrated against civilians. She was able to identify the beginning of her distress when her husband was arrested at their home soon after the birth of Heba. Ms A was hospitalized three times in her own country for disturbances that were not easy to diagnose; the first hospitalization occurred during the initial post-partum period shortly after the imprisonment of her husband. Ms A's sister, already in exile, was informed of the severity of her sister's disturbances, she planned Ms A's escape to France where she could receive care. Ms A left the country with her youngest daughter, Heba, who was four years old at the time, leaving three other children behind with her mother-in-law. Currently, Ms A has troubled memories about this period, yielding to a dissociative state.

At the initial referral, Heba was a small child and fearful at school and in consultation, not seeking contact either verbally with her mother or nonverbally with the clinical staff. Heba was quite silent and with poor appetite, sleeping problems including nightmares, and enuresis. She was later able to tell about war scenes present in her dreams. Heba tried to attune with her mother, even though Ms A appeared sad and not very reactive to her daughter's stimuli. Heba spoke in her mother tongue, not yet having mastered French.

Heba had experienced early chaotic events and developed an attachment relationship with a highly distressed mother who was not always available to interact with her. Heba eventually began to speak French during treatment while communicating with her mother in their native language. The child had to develop a relationship with a mother deeply affected by the traumatic experience, which elicited parentification. Ms A continues to progress slowly: she was severely affected by the lack of information about her husband and her other children over the previous three years. She fears their deaths, which causes an alternation between numbing and thought suppression.

Heba and her mother lived in various hostels and then in a community for asylum-seekers as independent accommodation was not an option for Ms A who was in need of constant reassurance. Heba exhibited an ambivalent affective style, seeking physical contact and showing difficulties in adjusting to interaction with people. Her mother was able to acknowledge her dependence on her daughter, who seemed better at decoding the demands of their environment. At the same time, she pointed out the level of her daughter's immaturity, which worried her particularly because of the imminence of puberty and all the issues relating to sexuality. "Heba will not listen to me, what will happen when she reaches ten?"

Even if the affective and cognitive development of Heba was delayed, she learned to read and write with remedial teaching. At the age of nine, Heba returned to normal schooling, but there is a considerable age gap between her and the other children in the class. A multidisciplinary intervention program was set up for Heba and her mother offering both individual and group treatments. The presence of an interpreter favored the development of a therapeutic alliance. Work with this family has been continuing in collaboration with social workers.

The clinical scenario above demonstrates that an infant or a young child may be overwhelmed by trauma. According to Bailly (2003), the trauma undermines the infant's *social theories*, which could also be called *life theories*. Traumatic events are related to an absence of primary love objects which leaves the child in external sensorial chaos (heat/cold, noise, light) and internal sensorial chaos (pain, hunger, thirst). Chaos may also be provoked by a maternal state of terror: both situations well illustrate the context of collective and war traumas when adults may no longer be able to contain and protect the child because they are overwhelmed by their own post-traumatic symptoms. Winnicott (2000) described the "harrowing primitive agony" that can occur at the stage of absolute dependency and can lead to psychotic-like defensive mechanisms. In this case the breakdown occurs when the self is not yet able to experience it or to retain it in memory. Winnicott observed (2004) that some adults feared this breakdown, which generated the defensive response as if the breakdown had already happened. For this reason, the author highlighted very long-term consequences resulting from early traumas and the importance of parental protection.

Bowlby provides a different understanding of children's cognitive development (1969, 1973, 1980). According to Bowlby, it is the interaction with the attachment figure that enables four-year-olds to construct themselves and their representations of self and others in a situation of distress. Attachment behavior is activated when the child is frightened, in danger or distressed. The attachment figure should then respond more or less adequately to their own emotions and to the child's emotions and intentions. When a traumatic experience occurs to both the mother and the child or to just the mother, the attachment figure may no longer be able to take on her reflexive function, and hence her protective function, thus the interaction is jeopardized (Fonagy et al., 1996).

Similar situations are present when a child is born after a period of imprisonment, torture or rape (Drell, Siegel, & Gaensbauer, 1993; Lachal, 2000; Marotte & Rousseau, 2003). The expression "PTSD *à deux*" describes a post-traumatic scenario in which parental response to trauma affects the child's well-being and initiates a dysfunctional interactive system which maintains the disorder in both members of the dyad (Scheeringa & Zeanah, 2001). Scheeringa and Zeanah developed the concept of "relational PTSD" describing a co-occurrence of a dyadic post-traumatic reaction where the symptoms of one exacerbate those of the other. The authors describe three relational modes:

– withdrawal/nonreceptiveness/unavailability: a situation that is often encountered when the parents have themselves previously experienced trauma;
– overprotection/constriction: the parents are overwhelmed by fear of another trauma and by guilt at not having been able to protect the child;

– reenactment of the traumatic scene/exposure to danger: the child's trauma is constantly reactivated by questions or triggers. The child is placed in situations where new traumas can occur.

Vulnerabilities specific to the children of migrants

Asylum children and adolescents present a cluster of specific vulnerabilities linked to the migratory experience which provides poorer resistance to harm and aggression (Anthony, Chiland, & Koupernik, 1978).

Most times, the children do not have a direct experience of migration, yet they are exposed to its consequences as a result of parental displacement and relocation in another country. The children live between two worlds that are not necessarily connected to one another: the "inner world," the world of the family, their mother tongue, their native culture; and the "outer world," the host country, the second language, and the host country's culture and society (Moro, 2003).

Parents are deprived of the cultural support that usually functions as a framework of thinking (Moro, 2003). Migration trauma, therefore, is linked to the loss of an internal cultural point of reference through which reality was formerly decoded and interpreted. Grieving for the culture of origin becomes more problematic to heal when migrants transit to parenthood.

The first pregnancy transforms a woman's identity, a process which reactivates regression and childhood conflicts and is defined by Bydlowski (1997) as a state of "psychic transparency." This identity crisis is accompanied by internal confusion, which is helped by the cultural group which codifies this life transition providing representations of parenting to support the couple (Moro et al., 1989). Migrant parents are prevented from benefiting from these cultural representations of parenting and are therefore more vulnerable to internal chaos (Moro et al., 1989) as the loss of the cultural framework leads to a loss of self-confidence in their inner ability to interpret thoughts, emotions, and bodily experiences.

After birth, mother and infant are embedded in interactive patterns where cultural markers are unstable and fragile as the mother lacks cultural support and is, therefore, more vulnerable in attuning with the child and providing care. In the aftermath of migration, this phenomenon is even more noticeable: the distance from a traditional family model, the cultural markers unsteady, and the external world insecure. Thus, parents transmit a kaleidoscopic vision of the world to their child, which generates experiences of anxiety and insecurity in the infant. Migrant parents cannot introduce the world in small doses as Winnicott (1969) described: the child faces the world from an insecure environment which very often does not prepare them for entering school. For this reason, entering school can be traumatic and being simultaneously a student in the school of the host country and a child of migrant parents who represent a different culture from the school system can undermine the child's ability to develop self-representation. Learning how to read and write is crucial to process the state of being in two different worlds and it can put the child at risk of academic failure.

Child development requires parental transmission of a coherent set of cultural representations via body care practices, interactive patterns, and parenting styles (Devereux, 1970; Gibello, 1988). Migration transforms the cultural context and creates more complex interpretative frameworks generating confusion, paradoxes, and conflicts. If one considers, in line with Devereux (1970), that "the human psyche and culture are inseparable twins," migration is a factor of vulnerability for migrant children.

Gibello put forward a link between trans-cultural situations and cognitive development impairments proposing the idea of "cultural containers," cognitive guides that are implicitly shared by all the members of a cultural group. They are responsible for the establishment of good thinking processes and a good communicative style in externalizing the "content of thoughts" within the group. Therefore, "implicit thought containers" vary across cultures: migrants are very often able to understand these containers, but not able to internalize them. For this reason, children acquire these implicit elements of the host culture on their own as they are not transmitted by their parents from the cradle. Consequently, shifting from one cultural framework to another may favor the onset of dysfunctional symbolization processes including cognitive, academic, social, and cultural aspects (Brinbaum & Kieffer, 2005). Moro (2003) proposes the concept of the "exposed child," that is a child who is exposed to a specific trans-cultural risk generated by the crossing-over of two cultural systems where filiations (what is transmitted by older generations) and cultural affiliations (which define the belonging to a group) are dissociated. Three periods are particularly sensitive regarding this vulnerability: early interactions, school entry, and adolescence; these are critical periods for affiliation to the host country. The other problematic issue is that this trans-cultural risk is not equally expressed among all children of migrants: some of them are more resilient and able to develop abilities in a trans-cultural context. The existence of such individual differences is explained by both internal and external factors. The child has personal resources that could contribute to their academic achievement and creative skills (Lachal, 2006; Schnapper, 1991). There is also the quality of family support and contact with other adults who function as bridges between the intra-family world and the external community and constitute special encounters for the child's exploration of the world. For example, an older sister or a professional can be a *resilience tutor*, enabling the child to compensate for the making-meaning of the world which was not provided by their parents. In line with this, balanced bilingualism plays a crucial role: early bilingualism could be an indication of mixed affiliations, established with the country of origin and with the receiving country at the same time, alongside the inscription of the child in his own affiliation (Moro, 2003; Rezzoug et al., 2007).

Group intervention for adolescents who have experienced extreme trauma

Ismael was 18 years old when he first arrived at the Avicenne Hospital trauma center, referred by a psychologist working with young adults. It was remarkable to me that he put a lot of himself into this relationship while he was not yet allowed to work in France.

That day, he was exhausted. He had not been able to sleep for nights because of repetitive nightmares in which he was reliving traumatic scenes from his past. Four years before, he and his family had been exposed to extreme trauma and destruction in their village in West Africa. Consequently, he experienced frequent daytime intrusions of horror, which he tried to overcome by avoiding being alone. Being alone was a source of intrusions and a result of a lack of social support from the host country's institutions. The combined effect of loneliness and exhausting, intrusive symptoms caused him to feel profound hopelessness and to have suicidal thoughts.

During the first therapy session, Ismael narrated his story in a monotone. The events were visited one after the other without any pause, creating in the therapist *emerging scenarios* defined by Christian Lachal (2006) as the part of the trauma that is transmitted to the therapist through a process of countertransference. He explained that he had a normal family life when rebels arrived in a village close to the country's borders. Several houses were burned, including his parents' house. He explained that his father was accused of supporting the government army, although he was simply a shopkeeper. According to the rebels, this accusation was sufficient justification for inflicting punishment: they raped Ismael and his parents in front of the younger boys. The children were allowed to leave while the parents were tortured and killed. Ismael lost his brothers in the forest. He could not remember what had happened in the rush, but it appeared that he and his younger brothers lost contact. He ran toward the border. For how many hours, he could not say. He fled in a trance, managing to reach the border and to survive. He was not able to give a timescale, but a woman finally rescued him. Exile started again when the war spilled over to the country he was living in, and when foreigners were hunted down and arrested; this is when the nightmares started. He decided to move on and escaped by boat to France.

Ismael was treated in group sessions alongside psychiatric support.

The trauma group sessions

This intervention model was developed over 20 years of experience of working with refugee patients and using a trans-cultural approach complementing psychoanalysis and anthropology. This trans-cultural psychotherapeutic approach was established in France by Tobie Nathan (1986) to treat first generations of migrants, and then by Marie Rose Moro and colleagues (2004) who have been treating second generations using the methodological principles of Georges Devereux (1985). Devereux put forward that any therapeutic relationship includes a psychic universality and a cultural encoding. To implement the model there is a group of five experienced therapists, trainees, and researchers, very often offering individual or couple treatments. The team works with a main therapist, several co-therapists from different cultural backgrounds, and usually an interpreter so that patients can use their mother tongue. The main therapist is the patient's direct interlocutor, *filtering* the communication among co-therapists, interpreter, and patient. The group enables shared representations and a shared therapeutic alliance. The presence of several co-therapists reduces the effects of numbness and daze linked to the trauma. Co-therapists suggest metaphors and narratives to symbolize what they understand of the patient's history. Thus the patient is *fed* with representations that can enable them to process their experiences through association and symbolization.

When the patient finds it difficult to disclose cultural beliefs and representations to a single therapist (i.e., experiences of possession or witchcraft) there may be heavy silences that can be better overcome by a team of professionals adopting a cross-cultural approach to trauma. Furthermore, when patients are extremely isolated, the group dimension can act as social support and as a symbolic realm of resources, memories, representations, and grieving rituals. Because the group provides genuine metaphoric and symbolic *nourishment*, patients gradually retrieve their narrative resources and bring back cultural strategies blocked by the traumatic experience (Baubet, 2008; Sturm, Baubet, & Moro, 2007). The analysis of countertransference is a decisive key in our work. Baubet (2008) points out that group therapy accompanies the patient toward a dynamic process against the "freezing" provoked by the trauma.

Migrant families in exile do not often access mental health specialists. The combination of environmental difficulties (unstable financial situation, poverty, isolation) and parental psychological distress (post-traumatic stress, depression) leave these families in the unchartered territory of need. Intervention requires working directly with the children and on the family system. It is crucial to offer proper support to traumatized parents to enable them to support their children. Furthermore, it is crucial to offer specifically designed therapies (individual or group) for migration-related post-traumatic stress where the trans-cultural dimension is integrated into the care strategy as a dynamic process enabling a co-construction of meaning with migrants, individuals between two worlds.

References

American Psychiatric Association (APA) (1980). *Diagnostic and Statistical Manual of Mental Disorders* (3rd ed.) (*DSM-III*). Washington, DC: Author.

Anthony, E. J., Chiland, C., & Koupernik, C. (Eds.) (1978/1982). *L'enfant dans sa famille, l'enfant vulnérable*. Paris: PUF.

Bailly, L. (1999). Psychotraumatisme de l'enfant: avancées cliniques et théoriques. *Nervure, 12*, 20–5.

Bailly, L. (2003). Traumatisme psychique chez le jeune enfant et théories sociales infantiles. In T. Baubet, C. Lachal, & M. R. Moro (Eds.), *Bébés et trauma* (pp. 59–67). Grenoble: La Pensée Sauvage.

Baubet, T. (2008). Effroi et métamorphose – Psychothérapie transculturelle des névroses traumatiques en situation d'impasse thérapeutique (Dissertation). Paris 13 University, Villetaneuse.

Baubet, T. & Moro, M. R. (2003). Cultures et soins du trauma psychique en situation humanitaire. In T. Baubet, K. Le Roch, & M. R. Moro (Eds.), *Soigner malgré tout. Vol. 1: Trauma, cultures et soins* (pp. 71–95). Grenoble: La Pensée Sauvage.

Baubet, T., Gaboulaud, V., Grouiller, K. et al. (2003). Facteurs psychiques dans les malnutritions infantiles en situation de post-conflit. Evaluation d'un programme de soins de dyades mères–bébés malnutris à Hébron (Territoires palestiniens). *Ann Med-Psychol, 161* (8), 609–13.

Bowlby, J. (1969/1978). *Attachement et perte. Vol. 1: L'attachement*. Paris: PUF.

Bowlby, J. (1973/1978). *Attachement et perte. Vol. 2: La séparation: Angoisse et colère*. Paris: PUF.

Bowlby, J. (1978/1980). *Attachement et perte. Vol. 3: La perte: tristesse et dépression*. Paris: PUF.

Brinbaum, Y., & Kieffer, A. (2005). D'une génération à l'autre, les aspirations éducatives des familles immigrées: ambition et persévérance. *Les dossiers d'éducation et formation, 72*, 53–75.

Bydlowski, M. (1997); La dette de vie: itinéraire psychanalytique de la maternité (p. 96). Paris: Le Fil Rouge (5th ed., 2005).

Devereux, G. (1970). *Essai d'ethnopsychiatrie générale*. Paris: Gallimard.

Devereux, G. (1972/1985). *Ethnopsychanalyse complémentariste*. Paris: Flammarion.

Drell, M. J., Siegel, C. H., & Gaensbauer, T. J. (1993). Post-traumatic stress disorder. In C. H. Zeanah (Ed.), *Handbook of infant mental health* (pp. 291–304). New York: Guilford Press.

Fazel, M., & Stein, A. (2002). The mental health of refugee children. *Archives of Disease in Childhood, 87*, 366–70.

Fonagy, P., Steele, M., Steele, H., Moran, G., & Higgitt, A. (1996). Fantômes dans la chambre d'enfant: étude de la répercussion des représentations mentales des parents sur la sécurité de l'attachement. *La Psychiatrie de l'Enfant, 39*(1), 63–83.

Freud, A. (1965). Le traumatisme psychique. In *L'enfant dans la psychanalyse* (pp. 205–14). Paris: Gallimard.

Freud, A., & Burlingham, D. (1943). *War and children*. New York: International Universities Press.

Freud, S. (1963). Principe de plaisir et névrose traumatique. In *Essais de psychanalyse*. Paris: Payot.

Frey, C. (2001). Post-traumatic stress disorder and culture. In A. T. Yilmaz, M. G. Weiss, & A. Riecher-Rössler (Eds.), *Cultural psychiatry: Euro-international perspectives* (pp. 103–16). Basel: Karger.

Gibello, B. (1988). Contenants de pensée, contenants culturels. La dimension créative de l'échec scolaire. In A. Yahyaoui (Ed.), *Troubles du langage et de la filiation chez le maghrébin de la deuxième génération.* Grenoble: La Pensée Sauvage.

Gonsalves, C. J. (1992). Psychological stages of the refugee process: a model for therapeutic intervention. *Professional Psychology: Research & Practice, 23,* 382–9.

Herman, J. L. (1992). Complex PTSD: A syndrome in survivors of prolonged and repeated trauma. *Journal of Traumatic Stress, 5*(3), 377–91.

Lachal, C. (2000). Le comportement de privation hostile. *L'Autre Cliniques Cultures et Société, 1*(1), 77–89.

Lachal, C. (2006). *Le partage du traumatisme. Contre-transferts avec les patients traumatisés.* Grenoble: La Pensée Sauvage.

Lachal, C., Ouss-Ryngaert, L., & Moro, M. R. (Eds.) (2003). *Comprendre et soigner le trauma en situation humanitaire.* Paris: Dunod.

Lustig, S. L., Kia-Keating, M., Knight, W. G. et al. (2004). Review of child and adolescent refugee mental health. *Journal of the American Academy of Child & Adolescent Psychiatry, 43*(1), 24–35.

Marotte, C., & Rousseau, C. (2003). Eclaboussures traumatiques et regards sur la filiation: les enfants nés du viol. In T. Baubet, C. Lachal, & M. R. Moro (Eds.), *Bébés et trauma* (pp. 135–49). Grenoble: La Pensée Sauvage.

Moro, M. R. (1994). *Parents en exil. Psychopathologie et migrations.* Paris: PUF.

Moro, M. R. (1998). *Psychothérapie transculturelle des enfants de migrants.* Paris: Dunod.

Moro, M. R. (2003). Parents and infants in changing cultural context: immigration, trauma and risk. *Infant Mental Health Journal, 24*(3), 240–64.

Moro, M. R. (2004). Transcultural approach in perinatality. *Journal de Gynecologie Obstetrique et Biologie de la Reproduction, 33*(1), 5–10.

Moro, M. R. (2007). *Aimer ses enfants ici et ailleurs. Histoires transculturelles.* Paris: Odile Jacob.

Moro, M. R., & Lebovici, S. (Eds.) (1995). *Psychiatrie humanitaire en ex-Yougoslavie et en Arménie.* Paris: PUF.

Moro, M. R., & Réal, I. (2004). La consultation transculturelle d'Avicenne, Bobigny, France. In M. R. Moro, Q. De La Noë, & Y. Mouchenik (Eds.), *Manuel de psychiatrie transculturelle: Travail clinique, travail social* (pp. 217–38). Grenoble: La Pensée Sauvage.

Moro, M. R., De la Noë, Q., & Mouchenik, Y. (Eds.) (2004). *Manuel de psychiatrie transculturelle: Travail clinique, travail social.* Grenoble: La Pensée Sauvage.

Moro, M. R., Nathan, T., Rabin-Jamin, J., Stork, H., & Si Ahmed, J. (1989). Le bébé dans son univers culturel. In S. Lebovici & F. Weil-Halpern (Eds.), *Psychopathologie du bébé* (pp. 698–99). Paris: PUF.

Nathan, T. (1986). *La folie des autres. Traité d'ethnopsychiatrie clinique.* Paris: Dunod.

Nathan, T. (1987). La fonction psychique du trauma. *Nouvelle Revue d'Ethnopsychiatrie, 8,* 7–9.

Nathan, T. (1990). Angoisse ou frayeur: un problème épistémologique de la psychanalyse. *Nouvelle Revue d'Ethnopsychiatrie, 15,* 21–38.

Papadopoulos, R. K. (2001). Refugee families: Issues of systemic supervision. *Journal of Family Therapy, 23,* 207–13.

Pury-Toumi, S. de (1990). Une maladie nommée susto. *Nouvelle Revue d'Ethnopsychiatre, 15*, 173–207.

Rezzoug, D., Baubet, T., Broder, G., Taïeb, O., & Moro, M. R. (2008). Addressing mother–infant relationship in displaced communities. *Child and Adolescent Psychiatric Clinics of North America, 17*(3), 551–8.

Rezzoug, D., De Plaën, S., Bensekhar-Bennabi, M. et al. (2007). Bilinguisme chez les enfants de migrants: mythes et réalités. *Le Français Aujourd'hui, 158*, 61–8.

Rousseau, C., & Drapeau, A. (1998). *The impact of culture on the transmission of trauma. International handbook of multigenerational legacies of trauma* (pp. 465–86). New York: Plenum Press.

Scheeringa, M. S., & Zeanah, C. H. (2001). A relational perspective on PTSD in early childhood. *Journal of Traumatic Stress, 14*, 799–815.

Schnapper, D. (1991). *La France de l'intégration. Sociologie de la nation en 1990*. Paris: PUF.

Sturm, G., Baubet, T., & Moro, M. R. (2007). Mobilizing social and symbolic resources in transcultural therapies with refugees and asylum seekers: the story of Mister Diallo. In B. Drozdek & P. Wilson (Eds.), *The voices of trauma: Treating survivors across cultures* (pp. 211–32). New York: Springer Science + Business Media.

van der Kolk, B. A. (1996). The complexity of adaptation to trauma. In B. A. van der Kolk, A. C. McFarlane, & L. Weisaeth (Eds.), *Traumatic stress: The effect of overwhelming experiences on mind, body, and society* (pp. 182–213). New York: Guilford Press.

Winnicott, D. W. (1969). *De la pédiatrie à la psychanalyse*. Paris: Payot.

Winnicott, D. W. (2000). Le concept de traumatisme par rapport au développement de l'individu au sein de sa famille. In *La crainte de l'effondrement et autres situations cliniques* (pp. 292–312). Paris: Gallimard.

Winnicott, D. W. (2004). *Les enfants et la guerre*. Paris: Payot.

Further Reading

Baubet, T., Marquer, C., Sturm, G., Rezzoug, D. & Moro, M. R. (2005). Un dispositive original, le "groupe trauma". *Rhizome, Bulletin National Santé Mentale et Précarité, 21*, 33–36.

Baubet, T., Abbal, T., Claudet, J. et al. (2004). Traumas psychiques chez les demandeurs d'asile en France: des spécificités cliniques et thérapeutiques. *Journal International de Victimologie, 2*(2), [1 screen]. Retrieved from www.jidv.com/BAUBET,T-JIDV2004_%202(2).html (accessed December 15, 2007).

Crocq, L. (2001). Perspective historique sur le trauma. In M. De Clerq & F. Lebigot (Eds.), *Les traumatismes psychiques* (pp. 23–64). Paris: Masson.

Crocq, L. (2002). Persée, la Méduse et l'effroi. *Stress & Trauma, 2*(3), 133–8.

Farwel, N. (2001). Onward through strength: Coping and psychological support among refugee youth returning to Eritrea from Sudan. *Journal of Refugee Studies, 14*, 1–69.

Lebigot, F. (2002). L'effroi du traumatisme psychique: le regarder en face ou s'en protéger. *Stress & Trauma, 2*(3), 139–46.

Mead, M. (1963). *Mœurs et sexualité en Océanie*. Paris: Plon.

Stern, D. (1985). *The Interpersonal World of the Infant: A view from psychoanalysis and development psychology*. Karnac Books: London (1989). New York. Basic Books.

Taïeb, O., Baubet, T., Pradère, J. et al. (2004). Traumatismes psychiques chez l'enfant et l'adolescent. *EMC-Psychiatrie, 1*(1), 23–32.

Terr, L. (1991). Childhood traumas: An outline and overview. *The American Journal of Psychiatry, 148*(1), 10–20.

Tomkiewicz, S., Manciaux, M. (1987). La vulnérabilité. In M. Manciaux, S. Lebovici, O. Jeanneret, E. A. Sand, & S. Tomkiewicz (Eds.), *L'enfant et sa santé. Aspects épidémiologiques, biologiques, psychologiques et sociaux* (pp. 737–42). Paris: Doin.

Chapter Five

Post-Traumatic Stress Related to Pediatric Illness and Injury

Elena Camisasca

Introduction

A new and useful framework for understanding key aspects of individual and family responses to the experience of children's medical illness, injury, and medical treatment refers to the construct of traumatic stress.
According to Kassam-Adams (2006):

> [A] traumatic stress framework complements traditional areas of pediatric psychology expertise and practice by bringing a specific and helpful new lens to the question of how illness, injury, or medical procedures affect children and families and has the potential to broaden the conceptualizations of the impact of medical events by drawing from a rich literature on the effects of other sudden or frightening experiences that may involve dimensions shared by many medical events, for example, life threat, physical risk, pain or anticipated pain, or exposure to the suffering of others (p. 338).

Since the use of this conceptual framework presupposes that pediatric medical events can be defined as *traumatic*, it is as well to remember the evolution of the diagnostic formulation of PTSD, and of the traumatic events associated with it, in the different editions of the *DSM*.

In particular, the formulation contained in *DSM-III* (APA, 1980) defined the traumatic event as a subjective experience understood as a "recognizable stressor that would evoke significant symptoms of distress in almost everyone," allowing many injuries and serious illnesses to be considered as traumatic. In contrast, *DSM-III-R* (APA, 1987) redefined a potentially traumatic stressor as

Post-Traumatic Syndromes in Childhood and Adolescence: A Handbook of Research and Practice, First Edition. Edited by Vittoria Ardino. © 2011 John Wiley & Sons, Ltd. Published 2011 by John Wiley & Sons, Ltd.

an event "outside the range of usual human experience" that would be distressing for almost everyone, including witnessing or learning of such an event experienced by family or a loved one. This definition, although it excludes the possibility that injuries/illnesses or other medical events might be considered traumatic stressors, inasmuch as they are common enough events to be human, introduces another interesting aspect. In fact, this definition conveys the idea that parents, or other members of the family of the victim of these events, can be psychologically affected as a repercussion. Finally, *DSM-IV* (APA, 1994) and, subsequently, *DSM-IV- TR* (APA, 2000) introduce a dual aspect into the definition of the traumatic event. It is, in fact, specified that the individual "has experienced, witnessed, or been confronted with an event or events that involve actual or threatened death or serious injury, or a threat to the physical integrity of oneself or others" and that the person "experienced fear, helplessness, or horror at the time of the event." This definition not only specifically includes the possibility that the injuries can be defined as traumatic stressors, but reiterates the possibility that these events may exert a traumatic effect on both sick subjects and family members.

From this there was an increasing attention to illness as a potential stress-inducing event in both adults and children/adolescents. It is, in fact, possible to maintain that, beginning in the 1980s with the studies on cancer survivors and their parents, there has been a continuous growth in studies which explore the presence of PTSD symptoms: first in injured adults and, more recently, in injured children, adolescents, and their parents.

Although this framework proposes to evaluate post-traumatic stress symptoms (PTSS) and/or traumatic stress disorders (Acute Stress Disorder [ASD] and Post-Traumatic Stress Disorder [PTSD]; APA, 1994), it underlines the importance of focusing on resilience processes (Kassam-Adams, 2006; Kazak et al., 2006), which are present in many children and their parents.

Likewise, it is important to emphasize that not all children/adolescents exposed to *traumatic* events develop PTSD or a related disorder. Some may overcome more effectively a traumatic event; others develop threshold post-traumatic-related symptoms (Keppel-Benson, Ollendick, & Benson, 2002). Two reviews on cancer survivors and their parents (Bruce, 2006; Taïeb et al., 2003) showed a prevalence of PTSS from moderate to severe intensity and/or compatible with a current PTSD (2%–21% of child survivors and 10%–30% of their parents). Similarly, studies on injured children and their parents found that prevalence rates of ASD symptoms and/or threshold ASD vary from 1.6% (Winston et al., 2005) to 28% of injured children (Winston et al., 2002) and from 4.7% (Winston et al., 2005) to 32% of their parents (Balluffi et al., 2004). Furthermore, rates of PTSS vary from 12.5% (Fein et al., 2002) to 34% of children (Stallard, Velleman, & Baldwin, 1998) and from 9% (Hall et al., 2006) to 17% and 23% of their parents (Landolt et al., 2003).

Recently, it has become evident that the discrepancy in prevalence rates is associated with a series of risk and protection factors that can increase or inhibit the emergence of post-traumatic symptomatology. A series of studies was carried out to explore the role of specific sociodemographic, contextual, relational, and individual variables responsible for the emergence of trauma-related symptomatology. This chapter reflects on the specific risks of pediatric illness as a traumatic event and on its subjective interpretation. Furthermore, the chapter puts forward the role of peri traumatic physiological distress responses and the protective role of family and social relational variables.

The chapter reviews the main findings in this area aiming at highlighting the impact of illness/injury-related traumatic stress on children and their parents, and the interplay of traumatic stress responses with other individual and family risk and protective factors.

Risk and protective factors in post-traumatic stress related to pediatric illness and injury

On the basis of the most recent literature, this study explores the predictive role of several factors implied in the onset of traumatic stress in pediatric illnesses and injuries. More specifically, sociodemographic variables are considered: contextual and individual factors prior to the traumatic exposure, the nature of the traumatic event, the subjective processing of the event, acute distress, physiological arousal reactions, and finally the parent–child relationship, family functioning, and social support.

Sociodemographic variables: gender, age, and socioeconomic status

The literature on pediatric illnesses does not show unique findings in terms of the role of specific sociodemographic variables (gender, age, family income) linked to the onset of PTSS.

Literature shows that being female is a key risk factor in children who survived cancer (see Bruce, 2006, for review); however, studies on injured children show discrepant findings: some confirm the predictive role of being female in both patients (Mirza et al., 1998; Stallard et al.,1998; Zatzick et al., 2006) and their parents (Balluffi et al., 2004; Landolt et al., 2003), but others do not confirm this result (Aaron, Zaglul, & Emery, 1999; Fein et al., 1991; Fein et al., 2002; Winston et al., 2005; Zink & McCain, 2002).

The role played by age was also inconsistent across different studies. The study by de Vries and colleagues (1999) on injured children and the study by Hobbie and colleagues (2000) on cancer survivors show that older children tend to exhibit higher rates of PTSS and PTSD than younger ones; however, similar studies failed to support the aforementioned findings (Aaron et al., 1999; Fein et al., 2002; Goldenberg Libov et al., 2002; Kazak et al., 1997;

Landolt et al., 2003; Nugent, Christopher, & Delahanty, 2006; Stallard et al., 1998; Taïeb et al., 2003; Winston et al., 2005; Zink & McCain, 2002).

Finally, while some studies do not show significant associations between socioeconomic status and PTSD symptoms in injured patients (Aaron et al., 1999; Keppel-Benson et al., 2002), others find that high family incomes are positively correlated with PTSS in the mothers of injured children and in children suffering from cancer (Goldenberg Libov et al., 2002; Landolt et al., 2003). This paradoxical result may be explained by hypothesizing that a higher income may result in higher work-related stress/pressure, which, in turn, increases the stress deriving from the illness and its treatment (Goldenberg Libov et al., 2002).

Environmental and individual factors prior to the traumatic event

An ecological study explored the role of specific contextual variables (e.g., stressful life events) and individual factors (prior psychopathology) present prior to the traumatic exposure.

Stressful life events
The hypothesis that both the quantity and the quality of stressful life events prior to a traumatic event constitute a risk factor for PTSD symptoms has not been empirically confirmed.

Some studies on cancer survivors (Barakat et al., 1997; Brown, Madan-Swain, & Lambert, 2003; Goldenberg Libov et al., 2002; Pelcovitz et al., 1998; Stuber et al., 1997) and on injured children (Daviss et al., 2000a; Stallard et al., 1998; Zatzick et al., 2006) show that the highest rates of PTSS are associated with a higher number of past and recent stressful life events; conversely, some studies did not find similar results in both samples either in cancer survivors (Barakat et al., 2000; Manne, DuHamel, & Redd, 2000) or in injured children (de Vries et al., 1999).

The retrospective study by Keppel-Benson et al. (2002) shows that injured children who had previously experienced a car accident reported *better* outcomes than did those who had not experienced any previous accidents. However, the authors underline the importance of further investigating a network of stressors that could contribute to children's outcomes.

A study conducted on 49 mothers of pediatric cancer survivors explored the different predictive weight of stressors of different magnitude (Goldenberg Libov et al., 2002) on PTSD symptoms. The data do not show significant associations between previous high-magnitude stressors (natural disaster or abuse) and rates of cancer-related PTSS. In contrast, there is a correlation between low magnitude stressors (marital distress and economic instability) and PTSS. However, the study by Daviss and colleagues (2000a) on 48 injured children and their parents shows that the children (especially females) with a diagnosis of full and partial PTSD, compared to subjects without PTSD, report a significantly higher rate of prior sexual abuse. Finally, the recent study by Zatzick and colleagues (2006), conducted on 97 injured adolescents (aged 12–18) and their parents, found that 40% of the parents and 30% of the injured adolescents had undergone at least four traumatic experiences before the last injury and that the pre-injury traumatic experiences constituted an important predictor of PTSS and depression symptoms in adolescents. The authors comment on the results, hypothesizing the existence of developmental trajectories including a history of prolonged traumatic exposure.

Pre-trauma psychopathology

A series of studies has analyzed the connection between behavioral problems prior to the traumatic event and PTSS in children and their parents. Research in the area highlighted both the role of internalizing behavior (Aaron, Zaglul, & Emery, 1999; Kazak et al., 1998; Mirza et al., 1998; Max et al., 1998) and of externalizing behavior (Daviss et al., 2000a; Daviss et al., 2000b) in the onset of PTSD symptoms in both children and their parents who experienced pediatric illness and injuries.

Mirza and colleagues (1998) in a study on 119 injured children (mean age 13.6 years) and Max and colleagues (1998) in a study on 50 children (6–14 years) with traumatic brain injury found that high levels of anxiety and depression are associated with post-traumatic symptomatology both at six weeks and at six months after the accident.

Internalizing symptoms have also played a role in the onset of PTSD in a study conducted on the mothers (N = 111) of children who are survivors of hematopoietic stem cell transplantation (Manne et al., 2004). The results indicate, in fact, a significant association between maternal anxiety/depression and PTSD symptoms measured 18 months after the conclusion of the treatment. The authors put forward two possible explanations: the first points out that post-traumatic reactions are an expression of preexisting psychiatric disturbances; the second contends that internalization leads to a focus on negative/aversive aspects of the traumatic event, which, in turn, favors the onset of persistent PTSS.

The relationship between pre-trauma internalizing behavior and PTSD is further investigated in two other studies where the mediating role of subjective appraisal of the event is shown. Aaron, Zaglul, and Emery (1999) carried out a study on 40 injured children showing the mediating role of peri traumatic fear responses. Findings indicate that children with frequent pre-trauma internalizing behaviors showed a more intense peri traumatic reaction at the moment of the injury, which, in turn, was associated with the development of PTSD symptoms. Kazak and colleagues (1998), in a study carried out on 640 parents of cancer survivors (who completed the treatment at least a year before), showed the mediating role of parents' appraisal of life threat and treatment intensity in determining the interaction between trait anxiety and PTSD symptoms.

Finally, two other studies carried out on injured children showed the predictive role of behavioral problems in the onset of ASD symptoms (Daviss et al., 2000b) and of PTSD symptoms at least one month after hospitalization (Daviss et al., 2000a). These studies hypothesized that the previous psychopathology (especially in terms of externalizing symptoms) could have increased the risk of children being injured.

The event typology and individual processing

Kazak and colleagues (2006) underline that, in medical settings, there are various events that could be potentially traumatic. These events, however, are defined only as *potentially traumatic* (PTE) since the same event may not elicit the same post-traumatic reactions in all children and families exposed to illness or injury (p. 344).

Indeed, the individual response to the event determines the intensity of the event in children who survived both cancer and injury. Reviews (Bruce, 2006; Taïeb et al., 2003) have shown *the role of individual differences in the onset of this symptomatology*. More specifically, Taïeb and colleagues (2003) show how beliefs about past and present life threats and perceptions of treatment intensity were more predictive of post-traumatic symptomatology than the medical conditions or procedures per se (e.g., type and stage of cancer, type and duration of treatment, and medical sequelae). Similarly, Bruce (2006) emphasizes how medical data about illness seriousness and type of treatment have failed to predict PTSS in cancer survivors and PTSD in their parents.

Research on injured children/adolescents and their parents does not provide consistent findings. In fact, whilst some studies underline how the gravity of the accident and the type of injury do not predict the onset of PTSD (Balluffi et al., 2004; Mirza et al., 1998; Nugent et al., 2006; Stallard et al., 1998; de Vries et al., 1999; Zinc & McCain, 2003), others (Keppel-Benson et al., 2002; Landolt et al., 1998; Rees et al., 2004) show the combined effect of medical data and individual responses. More specifically, a retrospective study (Keppel-Benson et al., 2002), carried out nine months after a road accident of 50 injured children (7–16 years) and their parents, shows that PTSD in injured children (14%) was closely associated both with injury severity and with the modalities of the accident (car passenger vs. pedestrian/bicyclist). Children who experienced more severe injuries and children who were injured while riding a bicycle or as pedestrians reported more symptoms. In a similar study conducted on children admitted to pediatric intensive care units (PICU) (N = 35) and to general pediatric units (N = 33) and on their parents, Rees and colleagues (2004) found that admission to PICU units constitutes a more severe traumatic event (children PTSD: 21% vs. 0%; parental PTSD: 27% vs. 7%) than admission to general pediatric departments. The authors also show significant correlations between PTSD, threat appraisal, and illness severity. Parental PTSD symptoms are significantly associated with the number of days spent in hospital by the child, illness severity, and appraisal of threat. Consistent with these results, Landolt and colleagues (1998) found a different prevalence of post-traumatic stress reactions in children (9%) and in parents (20%) admitted for minor illnesses (tonsillectomy, orchidopexy, excision of a cyst) requiring short admissions and no painful medical procedures (low-risk group: N = 11) compared to children (52%) and parents (68%) admitted for severe illnesses/injuries (cancer, burns, head injury, fractures of extremities) alongside prolonged stays and complex/painful medical procedures. Finally, in a further study analyzing the presence and possible predictors of PTSD in 209 pediatric patients (aged 6.5–14.5 years) across different conditions (injuries from accidents, new diagnosis of cancer or diabetes) and their parents, the authors (Landolt et al., 2003) showed that injured children reported more severe PTSS than children with a newly diagnosed chronic disease; furthermore, they showed that parents showed more serious post-traumatic reactions resulting from a cancer diagnosis than parents of children with diabetes or physical injuries. A significant association also emerged between parental PTSS and PTSD and medical parameters like the functional status of the child and the length of the hospitalization. The discrepancy in the results obtained in the parents and in children could be explained by the different interpretative nature of an injury and of a chronic illness. More specifically, children may interpret more easily accidents as extremely frightening and stressful events whereas they may be less able to interpret chronic illness as a threat to life due to their developing cognitive abilities. Furthermore, the sense of uncertainty about health states represents a key part of individual responses that may lead to PTSD in children and their parents (Lee, 2006; Lee et al., 2009; Mishel, 1990; Santacroce, 2002, 2003). A sense of uncertainty – or the inability to make meaning of illness – is characterized by four general features:

(a) ambiguity about the illness state; (b) lack of information about the illness, treatment, side effects and management; (c) complexity of information, care system, communication with healthcare providers; and (d) unpredictability of a person's prognosis, quality of life and ability to function (Santacroce, 2003, p. 46).

Nonetheless, uncertainty could be overcome differently across individuals who could interpret such a state as dangerous or beneficial. The individual response is determined by individual mental health, illness severity, treatment, and environmental factors, such as social support, relationship with healthcare providers, and the sociocultural context of illness.

Mishel (1990) hypothesized that individuals who consider chronic uncertainty as dangerous and feel themselves unable to cope with such uncertainty are more vulnerable to post-traumatic symptoms. Considering uncertainty as dangerous, individuals cope with the consequent unpleasant state by restricting/avoiding their self-awareness about uncertainty itself (Foa, Zinbarg, & Rothbaum, 1992).

The association between uncertainty and PTSD symptoms has been examined by Fuemmeler, Mullins, and Marx (2001) in a study carried out on a sample of 28 parents of 19 pediatric brain tumor patients. The authors studied both *perceived uncertainty due to the illness condition* and emotion-focused coping, hypothesizing that these two cognitive appraisal mechanisms would be associated with the severity of post-traumatic symptoms and general distress. Results indicate that perceived uncertainty constitutes an important correlate of both PTSS and general distress. Emotion-focused coping proved, on the other hand, to be associated only with increased general distress. In a further study carried out on parents of child cancer survivors (N = 47) and of children with diabetes mellitus type 1 (N = 31), the authors (Fuemmeler et al., 2005) show that the parents of cancer survivors demonstrate significantly higher levels of PTSS (32%) than parents of children with diabetes (10%), confirming the role of illness uncertainty and emotion-focused coping in the onset of symptoms both of PTSD and of general distress. A more recent study conducted on 45 long-term survivors of childhood cancer (aged 22–47 years) confirmed the aforementioned role of uncertainty in the onset of PTSD (Lee, 2006).

Cognitive processing involved in the interpretation of the event also plays a role in the maintenance of PTSD in children and adolescents; particularly, cognitive biases toward a negative perception of the event and its consequence may play a role when a pervasive and long-lasting sense of threat is perceived. Consequently, aiming at reducing the state of threat, individuals use dysfunctional cognitive strategies (thought suppression, avoidance, rumination, and dissociation) that are responsible for maintaining the problem (Ehlers & Steil, 1995; Steil & Ehlers, 2000).

The study by Aaron and colleagues (1999) on 40 children (mean age 13.6 years) victims of motor vehicle accidents (MVAs) found that a quarter of participants had developed PTSD, and demonstrated that peri traumatic fear alongside thought suppression constitute the predictors of PTSD a month after the trauma. Likewise, higher levels of fear and of thought suppression were associated with a worsening of the symptoms. Similarly, the study by Ehlers, Mayou, and Bryant (2003) on 86 children exposed to MVAs aged between five and 16 years confirmed the predictive role of thought suppression strategies and showed the role of brooding, of persistent dissociation, and of specific negative appraisals of the event in the onset of PTSD. Both negative appraisals of the trauma and of its consequences (negative interpretations of intrusive memories, such as "I'm going mad," self-detachment from others' behavior, and feelings of injustice about what happened) and thought control strategies (brooding, suppression, and dissociation) predict PTSD at three and six months after the event. Among thought control strategies, brooding proved to be the most strongly associated with PTSD across time. Stallard, Velleman, Langsford, and Baldwin (2001) conducted a study on distraction strategies that are considered to undermine the processing of traumatic memories. In particular, the study carried out on 97 MVAs aged between seven and 18 years demonstrated that the use of distraction strategies is associated with the presence of PTSD evaluated at six weeks after the accident; however, they were not associated with an assessment of PTSD at eight months after the trauma. Such findings challenge the investigation of thought control strategies in relation to PTSD and other anxiety and depression disorders.

Saxe and colleagues (2005) investigated, in a group of 72 severely burnt children (mean age 11.20 years), whether trauma characteristics (surface of the body burnt) and different reactions in the immediate aftermath (separation anxiety, dissociation, pain) are correlated with resulting PTSD symptoms. The results show the presence of two mutually independent developmental trajectories of PTSD. More specifically, two distinct trajectories emerge in which separation anxiety and dissociation play a mediating role between trauma severity (the extent of the burnt surface) and the onset of PTSD. The first trajectory shows that most severe burns cause higher levels of dissociation that, in turn, predict the onset of PTSD symptoms. The second trajectory shows that both the burn's severity and the level of peri-traumatic pain (experienced immediately after the burn) favor a stronger separation anxiety which, in turn, predicts the PTSS. The marked difference and independence of the two trajectories highlight the existence of two distinct bio-compartmental systems underlying the onset of PTSD. More specifically, the anxiety responses have been associated with the *fight-or-flight* responses activated by the sympathetic system. The dissociative systems, on the other hand, have been associated with the *freeze-or-immobilization* responses activated by the parasympathetic system. The authors have also hypothesized an evolutionary sequence in the appearance of these reactions. In conditions of immediate danger, the hyperarousal fight-or-flight responses are the first to appear. In contrast, the freeze-or-immobilization responses appear only afterwards, when the subjective evaluation indicates the presence of a danger that cannot be avoided or modified.

In a later work, Hall and colleagues (2006), referring to the stress-diathesis framework (Yehuda, 1999), explore – in 62 parents of children with burns (mean age 11.45 years) – the possible interaction between individual vulnerability factors (peri-traumatic anxiety and dissociation) and environmental factors (family conflict) in the onset of PTSD symptoms. The results demonstrate two distinct developmental PTSD trajectories. In the first trajectory, environmental factors (conflict with the extended families) and burn severity predict PTSS via dissociation (individual vulnerability factor). In other words, the parents of severely burnt children who are in conflict with their family members develop more serious dissociative responses that favor the onset of post-traumatic symptomatology. In the second trajectory, peri-traumatic anxiety (an individual vulnerability factor) predicts PTSD symptoms only indirectly, that is only through the mediation of increased conflict in the relationship with the child (environmental factor). In other words, the parents who develop high peri traumatic anxiety tend, after being discharged from hospital, to place restrictions on the child's autonomy with the objective of preventing the risk of new injuries. This behavior determines an increase of parent–child conflict which undermines trauma processing and favors the maintenance of PTSD symptoms.

Distress reactions and physiological arousal in the aftermath of trauma

A recent study on environmental risk factors conducted in an Emergency Department (ED) and Pediatric Intensive Care Unit (PICU) explored the role of *acute distress reactions* and *physiological arousal* in the onset of PTSS in pediatric patients and in their parents. This study combined with a few previous studies demonstrates that research on injured children and their parents confirms that undertaken with adults (see Harvey and Bryant, 2002, for a review). Specifically, research on injured children highlights the role of acute stress as a significant marker for prolonged emotional and psychological distress. Simultaneously, however, these studies indicate that a few individuals may develop PTSD without having previously met ASD criteria. In fact, a study conducted by Di Gallo, Barton, and Parry-Jones (1997) on 57 road traffic accident victims (aged 5–18 years) and their parents shows the role of acute stress symptoms experienced after the accident (2–16 days post-accident) in the onset of PTSS (12–15 weeks post-accident). The work by Fein and colleagues (2002) conducted on 69 violently injured patients (aged 12–24 years) reached similar conclusions indicating that the presence of ASD symptoms (measured in the immediate aftermath) is correlated with the severity of PTSD symptoms months after the event. Furthermore, a prospective study (Balluffi et al., 2004) carried out on parents (N = 272) of MVAs children (< 17 years) admitted to PICUs confirms the predictive role of the presence and severity of ASD symptoms in the onset of parental PTSD symptoms at least two months after discharge.

In a study conducted on 243 injured children (8–17 years), Kassam-Adams and Winston (2004) found that 8% of children met criteria for ASD and another 14% had threshold ASD one month after injury. Three months after the accident, 6% met the criteria for PTSD and another 11% had threshold PTSD. Similarly, Meiser-Stedman and colleagues (2005), in a study carried out on 93 injured children (10–16 years), found that 19.4% had ASD and that 24.7% met all ASD criteria, except dissociation, one month after injury. At six months after the injury, data indicate that 12.5% had PTSD and that ASD was a good predictor of later PTSD; however, dissociation was not significantly correlated with ASD.

These results are confirmed in a subsequent study by Bryant and colleagues (2007), conducted on 76 injured children (7–13 years), in which it emerged that 10% of the patients met ASD criteria and that, at six months post-trauma, 13% satisfied criteria for PTSD. Acute stress reactions that did not include dissociation provided better prediction of PTSD than full ASD criteria.

Regarding sympathetic reactions, available studies on pediatric patients have revealed that heart rate (Kassam-Adams et al., 2005; Nugent et al., 2006; Nugent et al., 2007) and levels of urinary cortisol (Delahanty et al., 2005), measured in the immediate aftermath constitute important predictors of PTSS. More specifically, Kassam-Adams and colleagues (2005) explored the reaction between cardiac frequency and PTSD in 190 children/adolescents (aged 8–17 years) hospitalized for traffic-related injury showing that high heart rate (measured within five minutes of arrival in the ED) predicted a small (but significant) proportion of variance in the severity of PTSD symptoms. Data indicate that children with a high heart rate met partial or full PTSD diagnosis at follow-up, at least three months after (28% vs. 12%) the accident. In particular, children with a high heart rate present more serious symptoms of hyperarousal (30% vs. 16%) but not of reexperiencing (44% vs. 31%) or of avoidance (13% vs. 9%). Attempting to replicate the above results, Nugent and colleagues (2006) showed how a single measurement of heart rate (at the moment of admission to the ED) cannot constitute a reliable parameter of evaluation as it may be influenced by a variety of factors (delay between time of traumatic injury and ED admission, medications, ED treatment). Therefore, in their study conducted on a sample of 82 children and adolescents (aged 8–18 years), the authors measured the heart rate at different moments in time (in the ambulance, upon admission to the ED, the first 20 minutes following admission, and at discharge). Findings suggest that the heart rate measured in the immediate aftermath (EMS) predicted PTSD symptoms both at six weeks and at six months after the event. In contrast, the heart rates at admission and discharge were not associated with subsequent PTSD symptoms.

Delahanty and colleagues (2005) explored the role of cortisol in the onset of PTSD to replicate a study conducted with abused children (Cicchetti & Rogosh, 2001), in which it emerged that abused children with PTSD had higher levels of salivary cortisol than children without PTSD. In their study carried out on 82 injured children (average age 13.04 years), the authors (Delahanty et al.) explored the association between the levels of urinary cortisol (measured within 12 hours after the trauma), acute PTSD symptoms, and depression symptoms (measured six weeks after the trauma). Data demonstrated an association between levels of urinary cortisol and PTSS symptoms six weeks after the trauma even when demographic variables (parental income and child's gender) and comorbid depression were controlled. Analyses controlling for gender, however, showed a predictive role of cortisol in the onset of PTSD in males but not in females. Finally, the recent work by Nugent and colleagues (2007) explores the role of both the two physiological indicators (heart rate and cortisol) and of parental PTSD in the onset of child PTSS. In the study carried out on 82 injured children (average age 13.04 years) and their parents, the authors hypothesized that the parents' acute PTSD symptoms may moderate the effect of the children's biological predictors (level of cortisol and heart rate) in the onset of child PTSS (at six months from the traumatic event). More specifically, they maintain that PTSD symptoms may perform a moderating role only in the case of biologically vulnerable children (i.e., with high initial physiological levels of biological predictors). Data confirmed the role of moderation of parental PTSD symptoms in the relation between biological predictors and child PTSS (six months after the trauma). However, children who did *not* present biological risk indicators developed PTSS through the moderation of their parents' responses to the trauma. Children with low levels of cortisol and heart rate prove to be more influenced by parental PTSS: they exhibit greater PTSS at high levels of parental PTSS and lower PTSS at low levels of parental PTSS.

Parents' response to the traumatic event: the association between parent and child post-traumatic stress reactions

The potential association between parents' and children's distress reactions gathered great scientific interest in the area of pediatric illnesses and injuries. However, available studies on the co-occurrence of parental post-traumatic symptoms and children with illness and injuries do not present consistent results. Some studies found correlations between the levels of parent and child PTSS/PTSD (Barakat et al., 1997; Daviss et al., 2000a, 2000b; Kazak et al., 1997; Pelcovitz et al., 1998; Stuber et al., 1996; de Vries et al., 1999); others have failed to report such relations (Bryant et al., 2004; Kazak et al., 2004; Landolt et al., 2003; Winston et al., 2002). Taking into account potential methodological pitfalls to explain such discrepancies (different age of the subjects examined, different timing of the evaluations, effect of complex interactions between the variables not the subject of analysis (Nugent et al., 2007)), scholars could identify some important points. In fact, the studies that examine acute distress levels, with the exception of the work by Daviss and colleagues (2000b), did not show significant associations between parental distress symptoms and child distress symptoms (Bryant et al., 2004; Winston et al., 2002). In contrast, the studies that analyze chronic distress report the existence of significant correlations between parents' and children's PTSD symptoms (Barakat et al., 1997, Kazak et al., 1997; Pelcovitz et al., 1998). Finally, prospective studies highlight the predictive role of parental ASD symptoms in their children's PTSD symptoms (Daviss et al., 2000a). The finding about the influence of parental distress on children's psychological well-being paved the way for two interpretative hypotheses (Nugent et al., 2007). The first hypothesis considers the effect of general levels of parental distress on children's development underlining that a distressed parent (i.e., more irritable, with poor physical and psychological resources, less attentive toward the child's needs) undermines the child's psychological well-being (Sawyer et al., 1998; Schwartz, Dohrenwend, & Levav, 1994). The second and more recent interpretative hypothesis specifically considers the role of parental PTSS in the development of child PTSS, suggesting that parental PTSS are more predictive of children's PTSD than parental distress.

The understating of the role of PTSS moved from a focus on the impact of general parental PTSS to a focus on specific aspects of PTSD which may influence the persistence of specific symptoms in some children more than others.

For example, children's avoidance of traumatic reminders may be influenced by parental avoidance responses. In fact,

> parents with PTSS caused by the child's injury might have difficulties in discussing the event with their child or might actively avoid activities or places associated with the event, preventing the child from habituating to these reminders. Alternatively, children may be sensitive to their parents' levels of distress and may avoid situations/discussions that could further distress their parents, thus reducing the child's exposure to, and subsequent habituation to, trauma-related stimuli (Nugent et al., 2007, p. 310).

In a recent study (Meiser-Stedman et al., 2006) carried out on 66 injured children and adolescents (mean age 13.8 years) and their parents, the authors analyzed the role of specific maladaptive parental cognitive styles in the relation between parental depression and child PTSS. More specifically, the authors hypothesized that this relation could be mediated by three specific parental cognitive styles (brooding, worry, and anxiety sensitivity). The results demonstrate that only parental worry mediated between parental depression and child PTSS. The authors explain the greater predictive weight of worry on child PTSS, demonstrating that worrisome parents can encourage avoidance and hypervigilance in their children, and act as an additional reminder of the trauma and its consequences. The other two aforementioned cognitive styles may not have been significantly correlated with later child PTSS because they represent internal processes and thereby may not be modeled by the child.

Current family functioning and social support

There are various studies that indicate the presence of a significant association between family functioning, social support, and PTSD symptoms in pediatric patients and in their parents.

Pelcovitz and colleagues (1998), in a study carried out on adolescent cancer survivors (N = 33), found that the subjects with PTSD perceived their families as more chaotic than the subjects without PTSD. The retrospective study carried out on 319 childhood cancer survivors and their parents (Barakat et al., 1997) demonstrated the protective role of family cohesion, satisfaction, and social support in the onset of maternal PTSD symptoms and of family cohesion alone for paternal PTSD symptoms. The protective role of satisfaction and communication within the family at the onset of child and parental PTSS symptoms was also shown in the study by Kazak and colleagues (1997) carried out on 130 childhood leukemia patients and their parents.

In contrast to this, in a study carried out on 90 mothers of children subjected to bone marrow transplants (Manne et al., 2002), the negative responses of family and friends (in terms of overtly critical and insensitive responses, avoidance, and withdrawal) constitute important risk factors in the onset of maternal PTSD symptoms (measured six months after the transplant).

In a subsequent study by Young and colleagues (2003), carried out on caregivers (N = 170) of pediatric transplant recipients, parents who reported feelings that family and social functioning (e.g., traveling, participating in social events, visiting with friends and relatives) was negatively affected by the transplant presented more severe PTSD symptoms. Furthermore, a parental negative attitude toward healthcare services increased parents' vulnerability to PTSD. The study by Brown and colleagues (2003) on 52 adolescent cancer survivors and their mothers showed that mothers' perception of family support was associated with fewer PTSS, whereas high levels of family conflict were associated with a greater number of PTSS. Finally, Keppel-Benson and colleagues (2002) confirmed the protective role of social support in injured children. The results of the study on 50 injured children indicated that children who were enabled to talk about the traumatic event (i.e., with emergency personnel, nurses, and doctors) and to be reassured about their future had fewer PTSD symptoms.

Methodological considerations

The above results seem to highlight some differences both in the prevalence of PTSS and PTSD and in the role of associated risk and protective factors. Several considerations could contribute to the understanding of present inconsistencies in the examined literature. A first consideration regards sampling, research design, and measures to assess PTSS and PTSD methods (Bruce, 2006; Saxe et al., 2003; Taïeb et al., 2003).

Regarding *sampling problems*, sample sizes of the examined studies varied considerably, ranging from 25 (Santacroce, 2002) to 640 (Kazak et al., 1998) participants. Therefore, findings may be subject to the Type I error affecting their reliability; conversely, in larger samples, reliability may be affected by the presence of heterogeneous samples in terms of age, type of illness or injuries, differences in prognosis, treatment modality, number of recurrences, length of hospitalization. Regarding *study design*, one limit was the paucity of prospective longitudinal *studies* that are the most appropriate to address questions about the severity and causality of the observed phenomena. Regarding the *assessment* of PTSD and PTSS, instruments and procedures used in the studies vary considerably, favoring erroneous comparisons: some studies used diagnostic interviews able to provide a diagnosis of PTSD; others used self-report questionnaires which can only measure PTSS. Finally, there is not yet a gold standard instrument to measure post-traumatic reactions in this age range.

Conclusions

Studies on risk and protective factors associated with PTSD symptoms in pediatric patients and their parents showed some discrepancies regarding the role of specific variables (sex, age, socioeconomic status, previous stressful life events, and objective nature of the event) and some shared findings underlining the role of individual and environmental-specific factors.

At an individual level, acute stress reactions and other peri traumatic physiological indicators play a decisive role (i.e., heart rate and cortisol) in favoring the onset of PTSS. Similarly, individual appraisals of the traumatic event constitute a decisive predictive factor in the onset of PTSS. Available studies have been increasing the background of understanding of pediatric illness-related trauma by including different aspects that could contribute to the advancement of knowledge. More specifically, studies explored different constructs and cognitive processes, such as health-related, fear/peri traumatic anxiety, coping strategies, specific cognitive strategies (brooding, worry, suppression, and dissociation). Altogether, these constructs could explain the process of individual misinterpretation of the traumatic symptoms.

Reviewed prospective studies highlighted the predictive role of parental distress reactions in the onset of the children's psychological dysfunction demonstrating an increasing understanding of this mechanism. Research moved from the general idea that distressed parents negatively influence children's adjustment to investigate different possible interpretations. Therefore, specific aspects of parents' post-traumatic symptomatology (e.g., avoidance of stimuli associated with trauma) and/or of parents' specific cognitive styles were explored to explain the onset of PTSS in children. Finally, studies agreed on emphasizing the protective role of social support and of the quality of family functioning considered both in structural terms (e.g., cohesion, chaotic nature) and in terms of communicative patterns within the family.

To conclude, I believe that future research will promote a more sophisticated framework to explore potential intersections between individual and relational factors (as in the study by Hall et al., 2006) and between individual cognitive and bio-behavioral factors.

References

Aaron, J., Zaglul, H., & Emery, R. E. (1999). Posttraumatic stress in children following acute physical injury. *Journal of Pediatric Psychology, 24,* 335–43.

American Psychiatric Association (APA) (1980). *Diagnostic and Statistical Manual of Mental Disorders* (3rd ed.) (*DSM-III*). Washington, DC: Author.

American Psychiatric Association (APA) (1987). *Diagnostic and Statistical Manual of Mental Disorders* (3rd ed.-Rev.) (*DSM-III-R*). Washington, DC: Author.

American Psychiatric Association (APA) (1994). *Diagnostic and Statistical Manual of Mental Disorders* (4th ed.) (*DSM-IV*). Washington, DC: Author.

American Psychiatric Association (APA) (2000). *Diagnostic and Statistical Manual of Mental Disorders* (4th ed., Text Rev.) (*DSM-IV-TR*). Washington, DC: Author.

Balluffi, A., Kassam-Adams, N., Kazak, A. et al. (2004). Traumatic stress in parents of children admitted to the pediatric intensive care unit. *Pediatric Critical Care Medicine, 5,* 547–53.

Barakat, L., Kazak, A. E., Gallagher, M. A., Meeske, K., & Stuber, M. L. (2000). Posttraumatic stress symptoms and stressful life events predict the long-term adjustment of survivors of childhood cancer and their mothers. *Journal of Clinical Psychology in Medical Settings, 7*, 189–96.

Barakat, L., Kazak, A., Meadows, A. et al. (1997). Families surviving childhood cancer: A comparison of posttraumatic stress symptoms with families of healthy children. *Journal of Pediatric Psychology, 22*, 843–59.

Best, M., Streisand, R., Catania, L., & Kazak, A. (2002). Parental distress during pediatric leukemia and parental posttraumatic stress symptoms after treatment ends. *Journal of Pediatric Psychology, 26*, 299–307.

Brown, R., Madan-Swain, A., & Lambert, R. (2003). Posttraumatic stress symptoms in adolescent survivors of childhood cancer and their mothers. *Journal of Traumatic Stress, 16*, 309–18.

Bruce, M. (2006). A systematic and conceptual review of posttraumatic stress in childhood cancer survivors and their parents. *Clinical Psychology Review, 26*, 233–56.

Bryant, R., Mayou, R., Wiggs, L., Ehlers, A., & Stores, G. (2004). Psychological consequences of road traffic accidents for children and their mothers. *Psychological Medicine, 34*, 335–46.

Bryant, R., Salmon, K., Sinclair, E., & Davidson, P. (2007). The relationship between acute stress disorder and posttraumatic stress disorder in injured children. *Journal of Traumatic Stress, 20*(6), 1075–9.

Cicchetti, D., & Rogosch, F. A. (2001). Diverse patterns of neuroendocrine activity in maltreated children. *Development and Psychopathology, 13*, 677–93.

Daviss, W., Mooney, D., Racusin, R. et al. (2000a). Predicting posttraumatic stress after hospitalization for pediatric injury. *Journal of the American Academy of Child & Adolescent Psychiatry, 39*(5), 576–83.

Daviss, W., Racusin, R., Fleischer, A. et al. (2000b). Acute stress disorder symptomatology during hospitalization for pediatric injury. *Journal of the American Academy of Child & Adolescent Psychiatry, 39*(5), 569–75.

Delahanty, D. L., Nugent, N. R., Christopher, N. C., & Walsh, M. (2005). Initial urinary epinephrine and cortisol levels predict acute PTSD symptoms in child trauma victims. *Psychoneuroendocrinology, 30*(2), 121–8.

Di Gallo, A., Barton, J., & Parry-Jones W. L. (1997). Road traffic accidents: early psychological consequences in children and adolescents. *The British Journal of Psychiatry, 170*, 358–62.

Ehlers, A., Mayou R., & Bryant, B. (2003). Cognitive predictors of posttraumatic stress disorder in children: results of a prospective longitudinal study. *Behaviour Research and Therapy 41*, 1–10.

Ehlers, A., & Steil, R. (1995). Maintenance of intrusive memories in posttraumatic stress disorder: a cognitive approach. *Behavioural and Cognitive Psychotherapy, 23*, 217–49.

Fein, J. A., Kassam-Adams, N., Vu, T., & Datner, E. M. (2001). Emergency department evaluation of acute stress disorder symptoms in violently injured youths. *Annals of Emergency Medicine, 38*, 391–6.

Fein, J., Kassam-Adams, N., Gavin, M. et al. (2002). Persistence of posttraumatic stress in violently injured youth seen in the emergency department. *Archives of Pediatric and Adolescent Medicine, 156*, 836–40.

Foa, E. B., Zinbarg, R., & Rothbaum, B. O. (1992). Uncontrollability and unpredictability in post-traumatic stress disorder: An animal model. *Psychological Bulletin, 112*(2), 218–38.

Fuemmeler, B. F., Mullins, L. L., & Marx, B. P. (2001). Posttraumatic stress and general distress among parents of children surviving a brain tumor. *Children's Health Care, 30,* 169–82.

Fuemmeler, B. F., Mullins, L.L., Van Pelt, J., Carpentier M., & Parkhurst J. (2005). Posttraumatic stress symptoms and distress among parents of children with cancer. *Children's Health Care, 34*(4), 289–303.

Goldenberg Libov, B., Nevid, J. S., Pelcovitz, D., & Carmony, T. M. (2002). Posttraumatic stress symptomatology in mothers of pediatric cancer survivors. *Psychology and Health, 17,* 501–11.

Hall, E., Saxe, G., Stoddard, F. et al. (2006) Posttraumatic stress symptoms in parents of children with acute burns. *Journal of Pediatric Psychology, 31*(4), 403–12.

Harvey, A. G., & Bryant, R. A. (2002). Acute stress disorder: A synthesis and critique. *Psychological Bulletin, 128,* 886–902.

Hobbie, W. L., Stuber, M., Meeske, K. et al. (2000). Symptoms of posttraumatic stress in young adult survivors of childhood cancer. *Journal of Clinical Oncology, 18,* 4060–6.

Kassam-Adams, N. (2006). Introduction to the Special Issue: Posttraumatic stress related to pediatric illness and injury. *Journal of Pediatric Psychology, 31*(4), 337–42.

Kassam-Adams N., Garcia-España, F., Fein, J., & Winston, F. K. (2005). Heart rate and posttraumatic stress in injured children. *Archives of General Psychiatry, 6,* 335–40.

Kassam-Adams, N., & Winston, F. K. (2004). Predicting child PTSD: The relationship between acute stress disorder and PTSD in injured children. *Journal of the American Academy of Child & Adolescent Psychiatry, 43,* 403–11.

Kazak, A. E., Alderfer, M., Rourke, M. T. et al. (2004). Posttraumatic stress disorder (PTSD) and posttraumatic symptoms (PTSS) in families of adolescent childhood cancer survivors. *Journal of Pediatric Psychology, 29,* 211–19.

Kazak, A. E., Barakat, L. P., Meeske, K. et al. (1997). Posttraumatic stress, family functioning, and social support in survivors of childhood leukemia and their mothers and fathers. *Journal of Consulting and Clinical Psychology, 65,* 120–9.

Kazak, A. E., Kassam-Adams, N., Schneider, S. et al. (2006). An integrative model of pediatric medical traumatic stress. *Journal of Pediatric Psychology, 31*(4), 343–55.

Kazak, A. E., Stuber, M. L., Barakat, L. P. et al. (1998). Predicting posttraumatic stress symptoms in mothers and fathers of survivors of childhood cancers. *Journal of the American Academy of Child & Adolescent Psychiatry, 37,* 823–31.

Keppel-Benson, J., Ollendick, T., & Benson M. (2002), Post-traumatic stress in children following motor vehicle accidents. *Journal of Child Psychology and Psychiatry, 43*(2), 203–12.

Landolt, M., Boehler, U., Schwager, C., Schallberger, U., & Nuessli, R. (1998). Posttraumatic stress disorder in paediatric patients and their parents: Findings from an exploratory study. *Journal of Paediatrics and Child Health, 34,* 539–43.

Landolt, M., Vollrath, M., Ribi, K., Gnehm, H., & Sennhauser, F. (2003). Incidence and associations of parental and child posttraumatic stress symptoms in pediatric patients. *Journal of Child Psychology and Psychiatry, 44*(8), 1199–207.

Lee, Y. L. (2006). The relationships between uncertainty and posttraumatic stress in survivors of childhood cancer. *Journal of Nursing Research, 14*(2), 133–42.

Lee, Y. L., Gau, B. S., Hsu, W. M., & Chang, H. H. (2009). A model linking uncertainty, posttraumatic stress, and health behaviors in childhood cancer survivors. *Oncology Nursing Forum, 36*(1), 20–30.

Manne, S., DuHamel, K., Nereo, N. et al. (2002). Predictors of PTSD in mothers of children undergoing bone marrow transplantation: The role of cognitive and social processes. *Journal of Pediatric Psychology, 27*, 607–17.

Manne, S., DuHamel, K., Ostroff, J. et al. (2004). Anxiety, depressive, and posttraumatic stress disorders among mothers of pediatric hematopoietic stem cell transplantation. *Pediatrics, 113*, 1700–8.

Manne, S., DuHamel, K., & Redd, W. H. (2000). Association of psychological vulnerability factors to post-traumatic stress symptomatology in mothers of pediatric cancer survivors. *Psycho-Oncology, 9*, 372–84.

Max, J. E., Castillo, C. S., Robin, D. A. et al. (1998). Predictors of family functioning following traumatic brain injury in children and adolescents. *Journal of the American Academy of Child & Adolescent Psychiatry, 37*, 83–90.

Meiser-Stedman, R., Yule, W., Dalgleish, T., Smith, P., & Glucksman, E. (2006). The role of the family in child and adolescent posttraumatic stress following attendance at an Emergency Department. *Journal of Pediatric Psychology, 31*(4), 397–402.

Meiser-Stedman, R., Yule, W., Smith, P., Glucksman, E., & Dalgleish, T. (2005). Acute stress disorder and posttraumatic stress disorder in children and adolescents involved in assaults or motor vehicle accidents. *The American Journal of Psychiatry, 162*, 1381–3.

Mirza, K. A. H., Bhadrinath, B. R., Goodyer, I. M., & Gilmour, C. (1998). Posttraumatic stress disorder in children and adolescents following road traffic accidents. *The British Journal of Psychiatry, 172*, 443–7.

Mishel, M. (1990). Reconceptualization of uncertainty in illness theory. *Image, 22*, 256–62.

Nugent, N., Christopher, N., & Delahanty, D. (2006). Emergency medical service and in-hospital vital signs as predictors of subsequent PTSD symptom severity in pediatric injury patients. *Journal of Child Psychology and Psychiatry. 47*(9), 919–26.

Nugent, N., Ostrowski, S., Christopher, N., & Delahanty, D. (2007). Parental posttraumatic stress symptoms as a moderator of child's acute biological response and subsequent posttraumatic stress symptoms in pediatric injury patients. *Journal of Pediatric Psychology, 32*(3), 309–18.

Pelcovitz, D., Libov, B., Mandel, F. et al. (1998). Posttraumatic stress disorder and family functioning in adolescent cancer. *Journal of Traumatic Stress, 11*, 205–21.

Rees G., Gledhill, J., Garralda, M. E., & Nadel, S. (2004). Psychiatric outcome following paediatric intensive care unit (PICU) admission: a cohort study. *Intensive Care Medicine, 30*, 1607–14.

Santacroce, S. (2002). Uncertainty, anxiety and symptoms of posttraumatic stress in parents of children recently diagnosed with cancer. *Journal of Pediatric Oncology Nursing, 19*, 104–11.

Santacroce, S. (2003). Parental uncertainty and posttraumatic stress in serious childhood illness. *Journal of Nursing Scholarship*, *35*(1), 45–51.

Sawyer, M., Streiner, D., Antoniou, G., Toogood, I., & Rice, M. (1998). Influence of family and parental adjustment on the later psychological adjustment of children treated with cancer. *Journal of the American Academy of Child & Adolescent Psychiatry*, *37*(8), 815–22.

Saxe, G., Stoddard, F., Hall, E. et al. (2005). Pathways to PTSD, Part I: Children with burns. *The American Journal of Psychiatry*, *162*, 1299–300.

Saxe, G., Vanderbilt, D., & Zuckerman, B. (2003). Traumatic stress in injured and ill children. *PTSD Research Quarterly*, *14*(2), 1–8.

Schwartz, S., Dohrenwend, B. P., & Levav, I. (1994). Nongenetic familial transmission of psychiatric disorders? Evidence from children of Holocaust survivors. *Journal of Health and Social Behavior*, *35*, 385–402.

Stallard, P., Velleman, R., & Baldwin, S. (1998). Prospective study of post-traumatic stress disorder in children involved in road traffic accidents. *British Medical Journal*, *317*, 1619–23.

Stallard, P., Velleman, R., & Baldwin, S. (2001). Recovery from post-traumatic stress disorder in children following road traffic accidents: the role of talking and feeling understood. *Journal of Community and Applied Social Psychology*, *11*, 37–41.

Steil, R., & Ehlers, A. (2000). Dysfunctional meaning of posttraumatic intrusions in chronic PTSD. *Behaviour Research and Therapy*, *38*, 537–58.

Stuber, M. L., Christakis, D., Houskamp, B., & Kazak, A. E. (1996). Posttraumatic symptoms in childhood leukemia survivors and their parents. *Psychosomatics*, *37*, 254–61.

Stuber, M., Kazak, A., Meeske, K. et al. (1997). Predictors of posttraumatic stress symptoms in childhood cancer survivors. *Pediatrics*, *100*, 958–64.

Taïeb, O., Moro, M. R., Baubet, T., Revah-Levy, A., & Flament, M. F. (2003). Post-traumatic stress symptoms after childhood cancer. *European Child and Adolescent Psychiatry*, *12*, 255–64.

de Vries, A. P. J., Kassam-Adams, N., Cnaan, A. et al. (1999). Looking beyond the physical injury: Posttraumatic stress disorder in children and parents after pediatric traffic injury. *Pediatrics*, *104*, 1293–9.

Winston, F. K., Baxt, C., Kassam-Adams, N. L., Elliott, M. R., & Kallan, M. J. (2005). Acute traumatic stress symptoms in child occupants and their parent drivers after crash involvement. *Archives of Pediatrics and Adolescent Medicine*, *59*(11), 1074–9.

Winston, F., Kassam-Adams, N., Vivarelli-O'Neill, C. et al. (2002). Acute stress disorder symptoms in children and their parents after pediatric traffic injury. *Pediatrics*, *109*(6), e90.

Yehuda, R. (1999). *Risk factors for posttraumatic stress disorder*. Washington, DC: American Psychiatric Press.

Young, G. S., Mintzer, L. L., Seacord, D. et al. (2003). Symptoms of posttraumatic stress disorder in parents of transplant recipients: Incidence, severity, and related factors. *Pediatrics*, *111*, 725–31.

Zatzick, D., Russo, J., Grossman, D. et al. (2006). Posttraumatic stress and depressive symptoms, alcohol use, and recurrent traumatic life events in a representative sample of hospitalized injured adolescents and their parents. *Journal of Pediatric Psychology,* *31*(4), 377–87.

Zink, K., & McCain, G. (2003), Post-traumatic stress disorder in children and adolescents with motor vehicle related injuries. *Journal for Specialists in Pediatric Nursing, 8*(3), 99–106.

Part III

Neurobiology, Memory, and Dissociative Processes

Chapter Six

Neuropsychological Underpinnings of PTSD in Children and Adolescents

Helen Z. MacDonald, Jennifer J. Vasterling, and Ann Rasmusson

Introduction

Approximately 15% to 20% of children and adolescents experience a traumatic event over the course of childhood (Breslau, 2002; Brown, 2002). Exposure to extreme stress can result in a broad array of cognitive, affective, and psychological sequelae that, when perpetuated, are associated with the development of Post-Traumatic Stress Disorder (PTSD). Attention and memory abnormalities are so central to PTSD that cognitive disturbances have been integrated into the diagnostic criteria. Specifically, hypervigilance and concentration impairments can be conceptualized as attentional abnormalities, whereas reexperiencing symptoms and psychogenic amnesia can be understood as over- and underactive aspects, respectively, of trauma memory.

For children, these neuropsychological abnormalities have the potential for causing major functional difficulties in academic and interpersonal settings. Cognitive dysfunction in children and adolescents with PTSD takes on a special significance due to the developmental stages involved. From a psychosocial perspective, children and adolescents are at critical periods of social, academic, and cognitive development, which may be particularly vulnerable to any cognitive abnormalities. From a neurobiological perspective, the brains of children and adolescents are not yet fully developed and may be expected to show a recovery course following trauma exposure different from that of adults (De Bellis, 1999 a and b). This chapter aims to summarize and critically review the literature on neuropsychological functioning in children and adolescents with PTSD, highlighting the specific neuropsychological correlates of PTSD within

Post-Traumatic Syndromes in Childhood and Adolescence: A Handbook of Research and Practice, First Edition.
Edited by Vittoria Ardino. © 2011 John Wiley & Sons, Ltd. Published 2011 by John Wiley & Sons, Ltd.

neurobiological and developmental perspectives. We will go on to discuss clinical implications and directions for future research.

Neurobiological context

There are multiple interconnected neurobiological systems involved in the activation and deactivation of the stress response and, subsequently, in the development and maintenance of PTSD. Although numerous neurobiological systems are involved in the stress response, three major systems are implicated in PTSD: The noradrenergic system, the serotonergic system, and the hypothalamic-pituitary-adrenal (HPA) axis. Although there is some evidence of noradrenergic and serotonergic dysregulation in trauma-exposed children and adolescents (De Bellis et al., 1999), we focus primarily on the HPA axis because of its emphasis within the child and adolescent PTSD literature (De Bellis, Hooper, & Sapia, 2005).

The HPA axis is a system of interconnected brain and peripheral structures that elaborate neuromodulators of the stress response. For example, the adrenal gland (part of the HPA axis) increases secretion of cortisol in response to stress. The flight-or-fight response is largely mediated by catecholamines released by the brainstem locus coeruleus and peripheral sympathetic nervous system. However, the stress-induced increase in cortisol secretion by the adrenal gland triggers a complex series of interrelated neuroendocrine events that facilitate and then help terminate the fight-or-flight response. This coordinated stress response, while beneficial in the short term, can have deleterious long-term consequences when perpetuated (McEwen, Gould, & Sakai, 1992; Sapolsky et al., 1990; Southwick et al., 1995). A post-traumatic stress reaction may occur when this system does not function properly, or when the stressor does not cease, resulting in overactivation of the coeruleus–SNS–catecholamine and HPA systems, leaving the individual in a constant state of hyperarousal, and rendering the stress response maladaptive. For example, overactive cortisol secretion in the context of chronic stress can contribute to neuronal cell death, decreased neuronal dendritic branching, and/or inhibition in neurogenesis in certain regions of the brain, including the hippocampus, the primary brain structure mediating declarative memory (Gould et al., 1998; Sapolsky, 2000; Teicher et al., 2003).

Neurobiological and neuropsychological responses to trauma exposure in children are best examined through a development lens. Human brains are highly malleable as they continue to develop postnatally (Johnson, 1999). The developing brain's plasticity has far-reaching implications; it can serve as a protective factor, such as in the case of exposure to a nurturing and healthy environment, or represent a risk factor for later psychopathology in the case of exposure to neglectful, abusive, or otherwise traumatic early experiences (Graham et al., 1999).

Animal research has shown that exposure to early adverse events results in sustained dysregulation of the HPA axis (Albeck et al., 1997; Ladd, Owens, & Nemeroff, 1996). However, the pattern of cortisol levels following trauma exposure in child and adolescent populations has been inconsistent. Some studies have found that exposure to extreme stress results in hypercortisolism (Gunnar & Vazquez, 2001), but others demonstrated hypocortisolism (Goenjian et al., 1996; Heim, Ehlert, & Hellhammer, 2000), with both dysfunctional patterns having implications for the development of PTSD (Gunnar & Vazquez, 2001; McEwen, 1998; Sapolsky, 1994). A study of infants adopted out of Romanian orphanages by Gunnar and colleagues (2001) found early deprivation in infancy to be associated with higher cortisol levels six to seven years later. In the first longitudinal study examining the relationship between PTSD, cortisol levels, and hippocampal volume in children, Carrion and colleagues (2007) found that PTSD symptoms and cortisol levels were negatively associated with changes in hippocampal volume over 12 to 18 months. The authors concluded that HPA axis activation following trauma exposure leads to heightened cortisol levels, which then results in toxicity to hippocampal neurons and impaired hippocampal inhibition of the HPA axis. In contrast, Goenjian and colleagues (1996) reported that five years after the 1988 earthquake in Armenia, adolescent participants with higher levels of PTSD symptoms showed lower mean baseline cortisol levels compared to less symptomatic adolescent participants. Further, Hart and colleagues report blunted cortisol reactivity in preschool-aged children with histories of maltreatment (Hart, Gunnar, & Cicchetti, 1995, 1996).

Expanding studies of HPA axis function to include other adrenally-derived neuroactive steroids and neuropeptides that modify cortisol output may help clarify the sources of difference between subpopulations of children and adolescents. Indeed, several of these modifying factors, including dehydroepiandrosterone (DHEA), allopregnanolone, and neuropeptide Y (NPY) are influenced by age and stage of reproductive development and are therefore candidates in explaining possible age and reproductive stage- or state-related differences in HPA axis adaptation to stress (Morgan et al., 2009; Rasmusson, Vythilingam, & Morgan, 2003; Rasmusson et al., 2006).

Although none of these modifying neurobiological factors has been examined in relation to cognitive functioning, they have been linked in multiple studies to PTSD symptoms and mood, and are thought to influence brain structural and functional adaptations to severe stress. DHEA, for example, increases HPA axis reactivity as it protects the brain, including the hippocampus, from some of the deleterious effects of cortisol and excitatory amino acid neurotransmitters released during stress (e.g., Bastianetto et al., 1999; Kaminska et al., 2000; Karishma & Herbert, 2002; Kimonides et al., 1998; Zhang et al., 2002).

DHEA levels are low from shortly after birth until adrenarche (a period of prepubertal sexual development beginning between ages five and seven).

DHEA levels then climb throughout adolescence and peak in early adulthood, after which they fall progressively to the much lower levels seen in old age. Allopregnanolone, a progesterone derivative, provides delayed negative feedback to the HPA axis and thus helps return post-stress cortisol levels to baseline (Barbaccia et al., 2001; Guo et al., 1995; Patchev et al., 1994; Patchev et al., 1996). Although allopregnanolone levels have not been thoroughly assessed over development, there is preliminary evidence that women with PTSD fail to show the more typical increase in allopregnanolone during the luteal (post-ovulation) phase of the menstrual cycle that women without PTSD show (A. Rasmusson and N. Epperson, personal communication, April 29, 2008), possibly contributing to the increase in cortisol seen in women with PTSD – a factor to be considered when studying female adolescents. Finally, NPY has been shown to inhibit HPA axis reactivity (Antonijevic et al., 2000). Since NPY release is influenced by testosterone, it too may play a more or less important role in HPA axis adaptation to stress depending on gender and, of relevance to this chapter, stage of reproductive development.

Extending beyond the pervasive effects of the HPA axis and the stress response across development on brain structure and function, current knowledge of brain plasticity suggests that functional brain specialization continues into childhood and adolescence and thus may also be shaped by the interactions of children and adolescents with their environments (Kempermann, Gast, & Gage, 2002; Kempermann, Kuhn, & Gage, 1997). In some parts of the brain, including the hippocampus, neurogenesis continues throughout adulthood (Kempermann et al., 2003). To this end, stressor exposure can be viewed as a neural insult, whereby children with exposure to extreme or chronic trauma may be more likely than other children to sustain long-lasting neurobiological and morphological deficits.

In the realm of functional brain abnormalities following exposure to trauma, Teicher and colleagues (2003) draw on animal literature to suggest that brain regions with the following three qualities increase risk for damage following early stress exposure: (1) lengthy postnatal development; (2) large number of glucocorticoid receptors; and (3) presence of postnatal neurogenesis. The hippocampus meets all of these criteria. Further, the hippocampus has projections to (a) the prefrontal cortex (PFC), which mediates higher order cognitive and neuropsychological functioning, including attention, working memory, executive functioning, and tonic suppression of amygdala reactivity; and (b) the amygdala, which mediates the highly conserved mammalian species specific defense response and plays a central role in fear conditioning (Goldstein et al., 1996). It has been hypothesized that the PFC is deleteriously impacted by stress both indirectly, through its connection to a damaged hippocampus, as well as directly, through stress-induced increases in cortisol and catecholamine levels, which lead to transient functional impairments (Murphy et al., 1996; Ramos & Arnsten, 2007) and structural reductions in neuronal connectivity (Sapolsky, 2000; Wooley, Gould, & McEwen, 1990).

Although there are exceptions (Bonne et al., 2001; Gilbertson et al., 2002; Schore, 2001), adults with PTSD have been shown to have significantly smaller hippocampi when compared to controls (Bremner et al., 1993; Bremner et al., 1995; Bremner et al., 1997; Bremner et al., 2003; Gilbertson et al., 2001; Gurvits et al., 1996; Stein et al., 1997; Villarreal et al., 2002). There is, however, limited research examining these questions in children and adolescents, and the results from preliminary empirical literature in this area reveal a pattern of findings different for children compared with adults.

For example, in contrast with the adult literature, Carrion and colleagues (2001) reported no significant volumetric differences in limbic structures between children with PTSD and controls, but found smaller total brain and cerebral volumes in PTSD participants. In addition, as compared to the control participants, the PTSD-diagnosed children demonstrated attenuation of frontal lobe asymmetry, a finding seen in other psychiatric populations, including adults with depression and schizophrenia (Kumar et al., 2000; Turetsky et al., 1995). De Bellis and colleagues (1999, 2001) have likewise found no evidence of volumetric differences in limbic structures between maltreated children with PTSD and healthy children, but have documented smaller intracranial and cerebral volumes associated with PTSD (De Bellis et al., 1999).

Pooling data from previously reported studies (De Bellis et al., 1999; De Bellis et al., 2002), Tupler and De Bellis (2006) found that participants with maltreatment-related PTSD had significantly larger hippocampi, controlling for cerebral volume, compared with healthy children. The authors speculated that developmental factors, allowing for hippocampal growth following trauma exposure and/or PTSD development, may contribute to these abnormalities, emphasizing that larger is not necessarily associated with more favorable behavioral outcomes (cf. Foster et al., 1999; Schumann et al., 2004).

In the only study examining the cerebellum, vermis, and brainstem in children with PTSD, De Bellis and Kuchibhatla (2006) examined structural volumes in 58 maltreated children and adolescents with PTSD, 13 non-traumatized children and adolescents with diagnoses of generalized anxiety disorder, and 98 healthy, non-abused children and adolescents. The results indicated that unadjusted means of the left, right, and total cerebellum were smaller in the PTSD group, remaining significant after adjusting for cerebral volume, IQ, gender, and socioeconomic status (SES). Further, cerebellar volumes correlated positively with age of trauma onset and negatively with duration of trauma, supporting the contention that the impact of exposure to stress in childhood and adolescence may be shaped by factors including age and/or length of traumatization.

In summary, these initial studies suggest that compared with non-traumatized children, children with PTSD may demonstrate structural brain differences, including smaller cerebellar, intracranial, and cerebral volumes, but possibly larger hippocampi. Such findings have implications for neuropsychological functioning and general scholastic performance in children and adolescents. As suggested by De Bellis, Hooper, and Sapia (2005), the hippocampus may be adversely affected by PTSD over time, with results not evident until later in adolescence or adulthood. Indeed, examination of factors that vary with developmental epoch and reproductive state or gender, and which influence HPA axis function, including neuromodulators and neuroprotectors such as DHEA, allopregnanolone, and NPY, will be important to assess in relation to brain structural and functional adaptation to traumatic stress.

Information-processing, cognitive, and neuropsychological correlates of PTSD

A robust body of literature has documented information-processing and neuropsychological abnormalities in adults with PTSD. Information-processing studies use experimental cognitive approaches to examine how trauma-relevant affective stimuli are processed cognitively. Many of these studies have used an emotional Stroop paradigm, which requires the respondent to name the color of ink in which words of varying emotional relevance are printed. Slower color naming is thought to indicate greater attentional resources devoted to the word meaning. Adults with PTSD perform more slowly in naming trauma-related words compared with either emotionally neutral words or emotionally cued words not related to the traumatic event, demonstrating an attentional "bias" toward threat-relevant stimuli (Bryant & Harvey, 1995; Buckley, Blanchard, & Hickling, 2002; Cassiday, McNally, & Zeitlin, 1992; Constans et al., 2004; Foa, Zinbarg, & Rothbaum, 1992; Kaspi, McNally, & Amir, 1995).

The research examining how emotionally neutral information is processed using traditional clinical neuropsychological tasks has largely demonstrated that adults with PTSD show deficits in attention, memory, and some types of executive functioning when compared with controls. These findings occur across samples, including combat veterans (Barrett et al., 1996; Beckham, Crawford, & Feldman, 1998; Bremner et al., 1993; Bremner et al., 1995; Gilbertson et al., 2001; Koso & Hansen, 2006; Samuelson et al., 2006; Uddo et al., 1993; Vasterling, Brailey, & Sutker, 2000; Vasterling et al., 1998; Vasterling et al., 2002; Yehuda, Grolier, & Tischler, 2005; Yehuda et al., 1995), prisoners of war (Sutker et al., 1991; Sutker et al., 1995), childhood abuse survivors (Bremner, Vermetten, & Afzal, 2004), rape survivors (Jenkins et al., 1998), and those with etiologically mixed trauma (Koenen et al., 2001). PTSD has also been robustly associated with poorer intellectual functioning (Brandes et al., 2002; Gil et al., 1990; Gilbertson et al., 2001; Gurvits, Lasko, & Schachter, 1993; Gurvits et al., 2000; Macklin et al., 1998; Vasterling et al., 1997; Vasterling et al., 2002), and, in particular, with lower verbal IQ scores (Vasterling et al., 1997). There are, however, exceptions to findings of neurocognitive impairment in adults with PTSD (Crowell, Kieffer, & Siders, 2002; Gurvits, Lasko, &

Schachter, 1993; Pederson, Maurer, & Kaminski, 2004; Stein et al., 1999; Twamley, Hami, & Stein, 2004).

Although the adult literature provides broad empirical support for associations between PTSD and neurocognitive and neuroanatomical abnormalities, limited research has examined information-processing and neuropsychological functioning in children and adolescents with PTSD.

Information-processing in children with PTSD

Only a few studies have examined information processing biases in children with PTSD. In the first of these studies, Moradi, Taghavi and colleagues (1999) administered the emotional Stroop task to 23 children and adolescents between the ages of nine and 17, meeting criteria for PTSD (secondary to motor vehicle accidents or interpersonal violence events) and a comparison group of 23 children and adolescents with no psychiatric diagnoses who were matched on age, sex, verbal IQ, and reading ability. Children with PTSD demonstrated slower color-naming performance overall as well as selectively slower color-naming performance for trauma-related words compared with non-emotional words and compared against the performance of the control group, suggesting an attentional bias to threat.

Dalgleish and colleagues (2001) attempted to replicate these findings with the attentional dot probe paradigm, using a sample of 24 children and adolescents with PTSD and 24 children and adolescents with no known psychiatric disorder or trauma history. In the dot probe task, word pairs appear – one word above the other – on a computer screen. The test pairs include one threatening word and one neutral word, and filler pairs include two neutral words. After the participant reads the top word on each trial, the word pair disappears from the screen. On test trials, a dot probe appears on the screen location previously occupied by one of the two test words. Participants then press a button as soon as they see the probe. Reaction time to the probe measures the visual attention to the word that the dot replaced. In this study, there were three types of emotional words presented: physical threat-related words (e.g., explosion), social threat-related words (e.g., rejection), and depression-related words (e.g., sad). Results revealed that the PTSD group showed greater attentional bias toward social threat-related words and away from depression-related words compared to the control group. There were no differences between the PTSD and control group in attention toward physical threat-related words. These findings suggest some degree of attentional bias toward threat, but unlike the adult literature, biases to a threat category (social threat) were not necessarily specific to the traumatic event.

Moradi and colleagues extended their findings of attentional biases in children and adolescents with PTSD by studying memory bias for negative material in children and adolescents with PTSD (Moradi et al., 2000). In this study,

24 children and adolescents with PTSD and 25 children and adolescents with no known psychiatric disorder or trauma history were presented with positively (e.g., pleasant), negatively (e.g., horror), and neutrally (e.g., lizard) valenced words. The negative words consisted of 12 depression-related words, 12 general threat words, and 12 trauma-related words. Following a 90-second filled delay, participants were given recall and recognition tests. Results revealed that the PTSD sample remembered fewer words overall compared with the control group. Further, there was an interaction effect whereby the PTSD group recalled more negative (trauma and general threat categories collapsed) words relative to positive and neutral words compared with the control group. There were no group differences on the recognition test, possibly due to ceiling effects, given that most participants performed well on the task. However, the findings generally provided initial support for a memory bias toward negatively, and away from positively and neutrally, valenced words in children and adolescents with PTSD.

Intellectual functioning and achievement in children with PTSD

There is an empirical basis supporting a relationship between PTSD and intellectual and achievement performance in children and adolescents (Breslau, Lucia, & Alvarado, 2006; Koenen et al., 2007; Saigh, Mroueh, & Bremner, 1997; Saigh et al., 2006). In an elegantly designed twin study, Koenen and colleagues (2003) examined the relationship between domestic violence exposure and environmentally mediated intellectual functioning. In their sample of 1,116 monozygotic and dizygotic twins, exposure to domestic violence was shown to have a dose–response relationship with IQ suppression. Compared to children with no exposure to domestic violence, on average, those with low, medium, and high levels of exposure showed suppression of IQ by one, five, and eight points, respectively. Independent of genetic influences, domestic violence accounted for 4% of the variance in children's IQ scores. Although it is difficult to determine the relative impact of trauma exposure versus PTSD from this study, the findings point to the generally elevated risk of poor outcomes in trauma-exposed child populations.

Using cross-sectional methodology, Saigh and colleagues demonstrated a specific association between IQ and PTSD, finding that children with PTSD scored lower on verbal IQ tests when compared with trauma-exposed children without PTSD and non-traumatized children (Saigh et al., 2006). Longitudinal research, however, suggests that intellectual functioning might alter risk of PTSD, rather than vary as a function of developing the disorder. Examining the relationship between PTSD and IQ in children, Breslau, Lucia, and Alvarado (2006) found that higher full-scale IQ scores on the Wechsler Intelligence Scale for Children–Revised at age six was protective against the development of PTSD later in adolescence. Similarly, in a prospective birth cohort study, Koenen and colleagues (2007) found that early childhood IQ, assessed by the Stanford-Binet, was strongly associated with the development of PTSD by age 26. Specifically, for each standard deviation increase in IQ score at age five, the risk of developing PTSD was reduced by 29% PTSD.

In the domain of achievement, adolescents with PTSD have also performed less proficiently on achievement tests compared with trauma-exposed adolescents without PTSD and non-traumatized adolescents (Saigh, Mroueh, & Bremner, 1997). It can be hypothesized that less favorable academic achievement can be attributed at least in part to structural and functional brain abnormalities and associated neuropsychological dysfunction associated with PTSD. For example, if the development of PTSD symptoms is associated with regional structural and functional weaknesses, neuropsychological functions associated with these regions would be expected to be likewise affected, in turn influencing achievement and scholastic performance. It should be noted that the literature in this field is sparse, however, and whereas Saigh and colleagues reported poorer achievement in children with PTSD, Sack and colleagues' (1995) longitudinal study of Cambodian youth resettled in the United States found no differences in the grade point averages of Cambodian youth with and without PTSD.

Neuropsychological functioning in children with PTSD

Although there are empirical studies investigating the relationships between PTSD symptomatology and specific domains of neuropsychological functioning in children, research in this area is currently preliminary. However, consistent with the adult literature, the extant child literature in this field indicates that children with PTSD tend to demonstrate neuropsychological deficits in the areas of attention, memory, and executive functioning (Beers & De Bellis, 2002; Moradi, Neshat Doost et al., 1999).

For example, Beers and De Bellis (2002) administered a comprehensive neuropsychological testing battery to 14 maltreated children with PTSD and 15 children matched on demographic variables, including IQ, without maltreatment histories or lifetime diagnoses of any Axis I disorder. Findings indicated differences in the areas of attention and abstract reasoning/executive functioning, with PTSD subjects demonstrating significant impairment on measures of distraction and impulsivity (standard Stroop color/word task, Digit Vigilance Test omission errors) as well as frontal lobe functioning measures, including hypothesis testing/problem solving (Wisconsin Card Sorting Test categories), and semantic organization (Controlled Oral Word Association Test Animal Naming). No differences were found in the domains of language or psychomotor speed. Although conclusions must be tempered by the lack of a trauma-exposed comparison group and the small sample size, findings provide support for the association between PTSD and impaired attentional and executive functioning in children and adolescents.

Whereas Beers and De Bellis' (2002) groups did not differ on measures of memory, the only other published study examining neuropsychological functioning in children with PTSD documented associations between PTSD and memory deficits. Moradi and colleagues assessed 18 children and adolescents aged 11 to 17 with PTSD secondary to motor vehicle accidents or interpersonal violence exposure and 22 children and adolescents matched on age, sex, and verbal IQ with no history of trauma or psychiatric disorder (Moradi, Neshat Doost et al., 1999). Compared with the control group, the PTSD group demonstrated general memory impairment as measured by the Rivermead Behavioural Memory Test. Whereas 55.6% of children and adolescents with PTSD were classified as having poor memory, and an additional 22.2% were classified as having impaired memory, only 13.6% of the control group was classified as having poor memory, and none of the control participants evidenced impaired memory. The PTSD group also demonstrated less proficient word reading than the control group, despite the groups having been matched on verbal IQ.

Taken together, the Moradi, Neshat Doost and colleagues (1999) and Beers and De Bellis (2002) findings suggest that PTSD may be associated with memory impairment in children and adolescents, as well as with poorer verbal functioning. These preliminary studies, though informative, are not as yet definitive and will require replication with trauma-exposed comparison samples, larger sample sizes, and across populations, including those exposed to different types of trauma and of different ages at the time of exposure.

Understanding the relationship between PTSD and neuropsychological functioning

As described above, in the face of exposure to extreme stress, an individual's biological system activates the fight-or-flight response. It can be reasoned, then, that perpetuation of such a stress response is associated with both the development of PTSD, as well as far-reaching neurobiological, neuropsychological, and neurobehavioral abnormalities. These alterations affect biological and anatomical systems related to arousal and fear, including the limbic system structures responsible for fear learning and sensitization (i.e., hippocampus and amygdala), the neurological structure responsible for arousal responses (i.e., the locus coeruleus), and the PFC, which is responsible for higher-order cognitive functioning, including inhibition of the limbic system (Bremner et al., 1999; Southwick et al., 2005; Sullivan & Gorman, 2002).

Studies demonstrating neuropsychological performance impairments in individuals with PTSD are generally consistent with the neuroanatomical literature, which documents limbic and paralimbic abnormalities in individuals with PTSD and trauma histories. Thus, it is expected that the corresponding functional domains in individuals with PTSD would be deleteriously affected. Although the literature examining neuropsychological functioning in children with PTSD is limited, there is evidence suggesting that, compared with non-traumatized children, those with PTSD demonstrate poorer performance on emotionally relevant information processing tasks, as well as on emotionally neutral neuropsychological functioning measures. Specifically, as reviewed above, children with PTSD demonstrate greater difficulty on measures of attention and some domains of executive functioning, results that are consistent with the brain regions found impaired in individuals with PTSD, including the PFC, hippocampus, and amygdala.

In addition to the direct effects of neural abnormalities, neuropsychological functioning might also be associated with specific behavioral symptoms. For example, research indicates that dissociative symptoms may be common among traumatized children, with reported rates of dissociation among traumatized children ranging from 19% to 73% (Silberg, 2000). Krystal and colleagues (1995) present a model whereby individuals with dissociative symptoms may demonstrate neuropsychological impairment in two areas. Firstly, these individuals may display more difficulty detaching focus from one stimulus in order to attend to a different relevant stimulus. Secondly, these individuals may demonstrate a poorer ability to focus their attention on a particular stimulus.

Additionally, reexperiencing cluster PTSD symptoms manifest through the intrusion of trauma-related material into consciousness, potentially diverting attention away from neutral information in the environment, and, therefore, the encoding of novel information that may counter the perception of threat (Elzinga & Bremner, 2002; McNally, 1991; Moradi, Neshat Doost et al., 1999; Wolfe & Schlesinger, 1997). Similarly, hypersensitivity and hypervigilance to trauma-related cues associated with heightened arousal may divert attentional resources from critical learning activities. That is, children may have greater difficulty attending to, organizing, or remembering new material, if they are focused on potential threats in their environments (Delaney-Black et al., 2002; Kolb, 1987; Siegel, 1995; Zigmond, Finlay, & Sved, 1995). This is consistent with information-processing conceptualizations of PTSD, which suggest that individuals with PTSD are biased toward threat-related stimuli at the expense of other stimuli (see Constans, 2007). Overall, therefore, there is a theoretical basis to suggest that there may be both direct neural and indirect behavioral influences on neuropsychological functioning in children and adolescents with PTSD.

Clinical implications

Neuropsychological deficits may represent a key correlate of PTSD with implications for children's functioning across contexts, including at home and school. Better understanding of the relationships between PTSD and associated neuropsychological deficits in children will potentially inform the development and implementation of critical prevention and intervention efforts that take more fully into account the myriad symptoms and impairments resulting from childhood trauma exposure (Dalgleish, Meiser-Stedman, & Smith, 2005).

Along with addressing the mental health needs of children with PTSD, these children may also warrant comprehensive neuropsychological evaluations and special attention in the classroom (Weber & Reynolds, 2004). As a result, parents and teachers would have the opportunity to gain insight into children's cognitive strengths and weaknesses, implement early intervention strategies as necessary, and remain vigilant to risk factors and developing concerns, specifically as related to neuropsychological functioning and scholastic performance.

The continuing postnatal brain development in early childhood and adolescence suggests that there may be an opportunity to reverse deleterious neuropsychological correlates of trauma exposure and PTSD symptom development. Psychotherapeutic interventions aimed at reducing PTSD symptoms may additionally result in improved neurocognitive functioning. In the context of academic functioning, classroom teachers, tutors, and parents can work with children with histories of trauma exposure to target specific areas of impairment.

Summary and future directions

The more extensive body of literature in the adult field, together with the preliminary research targeting children and adolescents, argues for continued examination of the complex relationships between trauma exposure, PTSD, and neuropsychological functioning in children. The field will in particular benefit from disentangling the relative risk of trauma exposure versus the emotional reaction to trauma exposure (i.e., PTSD) on the development of neuropsychological problems. For example, studies examining differences in neuropsychological functioning in children with PTSD, children with trauma exposure histories but without PTSD, and non-exposed children would address this question. Further, because of the high rates of comorbidity between PTSD and other psychiatric disorders, there is need for more work examining the contributions of comorbid mood, anxiety, and substance disorders to neuropsychological impairment in children and adolescents with PTSD.

Additional work is also needed to identify more specifically the pattern of neuropsychological deficits associated with trauma exposure and PTSD in children and adolescents (Dalgleish et al., 2005). Compared with reasonably well-replicated findings in the adult literature documenting associations between PTSD and neuropsychological functioning, the parallel body of research in child and adolescent samples remains in its infancy. Understanding better the specific cognitive processes that are altered and their longitudinal trajectory will help inform concrete educational interventions intended to help compensate for relative cognitive weaknesses and exploit windows of optimal benefit corresponding to periods of region-specific brain plasticity.

The extent to which the characteristics of trauma events, individual difference factors, and the interaction of trauma characteristics and individual differences affect neuropsychological functioning is also poorly understood. In their studies examining the effects of PTSD on neuropsychological functioning, Beers and De Bellis (2002) exclusively enrolled children with histories of maltreatment, whereas Moradi, Neshat Doost and colleagues' sample (1999) had experienced road traffic accidents or personal violence incidents. Although the former sample was likely exposed to repetitive trauma over a prolonged period, the Moradi and colleagues sample was likely comprised of a greater proportion of participants exposed to single, discrete trauma events. It could be reasoned that prolonged, repetitive trauma exposure, or long-term activation of the stress response, may have different implications for neuroanatomical alterations, and therefore neuropsychological functioning, than exposure to a single stressful event. Moreover, the individual developmental characteristics, such as the age at which a child is exposed to the trauma, may influence neuropsychological outcomes. Thus, the field will benefit from the systematic study of the influence of trauma-related variables, including type of trauma, age of trauma onset, time elapsed since trauma exposure, and duration/chronicity of trauma on neuropsychological functioning. Structural imaging studies have found associations between characteristics of the trauma exposure and degree of morphological abnormalities (De Bellis & Kuchibhatla, 2006), and thus we would expect to see corresponding differences in level of neuropsychological impairment. Finally, it will be important to take into account mitigating factors, such as environmental support, or individual characteristics that interact with trauma exposure to influence outcome (Kaufman et al., 2004; Kaufman et al., 2006).

In summary, children with PTSD appear to be at greater risk for information-processing, cognitive, and neuropsychological deficits in some areas compared to children without PTSD. Although the empirical research in this area is limited, the findings suggest that neurocognitive factors in traumatized children should be assessed and given attention in academic settings to minimize risk, bolster learning and development, and improve children's opportunity to thrive over the course of their lives.

References

Albeck, D. S., McKittrick, C. R., Blanchard, D. C., et al. (1997). Chronic social stress alters levels of corticotropin-releasing factor and arginine vasopressin mRNA in rat brain. *Journal of Neuroscience, 17*(12), 4895–903.

Antonijevic, I. A., Murck, H., Bohlhalter, S. et al. (2000). Neuropeptide Y promotes sleep and inhibits ACTH and cortisol release in young men. *Neuropharmacology, 39*, 1474–81.

Barbaccia, M. L., Serra, M., Purdy, R. H., & Biggio, G. (2001). Stress and neuroactive steroids. *International Review of Neurobiology, 46,* 243–72.

Barrett, D. H., Green, M. L., Morris, R., Giles, W. H., & Croft, J. B. (1996). Cognitive functioning and posttraumatic stress disorder. *The American Journal of Psychiatry, 153*(11), 1492–4.

Bastianetto, S., Ramassamy, C., Poirier, J., & Quirion, R. (1999). Dehydroepiandrosterone (DHEA) protects hippocampal cells from oxidative stress-induced damage. *Molecular Brain Research, 66,* 35–41.

Beckham, J. C., Crawford, A. L., & Feldman, M. E. (1998). Trail-making test performance in Vietnam combat veterans with and without posttraumatic stress disorder. *Journal of Traumatic Stress, 11*(4), 811–19.

Beers, S. R., & De Bellis, M. (2002). Neuropsychological function in children with maltreatment-related posttraumatic stress disorder. *The American Journal of Psychiatry, 159*(3), 483–6.

Bonne, O., Brandes, D., Gilboa, A. et al. (2001). Longitudinal MRI study of hippocampal volume in trauma survivors with PTSD. *The American Journal of Psychiatry, 158,* 1248–51.

Brandes, D., Ben-Schachar, G., Gilboa, A. et al. (2002). PTSD symptoms and cognitive performance in recent trauma survivors. *Psychiatry Research, 110*(3), 231–8.

Bremner, J. D., Randall, P., Scott, T. M. et al. (1995). MRI-based measurement of hippocampal volume in patients with combat-related posttraumatic stress disorder. *The American Journal of Psychiatry, 152*(7), 973–81.

Bremner, J. D., Randall, P., Vermetten, E. et al. (1997). Magnetic resonance imaging-based measurement of hippocampal volume in posttraumatic stress disorder related to childhood physical and sexual abuse: A preliminary report. *Biological Psychiatry, 41,* 23–32.

Bremner, J. D., Scott, T. M., Delaney, R. C. et al. (1993). Deficits in short-term memory in posttraumatic stress disorder. *The American Journal of Psychiatry, 150*(7), 1015–19.

Bremner, J. D., Southwick, S. M., Charney, D. S., Saigh, P. A., & Bremner, J. D. (1999). The neurobiology of posttraumatic stress disorder: An integration of animal and human research. In *Posttraumatic stress disorder: A comprehensive text.* (pp. 103–43). Needham Heights, MA: Allyn & Bacon.

Bremner, J. D., Vermetten, E., & Afzal, N. (2004). Deficits in verbal declarative memory function in women with childhood sexual abuse-related posttraumatic stress disorder. *Journal of Nervous and Mental Disease, 192*(10), 643–9.

Bremner, J. D., Vythilingam, M., Vermetten, E., et al. (2003). MRI and PET study of deficits in hippocampal structure and function in women with childhood sexual abuse and posttraumatic stress disorder. *The American Journal of Psychiatry, 160,* 924–32.

Breslau, N. (2002). Psychiatric morbidity in adult survivors of childhood trauma. *Seminar of Clinical Neuropsychiatry, 7*(2), 80–8.

Breslau, N., Lucia, V. C., & Alvarado, G. F. (2006). Intelligence and other predisposing factors in exposure to trauma and posttraumatic stress disorder. *Archives of General Psychiatry, 63,* 1238–45.

Brown, G. W. (2002). Measurement and the epidemiology of childhood trauma. *Seminar of Clinical Neuropsychiatry, 7*(2), 66–79.

Bryant, R. A., & Harvey, A. G. (1995). Processing threatening information in post-traumatic stress disorder. *Journal of Abnormal Psychology, 104*(3), 537–41.

Buckley, T. C., Blanchard, E. B., & Hickling, E. J. (2002). Automatic and strategic processing of threat stimuli: A comparison between PTSD, panic disorder, and nonanxiety controls. *Cognitive Therapy and Research, 26*(1), 97–115.

Carrion, V. G., Weems, C. F., Eliez, S. et al. (2001). Attenuation of frontal asymmetry in pediatric posttraumatic stress disorder. *Society of Biological Psychiatry, 50*, 943–51.

Carrion, V. G., Weems, C. F., & Reiss, A. L. (2007). Stress predicts brain changes in children: a pilot longitudinal study on youth stress, posttraumatic stress disorder, and the hippocampus. *Pediatrics, 119*(3), 509–16.

Cassiday, K. L., McNally, R. J., & Zeitlin, S. B. (1992). Cognitive processing of trauma cues in rape victims with post-traumatic stress disorder. *Cognitive Therapy and Research, 16*(3), 283–95.

Constans, J. I. (2007). Information processing in PTSD. In J. J. Vasterling & C. R. Brewin (Eds.), *Neuropsychology of PTSD: Biological, cognitive, and clinical perspectives* (pp. 105–30). New York: Guilford Press.

Constans, J. I., McCloskey, M. S., Vasterling, J. J., Brailey, K., & Mathews, A. (2004). Suppression of attentional bias in PTSD. *Journal of Abnormal Psychology, 113*(2), 315–23.

Crowell, T. A., Kieffer, K. M., & Siders, C. A. (2002). Neuropsychological findings in combat-related posttraumatic stress disorder. *Clinical Neuropsychologist, 16*(3), 310–21.

Dalgleish, T., Meiser-Stedman, R., & Smith, P. (2005). Cognitive aspects of posttraumatic stress reactions and their treatment in children and adolescents: An empirical review and some recommendations. *Behavioural and Cognitive Psychotherapy, 33*, 459–86.

Dalgleish, T., Moradi, A. R., Taghavi, M. R., Neshat-Doost, H. T., & Yule, W. (2001). An experimental investigation of hypervigilance for threat in children and adolescents with post-traumatic stress disorder. *Psychological Medicine, 31*(3), 541–7.

De Bellis, M. D., Baum, A. S., Birmaher, B. et al. (1999a). Developmental traumatology: I. Biological stress systems. *Biological Psychiatry, 45*, 1259–70.

De Bellis, M., Hall, J., Boring, A. M., Frustaci, K., & Moritz, G. (2001). A pilot longitudinal study of hippocampal volumes in pediatric maltreatment-related posttraumatic stress disorder. *Biological Psychiatry, 50*, 305–9.

De Bellis, M., Keshavan, M. S., Clark, D. et al. (1999b). Developmental traumatology: II. Brain development. *Biological Psychiatry, 45*, 1271–84.

De Bellis, M. D., Keshavan, M. S., Shifflett, H. et al. (2002). Brain structures in pediatric maltreatment-related posttraumatic stress disorder: a sociodemographically matched study. *Biological Psychiatry, 52*(11), 1066–78.

De Bellis, M. D., Hooper, S. R., & Sapia, J. L. (2005). Early trauma exposure and the brain. In J. J. Vasterling & C. R. Brewin (Eds.), *Neuropsychology of PTSD: Biological, cognitive, and clinical perspectives* (pp. 153–77). New York: Guilford Press.

De Bellis, M., & Kuchibhatla, M. (2006). Cerebellar volumes in pediatric maltreatment-related posttraumatic stress disorder. *Biological Psychiatry, 60*(7), 697–703.

Delaney-Black, V., Covington, C., Ondersma, S. J. et al. (2002). Violence exposure, trauma, and IQ and/or reading deficits among urban children. *Archives of Paediatric and Adolescent Medicine, 156,* 280–95.

Elzinga, B. M., & Bremner, J. D. (2002). Are the neural substrates of memory the final common pathway in posttraumatic stress disorder (PTSD)? *Journal of Affective Disorders, 70,* 1–17.

Foa, E. B., Zinbarg, R., & Rothbaum, B. O. (1992). Uncontrollability and unpredictability in post-traumatic stress disorder: an animal model. *Psychological Bulletin, 112*(2), 218–38.

Foster, J. K., Meikle, A., Goodson, G. et al. (1999). The hippocampus and delayed recall: bigger is not necessarily better? *Memory, 7*(5–6), 715–32.

Gil, T., Calev, A., Greenberg, D., Kugelmass, S., & Lerer, B. (1990). Cognitive functioning in post-traumatic stress disorder. *Journal of Traumatic Stress, 3,* 29–45.

Gilbertson, M. W., Gurvits, T. V., Lasko, N. B., Orr, S. P., & Pitman, R. K. (2001). Multivariate assessment of explicit memory function in combat veterans with posttraumatic stress disorder. *Journal of Traumatic Stress, 14*(2), 413–31.

Gilbertson, M. W., Shenton, M. E., Ciszewski, A. et al. (2002). Smaller hippocampal volume predicts pathological vulnerability to psychological trauma. *Nature Neuroscience, 5,* 1242–7.

Goenjian, A. K., Yehuda, R., Pynoos, R. S. et al. (1996). Basal cortisol, dexamethasone suppression of cortisol, and MHPG in adolescents after the 1988 earthquake in Armenia. *The American Journal of Psychiatry, 153*(7), 929–34.

Goldstein, L. E., Rasmusson, A. M., Bunney, B. S., & Roth, R. H. (1996). Role of the amygdala in the coordination of behavioral, neuroendocrine, and prefrontal cortical monoamine responses to psychological stress in the rat. *Journal of Neuroscience, 16*(15), 4787–98.

Gould, E., Tanapat, P., McEwen, B. S., Flugge, G., & Fuchs, E. (1998). Proliferation of granule cell precursors in the dentate gyrus of adult monkeys is diminished by stress. *Proceedings of the National Academy of Science USA, 95*(6), 3168–71.

Graham, Y. P., Heim, C., Goodman, S. H., Miller, A. H., & Nemeroff, C. B. (1999). The effects of neonatal stress on brain development: Implications for psychopathology. *Development and Psychopathology, 11*(3), 545–65.

Gunnar, M. R., & Vazquez, D. M. (2001). Low cortisol and a flattening of expected daytime rhythm: potential indices of risk in human development. *Development and Psychopathology, 13*(3), 515–38.

Guo, A. L., Petraglia, F., Criscuolo, M. et al. (1995). Evidence for a role of neurosteroids in modulation of diurnal changes and acute stress-induced corticosterone secretion in rats. *Gynecological Endocrinology, 9*(1), 1–7.

Gurvits, T. V., Gilbertson, M. W., Lasko, N. B. et al. (2000). Neurologic soft signs in chronic posttraumatic stress disorder. *Archives of General Psychiatry, 57*(2), 181–6.

Gurvits, T. V., Lasko, N. B., & Schachter, S. C. (1993). Neurological status of Vietnam veterans with chronic posttraumatic stress disorder. *Journal of Neuropsychiatry & Clinical Neurosciences, 5*(2), 183–8.

Gurvits, T. V., Shenton, M. E., Hokama, H. et al. (1996). Magnetic resonance imaging study of hippocampal volume in chronic, combat-related posttraumatic stress disorder. *Biological Psychiatry, 40,* 1091–9.

Hart, J., Gunnar, M., & Cicchetti, D. (1995). Salivary cortisol in maltreated children: Evidence of relations between neuroendocrine activity and social competence. *Development and Psychopathology*, 7(1), 11–26.

Hart, J., Gunnar, M., & Cicchetti, D. (1996). Altered neuroendocrine activity in maltreated children related to symptoms of depression. *Development and Psychopathology*, 8(1), 201–14.

Heim, C., Ehlert, U., & Hellhammer, D. H. (2000). The potential role of hypocortisolism in the pathophysiology of stress-related bodily disorders. *Psychoneuroendocrinology*, 25(1), 1–35.

Jenkins, M. A., Langlais, P. J., Delis, D., & Cohen, R. (1998). Learning and memory in rape victims with posttraumatic stress disorder. *The American Journal of Psychiatry*, 155(2), 278–9.

Johnson, M. H. (1999). Cortical plasticity in normal and abnormal cognitive development: Evidence and working hypotheses. *Development and Psychopathology*, 11(3), 419–37.

Kaminska, M., Harris, J., Gilsbers, K., & Dubrovsky, B. (2000). Dehydroepiandrosterone sulfate (DHEAS) counteracts decremental effects of corticosterone on dentate gyrus LTP. Implications for depression. *Brain Research Bulletin*, 52, 229–34.

Karishma, K. K., & Herbert, J. (2002). Dehydroepiandrosterone (DHEA) stimulates neurogenesis in the hippocampus of the rat, promotes survival of newly formed neurons and prevents corticosterone-induced suppression. *European Journal of Neuroscience*, 16, 445–53.

Kaspi, S. P., McNally, R. J., & Amir, N. (1995). Cognitive processing of emotional information in posttraumatic stress disorder. *Cognitive Therapy and Research*, 19(4), 433–44.

Kaufman, J., Yang, B. Z., Douglas-Palumberi, H. et al. (2004). Social supports and serotonin transporter gene moderate depression in maltreated children. *Proceedings of the National Academy of Science USA*, 101(49), 17316–21.

Kaufman, J., Yang, B. Z., Douglas-Palumberi, H. et al. (2006). Brain-derived neurotrophic factor-5-HTTLPR gene interactions and environmental modifiers of depression in children. *Biological Psychiatry*, 59(8), 673–80.

Kempermann, G., Gast, D., & Gage, F. H. (2002). Neuroplasticity in old age: sustained fivefold induction of hippocampal neurogenesis by long-term environmental enrichment. *Annals of Neurology*, 52(2), 135–43.

Kempermann, G., Gast, D., Kronenberg, G., Yamaguchi, M., & Gage, F. H. (2003). Early determination and long-term persistence of adult-generated new neurons in the hippocampus of mice. *Development*, 130(2), 391–9.

Kempermann, G., Kuhn, H. G., & Gage, F. H. (1997). More hippocampal neurons in adult mice living in an enriched environment. *Nature*, 386(6624), 493–5.

Kimonides, V. G., Khatibi, N. H., Svendsen, C. N., Sofroniew, M. V., & Herbert, J. (1998). Dehydroepiandrosterone (DHEA) and DHEA-sulfate (DHEAS) protect hippocampal neurons against excitatory amino acid-induced neurotoxicity. *Proceedings of the National Academy of Science*, 95(4), 1852–7.

Koenen, K. C., Driver, K. L., Oscar-Berman, M. et al. (2001). Measures of prefrontal system dysfunction in posttraumatic stress disorder. *Brain and Cognition*, 45, 64–78.

Koenen, K. C., Moffitt, T. E., Caspi, A., Taylor, A., & Purcell, S. (2003). Domestic violence is associated with environmental suppression of IQ in young children. *Development and Psychopathology, 15,* 297–311.

Koenen, K. C., Moffitt, T. E., Poulton, R., Martin, J., & Caspi, A. (2007). Early childhood factors associated with the development of post-traumatic stress disorder: Results from a longitudinal birth cohort. *Psychological Medicine, 37,* 181–92.

Kolb, L. C. (1987). A neuropsychological hypothesis explaining posttraumatic stress disorders. *The American Journal of Psychiatry, 144*(8), 989–95.

Koso, M., & Hansen, S. (2006). Executive function and memory in posttraumatic stress disorder: A study of Bosnian war veterans. *European Psychiatry, 21*(3), 167–173.

Krystal, J. H., Bennett, A. L., Bremner, J. D., Southwick, S., & Charney, D. S. (1995). A neuropsychological hypothesis explaining posttraumatic stress disorder. In M. J. Friedman, D. S. Charney, & A. Y. Deutsch (Eds.), *Neurobiological and clinical consequences of stress: From normal adaptation to PTSD*. Philadelphia, PA: Lippincott-Raven.

Kumar, A., Bilker, W., Lavretsky, H., & Gottlieb, G. (2000). Volumetric asymmetries in late-onset mood disorders: An attenuation of frontal asymmetry with depression severity. *Psychiatry Research and Neuroimaging, 100,* 41–7.

Ladd, C. O., Owens, M. J., & Nemeroff, C. B. (1996). Persistent changes in corticotropin-releasing factor neuronal systems induced by maternal deprivation. *Endocrinology, 137*(4), 1212–18.

Macklin, M. L., Metzger, L. J., Litz, B. T. et al. (1998). Lower precombat intelligence is a risk factor for posttraumatic stress disorder. *Journal of Consulting and Clinical Psychology, 66,* 323–6.

McEwen, B. S. (1998). Protective and damaging effects of stress mediators. *New England Journal of Medicine, 338*(3), 171–9.

McEwen, B. S., Gould, E. A., & Sakai, R. R. (1992). The vulnerability of the hippocampus to protective and destructive effects of glucocorticoids in relation to stress. *The British Journal of Psychiatry, 160,* 18–24.

McNally, R. J. (1991). Assessment of posttraumatic stress disorder in children. *Psychological Assessment: A Journal of Consulting and Clinical Psychology, 3,* 531–7.

Moradi, A. R., Neshat Doost, H. T., Taghavi, M. R., Yule, W., & Dalgleish, T. (1999). Everyday memory deficits in children and adolescents with PTSD: Performance on the Rivermead Behavioural Memory Test. *Journal of Child Psychology and Psychiatry, 40*(3), 357–61.

Moradi, A. R., Taghavi, M. R., Neshat Doost, H. T., Yule, W., & Dalgleish, T. (1999). Performance of children and adolescents with PTSD on the Stroop colour-naming task. *Psychological Medicine, 29*(2), 415–19.

Moradi, A. R., Taghavi, R., Neshat-Doost, H. T., Yule, W., & Dalgleish, T. (2000). Memory bias for emotional information in children and adolescents with post-traumatic stress disorder: A preliminary study. *Journal of Anxiety Disorders, 14*(5), 521–34.

Morgan III, C., Rasmusson, A., Pietrzak, R., Coric, V., & Southwick, S. (2009). Relationships among plasma dehydroepiandrosterone and dehydroepiandrosterone sulfate, cortisol, symptoms of dissociation, and objective performance in humans exposed to underwater navigation stress. *Biological Psychiatry, 66*(4), 334–40.

Murphy, B. L., Arnsten, A. F., Jentsch, J. D., & Roth, R. H. (1996). Dopamine and spatial working memory in rats and monkeys: pharmacological reversal of stress-induced impairment. *Journal of Neuroscience, 16*(23), 7768–75.

Patchev, V. K., Hassan, A. H., Holsboer, D. F., & Almeida, O. F. (1996). The neurosteroid tetrahydroprogesterone attenuates the endocrine response to stress and exerts glucocorticoid-like effects on vasopressin gene transcription in the rat hypothalamus. *Neuropsychopharmacology, 15*(6), 533–40.

Patchev, V. K., Shoaib, M., Holsboer, F., & Almeida, O. F. (1994). The neurosteroid tetrahydroprogesterone counteracts corticotropin-releasing hormone-induced anxiety and alters the release and gene expression of corticotropin-releasing hormone in the rat hypothalamus. *Neuroscience, 62*(1), 265–71.

Pederson, C. L., Maurer, S. H., & Kaminski, P. L. (2004). Hippocampal volume and memory performance in a community-based sample of women with posttraumatic stress disorder secondary to child abuse. *Journal of Traumatic Stress, 17*(1), 37–40.

Ramos, B. P., & Arnsten, A. F. (2007). Adrenergic pharmacology and cognition: focus on the prefrontal cortex. *Pharmacological Therapy, 113*(3), 523–36.

Rasmusson, A. M., Pinna, G., Paliwal, P. et al. (2006). Decreased cerebrospinal fluid allopregnanolone levels in women with posttraumatic stress disorder. *Biological Psychiatry, 60*(7), 704–13.

Rasmusson, A. M., Vythilingam, M., & Morgan, C. A. I. (2003). The neuroendocrinology of posttraumatic stress disorder: New directions. *CNS Spectrums, 8*(9), 651–67.

Sack, W. H., Clarke, G., & Seeley, J. (1995). Post-traumatic stress disorder across two generations of Cambodian refugees. *Journal of the American Academy of Child and Adolescent Psychiatry, 34*(9), 1160–66.

Saigh, P. A., Mroueh, M., & Bremner, J. D. (1997). Scholastic impairments among traumatized adolescents. *Behaviour Research and Therapy, 35*(5), 429–36.

Saigh, P. A., Yasik, A. E., Oberfield, R. A., Halamandaris, P. V., & Bremner, J. D. (2006). The intellectual performance of traumatized children and adolescents with or without posttraumatic stress disorder. *Journal of Abnormal Psychology, 115*(2), 332–40.

Samuelson, K. W., Neylan, T. C., Metzler, T. J. et al. (2006). Neuropsychological functioning in posttraumatic stress disorder and alcohol abuse. *Neuropsychology, 20*(6), 716–26.

Sapolsky, R. M. (1994). The physiological relevance of glucocorticoid endangerment of the hippocampus. *Annals of the New York Academy of Sciences, 746*, 294–304; discussion 304–7.

Sapolsky, R. M. (2000). Glucocorticoids and hippocampal atrophy in neuropsychiatric disorders. *Archives of General Psychiatry, 57*(10), 925–35.

Sapolsky, R. M., Uno, H., Rebert, C. S., & Finch, C. E. (1990). Hippocampal damage associated with prolonged and fatal stress in primates. *Journal of Neuroscience, 10*, 2897–902.

Schore, A. N. (2001). Effects of a secure attachment relationship on right brain development, affect regulation, and infant mental health. *Infant Mental Health Journal, 22*(1–2), 7–66.

Schumann, C. M., Hamstra, J., Goodlin-Jones, B. L. et al. (2004). The amygdala is enlarged in children but not adolescents with autism; the hippocampus is enlarged at all ages. *Journal of Neuroscience, 24*(28), 6392–401.

Siegel, D. J. (1995). Memory, trauma, and psychotherapy: A cognitive science view. *Journal of Psychotherapy Practice & Research, 4*(2), 93–122.

Silberg, J. L. (2000). Fifteen years of dissociation in maltreated children: where do we go from here? *Child Maltreatment, 5*(2), 119–36.

Southwick, S. M., Rasmusson, A., Barron, J., & Arnsten, A. (2005). Neurobiological and neurocognitive alterations in PTSD: A focus on norepinephrine, serotonin, and the hypothalamic-pituitary-adrenal axis. In J. J. Vasterling & C. R. Brewin (Eds.), *Neuropsychology of PTSD: Biological, cognitive, and clinical perspectives* (pp. 27–58). New York: Guilford Press.

Southwick, S. M., Yehuda, R., Morgan, C. A., III et al. (1995). Clinical studies of neurotransmitter alterations in posttraumatic stress disorder. In *Neurobiological and clinical consequences of stress: From normal adaptation to post-traumatic stress disorder* (pp. 335–49). Philadelphia, PA: Lippincott Williams & Wilkins.

Stein, M. B., Hanna, C., Vaerum, V., & Koverola, C. (1999). Memory functioning in adult women traumatized by childhood sexual abuse. *Journal of Traumatic Stress, 12*(3), 527–35.

Stein, M. B., Koverola, C., Hanna, C., Torchia, M. G., & McClarty, B. (1997). Hippocampal volume in women victimized by childhood sexual abuse. *Psychological Medicine, 27*, 951–9.

Sullivan, G. M., & Gorman, J. M. (2002). Finding a home for posttraumatic stress disorder in biological psychiatry: Is it a disorder of anxiety, mood, stress, or memory? *Psychiatric Clinics of North America, 25*(2), 463–8.

Sutker, P. B., Vasterling, J. J., Brailey, K., & Allain, A. N. (1995). Memory, attention, and executive deficits in POW survivors: Contributing biological and psychological factors. *Neuropsychology, 9*(1), 118–25.

Sutker, P. B., Winstead, D. K., Galina, Z. H., & Allain, A. N. (1991). Cognitive deficits and psychopathology among former prisoners of war and combat veterans of the Korean conflict. *The American Journal of Psychiatry, 148*(1), 67–72.

Teicher, M. H., Andersen, S. L., Polcari, A. et al. (2003). The neurobiological consequences of early stress and childhood maltreatment. *Neuroscience & Biobehavioral Reviews, 27*(1), 33–44.

Tupler, L. A., & De Bellis, M. (2006). Segmented hippocampal volume in children and adolescents with posttraumatic stress disorder. *Biological Psychiatry, 59*(6), 523–9.

Turetsky, B., Cowell, P. E., Gur, R. C., et al. (1995). Frontal and temporal lobe brain volumes in schizophrenia. *Archives of General Psychiatry, 52*, 1061–70.

Twamley, E. W., Hami, S., & Stein, M. B. (2004). Neuropsychological function in college students with and without posttraumatic stress disorder. *Psychiatry Research, 126*, 265–74.

Uddo, M., Vasterling, J. J., Brailey, K., & Sutker, P. B. (1993). Memory and attention in combat-related post-traumatic stress disorder (PTSD). *Journal of Psychopathology and Behavioral Assessment, 15*(1), 43–53.

Vasterling, J. J., Brailey, K., & Sutker, P. B. (2000). Olfactory identification in combat-related posttraumatic stress disorder. *Journal of Traumatic Stress, 13*(2), 241–53.

Vasterling, J. J., Brailey, K., Constans, J. I., & Borges, A. (1997). Assessment of intellectual resources in Gulf War veterans: Relationship to PTSD. *Assessment, 4*(1), 51–9.

Vasterling, J. J., Brailey, K., Constans, J. I., & Sutker, P. B. (1998). Attention and memory dysfunction in posttraumatic stress disorder. *Neuropsychology, 12*(1), 125–33.

Vasterling, J. J., Duke, L. M., Brailey, K. et al. (2002). Attention, learning, and memory performances and intellectual resources in Vietnam veterans: PTSD and no disorder comparisons. *Neuropsychology, 16*(1), 5–14.

Villarreal, G., Hamilton, D. A., Petropoulos, H. et al. (2002). Reduced hippocampal volume and total white matter volume in posttraumatic stress disorder. *Biological Psychiatry, 52*, 119–25.

Weber, D. A., & Reynolds, C. R. (2004). Clinical perspectives on neurobiological effects of psychological trauma. *Neuropsychology Review, 14*(2), 115–29.

Wolfe, J., & Schlesinger, L. (1997). Performance of PTSD patients on standard tests of memory. Implications for trauma. In R. Yehuda & A. C. McFarlane (Eds.), *Psychobiology of posttraumatic stress disorder* (pp. 208–18). New York: New York Academy of Sciences.

Wooley, C. S., Gould, E., & McEwen, B. S. (1990). Exposure to excess glucocorticoids alters dendritic morphology of adult hippocampal pyramidal neurons. *Brain Research, 531*, 225–31.

Yehuda, R., Grolier, J. A., & Tischler, L. (2005). Learning and memory in aging combat veterans with PTSD. *Journal of Clinical and Experimental Neuropsychology, 27*(4), 504–15.

Yehuda, R., Keefe, R. S. E., Harvey, P. D. et al. (1995). Learning and memory in combat veterans with posttraumatic stress disorder. *The American Journal of Psychiatry, 152*(1), 137–9.

Zhang, L., Li, B., Ma, W. et al. (2002). Dehydroepiandrosterone (DHEA) and its sulfated derivative (DHEAS) regulate apoptosis during neurogenesis by triggering the Akt signaling pathway in opposing ways. *Molecular Brain Research, 98*, 58–66.

Zigmond, M. J., Finlay, J. M., & Sved, A. F. (1995). Neurochemical studies of central noradrenergic responses to acute and chronic stress: Implications for normal and abnormal behavior. In M. J. Friedman, D. S. Charney, & A. Y. Deutch (Eds.), *Neurobiological and clinical consequences of stress: From normal adaptation to posttraumatic stress disorder* (pp. 45–60). Philadelphia, PA: Lippincott-Raven.

Chapter Seven

Why and How People Forget. Why and How People Forget Sexual Abuse. The Role of Traumatic Memories

Kathryn A. Becker-Blease, Anne P. DePrince,
and Jennifer J. Freyd

Introduction

Cases of child sexual abuse brought to the attention of researchers and clinicians reveal a complicated picture of memory for abuse. The accounts of survivors of Catholic priest abuse, including the widely reported story of Paul Busa, made the complexity of these stories known to the public in a new way (e.g., see Stern, 2002). As reported in the media, in February 2002, military security officer Paul Busa read a newspaper report about allegations of sexual abuse against Paul Shanley, a priest. The account triggered memories of being sexually abused by Shanley in the 1980s. Three years later, Shanley was convicted of raping Busa when he was a six-year-old boy. In addition to the evidence, which was sufficient to convict Shanley of abusing Busa, there was reason to believe that Shanley had abused many children throughout his career. According to newspaper reports, allegations of sexual abuse arose as early as a year after he was ordained as a priest, over 20 years before the incidents for which he was convicted. In 2002, when charges were pending against Shanley, 30 accusers had been identified. Over the years Shanley had made public comments supportive of sexual abuse of minors, and reportedly admitted being "attracted to adolescents" and having sexually abused four boys. Busa gave a similar account of repeated sexual abuse as two other boys who attended the same church, but much attention was paid to the fact that Busa did not have continuous memories of the abuse (Stern, 2002).

Post-Traumatic Syndromes in Childhood and Adolescence: A Handbook of Research and Practice, First Edition.
Edited by Vittoria Ardino. © 2011 John Wiley & Sons, Ltd. Published 2011 by John Wiley & Sons, Ltd.

These cases led the court, the public, and researchers to ask (at least) three questions: (1) *What* is the phenomenon? That is: Do people actually fail to recall sexual abuse? Do they have access to some parts of memories some of the time or are events completely unavailable? (2) *Why* do people fail to recall abuse? That is: Are people motivated not to recall abuse because the memories are too painful, terrifying, or threatening to relationships? (3) *How* do people *not* recall abuse? That is: What are the particular mechanisms by which people fail to recall abuse?

While these three questions are ultimately related, disentangling them is important for the progress of good science. This is because conflating these questions increases the chances that we will erroneously use answers to one question to confirm or dismiss answers to another question. For example, if we fail to identify the proper mechanisms by which people fail to recall abuse (*how* question), it may be tempting to disregard the phenomenon itself (*what* question) or the motivation to forget (*why* question). However, failure to identify the mechanism(s) by which a phenomenon emerges does not negate the phenomenon itself; nor does it disconfirm hypotheses about why the phenomenon may occur in the first place. In this chapter, we address each of these questions in turn, and conclude with recommendations for future research on memory for sexual abuse and other trauma.

The basics of human memory

Before embarking on a discussion of *what*, *why*, and *how*, we offer a brief overview of memory systems. Traditional models of memory describe a generic three-step process. First, information is encoded, then stored, and later retrieved. This process has also been called the library model, because it is similar to the process of receiving and labeling books with call numbers (encoding), placing books on stacks (storage), and finding and checking books out (retrieval). Cognitive psychology and neuroscience have elaborated on this model in recent years, finding that there are many kinds of memory at work simultaneously. Humans depend upon procedural memory (e.g., for riding a bike), sensory memory (e.g., for smells), declarative memory (e.g., for facts), and many other kinds of memory all at the same time. While often these different kinds of memories are linked together, they depend on somewhat separate neural and cognitive systems.

Memory impairment, then, can occur under at least three conditions: during encoding (failure to perceive or failure to consolidate), during retrieval, or during both encoding and retrieval (Freyd, 1996). While the field has at times treated all unawareness as equal, a more accurate picture of memory for trauma may be that some unawareness occurs because memories were never consolidated due to the effects of terror-inducing stressors, while other memories are inaccessible at a particular moment in time. Memories that are never consolidated have not entered the system in a way that the memory event has been integrated and can later be recalled. Inaccessible memories, on the other hand, may have entered the system, but are inaccessible at the level of recall. Through these important distinctions, we notice multiple explanations for why unawareness might occur, which we will discuss in reviewing approaches to why and how questions.

Describing the phenomena: do people really forget sexual abuse?

There is enough empirical evidence to know that, in some cases, people do forget child sexual abuse. Across studies, roughly one third of adults tend to report some period for which they did not have full access to memory for a childhood traumatic event, though criteria for amnesia, from partial to full, varies from study to study (e.g., Elliott & Briere, 1995; Feldman-Summers & Pope, 1994; Herman & Shatzow, 1987; Loftus, Polonsky, & Fullilove, 1994; Williams, 1994). This body of work includes studies using both prospective (e.g., Williams, 1994, 1995) and retrospective (Elliott, 1997; Feldman-Summers & Pope, 1994; Freyd, DePrince, & Zurbriggen, 2001; Schultz, Passmore, & Yoder, 2003; Sheiman, 1999; Stoler, 2000) research methods; and includes documentation of amnesia for corroborated cases of abuse (Cheit, 2005). As noted by Brown, Scheflin, and Whitfield in their 1999 literature review: "in just this past decade alone, 68 research studies have been conducted on naturally occurring dissociative or traumatic amnesia for childhood sexual abuse. Not a single one of the 68 data-based studies failed to find it" (p. 126).

As these studies demonstrate, the phenomenon of forgetting is diverse. For example, some people report relatively complete forgetting for sexually abusive events that occurred in childhood followed by remembering that ranges from relatively incomplete to complete. Still others report continuous, but incomplete memories. That is, they report always knowing what happened to them, but memories for aspects of the experience – for example, the emotions they felt at the time – are not accessible. There are many other permutations of discontinuous and/or incomplete memories that survivors, clinicians, and researchers may or may not label consistently as "forgotten" or "recovered" (e.g., Fivush, 2004). Some people report the experience of being surprised to "discover" they have memories of abuse that in fact they had discussed previously with other people. Schooler (2001) suggests that some people retain memories, but gain a new level of meta-awareness of the memories that is so surprising it leads them to believe they are recovering the memories themselves for the first time.

Survivors' experiences are diverse, and so are the names people use to describe the phenomenon of memory disturbance following trauma. This leads directly to the question: what should we call this phenomenon? As Freyd (1996) noted, "Whatever we call it – repression, dissociation, psychological defense, denial, amnesia, unawareness, or betrayal blindness – the failure to know some significant and negative aspect of reality is an aspect of human experience that remains at once elusive and of central importance" (p. 16). Drawing on Freyd, DePrince, and Gleave's (2007) recent discussion of terminology, we use the term *unawareness* to refer to the phenomenon of information inaccessibility. In using this term, we intentionally avoid any inferences about *how* (i.e., mechanism) information becomes inaccessible (e.g., dissociation, everyday forgetting, encoding failures), instead emphasizing *why* (i.e., motivation) information may become inaccessible.

As we move on to discuss the *why* and *how* questions, we will structure our discussion around two major approaches to traumatic stress studies. The first highlights the role of fear in understanding post-traumatic responses and memory; the second highlights the role of betrayal.

Why do people forget? Why might fear lead to unawareness?

Researchers and clinicians have long assumed that terror plays a central role in human responses to traumatic events. In fact, the very definition of Post-Traumatic Stress Disorder (PTSD) requires that the individual react with overwhelming fear, helplessness, or horror (APA, 1994) to meet the diagnostic criteria. Different people who have experienced terrifying events report different types of memory disturbance, including both memory intrusions and unawareness. It could be that "difficulty forgetting (or letting go of) a horrifying experience may simply be the opposite side of the same coin of difficulty remembering (accepting or acknowledging) a horrifying experience" (Widiger & Sankis, 2000, p. 391). Indeed, PTSD has been characterized as "the reciprocal oscillation between reexperiencing and avoidance" (Leskin, Kaloupek, & Keane, 1998, p. 986).

In the face of divergent views about the relationship between un- and hyperawareness in PTSD, we pause here to ask *why* might fear be associated with unawareness, particularly if we are more generally used to thinking of it as associated with memory intrusions or *hyper*-awareness? One explanation is that emotional arousal can have surprising and seemingly contradictory effects on memory. As noted in his recent review, Brewin (2003) examines evidence demonstrating that emotional arousal can be linked with *both* improved and impoverished memory for events. Thus, one logical route to memory impairment is to argue that overwhelming fear disrupts memory processes, thereby resulting in unawareness.

Why might betrayal lead to unawareness?

Freyd (1996) proposed betrayal trauma theory to account for the particular motivations that might lead to unawareness following sexual abuse. Betrayal trauma theory posits that there is a social utility in remaining unaware of abuse perpetrated by a caregiver. In cases where betrayals occur, the victim may be motivated by the attachment to the caregiver to be unaware of the abuse. This type of memory impairment does not require that the memory for the event did not enter the system; rather, the theory supposes that autobiographical awareness of the event is dissociated or isolated from conscious awareness. This model does not require that memory impairment occurs at any particular stage; rather, the memory impairment can occur at encoding, consolidation, or retrieval.

Betrayal trauma theory was forged from an interdisciplinary view of human psychology (Figure 7.1). Drawing on evolutionary perspectives, Freyd (1996) reviewed evidence that humans have evolved to be excellent cheater detectors; under most circumstances, an ability to detect cheaters allows humans to withdraw from relationships in which they will likely be harmed by the cheater. Under some circumstances, however, detecting betrayals may actually be counterproductive to survival goals. In cases where a victim is dependent on a caregiver, survival may require that she/he remains unaware of the betrayal in order to maintain an attachment that is otherwise necessary for survival. In childhood sexual abuse, for example, a child who is aware that she/he is being abused by a parent may withdraw from the relationship (e.g., withdraw in terms of proximity or emotionally). For a child who depends on a caregiver for basic survival, withdrawing may actually be at odds with long-term survival. In this example, the child's survival would be better ensured by remaining blind to the betrayal and isolating knowledge of the event from conscious awareness.

Freyd (1996) reported on the re-analyses of four major data sets to test the betrayal trauma prediction that higher levels of memory impairment for

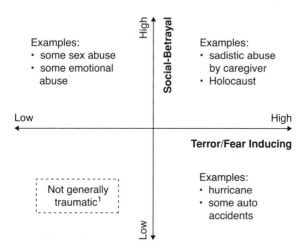

Figure 7.1 The two-dimensional model of trauma. © Jennifer J. Freyd, 1996. Reprinted with permission

Footnote 1. This is not to discount cases of sexual abuse in which a child is victimized by another child, or cases in which no interpersonal contact occurs (e.g. exposure to online pornography, or taking pictures of children for the purpose of producing child pornography without the child's knowledge).

childhood sexual abuse would differ depending on the victim–perpetrator relationship (see Figure 7.1). Three of these data sets were retrospective (Cameron, 1993; Feldman-Summers & Pope, 1994; Loftus, Polonsky, & Fullilove, 1994) and one was prospective (Williams, 1994). Within these data sets, the only information available on the victim–perpetrator relationship was an indication of whether the perpetrator was a family member or not. Freyd (1996) predicted that higher levels of reported memory impairment would be found for those people whose perpetrator was a family member compared to those whose perpetrator was a non-family member. In three of the re-analyses, higher levels of memory impairment were found when the perpetrator was a family member compared to cases when the perpetrator was a non-family member. In one study, no differences in memory impairment between family and non-family perpetration were found (Loftus, Polonsky, & Fullilove, 1994).

The re-analyses conducted by Freyd (1996) were an important first step in testing betrayal trauma theory. However, Freyd's original re-analyses (1996) assumed that a family member was equivalent to a caregiver. This may frequently be the case, but likely a subset of people may be abuse by a family member who is not a caregiver (e.g., abused by a father who is separated from the family and not responsible for caregiving). Likewise, perpetrators categorized as non-family members may provide care and be trusted, making abuse a betrayal; for example, coaches and clergy who provide emotional care to children, but are not family members. In such cases, betrayal trauma theory would predict memory impairment, but this would not be captured with the simple distinction of family member versus non-family member.

Support for betrayal trauma theory was found when the perpetrator–victim relationship was defined by caregiver status in a sample of participants at the University of Oregon (Freyd, DePrince, & Zurbriggen, 2001). Undergraduates were asked to complete a modified version of the Abuse and Perpetration Inventory (Lisak et al., 2000), called the Betrayal Trauma Inventory (BTI; Freyd et al., 2001), which specified the victim–perpetrator relationship along dimensions not previously examined. For example, this modified measure asks respondents to indicate who the perpetrator was ("What was the person's relationship to you; for example, friend, father, sister, uncle, etc.?"), as well as asks the respondent to identify whether or not the perpetrator was a caregiver. Caretaker status of the perpetrator, therefore, was determined by the participants' response to the item, "Was this person responsible for caring for you; for example, providing you with food or shelter?" Analyses revealed significantly more reported memory impairment when the perpetrator was a caregiver than when the perpetrator was a non-caregiver for sexual and physical abuse events. This was the first study to look at reported memory impairment by caretaker for sexual, physical, and emotional abuse. The pattern of memory impairment was consistent across sexual and physical abuse: more memory impairment was reported when the perpetrator was identified as a caregiver versus when the perpetrator was identified as a non-caregiver.

This pattern has now been replicated by others. For example, Shultz and colleagues (2003) found that participants reporting memory disturbances (relative to those who did not) indicated closer relationships with the perpetrator(s). Sheiman (1999) reported that, in a sample of 174 students, those participants who reported memory loss for child sexual abuse were more likely to experience abuse by people who were well known to them, compared to those who did not have memory loss. Interestingly, general autobiographical memory loss measured in a large epidemiologic study was strongly associated with a history of childhood abuse; further, increased memory loss was associated with sexual abuse by a relative (Edwards et al., 2001).

What is the mechanism: how do people forget sexual abuse? How might fear lead to unawareness?

Turning to the *how* question, we discuss three possible fear-related routes to unawareness: (1) disruptions in encoding and consolidation; (2) dual representation models; and (3) avoidance.

Disruptions in encoding and consolidation of memories

Overwhelming fear may cause encoding disruptions in at least two ways. First, effects of emotional arousal at the time of the event may disrupt information entering the nervous system. Emotional arousal, for example, may cause a narrowing of attention resulting in either lack of or shallow encoding of important aspects of the trauma. As in the picnic example described below, if aspects of the event are not encoded (or are encoded only in a shallow way), they will be unavailable for retrieval later. Similarly, peritraumatic dissociative responses to the overwhelming fear may disrupt encoding of the aspects of the event. Indeed, fear at the time of the event has been associated with peritraumatic dissociation (Gershuny, Cloitre, & Otto, 2003).

Secondly, fear and corresponding stress may impair brain regions responsible for important memory functions, thus leading to unawareness. That is to say, overwhelming fear places the individual under demands of chronic stress. When an individual experiences a traumatic event that invokes terror, the system is driven to make changes to deal with the fear; these alterations may ultimately lead to neurobiological consequences which, in turn, interact with memory systems. When fear is the primary response to trauma, the systems likely to be involved with memory impairment will be those that are affected by the deleterious impact of stress, such as the hippocampus and related structures. The hippocampus is a brain structure located in the limbic system which has been associated with memory consolidation (Zola-Morgan & Squire, 1993), and which has been shown to be particularly vulnerable to the deleterious effects of stress (see Sapolsky, 1992). Not surprisingly, then, theorists and researchers have been interested in the interplay between fear, stress, and the hippocampus to provide an explanation of how fear may result in unawareness. For example,

Bremner (2001) argued that hippocampal dysfunction in individuals diagnosed with PTSD may result in an impaired ability to integrate memories for trauma at retrieval. In addition, chronic dysregulation of systems related to the stress response may also affect memory retrieval (Bremner, 2001).

Indeed, hippocampal correlates of trauma generally (and sexual abuse specifically) have been replicated fairly extensively. For example, a handful of studies demonstrate differences in hippocampal volume size in individuals exposed to traumatic events, including sexual abuse (e.g., Bremner et al., 1995; Bremner, et al., 1997; Gurvits et al., 1996; Stein et al., 1997). When differences in hippocampal function first emerged, it was generally assumed that the lower volumes were a consequence of the chronic stress caused by the trauma and its aftermath. Drawing on more recent twin studies, however, researchers have recently begun to suggest that smaller hippocampal volume may actually represent a risk factor for the development of PTSD (e.g., Pitman et al., 2006).

While the recent twin work causes the field to revisit interpretations of what the smaller hippocampal volume means (e.g., risk factor for or consequence of PTSD), links between fear-inducing traumas that cause PTSD and smaller hippocampal volume continue to provide a viable route to disruptions in memory. Because the hippocampus is responsible for important integrative functions, it would not be surprising to find that memory dysfunction – in the forms of hyper- and unawareness of memories – is mediated, in part, by the hippocampus.

Dual representation models of memory

The second fear-related route to memory impairment invokes dual representation theories of memory. Specifically, Brewin and colleagues (e.g., Brewin, 2003; Brewin, Dalgleish, & Joseph, 1996) have proposed a dual representation theory of PTSD, which suggests that trauma-related memories for emotionally arousing events are stored as verbally accessible and situationally accessible memories (VAMs and SAMs). VAMs include trauma narratives that the individual can consciously bring into awareness and articulate. VAMs and declarative memory are similar insofar as both include knowledge about which we can make statements. Brewin and colleagues argue that VAMs are integrated with other autobiographical information, interact with processes to develop meaning, and can be updated and recognized as existing at a particular point in time relative to the past, present, and future. SAMs, on the other hand, include lower-level perceptual information about the trauma scene and/or about somatic experiences during the trauma. SAMs are not verbally accessible and are more closely akin to non-declarative memories. SAMs are, in a sense, time-locked to the trauma; the memories do not get updated based on other information in autobiographical memory or based on time or context (e.g., relative to the past, present, and future).

Brewin and colleagues have generally used the dual-representation theory as a model for understanding intrusive flashbacks, arguing that flashbacks represent

SAMs that are neither linked to other aspects of autobiographical memory nor verbal expression. As noted by Brewin and colleagues (1996), hormones released in response to acute traumas "may act to diminish neural activity in anatomical structures serving conscious processing and to enhance activity in structures serving non-conscious perceptual and memory processes" (p. 676). While SAMs may give rise to the experiences of intrusive memories, they may also give rise to the experience that one does not *know* what happened in a verbally accessible way, which in turn may increase the likelihood of actual unawareness or reports of unawareness. Indeed, Brewin and colleagues (1996) argue that premature inhibition of processing trauma memories may result in impaired memory for the trauma or trauma-related material. Thus, the dual representation view of PTSD provides another route by which people may come to experience and report unawareness.

Avoidance

The third fear-related route to unawareness invokes classic approaches to anxiety. To the extent that fear-related memories are painful and aversive, anxiety models suggest that the individual will increasingly avoid both external and internal reminders of the trauma (notably, Brewin et al., 1996, also predict avoidance when memories are prematurely inhibited). In turn, the memories may not be processed in ways that integrate them with other autobiographical memories, increasing the likelihood of unawareness.

How might betrayal be related to unawareness?

We discuss three possible betrayal-related routes to unawareness: (1) retrieval-induced forgetting; (2) silencing and nondisclosure; and (3) related coping and/or symptoms.

Retrieval-induced forgetting

Retrieval-induced forgetting may be especially relevant under circumstances where a child must contend with a caregiver who is also abusive. Specifically, Anderson (2001) has applied models of active forgetting to memory impairment for betrayal traumas. Drawing on a strong empirical research program, Anderson (2001) proposes that human cognition includes the ability to actively inhibit information. The ability to inhibit information is necessary to human cognitive functioning; that is, we must be able to forget information, particularly when trying to learn new information.

In a series of laboratory tasks, Anderson (2001) and colleagues have illustrated that under certain circumstances, individuals will actively inhibit information from recall in order to retrieve related information. Anderson (2001) proposes that retrieval-induced forgetting is caused by inhibitory mechanisms that can be studied empirically. For example, participants in a laboratory task are asked to study words that fall into categories (e.g., *banana* and *orange* are members of the category *fruit*). Using a retrieval practice paradigm, participants are asked to rehearse certain word-pairs, such as *fruit–banana*. Following this, the participants are tested for their memory for a previously introduced, but not practiced, item (e.g., *orange*). Researchers were interested in participants' memory for *banana* (also in the category *fruit*, but not practiced) versus memory for *house* (not in the category *fruit*, but not practiced). Participants showed poorer memory for words drawn from the same category they had practiced than those drawn from a different category (e.g., house) (Anderson & Bjork, 1994). Anderson and colleagues have argued that memory mechanisms allow us to suppress banana when we are trying to remember *fruit–orange* because *banana* would otherwise compete with *orange*; therefore, retrieval-induced forgetting mechanisms suppress *banana*. When subsequently tested for *banana*, memory for items has been inhibited.

Extending this work to trauma, Anderson (2001) proposed that betrayal traumas (e.g., child abuse by a caregiver) may create dynamics in which retrieval-induced forgetting is possible. Drawing on betrayal trauma theory, Anderson suggests that children who are abused by caregivers take in a great deal of information – good and bad – about their abusive caregivers. As Freyd (1996) has proposed, a child abused by a caregiver may be at an advantage to remain unaware of the abuse in order to preserve the attachment. In such a case, the child would be motivated to rehearse and remember non-abuse-related information about the caregiver and forget abuse-related information. A parallel can be drawn between the laboratory model of retrieval-induced forgetting (e.g., Anderson, 2001) and cases where a child is motivated to rehearse and remember non-abuse-related information about the caregiver. Specifically, as the child rehearses non-abuse-related information, he/she may actively suppress completing information about abuse. A retrieval-induced forgetting model provides the first empirical support for the processes that lead to memory impairment in betrayal trauma theory. Caution must be taken in generalizing from laboratory tasks to real world events; Anderson's (2001) model provides a useful framework for delineating possible mechanisms that underlie forgetting, but does not have the ecological validity to speak directly to the phenomenon of memory impairment for trauma.

Another recent study addressed the question of whether even highly valenced violent and sexual information could be forgotten and later recalled. Smith and Moynan (2008) asked participants to memorize lists of words that included expletives and words related to death and disease, followed by either an interference task or a control task. Participants were then given a free recall task. On the free recall task, participants in the experimental condition remembered significantly fewer words, including the highly charged expletives and words related to death and disease. After the free recall test, participants were given retrieval cues. On the cued recall test, no differences in memory for the original lists of words emerged. In sum, participants were able to encode highly charged words, to forget those words, and later recall the words when the appropriate cues were available. This study is unique in that it provides direct laboratory evidence that even emotionally charged, violent, and sexual material can be forgotten and recalled.

Silencing and nondisclosure

While the retrieval-induced forgetting approach offered an active route whereby rehearsing one set of associations inhibits another set of associations, more passive processes may also lead to unawareness. In particular, nondisclosure of events may have important effects on memory (and as noted previously, nondisclosure could occur because of avoidance of fear-related affect). As reviewed by Foynes, Freyd, and DePrince (2009), most survivors of sexual abuse either do not disclose or wait long periods of time to disclose sexual abuse. In fact, a recent review found nondisclosure rates in sexual abuse as high as 46–69% (London et al., 2005). Less than one in four survivors disclose immediately following abuse (Paine & Hansen, 2002).

Why don't children disclose abuse, especially when they are exposed to child abuse prevention campaigns that encourage them to "tell a trusted adult"? Children who have been confused and betrayed by an adult (and/or by non-offending adults as well) have good reason to be wary of all adults. If the child is not believed, they risk disrupting attachments to caregivers and retaliation from the perpetrator. Indeed, data suggest that when disclosure of a negative experience results in *negative* feedback, *non* disclosure actually predicts better outcomes (Lepore, Ragan, & Jones, 2000; Major et al., 1990). In very real ways, sexual abuse narratives continue to be silenced within families and, societies, and by survivors themselves (Fivush, 2004).

In the context of the striking rates of nondisclosure, shareability theory (Freyd, 1983, 1996) offers additional explanations for unawareness of abuse. Shareability theory was first developed to explain mental processing about a single event can be continuous and fine-grained as well as discrete and categorical. Shareability theory posits that mental processing is affected by the fact that humans are socially dependent on each other. According to shareability theory, people recode fine-grained perceptual information about events to a more discrete and abstract form so that the information can be shared with other people. A person's internal representation of an event may be highly continuous and full of sensory details that differ substantially from the representation of the event that is shared with another person.

Through the process of sharing, according to shareability theory, those aspects of the event that are hard to share with others are likely to be dropped from memory or recoded into more discrete concepts as the event is shared with other people. For example, a person may have an internal memory of a picnic on a hot day that includes the smell of flowers, the sensation of the sun on skin, conversations with other people, and similar. In telling someone else about the picnic, the person is likely to say it was a hot day, or give an approximate temperature in degrees rather than attempt to explain the sensation of being under the hot sun. In other words, fine-grained details become more discrete. Telling another who was present and the topic of conversation is easy to share with words and are details that are likely to remain as the story is told. The smell of the flowers is difficult to convey to another person, as well as usually being less relevant to the listener, and may be dropped from the story altogether. As memories are told and retold, shareability theory posits that they become more and more concrete and shareable in just this way.

Shareability theory, then, predicts that memory for events that have never been discussed will be qualitatively different from those that have been shared with others. Sexual abuse is very unlikely to be shared with others, and thus is unlikely to undergo the process of becoming more discrete and shareable. The original sensory and other fine-grained details are likely to remain intact, and the memory is likely to not be in a form that is immediately shareable with others. Placing memory for unspoken events within the context of shareability theory provides one way of understanding how memory for sexually abusive events may be processed differently from other memories that are shared with others.

In applying shareability theory to memory for trauma, disclosure becomes an increasingly important factor to assess. For example, Goodman and colleagues (2003) reported that "relationship betrayal" was not a statistically significant predictor of forgetting in a sample of adults who had been involved in child abuse prosecution cases during childhood. The prosecution process would have required children to communicate about the sexual abuse, which may have resulted in less memory decline because of changes in the structure of the memory; as well as opportunities to rehearse the memory. Thus, disclosure may have played an important role in the development and maintenance of memories for the sexual abuse. However, it is also possible that the motivation to be unaware was removed because the children (presumably) did not need to remain dependent upon perpetrators who were being charged with a crime (see commentaries by Freyd, 2003, and Zurbriggen & Becker-Blease, 2003 for additional discussion).

Developmental research on autobiographical memory sheds light on why young children are likely to have a particularly hard time developing a coherent narrative for sexual abuse memories. Robyn Fivush and colleagues have found that parents play an important role in providing recall cues to help children remember relevant details of memories (Fivush, 2007; Fivush et al., 1997). Parents who provide meaningful narration before, during, and after events can help their children retrieve memories, as well as help them organize memories, and learn which aspects of memories are most important for others to understand what happened. Parents who are skilled at helping children construct narratives of everyday events tend to be better at helping children understand stressful events, such as a trip to the emergency room or being in a natural disaster (Sales, Fivush, & Peterson, 2003; Ackil, Van Abbema, & Bauer, 2003). When parents talk to their children about these events, they use a slightly different style than when discussing everyday events. Rather than creating a shared positive memory, parents use language to help children understand stressful events and why they happened (Fivush, 2007). The fact that parents change their strategy when talking about memories of stressful events that involve high levels of fear and physical danger tells us something about the power of communication in how young children perceive and recall these kinds of events.

How do parents talk with children about sexual abuse? We do not yet have the answer to that question, but children are very unlikely to have the same meaningful narrative to accompany memories of sexual abuse as they might for everyday or even other kinds of stressful events. Perpetrators and non-offending adults are likely either to not talk about the abusive event at all or to provide a confusing narrative (e.g., telling children that they initiated the abuse). We can speculate that an inconsistent pattern, providing elaborate narratives for most events but not abusive events, may influence memory retrieval and organization even further.

Fivush (2004) further posits that not talking about sexual abuse narratives affects a survivor's sense of self. Based on a study of 12 sexual abuse survivors, she found that survivors who reported "continuous memory" (i.e., always recalled the events, but the level of detail may have changed over time) were more likely than those who abruptly became aware of previously inaccessible memories to provide a coherent narrative of the abuse events, and were more likely to describe an integrated sense of self. Those with a less integrated sense of self indicated that it was hard for them to accept that the abuse they remembered actually happened to them. This line of investigation brings in the question not only of basic memory processes, but the roles of schemas and self-concept in integrating experiences into a memorable and consistent set of autobiographical memories.

This research also points to the role of other adults – perpetrators – in the formation of children's memories. We should remember that most sexual abuse involves interpersonal interactions between a child victim and an older perpetrator. Unlike witnesses to crime or victims of natural disasters, or even most physical abuse victims, sexual abuse victims are often targeted and manipulated by another person who depends on the victim's silence.

Many perpetrators take careful steps to prevent children from disclosing abuse. They choose potential victims who are socially isolated, have poor relationships with parents, and who lack confidence (Elliott, Browne, & Kilcoyne, 1995). They often introduce sex slowly, and stop if children show signs that they might tell someone, and they scare children with stories of what will happen if they do tell (e.g., the child will go into foster care, the perpetrator will go to jail, the perpetrator will hurt the child, etc.). In light of the foregoing discussion about shareability and children's needs to discuss events with adults in order to form coherent memories, every step perpetrators take to ensure nondisclosure is a step toward amnesia for the event. In other words, perpetrators' grooming activities are so frequently successful, in part, because they prevent children from developing coherent memories that could be told.

Some perpetrators take an even more direct route to disorient victims and prevent the development of coherent memories. They drug their victims by giving them drugs or alcohol with or without their knowledge. The victims of Dennis Gray, a former priest, explain in the documentary *Twist of Faith* (Dick, 2006) how Gray invited adolescent boys to a cabin where alcohol was freely available. One survivor described getting drunk and waking up the next morning in Gray's bed, not knowing what happened the night before. This technique works on three levels. First, boys are given gifts and made to feel special and grown up. Second, the gifts are illegal, so the boys would have to admit to illegal activity in order to report the abuse. For both of these reasons, the boys were reluctant to disclose, and thus less likely to have complete memories. Third, the alcoholic substances themselves induce amnesia, preventing them from giving a coherent report.

One of the ways that offender behavior confuses children and makes it hard for them to develop a coherent memory or disclose is the way in which many act one way during the abuse and another way in everyday life. In *Twist of Faith*, a survivor described his confusion when, minutes after raping him, his priest Dennis Gray led a group of people in Sunday Mass. It was a surreal experience, and he could not reconcile the two back-to-back events. How do offenders manage that kind of Jekyll and Hyde act? Some are likely psychopaths who blatantly manipulate people for their own desires. Others, though, may make use of some of the same dissociative strategies that victims use to get through victimization. That is, some offenders may dissociate, or block out, perpetration experiences during the times when they are living their everyday lives. In fact, lack of memory for perpetration is a significant issue in treatment. Some offenders do not deny that they committed sexual crimes for which they were convicted, but claim no personal memories for the event (Marshall et al., 2005). In a separate study of 17 convicted sex offenders, Becker-Blease and Freyd (2007) found that half reported some amnesia for at least one perpetration event, and forgetting perpetration was related to dissociating during the event.

Related coping and/or symptoms

Betrayal traumas may be associated with psychobiological responses, efforts at coping, or psychological symptoms that, in turn, are also associated with memory disruption. For example, traumas high in betrayal appear to be associated with dissociation (see Somer, Chapter 8 in this book for a review on dissociation and trauma). Maltreated preschoolers have been shown to have higher dissociation scores than non-maltreated peers (Hulette, Fisher et al., 2008; Hulette, Freyd et al., 2008). Chu and Dill (1990) reported that childhood physical and/or sexual abuse by family members (but not abuse by non-familial members) was significantly related to increased DES (Dissociative Experiences Scale) scores in psychiatric inpatients. Similarly, significant correlations between symptoms of pathological dissociation and intra-familial (but not extra-familial) trauma have been observed among delinquent juveniles (Plattner et al., 2003). Among undergraduates, DePrince (2005) found that the presence of betrayal trauma before the age of 18 was associated with pathological dissociation after age 18.

Phenomenologically, dissociation involves alterations in attention and memory (see DePrince & Freyd, 2007, for review). Indeed, laboratory-based studies have identified attentional conditions under which high levels of dissociation are associated with worse recall of trauma-related relative to neutral stimuli when compared to low dissociators, which show the opposite pattern (see DePrince & Freyd, 2001, 2004; DePrince, Freyd, & Malle, 2007).

Attachment theorists posit that inconsistent care from caregivers may lead children to develop cognitive strategies to avoid rejection in the future (Kirsh & Cassidy, 1997; Main & Solomon, 1990). As such, these theories are consistent with fear-based theories that emphasize avoidance of overwhelming stimuli. These theories are especially applicable to betrayal trauma theory, however, since betrayal trauma theory specifically implicates attachment processes in the motivation for amnesia. Specifically, according to betrayal trauma theory, children remain unaware of abuse because it allows them to maintain functional attachment systems with caregivers.

Some researchers have pointed to attachment theory as an important framework for understanding children's memory for trauma (Alexander, Quas, & Goodman, 2002). As reviewed by Alexander and colleagues, several studies have shown that attachment classification predicted how well children recalled a number of stories designed to evoke representations of caregivers (e.g., stories about a child asking for help after being injured) or had a negative or positive valence (Alexander & Edelstein, as cited in Alexander, Quas, & Goodman, 2002; Belsky, Spritz, & Crnic, 1996; Kirsh & Cassidy, 1997). This line of research suggests that children attend to, and therefore construct memories based upon, information consistent with their view of relationships between themselves and caregivers. In a study of abused children, Becker-Blease, Freyd, and Pears (2004) found that abused preschoolers remembered fewer negatively charged, attachment-related pictures compared to non-abused children in a divided attention task. Valentino and colleagues (2008) found that abused children, relative to neglected and non-maltreated children, had poorer memory overall for positive and negative words, some of which were associated with mothers. One of the authors' explanations for the finding is that the procedure, which highlighted the mother-relevant information, activated the children's attachment system, leading to overall memory impairment for all the words in the task. Clearly, more research is needed to pull together emerging lines of research in the area of attachment and memory.

Thus, links between dissociation, attachment, and basic cognitive processes involved in attention and memory may provide another route by which unawareness can emerge following traumatic events, especially those high in betrayal.

Assumptions in both terror and betrayal approaches

Both fear and betrayal perspectives make assumptions that are important to keep in mind as the field moves forward. For example, a focus on terror and PTSD resulting from traumatic events has likely driven the way that the field has looked at childhood trauma and its effects to date (e.g., for a review, see Finkehor & Kendall-Tackett, 1997). With a focus on PTSD, Finkelhor and Kendall-Tackett (1997) have argued that the field as a whole has concentrated on extremes of victimization in children and paid relatively little attention to effects outside of PTSD. Further, the focus on PTSD has also resulted in relatively little research attention being paid to forms of childhood trauma that do not necessarily lead to PTSD, such as abandonment and neglect (Finkelhor & Kendall-Tackett, 1997). Likely, it is the case that researchers have focused primarily on events that are very high in terror (e.g., severe physical abuse) and less so on events that are lower in terror (e.g., some neglect) because the predominant models for studying post-traumatic responses have been derived from the PTSD research tradition that assumes terror and fear to be central.

The betrayal trauma approach assumes that it is not necessary for victims to be consciously aware of the feeling of betrayal; however, appraisal processes have been very important in models of post-traumatic distress. Instead, betrayal is defined by the relationship between victim and perpetrator. We applaud that the betrayal perspective emphasizes that the context of traumatic events must be examined to determine whether the trauma involved an interpersonal violation and if so, the degree to which this violation was a betrayal of a human ethic. However, we should not lose sight of the important role that appraisals appear to play in long-term attempts at meaning-making and coping.

Conclusions

As our understanding of memory for trauma advances, the field must start to differentiate between mechanisms (*how*) and motivations (*why*) that can lead to memory impairment. This chapter set out to identify two ways in which memory can be unavailable: failure to consolidate information under conditions of terror versus knowledge isolation resulting in unawareness of trauma in order to preserve necessary attachments.

The study of sexual abuse may benefit more than other types of trauma from analyses that differentiate between fear and betrayal. Some events, like most natural disasters, are almost purely fear-inducing. Other events, such as physical abuse, almost always involve fear and betrayal. Sexual abuse can take many forms, from almost purely terrifying, as in the case of a stranger rape, or an almost pure betrayal, as when a father has his children pose for pornographic pictures. Of course, sexual abuse very often involves both fear and betrayal. Studies that measure not only the presence or absence of sexual abuse, but also factors that contribute to fear and betrayal may discover important differences in when and how memories for the abuse are remembered.

References

Ackil, J. K., Van Abbema, D. L., & Bauer, P. J. (2003). After the storm: Enduring differences in mother–child recollections of traumatic and non-traumatic events. *Journal of Experimental Child Psychology, 84,* 286–309.

Alexander, K. W., Quas, J. A., & Goodman, G. A. (2002). Theoretical advances in understanding children's memory for distressing events: The role of attachment. *Developmental Review, 22,* 490–519.

American Psychiatric Association (APA) (1994). *Diagnostic and Statistical Manual of Mental Disorders* (4th ed.) (*DSM-IV*). Washington, DC: Author.

Anderson, M. A. (2001). Active forgetting: Evidence for functional inhibition as a source of memory failure. In J. J. Freyd & A. P. DePrince (Eds.), *Trauma and cognitive science: A meeting of minds, science, and human experience* (pp. 185–210). New York: Haworth Press. (Published simultaneously as a Special Issue of the *Journal of Aggression, Maltreatment, and Trauma.*)

Anderson, M. C., & Bjork, R. A. (1994). Mechanisms of inhibition in long-term memory: A new taxonomy. In D. Dagenbach & T. Carr (Eds.), *Inhibitory processes in attention, memory, and language* (pp. 265–325). San Diego, CA: Academic Press.

Becker-Blease, K. A., Freyd, J. J., & Pears, K. C. (2004). Preschoolers' memory for threatening information depends on trauma history and attentional context: Implications for the development of dissociation. *Journal of Trauma & Dissociation,* 5(1), 113–31.

Becker-Blease, K., & Freyd, J. J. (2007). Dissociation and memory for perpetration among convicted sex offenders. *Journal of Trauma and Dissociation, 8*(2), 69–80.

Belsky, J., Spritz, B., & Crnic, K. (1996). Infant attachment security and affective-cognitive information processing at age 3. *Psychological Science, 7*(2), 111–14.

Bremner, J. D. (2001). A biological model for delayed recall of childhood abuse. In J. J. Freyd & A. P. DePrince (Eds.), *Trauma and cognitive science: A meeting of minds, science, and human experience* (pp. 165–84). New York: Haworth Press. (Published simultaneously as a Special Issue of the *Journal of Aggression, Maltreatment, and Trauma.*)

Bremner, J. D., Randall, P., Scott, T. M. et al. (1995). MRI-based measurement of hippocampal volume in patients with combat-related posttraumatic stress disorder. *The American Journal of Psychiatry, 152,* 973–80.

Bremner, J. D., Randall, P., Vermetten, E. et al. (1997). Magnetic resonance imaging-based measurement of hippocampal volume in posttraumatic stress disorder related to childhood physical and sexual abuse – A preliminary report. *Biological Psychiatry,* 41, 23–32.

Brewin, C. R. (2003). *Posttraumatic Stress Disorder: Malady or myth?* New Haven, CT: Yale University Press.

Brewin, C. R., Dalgleish, T., & Joseph, S. (1996). A dual representation theory of posttraumatic stress disorder. *Psychological Review, 103,* 670–86.

Brown, D., Scheflin, A. W., & Whitfield, C. L. (1999). Recovered memories: The current weight of the evidence in science and in the courts. *Journal of Psychiatry & Law, 27*, 5–156.

Cameron, C. (1993, April). Recovering memories of childhood sexual abuse: A longitudinal report. Paper read at the Western Psychological Association Convention, Phoenix, Arizona.

Cheit, R. E. (2005). *The Recovered Memory Project*. Retrieved from www.brown.edu/PublicPolicy/Recovmem (accessed February 17, 2010).

Chu, J. A., & Dill, D. L. (1990). Dissociative symptoms in relation to childhood physical and sexual abuse. *The American Journal of Psychiatry, 147*, 887–92.

Dick, Kirby (2006). *Twist of Faith*. HBO Documentary Films.

DePrince, A. P. (2005). Social cognition and revictimization risk. *Journal of Trauma and Dissociation, 6*, 125–41.

DePrince, A. P., & Freyd, J. J. (1999). Dissociation, attention and memory. *Psychological Science, 10*, 449–52.

DePrince, A. P., & Freyd, J. J. (2001). Memory and dissociative tendencies: The roles of attentional context and word meaning. *Journal of Trauma and Dissociation, 2*, 67–82.

DePrince, A. P., & Freyd, J. J. (2004). Forgetting trauma stimuli. *Psychological Science, 15*, 488–92.

DePrince, A. P., & Freyd, J. J. (2007). Trauma-induced dissociation. In M. J. Freidman, T. M. Keane, & P. A. Resick (Eds.), *Handbook of PTSD: Science and practice* (pp. 135–50). New York: Guilford Press.

DePrince, A. P., Freyd, J. J., & Malle, B. F. (2007). A replication by another name: A response to Devilly et al. (2007). *Psychological Science, 18*, 218–19.

Edwards, V. J., Fivush, R., Anda, R. F. et al. (2001). Autobiographical memory disturbances in childhood abuse survivors. *Journal of Aggression, Maltreatment, & Trauma, 4*, 247–64.

Elliott, D. (1997). Traumatic events: Prevalence and delayed recall in the general population. *Journal of Consulting and Clinical Psychology, 65*(5), 811–20.

Elliott, D. M., & Briere, J. (1995). Posttraumatic stress associated with delayed recall of sexual abuse: A general population study. *Journal of Traumatic Stress, 8*, 629–47.

Elliott, M., Browne, K., & Kilcoyne, J. (1995). Child sexual abuse prevention: What offenders tell us. *Child Abuse & Neglect, 19*(5), 579–94.

Erikson, M. H. (1938). Negation or reversal of legal testimony. *American Medical Association Archives of Neurology and Psychiatry, 40*, 548–53.

Feldman-Summers, S., & Pope, K. S. (1994). The experience of "forgetting" childhood abuse: A national survey of psychologists. *Journal of Consulting and Clinical Psychology, 62*, 636–9.

Finkelhor, D., & Kendall-Tackett, K. (1997). A developmental perspective in the childhood impact of crime, abuse, and violent victimization. In D. Cicchetti & S. L. Toth (Eds.), *Developmental perspectives on trauma: Theory, research and intervention* (pp. 1–32). Rochester: University of Rochester Press.

Fivush, R. (2004). The silenced self: Constructing self from memories spoken and unspoken. In D. R. Beike, J. M. Lampinen, & D. A. Behrend (Eds.), *The self and memory* (pp. 75–93). New York: Psychology Press.

Fivush, R. (2007). Maternal reminiscing style and children's developing understanding of self and emotion. *Journal of Clinical Social Work, 35*, 37–45.

Fivush, R., Pipe, M. E., Murachver, T., & Reese, E. (1997). Events spoken and unspoken: implications of language and memory development for the recovered memory debate. In M. A. Conway (Ed.), *Recovered memories and false memories: Debates in psychology* (pp. 34–62). Oxford: Oxford University Press.

Foynes, M., Freyd, J. J., & DePrince, A. P. (2009). Child abuse: Betrayal and disclosure. *Child Abuse & Neglect, 33*(4), 209–17.

Freyd, J. J. (1983). Shareability: The social psychology of epistemology. *Cognitive Science, 7*, 191–210.

Freyd, J. J. (1996). *Betrayal trauma theory: The logic of forgetting childhood abuse.* Cambridge, MA: Harvard University Press.

Freyd, J. J. (2003). Memory for abuse: What can we learn from a prosecution sample? *Journal of Child Sexual Abuse, 12*, 97–103.

Freyd, J. J., DePrince, A. P., & Gleaves, D. (2007). The State of Betrayal Trauma Theory: Reply to McNally (2007) – Conceptual issues and future directions. *Memory, 15*, 295–311.

Freyd, J. J., DePrince, A. P., & Zurbriggen, E. L. (2001). Self-reported memory for abuse depends upon victim–perpetrator relationship. *Journal of Trauma and Dissociation, 2*, 5–16.

Gershuny, B. S., Cloitre, M., & Otto, M. W. (2003). Peritraumatic dissociation and PTSD severity: Do event-related fears about death and control mediate their relation? *Behaviour Research and Therapy, 41*, 157–66.

Goodman, G. S., Ghetti, S., Quas, J. A. et al. (2003). A prospective study of memory for child sexual abuse: New findings relevant to the repressed-memory debate. *Psychological Science, 14*, 113–18.

Gurvits, T. V., Shenton, M. E., Hokama, H. et al. (1996). Magnetic resonance imaging study of hippocampal volume in chronic, combat-related posttraumatic stress disorder. *Biological Psychiatry, 40*, 1091–9.

Herman, J. L., & Shatzow, E. (1987). Recovery and verification of memories of childhood sexual trauma. *Psychoanalytic Psychology, 4*, 1–14.

Hulette, A. C., Fisher, P. A., Kim, H. K., Ganger, W., & Landsverk, J. L. (2008). Dissociation in foster preschoolers: A replication and assessment study. *Journal of Trauma & Dissociation, 9*(2), 173–90.

Hulette, A. C., Freyd, J. J., Pears, K. C. et al. (2008). Dissociation and posttraumatic symptoms in maltreated preschool children. *Journal of Child and Adolescent Trauma, 1*(2), 93–108.

Kirsh, S., & Cassidy, J. (1997). Preschoolers' attention to and memory for attachment-relevant information. *Child Development, 68*(6), 1143–53.

Lepore, S. J., Ragan, J. D., & Jones, S. (2000). Talking facilitates cognitive-emotional processes of adaptation to an acute stressor. *Journal of Personality & Social Psychology, 78*(3), 499–508.

Leskin G. A., Kaloupek D. G., & Keane T. M. (1998). Treatment for traumatic memories: Review and recommendations. *Clinical Psychology Review, 18*, 983–1002.

Lisak, D., Conklin, A., Hopper, J. et al. (2000). The Abuse-Perpetration Inventory: Development of an assessment instrument for research on the cycle of violence. *Family Violence & Sexual Assault Bulletin*, Spring–Summer, 21–30.

Loftus, E. F., Polonsky, S., Fullilove, M. T. (1994). Memories of childhood sexual abuse: Remembering and repressing. *Psychology of Women Quarterly, 18*, 67–84.

London, K., Bruck, M., Ceci, S. J., & Shuman, D. W. (2005). Disclosure of child sexual abuse: What does the research tell us about the ways that children tell? *Psychology, Public Policy, & Law, 11*(1), 194–226.

Main, M., & Solomon, J. (1990). Procedures for identifying infants as disorganized/disoriented during the Ainsworth Strange Situation. In M. Greenberg, D. Cicchetti, & E. M. Cummings (Eds.), *Attachment in the preschool years: Theory, research and intervention* (pp. 121–60). Chicago: University of Chicago Press.

Major, B., Cozzarelli, C., Sciacchitano, A. M., Cooper, M., & Testa, M. (1990). Perceived social support, self-efficacy, and adjustment to abortion. *Journal of Personality & Social Psychology, 59*(3), 452–63.

Marshall, W. L., Serran, G., Marshall, L. E., & Fernandez, Y. M. (2005). Recovering memories of the offense in "amnesic" sexual offenders. *Sexual Abuse: A Journal of Research and Treatment, 17*, 31–8.

Paine, M. L., & Hansen, D. J. (2002). Factors influencing children to self-disclose sexual abuse. *Clinical Psychology Review, 22*(2), 271–95.

Pitman, R. K., Gilbertson, M. W., Gurvits, T. V. et al. (2006). Clarifying the origin of biological abnormalities in PTSD through the study of identical twins discordant for combat exposure. In R. Yehuda (Ed.), *Psychobiology of Posttraumatic Stress Disorder: A decade of progress* (pp. 242–54). Malden, MA: Blackwell Publishing.

Plattner, B., Silvermann, M. A., Redlich, A. D. et al. (2003). Pathways to dissociation: Intrafamilial versus extrafamilial trauma in juvenile delinquents. *The Journal of Nervous and Mental Disease, 191*, 781–8.

Sales, J. M., Fivush, R., & Peterson, C. (2003). Parental reminiscing about positive and negative events. *Journal of Cognition and Development, 4*, 185–209.

Sapolsky, R. M. (1992). *Stress, the aging brain, and the mechanisms of neuron death.* Cambridge, MA: MIT Press.

Schooler, J. W. (2001). Discovering memories of abuse in the light of meta-awareness. *Journal of Aggression, Maltreatment & Trauma, 4*(2), 105–36.

Schultz, T. M., Passmore, J., & Yoder, C. Y. (2003). Emotional closeness with perpetrators and amnesia for child sexual abuse. *Journal of Child Sexual Abuse, 12*, 67–88.

Sheiman, J. A. (1999). Sexual abuse history with and without self-report of memory loss: Differences in psychopathology, personality, and dissociation. In L. M. Williams & V. L. Banyard (Eds.), *Trauma and memory* (pp. 139–48). Thousand Oaks, CA: Sage.

Smith, S. M., & Moynan, S. C. (2008). Forgetting and recovering the unforgettable. *Psychological Science, 19*(5), 462–8.

Stein, M. B., Koverola, C., Hanna, C., Torchia, M. G., & McClarty, B. (1997). Hippocampal volume in women victimized by childhood sexual abuse. *Psychological Medicine, 27*, 951–9.

Stern, S. (2002, May 9). "Repressed memory" key to lawsuits. *The Christian Science Monitor.* Retrieved from www.csmonitor.com/2002/0509/p01s01-usju.html?s=r101a (accessed June 12, 2008).

Stoler, L. R. (2000). Recovered and continuous memories of childhood sexual abuse: A quantitative and qualitative analysis (Doctoral Dissertation, University of Rhode Island). [Purchase as UMI Proquest Dissertation #9988236 at wwwlib. umi.com/dissertations.]

Valentino, K., Cicchetti, D., Rogosch, F. A., & Toth, S. L. (2008). True and false recall and dissociation among maltreated children: The role of self-schema. *Development and Psychopathology, 20*(1), 213–32.

Widiger, T., & Sankis, L. (2000). Adult psychopathology: Issues and controversies. *Annual Review of Psychology, 51,* 377–404.

Williams, L. M. (1994). Recall of childhood trauma: A prospective study of women's memories of child sexual abuse. *Journal of Consulting and Clinical Psychology, 62,* 1182–6.

Williams, L. M. (1995). Recovered memories of abuse in women with documented child sexual victimization histories. *Journal of Traumatic Stress, 8,* 649–74. (For additional analyses, see Freyd, 1996.)

Zola-Morgan, S., & Squire, L. R. (1993). Neuroanatomy of memory. *Annual Review of Neuroscience, 16,* 547–63.

Zurbriggen, E. L., & Becker-Blease, K. (2003). Predicting memory for childhood sexual abuse: "Non-significant" findings with the potential for significant harm. *Journal of Child Sexual Abuse, 12,* 113–21.

Chapter Eight

Dissociation in Traumatized Children and Adolescents

Eli Somer

Introduction

This chapter explores childhood dissociation, its use as a defensive response during child abuse, and its ensuing dissociative psychopathology. For the purposes of this chapter dissociation is assumed to be a normal childhood ability that develops as a psychological defense mechanism in the face of extreme or prolonged and inescapable physical, sexual, and emotional traumas. It works as a shield against the conscious experience of overwhelming stress by producing psychological and/or physical analgesia, emotional calming, and a breakdown of the normally integrated experiential components of behavior, affect, sensation, knowledge, and identity.

Following Spiegel and Cardeña (1991), I refer to dissociation "as a structured separation of mental processes (e.g., thoughts, emotions, cognition, memory, and identity) that are ordinarily integrated" (p. 367).

Normal childhood dissociation

Childhood dissociation is a normal phenomenon familiar to many parents. Children often show their ability to dissociate when they lose themselves in daydreaming, when they talk to imaginary friends or immerse themselves in prolonged fantasy games. The plasticity of the child's reality is often a source of joy and amusement to both the youngsters and their families. Children bask in their imaginativeness when they make believe they are different. For example, they can pretend in role-play that they are Daddy, a doctor or a

Post-Traumatic Syndromes in Childhood and Adolescence: A Handbook of Research and Practice, First Edition. Edited by Vittoria Ardino. © 2011 John Wiley & Sons, Ltd. Published 2011 by John Wiley & Sons, Ltd.

princess. They can also "make" others and their environment change, for example, by imagining that their dolls and toys can talk or by the pretense that their friends are soldiers, shop attendants or hairdressers. Children can also get completely absorbed in their activities and become totally oblivious to their surroundings. The "make-believe world" children develop does not interfere with their reality testing. Healthy, playful childhood dissociation is marked by an appreciation of the difference between what fantasy is and what is real.

Children, like adults, can find themselves reading entire paragraphs without knowing what they have read because their minds have gone somewhere else. In its common form, normal dissociation includes staring while daydreaming, *zoning out* or doing things on *autopilot*, for example, when children may think about what they are going to do after class and miss something important said by the teacher. This form of dissociation occurs more often during boredom or monotonous activities. In this sense, dissociation offers an ability to do more than one thing at a time. While the child may be half-hearing what is happening in a boring class, his or her mind can wander off somewhere else. These instances of normal dissociation can also be observed in nature where, for example, mammal cubs can be seen playfully engaged in "make-believe" hunting or mating games, completely unaware of a nearby predator their mother is attentively monitoring. These instances of normal dissociation do not interfere with the child's development and social and academic progress.

Almost all children also daydream, a form of normal imaginary dissociation from reality. In daydreams, the child forms a mental image of a past experience, often a pleasant one, or of a situation that he or she has never actually experienced. Daydreams may be triggered by a situation, a memory or a sensory input (sight, taste, smell, sound, touch). The daydreaming child may use these mental pictures to satisfy wishes, to escape from a boring reality temporarily or to overcome a frustrating situation. Children often talk or act out the scenario envisioned during their daydreams. Many young children include an imaginary playmate in the mental images of daydreaming. Toward preadolescence an internalizing process of daydreaming begins. Older children create private mental images and are less likely to talk or physically participate in their daydreams (Gold & Henderson, 1990).

Children, like adults, can also distract themselves and block out an unpleasant thought or feeling without harming their overall functioning. In this sense, normal dissociation works very much like instances in medical hypnosis, when children are instructed to focus their attention on distracting images or activities during potentially painful procedures to alleviate their discomfort.

Normal childhood dissociative abilities peak during latency years and decline during adolescence. When childhood trauma intersects this developmental window of proneness to normal dissociation, some children are thought to harness their innate normal abilities to generate effective ways of coping.

Dissociation as an adaptive response during childhood trauma

The first to recognize the association between pathological dissociation and trauma was Pierre Janet (1859–1947). In his first book on psychology, *L'Automatisme psychologique* (Psychological Automatism), Janet described his dissociation theory and a variety of psychological phenomena observed in hysteria, hypnosis, and possession states (Janet, 1889). Currently, two major theories describe best the pathogenesis of adaptive childhood dissociation in the face of child abuse: betrayal trauma theory (Freyd, 1996) and the Discrete Behavioral States model (Putnam, 1997).

Betrayal trauma theory suggests that violence perpetrated by a care-giving individual on whom the child is dependent will be associated with psychological dysfunctions manifested in memory or dissociation aimed at aiding the child in maintaining the essential attachment, despite its abusive nature. This theory has been supported by several studies demonstrating that childhood abuse by family members is related to elevated dissociative symptoms, while stranger abuse is not (e.g., Chu & Dill, 1990; DePrince, 2005; Plattner, Silvermann, & Redlich, 2003). The Discrete Behavioral States model posits that pathological dissociation stems from the child's inability to learn to integrate mental states. Putnam (1997) reminds us that in normal development, parents are instrumental in teaching infants to move smoothly between emotional states, for example, when children are shown ways to calm down and shift from a distressed to a neutral state. Infants communicate their needs mainly through alterations of behavioral states. For instance, crying is a common behavioral state infants enter to signal distress, motivating their parents to alleviate the distress by providing a need, by soothing or distracting. Maltreating parents are less attentive to their children's needs and therefore are less likely to offer emotional regulation and to model it. In response to punitive and harsh exploitative parenting, traumatized children compensate for their deficient self-modulating capacities by phobic avoidance, suppression of intrusive affects and images, and, finally, the disavowal and encapsulation of trauma-induced behavioral states – a process that can result in the pathological dissociation of trauma-induced mental states from normal conscious awareness.

The descriptor *pathological* is added to the term *dissociation* to describe dissociation that was first employed as a helpful reaction retrieved from the child's normal repertoire of behaviors and that was effective in regulating caretaker betrayal and inescapable harsh treatment. This defensive reaction evolves into a disorder when it becomes automated and develops into the main defense against all stressors. The psychopathologization of normal defensive dissociation encompasses several processes, among them: defensive automated behavior, compartmentalization of threatening mental materials, and the estrangement from the suffering self.

The pathologization of adaptive dissociation during child abuse

Compartmentalization

This form of dissociation can be described as a separation of discrete experiences and memories to the extent that they are not integrated in one's knowledge. Compartmentalized memory is a familiar occurrence to many of us who seem unable to recall information stored in a particular context if it is not retrieved in the same context. For example, one may decide while cooking to check a particular issue on the Internet, yet at their desk, they are unable to recall what was it that they wanted to do and only remember it when they return to check the cooking food in the kitchen. This form of dissociation is also known as state-dependent memory. The capacity to store psychological records of horrific experiences in "mental files" that are normally inaccessible to conscious awareness can allow children to avoid irresolvable cognitive dissonances and conflicts associated with bad experiences caused by beloved caretakers. Compartmentalized experiences often behave like classically (Pavlovian) conditioned stimuli (e.g., salivation in Pavlov's dogs) that are elicited following later exposure to the conditioned stimulus (e.g., the bell in Pavlov's experiment). Following is an illustrative example:

> Rose, was only six years old when her sadistic father used to take her to the home's basement demanding that she role-play with him a series of ritualized acts in which he played a Nazi concentration camp guard and she was coerced into role-playing his inmate sex-slave. Rose had never heard of the term *Nazi* before. Although, she had developed amnesia for the complex exploitative rituals, she had always wondered about the sexual sensations she would experience later in life when exposed to information on concentration camps. The connection was only uncovered in therapy, 25 years following the abuse.

Compartmentalized memories often contain unprocessed, raw experiences that can present as disorienting flashbacks and reenactments.

Automatization

Highway hypnosis is a common example of the mind's capability of employing more than one stream of consciousness during routine or repetitive tasks. This withdrawal of attention from routine tasks does not diminish from quality performance of automated tasks because meta-cognitive monitoring processes usually switch awareness back to the task when deviation from safe or adequate performance is risked. An extreme example of an automated behavior is dissociated automatism. The condition, often involving complex behaviors, has been observed under stressful conditions among individuals later assessed to display post-traumatic and dissociative disorders (Erdreich, 1994). The normal capacity to engage in behavior that is outside conscious awareness is probably quite adaptive in circumstances where children must perform complex behaviors when traumatized. For example:

> Joan was four years old when her older brother begun teaching her *games* that involved nudity and touching. As the exploitation deteriorated, the brother introduced several habits including asking Joan to fetch a towel and Vaseline from the bathroom and to prepare the bed for her abuse. Joan had learned to switch off emotionally as soon as her brother called her into his room. Although her behaviors were completely compliant with her brother's expectations, she used to switch off her conscious awareness and go into her fantasy life while cooperating with her brother.

In this case the child was forced to perform a series of complex acts that were extremely traumatic. To survive and to also maintain her attachment to her brother, Joan learned to perform the requested behaviors well. However, to maintain sanity, she also had maintained unawareness of her actions. Dissociated automatism permitted these contradictory needs to be met simultaneously. I have encountered similar patterns of behavior among mental health workers acting as first-responders during terror attacks and shelling of civilian targets. Some of these professionals reported that under horrific circumstances of involving the need to manage the sounds, sights, and smells of injury and death they reverted to automatic, emotionless behaviors and, later, memory problems associated with these instances (Somer et al., 2004).

Depersonalization

Normal depersonalization may occur in fantasy child play when youngsters embellish reality or mold it for a better fit with emotional or creative play needs. This phenomenon is probably related to commonly familiar daydreaming. In his seminal book *Daydreaming*, Singer (1966) reported that 96% of presumably normal, fairly well-educated American adults engaged in some form of daydreaming daily. This mental activity was reported to occur chiefly when one is alone (e.g., in bed before sleep) and was said to focus principally on planning for future actions and reviewing interpersonal contacts. There has been a fruitful effort to quantify the traits associated with daydreaming. In the context of a study of excellent hypnotic subjects, Wilson and Barber (1981, 1983) serendipitously discovered a group of avid daydreamers later characterized as "fantasy-prone personalities." These individuals were said to share the tendency to "live much of the time in a world of their own making – in a world of imagery, imagination, and fantasy" (Wilson & Barber, 1981, p. 31). Extensive or maladaptive daydreaming might be related to childhood emotional neglect or abuse that motivates victims to divorce from the threatening world and from their material entity (Somer, 2002). Depersonalization may represent a coalescence of imagination-based coping mechanisms to escape from aversive early life circumstances into a stable personality style marked by flight into fantasy and high psychological absorption. Following is a clinical example:

His school counselor referred Dan, an 11-year-old boy, for evaluation because of poor scholastic performance. The boy was described as inattentive and as "spacing out" extensively. A social services report indicated that Dan has been exposed to violent inter-parental conflicts that often involved blaming the child for the couple's misfortunes. Dan described a rich inner world in which he preferred to live. In it he was older and his family was harmonious and loving. Dan had spent all his free time fantasizing daily life in his alternate family. Often he would slip into comforting daydreaming during boring or stressful times.

This child used his normal imagination capacities to alter inescapable, harsh living conditions and to modify an emotionally harmful reality. Using his normal mental resources, he changed his helpless experience of dejection into one of control and emotional soothing. However, the relief experienced by his resourcefulness reinforced his motivation to elaborate his alternate imaginary life at the expense of engaging in academic and social life in his real world.

From ego states to identity confusion/alteration

According to Watkins and Watkins (1996), human personality develops through two basic processes, namely differentiation and integration. These processes operate both concurrently and intermittently. Through integration a child learns to put together concepts such as dog, mouse, cat, rabbit, and horse and therefore build units that are more complex called "animals." By differentiation, the child separates general concepts into more specific meanings, such as learning to distinguish between a mouse and a dog (Watkins & Watkins, 1993). Therefore, the child, by refining these concepts, develops more adaptive control of the environment. As integration may be considered a "putting together" process, differentiation may be called a "separating" process. Through putting together and separating human behavior, an experience evolves. Normal differentiation permits individuals to display one set of experiences and behaviors at a party and another at the office. Differentiation is adaptive, and some separation of personality segments should make for better personality functioning. For example, a girl could display docile, nurturance-seeking behavior when visiting her grandmother but show independence and self-assurance at school. This is an example of adaptive differentiation of a personality into distinct yet integrated ego-states. Watkins and Watkins (1990) expanded their use of the term *dissociation* and defined the normal separating or differentiating process as dissociation. Many of the major theorists of personality have also proposed that the mind is made up of many subselves. For example, Berne (1961) talked of ego states, Jung (Progoff, 1973) of complexes, and Angyal (1965) of subsystems.

An important characteristic of an ego state is that it was often developed to enhance the child's ability to adapt and cope with a specific problem or situation. Thus, one ego state may have taken over the overt, executive position when dealing with parents, another on the playground, and a different one during athletic contests. During child abuse, the specific situation is usually intolerable and inescapable. Ego states are often formed to help the child in coping with a variety of challenges. One ego state can help protect the primary alter from physical pain, another specializes in containing fear, a third one might learn to contain the sexual feelings. This process of differentiation can make it easier for the host personality to deal with the perpetrator during the abuse and after it, while carrying on with normal life in the family, with friends, and at school.

Stephanie was four years old when her alcoholic, neglectful, single mother begun abusing her physically as punishment for being untidy or for crying and expressing emotional needs. In an attempt to internalize the mother's orders, she would rehearse the commands and reprimands to the extent that her mother's messages were well assimilated into a distinct *Maternal Introject Ego State* that had echoed the mother's words and criticisms, internally. Since tears, crying, and clinging were prohibited, Stephanie had to learn to repress and disown her pain. Her mode of adaptation was the development of a *Frightened Child Ego State*, which had cried inside only. As she grew older, Stephanie had identified some new feelings associated with her need to resist her mother's hurtful behavior. Because expressing anger toward her only parent was too risky, Stephanie learned to contain her livid and rebellious feelings into an *Angry/Defiant Child Ego State* that had emerged exclusively at school.

This example illustrates the adaptive nature of normal personality differentiation in the face of overpowering childhood experiences. The *Maternal Introject Ego State* had effectively recorded the mother's demands and reminded the child continuously what expected behaviors are helpful in evading punishment. The *Frightened Child Ego State* had been adaptive in its isolation of the victim's overt neediness to allow safer internal ventilation of emotional pain.

The *Angry/Defiant Child Ego* State helped in containing forbidden affect at home, yet provided an outlet for more empowering experiences under less toxic circumstances. Under chronic abusive conditions ego states can develop more opaque boundaries and greater autonomy and investment in separateness. These psychological elaborations can be at odds with the initial adaptive function of the ego states, for instance, *Maternal Introject Ego States* could develop into internal persecutor ego states and the normal ego state differentiation may well evolve into a pathological form of dissociation, for example, Dissociative Identity Disorder (DID).

Childhood dissociative disorders

It is generally acknowledged that severe dissociative psychopathology originates in childhood. For example, in a review of 100 adult clients diagnosed with DID (then termed Multiple Personality Disorder, MPD), 89% of the clients indicated their first alter personality appeared prior to age 12 (Putnam et al., 1986). Early identification and treatment of childhood dissociative disorders may prevent the development of more complicated and broader psychopathology in adulthood. Waters and Silberg (1996a) have suggested that the treatment of youngsters diagnosed with dissociative disorders may be less complex and of shorter duration than the treatment of the adult client. It is, therefore, vital that pediatric mental health professionals familiarize themselves with assessment and treatment skills that would promise effective help for abused children.

Impediments to the identification of childhood dissociative disorders

Because dissociative disorders have been widely associated with the more severe and controversial forms of dissociative psychopathology, unless bizarre behavior is displayed, most clinicians tend to discount the likelihood of dissociative disorders presenting in children. As noted earlier, many forms of dissociation are normal among children. This may lead even perceptive clinicians to inhibit their identification of disordered patterns. Since dissociative experiences are often ego-syntonic among youngsters, many children do not realize that coping patterns with stress are unusual and would, therefore, tend not to complain about their dissociative tendencies. Finally, childhood dissociative symptoms patterns are often identified as disorders that are more common among children. Among the most common diagnoses provided to children who have been later recognized as suffering from dissociative psychopathology are attention deficit/hyperactivity disorder, mood disorder, and conduct disorder.

Symptom classification

The *Diagnostic and Statistical Manual for Mental Disorders-Revised* (*DSM-IV-TR*, APA, 2000) classifies the dissociative disorders into Dissociative Amnesia,

Dissociative Fugue (with a primary disturbance in memory for both with an additional feature for Dissociative Fugue of travel to a new location and the assumption of a new identity), Depersonalization Disorder (with a primary disturbance of detachment from one's thoughts or body), Dissociative Identity Disorder (DID), and Dissociative Disorder Not Otherwise Specified (DDNOS) (with a primary disturbance in identity). Dell (2001) described several disadvantages of the *DSM-IV-TR* criteria for dissociative disorders. He argued that the *DSM-IV-TR* criteria for DID: are out of step with the state-of-the-art of psychiatric classification; have poor content validity; throw away important information; have poor reliability; and cause frequent misdiagnoses. A set of core dissociative symptoms has been identified as essential elements of the broader spectrum of dissociative psychopathology.

While a complete examination of the entire spectrum of childhood dissociative symptomatology and its treatment is beyond the scope of this chapter, a more focused account of common childhood dissociative symptoms might be suitable. Focusing on childhood core symptoms and processes is warranted because the characteristics of dissociation found in children fall even less into the DSM diagnostic categories than do those of adults (Silberg, 2000). Putnam (1997) offered a more phenomenological description of dissociation. He divided the primary dissociative symptom clusters into (1) amnesia and memory symptoms (e.g., fragmentary autobiographical recall, amnesia and time loss, perplexing fluctuations in skills, fugue states), and (2) dissociative process symptoms (e.g., depersonalization, derealization, passive influence/interference experiences, dissociative auditory hallucinations, dissociative "thought disorder," alter personality states, and switching behaviors).

Memory symptoms

Fragmentary autobiographical recall

Most children form their first enduring childhood memories after age three. The infant's mind is simply not mature enough to create long-lasting autobiographical memories. In particular, it is not until the age of three or four that toddlers have a mature hippocampus and prefrontal cortex. These regions of the brain are known to be associated with the formation of autobiographical memories of the type notably missing from adult recollection of early childhood (Newcombe et al., 2000). The incomplete development of language in young children may be another cause of childhood amnesia in that infants do not have the language capacity to encode autobiographical memories in a manner that their language-based adult selves can interpret correctly. Autobiographical memory gaps observed in dissociative youngsters often relate to age-demarcated or other specific patterns of forgetting. For example: localized amnesia, selective amnesia, and systematized amnesia (Van der Hart & Brom, 2000). Localized amnesia is a gap in memory in which the child fails to recall events that occurred during a circumscribed period of time. Following is an illustration previously reported in an article on the treatment of a Holocaust child survivor (Somer, 1994):

> Bronya was a 58-year-old woman, born in Poland, who survived the Holocaust, amongst others, and a year-long internment in Auschwitz. She was 11 years old when she saw the American liberators enter the gates of Auschwitz. My diagnostic impression was one of Post-Traumatic Stress Disorder, chronic, with dissociative features and psychosomatic correlates. The patient was amnesic to almost the entire duration of her imprisonment in Auschwitz. Fragmentary recall was devoid of any affect. The patient had only scarce memories of the years prior to her internment in the death camp. She felt as if her life began only following her liberation.

Selective amnesia is a condition in which the child can recall some, but not all, of the events during a circumscribed period of time, for example, an abused girl may recall only some parts of a series of violent, sexually abusive incidents, but not the actual penetration. Systematized amnesia occurs in cases where the child loses memory for certain categories of information, such as all memories relating to a particular person, or certain activities with that person (e.g., a child can remember her father used to take her on outings every Saturday between ages five and 10, but have no recollection on what transpired on these occasions).

Amnesias and time loss

Children often notice disruptions in their sense of time when they repeatedly experience "waking up" in the middle of an activity with no recollection of when or why they started that behavior or when they notice time (sometimes hours) has gone by without them knowing what they did during the lost time. These children can be observed to be "spacing out" or staring motionlessly for prolonged periods of time. Some dissociative children are less able to recall detailed information related to specific circumstances. For example, memory regarding time they spent with an uncle is always sketchy and vague. Another instance of lost time relates to disremembered behavior:

> Carolyn, a timid 10-year-old girl, had been getting herself in trouble during the two months preceding her referral for evaluation. Her teachers had become perplexed by the emergence of complaints by schoolmates concerning behaviors that were out of character for Carolyn: pushing and hitting younger girls. She has been observed pushing these girls from

behind, causing them bleeding injuries. Sobbing and appearing offended and baffled, Carolyn denied that she would ever do anything of the sort. The teacher reprimanded the girl for her blatant lying.

Disremembered behaviors could also manifest themselves in the finding of unexpected possessions that the child does not remember receiving or acquiring, or when new artwork is found that is not in line with the typical style or skill of the child or which the child denies doing.

Puzzling variations in skills

Another common form of dissociative memory dysfunction among children is manifested in inexplicable changes in ability and recall of acquired knowledge. Children showing this type of behavior can be suspected of suffering from motivational problems, learning disabilities or plainly lying. Following is a typical example:

Sharon, a 10-year-old bright, female fourth-grader, long known to the local social welfare services as a neglected child from a poor, single-parent family, had been observed on occasions to scavenge school trash cans for food. Her teacher reported to the school psychologist that the girl would suddenly appear to be unable to read or perform simple math, tasks that she had mastered well by second grade. Sharon attempted to compensate for her sudden loss of ability by refusing to perform or by claiming she was sick to her stomach. Sharon confided to the school psychologist that she actually forgot, at times, how to read or do simple calculations and that she felt shamed by what she termed "stupidness attacks."

Putnam (1997) states that seemingly random fluctuations in knowledge and skills can create suspicion about the plausibility of such skills disappearing suddenly and may contribute to a false impression that the child is lying.

Fugue states

During a fugue, the child may appear normal and attract no attention. The condition is suspected when a child seems confused over his identity or puzzled about his past. Dissociative fugue involves episodes of amnesia in which the inability to recall some or all of one's past and either the loss of one's identity or the formation of a new identity occur with sudden, unexpected, purposeful travel away from home. The length of a fugue may range from hours to weeks, but it is usually of short duration, particularly among children.

> Yossi, a 14-year-old youngster, was stopped by a military patrol as he was wandering dangerously close to a minefield near the Israeli–Syrian border. The youngster reacted with belligerence and had to be restrained for questioning. Initially, the boy was unable to provide coherent responses as to his identity and home address. Not more than 30 minutes into the interrogation, Yossi suddenly froze and his facial expression changed from angry and defiant to shocked and frightened. He began weeping, claiming he had no recollection of how he got to the border. The last thing he remembered was being scolded at school for not having prepared his homework properly.

His maternal grandmother had raised Yossi after his violent abusive father murdered his mother. A later psychological evaluation determined a diagnosis of DID. Yossi's example is not atypical in that fugue states often reflect switches in executive control that occur when an alternate personality takes over in DID.

Dissociative process symptoms

Depersonalization and derealization

This process involves an *alteration* in the child's perception or experience of the self so that she or he feels *detached* from, and as if the child is an *outside* observer of, his or her body. Dissociative youngsters may report that they feel or watch themselves act, while having no control over what transpires. Derealization, an alteration in the perception or experience of the external world so that it seems strange or unreal, frequently accompanies depersonalization symptoms. These symptoms can distort the child's visual perception (e.g., seeing the world in faded colors, dimly lit, through a bubble or fog, hearing sounds as muffled, etc.), but they do not impair sight or reality testing. Nevertheless, many youngsters who suffer from depersonalization also experience a numbing sense of estrangement and detachment from their emotions and feelings that in itself can be distressful and conducive to depression.

Passive influence/interference experiences

Passive influence experiences, also known as Schneiderian first-rank symptoms, have long been considered accurate markers for schizophrenia. However, these symptoms are now regarded as core characteristics of severe dissociative psychopathology (Dell, 2001); they are more common in severe dissociative disorders and are not a useful indicator of psychosis when a differential diagnosis is conducted. Passive influence/interference symptoms comprise feelings, impulse actions or thoughts that feel to the child as if they are imposed from an external source, including the delusion that thoughts are being inserted into the mind or *taken out* of the mind by someone else. They are also called *made* feelings, *made* impulses, *made* actions. Children who experience these core dissociative symptoms may also report thought blocking. The child may experience a break in the flow of thoughts, believing that the missing thoughts have been withdrawn from the mind by some unknown agency. However, unlike schizophrenics, dissociative individuals often claim that the experience feels like an internal struggle for control.

Dissociative auditory hallucinations

Hearing voices is the second common source for misdiagnosis of dissociative children. However, auditory hallucinations in dissociative pathology usually refer to a traumatic scenario, an inner conversation among personality states (to be described later) or alters' attempts to influence the identity in apparent executive control. They are usually coherent. When fragmentary, it is usually because they have not been heard completely. Auditory hallucinations of dissociative disorder patients are heard as emanating from inside the head in over 80% of cases. For schizophrenics, over 80% are heard as emanating from outside of the head (Kluft, 2003). Many internal voices heard by dissociative children are internal arguments or comments (often pejorative) on the child's behavior, but they can also be weeping voices or voices offering soothing solace. The voices often are consistent in their style, tone, gender, age, and internal role, and should be considered as powerful markers for the existence of distinct personality states (or alters), indicators of a DID. Auditory hallucinations in DID usually refer to a traumatic scenario.

Dissociative "thought disorder"

Incoherence and true loosening of associations do not characterize thought disorder among dissociative children. Dissociative youngsters may report the presence of inner voices and express vocally inner conversations among alters. When their speech sounds fragmentary, it is usually because alters may have not been heard completely. Harrow and Prosen (1978) discovered that many instances of thought disorder arose because the individual had "intermingled" associations from past events with the current context, but had failed to explain this to listeners. Dissociative thought disorder may occur if the child does not disclose the nature of his or her inner world or personal associations. The intrusion of past traumatic material may also be involved in this process. When a traumatized young person experiences a flashback, his or her *thought-disordered* speech might be appropriate to the reexperienced trauma but inappropriate in the present context.

Since some of the dissociative process symptoms can be confused with psychotic signs, differential diagnosis should also consider the following additional points:

1. Unlike schizophrenia, dissociative disorders present no negative symptoms.
2. Deteriorated behavior is uncommon in dissociative disorders unless there has been prolonged hospitalization.
3. Hypnotizability is usually high in dissociative disorders and low in schizophrenia.
4. Suggestive techniques often can modify *psychotic* symptoms.
5. Disorganized behavior and thought in dissociative disorders are mostly the result of switching behaviors and processes between alter personality states.
6. Almost all children and adolescents with dissociative disorders have been severely traumatized and probably also suffer from PTSD. Most schizophrenic kids do not.

Alter personality states

The *DSM-IV-TR* (APA, 2000) uses the term "alter" to describe the distinct identities or personality states that the individual with DID experiences. To be classified as a "personality state," the following conditions must be met: a consistent and ongoing set of response patterns to given stimuli; a significant confluent history; a range of emotions available (anger, sadness, joy, and so on); a range of intensity of affect for each emotion (for example, anger, ranging from neutrality to frustration and irritation to anger and rage). This is the most dramatized aspect of dissociative disorders. The skepticism this clinical phenomenon elicited in the mental health field was, probably, a major motivation behind the name change from Multiple Personality Disorder (MPD) to Dissociative Identity Disorder (DID). Persons with DID usually have one personality that controls the body and its behavior. Professionals refer to this alter as the "host." This is generally not the person's original personality or birth personality. The host is often initially unaware of the other identities and typically loses time when they appear. The host is the identity that most often presents itself in treatment, usually after developing symptoms, such as school performance, attention deficit problems or depression. The number of alters in any given case can vary widely. Although poly-fragmented cases with dozens of alter personalities have been reported in survivors of sadistic abuse, the mode is three and the median typically eight to 10 (Putnam, 1997). Patients vary with regard to their alters' awareness of one another. Some alters may acknowledge the existence of others, different alters can be completely oblivious to the existence of an internal structural fragmentation. Alters are often of different genders, i.e., boys can have female alters and girls can have male. Other types of alters include children, protectors, and persecutors. Youngsters who appear to assume whole new physical postures, voices, vocabularies, preferences, moods, knowledge, skills, or handwritings should be assessed for alter state personality activity, also known as *switching*.

Switching behaviors

Experts refer to the phase of transition between alters as a *switch*. While the appearance of switching may exist in rapid-cycling bipolar disorder and in panic attacks, they are central features in severe dissociative psychopathology. Specific circumstances or stressful situations may bring out particular identities. Some young patients may display erratic performance in school, in sports or in social circumstances caused by the emergence of alternate personalities during stressful situations. Each alternate identity takes control one at a time, denying control to the others. Conflict with regard to the executive control of the patient or with regard to participation in therapy is often an essential process. Switches may be manifested by a variety of signs with individual variations typical of each youngster. Examples of observable switching behaviors include: an eye-roll or rapid blinking, a sudden change in mannerism, an abrupt derailment of thought, an expression of puzzlement usually coupled with grounding behaviors (e.g., visual scanning of the office), a postural shift or a sudden change in voice pitch.

Treatment principles and phases

Based on Kluft (1993), Waters and Silberg (1996b) formulated principles that distinguish effective therapy with dissociative children and adolescents. Therapists are cautioned to remain alert to issues of ongoing safety and to employ sensitivity and wisdom when working with the potentially conflicting interests of families, police, and child protection services.

1. Although some professional contact outside therapy is sometimes needed (e.g., a house visit), therapists should maintain firm professional boundaries and avoid dual relationships with their youngster clients and their families.
2. The therapist must maintain a solid therapeutic bond not only with the child but equally importantly with the parents, who often are the gatekeepers of the therapy. If the family environment is judged to be inappropriate for the child, the therapist should work toward securing a safer setting (e.g., residential shelter or foster care).
3. The therapist should hold the youngster (all personality alters included) accountable for his or her behavior. Rules should be conveyed to "all inside" and denial of responsibility of actions performed outside consciousness should provide opportunities for enhancing internal communication and control.

4. Children cannot be expected to give up dissociative defenses as long as they continue to live in abusive circumstances. For treatment to be effective the child must be in a safe and preferably nurturing environment.
5. Dissociative minors in therapy are dependent on many adults within and outside the family. Effective treatment with youngsters must comprise a multidisciplinary team to address the many needs and issues involved with resolving the traumatic outcome in the life of the young patient.
6. Therapeutic goals should work toward developmentally appropriate behavior, activities, and skills, including participation in sports, clubs, youth movements (e.g., girl scouts), creative activities, and hobbies.

Trauma experts agree that, regardless of patient age, trauma work should follow a progression in a three-phase process. The first phase involves assessment, accurate identification of the child's unique symptom clusters, reassurance and education about the traumatic disorder and its treatment, and relationship-building with the child, family, and the professional team. The initial phase does not end before safety and stabilization in the child's life are achieved. The second treatment phase involves the development of a narrative of the traumatic events and processing of the harmful experiences. The third phase of therapy involves integration of the dissociated processes and personality structures, and the development of age-appropriate, healthy ways of coping.

Conclusion

Accurate identification, assessment and treatment of dissociative children and adolescents are not straightforward professional challenges. Firstly, children display a wide array of dissociative-like behaviors that are not necessarily pathological. Secondly, the very nature of many dissociative defenses is covert and often hidden from the untrained clinical observer. Thirdly, many dissociative symptoms mimic more familiar psychological disorders. Fourthly, some dissociative symptoms have been sensationalized and created grave skepticism in some professional circles regarding the validity of dissociative disorders as a whole, and also sadly, the veracity of the uncovered trauma memories themselves. Making a correct diagnosis of children and adolescents with dissociative disorders offers these suffering children the only hope for effective treatment. Proper identification and treatment of traumatized children are perhaps their only hope to move away from their painful past. The promise of healing and recovery from perpetual pain caused by child abuse and neglect is not only a satisfying act of professionalism, but also an expression of sublime justice for the young patient: extracting the child victim from the perpetual pain they were trapped in.

References

American Psychiatric Association (APA) (2000). *Diagnostic and Statistical Manual for Mental Disorders* (4th ed., Text Rev.) (*DSM-IV-TR*). Washington, DC: Author.

Angyal, A. (1965). *Neurosis and treatment.* New York: John Wiley & Sons, Inc.

Berne, E. (1961). *Transactional analysis in psychotherapy.* New York: Grove.

Chu, J. A., & Dill, D. L. (1990). Dissociative symptoms in relation to childhood physical and sexual abuse. *The American Journal of Psychiatry, 147,* 887–92.

Dell, P. F. (2001). Why the diagnostic criteria for dissociative identity disorder should be changed. *Journal of Trauma & Dissociation, 2*(1), 7–37.

DePrince, A. P. (2005). Social cognition and revictimization risk. *Journal of Trauma & Dissociation, 6,* 125–41.

Erdreich, M. (1994). Sectorial automatism: A further development. *Medicine and Law, 13*(1–2), 167–75.

Freyd, J. (1996). *Betrayal trauma: The logic of forgetting childhood abuse.* Cambridge, MA: Harvard University Press.

Gold, S. R., & Henderson, B. B. (1990). Daydreaming and curiosity: Stability and change in gifted children and adolescents. *Adolescence, 25,* 701–8.

Harrow, M., & Prosen, M. (1978). Intermingling and disordered logic as influences on schizophrenic "thought disorders." *Archives of General Psychiatry, 35,* 1213–18.

Janet, P. (1889). *L'Automatisme psychologique.* Paris: Félix Alcan. (New ed.: Société Pierre Janet, Paris, 1973.)

Kluft, R. P. (1993). Basic principles in conducting the psychotherapy of multiple personality disorder. In R. P. Kluft & C. C. Fine (Eds.), *Clinical perspectives on multiple personality disorder* (pp. 19–49). Washington, DC: American Psychiatric Press.

Kluft, R. P. (2003). Current issues in Dissociative Identity Disorder. *Bridging Eastern and Western Psychiatry, 1*(1), 71–87.

Newcombe, N., Drummey, A., Fox, N., Lai, E., & Ottinger-Alberts, W. (2000). Remembering early childhood: How much, how, and why (or why not). *Current Directions in Psychological Science, 9,* 55–8.

Plattner, B., Silvermann, M. A., & Redlich, A. D. (2003). Pathways to dissociation: Intrafamilial versus extrafamilial trauma in juvenile delinquents. *Journal of Nervous and Mental Disease, 191,* 781–8.

Progoff, I. (1973). *Jung's psychology and its social meaning.* Garden City, NY: Anchor.

Putnam, F. W. (1997). *Dissociation in children and adolescents: A developmental perspective.* New York: Guilford Press.

Putnam, F. W., Guroff, J. J., Silberman, E. K., Barban, L., & Post, R. M. (1986). The clinical phenomenology of multiple personality disorder: A review of 100 recent cases. *Journal of Clinical Psychiatry, 47,* 285–93.

Silberg, J. (2000). Fifteen years of dissociation in maltreated children: Where do we go from here? *Child Maltreatment, 5,* 119–36.

Singer, J. L. (1966). *Daydreaming.* New York: Random House.

Somer, E. (1994). Hypnotherapy and regulated uncovering in the treatment of older survivors of Nazi persecution. *Clinical Gerontologist, 14,* 47–65.

Somer, E. (2002). Maladaptive daydreaming: A qualitative inquiry. *Journal of Contemporary Psychotherapy, 32*(2), 195–210.

Somer, E., Buchbinder, E., Peled-Avram, M., & Ben-Yizhack, Y. (2004). The stress and coping of Israeli emergency room social workers following terrorist attacks. *Qualitative Health Research, 14*(10), 1077–93.

Spiegel, D., & Cardeña, E. (1991). Disintegrated experience: The dissociative disorders revisited. *Journal of Abnormal Psychology, 100*, 366–78.

Van der Hart, O., & Brom, D. (2000). When the victim forgets: Trauma-induced amnesia and its assessment in Holocaust survivors. In A. Y. Shalev, R. Yehuda, & A. C. McFarlane (Eds.), *International handbook of human response to trauma* (pp. 233–48). New York: Plenum.

Waters, F. S., & Silberg, J. L. (1996a). Promoting integration in dissociative children. In J. L. Silberg & F. S. Waters (Eds.), *The dissociative child* (pp. 167–90). Lutherville, MD: Sidran.

Waters, F. S., & Silberg, J. L. (1996b). Therapeutic phases in the treatment of dissociative children. In J. L. Silberg & F. S. Waters (Eds.), *The dissociative child* (pp. 135–65). Lutherville, MD: Sidran.

Watkins, J. G., & Watkins, H. H. (1990). Dissociation and displacement: Where goes the "ouch"? *American Journal of Clinical Hypnosis, 33*, 1–10.

Watkins, J. G., & Watkins, H. H. (1993). Accessing the relevant areas of maladaptive personality functioning. *American Journal of Clinical Hypnosis, 35*, 277–84.

Watkins, J. G., & Watkins, H. H. (1996). Overt-covert dissociation and hypnotic ego state therapy. In L. K. Michelson & W. J. Ray (Eds.), *Handbook of dissociation: Theoretical, empirical, and clinical perspectives* (pp. 431–47). New York: Plenum.

Wilson, S. C., & Barber, T. X. (1981). Vivid fantasy and hallucinatory abilities in the life histories of excellent hypnotic subjects ("somnambulers"): Preliminary report with female subjects. In E. Klinger (Ed.), *Imagery. Vol. 2: Concepts, results, and applications* (pp. 133–49). New York: Plenum.

Wilson, S. C., & Barber, T. X. (1983). The fantasy-prone personality: Implication for understanding imagery, hypnosis, and parapsychological phenomena. In A. A. Sheikh (Ed.), *Imagery: Current theory, research, and application* (pp. 340–90). New York: John Wiley & Sons, Inc.

Part IV

Forensic Aspects

Chapter Nine

The Role of PTSD in Understanding Child Allegations of Sexual Abuse

Paola Di Blasio, Sarah Miragoli, and Rossella Procaccia

Introduction

Empirical and clinical findings have demonstrated that violence can have severe psychological and physical consequences for victims. Amongst the various forms of interpersonal violence, child sexual abuse has proven to be the most serious (for a review, see Sachs-Ericsson et al., 2009) in terms of internalization and externalization (Quas, Goodman, & Jones, 2003; Sternberg et al., 2006; Walrath et al., 2003) and Post-Traumatic Stress Disorder (PTSD) symptomatology (Feerick & Snow, 2005; Hetzel & McCanne, 2005).

Child sexual abuse also raises many problematic areas when the child has to testify in court, such as potential secondary forms of victimization when children have to relate their traumatic experience (Glaser & Spencer, 1990; Goodman & Jones, 1988; Goodman et al., 1992; Quas et al., 2005; Whitcomb, 2003; Whitcomb et al., 1994). Another problematic area concerns the impact of PTSD on children's allegations. In fact, although the association between traumatic sexual experiences and symptoms of PTSD is well established, little is known about how post-traumatic symptoms may impact on a child's ability to testify in court. Furthermore, little is known about whether the content and structure of child abuse allegations are affected by the presence/absence of PTSD symptoms.

In a court setting, the reliability of child witnessing is tested through the children's ability to recall their experiences in the form of explicit, distinct memories and in a narrative framework where time and space are coherently anchored alongside meaningful contextual details (Dent, 1977; Spencer & Flin, 1990; Whitcomb, Shapiro, & Stellwagen, 1985). Children's narratives that provide a

Post-Traumatic Syndromes in Childhood and Adolescence: A Handbook of Research and Practice, First Edition. Edited by Vittoria Ardino. © 2011 John Wiley & Sons, Ltd. Published 2011 by John Wiley & Sons, Ltd.

coherent account of the trauma also present a greater quantity of correct information, confirming the close link between contents of the autobiographical memory and narrative ability (Kleinknecht & Beike, 2004; Kulkofsky, Wang, & Ceci, 2008; Saywitz & Snyder, 1996; Saywitz, Snyder, & Lamphear, 1996). Because narratives and autobiographical memory are closely intertwined, narratives are emotionally charged and mirror the map of logically connected events (Damasio, 1999). Furthermore, narratives supply a logical framework of associations that enable more accurate information-processing and a clearer organization of memory (Bolan, Haden, & Ornstein, 2003; Haden et al., 2001; McGuigan & Salmon, 2004).

This empirical chapter presents a study aiming to investigate whether PTSD symptoms impact on the reliability of child abuse allegations via a specific structure of narratives that could mirror the presence of post-traumatic symptoms. A study conducted by Mossige and colleagues (1997) demonstrated that the abuse accounts of 10 children were different when compared in terms of elaboration and structure. The accounts of abuse seemed merely descriptive, incomplete, confused, and contradictory and also not organized into interconnected sequences. Data from an exploratory study carried out by three authors (Di Blasio, Ionio, & Procaccia, 2004) showed that sexually abused children with PTSD symptoms provided briefer accounts and more references to their emotions and to tactile, gustatory, and olfactory perceptions. In addition, children with PTSD had greater difficulty in considering themselves as central to the narrative account of the abuse. This preliminary research, however, presented two limitations in terms of sample size (a low number of depositions) and variation in the age range of victims. For this reason, specific characteristics of narratives based on the presence/absence of PTSD could not be determined. In this chapter, a further study is reviewed which presents results from a higher number of depositions in order to better understand the role of PTSD in shaping children's allegations of abuse.

The influence of age

Three-year-old children are capable of codifying, remembering, and relating past events (Fivush, 1993), especially if they have to remember central and salient aspects of personal experiences (Ceci & Friedman, 2000; Goodman et al., 1990). However, it is not until they reach school age that children are able to produce more articulate narratives (Berliner et al., 2003; Eisen et al., 2002; Ghetti et al., 2002) and provide coherent contents (regarding actions, interactions, and mental states), and to monitor the sources of their memories (Baker-Ward, Ornstein, & Principe, 1997; Fivush, Haden, & Adam, 1995; Poole & Lindsay, 2002; Quas & Schaaf, 2002; Quas et al., 1999; Schneider & Pressley, 1997).

Under stressful and traumatogenic conditions (Chen et al., 2000), age is a good predictor of narrative accuracy, completeness demonstrating an acquired metacognitive understanding, and ability to make meaning (Berliner et al., 2003; Eisen et al., 2002; Ghetti et al., 2002; Lamb, Sternberg, & Esplin, 2000; Lamb et al., 2003). Younger children do not possess adequate cognitive mechanisms to frame their traumatic experience and, therefore, to conceptualize semantically what happened (Ehlers et al., 1998). For this reason, they concentrate on emotional states rather than external spatial or temporal details (Fivush et al., 2002) producing richer narratives in terms of sensory and emotional elements and yet poor narratives in terms of spatial-temporal contextualization. An analysis of court allegations of 250 sexually abused children between the ages of four and ten revealed that age was also responsible for an increasing number of time references (Orbach & Lamb 2007).

The influence of trauma

Mnemonic and narrative abilities are impacted by the emotional charges linked to life experiences (Engelberg & Christianson, 2002; Ochsner, Zaragoza, & Mitchell, 1999; van der Kolk, 1999; Yuille & Tollestrup, 1992). However, the interplay among memory, narrative, and stress is not linear for several reasons. Firstly, different types of stressors hold different degrees of stress severity that are not always comparable and that vary across individuals (Bohanek, Fivush, & Walker, 2005; Byrne, Hyman, & Scott, 2001; Peace & Porter, 2004). Some individuals can develop more severe fear reactions and post-traumatic stress reactions in responding to a trauma like being abused, others may overcome the traumatic experience without developing PTSD. This discrepancy depends upon the way in which experience is processed and recalled by the memory system when it has to be reported and narrated (Cordon et al., 2004). The multiplicity of factors involved in explaining the relationship between trauma and individual appraisal of the trauma may explain why research has not yet succeeded in fully explaining the interaction between memory, narrative, and traumatic reactions. Some studies have demonstrated that both adults and children provide more accurate recalls of their experiences if at the time of storing information they were moderately or highly stressed or if the event had a strong emotional impact at a personal level (Eisen et al., 1998; Engelberg & Christianson, 2002; Goodman et al., 1991; Ochsner, Zaragoza, & Mitchell, 1999; Peterson & Whalen, 2001; Yuille & Tollestrup, 1992). Other studies, however, have shown that stress also has the power to block and inhibit memory (Baker-Ward et al., 1993; Howe, Courage, & Peterson, 1996; Peterson & Bell, 1996).

The emotional valence of sexual traumatic experiences could also explain why narratives (more than other types of trauma, such as traffic accidents, natural disasters, physical violence) are characterized by a greater number of omission errors (Bidrose & Goodman, 2000) and poor reflections and making-meanings of the event. Such narratives are also characterized by denial, silence, and minimization as it appears evident in cases of abuse and/or maltreatment (Bidrose & Goodman, 2000; Sjoberg & Lindblad, 2002). Children desire to forget and to avoid painful memories as Becker-Blease, DePrince, and Freyd explain in Chapter 7 of this book; this aspect may also have an impact on narrative accounts of child sexual abuse. For example, children who underwent stressful and embarrassing medical procedures (like the Voiding cystourethrogram (VCUG)) and felt sad, embarrassed, and disturbed by this experience are more vulnerable to provide errors when they are asked to narrate their traumatic experience than subjects who experience low or moderate levels of embarrassment (Goodman et al., 1994, 1997). Furthermore, even when the memory of the event is not affected (Alexander et al., 2002; Shaaf et al., 2008), narrative accounts may be independently affected by emotions.

The influence of PTSD

Post-Traumatic Stress Disorder (APA, 1994) is characterized by a combination of symptoms which influence the individual's emotional and cognitive abilities. Reexperiencing symptoms cyclically breaks into the internal world with strong and unexpected negative emotions, leading to a state of severe and persistent threat affecting cognitive resources and emotional stability (Ehlers & Clark, 2000). Concomitant and opposite avoidance symptoms apparently enable the mind to remove reminders of the trauma. Consequently, individuals have difficulty both in integrating negative emotions and in processing highly disturbing traumatic memories resulting in a fragmentation of memory (Foa, Molnar, & Cashman, 1995; van der Kolk, 1996). PTSD symptoms may also characterize narratives of trauma as disorganized, poor in details, and lacking a spatial and temporal frame (Amir et al., 1998; Esterling et al., 1999; Foa et al., 1995; Halligan, Clark, & Ehlers, 2002; Koss et al., 1996; van der Kolk & Fisler, 1995).

Outcome studies have shown that narratives of individuals with PTSD symptoms present negative feelings, repetition of identical sentences, lack of time connections, and interruptions which undermine the complete and coherent development of the memory and narrative (Foa & Riggs, 1993; Tromp et al., 1995). Similar results are found in studies on autobiographical memory in traumatized children and adolescents. The presence of PTSD is associated with poor performance of short- and long-term memory, a greater number of errors in answers to specific and suggestive questions (Moradi et al., 1999), selective memory for emotionally negative information (Moradi et al., 2000), and impairment in the retrieving of autobiographical semantic memories associated with intrusion and avoidance of the trauma, in child cancer traumatized survivors (Moradi et al., 2008). Even if the general quality of the account is not affected, narratives of children with PTSD produced poorer and more fragmented information (Ehlers, Mayou, & Bryant, 2003; McDermott Sales et al., 2005; Stallard, 2003).

As stated elsewhere in this book, Scheeringa, Zeanah, Drell, and Larrieu (1995) argued that many children with PTSD symptoms may not meet criteria for a full diagnosis as an adult would because they still lack specific developmental capabilities. Furthermore, children probably perceive, codify, and express memories differently from adults and have greater difficulty in processing language, in manifesting emotions, and in spatio-temporal coordination (Kenardy et al., 2007). Likewise, dissociative contents that predict the onset of PTSD in adults (Harvey & Bryant, 2002; Kenardy et al., 2007; Koopman, 2000; Murray, Ehlers, & Mayou, 2002) are relatively insignificant in children. In fact, a study by Kenardy and colleagues (2007) showed that even when children's accounts contain elements similar to those of adults (temporal disorganization, lack of emotions, and amnesia), only the temporal disorganization predicts PTSD after four to seven weeks (Kenardy et al., 2007).

The present study

This study aimed to investigate how PTSD symptoms impact on children's narratives of their abuse. The authors did not expect age to influence the ability to report details of the traumatic experience (in terms of spatio-temporal contextualization and the elements useful for the identification of the perpetrator). However, they expected that PTSD symptoms would have impacted on their ability to refer to mental states. Finally, the authors hypothesized that children with PTSD symptoms would provide greater references to emotional content resulting from an impaired affect regulation (Dunmore et al., 1999, 2001) and from overwhelming post-traumatic intrusions (van der Kolk, 1996). In addition, due to the alternation of reexperiencing and avoidance symptoms (Carlson et al., 1997; Horowitz, 1986; van der Kolk, 1996; van der Kolk & Fisler, 1995) we expected children with PTSD to have greater difficulty in reporting specific details of the perpetrator and abuse-related behavior.

Method

Participants
The study was carried out on 80 allegations by sexually abused children provided during legal proceedings that resulted in a conviction of the perpetrators. The mean age of the child witnesses (53 females and 27 males), was, at the time of the allegation, nine years (SD = 4 years; range: 4–17 years). Regarding the characteristics of the traumatic experience, 48.8% (N = 39) of children experienced intra-familial sexual abuse, 28.8% (N = 23) experienced abuse outside the family, and 22.5% (N = 18) experienced both domestic abuse and extra-familial abuse; 56.2% (N = 45) of children experienced penetration (genital, anal and/or oral) and the remaining 43.8% (N = 35) experienced sexual violence without penetration. Five children with mental health issues

and language impairments were excluded from the study. Twenty-eight children (48.3%) met the criteria for a diagnosis of full PTSD whereas 30 children did not present post-traumatic symptoms.

Content analysis

Each allegation was audio-recorded and transcribed verbatim. Subsequently, content analysis was conducted on the transcript parts where victims referred to the offence. Such parts were coded according to a coding system adapted from the literature on traumatic memories and narratives. Analysis categories are described in Table 9.1 on the next page.

Scoring of the allegations

Two independent coders analyzed and coded all the allegations achieving an interrater agreement of 87% reliability, with a range of 74.5% to 96.4%. All discrepancies between the two coders were resolved through discussions and with the aid of another experienced coder. The weight of all categories was measured by a word-count of terms used by children to describe their experience of abuse (*length of narrative*). The number of words of categories two and three and the number of propositions in categories four and eight were then transformed into percentages by dividing the total number of words or sentences of each category by the total number of words used by the child to describe the traumatic experience.

Results

Data analysis was organized into two parts. The first part was carried out on all 80 depositions. Descriptive data are presented, including the influence of age on the content of allegations. The second part was carried out on a subgroup of 58 allegations to investigate the relation between presence and absence of PTSD. Regression statistics analyzed the predictive power of age and PTSD.

Descriptive statistics

Child abuse reports showed a consistent use of information referring to the self and direct experience (Table 9.2) (M = 4.41). Likewise, reports present terms referring to time (M = 4.12) and to spatial (M = 2.12) and causal coordinates (M = 1.99) that witness an attempt to contextualize the event. The recall of the experience was mediated by memories of visual elements (M = 2.70) rather than auditory, tactile, and gustatory memories. Visual memories were used by children to describe the behavior of the perpetrator (M = 2.29) alongside other details to describe physical features of the perpetrator (M = 0.41).

Contents referring to other categories are present in lower percentages. This phenomenon could be explained by the nature of forensic allegations that aim to orient narratives toward factual data. Information derived from the

Table 9.1 Categories used for the analysis of the content of the depositions

---

Quantitative analysis: effected by means of word-count

---

1   *Length of narrative:* the total number of words (verbs, adjectives, substantives, etc.) used to describe abuse episodes (Foa, Molnar, & Cashman, 1995; Peterson & McCabe, 1983).

2   *Focus on self:* the number of words **focused on self** (*me*, *myself*, *my*, *mine*, etc.) (Klein & Janoff-Bulman, 1996) (e.g., "He asked *me* to play a game with him and *I* accepted: he seemed a nice person to *me* and *I* trusted him").

3   *Contextual embedding:* the number of words used to mark **temporal** (*then*, *when*, *while*, *until*, *next*, *before*, *after*, etc.), **spatial and causal** relations (*because*, *so*, *in order to*, *therefore*, *consequently*, etc.) (Fivush, Haden, & Adam, 1995; Peterson & Biggs, 1998; Peterson & McCabe, 1991; Weingarten, 1995) (e.g., "We were in the *living room*, *then* he arrived and took me to the *bedroom* for us to be alone").

   Qualitative analysis: At a qualitative level, we examined the type of content by means of five categories and subcategories. The depositions, each about 20 pages long, were broken down into propositions. A proposition was defined as a subject–verb construction (Peterson & McCabe, 1983) and each proposition, containing references to abuse, was then coded into one of the following categories or subcategories, adapted from previous research.

4   *Perceptions of perpetrator*: considers the various sensorial channels by means of which the memory codifies the information on the perpetrator, and takes account of the fact that frequently traumatic memories are codified in the form of images and sensorial sensations (van der Kolk & Fisler, 1995; Ward & Carroll, 1997; Weingarten & Cobb, 1995; Whitfield, 1995). This category includes propositions, which provide descriptions about **visual perception** in connection with the perpetrator: **perpetrator's behavior** (e.g., "*He took my hand,*" "*that day he arrived running*"); **identity of perpetrator** (age, gender, face, dress); **auditory channel (voice of the perpetrator** like intonation, pronunciation, and accent (e.g., "*He spoke very fast,*" "*He was coughing and his voice was affected by a cold*"); direct or indirect **conversation with the perpetrator** or with the **others** (e.g. "*He told me to stay still,*" "*I heard my mother telling him to leave me alone*"); and **sensory perceptions:** tactile, gustatory, and olfactory (e.g., "He had a *beard* and always wore a *dark T-shirt*," "He *smelt of aftershave*," "I remember his *footsteps* when he was climbing the stairs to my room").

5   *Emotions* (Lisak, 1994; Roth & Newman, 1991; Ward & Carroll, 1997): this category consists of propositions including autoreferential **emotions** linked to the abusive event (fear, anger, estrangement, shame, guilt, sadness, powerlessness, self-deprecation, betrayal, disgust). Often the subjects do not explicitly indicate the individual emotion (e.g., "I was *very afraid*") but use sentences from which it is possible to deduce the corresponding emotion of fear (e.g. "*I was trembling and I couldn't escape*").

6   *Metamemory:* this category includes propositions that **admit not remembering**, or express **doubts and uncertainty about evidence** (e.g. "*I don't remember well how it began,*" "*They wouldn't have believed me*").

(*Continued*).

Table 9.1 Categories used for the analysis of the content of the depositions (*Continued*)

Quantitative analysis: effected by means of word count

---

7   *Self-reflective ability:* this category includes propositions that provide evaluative commentary on self or on perpetrator (expressions of **self-awareness and attribution of mental state to perpetrator**) (Fonagy & Target, 1997, 1998; Fonagy et al., 1999) (e.g., "I thought that if I had talked to someone *he would have hurt me and that he behaved in that way to punish me*," "before I was *trusting*, but not now," or "at that moment I *was thinking that* ...").

8   *Interaction:* this category includes propositions that describe **actions** and **interactions** that occurred **with the perpetrator** or between perpetrator and **other victims** (e.g. "*He took me to his room, he took off his T-shirt and I didn't move*"). This category refers to the concatenation of actions of the perpetrator and reactions of the victim, and codifies elements which can be partly superimposed on the subcategory perpetrator's behavior which only refers to the perpetrator.

---

episodic memory (who, what, where, when) serves, in fact, the purposes of the trial to find objective evidence of the alleged offence. References to emotions ($M = 0.46$), to self-reflection (0.43), to metamemory (0.40), and to interaction (0.13) are, therefore, rather limited. Terms referring to fear ($M = 0.14$) generally prevail, as do terms referring to the child's own mental state ($M = 0.28$) over terms referring to the perpetrator's mental state ($M = 0.15$).

Age and content of the deposition

To verify whether age had an impact on the content of the allegations, transcripts were subdivided into three groups according to the age of the child at the time of their witnessing in court: group (1) preschoolers (4–6 years, N = 15); (2) school-age children (7–10 years, N = 39), and (3) preadolescents and adolescents (11–17 years, N = 26).

An ANOVA was conducted between contents of the depositions across the three age groups (Table 9.3). Data indicated that the contents of the depositions did not present a significant relationship with age, meaning that younger children are also able to provide useful details during criminal proceedings. However, age influenced both the length of the narrative and its quality. Younger children provided briefer accounts ($M = 1,150$) than school-age children ($M = 1,812$) and adolescents ($M = 2,663$). Along similar lines, visual descriptions of the perpetrator's behavior are more detailed in preschoolers ($M = 1.84$) and school-age children ($M = 2.57$). Furthermore, narratives of preschoolers are richer in terms of tactile ($M = 0.37$) and sensorial ($M = 0.39$) details than those of adolescents ($M = 0.09$).

Table 9.2 Descriptive statistics of content of the depositions (N = 80)

Categories and subcategories		Mean of words (*SD*)	Range
1	*Length of depositions*	Number of words	2,103 (*1,581*) **Mean (*SD*) % by total word**	151–8785
2	*Focus on self*	Focus on the self	4.41 (*1.41*)	2.14–8.68
3	*Contextual embedding*	Time connectors	4.12 (*1.29*)	1.32–7.62
		Spatial connectors	2.12 (*0.85*)	0.87–5.88
		Casual connectors	1.99 (*0.78*)	0.16–5.00
		Total contextual embedding	8.23 (*1.96*)	3.34–14.1
4	*Perceptions of perpetrator*	Behavior of perpetrator	2.29 (*0.97*)	0.00–4.34
		Identity of perpetrator	0.41 (*0.39*)	0.00–1.78
		Total visual	2.70 (*1.28*)	0.00–5.78
		Perpetrator's voice	0.06 (*0.02*)	0.00–0.52
		Conversations with perpetrator	0.50 (*0.37*)	0.00–1.68
		Conversations with others	0.05 (*0.13*)	0.00–0.64
		Total auditory memory	0.61(*0.37*)	0.00–1.68
		Total tactile, gustatory and olfactory perceptions	0.23 (*0.35*)	0.00–1.99
		Total perceptions of perpetrator	2.97 (1.29)	0.63–6.62
5	*Emotions*	Fear	0.13 (*0.19*)	0.00–1.12
		Anger	0.05 (*0.16*)	0.00–1.32
		Estrangement	0.01 (*0.05*)	0.00–0.42
		Powerlessness	0.06 (*0.11*)	0.00–0.90
		Shame	0.02 (*0.05*)	0.00–0.28
		Guilt	0.01 (*0.08*)	0.00–0.56
		Betrayal	0.03 (*0.09*)	0.00–0.63
		Self-deprecation	0.05 (*0.12*)	0.00–0.79
		Sadness	0.06 (*0.12*)	0.00–0.66
		Disgust	0.03 (*0.14*)	0.00–1.32
		Total memory of emotions	0.46 (*0.56*)	0.00–3.31
6	*Metamemory*	Admission not to remember	0.28 (*0.55*)	0.00–2.74
		Doubts and uncertainty about evidence	0.12 (*0.14*)	0.00–0.96
		Total metamemory	0.40 (*0.62*)	0.00–2.89

(*Continued*).

Table 9.2 Descriptive statistics of content of the depositions (N = 80) (*Continued*)

Categories and subcategories		Mean of words (*SD*)	Range
7 *Self-reflective ability*	Self-awareness	0.28 (*0.23*)	0.00–1.09
	Attribution of mental state to perpetrator	0.15 (*0.15*)	0.00–0.68
	Total self-reflective ability	0.43 (*0.32*)	0.00–1.78
8 *Interaction*	Interactions with the perpetrator	0.12 (*0.19*)	0.00–1.30
	Interactions with others	0.01 (*0.06*)	0.00–0.42
	Total interactions	0.13 (*0.28*)	0.00–1.30

The ability to refer to mental states becomes more sophisticated as children grow older. Self-reflective capacities and awareness of one's mental states become increasingly richer from preschool age (M = 0.17 and M = 0.27), to school age (M = 0.26 and M = 0.41), to adolescence (M = 0.37 and M = 0.54). Verbal expressions reflect the capacity of the victim to make meaning of others' behavior with the aid of volitive, motivational, and emotional contents.

PTSD and content of depositions

Most studies on child abuse allegations have neglected to investigate the role of PTSD symptomatology. The study presented here analyzed 58 depositions subdivided into 28 cases where PTSD symptoms were present and 30 cases where PTSD symptoms were not. A chi^2 test between absence/presence of PTSD and age ($\chi^2 = 4,451$; DOF = 2; p = 0,108) indicates a non-significant relationship between the two variables. An independent t-test comparing contents of the testimony and the absence/presence of PTSD is shown in Table 9.4.

The analysis shows a non-significant difference regarding the total number of words (length of deposition), the temporal and causal contextualization of the events, the use of auditory and visual perceptive contents to describe the perpetrator, emotional references, and references to metamemory and reflective capacities. Therefore, the presence of PTSD per se does not have an impact on allegations as children were able to place events in an appropriate timeframe, to make consequential links, and to remember the key features of the perpetrator.

However, there are some problematic areas where PTSD symptoms do play a role. Firstly, children without PTSD produce narratives that are more focused on the *self* and use a greater number (M = 4.51 vs. M = 3.84) of personal pronouns, which are linguistically useful to clarify and delimit the identities of the participants. Post-Traumatic symptomatology also has an impact on the possibility of developing a coherent narrative structure, especially concerning

Table 9.3 Mean values of deposition content and age (N = 80)

Categories and subcategories		4–6 years (N = 15) Mean (SD)	7–10 years (N = 39) Mean (SD)	11–17 years (N = 26) Mean (SD)	F$_{(2\,77)}$	p
1. Length of deposition	Number of words	1150.40 (720.57)	1811.87 (128.74)	2662.50 (1976.23)	5.91	0.004
		% Mean (SD)	**% Mean (SD)**	**% Mean (SD)**		
2. Focus on self	Total focus on self	4.20 (1.13)	4.59 (1.29)	4.26 (1.72)	0.62	n.s.
3. Contextual embedding	Total contextual embedding	8.50 (2.09)	8.46 (1.84)	7.76 (2.06)	1.17	n.s
4. Perceptions of perpetrator	Total perceptions of perpetrators		2.66 (1.64)	2.67 (1.07)	2.41	0.090
	Total visual	2.26 (1.44)	3.00 (1.09)	2.52 (1.08)	2.67	n.s.
	Behavior of perpetrator	1.84 (1.13)	2.57 (0.93)	2.30 (0.98)	3.55	0.033
	Total auditory	0.53 (0.43)	0.62 (0.39)	0.58 (0.34)	0.26	n.s.
	Total tactile, gustatory and olfactory perceptions	0.39 (0.59)	0.25 (0.31)	0.09 (0.13)	3.88	0.025
	Total tactile perceptions	0.37 (0.59)	0.22 (0.30)	0.58 (0.34)	3.58	0.033
5. Emotions	Total emotions	0.44 (0.81)	0.51 (0.51)	0.42 (0.50)	0.20	n.s.
6. Metamemory	Total metamemory	0.19 (0.33)	0.55 (0.77)	0.32 (0.44)	2.20	n.s.
8. Self-reflective ability	Total self-reflective ability	0.27 (0.29)	0.41 (0.33)	0.54 (0.33)	3.38	0.039
	Self-awareness	0.17 (0.21)	0.26 (0.21)	0.37 (0.25)	3.91	0.024
9. Interaction	Total interactions	0.08 (0.20)	0.11 (0.25)	0.20 (0.35)	1.06	n.s.

Table 9.4   Mean values of the contents of the deposition and PTSD (N = 58)

Categories and subcategories		PTSD (N = 28) Mean (*SD*)	NO PTSD (N = 30) Mean (*SD*)	t (56)	p
1. Length of deposition	Number of words	2025.96 (*1599.09*) % Mean (*SD*)	1935.57 (*1503.08*) % Mean (*SD*)	0.22	n.s.
2. Focus on self	Total focus on self	3.84 (*0.95*)	4.51 (*1.60*)	1.97	0.055
3. Contextual embedding	Total contextual embedding	7.69 (*1.65*)	8.46 (*2.14*)	1.52	n.s.
	Spatial connectors	1.91 (*0.49*)	2.39 (*1.14*)	2.09	0.043
4. Perceptions of perpetrator	Total perceptions of perpetrator	3.25 (*1.35*)	2.89 (*1.29*)	1.03	n.s.
	Total tactile, gustatory, olfactory	0.35 (*0.47*)	0.13 (*0.15*)	2.7	0.024
	Tactile perceptions	0.34 (*0.46*)	0.10 (*0.13*)	2.61	0.014
5. Emotions	Total emotions Shame	0.42 (*0.61*) 0.05 (*0.08*)	0.29 (*0.41*) 0.01 (*0.02*)	0.91 2.61	n.s. 0.014
	Betrayal	0.00 (*0.00*)	0.06 (*0.14*)	2.27	0.031
	Sadness	0.07 (*0.13*)	0.02 (*0.05*)	2.06	0.044
6. Metamemory	Total metamemory	0.22 (*0.41*)	0.29 (*0.51*)	0.54	n.s.
8. Self-reflective ability	Total self-reflective ability	0.53 (*0.37*)	0.39 (*0.27*)	1.66	n.s.
9. Interaction	Total interaction Interactions with the perpetrator	0.02 (*0.05*) 0.02 (*0.05*)	0.17 (*0.34*) 0.16 (*0.33*)	2.34 2.22	0.026 0.034

spatial contextualization of abusive events (t = 2.09 df = 56 p<.05), the general description of the *interactions* (t = 2.34 df = 56 p<.03) and, in particular, the *interactions with the perpetrator* (t = 2.22 df = 56 p<.04). Children without PTSD symptoms were more able to define spatial coordinates of the traumatic event (M = 2.39 vs. M = 191) and to produce a more vivid account of the interactions (M = 0.17 vs. M = 0.02) and, in particular, the interactions with the perpetrator (M = 0.16 vs. M = 0.02). Conversely, children with PTSD provided more sensory details (tactile, olfactory, and gustatory) (M = 0.35 vs. M = 0.13; t = 2.37 df = 56 p<.03), especially of tactile perception (M = 0.34 vs. M = 0.10; t = 2.61 df = 56 p<.02). Finally, regarding the *emotions*, there were significant differences in the ability to express *shame* (t = 2.61 df = 56 p<.02), *sadness* (t = 2.06 df = 56 p<.05), and *betrayal* (t = .27 df = 56 p<.04). Allegations of children with PTSD contain more references to shame (M = 0.05 vs. M = 0.01) and to sadness (M = 0.07 vs. M = 0.02); allegations of children without PTSD included more references to betrayal (M = 0.06 vs. M = 0.01).

Age or PTSD?

To understand whether the testimony was influenced by age or by the presence/absence of post-traumatic symptomatology, multiple block regressions were conducted. Age and PTSD were considered to be the independent variables, whereas the content of allegations was considered to be the dependent variable. Table 9.5 presents significant results.

Data highlight the predictive power of the PTSD with respect to age. PTSD was the only predictor of contents relating to: *spatial contextualization* (R = 0.38 $F_{(1, 56)}$ = 3.29 p<.05, R^2 = 0.11), *tactile sensations* considered separately (R = 0.38 $F_{(1, 56)}$ = 4.56 p<.02, R^2 = 0.14), and combined with the *gustatory and olfactory sensations* (R = 0.36 $F_{(1, 56)}$ = 4.02 p<.02, R^2 = 0.13), the emotion of shame (R = 0.40 $F_{(1, 56)}$ = 5.36 p<.01, R^2 = 0.16), and *interactions* (R = 0.33 $F_{(1, 56)}$ = 3.38 p<.04, R^2 = 0.11). In contrast, age is the only significant predictor both for the *length of the account* (R = 0.27 $F_{(1, 56)}$ = 4.32 p<.04, R^2 = .07) and for the *reflective abilities* in the sense of self-awareness (R = 0.42 $F_{(1, 56)}$ = 6.02 p<.001).

Discussion

In line with the literature on narratives of child sexual abuse (Berliner et al., 2003; Eisen et al., 2002; Ghetti et al., 2002; Lamb, Sternberg, & Esplin, 2000; Lamb et al., 2003), the study presented here confirmed that age influenced the complexity and content of children's accounts. Data on all 80 allegations show that the length of the account (in terms of the overall number of words used) and its lexical and conceptual organization are affected by

Table 9.5   Results of the regression analysis of the contents of the depositions with Age and PTSD as predictors

Predictors		Criterion		*Beta*	t	Sig.
Length of deposition	Number of words	**Age**		**0.28**	**2.13**	**0.04**
		PTSD		0.08	0.57	0.57
Contextual embedding	Spatial connectors	Age		−0.20	−1.52	0.13
		PTSD		**−0.30**	**−2.29**	**0.03**
Perceptions of perpetrator	Total tactile, gustatory and olfactory perceptions	Age		−0.18	−1.42	0.16
		PTSD		**0.28**	**2.19**	**0.03**
	Total tactile perceptions	Age		−0.17	−1.33	0.19
		PTSD		**0.31**	**2.46**	**0.02**
Emotions	Shame	Age		0.22	1.79	0.08
		PTSD		**0.37**	**3.00**	**0.001**
Self-reflective ability	Self-awareness	**Age**		**0.41**	**3.28**	**0.001**
		PTSD		0.21	1.67	0.10
Interaction	Total interactions	Age		0.16	1.26	0.21
		PTSD		**−0.26**	**−2.01**	**0.05**

children's linguistic and cognitive development; findings mainly discriminate preschoolers (4–6 years) from school-age children (7–10 and 11–17 years). Advanced communicative skills depend on the ability to understand intentions and beliefs and, in turn, to infer one's and others' mental states (Astington, Harris, & Olson, 1988). For this reason, only school-age children are able to produce more sophisticated allegations referring to mental states.

The analysis of the influence of post-traumatic symptomatology on autobiographical memory indicates that the narratives of children with PTSD display some deficits that do not affect the general validity of children's allegations; however, the same deficits make the allegations less effective. This lesser efficacy is caused by the lack of references to self and of core elements of the narrative, like the description of the events in terms of actions and reactions (specifically, the total interactions, and the interactions with the abuser) and the spatial collocation of the events. The children with acute PTSD employed fewer words which evoke a *focus on self* as the actor, and infrequently they adopted expressions and sentences in which *I*, *me*, *myself*, *my* are present. However, they used a more impersonal style of narrative in which the victim did not emerge as the agent or the thinker. Klein and Janoff-Bulman (1996), in a study on the accounts of abused adults, noted that the focus on self was reduced in the stories of adults with a history of child abuse. In fact, such adults used significantly more third-person than first-person pronouns, indicating a greater emphasis on others than on self, suggesting that their personal history was transformed into the history of *others*.

When, however, the effects of age and PTSD were jointly analyzed, PTSD symptoms were more predictive in terms of both specific and distinct contents. PTSD accounted for poor narratives in terms of spatial contextualization and information about the relationship with the abuser. Furthermore, narratives of children with PTSD presented a richer content in terms of olfactory, gustatory, and tactile sensorial memory and shame. Children are, therefore, able to produce reflective accounts to regulate and monitor verbal flows in their narratives of abuse. Post-Traumatic symptomatology, however, specifically favors sudden and unexpected use of gustatory and tactile sensorial memories (Beaudreau, 2007; van der Kolk, 1999; van der Kolk & Fisler, 1995, 1996). Brewin and Holmes (see review 2003) argue that traumatic memory in PTSD cases functions to relieve from flashbacks. Yet, flashbacks are dominated by sensory details, such as vivid visual images, and may include sounds and other involuntary fragmentary sensations triggered by specific reminders of the trauma, such as the sound of a police siren or the smell of smoke, or particular thoughts or images relating to the event (p. 341). Children with PTSD are, therefore, less able to overcome shame and to recall specific aspects of the occurred interactions with the abuser and of locations where the traumatic experience happened.

To summarize, PTSD affects autobiographical narrative regarding shame because children at that point recall the involvement with the abuser. Aspects that are particularly difficult to recall come to the child's mind through sensorial details that intrude in the form of reexperiencing symptoms. The results of this research thus highlight the need to differentiate child sexual abuse experiences in terms of specific cognitive and emotional mechanisms involved with PTSD symptoms. Although all the depositions examined here were considered to be reliable during the criminal proceedings and all perpetrators were found guilty, children's accounts are fragmented and qualitatively different in PTSD cases. Therefore, ethical considerations are the issue if professionals consider the potential risk of revictimizing children who have not healed their traumatic experiences. It is the authors' opinion that children with current PTSD symptoms should be treated prior to testifying in court.

The study presents some limitations. First of all, PTSD symptoms were not assessed via validated assessment tools. The use of a checklist would enable the analysis of partial PTSD symptoms and the interplay between the categories of symptoms (intrusive, avoidance, and hyperarousal), and the exploration of other associated dimensions (e.g., dissociation symptoms, anxiety, anger). The absence of this information prevented us, for example, investigating, as Kenardy and colleagues (2007) showed in their study on hospitalized children who were the victims of accidents, the relationship between intrusive post-traumatic symptoms and the quality of the trauma narrative. However, the fact that there is no research (apart from the clinical study by Mossige on subjects under treatment) on the relation between children's allegations of sexual abuse and their PTSD symptoms makes these preliminary results interesting.

Furthermore, it could also be useful to understand which specific elements of the deposition are compromised by PTSD and by other factors. For example, abused children are more vulnerable to disorganized attachment styles (Alexander, 1992; Bacon, 2001; Cicchetti & Toth, 1995; Holmes, 1999; Lyons-Ruth & Jacobitz, 1999) that are correlated with greater difficulty in telling a story, less coherence, and more problematic access to memories, especially in preschoolers. On the one hand, therefore, PTSD could be responsible for "flashbacks" and related sensory details in the narratives; on the other hand, disorganized or insecure attachment could affect the coherence of the account.

To conclude, future studies should investigate the role of PTSD in a wider sample of child abuse allegations controlling for consistent age ranges. Secondly, children who produced a narrative should be assessed with PTSD validated measures. Finally, other dimensions should also be explored, such as attachment relationships that have been shown to be crucial in shaping individuals' narratives of their life experience.

References

Alexander, K. W., Quas, J. A., & Goodman, G. S. (2002). Theoretical advances in understanding children's memory for distressing events: The role of attachment. *Developmental Review, 22,* 490–519.

Alexander, P. (1992). Application of attachment theory to the study of sexual abuse. *Journal of Consulting and Clinical Psychology, 60,* 185–95.

American Psychiatric Association (APA) (2000). *Diagnostic and Statistical Manual of Mental Disorders* (4th ed., Text Rev.) (*DSM-IV-TR*). Washington, DC: Author.

Amir, N., Stafford, J., Freshman, M. S., & Foa, E. B. (1998). Relationship between trauma narratives and trauma pathology. *Journal of Traumatic Stress, 11*(2), 385–92.

Astington, J., Harris, P., & Olson, D. (1988). *Developing theories of mind.* New York: Cambridge University Press.

Bacon, H. (2001). Attachment, trauma, and child sexual abuse: An exploration. In S. Richardson & H. Bacon (Eds.), *Creative responses to child sexual abuse: Challenges and dilemmas.* London: Jessica Kingsley.

Baker-Ward, L., Gordon, B. N., Ornstein, P. A., Larus, D. M., & Clubb, P. A. (1993). Young children's long-term retention of a pediatric examination. *Child Development, 64,* 1519–33.

Baker-Ward, L., Ornstein, P. A., & Principe, G. (1997). Revealing the representation: Evidence from children's reports of events. In P. van den Broek & P. Bauer (Eds.), *Developmental spans in event comprehension and representation: Bridging fictional and actual events* (pp. 79–107). Hillsdale, NJ: Erlbaum.

Beaudreau, S. (2007). Are trauma narratives unique and do they predict psychological adjustment? *Journal of Traumatic Stress, 20*(3), 353–7.

Berliner, L., Hyman, I., Thomas, A., & Fitzgerald, M. (2003). Children's memory for trauma and positive experiences. *Journal of Traumatic Stress, 16*(3), 229–36.

Bidrose, S., & Goodman, G. (2000). Testimony and evidence: A scientific case study of memory for child sexual abuse. *Applied Cognitive Psychology, 14,* 197–213.

Bohanek, J. G., Fivush, R., & Walker, E. (2005). Memories of positive and negative emotional events. *Applied Cognitive Psychology, 19*(1), 51–66.

Bolan, A. M., Haden, C. A., & Ornstein, P. A. (2003). Boosting children's memory by training mothers in the use of elaborative conversational style as an event unfolds. *Journal of Cognition and Development, 4,* 39–65.

Brewin, C. R., & Holmes, E. A. (2003). Psychological theories of posttraumatic stress disorder. *Clinical Psychology Review, 23,* 339–76.

Byrne, C. A., Hyman, I. E., & Scott, K. L. (2001). Comparisons of memories for traumatic events and other experiences. *Applied Cognitive Psychology, 15*(7), 119–33.

Carlson, E., Furby, L., Armstrong, J., & Shales, J. (1997). A conceptual framework for the long-term psychological effects of severe and chronic childhood abuse. *Child Maltreatment, 2,* 272–95.

Ceci, S. J., & Friedman, R. D. (2000). The suggestibility of children: Scientific research and legal implications. *Cornell Law Review, 86,* 33–108.

Chen, E., Zeltzer, L. K., Craske, M. G., & Katz, E. R. (2000). Children's memories for painful cancer treatment procedures: Implications for distress. *Child Development, 71,* 933–47.

Cicchetti, D., & Toth, S. L. (1995). Child maltreatment and attachment organisation: Implications for intervention. In S. Goldberg, R. Muir, & J. Kerr (Eds.), *Attachment theory: Social developmental and clinical perspectives.* Hillsdale, NJ: Analytic Press.

Cordon, I., Pipe, M., Sayfan, L., Melinder, A., & Goodman, G. (2004). Memory for traumatic experiences in early childhood. *Developmental Review, 24,* 101–32.

Damasio, A. R. (1999). *The feeling of what happens. Body and emotion in making of consciousness.* New York: Harcourt Brace.

Dent, H. (1977). Stress as a factor influencing person recognition in identification parades. *Bulletin of the British Psychological Society, 30,* 339–40.

Di Blasio, P., Ionio, C., & Procaccia, R. (2004). Traumatic narratives: Analysis of child abuse allegations. In A. A. V. V., *Forensic Psychology and Law* (pp. 103–14). Krakow: Institute of Forensic Research Publishers.

Dunmore, E., Clark, D. M., & Ehlers, A. (1999). Cognitive factors involved in the onset and maintenance of post-traumatic stress disorder (PTSD) after physical or sexual assault. *Behaviour Research and Therapy, 37*(9), 809–29.

Dunmore, E., Clark, D. M., & Ehlers, A. (2001). A prospective investigation of the role of cognitive factors in persistent Post-Traumatic Stress Disorder (PTSD) after physical or sexual assault. *Behaviour Research and Therapy, 39*(9), 1063–84.

Eisen, M. L., Goodman, G. S., Qin, J., & Davis, S. L. (1998). Memory and suggestibility in maltreated children: New research relevant to evaluating allegations of abuse. In S. Lynn & K. McConkey (Eds.), *Truth in memory* (pp. 163–89). New York: Guilford.

Ehlers, A., & Clark, D. (2000). A cognitive model of post-traumatic stress disorder. *Behaviour Research and Therapy, 38,* 319–45.

Ehlers, A., Clark, D. M., Dunmore, E. et al. (1998). Predicting response to exposure treatment in PTSD: The role of mental defeat and alienation. *Journal of Traumatic Stress, 11*, 457–71.

Ehlers, A., Mayou, R. A., & Bryant, B. (2003). Cognitive predictors of post-traumatic stress disorder in children: Results of a prospective longitudinal study. *Behaviour Research and Therapy, 41*(1), 1–10.

Eisen, M. L., Qin, J., Goodman, G. S., & Davis, S. L. (2002). Memory and suggestibility in maltreated children: Age, stress arousal, dissociation and psychopathology. *Journal of Experimental Child Psychology, 83*, 167–212.

Engelberg, E., & Christianson, S. (2002). Stress, trauma, and memory. In M. Eisen, J. Quas, & G. S. Goodman (Eds.), *Memory and suggestibility in the forensic interview*. Mahwah, NJ: Lawrence Erlbaum Associates.

Feerick, M. M., & Snow, K. L. (2005). The relationships between childhood sexual abuse, social anxiety, and symptoms of Post-Traumatic Stress Disorder in women. *Journal of Family Violence, 20*(6), 409–19.

Fivush, R. (1993). Emotional content of parent–child conversations about the past. In C. A. Nelson (Ed.), *The Minnesota Symposium on Child Psychology: Memory and affect in development* (pp. 39–77). Hillsdale, NJ: Erlbaum.

Fivush, R., Haden, C., & Adam, S. (1995). Structure and coherence of preschoolers' personal narratives over time: Implications for childhood amnesia. *Journal of Experimental Child Psychology, 60*, 32–56.

Fivush, R., Hazzard, A., Sales, J., Sarfati, D., & Brown, T. (2002). Creating coherence out of chaos? Children's narratives of emotionally negative and positive events. *Applied Cognitive Psychology, 16*, 1–19.

Foa, E. B., Molnar, C., & Cashman, L. (1995). Change in rape narratives during exposure therapy for posttraumatic stress disorder. *Journal of Traumatic Stress, 8*, 675–90.

Foa, E. B., & Riggs, D. S (1993). Post-traumatic stress disorder in rape victims. In J. Oldham & A. Tasman (Eds.), *Annual Review of Psychiatry* (v. *12*, pp. 273–303). Washington, DC: American Psychiatric Association.

Fonagy, P., & Target, M. (1997). Attachment and reflective functioning: Their role in self organization. *Development and Psychopathology, 9*, 679–700.

Fonagy, P., & Target, M. (1998). Mentalization and the changing aims of child psychoanalysis. *Psychoanalytic Dialogues, 8*, 87–114.

Fonagy, P., Target, M., Miller, J., & Moran, G. S. (1999). *Contemporary psychodynamic child therapy. Theory and technique*. New York: Guilford Press.

Ghetti, S., Goodman, G. S., Eisen, M. L., Qin, J., & Davis, S. L. (2002). Consistency in children's reports of sexual and physical abuse. *Child Abuse & Neglect, 26*, 977–95.

Glaser, D., & Spencer, J. (1990). Sentencing, children's evidence and children's trauma. *Criminal Law Review*, 371–82.

Goodman, G. S., Bottoms, B. L., Schwartz-Kenney, B. M., & Rudy, L. (1991). Children's testimony about a stressful event: Improving children's reports. *Journal of Narrative and Life History, 1*, 69–99.

Goodman, G., & Jones, D. (1988). The emotional effects of criminal court testimony on child sexual assault victims: A preliminary report. In G. Davies & J. Drinkwater (Eds.), *The child witness: Do the courts abuse children?* Leicester: The British Psychological Society.

Goodman, G., Pyle-Taub, E., Jones, D. et al. (1992). Emotional effects of criminal court testimony on child sexual assault victims. *Monographs of the Society for Research in Child Development, 57,* 1–42.

Goodman, G. S., Quas, J., Batterman-Faunce, J., Riddelsberg, M., & Kuhn, J. (1994). Predictors of accurate and inaccurate memories of traumatic events experienced in childhood. *Consciousness and Cognition, 3,* 269–94.

Goodman, G. S., Quas, J., Batterman-Faunce, J., Riddelsberg, M., & Kuhn, J. (1997). Children's reaction to and memory of stressful event: Influences of age, anatomical dolls, knowledge, and parental attachment. *Applied Developmental Science, 1*(2), 54–75.

Goodman, G. S., Rudy, L., Bottoms, L., & Aman, C. (1990). Children's concerns and memory: Issues of ecological validity in the study of children's eyewitness testimony. In R. Fivush & J. A. Hudson (Eds.), *Knowing and remembering in young children* (pp. 249–84). New York: Cambridge University Press.

Haden, C. A., Ornstein, P. A., Eckerman, O. C., & Didow, S. M. (2001). Mother–child conversational interactions as events unfold: Linkages to subsequent remembering. *Child Development, 72,* 1016–31.

Halligan, S. L., Clark, D. M., & Ehlers, A. (2002). Cognitive processing, memory, and the development of PTSD symptoms: Two experimental analogue studies. *Journal of Behavior Therapy and Experimental Psychiatry, 33,* 73–89.

Harvey, A. G., & Bryant, R. A. (2002). Acute stress disorder: A synthesis and critique. *Psychological Bulletin, 128,* 886–902.

Hetzel, M. D., & McCanne, T. R. (2005). The roles of peri-traumatic dissociation, child physical abuse, and child sexual abuse in the development of post-traumatic stress disorder. *Child Abuse & Neglect, 29*(8), 915–30.

Holmes, J. (1999). Attachment theory and abuse: A developmental perspective. In U. McLusky & C. A. Hooper (Eds.), *Psychodynamic perspectives on abuse.* London: Jessica Kingsley.

Horowitz, M. (1986). Stress-response syndromes: A review of posttraumatic and adjustment disorders. *Hospital & Community Psychiatry, 37,* 241–9.

Howe, M. L., Courage, M. L., & Peterson, C. (1996). How can I remember when I wasn't there?: Long-term retention of traumatic experiences and emergence of the cognitive self. In K. Pezdek & P. Banks (Eds.), *The recovered memory/false memory debate* (pp. 121–49). San Diego, CA: Academy Press.

Kenardy, J., Smith, A., Spence, S. H. et al. (2007). Dissociation in children's trauma narratives: An exploratory investigation. *Journal of Anxiety Disorders, 21*(3), 456–66.

Klein, I., & Janoff-Bulman, R. (1996). Trauma history and personal narratives: Some clues to coping among survivors of child abuse. *Child Abuse & Neglect, 20,* 45–54.

Kleinknecht, E., & Beike, D. R. (2004). How knowing and doing inform an autobiography: Relations among preschoolers' theory of mind, narrative, and event memory skills. *Applied Cognitive Psychology, 18,* 745–64.

Koopman, C. (2000). New DSM-IV diagnosis of acute stress. *The American Journal of Psychiatry, 157,* 1888.

Koss, M. P., Figueredo, A. J., Bell, I., Tharan, M., & Tromp, S. (1996). Traumatic memory characteristics: A cross-validated meditational mode of response to rape among employed women. *Journal of Abnormal Psychology, 105,* 421–32.

Kulkofsky, S., Wang, Q., & Ceci, S. J. (2008). Do better stories make better memories? Narrative skills and memory accuracy in preschool children. *Applied Cognitive Psychology*, *22*, 21–38.

Lamb, M. E., Sternberg, K. J., & Esplin, P. W. (2000). Effects of age and delay on the amount of information provided by alleged sex abuse victims in investigative interviews. *Child Development*, *71*(6), 1586–96.

Lamb, M. E., Sternberg, K. J., Orbach, Y. et al. (2003). Age differences in young children's responses to open-ended invitations in the course of forensic interview. *Journal of Consulting and Clinical Psychology*, *71*(5), 926–34.

Lisak, D. (1994). The psychological impact of sexual abuse: Content analysis of interviews with male survivors. *Journal of Traumatic Stress*, *7*, 525–48.

Lyons-Ruth, K., & Jacobitz, D. (1999). Attachment disorganisation: Unresolved loss, relational violence, and lapses in behavioural and attentional strategies. In J. Cassidy & P. R. Shaver (Eds.), *Handbook of attachment: Theory, research and clinical applications*. London: Guilford Press.

McDermott Sales, J., Fivush, R., Parker, J., & Bahrick, L. (2005). Stressing memory: Long-term relations among children's stress, recall and psychological outcome following Hurricane Andrew. *Journal of Cognition and Development*, *6*(4), 529–45.

McGuigan, F., & Salmon, K. (2004). The time to talk: The influence of the timing of adult–child talk on children's event memory. *Child Development*, *75*(3), 669–86.

Moradi, A. R., Doost, H., Taghavi, M., Yule, W., & Dalgleish, T. (1999). Everyday memory deficits in children and adolescents with PTSD: Performance on the Riverhead Behavioural Memory Test. *Journal of Child Psychology and Psychiatry and Allied Disciplines*, *40*(3), 357–61.

Moradi, A. R., Herlihy, J., Yasseri, G. et al. (2008). Specificity of episodic and semantic aspects of autobiographical memory in relation to symptoms of post-traumatic stress disorder (PTSD). *Acta Psychologica*, *127*(3), 645–53.

Moradi A. R., Taghavi R., Neshat-Doost H. T., Yule, W., & Dalgleish, T. (2000). Memory bias for emotional information in children and adolescents with post-traumatic stress disorder: A preliminary study. *Journal of Anxiety Disorders*, *14*(5), 521–34.

Mossige, S., Jensen, T. K., Gulbrandsen, W., Reichelt, S., & Tjersland, O. A. (2005), Children's narratives of sexual abuse What characterizes them and how do they contribute to meaning-making? *Narrative Inquiry*, *15*(2), 377–404.

Murray, J., Ehlers, A., & Mayou, R. A. (2002). Dissociation and post-traumatic stress disorder: Two prospective studies of motor vehicle accident survivors. *British Journal of Psychiatry*, *180*, 363–8.

Ochsner, J. E., Zaragoza, M. S., & Mitchell, K. J. (1999). The accuracy and suggestibility of children's memory for neutral and criminal eyewitness events. *Legal and Criminological Psychology*, *4*, 79–92.

Orbach, Y., & Lamb, M. E. (2007). Young children's references to temporal attributes of allegedly experienced events in the course of forensic interviews. *Child Development*, *78*(4), 1100–20.

Peace, K. A., & Porter, S. (2004). A longitudinal investigation of the reliability of memories for trauma and other emotional experiences. *Applied Cognitive Psychology*, *18*, 1143–59.

Peterson, C., & Bell, M. (1996). Children's memory for traumatic injury. *Child Development, 67*, 3045–70.

Peterson, C., & Biggs, M. (1998). Stitches and casts: Emotionally and narrative coherence. *Narrative Inquiry, 8*, 51–76.

Peterson, C., & McCabe, A. (1983). *Developmental psycholinguistics: Three ways of looking at a child's narrative.* New York: Plenum.

Peterson, C., & McCabe, A. (1991). Linking children's connective use and narrative macrostructure. In A. McCabe & C. Peterson (Eds.), *Developing narrative structure* (pp. 29–53). Hillsdale, NJ: Lawrence Erlbaum Associates.

Peterson, C., & Whalen, N. (2001). Five years later: Children's memory for medical emergencies. *Applied Cognitive Psychology, 15*, 7–24.

Poole, D. A., & Lindsay, D. S. (2002). Children's suggestibility in the forensic context. In M. Eisen, J. Quas, & G. Goodman (Eds.), *Memory and suggestibility on the forensic interview* (pp. 355–81). Mahwah, NJ: Lawrence Erlbaum Associates.

Quas, J., Goodman, G., Bidrose, S. et al. (1999). Emotion and memory: Children's long term remembering, forgetting, and suggestibility. *Journal of Experimental Child Psychology, 72*(4), 235–70.

Quas, J., Goodman, G., Ghetti, S. et al. (2005). Childhood sexual assault victims: Long-term outcomes after testifying in criminal court. *Monographs of the Society for Research in Child Development, 70*, 1–129.

Quas, J. A., Goodman, G. S., & Jones, D. P. H. (2003). Predictors of attributions of self-blame and internalizing behavior problems in sexually abused children. *Journal of Child Psychology and Psychiatry, 44*(5), 723–36.

Quas, J., & Schaaf, J. (2002). Children's memories of experienced and non-experienced events following repeated interviews. *Journal of Experimental Child Psychology, 83*, 304–38.

Roth, S., & Newman, E. (1991). The process of coping with sexual trauma. *Journal of Traumatic Stress, 4*, 279–97.

Sachs-Ericsson, N., Cromer, K., Hernandez, A., & Kendall-Tackett, K. (2009). A review of childhood abuse, health, and pain-related problems: The role of psychiatric disorders and current life stress. *Journal of Trauma and Dissociation, 10*(2), 170–88.

Saywitz, K. J., & Snyder, L. (1996). Narrative elaboration: Test of a new procedure for interviewing children. *Journal of Consulting and Clinical Psychology, 67*, 1347–57.

Saywitz, K. J., Snyder, L., & Lamphear, V. (1996). Helping children tell what happened: A follow-up study of the narrative elaboration procedure. *Child Maltreatment, 1*(3), 200–12.

Schaaf, J. M., Alexander, K.W., & Goodman, G. S. (2008). Children's false memory and true disclosure in the face of repeated questions. *Journal of Experimental Child Psychology, 100*, 157–85.

Scheeringa, M. S., Zeanah, C. H., Drell, M. J., & Larrieu, J. A. (1995). Two approaches to the diagnosis of post-traumatic stress disorder in infancy and early childhood. *Journal of the American Academy of Child and Adolescent Psychiatry, 34*, 191–200.

Schneider, W., & Pressley, M. (1997). *Memory development between two and twenty.* Mahwah, NJ: Lawrence Erlbaum Associates.

Sjoberg, R., & Lindblad, F. (2002). Limited disclosure of sexual abuse in children whose experiences were documented by videotape. *The American Journal of Psychiatry, 159*(2), 312–14.

Spencer, J., & Flin, R. (1990). *The evidence of children: The law and psychology*. London: Blackstone.

Stallard, P. (2003). A retrospective analysis to explore the applicability of the Ehlers and Clark (2000) Cognitive Model to explain PTSD in children. *Behavioural and Cognitive Psychotherapy, 31*(3), 337–45.

Sternberg, K. J., Lamb, M. E., Guterman, E., & Abbott, C. B. (2006). Effects of early and later family violence on children's behavior problems and depression: A longitudinal, multi-informant perspective. *Child Abuse and Neglect, 30*(3), 283–306.

Tromp, S., Koss, M., Figueredo, A. J., & Tharan, M. (1995). Are rape memories different? A comparison of rape, other unpleasant, and pleasant memories among employed women. *Journal of Traumatic Stress, 4*, 607–27.

van der Kolk, B. A. (1996). The complexity of adaptation to trauma: Self-regulation, stimulus discrimination, and characterological development. In B. A. van der Kolk, A. C. McFarlane, & L. Weisaeth (Eds.), *Traumatic stress: The effects of overwhelming experience on mind, body, and society*. New York: Guilford Press.

van der Kolk, B. A. (1999). Trauma and memory. In B. A. van der Kolk, A. C. McFarlane, & L. Weisaeth (Eds.), *Traumatic stress: The effects of overwhelming experience on mind, body, and society* (pbk) (pp. 279–302). New York: Guilford Press.

van der Kolk, B. A., & Fisler, R. (1995). Dissociation and the fragmentary nature of traumatic memories: Overview and exploratory study. *Journal of Traumatic Stress, 8*(4), 505–25.

van der Kolk, B. A., & Fisler, R. (1996). Dissociation and the fragmentary nature of traumatic memories: Overview. *British Journal of Psychotherapy, 12*, 352–61.

Yuille, J. C., & Tollestrup, P. A. (1992). A model of diverse effects of emotion on eyewitness memory. In S. Christianson (Ed.), *The handbook of emotion and memory: Research and theory*. Hillsdale, NJ: Lawrence Erlbaum Associates.

Walrath, C., Ybarra, M., Holden, E. W. et al. (2003). Children with reported histories of sexual abuse: Utilizing multiple perspectives to understand clinical and psychosocial profiles. *Child Abuse & Neglect, 27*(5), 509–24.

Ward, G., & Carroll, M. (1997). Reality monitoring for sexual abuse memories. *Applied Cognitive Psychology, 11*, 293–304.

Weingarten, E. K., & Cobb, S. (1995). Timing disclosure sessions: Adding a narrative perspective to clinical work with adult survivors of childhood sexual abuse. *Family Process, 34*, 257–69.

Whitcomb, D. (2003). Legal interventions for child victims. *Journal of Traumatic Stress, 16*(2), 149–57.

Whitcomb, D., Goodman, G., Runyan, D., & Hoak, S. (1994). *The emotional effects of testifying on sexually abused children*. Washington, DC: US Department of Justice.

Whitcomb, D., Shapiro, E., & Stellwager, L. (1985). *When the victim is a child: Issues for judges and prosecutors*. Washington, DC: National Institute of Justice.

Whitfield, C. L. (1995). The forgotten difference: Ordinary memory versus traumatic memory. *Consciousness & Cognition, 4*, 88–94.

Chapter Ten

Exposure to Violence, Post-Traumatic Symptomatology, and Criminal Behaviors

David W. Foy, James Furrow, and Shauna McManus

Introduction

In this chapter we will present a review of studies on relationships between exposure to violence, post-traumatic symptomatology, and criminal behaviors among male juvenile offenders. We will use the central findings from these studies to increase knowledge among professionals in mental health or corrections settings of the linkage between violence exposure in both family and community contexts, post-trauma symptoms, and violent or criminal behavior. We will emphasize that recent studies show extensive prevalence rates for violence exposure and PTSD or post-trauma symptoms among delinquents. An interactional conceptual model will be used to demonstrate how protective factors, as well as familiar risk factors, need to be considered in developing treatments to improve mental health and recidivism outcomes. Next, a Positive Youth Development (PYD) perspective (Damon, 2004) will be used to emphasize the need to strengthen family and community supports to improve psychological adjustment in juvenile offenders. Advances in treatments for post-traumatic symptoms amongst adolescents will be described. Finally, we recommend an expanded treatment focus to include both specific treatments for reducing post-trauma symptoms, as well as improving PYD-based supports for juvenile offenders.

Post-Traumatic Syndromes in Childhood and Adolescence: A Handbook of Research and Practice, First Edition. Edited by Vittoria Ardino. © 2011 John Wiley & Sons, Ltd. Published 2011 by John Wiley & Sons, Ltd.

Brief literature review

We reviewed and updated the literature for recent findings on linkages between violence exposure, post-trauma symptoms, and criminal behaviors in male juvenile offenders. Overall, there were two key findings:

1. early exposure to familial or community trauma is related to increased risk for delinquency; and
2. delinquent youths exhibit high rates of PTSD.

Notably, these findings have been consistently reported both in the United States and internationally.

Our review revealed studies that consistently found significant links between childhood trauma exposure and risk for delinquency (Vermeiren, 2003) such that children who are victims of violence are more prone to delinquent activities (Siegfried, Ko, & Kelly, 2004). For example, Smith and Thornberry (1995) found that children maltreated before age 12 were significantly more likely to be arrested and to report more serious, violent delinquency when gender, ethnicity, family structure, and social class were controlled. In addition, Widom and Maxfield (2001) conducted a longitudinal study of nearly 2,000 students and found that childhood abuse or neglect increased the likelihood of arrest as a juvenile by 59% and as an adult by 28%. Another study examined a heterogeneous sample of 116 incarcerated male adolescents and confirmed that exposure to community violence and family functioning are predictive of psychological distress in delinquent youth (Ball et al., 2007).

Among studies examining the relationship between PTSD and delinquency, high rates for the disorder have been reported among youths in the juvenile justice system both in the United States and internationally. In one of the first studies to investigate community violence (CV) as a source of traumatic exposure in delinquent males, Burton and colleagues (1994) found that CV was positively correlated with PTSD severity, and that 25% of the juvenile offenders met full criteria for a PTSD diagnosis. A later study of 51 delinquent males in Massachusetts reported that 92% of the youths endorsed previous exposure to malevolent environmental factors and 18% met for PTSD (Erwin et al., 2000); and In another large epidemiological study of juvenile detainees in Chicago, Abram and colleagues (2004) found that 92.5% of the participants had experienced one or more traumas and that 11.2% of the sample met criteria for PTSD in the past year. In a follow-up study, researchers reported that 93% of the study participants diagnosed with PTSD had at least one comorbid psychiatric disorder (Abram et al., 2007). The implication is that PTSD and other comorbid disorders are often missed because traumatic experiences are rarely included in standard screens or volunteered by detained youths.

In order to gain a more global understanding of the prevalence of PTSD in youth offender populations, we extended our review to include studies conducted internationally. Baldry (2007) surveyed 532 Italian students and found that children who are abused or exposed to domestic violence are likely to become involved in aggressive or delinquent behavior. In a study of 370 male juvenile delinquents in Russia, Ruchkin and colleagues (2002) reported that 42% fulfilled partial diagnostic criteria and 25% met full criteria for PTSD. Among 251 juvenile offenders in Japan, Yashinaga and colleagues (2004) found that 36% of the delinquents reported experiences of exposure to overwhelming traumatic events. In addition, a study of 105 young offenders in the United Kingdom reported that as well as ethnic origin and historical variables, intrusion and rumination characteristics related to the crimes they committed explained an additional 48% of variance of the PTSD symptom severity (Evans et al., 2007).

At this point there are many studies that show consistency in linking childhood violence exposure with increased risk for delinquency. However, Vermeiren (2003) argues that the pathways responsible for resilience or vulnerability to criminality are largely unidentified and the potential mediating role of PTSD symptomatology remains unclear. Recent research has suggested the influence of caregiver-adult support and control (Ball et al., 2007), negative affect, and delinquent peer exposure (Maschi, Bradley, & Morgen, 2008) as potential moderating factors. In a study designed to address these limitations, Wood and colleagues (2002) used a matched sample of 200 inner-city high school students and 200 incarcerated youths to compare measures of violence exposure and PTSD rates. These researchers reported that both CV exposure and PTSD rates were significantly higher in the incarcerated males and females. Most notably, significantly more incarcerated adolescents (40%) met PTSD diagnostic criteria, than the 23% who were diagnosed positive in the high school sample. Wood and her colleagues (2002, p. 128) concluded that,

> Within the incarcerated group, adolescents who report higher levels of delinquent activity (in the form of gun possession and gang involvement) also report higher levels of some forms of violence exposure. Incarcerated youth with more serious delinquent histories displayed higher levels of PTSD symptomatology, as well.

Similar patterns were recently reported by Kilpatrick (2006) from a large national survey of nearly 2,000 adolescents where significant relationships were found for violence exposure, PTSD, and violence perpetration. Overall, these findings are persuasive in demonstrating that both violence exposure and PTSD are linked to increased risk for violence or delinquency. Future longitudinal research investigating potential mechanisms or mediating variables in this relationship is needed.

Toward an interactional prevention model

Prevention and risk models

Primary, secondary, and tertiary prevention programs target reduction in youth delinquency and violence through a broad array of interventions designed to impact youth and their immediate environments (Office of the Surgeon General, 2001). The preponderance of these programs maintain a "deficit model" focusing on the reduction of juvenile offending and the factors that put youths "at risk" for delinquent behavior. This emphasis is consistent with an impressive base of empirical support identifying personal and social factors associated with aggression and youth violence (Hann & Borek, 2001) and a "problem-focused" juvenile justice system (Barton & Butts, 2008).

Increasingly, risk-based models of delinquency suggest that youth risk for aggression and violence is better informed by a confluence of factors at a personal, familial, and community level. Personal factors associated with aggressive and violent behavior in youth include: biological or genetic risk factors (DiLalla & Gottesman, 1991), social-cognitive deficits, inflated self-esteem, and involvement in drug and alcohol use (Stiffman, Dore, & Cunningham, 1996). Juvenile weapon possession represents a significant risk factor of criminal behavior, particularly when associated with gang-related activity (Brown, 2004).

Social factors include familial and parental influences, including poor child-rearing practices, inadequate supervision, lack of parental involvement, poor or punitive discipline (Patterson et al., 1998), and antisocial parents (Moffitt, et al., 2002). Tolan, Gorman-Smith, and Henry (2003) suggest that poor parenting practices heighten the likelihood of youth involvement in deviant peer groups, which in turn increase the risk for violent and criminal behavior (Thornberry, 1998). The absence of peers (i.e., social isolation) and peer rejection represent a similar risk (Coie et al., 1995). The salience of deviant peer affiliation and delinquency is heightened in communities characterized by declining social control and reduced socioeconomic resources (Leventhal & Brooks-Gunn, 2000; Wikstrom & Loeber, 2000). Taken together these findings suggest that youth violence is multi-determined and subject to a dynamic interaction of risk factors across a young person's developmental context.

Prevention and positive youth development

There is growing recognition that prevention policies need to be guided by more than simple *at risk* models to address the complex problems and solutions needed to deal with violent behavior (Farrington, 2000). Recent advances in developmental psychology provide an alternative to an exclusive *deficit* model by identifying health promotion and positive development strategies that are ecologically derived (Weisz et al., 2005). A PYD approach to juvenile delinquency requires moving beyond prevention strategies that focus solely on protective factors and personal resilience to endorse an approach that emphasizes a youth's "manifest potentialities" through education and engagement with opportunities for contribution (Barton & Butts, 2008; Damon, 2004).

From a PYD perspective, prevention strategies need to strengthen the developmental infrastructure supporting youth in a given community. Eccles and Gootman (2002) underscore the necessary contribution of personal and social resources in the promotion of adolescent health and well-being. Healthy development requires ongoing adaptive responses in the relationship of a developing individual and the community to which he or she belongs (Lerner, Dowling, & Anderson, 2003). A developmentally responsive environment promotes the expression of personal initiative, a hallmark of positive youth development, which is often associated with acts of community involvement or service (Larson, 2000). These positive contexts offer an alternative to more "risky" social contexts that leave youths at greater vulnerability for violence exposure, delinquency, and psychological distress (Richards et al., 2004).

Protective factors and PYD

The deleterious effects of youth exposure to community violence can be mitigated by protective resources within a child's developmental context. Families and schools provide resources for aiding children in bringing a moral sense to their exposure to danger (Garbarino, 2001). For example, Ozer and Weinstein (2004) found that a youth's experience of parental and teacher support, along with reduced constraints for discussing violence exposure, demonstrated a protective and stabilizing effect for urban at-risk youth. Resilience and protective effects may serve adaptive functions which buffer against environmental risks, but these factors do not inherently ensure health and developmental success (Freitas & Downey, 1988). As Karen Pittman suggests: "problem-free is not fully prepared" (Benson & Pittman, 2001, p. 172). Therefore, an integrated prevention approach warrants a focus on these protective resources, along with a "promotive" emphasis that builds resources associated with positive developmental outcomes (Scales et al., 2000).

Prevention efforts focusing on the development of personal values and identity provide one example of strategies that increase resilience and enhance personal growth and well-being. Bonanno (2004) identifies "hardiness" as a resilience factor enabling a person to limit the harmful effects of traumatic exposure. Hardiness reflects the values and beliefs one has about their life, including the ability to grow and learn from negative life experiences. Similarly, Jessor and colleagues (1995) found that the demonstration of a child's self-responsibility through standing up for what he/she believes was related to that child's espousal of an intolerant attitude toward deviance and violent behavior. Other studies find that students with high achievement motivation and commitment to school report gains on psychological indicators and decreased involvement in problem behavior, including causing harm to others (Allen, Leadbeater, & Aber, 1990; Connell et al., 1995). Seginer (2008) concludes that efforts to promote hardiness through self-development and emotional health remain significant in developing and maintaining a hopeful future orientation among youth facing adversity.

Current research directions in developmental psychology need to examine the role of developmental assets in promoting positive outcomes among youth. New research on developmental pathways, delinquency, and violence offers direction in the study of alternate pathways leading to positive outcomes for youths facing similar environmental challenges and risk factors (Lerner & Galambos, 1998). This approach considers the individual characteristics of the adolescent together with the immediate environment, potentialities, and limitations found in the larger social context. Future research needs to examine the role of developmental resources in promoting resilience, reducing risk for violent behavior, and optimizing developmental outcomes among youth (Barton & Butts, 2008).

Advances in PTSD treatment for adolescents

The National Child Traumatic Stress Network (NCTSN) was inaugurated in 2001 in the USA to promote the development and dissemination of effective treatments for youth trauma survivors. The NCTSN website (www.nctsn.org) offers up-to-date, downloadable information about assessment and treatment methods for use by mental health professionals working within the juvenile justice system. There is a current emphasis on promoting the use of empirically validated treatments as "best practices." These include trauma-focused interventions for youth that feature the cognitive-behavioral techniques (CBT) of therapeutic exposure, cognitive restructuring, and self-management skills enhancement (Cohen, Berliner, & March, 2000). Commendably, these cognitive-behavioral techniques have already received consideration by juvenile justice professionals.

One of the first studies to examine the effectiveness of CBT group therapy for treating incarcerated male juveniles was conducted by Ovaert, Cashel, and Sewell (2003), who administered pre- and post-treatment measures to 10 successive cohorts receiving group therapy. Their findings indicated that 78.5% of the juveniles screened prior to group enrollment met criteria for PTSD and that CBT-treated groups showed a greater reduction in symptoms than comparison groups. In the study, those juveniles exposed only to trauma related to gang and community violence had higher levels of PTSD; however, they responded to treatment better than those who had also experienced childhood physical and/or sexual abuse.

Positive youth development strategies and PTSD treatment

It is commendable that effective trauma treatments for youths are becoming more widely available. However, there are several limitations concerning their use in juvenile justice settings. First, mental health professionals need knowledge and skills in both trauma psychology and CBT in order to competently provide these services. These therapy skills are complex and may not have been included in current professionals' graduate school training. Fortunately, training opportunities are available through workshops at the bi-annual confer-ence of the European Society for Traumatic Stress Studies, as well as the annual meetings of the International Society for Traumatic Stress Studies. In addi-tion, didactic training in trauma-focused cognitive-behavioral skills for youth is available through the NCTSN website (www.nctsn.org).

Another significant limitation to these treatments is that the rehabilitation needs of many juvenile offenders go well beyond a narrow focus on reducing trauma-related symptoms. It is also important for treatment efforts to include broader therapeutic needs for making meaning of the challenges and adver-sities in their lives and establishing hopeful expectations and plans for their futures.

More recent attention to resilience among youth may help augment earlier perspectives on the relationship of trauma exposure and delinquency. Contri-butions from the specialty areas of post-traumatic growth and positive youth development are important. They represent potential resources for identifying and supporting those developmental processes that restore or sustain a positive developmental trajectory for youth in adverse environments.

Resilience and thriving are common descriptions used to identify the adapt-ability of youth to adverse demands in their personal and social environment. Increasingly, the capacity for resilience is understood as an "ordinary" human process (Bonanno, 2004; Masten, 2001). Further, a person's ability to endure and respond positively to a traumatic event describes "Post-Traumatic Growth" (Tedeschi & Calhoun, 2004). While the actual nature of the stimulus for this growth has been questioned (Aldwin & Levenson, 2004), there is general recognition in the broader developmental literature that positive developmen-tal trajectories in youth are indicative of children whose lives are characterized by a higher level of functioning following developmental challenges or event(s) (Carver, 1998).

Interventions that promote growth and thriving among delinquents exposed to community violence need to accentuate protective factors to buffer the neg-ative effects of exposure to traumatic and other developmental risk factors. Fostering these *protective factors* could moderate the adverse effects of harsh developmental conditions. Various models have been proposed that describe the social ecology of resilience and the influence that these protective effects demonstrate in reducing the likelihood of negative behavior following risk exposure (e.g., Jessor et al., 1995; Resnick et al., 1997; Stouthamer-Loeber et al., 2002). Similarly, these protective factors also represent developmental resources associated with positive development in all youths (Benson et al., 1998). The focus on protective factors and developmental resources bolsters intervention strategies by including both reduction of risk and promotion of health among delinquent youths. The goal is to reduce risk for further negative developmental outcomes after release from incarceration. Promoting the re-sources necessary for the development of personal meaning and positive future orientation are key elements of this approach.

Garbarino (2001) posits that youth responses to adversity can take one of two forms. For some it can lead to hopelessness, despair or violence; for others, this adversity becomes a key aspect in the development of personal meaning. Meaning is often constructed as a part of a personal narrative or life story, which begins to unfold in mid- to late adolescence (Habermas & Bluck, 2000), as youths engage in autobiographical reasoning to integrate their sense of the present in the context of a past and future. The development of a hopeful future orientation partially depends upon realistic self-reappraisals in relation to difficulties in the past and present.

Studies on juvenile offenders demonstrate a relationship between their negative behavior and personal beliefs about their future. When delinquent youths are asked to talk about their future, the descriptions are often characterized by their fears about their future (Trommsdorff & Lamm, 1980). They also may express uncertainty and limited expectations about career and educational aspirations (Sutherland & Shepherd, 2001). Importantly, youth in at-risk populations who had future plans were less likely to engage in problem behaviors (Quinton et al., 1993). In another study, youths who possessed more positive orientations to the future demonstrated higher levels of academic performance and social functioning (Peetsma, 2000). Accordingly, an integrated treatment approach for incarcerated youths needs to emphasize these positive youth developmental resources to increase the likelihood for successful return to the community upon release.

Conclusion and future directions

Currently, it is clear that there are strong associations between violence exposure, PTSD, and delinquency. "Cycles of violence" explanations are empirically supported by many studies showing that, indeed, "violence begets violence." Child victims are more likely to be adolescent perpetrators, and recent studies have highlighted that PTSD is linked to more severe violent behaviors among male offenders. How the presence of PTSD symptoms may mediate the relationship between earlier violence exposure and violent behavior among delinquents has not yet been elucidated. It may be that some PTSD-related symptoms (e.g., hyperarousal, fear of trauma reminders or recurrence, hypervigilance, and mistrust) make violent responses more likely. Indirect effects of PTSD could include increased risk for engaging in violence-related activities such as weapon-carrying gang involvement, and alcohol or drug abuse. Effective trauma-focused treatments are available for adolescent trauma survivors, and there are accessible means to provide the necessary knowledge and skills for professionals to use them with delinquents. We believe that rehabilitation efforts for juvenile offenders will be improved by integrating trauma-focused cognitive-behavioral treatment and positive youth development concepts. For example, the key PYD element of engaging community resources can be used to increase a personal sense of meaning and a hopeful future. Finally, future research should take into consideration methodological limitations of current studies. Given the high prevalence of trauma exposure and PTSD in juvenile justice populations, systematic assessment of offenders' trauma histories and PTSD diagnostic screening are needed to set the stage for improving rehabilitation services and lowering recidivism for delinquents.

References

Abram, K. M., Teplin, L. A., Charles, D. R. et al. (2004). Posttraumatic stress disorder and trauma in youth in juvenile detention. *Archives of General Psychiatry, 61*, 403–10.

Abram, K. M., Washburn, J. J., Teplin, L. A. et al. (2007). Posttraumatic stress disorder and psychiatric comorbidity among detained youths. *Psychiatric Services, 58*, 1311–16.

Aldwin, C. M., & Levenson, M. R. (2004). Posttraumatic growth: A developmental perspective. *Psychological Inquiry, 15*, 19–21.

Allen, J. P., Leadbeater, B. J., & Aber, J. L. (1990). The relationship of adolescents' expectations and values to delinquency, hard drug use, and unprotected sexual intercourse. *Development and Psychopathology, 2*, 85–98.

Baldry, A. C. (2007). "It does affect me": Disruptive behaviors in preadolescents directly and indirectly abused at home. *European Psychologist, 12*(1), 29–35.

Ball, J., Jurkovic, G., Barber, N. et al. (2007). Relation of community violence exposure to psychological distress in incarcerated male adolescents: Moderating role of caregiver-adult support and control. *Journal of Aggression, Maltreatment & Trauma, 15*(2), 79–95.

Barton, W. H., & Butts, J. A. (2008). *Building on strength: Positive youth development in juvenile justice programs.* Chicago, IL: Chapin Hall Center for Children, University of Chicago.

Benson, P. L., & Pittman, K. J. (2001). *Trends in youth development.* New York: Springer.

Benson, P. L., Leffert, N., Scales, P., & Blyth, D. A. (1998). Beyond the "village" rhetoric: Creating healthy communities for children and adolescents. *Applied Developmental Science, 2*, 138–59.

Bonnano, G. A. (2004). Loss, trauma, and human resilience. *American Psychologist, 59*, 20–8.

Brown, B. (2004). Juveniles and weapons: Recent research, conceptual considerations, and programmatic interventions. *Youth Violence and Juvenile Justice, 2*, 163–84.

Burton, D., Foy, D., Bwanausi, C., Johnson, J., & Moore, L. (1994). The relationship between traumatic exposure, family dysfunction, and Posttraumatic Stress Symptoms in male juvenile offenders. *Journal of Traumatic Stress, 7*(1), 83–93.

Carver, C. S. (1998). Resilience and thriving: Issues, models, and linkages. *Journal of Social Issues, 54*, 45–266.

Cohen, J. A., Berliner, L., & March, J. S. (2000). Treatment of children and adults. In E. Foa, T. Keane, & M. Friedman (Eds.), *Effective Treatments for PTSD* (pp. 106–38). New York: Guilford Press.

Coie, J. D., Terry, R., Lenox, K., Lochman, J., & Hyman, C. (1995). Childhood peer rejection and aggression as predictors of stable patterns of adolescent disorder. *Development and Psychopathology, 7*, 697–713.

Connell, J. P., Halpern-Felsher, B. L., Clifford, E., & Crichlow, W. (1995). Hanging in there: Behavioral, psychological, and contextual factors affecting whether African-American adolescents stay in high school. *Journal of Adolescent Research, 10*, 41–63.

Damon, W. (2004). What is positive youth development? *The Annals of the American Academy of Political and Social Science, 591*, 13–24.

DiLalla, L. F., & Gottesman, I. I. (1991). Biological and genetic contributors to violence – Widom's untold tale. *Psychological Bulletin, 1*, 125–29.

Eccles, J., & Gootman, J. A. (Eds.) (2002). *Community programs to promote youth development.* Washington, DC: National Academy Press.

Erwin, B. A., Newman, E., McMackin, R. A., Morrissey, C., & Kaloupek, D. G. (2000). PTSD, malevolent environment, and criminality among criminally involved male adolescents. *Criminal Justice and Behavior, 27*(2), 196–215.

Evans, C., Ehlers, A., Mezey, G., & Clark, D. M. (2007). Intrusive memories and ruminations related to violent crime among young offenders: Phenomenological characteristics. *Journal of Traumatic Stress, 20*(2), 183–96.

Farrington, D. P. (2000). Explaining and preventing crime: The globalization of knowledge. The American Society of Criminology 1999 presidential address. *Criminology, 38*, 1–24.

Freitas, A. L., & Downey, G. (1998). Resilience: A dynamic perspective. *International Journal of Behavioral Development, 22*, 263–85.

Garbarino, J. (2001). An ecological perspective on the effects of violence on children. *Journal of Community Psychology, 29*, 361–78.

Habermas, T., & Bluck, S. (2000). Getting a life. The emergence of the life story in adolescence. *Psychological Bulletin, 126*, 748–69.

Hann, D. M., & Borek, N. T. (Eds.) (2001). *NIMH taking stock of risk factors for child/youth externalizing behavior problems.* Washington, DC: US Government Printing Office.

Jessor, R., Van Den Bos, J., Vanderryn, J., Costa, F. M., & Turba, M. S. (1995). Protective factors in adolescent problem behavior: Moderator effects and developmental change. *Developmental Psychology, 31*, 923–33.

Kilpatrick, D. G. (2006). Common risk factors for different forms of violence: Findings from the National Survey of Adolescents. Paper presented at annual convention of the American Psychological Association, New Orleans, August.

Larson, R. W. (2000). Toward a psychology of positive youth development. *American Psychologist, 55*, 170–83.

Lerner, R. M., Dowling, E. M., & Anderson, P. M. (2003). Positive youth development: Thriving as the basis of personhood and civil society. *Applied Developmental Science, 7*, 172–80.

Lerner, R. M., & Galambos, N. L. (1998). Adolescent development: Challenges and opportunities for research, programs, and policies. *Annual Review of Psychology, 49*, 413–46.

Leventhal, T., & Brooks-Gunn, J. (2000). The neighborhoods they live in: The effects of neighborhood residence on child and adolescent outcomes. *Psychological Bulletin, 126*, 209–337.

Maschi, T., Bradley, C. A., & Morgen, K. (2008). Unraveling the link between trauma and delinquency: The mediating role of negative affect and delinquent peer exposure. *Youth Violence and Juvenile Justice, 6*(2), 136–57.

Masten, A. S. (2001). Ordinary magic: Resilience processes in development. *American Psychologist, 56*, 227–38.

Moffitt, T. E., Caspi, A., Harrington, H., & Milne, B. J. (2002). Males on the life-course-persistent and adolescence-limited antisocial pathways: Follow-up at age 26 years. *Developmental Psychopathology, 14*(1), 179–207.

Office of the Surgeon General (2001). *Youth violence: A report of the Surgeon General.* Washington, DC: US Department of Health and Human Services.

Ovaert, L. B., Cashel, M. L., & Sewell, K. W. (2003). Structured group therapy for posttraumatic stress disorder in incarcerated male juveniles. *American Journal of Orthopsychiatry, 73*(3), 294–301.

Ozer, E. J., & Weinstein, R. S. (2004). Urban adolescents' exposure to community violence: The role of support, school safety, and social constraints in a school-based sample of boys and girls. *Journal of Clinical Child and Adolescent Psychology, 33*, 463–76.

Patterson, G. R., Forgatch, M. S., Yoerger, K. L., & Stoolmiller, M. (1998). Variables that initiate and maintain an early-onset trajectory for juvenile offending. *Development and Psychopathology, 10*, 531–47.

Peetsma, T. (2000). Future time perspective as a predictor of school investment. *Scandinavian Journal of Educational Research, 44*, 177–92.

Quinton, D., Pickels, A., Maughan, B., & Rutter, M. (1993). Partners, peers, and pathways: Assortative pairing and continuities in conduct disorder. *Development and Psychopathology, 5*, 763–83.

Resnick, M. D., Bearman, P. S., Blum, R. W. et al. (1997). Protecting adolescents from harm: Findings from the National Longitudinal Study on Adolescent Health. *Journal of the American Medical Association, 278*, 823–32.

Richards, M. H., Larson, R., Miller, B. V. et al. (2004). Risky and protective contexts and exposure to violence in urban African-American young adolescents. *Journal of Clinical Child and Adolescent Psychology, 33*, 138–48.

Ruchkin, V. V., Schwab-Stone, M .E., Koposov, R. A., Vermeiren, R., & Steiner, H. (2002). Violence exposure, posttraumatic stress, and personality in juvenile delinquents. *Journal of the American Academy of Child and Adolescent Psychiatry, 41*(3), 322–9.

Scales, P. C., Benson, P., Leffert, N., & Blyth, S. (2000). Contribution of developmental assets to the prediction of thriving among adolescents. *Applied Developmental Science, 4*, 27–46.

Seginer, R. (2008). Future orientation in times of threat and challenge: How resilient adolescents construct their future. *International Journal of Behavioral Development, 32*, 272–82.

Siegfried, C. B., Ko, S. J., & Kelley, A. (2004). *Victimization and juvenile offending.* Los Angeles: National Child Traumatic Stress Network.

Smith, C., & Thornberry, T. P. (1995). The relationship between childhood maltreatment and adolescent involvement in delinquency. *Criminology 33*, 451–81.

Stiffman, A. R., Dore, P., & Cunningham, R. M. (1996). Violent behavior in adolescents and young adults: A person and environment model. *Journal of Child and Family Studies, 5*, 487–501.

Stouthamer-Loeber, M., Loeber, R., Wei, W., Farrington, D. P., & Wikstrom, P. H. (2002). Risk and promotive effects in the explanation of persistent serious delinquency in boys. *Journal of Consulting and Clinical Psychology*, *70*, 111–23.

Sutherland, I., & Shepherd, J. P. (2001). Social dimensions of adolescent substance use. *Addiction*, *96*, 445–58.

Tedeschi, R. G., & Calhoun, L. G. (2004). Target article: Posttraumatic growth: Conceptual foundations and empirical evidence. *Psychological Inquiry*, *15*, 118.

Thornberry, T. P. (1998). Membership in youth gangs and involvement in serious and violent offending. In R. Loeber & D. Farrington (Eds.), *Serious and violent juvenile offenders: Risk factors and successful interventions* (pp. 147–66). Thousand Oaks, CA: Sage Publications.

Tolan, P. H., Gorman Smith, D., & Henry, D. B. (2003). The developmental ecology of urban males' youth violence. *Developmental Psychology*, *39*, 274–291.

Trommsdorff, G., & Lamm, H. (1980). Future orientation of institutionalized and noninstitutionalied delinquents and nondelinquents. *Journal of Social Psychology*, *10*, 247–78.

Vermeiren, R. (2003). Psychopathology and delinquency in adolescents: A descriptive and developmental perspective. *Clinical Psychology Review*, *23*, 277–318.

Weisz, J. R., Sandler, I. N., Durlak, J. A., & Anton, B. S. (2005). Promoting and protecting youth mental health through evidence-based prevention and treatment. *American Psychologist*, *66*, 628–48.

Widom, C. S., & Maxfield, M. G. (2001). An update on the "cycle of violence." *National Institute of Justice: Research in Brief*. Washington, DC: US Department of Justice, National Institute of Justice, February, 2001 NCJ 184894.

Wikstrom, P. O., & Loeber, R. (2000). Do disadvantaged neighborhoods cause well-adjusted children to become adolescent delinquents? *Criminology*, *38*, 1109–42.

Wood, J. L., Foy, D. W., Layne, C. M., Pynoos, R. S., & James, C. B. (2002). An examination of the relationships between violence exposure, posttraumatic stress symptomatology, and delinquent activity: an "ecopathological" model of delinquent behavior among incarcerated adolescents. *Journal of Aggression, Maltreatment and Trauma*, *6*(1), 127–47.

Yashinaga, C., Kadomoto, I., Otani, T., Sasaki, T., & Kato, N. (2004). Prevalence of post-traumatic stress disorder in incarcerated juvenile delinquents in Japan. *Psychiatry Clinical Neuroscience*, *58*(4), 383–38.

Chapter Eleven

Post-Traumatic Stress in Antisocial Youth: A Multifaceted Reality

Vittoria Ardino

Introduction

Antisocial youth very often live in a milieu of risk where social exclusion and early traumatization are central features of their developmental trajectories. Research undertaken to investigate possible interconnections between trauma and criminal behavior shows a clear interaction between psychopathological outcomes and antisocial tendency (Abram et al., 2004; Cauffman et al., 1998; see also Foy and colleagues, Chapter 10, for a review).

In 1935, Aichhorn highlighted for the first time that trauma contributes to developmental disruptions across the lifespan. Twenty years later, Minuchin and Guerny (1967) emphasized that "a multitude of children in institutions, and urban ghettos, share thinking, coping, communicative, and behavioral styles that can be traced back to the family where they were born" (p. 193). In 1989, Widom and colleagues conducted a pioneering study on 900 children abused before age 11. The authors outlined more clearly the interaction between early trauma and antisocial conduct, reporting that such children are more at risk of arrest in adolescence (Maxfield & Widom, 1996). Nowadays, the work of Widom and colleagues is supported by a series of new studies that further demonstrate how antisocial adolescents who enter a criminal career very often have a history of serious victimization, and this history is often part of an intergenerational story of violence (Erwin et al., 2000; McGruder-Johnson et al., 2000; Scarpa, 2001).

Research on the impact of traumatic events has demonstrated that traumatic exposures seriously affect adolescents' functioning (Erwin et al., 2000; McGruder-Johnson, et al., 2000); their behavior, emotions, and cognition

Post-Traumatic Syndromes in Childhood and Adolescence: A Handbook of Research and Practice, First Edition.
Edited by Vittoria Ardino. © 2011 John Wiley & Sons, Ltd. Published 2011 by John Wiley & Sons, Ltd.

are altogether negatively redefined by post-traumatic poor self-regulation and information-processing. Briere (2002) defined *emotion regulation* as "the capacity of individuals to control and tolerate intense negative emotions without avoidance behaviors, such as dissociation, substance misuse or other behaviors to reduce tension" (p. 180). Likewise, van der Kolk and Fisler (1994) contend that one of the most undermining effects of early victimization is the inability to manage intense emotions and control impulses. The lack of such a socioaffective repertoire may result in antisocial behaviors, such as aggression, substance abuse, and criminal behavior (Lynam et al., 2000; White et al., 1994).

Thus, if adolescent victims of trauma often engage in antisocial behavior, trauma and criminal behavior may share a similar developmental platform, which could benefit from an integrated theoretical understanding linking the developmental criminology framework and psychotraumatology.

Following on from Foy and colleagues in the previous chapter, which highlighted the state-of-the-art in this area and a prevention model for traumatized youths with antisocial behavior, this chapter explores the connections between antisociality and developmental victimization in at-risk adolescents with a focus upon post-traumatic reactions and specific self-regulatory mechanisms that facilitate these interconnections.

Trauma and criminal behavior in adolescence: open questions

Several studies have demonstrated that PTSD reaches higher rates in adolescents in the criminal justice system than in other samples of traumatized youths (Burton et al., 1994; Steiner, Garcia, & Matthews, 1997; Vermeier, 2003), highlighting that children exposed to intrafamilial and community violence are at greater risk of conduct disorders (Briggs-Gowan et al., 2003; Kolko, Moser, & Weldy, 1990). More specifically, criminal youths are often exposed to traumatic events as a result of living in difficult social environments (Garbarino, 2001); being a victim of abuse or witnessing violence are both risk factors for the development of PTSD and criminal behavior (Dziuba-Leatherman & Finkelhor, 1994).

Therefore, it can be argued that the link between trauma and violent behaviors is supported by empirical work; however, there are many questions left unexplored and a lack of an integrated theoretical model which brings together neurobiology, cognition, and behavior involved in both traumatic exposure and antisociality. In particular, more work is needed to explain how PTSD specifically contributes to the passage from a conduct disorder in preadolescence to antisocial conduct in adolescence and, in turn, to criminal behavior in early adulthood and adulthood. Secondly, it is not clear in what ways trauma and

PTSD impact on impulsivity and affect regulation mechanisms that may also be responsible for criminal behavior.

Neurobiological mechanisms

Prolonged traumatic exposures interfere with neurobiological development (see MacDonald, Vasterling, and Rasmusson, Chapter 6, on this topic) and with the ability to integrate sensorial, emotive, and cognitive information into a coherent frame (Ford, 2002). Neurobiological deficits characterizing traumatized youth are also a common trait in antisocial behavior. This implies that trauma and criminal behavior may share crucial aspects of neurobiological dysfunctioning.

The crystallization of internal states' regulation is central to PTSD. Dramatic, rapid, unpredictable or threatening changes in the environment activate "stress-response" systems. These brain-mediated responses employ a set of central and peripheral nervous system, neuroendocrine, and immune responses that promote adaptive "survival" functions, and, later, a return to equilibrium or homeostatic patterns. Events that disrupt homeostasis are, by definition, stressful. If this stress is severe, unpredictable, prolonged or chronic, the compensatory mechanisms can become overactivated, or fatigued and incapable of restoring the previous state of equilibrium or homeostasis. Trauma negatively impacts on the physiological regulation of stress in the hypothalamic-pituitary-adrenal axis (HPA), a physiological feedback loop including the hypothalamus, pituitary gland, and hyphysis (for a review of how HPA is affected by PTSD, see MacDonald and colleagues, Chapter 6). Activated hormones are corticotrophin factor (CRF), arginine (AVP), and adrenocorticotrophin factor (ACTH). The cycle is completed when cortisol negatively feeds back to the hypothalamus and hyphysis. Cortisol-releasing factor determines an increase of glucose in the blood and immune system resulting in a blockage of immunotransmitters. The HPA axis plays a crucial role in monitoring and controlling stress responses (Yehuda et al., 1995a, b), demonstrating that some stressors increase glucocorticoids in the blood (Sapolsky et al., 1997) and, in turn, cause an increase of cortisol in the system (Coplan et al., 1996; Ladd et al., 1996; Levine, 1994; Plotsky & Meaney, 1993; Smith & Vale, 2006; Takahashi, Palmer, & Gage, 1998). Other studies produced opposite, results showing a decrease of cortisol and consequent ability to cope with stress (Severs & Daniels-Severs, 1973; Young & Akil, 1985).

For this reason, traumatized children are unable to learn how to plan their behaviors in such a way as to adapt to the environment because their early attachment experiences mold their growing brain based on extreme reactions. In turn, extreme reactions can result in dissociative states and aggressive behaviors "switching" from a fear stimuli to a "fight-or-flight or freezing" response even in the absence of real danger (Henry & Moffitt, 1997). Chronic and early victimization could be considered as a type III trauma, an extreme manifestation of multiple traumatic experiences that are perceived as a continuous and serious threat (Solomon & Heide, 1999). Changes in the brain influence emotion, cognition, and social functioning, such as emotion regulation, interaction with others, and empathy (Lipschitz, Morgan, & Southwick, 2002; Moffitt & Silva, 1988). Victims of type III trauma respond to environmental stimuli mostly using the limbic areas of the brain preventing a higher cortex elaboration which is responsible for cognitive information-processing of the experience. Such primitive functioning leads to a myriad of impulse dyscontrol and anger-related problems (Heide & Solomon, 2006) are also based on neurobiological deficits responsible for maintaining an excess of cortisol in the hippocampus area of the brain (Makino et al., 1995a, b; Sapolsky, Krey, & McEwen, 1984; Smith & Vale, 2006) and a related deficit of the neurogenesis (Duman et al., 1997; Gould et al., 1998; Nibuya, Morinobu, & Duman, 1995; Smith et al., 1995).

Psychophysiology and attachment

The chronic inability to modulate emotions, behaviors, and impulses leads to a variety of psychosocial problems, including aggression against the self and others (van der Kolk & Fisler, 1994). Secure attachment with a primary caregiver is critical if children are to learn self-control. Attachment and nurturing behaviors (eye contact, reciprocal smiling, holding, rocking, touching) help to maintain the infant's homeostatic balance both emotionally and physically (Hofer, 1995; van der Kolk, 1996). This is a process that caregivers and babies accomplish together. This mutual regulatory process breaks down under conditions of anxious and disrupted attachment. Depressed, substance-abusing, or otherwise neglectful and abusive caregivers are not attuned to their infant's emotions and needs, leaving the baby without the necessary regulatory support (Robinson & Glaves, 1996). The first 33 months (fetal stage and first two years) is the time of most rapid brain growth; the period when the quality of the caregiving environment profoundly affects the structure and function of the developing brain. Trauma affects the young at many levels of biological functioning. Threats to the infant and young child that are of sufficient intensity, duration, or frequency, such as abuse, neglect, and anxious-disorganized attachment, trigger an alarm reaction ("fight-or-flight, freeze"). This instinctual reaction to real or perceived danger is a normal response to acute stress. Traumatic experiences during infancy and childhood, however, can trigger prolonged alarm reactions, which alter the neurobiology of the brain and central nervous system. Lack of secure attachment and exposure to traumatic stress alter the nervous system, predisposing the child to be impulsive, overreactive, and violent behaviors (Perry, 1994 1996). These children often develop symptoms of Post-Traumatic Stress Disorder, including: (1) recurring intrusive recollections, such as dreams or flashbacks; (2)

persistent avoidance of stimuli associated with the trauma and numbing of general responsiveness; and (3) hyperarousal, such as hypervigilance, startle response, sleep difficulties, irritability, anxiety, and hyperactivity (Perry, 1994).

The limbic system is the part of the brain that controls emotion, impulses, and maternal functions. The cortex is involved in higher mental functions, such as logic and planning. The orbitofrontal cortex connects these two parts of the brain and is a key area that is crucial to both attachment and emotional regulation. The orbitofrontal cortex blends input from the environment with visceral signals from inside the body and is especially sensitive to facial expressions (e.g., mother's smile). Compromised attachment, resulting from abusive and/or unresponsive caregiving, can inhibit the proper development of this brain system – the result of which is often impulsivity and violence (Schore, 1994, 1996).

Children with maltreatment-related PTSD also demonstrated significant deficits within the domains of attention and abstract reasoning/executive function when compared with sociodemographically similar healthy children who had not been maltreated. The children with PTSD were more susceptible to distraction and demonstrated greater impulsivity, making more errors on a task of sustained attention. Children with PTSD also demonstrated deficits on two tests designed to measure frontal lobe function. Neuroimaging studies indicate that PTSD in children is associated with diffuse CNS effects (i.e., smaller cerebral volumes and corpus callosum areas) but no anatomical changes in limbic structures. Functional imaging procedures indicate that medial prefrontal cortical dysfunction may be associated with both adult and pediatric PTSD. The neuropsychological consequences of PTSD-related brain alterations are also of central importance to further understanding the relationship between trauma and criminal behavior. In fact, the importance of recognizing PTSD in offenders is underscored by personality assessment showing the negative effect of PTSD on impulsivity, aggression, and negative emotions (e.g., anxiety and depression; Cauffman et al., 1998; Steiner et al., 1997). Later affect dysregulation and impulse dyscontrol difficulties are not only shown to have stemmed from childhood or adolescent disruptive experiences, but self-regulation problems have also consistently been found to be related to reoffending risk (Andrews & Bonta, 1998; Friendship & Thornton, 2002; Grann & Wedin, 2002). Such experiences may lead to both risky behaviors and to an increased risk of exposure to traumatic events and to subsequent PTSD. Very often, PTSD may prompt individuals to engage in greater risk-taking behavior to seek out dangerous and sensational situations as part of a compulsive need for reexposure to trauma (Joseph et al., 1997; see later in this chapter). The antisocial acting-out of unresolved childhood trauma is a consistent feature in the behavior of criminals and may also find an explanation in criminology theories. In particular, children's and adolescents' aggressive and antisocial behaviors are often paired with a deficit of activity in the HPA axis (Loeber el al., 2000; Raine, 1993, 2002; van Goozen et al., 2000) with low basal levels of arousal.

According to the "fearlessness" theory (Raine, 1993; Raine et al., 1998), low levels of arousal are markers for low levels of fear. Lack of fear would predispose to antisocial and violent behavior because such behavior (e.g., fights and assaults) requires a degree of fearlessness to execute, whereas lack of fear, especially in childhood, would help explain poor socialization because low fear of punishment would reduce the effectiveness of conditioning. Fearlessness theory receives support from the fact that autonomic underarousal also provides the underpinning for a fearless or uninhibited temperament in infancy and childhood (Fowles, Kochanska, & Murray, 2000; Scarpa et al., 1997).

A second theory explaining reduced arousal is stimulation-seeking theory (Eysenck, 1977; Quay, 1965; Raine, 1993; Raine et al., 1998). This theory argues that low arousal represents an unpleasant physiological state, and that antisocial individuals seek stimulation in order to increase their arousal levels to an optimal or normal level. Antisocial behavior is thus viewed as a form of stimulation-seeking in that committing a burglary, assault, or robbery could be stimulating for some individuals. Stimulation-seeking and fearlessness theories may be complementary perspectives in that a low level of arousal may predispose to crime because it produces some degree of fearlessness, and also because it encourages antisocial stimulation-seeking. Indeed, behavioral measures of stimulation-seeking and fearlessness, both taken at age three in a large sample, predict aggressive behavior at age 11 (Raine et al., 1998).

Research on links between hormones and antisocial, aggressive behavior illustrates the complexities of biology–behavior relationships, and clearly demonstrates the influence of the social context on biological functioning. Despite the clear evidence that contextual and environmental influences alter both testosterone and cortisol levels, a few researchers have tested for biosocial interactions between chronic traumatization and antisocial behavior. Further studies are needed to investigate whether low arousal as explained by criminological theories could be the result of early traumatization or PTSD symptoms that, as stated earlier, shape psychophysiology of youths in such a way as to increase their proneness to antisocial behavior.

Trauma reenactment and antisocial behavior

A trauma experienced as the result of abuse or neglect, inflicted by a primary caregiver, which disrupts the normal development of secure attachment may lead to the disorganization of attachment (Carlson & Sroufe, 1995; Lyons-Ruth & Jacobvitz, 1999; Main & Hesse, 1990; Solomon & George, 1999), which is associated with a number of developmental problems, including dissociative symptoms (Carlson & Kashani, 1988), as well as depressive, anxiety, and acting-out symptoms (Lyons-Ruth, 1996; Lyons-Ruth, Alpern, & Repacholi, 1993). Acting-out symptoms may explain why many children with histories of maltreatment are violent (Robins, 1978) and aggressive (Prino & Peyrot,

1994) and as adults are at risk of developing a variety of psychological problems (Schreiber & Lyddon, 1998) and personality disorders, including antisocial personality disorder (Finzi et al., 2000).

The relation between violence exposure and the perpetration of violence and aggression against others has been documented in several studies (Bell & Jenkins, 1991; Burton et al., 1994; Farrell & Bruce, 1997; Flannery, Singer & Wester, 2001; Flannery et al., 1998; Jenkins & Bell, 1994; Lipschitz et al., 2000; Pelcovitz et al., 1994; Widom, 1989; Williamson, Borduin, & Howe, 1991) as discussed by Foy and colleagues in Chapter 10 of this volume.

After having been traumatized multiple times, the imprint of the trauma becomes lodged in many aspects of the child's make-up. This is manifested in numerous ways: for example, as fearful reactions, aggressive and sexual acting-out, avoidance, and uncontrolled emotional reactions. Unless this tendency to repeat the trauma is recognized, the response of the environment is likely to be a replay of the original traumatizing, abusive, but familiar, relationships. Because these children are prone to experience anything novel, including rules and other protective interventions, as punishments, they tend to regard their teachers and therapists who try to establish safety as perpetrators.

Tyson and Goodman (1996) define "reenactment" as "the unconscious re-experiencing and behavioral recreating of past events in the current therapy setting and in the person's daily life" (p. 536). These disruptions in awareness and self-regulation come on suddenly and unpredictably in any social setting. Awareness of the feelings of terror, helplessness, betrayal, and pain often returns in uncontrolled bursts of reenactments, nightmares, and flashbacks, only to be blocked off again as the traumatized person returns to a frozen state of affectless numbness. Post-Traumatic stress reactions have been conceptualized as alternating phases of increased arousal (e.g., anxiety) and "emotional numbing and constriction of ideas" (Horowitz, 1993, p. 49). Such emotional dysregulation might play a very important role in the relationship between violence exposure and violent behaviors. Specifically, the emotional disengagement and hyper-arousal associated with PTSD might partially mediate the relation between trauma exposure and violent behavior in youth. The roles of emotional numbing and arousal might be particularly salient in the violence exposure–behavior relationship. Conceptually, the emotional disengagement and hyperarousal often seen with PTSD might be associated with a lack of empathy and inability to control impulses seen in many conduct-disordered youth. Although the possible mediational roles of numbing and arousal have not been tested directly, emotional detachment has been linked to violent crimes (Steiner et al., 1997), and a previous examination of children exposed to war has shown a moderate positive association between arousal symptoms and aggression (Allwood, Bell-Dolan, & Husain, 2000). In addition, Ruchkin and colleagues (2002) found that in a sample of 370 incarcerated Russian youths, trauma symptoms partially mediated the relationship between violence exposure (as witness or victim) and self-reported delinquent and aggressive behaviors as measured by the Youth Self-Report (Achenbach, 1991). However, Farrell and Bruce (1997) found that post-trauma distress did not mediate the relationship between violence exposure-violent behavior as measured on three occasions. Of note, Farrell and Bruce's study of primarily low-income African-American youth had several methodological shortcomings: (1) distress was measured by six items Youth Violence Exposure and Response of general anxiety and depression (e.g., "I worry too much about things that aren't important"); and (2) violent behavior was measured by the presence and frequency of only four behaviors within a 30-day period (e.g., "been in a fight in which someone was hit," "threatened to hurt a teacher"). The limited conceptualization of post-trauma distress and post-trauma violence in the latter study might account for the null finding. Therefore, the specific role of PTSD symptoms in the violence exposure–violent behavior link requires further study.

Although the exact mechanisms involved in post-trauma cognitive biases are unknown, Schachter's two-factor theory may provide some links. Schachter's theory posits that under ambiguous circumstances, physiological arousal can be experienced as either anger or euphoria (as cited in Bandura, 1986). In addition, youth anxiety has been associated with hostile attributions of ambiguous situations (Bell-Dolan, 1995). Conceptually, for youths with a history of violence exposure, the arousal symptoms that are common to PTSD might be interpreted as anger brought on by provocation. Thus, PTSD symptoms might have a direct relationship with aggressive cognitive biases, which in turn might be linked to post-trauma aggressive behaviors. Indeed, using a stepwise regression analysis, Lehmann (1997) demonstrated that adding negative attributions after the trauma exposure predictors accounted for an additional 54% of the variance between violence exposure and trauma response.

The role of aggressive cognitions

Early victimization paves the way to impulsive and attention-seeking behaviors. Traumatized children are restless, irritable, have a short attention span, demand instant gratification, and have little frustration tolerance by the preschool years. By age five, they are angry, oppositional, and show lack of enthusiasm for learning. Their inability to control impulses and emotions leads to aggressive acting-out and lack of enduring relationships.

Such children are also prone to develop beliefs about themselves, relationships, and life in general, based on the nature of early victimization which will affect how the child interprets events, stores information in memory, and perceives social situations. Therefore, they miss the internalization of important prosocial values, attitudes, and behaviors that are usually learned in the context of secure attachment relationships via four psychological processes:

(1) *Modeling* by parents or other attachment figures, (2) *internalizing* the values and behavior of parents or other attachment figures, (3) experiencing

synchronicity and *reciprocity* in early attachment relationships, and (4) developing a positive *sense of self*. When the family and the community do not promote secure attachment and appropriate socialization experiences but promote prolonged exposure to violence, the child is at risk for developing not only conduct disorders, but also a more pervasive lack of morality. Empathic parents rear empathic children. Children with compromised and disrupted attachments lack the models of empathy and compassion and tend to be cruel, controlling, and selfish. They have internalized antisocial values and standards, such as sadistic power, dishonesty, selfishness, and aggressive control. Their inner voice does not include a conscience or feelings of remorse. Lacking a secure foundation, a weak and negative self-identity has been created, and the child assumes a fearful and punitive orientation. There is no room for empathy or caring as the child must survive in a world perceived as lonely and threatening (Zahn-Waxler et al., 1992). This constellation of risk factors may predispose children and adolescents to adopt chronic forms of traumatic processing that involve a failure to prevent trauma reminders from constantly activating memory representations and bringing them into consciousness. This outcome can be linked to overaccommodation, in which the person reacts to the trauma by labeling a wide variety of innocuous situations as potentially threatening, unpredictable, or unfair. Alternatively, the person may label themselves as weak, bad, or inadequate. This form of catastrophic interference can have a number of adverse effects. One is to vastly increase the number of cues that will potentially elicit cognitions related to the trauma, thereby inducing a constant sense of current threat (Brewin, 2000; Ehlers & Clark, 2000). Another adverse effect may be to generate secondary emotions such as anger and guilt, which in turn increase the aversiveness of flashbacks and prompt ruminative responses. Ruminations include evaluative thoughts that assign blame and elaborative thoughts involving feared or worst-outcome scenarios (Merckelbach et al., 1998; Reynolds & Brewin, 1998). These responses are associated with a poor outcome (Ehlers, Mayou, & Bryant, 1998) and further investigations are needed to better understand how such cognitions may bridge trauma and criminal behavior in antisocial youths. One possibility is that flashbacks, ordinary memories, and ruminations provide cues that trigger each other, maintaining the urge to act to "switch off" such disturbing thoughts. The high degree of accessibility of thoughts and vivid memories is in turn likely to increase the estimated probability of such traumatic events occurring again (MacLeod & Campbell, 1992), thus maintaining the sense of threat (Borkovec & Lyonfields, 1993). Alternatively, the emotions generated by these appraisals may use up resources shared with inhibitory mechanisms and interfere with their effectiveness.

Prematurely inhibited processing may be linked to the counterpart of catastrophic interference leading to a conscious construction and rehearsal of a restricted, minimized, and likely distorted version of the traumatic event. One effect of selectively rehearsing a partial and distorted version of events may be to limit the number of weak trauma cues that are likely to accidentally activate trauma memories.

Current cognitive developmental models may integrate clinical under-standing of the trauma role in the genesis of criminal behavior. Such theories suggest that exposure to violence may alter cognitive processes in two ways that increase youths' vulnerability to subsequent violent behaviors. First, the social information-processing model suggests that exposure to violence may result in processing biases, such as aggressive attention biases and hostile attribution biases, which may in turn lead to aggressive behaviors (Coie & Dodge, 1997; Shahinfar, Kupersmidt, & Matza, 2001). For example, maltreated children have been shown to be more vigilant to aggressive stimuli (Reider & Cicchetti, 1989; Steinberg & Dodge, 1983) than non-maltreated children, and in one study of preschoolers, social information-processing variables were shown to fully mediate the relationship between physical abuse and later violent behaviors with peers (Dodge, Bates, & Pettit, 1990). In support of the social information-processing mediational model, Dodge and colleagues (1990) state, "... early physical harm has its effect on a child's aggressive behavioral development largely by altering the child's patterns of processing social information" (p. 1682).

Secondly, the social learning model posits that youths exposed to violence may learn that violence serves an instrumental function and may consequently develop a cognitive style in which violence is a permissible way of getting what is wanted and/or needed (Bandura, 1973, 1986; Patterson, 1982). Empir-ical support has also been found for this theory. In a sample of adolescent males incarcerated for violent crimes (N = 213), Spaccarelli, Coatsworth, and Bowden (1995) found that boys who had been exposed to family violence expressed the belief that the use of violence enhanced their reputation or self-image much more so than boys who were not exposed to such violence. Funk and colleagues (1999) also demonstrated that youths who were victimized by violence had higher pro-violence attitudes than youths not victimized by vio-lence. In one of the few studies to directly examine the potential mediational role of cognitive processes, Schwartz and Proctor (2000) employed a structural equation model in which they examined the relation of violence exposure to aggressive behaviors with social-cognitive biases as a mediator. Schwartz and Proctor (2000) found that social-cognitive biases were a significant mediator for 4th through 6th grade youths who witnessed violent behavior. However, the mediational effects were not significant for youths who were victimized by violence. Conversely, Halliday-Boykins and Graham (2000) found that incar-cerated youths' aggressive beliefs and hostile attributional biases were positively associated with violent victimization and violent behavior. Yet, no relationship was found for aggressive beliefs or hostile attributional biases with witnessing violence or vicarious violence exposure. The conflicting patterns found in these two studies might be partly due to sampling differences (e.g., community versus incarcerated youths).

The perception of the world and the self

As mentioned earlier, children and adolescents who suffer from PTSD have several deficits in their cognitive processing of information. Fear of traumatic events suddenly intrudes into the child's mind, leading to avoidance and defiant behaviors. It is not, therefore, surprising that such mental configuration alters the perception of others and of the world. Affect regulation problems promote a view of the self as helpless, damaged, and ineffective (van der Kolk & Fisler, 1995).

Children and adolescents who have been victims of trauma organize their perspectives on the world around their traumatic experience, altering their future interpretation of experience toward expectations of negative events (Kardiner, 1941, p. 82). Early victimization, in fact, is associated with low self-esteem, fear of rejection, and conceptions of the world as a dangerous place (Foa et al., 1999; Janoff-Bulman, 1989; McCann & Pearlman, 1990). When such beliefs are developed early in life, they could be framed into complex relational schemata (Baldwin et al., 1993) or internal working models that promote negative views of the self and expectations of future traumatic events. Furthermore, the aforementioned schemata are easily triggered by stimuli that evoke the past traumatic experience, leading to traumatic reenactments via fear and anger (Baldwin et al., 1993; Briere, 2002). Underlying such reenactments there is poor affect regulation. Poor affect regulation pressures children to learn from external stimuli how to avoid and lessen trauma-related distress. Such learned behaviors may include substance misuse and other behaviors aimed at reducing tension, such as compulsive actions (Briere & Elliott, 2003), self-harm (Briere & Gil, 1998), and suicide attempts (Zlotnick et al., 1997). These acting-out behaviors are distracting strategies to heal the trauma and to avoid overwhelming affects.

Going back to the strategies to interpret realities, poor affect regulation makes individuals with PTSD less able to make meaning of events, and therefore, they tend to be more vigilant and alarmed in the event of potential threats. This trait promotes a failure of metacognition abilities (thinking about thinking, monitoring one's own thoughts, and planning actions), which are also at the core of violent offending. Violent young offenders, in fact, have difficulty in foreseeing the consequences of their behaviors and in finding alternate strategies to solve threatening situations (Fonagy & Target, 2000). Therefore, all the psychological mechanisms at issue here create a feedback loop which enables traumatized youths to "feel" and to "avoid" emotions related to the traumatic pain and to the offence.

Developmental trauma and developmental criminology

Traumatic experiences play a key role in criminal careers of young generations. However, mechanisms of this relationship remain unchartered territory to be explored in future studies, including dissociation, which may be involved in impulse dyscontrol (Armstrong et al., 1997).

The interplay among early victimization, PTSD, and delinquency requires a reframing of the social context of at-risk youth who often remain "frozen" in the "here-and-now" of trauma. Youths exposed to violence feel continuous reenactments of their trauma, which may expose them to a criminogenic environment and to the risk of chronic victimizations. Chronically victimized youth are, therefore, at risk of becoming *life-course persistent offenders* (adolescents who are more vulnerable to a life-course criminal career) (Moffitt, 1993), as a result of a complex interaction between neurobiological deficits, biased interpretations of reality, and post-traumatic symptoms. Psychotraumatology and developmental criminology are urged to work toward an integrated theoretical understanding and empirical investigation to shed light on the aforementioned complex interactions. For example, *life-course offenders* may respond differently to traumatic experiences from *adolescent-limited offenders* (young offenders who desist when they enter adulthood). Many studies demonstrate that early traumatization elicits antisocial behavior (Babinski, Hartsough, & Lambert, 1999; Coleman, 2005). Some theoretical models attempt to explain this association (Haapasalo & Pokela, 1999) focusing on security of attachment, imitation of parental aggression and violence, and development of dysfunctional information-processing strategies (Dodge et al., 1990). Two other models – the "post-traumatic" and the "affect-regulation" – are centered on biological deficits resulting from trauma.

If the aforementioned dysfunctional areas become chronic early in life, they may favor early onset of antisocial conduct, which is a key risk factor in developmental trajectories of *life-course* offenders, who display conduct disturbances and aggression before the age of 11 (Moffitt, 1993; Moffitt et al., 1996). Furthermore, neurobiological differences between *life-course* and *adolescent-limited* offenders could also contribute to better explaining a different configuration of post-traumatic symptoms in the two groups.

The cognitive processes of delinquents with PTSD symptoms are very often focused on intrusions of their victimizations. Their information-processing tends to be confused, fragmented, and oriented to interpretative biases (Rutter, 1997). This could partially explain why incarceration – a stressful event – often reactivates the trauma and, therefore, facilitates the maintenance of antisocial behavior if post-traumatic symptoms are not adequately addressed. Isolating post-traumatic symptoms in a confused realm of understanding leads to empirical errors and to inadequate intervention programs that may be ineffective in reducing reoffending in such populations (Vermeiren et al., 2002).

References

Abram, K., Teplin, L. Charles, D. et al. (2004). Posttraumatic stress and trauma in youth in juvenile detention. *Archives of General Psychiatry, 61*, 403–10.

Achenbach, T. M. (1991). *Manual for the child behavior checklist/4–18 and 1991 profile*. Burlington, VT: University of Vermont, Department of Psychiatry.

Aichhorn, A. (1935). *Wayward youth*. New York: Viking Press.

Allwood, M. A., Bell-Dolan, D., & Husain, S. A. (2002). Children's trauma and adjustment reactions to violent and non-violent war experiences. *Journal of the American Academy of Child and Adolescent Psychiatry, 41*, 450–57.

Andrews, D. A., & Bonta, J. (1998). *The Psychology of Criminal Conduct* (2nd ed.). Cincinnati, OH: Anderson.

Armstrong, J., Putnam, F., Carlson, E. Libero, D., & Smith, S. (1997). Development and validation of a measure of adolescent dissociation: The Adolescent Dissociative Experiences Scale. *The Journal of Nervous & Mental Disease, 185*(8), 491–97.

Babinski, L. M., Hartsough, C. S., & Lambert, N. M. (1999). Childhood conduct problems, hyperactivity–impulsivity, and inattention as predictors of adult criminal activity. *Journal of Child Psychology and Psychiatry and Allied Disciplines, 40*, 347–55.

Baldwin, M. W., Fehr, B., Keedian, E., Seidel, M., & Thomson, D. W. (1993). An exploration of the relational schemata underlying attachment styles: Self-report and lexical decision approaches. *Personality and Social Psychology Bulletin, 19*(6), 746–54.

Bandura, A. (1973). *Aggression: A social learning analysis*. Englewood Cliffs, NJ: Prentice-Hall.

Bandura, A. (1986). *Social foundation of thought and action: A social cognitive theory*. Englewood Cliffs, NJ: Prentice-Hall.

Beers, S. R., & De Bellis, M. D. (2002). Neuropsychological function in children with maltreatment-related Posttraumatic Stress Disorder. *The American Journal of Psychiatry, 159*, 483–6.

Bell, C. C., & Jenkins, E. J. (1991). Traumatic stress and children. *Journal of Health Care for the Poor and Underserved, 2*(1), 175–88.

Bell-Dolan, S. (1995). Social cue interpretation of anxious children. *Journal of Clinical Child Psychology, 24*, 1–10.

Borkovec, T. D., & Lyonfields, J. D. (1993). Worry: Thought suppression of emotional processing. In H. W. Krohne (Ed.), *Attention and avoidance: Strategies in coping with aversiveness* (pp. 101–18). Ashland, OH: Hogrefe & Huber.

Brewin, C., R., & Valentine, J. D. (2000). A meta-analysis of risk factors for posttraumatic stress disorder in adults exposed to trauma. *Journal of Consulting and Clinical Psychology, 68*, 748–66.

Briere, J. (2002). Treating adult survivors of severe childhood abuse and neglect: Further development of an integrative model. In J. E. Myers, L. Berliner, J. Briere et al. (Eds.), *The APSCAC handbook on child maltreatment* (2nd ed., pp. 175–203). Thousand Oaks, CA: Sage.

Briere, J., & Elliott, D. M. (2003). Prevalence and psychological sequelae of self-reported childhood physical and sexual abuse in a general population sample of men and women. *Child Abuse & Neglect, 27*(10), 1205–22.

Briere, J., & Gil, E. (1998). Self-mutilation in clinical and general population samples: Prevalence, correlates, and functions. *American Journal of Orthopsychiatry, 68*(4), 609–20.

Briggs-Gowan, M. J., Owens, P. L., Schwab-Stone, M. E. et al. (2003). Persistence of psychiatric disorders in pediatric settings. *Journal of the American Academy of Child & Adolescent Psychiatry, 42*(11), 1360–9.

Burton, D., Foy, D., Bwanausi, C., Johnson, J., & Moore, L. (1994). The relationship between traumatic exposure, family dysfunction, and post-traumatic stress symptoms in male juvenile offenders. *Journal of Traumatic Stress, 7*(1), 83–93.

Carlson, G. A., & Kashani, J. H. (1988). Phenomenology of major depression from childhood through adulthood: analysis of three studies. *American Journal of Psychiatry, 145*, 1222–5

Carlson, E. A., & Sroufe, L. A. (1995). Contribution of attachment theory to developmental psychology. In D. Cicchetti & D. Cohen (Eds.), *Developmental psychopathology. Vol. 1: Theory and methods* (pp. 581–617). New York: John Wiley & Sons, Inc.

Cauffman, E., Feldman, S., Watherman, J., & Steiner, H. (1998). Posttraumatic Stress Disorder among female juvenile offenders. *Journal of American Academy of Child and Adolescent Psychiatry, 37*, 1209–16.

Coie, J. D., & Dodge, K. A. (1998). Aggression and antisocial behavior. In W. Damon (Series Ed.) & N. Eisenberg (Vol. Ed.), *Handbook of child psychology. Vol. 3: Social emotional and personality development* (5th ed., pp. 779–862). New York: John Wiley & Sons, Inc.

Coleman, D. (2005). Trauma and incarcerated youth. *Journal of Evidence-Based Social Work, 2*(3), 113–124.

Coplan, J. D., Andrews, M.W., Rosenblum, L.A., et al. (1996). Persistent elevations of cerebrospinal fluid concentrations of corticotropin-releasing factor in adult nonhuman primates exposed to early-life stressors: implications for the pathophysiology of mood and anxiety disorders. *Proceedings of the National Academy of Sciences of the United States of America, 93*(4), 1619–23

Dodge, K. A., Bates, J. E., & Pettit, G. S. (1990). Mechanisms in the cycle of violence. *Science, 250*, 1678–83.

Duman, R. S., Heninger, G. R., Nestler, E. J. (1997). A molecular and cellular theory of depression. *Archives of General Psychiatry, 54*, 597–606

Dziuba-Leatherman, J., & Finkelhor, D. (1994). How does receiving information about sexual abuse influence boys' perceptions of their risk? *Child Abuse and Neglect, 18*(7), 557–68.

Ehlers, A., & Clark, D. M. (2000). A cognitive model of posttraumatic stress disorder. *Behaviour Research and Therapy, 38*(4), 319–45.

Ehlers, A., Mayou, R., & Bryant, B. (1998). Psychological predictors of chronic post-traumatic stress disorders after motor vehicle accidents. *Journal of Abnormal Psychology, 107*(3), 508–19.

Erwin, B. A., Newman, E., McMackin, R. A., Morrissey, C., & Kaloupek, D. G. (2000). PTSD, malevolent environment, and criminality among criminally involved male adolescents. *Criminal Justice and Behavior, 27*, 196–215.

Eysenck, H. J. (1977). Psychosis and psychoticism: A reply to Bishop. *Journal of Abnormal Psychology, 86*, 427–30.

Farrell, A. D., & Bruce, S. E. (1997). Impact of exposure to community violence on violent behavior and emotional distress among urban adolescents. *Journal of Clinical Child Psychology, 26*, 2–14.

Finkelhor, D., & Dziuba-Leatherman, J. (1994). Children as victims of violence: A national survey. *Pediatrics, 94*(4), 413–20.

Finzi, R., Cohen, O., Sapir, Y., & Weizman, A. (2000). Attachment styles in maltreated children: A comparative study. *Child Psychiatry and Human Development, 31*(2), 113–28.

Flannery, D. J., Singer, M., & Wester, K. (2001). Violence exposure, psychological trauma, and suicide risk in a community sample of dangerously violent adolescents. *Journal of the American Academy of Child & Adolescent Psychiatry, 40*(4), 435–42.

Flannery, D. J., Singer, M., Williams, L., & Castro, P. (1998). Adolescent violence exposure and victimization at home: Coping and psychological trauma symptoms. *International Review of Victimology, 6*(1), 29–48.

Fonagy, P., & Target, M. (2000). Mentalisation and changing aims of child's psychoanalysis. In K. von Klitzing, P. Tyson, & D. Burgin (Eds.), *Psychoanalysis in childhood and adolescence* (pp. 129–39). Basel: Karger.

Foa, E. B., Ehlers, A., Clark, D. M., Tolin, D. F. & Orsillo, S. M. (1999). The post-traumatic cognitions inventory (PTCI): Development and validation. *Psychological Assessment, 11*(3), 303–14.

Ford, J. D. (2002). Traumatic victimization in childhood and persistent problems with oppositional defiance. *Journal of Aggression, Maltreatment and Trauma, 6*(1), 25–58.

Fowles, D. C., Kochanska, G., & Murray, K. (2000). Electrodermal activity and temperament in preschool children. *Psychophysiology, 37*, 777–87.

Funk, J. B., Elliott, R., Urman, M. L., Flores, G. T., & Mock, R. M. (1999). The attitudes towards violence scale: A measure for adolescents. *Journal of Interpersonal Violence, 14*, 1123–36.

Garbarino, J. (2001). An ecological perspective on the effects of violence on children. *Journal of Community Psychology, 29*(3), 361–78.

Gould, E., Tanapat, P., McEwen, B. S., Flugge, G., & Fuchs, E. (1998). Proliferation of granule cell precursors in the dentate gyrus of adult monkeys is diminished by stress. *Proceedings of the National Academy of Sciences, 95*, 3168–71.

Grann, M., & Wedin, I. (2002). Risk factors for recidivism among spousal assault and spousal homicide offenders. *Psychology, Crime & Law, 8*(1), 5–23.

Haapasalo, J., & Pokela, E. (1999). Child-rearing and child abuse antecedents of criminality. *Aggression and Violent Behavior, 4*, 107–27.

Halliday-Boykins, C. A., & Graham, S. (2000). At both ends of the gun: Testing the relationship between community violence exposure and youth violent behavior. *Journal of Abnormal Child Psychology, 29*(5), 383–402.

Heide, K. M., & Solomon, E. P. (2006). Biology, childhood trauma, and homicide: Rethinking justice. *International Journal of Law & Psychiatry, 29*, 220–33.

Henry, B., & Moffitt, T. E. (1997). Neuropsychological and neuroimaging studies of juvenile delinquency and adult criminal behavior. In D. M. Stoff, J. Breiling, & J. D. Maser (Eds.), *Handbook of antisocial behavior* (pp. 280–8). New York: John Wiley & Sons, Inc.

Hofer, M. A. (1994). Early social relationships as regulators of infant physiology and behavior. *Acta Paediatrica, 397*(Suppl.), 9–18.

Horowitz, M. J. (1993). Stress-response syndromes: a review of posttraumatic stress and adjustment disorders. In J. P. Wilson & B. Raphael (Eds.), *International Handbook of Traumatic Stress Syndromes*. New York: Plenum Press.

Janoff-Bulman, R. (1989). Assumptive worlds and the stress of traumatic events: Applications of the schema construct. *Social Cognition, Special Issue: Social Cognition and Stress, 7*, 113–36.

Jenkins, E. J., & Bell, C. C. (1994). Violence among inner city high school students and post-traumatic stress disorder. Anxiety disorders in African Americans. In S. Friedman (Ed.), *Anxiety disorders in African Americans* (pp. 76–88). New York: Springer.

Joseph, S., Dalgleish, T., Thrasher, S., & Yule, W. (1997). Impulsivity and post-traumatic stress. *Personality and Individual Differences, 22*(2), 279–81.

Kardiner, A. (1941). *The traumatic neuroses of war*. New York: Hoeber.

Kolko, D. J., Moser, J. T., & Weldy, S. R. (1990). Medical/health histories and physical evaluation of physically and sexually abused child psychiatric patients: A controlled study. *Journal of Family Violence, 5*, 249–67.

Ladd, O. C., Huot, R. L., Thrivikraman, K. et al. (1996). Long-term behavioral and neuroendocrine adaptations to adverse early experience. In E. A. Mayer & C. B. Saper (Eds.), *Progress in Brain Research* (Vol. 122, pp. 81–103). New York: Elsevier.

Lehmann, P. (1997). The development of posttraumatic stress disorder (PTSD) in a sample of child witnesses to mother assault. *Journal of Family Violence, 12*, 241–6.

Levine, S. (1994). The ontogeny of the hypothalamic-pituitary-adrenal axis. The influence of maternal factors. *Annals of the New York Academy of Sciences, 746*, 275–88.

Lipschitz, D. S., Morgan, C. A., Southwick, S. M. (2002). Neurobiological disturbances in youth with childhood trauma in youth with conduct disorder. *Journal of Aggression, Maltreatment & Trauma, 6*(1), 149–74.

Lipschitz, D. S., Rasmusson, A. M., Anyan, W., Cromwell, P., & Southwick, S. M. (2000). Clinical and functional correlates of posttraumatic stress disorder in urban adolescent girls at a primary care clinic. *Journal of American Academy of Child and Adolescent Psychiatry, 39*(9), 1104–11.

Loeber, R., Green, S. M., Lahey, B. B., Frick, P. J., & McBurnett, K. (2000). Findings on disruptive behavior disorders from the first decade of the Developmental Trends Study. *Clinical Child and Family Psychology Review, 3*, 37–60.

Lynam, D. R., Caspi, A., Moffitt, T. E. et al. (2000). The interaction between impulsivity and neighborhood context on offending: the effects of impulsivity are stronger in poorer neighborhoods. *Journal of Abnormal Psychology, 109*, 563–74.

Lyons-Ruth, K. (1996). Attachment relationships among children with aggressive behavior problems: The role of disorganized early attachment patterns. *Journal of Consulting and Clinical Psychology, 64*(1), 64–73.

Lyons-Ruth, K., Alpern, L., & Repacholi, B. (1993). Disorganized attachment classification and maternal psychosocial problems as predictors of hostile-aggressive behavior in preschool classroom. *Child Development, 64*, 572–85.

Lyons-Ruth, K., & Jacobvitz, D. (1999). Attachment disorganization: Unresolved loss, relational violence, and lapses in behavioral and attentional strategies. In J. Cassidy & P. R. Shaver (Eds.), *Handbook of attachment: Theory, research, and clinical applications* (pp. 520–54). New York: Guilford Press.

McCann, L. I., & Pearlman, L. A. (1990). Vicarious traumatization: A framework for understanding the psychological effects of working with victims. *Journal of Traumatic Stress*, 3(1), 131–49.

McGruder-Johnson, A. K., Davidson, E. S., Gleaves, D. H., Stock, W., & Finch, J. F. (2000). Interpersonal violence and posttraumatic symptomatology: The effects of ethnicity, gender, and exposure to violent events. *Journal of Interpersonal Violence*, 15(2), 205–21.

MacLeod, C., & Campbell, L. (1992). Memory accessibility and probability judgments: An experimental evaluation of the availability heuristic. *Journal of Personality and Social Psychology*, 63(6), 890–902.

Main, M., & Hesse, E. (1990). Parents' unresolved traumatic experiences are related to infant disorganized attachment status: Is frightened and/or frightening parental behavior the linking mechanism? In M. T. Greenberg, D. Cicchetti, & E. M. Cummings (Eds.), *Attachment in the preschool years: Theory, research, and intervention* (pp. 161–82) (The John D. and Catherine T. MacArthur Foundation Series on Mental Health and Development). Chicago: University of Chicago Press.

Makino, S., Schulkin, J., Smith, M.A., Pacak, K., Palkovits, M., Gold, P.W. (1995a). Regulation of corticotropin-releasing hormone receptor messenger ribonucleic acid in the rat brain and pituitary by glucocorticoids and stress. *Endocrinology*. 136, 4517–25.

Makino, S., Smith, M.A., Gold, P.W. (1995b). Increased expression of corticotropin-releasing hormone and vasopressin messenger ribonucleic acid (mRNA) in the hypothalamic paraventricular nucleus during repeated stress: association with reduction in glucocorticoid receptor mRNA levels. *Endocrinology*. 136, 3299–309.

Maxfield, G. M., & Widom, C. (1996). The cycle of violence revisited 6 years later. *Archives of Pediatric & Adolescent Medicine*, 150(4), 390–5.

Merckelbach, H., Muris, P., Horselenberg, R., & Rassin, E. (1998). Traumatic intrusions as "worse case scenarios". *Behaviour Research and Therapy*, 36, 1075–9.

Minuchin, R., & Guerny, G. (1967). *Families of the slums*. New York: Viking Press.

Moffitt, T. E. (1993). Adolescence-limited and life-course-persistent antisocial behavior: A developmental taxonomy. *Psychology Review*, 100, 674–701.

Moffitt, T. E., Caspi, A., Dickson, N., Silva, P., & Stanton, W. (1996). Childhood-onset versus adolescent-onset antisocial conduct problems in males: Natural history from ages 3 to 18 years. *Development and Psychopathology*, 8, 399–424.

Moffitt, T. E., & Silva, P. A. (1988). Self-reported delinquency, neuropsychological deficit, and history of attention deficit disorder. *Journal of Abnormal Child Psychology*, 16, 553–69.

Nibuya, M., Morinobu, S., & Duman, R. S. (1995). Regulation of BDNF and trkB mRNA in rat brain by chronic electroconvulsive seizure and antidepressant drug treatments. *Journal of Neuroscience*, 15, 7539–47.

Patterson, G. R. (1982). *A social learning approach: 3. Coercive family process*. Eugene, OR: Castalia.

Pelcovitz, D., Kaplan, S., Goldenberg, B. et al. (1994). Post-Traumatic Stress Disorder in physically abused adolescents. *Journal of the American Academy of Child and Adolescent Psychiatry*, 33(3), 305–12.

Perry, B. D. (1996). *Maltreated Children: Experience, Brain Development and the Next Generation*. New York and London: W.W. Norton.

Plotsky, P. M., & Meaney, M. J. (1993). Early, postnatal experience alters hypothalamic corticotrophin-releasing factor (CRF) mRNA, median eminence CRF content and stress-induced release in adult rata. *Molecular Brain Research*, *18*, 195–200.

Prino, C. T., & Peyrot, M. (1994). The effect of child physical abuse and neglect on aggressive, withdrawn, and prosocial behavior. *Child Abuse and Neglect*, *18*(10), 871–84.

Quay, H. C. (1965). Psychopathic personality as pathological stimulation-seeking. *The American Journal of Psychiatry*, *122*, 180–83.

Raine, A. (1993). *The psychopathology of crime: Criminal behavior as a clinical disorder*. San Diego, CA: Academic Press.

Raine, A., Reynolds, C., Venables, P. H., Mednick, S. A., & Farrington, D. P. (1998). Fearlessness, stimulation-seeking, and large body size at age 3 years as early predispositions to childhood aggression at age 11 years. *Archives of General Psychiatry*, *55*, 745–51.

Raine, A. (2002). Biosocial studies of antisocial and violent behavior in children and adults: A review. *Journal of Abnormal Child Psychology*, *30*, 311–26.

Reider, C., & Cicchetti, D. (1989). Organizational perspective on cognitive control functioning and cognitive-affective balance in maltreated children. *Developmental Psychology*, *25*, 382–93.

Reynolds, M., & Brewin, C. R. (1998). Intrusive cognitions, coping strategies and emotional responses in depression, post-traumatic stress disorder and a non-clinical population. *Behaviour Research and Therapy*, *36*(2), 135–47.

Robins, L. N. (1978). Study childhood predictors of adult antisocial behaviour: Replications from longitudinal studies. *Psychological Medicine*, *8*(4), 611–22.

Robinson, J., & Glaves, L. (1996). Supporting emotion regulation and emotional availability through home visitation. *Bulletin of Zero to Three*, *27*(1), 31–5.

Ruchkin, V., Schwab-Stone, M., Koposov, R., & Steiner, H. (2002). Violence exposure, posttraumatic stress and personality in juvenile delinquents. *Journal of the American Academy of Child and Adolescent Psychiatry*, *41*, 322–9.

Rutter, M. (1997). Antisocial behavior: developmental psychopathology perspectives. In D. M. Stoff, J. Breiling, & J. D. Maser (Eds.), *Handbook of antisocial behavior* (pp. 115–24). New York: John Wiley & Sons, Inc.

Sapolsky, R. M., Alberts, S. C., Altmann, J. (1997). Hypercortisolism associated with social subordinance or social isolation among wild baboons. *Archives of General Psychiatry*, *54*, 1137–43

Sapolsky, R., Krey, L., & McEwen, B. (1984). Glucocorticoid-sensitive hippocampal neurons are involved in terminating the adrenocortical stress response. *Proceedings of the National Academy of Science*, *87*, 6174–7.

Scarpa, A. (2001). Community violence exposure in a young adult sample: Lifetime prevalence and socioemotional effects. *Journal of Interpersonal Violence*, *16*(1), 36–53.

Scarpa, A., Raine, A., Venables, P. H., & Mednick, S. A. (1997). Heart rate and skin conductance in behaviourally inhibited Mauritian children. *Journal of Abnormal Psychology*, *106*, 182–190.

Schore, A. N. (1994). *Affect regulation and the origin of the self: The neurobiology of emotional development*. Mahweh, NJ: Erlbaum.

Schore, A. N. (1996). The experience-dependent maturation of a regulatory system in the orbital prefrontal cortex and the origin of developmental psychopathology. *Development and Psychopathology, 8*, 59–87.

Schreiber, R., & Lyddon, W. J. (1998). Parental bonding and current psychological functioning among childhood sexual abuse survivors. *Journal of Counseling Psychology, 45*(3), 358–62.

Schwartz, D., & Proctor, L. J. (2000). Community violence exposure and children's social adjustment in the school peer group: The mediating roles of emotion regulation and social cognition. *Journal of Consulting and Clinical Psychology, 68*(4), 670–83.

Severs, W. B., & Daniels-Severs, A. E. (1973). Effects of angiotensin on the central nervous system. *Pharmacological Reviews, 25*(3), 415–49.

Shahinfar, A., Kupersmidt, J. B., & Matza, L. S. (2001). The relation between exposure to violence and social information processing among incarcerated adolescents, *Journal of Abnormal Psychology, 110*(1), 136–41.

Smith, M. A., Makino, S., Kvetnansky, R., & Post, R. M. (1995). Stress and glucocorticoids affect the expression of brain-derived neurotrophic factor and neurotrophin-3 mRNAs in the hippocampus. *The Journal of Neuroscience, 15*(3), 1766–77.

Smith, S. M., Vale, W. W. (2006). The role of the hypothalamic-pituitary-adrenal axis in neuroendocrine responses to stress. *Dialogues in Clinical Neuroscience 8*, 383–95.

Solomon, E. P., & Heide, K. M. (1999). Type III Trauma: Toward a more effective conceptualization of psychological trauma. *International Journal of Offender Therapy and Comparative Criminology, 43*(2), 202–10.

Solomon, J., & George, C. (1999). The place of disorganization in attachment theory: Linking classic observations with contemporary findings. In J. Solomon & C. George (Eds.), *Attachment disorganization* (pp. 3–31). New York: Guilford Press.

Spaccarelli, S., Coatsworth, J. D., & Bowden, B. S. (1995). Exposure to serious family violence among incarcerated boys: Its association with violent offending and potential mediating variables. *Violence and Victims, 10*, 163–82.

Steinberg, M. S., & Dodge, D. K. (1983). Attributional bias in aggressive adolescent boys and girls. *Journal of Social & Clinical Psychology, 1*(4), 312–21.

Steiner, H., Garcia, I. G., & Matthews, Z. (1997). Posttraumatic stress disorder in incarcerated juvenile delinquents. *Journal of the American Academy of Child and Adolescent Psychiatry, 36*, 357–65.

Takahashi, J., Palmer, T. D., & Gage, F. H. (1998). Retinoic acid and neurotrophins collaborate to regulate neurogenesis in adult-derived neural cell cultures. *Journal of Neurobiology, 38*, 65–81.

Tyson, A. A., & Goodman, M. (1996). Group treatment for adult women who experienced childhood sexual trauma: Is telling the story enough? *International Journal of Group Psychotherapy, 46*(4), 535–42.

Van der Kolk, B. A., & Fisler, R. (1994). Childhood abuse & Neglect and loss of self-regulation. *Bulletin of Menninger Clinic, 58*, 145–68.

van der Kolk, B. A., & Fisler, R. (1995). Dissociation and the perceptual nature of traumatic memories: review and experimental confirmation. *Journal of Traumatic Stress, 8*(4), 505–25.

van der Kolk, B. A. (1996). The body keeps score. Approaches to the psychobiology of posttraumatic stress disorder. In B. A. van der Kolk, A. C. McFarlane, & L.

Weisaeth (Eds.), *Traumatic stress: The effects of overwhelming experience on mind, body, and society* (pp. 214–241). New York: Guilford Press.

van Goozen, S., Matthys, W., Cohen-Kettenis, P. et al. (1998). Salivary cortisol and cardiovascular activity during stress in oppositional-defiant disorder boys and normal controls. *Biological Psychiatry, 43*(7), 531–9.

Veirmeiren, R. (2003). Psycopathology and delinquency in adolescents: A descriptive and developmental perspective. *Clinical Psychology Review, 23,* 277–318.

Vermeiren, R., Schwab-Stone, M., Ruchkin, V., De Clippele, A., & Deboutte, D. (2002). Predicting recidivism in delinquent adolescents from psychological and psychiatric assessment. *Comprehensive Psychiatry, 43*(2), 142–9.

Widom, C. S. (1989). Does violence beget violence? A critical examination of the literature. *Psychological Bulletin, 106,* 3–28.

Williamson, J. M., Borduin, C. M., & Howe, B. A. (1991). The ecology of adolescent maltreatment: A multilevel examination of adolescent physical abuse, sexual abuse, and neglect. *Journal of Consulting and Clinical Psychology, 59*(3), 449–57.

Yehuda, R., Keefer, R. S. E., Harvey, P. D. et al. (1995a). Learning and memory in combat veterans with posttraumatic stress disorder. *The American Journal of Psychiatry, 152,* 137–9.

Yehuda, R., Boisoneau, D., Lowy, M. T., Giller, E. L. Jr. (1995b). Dose-response changes in plasma cortisol and lymphocyte glucocorticoid receptors following dexamethasone administration in combat veterans with and without PTSD. *Archives of General Psychiatry, 52,* 583–93.

Young, E. A., & Akil, H. (1985). Corticotropin-releasing factor stimulation of adrenocorticotropin and beta-endorphin release: Effects of acute and chronic stress. *Endocrinology, 1*(17), 23–30.

Zahn-Waxler, C., Radke-Yarrow, M., Wagner, E., & Chapman, M. (1992). Development of concerns for others. *Developmental Psychology, 28*(1), 126–36.

Zlotnick, C., Donaldson, D., Spirito, A., & Pearlstein, T. (1997). Affect regulation and suicide attempts in adolescent inpatients. *Journal of the American Academy of Child & Adolescent Psychiatry, 36*(6), 793–8.

Further Reading

Sapolsky, R. M. (2000). Glucocorticoids and hippocampal atrophy in neuropsychiatric disorders. *Arch Gen Psychiatry, 57,* 925–35.

Sapolsky, R. M. (2003). Stress and plasticity in the limbic system. *Neurochem Res, 28,* 1735–42.

Part V

Psychosocial Interventions

Chapter Twelve

Schools as a Context of Trauma Prevention

Barbara Oehlberg

Trauma comes to school: The neurobiological legacy

Many children bring unprocessed traumatic memories with them into their classrooms and schools. Although teachers are not clinicians and schools are not mental health agencies, child traumatic stress is an educational issue because it interferes with students' opportunity to learn up to their potential.

Certainly, schools cannot address child traumatic stress alone but they have a significant role in alleviating the stress of trauma and promoting resilience while performing their mandate to generate the academic achievement of students and prepare them for meaningful citizenship.

Schools, preschool to 12, are strategically positioned to recognize child traumatic stress in children while the brain is still very malleable, introduce transformative activities that fit into core curriculum subjects, and break the cycle of intergenerational PTSD. Schools offer an existing network for expanded delivery of child traumatic stress relief, especially for children who may not have access to clinical therapy because of finances or adult apprehensions. After-school programs also offer significant opportunities for addressing traumatic stress because of their flexibility and freedom from academic mandates.

Attachment trauma

Children who have not been afforded the opportunity to complete the attachment process during early childhood have reduced capacities for self-regulation, stress management, and empathy according to Allan Schore, who refers to this as attachment trauma (Schore, 2001). Early relationships that are predictable

Post-Traumatic Syndromes in Childhood and Adolescence: A Handbook of Research and Practice, First Edition. Edited by Vittoria Ardino. © 2011 John Wiley & Sons, Ltd. Published 2011 by John Wiley & Sons, Ltd.

and include ample eye contact, smiling faces, and touching stimulate critical development of the prefrontal cortex, considered the executive manager of the neurological system. Perceived rejections and separations will continue to be a sensitive issue for these children and youth if not addressed by informed adults in childhood (Stien & Kendall, 2004).

Children with an underdeveloped prefrontal cortex often present disruptive and unsettling behaviors in the classroom because they were not afforded the opportunity to develop the neurological structure necessary for self-regulation. Unfortunately, these behaviors can be misinterpreted as misbehaviors and are reacted to with disciplinary actions, which then are interpreted by the child as another rejection, setting in motion a pattern of emotional insecurity and behavioral issues that greatly interfere with learning and achievement for the rest of the student's educational experience. Social and relationship issues can become lifelong struggles for children who were denied the opportunity to attach and, in certain cases, may favor the entry of those children into the criminal justice system, as noted by Foy and colleagues and Ardino in Chapters 10 and 11 this book.

Children who have not completed attachment have greater susceptibility to develop PTSD following a traumatic experience, yet another complication over which they have no control (Cozolino, 2006).

Strengthening children's self-regulation

Becky A. Bailey has created very compelling activities involving teacher, parent, sibling, or classmates with a young child which include direct, intentional eye contact and hand touching, which can stimulate the production of calming hormones. The activities also nurture prefrontal brain development for young students with incomplete attachments. Through these activities, called "I love you rituals," children's self-regulation can be enhanced (Bailey, 2000). Encouraging parents and siblings to engage in these fun activities with young children can even augment their own capacity to attach, thereby breaking the cycle of attachment issues.

Examples from Becky A. Bailey

A wonderful woman who lived in a shoe
(Hold the child's hand in yours and rock back and forth)
A wonderful woman lived in a shoe.
She had so many children she knew exactly what to do.
She held them, she rocked them, and tucked them in bed.
"I love you, I love you," is what she said.

Twinkle, twinkle little star
(Hold up fingers and tap the child's with yours)
Twinkle, twinkle little star,

What a wonderful child you are!
With bright eyes and nice round cheeks,
A talented child from head to feet.
Twinkle, twinkle little star,
What a wonderful child you are!

Examples from the author

Deedle, deedle dumpling
Deedle, deedle dumpling, my sweet child
Wants to be cuddled all through the day.
Deedle, deedle dumpling, my sweet child
Simply wants to play.
(Cup child's hands and wave side to side)

Hickety pickety
Hickety, picket, my best little friend.
I love to watch you coo and bend.
With your sweet, sweet giggles and smile so bright,
Hickety picket, my best little friend.
(Clap child's hand with yours to the beat)

Having experienced or witnessed violence

Early childhood experiences of fear and terror are recorded without words or narrative. These implicit memories are stored in the amygdala within the limbic area and cause perceptions of helplessness along with over-sensitized fear-alarm reactions whenever the child/youth perceives a threat (Cozolino, 2006). Such fear reactions are prompted by an automatic shift out of the neocortex into the limbic area for the survival purposes of fight-or-flight or freeze.

Survival reactions, generated by unprocessed memories of terror and loss, directly complicate learning and classroom climates. These students are not able to communicate their sense of fear and doom with words, but do so through behavioral outbursts and class disruptions. Such behaviors can be interpreted by uninformed adults as disrespect and defiance. They can even be misdiagnosed as ADHD and oppositional defiance which will lead to interventions and medications that fail to address the root cause (Perry, 2004).

Students with traumatic stress pay particular attention to teachers or school personnel who are beginning to lose control of themselves, indicated by a changed breathing pattern, facial expressions, and tone of voice. These cues will trigger perceptions of vulnerability for students with unprocessed traumatic memories. These survival reactions by students following a perceived threat are neither rational nor by choice as they are not generated by a cortical process; nor are they acceptable. They are sensory reactions generated by the limbic system and appear to be anger rather than fear. One student's fear-alarm reaction can trigger and spread to other students with unprocessed traumatic stress, creating a classroom climate in which little learning ensues (Oehlberg, 2006).

The learning process for students with traumatic stress is further compromised by their inability to focus. Perry states that these students hear about half the words their teacher says, causing them to fall behind year after year (2004). Traumatized students are unable to problem-solve or participate in their own safety after they have down-shifted out of their neocortex when threatened. Regretfully, this sense of helplessness can prompt some teens to be more afraid of life than death, making it extremely difficult to be educationally motivated.

School climate and disciplinary policies

Educators who are not trauma-informed can unwittingly escalate a student's stress through disciplinary policies that perhaps were successful a generation ago when children perceived the world as safer. Today's children and teens are neurologically wired differently due to viewing repeated electronic images of violence and death during early childhood. As a result, more students interpret disciplinary actions as a rejection and threat, causing increased alienation and despair which are counterproductive to generating resilience and academic achievement (Perry, 1997).

Students with traumatic stress do best in emotionally secure school environments that are predictable and free from shaming. Their distress is activated when adults attempt to control individuals, rather than control the environment. Emotionally secure climates assure that every student has a right to feel safe and valued, and experience mutual respect from adults and peers (Perry, 2004).

Confrontational tactics by adults in authoritative roles can trigger explosive, aggressive outbursts, especially from preteens and teens with traumatic stress. When attending adults communicate their own alarm and apprehension, verbally or nonverbally, the panic of distressed students is provoked due to their implicit memories of childhood terror. Students with traumatic stress immediately recognize when an attending adult has dropped out of their neocortex and feels helpless and challenged, triggering the student's fear-alarm reaction.

The more often the fear-alarm reaction is activated, the more difficult it will be to diffuse and transform these unprocessed memories. Because of the significant role that educators play in the lives of students who come to school with over-sensitized fear-alarm reactions, schools have an obligation to assure all personnel become trauma-informed. This is essential for academic achievement and mental health purposes.

The bullying issue

The issue of bullying and traumatic stress are dramatically linked, both before and after incidents. All persons involved struggle from the sense of helplessness and vulnerability but present differing reactions, activated by rejections, real or perceived, be they male or female. Traumatic stress can occur within bystanders as well, depending on their previous experiences of fears and losses.

As schools struggle with this issue, they are discovering that standard disciplinary actions are not very effective. The aspect of revenge, an integral component of normal reactions to trauma, complicates the bullying issue, especially where students have access to guns.

Richard Kagan offers a stunning explanation of the goal of bullying behavior which offers alternative insights for prevention and intervention (Kagan, 2004). When the aggressor sees fear in the eyes of the targeted person, it affords him/her some relief from their own internal fears and sense of helplessness. Schools could be more effective in intervening in bullying issues if they intentionally create ways for both the perpetrators and targets to feel more included, valued, and positively empowered. Offer them opportunities to help build school climates that assure emotionally security for everyone. Integrate and empower them in ways that benefit all without creating new victims (Malchiodi, 2008).

Anger management, conflict management, and peacemaking skills

Since schools are institutions built around teaching, it's not surprising that they focus on "teaching" students acceptable behaviors. However, the majority of behavior problems in schools are generated by 10–12% of the students, youngsters who most likely have experienced traumatic family violence, chaos, or multiple losses. Cognitive teaching will have no effect on the memories of terror and rejection stored in their amygdala. As indicated earlier, words do not connect with the limbic area (Levine & Kline, 2007).

This does not mean schools should not engage in developing these important skills. However, unless students with traumatic stress are afforded the tools for diffusing and transforming frozen memories first, we set them up to fail. Unless schools make it possible for students to process their frozen memories of fear and rejection they will still be prone to aggressive eruptions when they perceive a threat.

Classroom activities for trauma transformation

The healing or recovery process for children with traumatic stress fits comfortably and naturally into the educational process of most schools. It requires no additional equipment, but it does require trauma-informed personnel, including support staff and nonprofessionals.

Healing activities can be integrated into core curriculum subjects, especially language arts and social studies, without reducing subject contact time.

Actually, the activities enhance the meaning and relevance of these subjects for students with traumatic memories, providing new motivation for students who tend to be difficult to reach and teach. Schools can significantly intervene and break the cycle of traumatic stress that can lead to PTSD.

Because traumatic memories are stored in the amygdala, not in the neocortex, students cannot access them through cognitive methods in order to diffuse and process them. Initial connection with the memory requires a psychomotor process, primarily movement of the hands. The cathartic activities of drawing and creative writing fulfill these requirements and fit productively into elementary curricula and classrooms. Participating in music, drama, and dance naturally offers the same opportunities.

Games and play also offer psychomotor activity and are particularly suited to preschool, kindergarten, and the early grades (Oehlberg, 1996). The younger the child, the greater the chances for meaningful intervention due to the malleability of the brain in children under the age of eight. Recovery requires more time and patience after puberty.

The key to transforming traumatic memories is to offer classroom assignments that afford students the opportunity to create endings to scenarios that provide greater fairness, empowerment, and hope. Through play, art, and journaling, students, both those with and without traumatic memories, benefit when encouraged to choose the words and/or actions for characters in a story, including the most powerful and the most threatened characters. This permits the student to begin to transform the traumatic encoding of helplessness and introduces the language of possibilities for them.

These characters have to be fictional and second party, not the student himself or herself. Through the symbolic or metaphorical processing of imaginary situations of threat, rejection, and helplessness, students can access their neocortex through an alternate pathway and avert the imprinted barrier of shocking fear, thereby finding relief and freedom from internalized traumatic stress and helplessness.

Students with traumatic stress often are unaware of their need to externalize these frozen memories or that they are engaging in a transformative process, as it should be. There is no reason to label these students or separate them out from classmates.

Healing activities for early childhood education, preschool to grade three

Play, games, and art activities offer the most natural and comfortable cathartic endeavors for young students. Art activities allow them to symbolically share observations and experiences for which they may not have the words needed to tell the story. The paper the drawing is on has edges, which means the memory is contained within the sheet and the child now has control of the memory and the drawing. This is empowering. Some students find great satisfaction in putting the drawings through a shredder.

- Suggest students show with colored lines, shapes, or scribbles what anger feels like inside their tummy or chest. Other descriptions can be for sadness, fear, being left out, jealousy, embarrassment, loved, confident or happy (Steele, 1997).
- Suggest students take a red crayon and color out all the anger within them; a blue crayon for coloring out all the sadness within them.
- Provide students with a graphic human outline, racial- and gender-neutral. Encourage them to color the area of the body where they might feel the sensations of anger, fear, stress, joy, or sadness and select a color that best describes the sensation.
- Encourage students to select an animal they admire and draw that animal, clearly showing why they like it. Have them write or tell why the animal of their choice is so special to them.
- Offer imaginary, magical, "if-only" glasses. Ask what they would choose to change or make different by wearing them. Ask them to draw or write how the world would be different when seen through their "if-only" glasses.
- Offer imaginary magical Band-aids that could heal any hurt applied to, even inside hurts. Ask them to draw or write how their lives, or the world, would be made better by the magical Band-aid.
- Offer students a tool box to be used for fixing the world. Ask them to draw or write about which tools would be in the box and how the world would be made better by them (Oehlberg, 2006).

Healing activities for intermediate and middle school

Language arts
Creative writing and journaling offer the most natural and purposeful assignments in language arts for intermediate and middle school students. Keep the writing guidelines flexible to afford the greatest opportunities for students to develop a story-line that provides them symbolic relief and empowerment. Creative writing and journaling afford students the opportunity to transform implicit memories and address mental health implications without triggering their own traumatic stress, providing the suggested topics are hypothetical.

Examples of creative writing or journaling topics (Oehlberg, 2006):

- Issues of loss and being invisible:
  A young Native American who has discovered a way to make shoes or sandals that have the ability to make adults walk in children's shoes and sense their hurts, loneliness or invisibility. Expand on how this could change the lives of children.

- Issues of rejection:
  A robot that was stamped "defective" at the factory. What does the robot do to feel valued and purposeful?
- Issues of brokenness:
  An elderly lady provides the children in her neighborhood with a doll hospital. How might the neighborhood and the children be changed by this gift?
- Issues of betrayal or broken promises:
  A suitcase is found that has been used to store broken promises to children. How might this find change children's lives when the contents of the suitcase are revealed?
- Issues of hope, empowerment, and healing:
  A scientist has developed a pill that can cure or erase children's memories of being shamed. Who would the scientist give the pills to and what changes would this bring to those children?

Combine language arts and the art of drawing in small team assignments (Oehlberg, 2006). For example, create print and illustrated ad campaigns for:

- Children's rights.
- Save the whales.
- A home security system for emotional security.

Create comic books about:

- A youngster who invents a happy dream machine.
- A bicycle that will take children to places where they are totally safe and adults respect and love them.

Social studies

Offering seed-ideas that correlate to social studies topics or historical periods provides students with deeper insights into the subject and ways to symbolically shape the world they are currently part of. To metaphorically address systemic and individual historical injustices that have afflicted children in every society throughout the ages and reframe them into stories of more desirable endings of fairness and being valued can bring empowerment and hope to students with unprocessed traumatic stress (Oehlberg, 2006).

Examples:
Historical cartoons or comic books as small group activities involving art and creative writing:

- A 14-year-old who worked in the coal mines of Wales six days a week, 10 hours a day in 1851.
- Children bussed out of London to rural communities for safety during the Blitz in 1941.

- How Eleanor Roosevelt labored to have the United Nations develop an International Children's Emergency Fund (UNICEF) in the 1950s.
- Sadako and her inspiring paper crane story in Japan in 1946.

Media projects for history or social studies:

Assign students to write the scripts for a fictional radio interview of 10 minutes with the children or characters in the following historic events and shape an ending that would be empowering for that child/character (Oehlberg, 2006).

1730: An 11-year-old who is an apprentice to a London or Boston cabinetmaker misses his family.
1838: Two Cherokee youngsters who walked with their family and relatives on the Trail of Tears from Tennessee to Oklahoma.
1918: A youngster whose father has returned from World War I after being gassed and is blind.
1971: A youngster in the townships of South Africa whose father works in the diamond mines and is allowed to come home to visit only twice a year.

Write the scripts (and record if desired) for 90-second public service announcements on the following topics:

- Promoting the rights of all children.
- Developing youth leadership skills.
- Embracing diversity.
- Overcoming fears of immigrants.

Feel free to change these characters or situations to better match the needs or interests of students (Oehlberg, 2006).

Healing activities for high school students or adolescents

Processing implicit memories of terror and rejections become improbable after puberty due to reduced malleability of the limbic and mid-brain areas. Nevertheless, students can achieve relief from their traumatic stress by engaging in the same or similar creative writing and art activities offered for middle school students. Actual brain changes will be less likely, however. Observing positive behavioral or academic changes may require extra patience and repeated activities.

Conclusion

The role of educators and schools in the context of preventing PTSD is very real, beneficial, and essential for individual students and the future of society.

Schools cannot be expected to achieve this critical task alone, but require the coordinated support of the community in generating the attitude that students can be aided in successfully recovering from traumatic stress. Key to this goal will be an intentional commitment to trauma-informed staff development and teacher training courses.

Accepting the notion that students with traumatic stress are profoundly sensitive to perceived threats is the critical first step to becoming trauma-informed. The resulting changes in disciplinary policies and ultimately school climates would be freeing and productive for both students and staff.

Believing that compassion, warmth, and love have the power to change the brain can become the legacy of trauma-informed schools and educators. Trauma does not have to be a lifetime sentence (Cozolino, 2006).

References

Bailey, B. A. (2000). *I love you rituals*. New York: HarperCollins.

Cozolino, L. (2006). *The neuroscience of human relationships: Attachment and the developing brain*. New York: W. W. Norton & Co.

Kagan, R. (2004). *Rebuilding attachments with traumatized children*. New York: Haworth Press.

Levine, P. A., & Kline, M. (2007). *Trauma through a child's eyes*. Berkeley, CA: North Atlantic Books.

Malchiodi, C. A. (2008). *Creative interventions with traumatized children*. New York: Guilford Press.

Oehlberg, B. (1996). *Making it better: Activities for children living in a stressful world*. St. Paul, MN: Redleaf Press.

Oehlberg, B. (2006). *Reaching and teaching stressed and anxious learners in Grades 4–8*. Thousand Oaks, CA: Corwin Press.

Perry, B. D. (1997). Incubation in terror: Neurodevelopmental factors in the cycle of violence. In J. Osofsky (Ed.), *Children, youth, and violence*. New York: Guilford Press.

Perry, B. D. (2004). The fear response: The impact of childhood trauma. [Video, Series No. 1.] The Child Trauma Academy, at www.childtrauma.org (accessed February 23, 2010).

Schore, A. N. (2001). Effects of a secure attachment relationship on right brain development, affect regulation, and infant mental health. *Infant Mental Health Journal*, 22(1 & 2), 7–66.

Steele, W. (1997). *Trauma Intervention Program for children and adolescents*. Grosse Pointe, MI: The National Institute for Trauma and Loss in Children.

Stien, P. T., & Kendall, J. (2004). *Psychological trauma and the developing brain*. Binghamton, NY: Haworth Press.

Chapter Thirteen

A City-Wide School-Based Model for Addressing the Needs of Children Exposed to Terrorism and War

Ruth Pat-Horenczyk, Danny Brom, Naomi Baum, Rami Benbenishty, Miriam Schiff, and Ron Avi Astor

Introduction

This chapter describes a broad-based school program for providing services for children in the wake of terrorism and war in Israel. The model was developed after the escalation of political violence in the Middle East with the outbreak of the Second Intifada in September 2000. It was implemented after the Second Lebanon War, when 4,000 rockets hit several cities in the north of Israel during the late summer of 2006. This chapter outlines the development of the model as well as its various components, including its limitations. We also indicate the challenges that may be faced in future adaptations of the model by other communities exposed to political conflicts, community violence, and natural disasters.

Current community-wide, post-trauma models often do not address the needs of children in an entire city. Even more important is the fact that variations in the incidence and prevalence of both post-traumatic stress and resilience *in different schools* in the same city are sorely neglected conceptual areas in the post-trauma literature. This limits our ability to funnel scarce physical and mental health resources to the locations that need it the most and to the children who are most vulnerable. Our model was developed with the goal of reaching each school and child in any given city or region, following a traumatic event such as war.

Post-Traumatic Syndromes in Childhood and Adolescence: A Handbook of Research and Practice, First Edition.
Edited by Vittoria Ardino. © 2011 John Wiley & Sons, Ltd. Published 2011 by John Wiley & Sons, Ltd.

Background and assumptions

One of the distinguishing aspects of catastrophic events and ongoing exposure to various types of violence is that the traumatic experiences are not limited to a few individuals or families, but tend to involve entire communities. A major tenet of our model, therefore, is that, in order to prevent or reduce the negative impact of disasters on children, it is essential to adopt an ecological approach (Bronfenbrenner, 1979). Accordingly, we assume that the consequences of children's exposure to political violence are based on the interaction among several relevant subsystems, i.e., the individual child, the family, the school, neighborhood, and the entire social service system (Kataoka et al., 2003).

Recently, other researchers have recognized the need for a conceptual integration of the city and schools. These studies have included screening for post-disaster trauma symptoms and resulting interventions in school systems as the result of: (a) natural disasters, e.g., Hurricane Andrew (Chemtob, Nakashima, & Hamada, 2002); (b) terrorist attacks, e.g., 9/11 (Hoven, Duarte, & Mandell, 2003); (c) inner-city violence (Stein et al., 2003); and (d) the war in Bosnia (Layne et al., 2001). Our model has been influenced also by previous clinical experience with school-based interventions in the face of terrorism in Israel (Baum, 2005; Pat-Horenczyk, 2005) and the burgeoning literature on building resilience in the school system (Masten, 2007).

More specifically, the model we present here developed in the face of terrorism and war integrates community and clinical interventions for mitigating their impact as well as enhancing personal and communal resilience. Thus, it is geared at serving the entire school population, which is mostly resilient, but also at clinically targeting the most vulnerable or impacted children.

An additional assumption of the model is that any intervention must be tailored to the specific needs of a particular school and district, based on the current circumstances of the children and the school staff. For example, even in situations in which an entire city or district has been directly exposed to war, the death of one or more children or parents in a particular school drastically changes the needs of this school in comparison with other schools which have not sustained similar losses. We have learned that while there is much that is shared by communities that are exposed to violence and catastrophic events, in each case there are many unique contextual characteristics that have immediate implications for assessment and intervention strategies. Specific adaptations also are needed to work with a variety of age groups from kindergarten to high school. Similarly, any intervention must be sensitive to the specific needs of culturally diverse communities.

The model is also built on the conviction that effective implementation of long-term programs is conditional upon building capacity within the local educational system. Immediate responses after a traumatic event and development of innovative programs are often conducted by organizations that are not part of the regular school system, such as nongovernmental organizations (NGOs) and university departments. The work of these organizations is commonly characterized by versatility and the possibility of quick responses to new situations, but is also limited in time, budget, and capacity. Thus, the question of the sustainability of such projects becomes a crucial one. The model, therefore, includes the ecological environment with the goal of building capacity within the local educational system and independent sustainability of the model over time. Consequently, we involve the local school and municipality staff from the planning phase of the program and transfer more and more tasks to local staff as the process progresses.

Finally, we believe that research and evaluation are integral parts of the change process and provide important empirical evidence that advances both scientific knowledge and clinical practice. Thus, the model is built on the supposition that ongoing collaboration between academic scholars and practitioners is mutually beneficial, in that clinical and community interventions are informed by the knowledge gained from research. The scholarly work has helped us to identify the most relevant risk and protective factors, to develop valid instruments with which to assess them, and to implement the most effective evidence-based intervention practices. The results obtained from the field, in turn, provide feedback and evidence as to the feasibility and efficacy of the model and lead to further research and more refined conceptualizations. We found this approach both stimulating and empowering for the school staff and community professionals, by helping them base their interventions on scientific evidence, rather than solely on practical wisdom. The approach was also extremely enriching for the scholars, whose research directions were constantly fertilized by the results from the field. In addition, we have found that continuous monitoring and data collection are pivotal, in the context of social challenges, for planning new, flexible, and relevant responses to the changing needs within the school system.

Implementation of the model

The model consists of seven components that reflect a nested ecological social environment. The components include (a) screening at the individual and school levels for post-traumatic stress as well as protective factors; (b) working with teachers on building resilience; (c) building the resilience of parents; (d) the implementation of school-based interventions; (e) identifying and training school mental health personnel; (f) working with local governmental authorities in order to build community capacity and ensure sustainability; and (g) continuous monitoring of the evolving needs and effectiveness of the various components.

Based on the work published by the Institute of Medicine (1994), we incorporated into our model three different types of intervention aimed at improving the mental health of students: universal, selective, and indicated. *Universal interventions* target all students; *selective interventions* are addressed only to high-risk students; and *indicated interventions* address the needs of students on the brink of risk, when signs of problem behavior begin to emerge (Power, 2003). Inherent in these three models is the desire to promote maximum health and resilience (Baum et al., 2009), on the one hand, while also intervening, and possibly, offering treatment in the case of risk or psychopathology, on the other hand.

The model is also predicated on the assumption that addressing the difficulties of significant adults in children's lives, i.e., parents and teachers who may also be affected by a disastrous event, is an integral part of addressing the needs of children. Therefore, teachers and parents, whose distress is a risk factor for children's distress, are legitimate targets for intervention.

School-based screening for post-traumatic distress

We developed our screening strategy based on previous large-scale, school-based screening efforts (for school intervention, see also Oehlberg, Chapter 12 in this book). These school-based screenings have shown that neither teachers nor parents know how to identify post-traumatic distress in children (Chemtob et al., 2002), and that the majority of students (about two-thirds) suffering from post-traumatic symptoms are not referred for any mental health services (Hoven et al., 2003). Thus, the aim of the school-based screening was to identify students suffering from post-traumatic symptoms, functional impairment, and related distress and refer them for appropriate and effective school-based interventions. An additional purpose of the screening was to assess a variety of existing risk and protective factors among the student population that are relevant for their ability to cope in the aftermath of traumatic events (Pat-Horenczyk et al., 2008).

Since the outbreak of the Second Intifada in September 2000, and based on a sample of nearly 7,000 students throughout Israel, we have shown the feasibility and effectiveness of our school-based screening in identifying students in need of some form of intervention. We have found that more than 32% reported personal exposure to terrorist attacks, and an additional 22% reported near-miss experiences (Pat-Horenczyk et al., 2007). Although more than two-thirds of the youths reported extreme fear and helplessness, only 7.6% of them reported post-traumatic symptoms that would meet the *DSM-IV* criteria for PTSD.

The school-based screening, including the assessment of coping strategies and social support, has led to some important findings. One is the ability to assign students to various school-based interventions according to their combined profiles of risk and protective factors. We also have found that while girls tend to express their distress in more severe post-traumatic symptoms, boys show more impaired functioning in school, family, and social domains (Pat-Horencyzk, Abramovitz et al., 2007). Another important finding points to the relationship between post-traumatic distress and increased risk-taking behavior among adolescents (Pat-Horenczyk, Peled et al., 2007). Surprisingly, we also learned that some students exposed to terrorism only through media coverage also developed post-traumatic symptoms (Pat-Horenczyk, 2005).

A city-wide screening of 1,015 students in grades 4 to 12 in the northern Israeli city of Nahariya, a year after the Second Lebanon War, gave us additional insight. In a city that had experienced extensive damage from rockets, we asked students directly to what extent they would like to get help coping with the aftermath of the war. We learned that the extent to which they wanted help was a significant predictor of their distress over and above other known risk and protective factors. Based on this self-report question, 25% of the children and 5% of the adolescents indicated that they were interested in getting help. An additional 16% of the adolescents were "not sure" whether they wanted help (Brom et al., 2007).

Building resilience with teachers

Our intervention began by working with teachers and focused specifically on how they themselves were coping with the massive exposure to terrorism and on how they could strengthen their own resilience as well as that of their students. Teachers expressed the need for concrete tools and structured activities they could practice in the classroom. These tools served two purposes: they empowered teachers and gave them a sense of control and confidence; they also helped them to introduce difficult and painful subjects in the classroom that they had hitherto avoided. In so doing, the teachers were able to change the classroom environment into one that encouraged communication regarding the range of emotions that all were experiencing and, thus, became a center of social support and caring.

All our interventions were accompanied by pre-and post-evaluations designed to assess teacher satisfaction and changes in skills, knowledge, and attitudes. Data from more than 900 teachers who participated in resilience-building programs indicated a significant increase in knowledge, skills, and a greater willingness to implement the program.

Building resilience with parents

Involving the children's parents is often the most neglected component of school-based interventions. Hence, there is a dearth of knowledge regarding the feasibility and effectiveness of parental involvement in school-based interventions. Yet, in order to create a truly resilient environment for the children, it is not enough to change the classroom environment. We have been most successful at recruiting parental involvement in the preschools, running many four-session parent groups entitled *Resilient Parent–Resilient Child*. In contrast, parental participation at the elementary and high school level has proven more difficult to obtain. At those levels, we have been most successful in involving parents by initiating single-event parents' nights. This one-time session includes a lecture to parents on the subject of how adults and children cope during prolonged periods of stress and exposure to trauma, as well as teaching parents how to communicate with children about stress and trauma. Parents' nights also proved to be an ideal time to present information about the screening program and to obtain informed consent from parents.

School-based treatment modalities

The screening component of the model showed us the importance of developing appropriate school-based interventions to address the needs of the most affected students within the school system in a non-stigmatizing way. Hence, we developed two modules of school-based interventions. The first is entitled *Journey to Resilience* and is geared to students who manifest post-traumatic symptoms and general distress that does not reach the clinical level. For this group, we developed a protocol for a six-session intervention, which is facilitated by trained guidance counselors. The intervention includes sessions on psychoeducation about normal reactions and coping with trauma and stress, practicing stress management techniques, including relaxation and cognitive restructuring, and enhancing peer group support and self-care (Pat-Horenczyk et al., 2004). We have successfully trained nearly 400 guidance counselors with this protocol and they have implemented it in hundreds of groups across Israel in the last few years.

The second module is a school-based group treatment geared to students who have been screened and identified as having PTSD. This 12-session intervention is conducted by trained school psychologists (Pat-Horenczyk et al., 2004). The treatment module includes the employment of specific techniques to process the traumatic event and its consequences, along with units on psychoeducation, relaxation, and relapse-prevention. A pre- and post-assessment of the group treatment module has indicated a decrease in post-traumatic symptoms, particularly in symptoms of hyperarousal.

Training school mental health professionals

School mental health professionals in Israel have become increasingly aware of the need to be trained in specific tools designed to help them provide appropriate interventions in the wake of a terrorist attack. Because the school system is often eager to show that everything is *back to normal* and encourages teachers to go about their daily routine, school mental health practitioners often have sole responsibility for taking care of the lingering consequences of such a major traumatic event.

In the Israeli system, school psychologists and guidance counselors address different mental health needs. Our model provides for psychologists to be trained in specific skills needed for conducting teacher resilience workshops. They also are trained to provide more specialized treatment to individuals and to follow the 12-session group treatment protocol. Guidance counselors are also key players in the program. They act as mental health advocates in schools and mobilize existing resources to better cope with trauma and disaster. Their trauma and resilience training includes ongoing supervision in the process of the implementation of the school-based intervention and in building resilience. This multilayered system of care for children in the educational system is an important component in the implementation of our school-based intervention program. School psychologists who have participated in the trauma and re-silience training have reported a significant increase in their professional skills level and in their own ability to cope with stress. Similarly, guidance counselors whom we have trained have been highly motivated to employ the school-based group intervention (Baum et al., 2009).

Building system-wide capacity and sustainability

In order to ensure proper implementation of the program, including its sustain-ability, strong working relationships need to be established with municipalities or school districts, supervisors of boards of education, and school principals. After meeting and gaining commitment from educational leaders and policy makers in the Israeli Ministry of Education, we informed all levels of school administration, staff, and parents about the project.

After we established a working relationship with the principal and a leading team in each school, we explained the program, set up timelines, and clarified expectations and responsibilities for both the research team and the school staff. It has become our practice to train psychologists from the local school system in conducting resilience-building workshops, so that this skill becomes institutionalized. Additionally, in order to treat the children who are identified through the screening, local therapists are selected in coordination with the school's psychological services and are trained in trauma-focused therapy.

Experience has taught us that a city-wide approach is most likely to be effective in contributing to the long-term sustainability of the program. Prior city-wide studies of school violence, PTSD, and substance abuse in the face of prolonged exposure to terrorism in a number of Israeli cities (Schiff, 2006; Schiff et al., 2007) have already been instrumental in guiding local policy (Benbenishty, Khoury-Kassabri, & Astor, 2005).

Continuous monitoring of needs in affected communities

Community needs change dynamically after disasters and war, and create a constant challenge to flexibly adjust the community's mental health response. Continuous monitoring through research and ongoing feedback from the field to policy makers can guide the tailoring of programs to the most affected groups. An additional function of the continuous monitoring is to highlight new emerging needs and stimulate the development of appropriate new responses.

A recent example of such an interactive process is a survey we conducted after the Second Lebanon War among Israeli children and youths which was designed to assess psychological distress and needs. The sample consisted of 6,679 Jewish and Arab 4th to 11th grade students in the north of Israel. The survey examined several types of stressors (e.g., degree of exposure to war and prior trauma history) and individual and social protective factors (e.g., perceived teacher support and life satisfaction). It also assessed levels of post-traumatic symptoms, anxiety, and depression, as well as functional impairment.

We found that 4% of elementary school students and 3.4% of junior high school students reported symptoms meeting criteria for PTSD. The study also corroborated the impressions of educational staff that there had been a substantial increase in school violence and in substance abuse. Self-reports of violence were more prevalent among boys than girls. Arab students reported a greater prevalence of serious violence directed at students and teachers than did Jewish students. For example, 2.8% of the Jewish students reported that they had hit or pushed a teacher compared to 10.7% of the Arab students. Half of the Jewish students and about one-fifth of the Arab students reported that they drank alcohol; about a quarter of the Arab students and about 15% of the Jewish students reported sniffing volatile substances. These data proved to be valuable for policy makers and pointed to the specific need to address the school violence and substance abuse issues within the comprehensive resilience-building programs (Schiff et al., 2007).

The study also was instrumental in identifying high-risk groups in need of more intensive intervention. For instance, we found that Israeli Arab youths were much more vulnerable to post-traumatic symptomatology and reported fewer protective factors than Jewish youths who had experienced similar levels of exposure to the war.

Lessons learned

During the years of the development of the school-based intervention program we have learned the crucial importance of involving the professional resources that are available in the community. If intervention programs are to have a lasting impact beyond their initial implementation, they must aim at building the capacity within the local community to disseminate the program. In order to increase community-wide motivation to implement new programs, all stakeholders in the community need to be involved in the coordination of the program's activities and feel ownership of the process. This requires researchers and NGOs to make a clear policy decision to avoid fostering dependence on external resources and instead empower the existing community infrastructure.

It has also become clear that there is a better chance of a community taking over the program if it builds on existing relationships within the community and creates new dialogue among the participating organizations. Once people experience the benefits of the integrative program and appreciate the additional benefits of the collaboration, sustainability becomes a possibility. Conversely, when new programs are forced onto the system without preparatory dialogue, they often meet resistance on the part of the community's professionals. For example, the involvement of the School Psychological Service in the implementation of the school-based intervention program created an opportunity to integrate a new project into the existing services and strengthen the community's resources. Once the recognition of the need grows, there is a better chance for the program to be perceived as an essential part of the psychosocial services landscape.

We have learned that combined efforts to implement the various components of the model are likely to have a much more substantial impact on the system than the mere additive value of each of the components. In other words, the implementation of the model as a whole and the fact that parents, teachers, mental health personnel, and the children themselves are all direct beneficiaries of the program create a new language within the school environment. For example, the importance of self-care for parents and teachers can be acknowledged and defined as a necessary ingredient for the success of such intervention programs. The concepts of building resilience and the importance of providing services for vulnerable children based on ongoing data collection and monitoring may become a consensual standard for the care for children after trauma. This new language of child care as a societal priority is an important part of community resilience.

Dilemmas and challenges

Privatization of services is a major challenge in western societies, where governments are often accused of failing to meet their responsibilities to effectively respond to disasters and terrorism. NGOs often are much quicker in responding to rapidly changing situations. This unique relationship between government and NGOs creates a challenge for designing and implementing programs. On the one hand, the versatility of NGOs can provide governmental mental health systems with new options, but on the other hand, NGOs are often funded for specific and time-limited projects, and therefore may lose their long-term interest or ability in sustaining their involvement. The comprehensive program presented in this chapter is based on a clear strategic decision to use the respective strengths of the NGO and the governmental education system. Both have their separate tasks, recognition of which can foster mutual respect and collaboration.

Parents are crucial partners in programs designed to advance the care for children. However, they become the neglected party in many interventions. A known phenomenon is that recruitment of parents in school-based programs gets more difficult the older the children are. In early childhood it is relatively easy to have parents respond to programs that affect their children. In high schools it is a very serious challenge. Yet, parental involvement is crucial, not least for obtaining consent for the school-based screening, which is a basic element in the implementation of school-based interventions.

The roles that schools fulfill are changing according to their sociopolitical environment. In the aftermath of trauma and disaster, schools are a major force for the well-being of children. However, they are often overburdened in the immediate aftermath of trauma or disaster and, thus, they tend to show a keen interest in intervention programs. Yet, as time passes and the burden of daily routine takes over, motivation to be involved tends to decrease. We are trying out different ways of boosting the motivation of school staff, through supporting more counseling hours and other forms of activities that enhance professionalism.

Finally, the need for cultural adaptation and the effort to reach out to vulnerable populations, such as minorities, immigrants, and groups with special needs, is a constant challenge. In more traditional cultures, it might be easier to implement intervention programs, once the spiritual or community leadership is convinced of their value. We have seen that in populations with more traditional family structures, the adherence to the program and the response rate for the screening are much higher than in more westernized populations. The partnership between school staff and those who design the programs is crucial for the flexible adaptation of services to the varying needs of children.

The model for post-trauma intervention presented here is unique in the sense that it has the potential to identify each student in a given school who is experiencing either PTSD or school-related difficulties. It also has the potential to target specific grade levels, gender groups or ethnic subgroups that are more heavily affected. Because the survey administration is a relatively quick method to apply (compared with clinical screening of each child), it can be used multiple times to help identify every potentially needy child in every school within a given city or region. This allows all of a system's resources, NGO supports, and all available trained professionals to effectively reach out to the schools and the children that need it the most.

Future development of the model and its implementation need to be directed at determining the immediate and long-term effects of each type of intervention in various types of community disasters. Attention also needs to be given to the extent to which each type of intervention enhances participants' sense of competence and well-being, beyond the focus on the measurement of post-traumatic distress. Lastly, the model presented in this chapter is likely to be useful in societies in which violence has become an ongoing phenomenon in children's lives.

References

Baum, N. (2005). Post-traumatic distress in adolescents exposed to ongoing terror: Findings from a school-based screening project in the Jerusalem area. In Y. Daniely, D. Brom, J. Sills, & M. I. Holland (Eds.), *The trauma of terrorism: Sharing knowledge and shared care, An international handbook* (pp. 487–98). Binghamton, NY: Haworth Press.

Baum, N. L., Rotter, B., Reidler, E., & Brom, D. (2009). Building resilience in schools in the wake of Hurricane Katrina. *Journal of Child & Adolescent Trauma, 2*(1), 62–70.

Benbenishty, R., Khoury-Kassabri, R., & Astor, R. A. (2005). *Violence in the school system 2005.* Jerusalem: Hebrew University School of Social Work.

Brom, D., Pat-Horenczyk, R., Baum, N. et al. (2007). Children in the wake of the Second Lebanon War: Findings of the city-wide school-based screening process in Nahariya. Unpublished report.

Bronfenbrenner, U. (1979). *The ecology of human development: Experiments by nature and design.* Cambridge, MA: Harvard University Press.

Chemtob, C., Nakashima, J., & Hamada, R. (2002). Psychosocial intervention for post-disaster trauma symptoms in elementary school children. *Archive of Pediatric Adolescent Medicine, 156,* 211–16.

Hoven, C., Duarte, C., & Mandell, D. (2003). Children's mental health after disasters: The impact of the World Trade Center attack. *Current Psychiatry Reports, 5*(2), 101–7.

Institute of Medicine (1994). *Reducing risks for mental disorders: Frontiers for preventive intervention research.* Washington, DC: National Academy Press.

Kataoka, S., Stein, B., Jaycox, L. et al. (2003). A school-based mental health program for traumatized Latino immigrant children. *American Academy of Child and Adolescent Psychiatry, 42*(3), 311–18.

Layne, C. M., Pynoos, R. S., Saltzman, W. R. et al. (2001). Trauma/grief-focused group psychotherapy: School-based postwar intervention with traumatized Bosnian adolescents. *Group Dynamics, 5,* 277–90.

Masten, A. (2003). Commentary: Developmental psychopathology as a unifying context for mental health and education models, research, and practice in schools. *School Psychology Review, 32*(2), 169–73.

Masten, A. (2007). Resilience in developing systems: Progress and promise as the fourth wave rises. *Development and Psychopathology, 19,* 921–30.

Pat-Horenczyk, R. (2005). Post-traumatic distress in adolescents exposed to ongoing terror: Findings from a school-based screening project in the Jerusalem area. In Y. Daniely, D. Brom, J. Sills, & M. I. Holland (Eds.), *The trauma of terrorism: Sharing knowledge and shared care, an international handbook* (pp. 335–47). Binghamton, NY: Haworth Press.

Pat-Horenczyk, R., Abramovitz, R., Peled, O. et al. (2007). Adolescent exposure to recurrent terrorism in Israel: Posttraumatic distress and functional impairment. *American Journal of Orthopsychiatry, 7*(1), 76–85.

Pat-Horenczyk, R., Berger, R., Kaplinsky, N., & Baum. N. (2004). The journey to resilience: Coping with ongoing stressful situations. Protocol for guidance counselors (adolescents' version). Unpublished manuscript.

Pat-Horenczyk, R., Peled, O., Miron, T. et al. (2007). Risk-taking behaviors among Israeli adolescents exposed to recurrent terrorism. *The American Journal of Psychiatry, 164*(1), 66–72.

Pat-Horenczyk, R., Rabinowitz, R., Rice, A., & Tucker-Levin, A. (2008). The search for risk and protective factors in childhood PTSD: From variables to processes. In D. Brom, R. Pat-Horenczyk, & J. Ford (Eds.), *Treating traumatized children: Risk, resilience, and recovery.* Hove, East Sussex: Routledge.

Power, T. (2003) Promoting children's mental health: Reform through interdisciplinary and community partnerships. *School Psychology Review, 32*(1), 3–16.

Schiff, M. (2006). Living in the shadow of terrorism: Psychological distress and alcohol use among religious and non-religious adolescents in Jerusalem. *Social Science and Medicine, 62,* 2301–12.

Schiff, M., Zweig, H., Benbenishty, R., & Hasin, D. S. (2007). Exposure to terrorism and Israeli youth's cigarettes, alcohol, and cannabis use. *American Journal of Public Health, 97,* 1852–8.

Stein, B. D., Jaycox, L. H., Kataoka, S. H. et al. (2003). A mental health intervention for school children exposed to violence. *Journal of the American Medical Association, 290,* 603–11.

Chapter Fourteen

Helping Children after Mass Disaster: Using a Comprehensive Trauma Center and School Support

Brigitte Lueger-Schuster

Introduction

Major disasters can strike children of all ages leading to phased psychosocial responses: the event, the evolution of the event, parental and siblings' reactions to the event, teachers' response, availability of social support, and the child's individual characteristics, such as resilience and vulnerability.

How children cope with disasters influences their mental functioning as children and as adults. This chapter presents an overview of psychosocial interventions in mass disasters underpinned by scientific findings, and provides an example of the intervention model, which was adopted by the author in the aftermath of the Beslan[1] massacre.

The impact of mass disasters on children

Children respond to trauma in a different way from adults. As stated elsewhere in this book, *ICD-10* (International Statistical Classification of Diseases and Related Health Problems; WHO, 2005) and *DSM-IV* (APA, 1994) offer diagnostic criteria to classify trauma-related disorders; however both

---

[1] Project holder: Hilfswerk Austria, financed by Austria Developmental Agency (ADA), leader of expert team: Katharina Purtscher; visiting experts: Maria Steinbauer, Peter Ruggenthaler, Brigitte Lueger-Schuster. Duration of Austrian funding: 2004–2006.

Post-Traumatic Syndromes in Childhood and Adolescence: A Handbook of Research and Practice, First Edition. Edited by Vittoria Ardino. © 2011 John Wiley & Sons, Ltd. Published 2011 by John Wiley & Sons, Ltd.

diagnostic systems are principally based on adults' reactions to type I traumas. Although DSM and ICD attempted to provide a spectrum of symptoms representing children's reactions, such as regression and traumatic play, there is an ongoing debate about the adequacy of the official diagnostic criteria to classify children's post-traumatic reactions. Most critiques put forward the poor link between developmental stage and expression of symptoms as well as the interaction between children's developmental changes in terms of cognitive abilities, personality, and social challenges, and their expression of symptoms.

The aforementioned critical issues could also be applied to the understanding of children's reactions to mass disasters (Meichenbaum, 1994). Major disasters fall within the dimensions of unusual stress as defined within the criteria of PTSD, which include natural and technological disasters, war, the child's witnessing the accidental or violent death of a significant adult, being kidnapped, and other stressors of similar severity. Frederick (1980) has claimed that victims react differently to man-made versus natural disasters; and Beigel and Berren (1985) have suggested that diverse emotional reactions to different natural disasters depend on the victim's belief about what caused the disaster, the degree of violence it produced, and the extent to which the victim was involved with its effects. Other additional factors have also been offered as explanations for children's very different responses to disasters. Two of these are intra-psychic: (1) the developmental level of the child, and (2) the child's premorbid mental health, some children being resilient and others, vulnerable. More vulnerable victims of mass disasters develop PTSD symptoms in the first weeks or months after the event. Such symptoms include worries, fears, and anxieties about the safety of self and others, and worries about reexperiencing the event. Furthermore, children may also present behavioral changes, such as increased arousal, poor concentration, and attention problems (which could lead to a misdiagnosis of ADHD in school-age children). Other symptoms include outbursts of anger or irritability, poor academic achievement, and withdrawal. Physical reactions include headaches, gastrointestinal problems, vague aches and pains, and sleep problems usually related to nightmares of trauma-related material (younger children may present nightmares not specifically related to the traumatic event). Intrusions could be expressed via post-traumatic play, repetitive thoughts about death, dying, suicidal ideas, and/or plans.

Although children's reactions to mass disasters have been explored in several studies, scientific knowledge of the impact upon the younger members of our community is limited. The literature is evolving, and there is a small number of valuable studies that can inform a response to the mental health needs of this younger population, for example, the intervention undertaken by the author following Beslan. For the purposes of this chapter available epidemiological data on children's and adolescents' mental health after a traumatic experience are presented first, followed by epidemiological data focused on child victims of mass disasters.

Epidemiological data on children and mass disasters

Epidemiological research points out that a large majority of children and adolescents are exposed to at least one or more traumatic events in their lifetime (Fairbrother et al., 2003). The risk for developing a PTSD or other related disorder can be assessed as high, especially for those with multiple traumatic experiences.

In a recent epidemiological study, Fairbank (2008) identified four epidemiological categories that are informative of children's and adolescents' reactions to a spectrum of traumatic experiences. The identified categories are:

1. estimation of the prevalence and impact of different traumatic experiences on the general population of youth using national samples;
2. estimation of exposure severity and impact of specific disasters based on school samples;
3. estimation of the prevalence of child abuse based on data from child protection services;
4. research on vulnerable groups of children, such as children in foster care.

Falling in the first category, the Developmental Victimization Study (Finkelhor et al., 2005) found 34 different forms of victimization in a representative sample of 2,030 children aged from two to 17 years. Furthermore, 71% of the sample had been exposed to one or more incidents in the preceding year. Likewise, almost 70% of the sample had been victims of a multiple exposure (three incidents over the preceding year). In Europe, Perkonigg and colleagues (2000) conducted a longitudinal study on 3,021 German adolescents aged 14 to 24; 21.4% reported a *lifetime* exposure, meeting the *DSM-IV* A1 criterion. Male adolescents were more vulnerable to multiple exposures compared to female adolescents (26% against 17.7%). When Criterion A2 was introduced, the percentage decreased to 18.6% for males and 15.5% for females. The prevalence of PTSD in the general population was 1% for males and 2.2% for females. In a follow-up study by Perkonigg and colleagues (2005), the authors reported that more than 50% of the cohort with PTSD at baseline remained symptomatic for more than three years. In the National Comorbidity Survey (Kessler et al., 1995) the lifetime prevalence of PTSD was found to be 7.8% in the general population; however, out of a total percentage of 60%, 51% of females were exposed to a traumatic event against 7% for males. Breslau and colleagues (2004) found in a large US urban population of adolescents a lifetime exposure of 82.5% and a lifetime prevalence of 7.9% for females and 6.3% for males. In the second category – focused on school samples – Fairbank (2008) analyzed the psychosocial and psychiatric sequelae of disasters. For example, Hoven and colleagues (2005) assessed the needs of public school students in New York City after the 9/11attacks. The prevalence of PTSD six months after the attack was between 6% and 10% alongside a percentage of agoraphobia of 14.8%, conduct disorder of 12.8%, separation anxiety of 12.3%, and alcohol problems of 4.5%. Fairbank (2008) also presented other studies focused on the sequelae of hurricanes, bush fires, and earthquakes. The PTSD prevalence rate was between 8% and 75% up to 18 months after the disaster.

Galea, Nandi, and Vlahov (2005) comprehensively and systematically reviewed epidemiologic evidence about PTSD following disasters; they pointed out that although comparable international data are not available, many individuals across the world have been exposed to different forms of collective traumas, such as war, terror, natural disasters, and displacement. The review put forward the need to identify specific characteristics across different typologies of collective traumas and therefore, the importance of differentiating natural disasters from man made or technological disasters and terror, as the dynamics and implications vary greatly according to the type of disaster. The prevalence of PTSD after man-made/technological disasters similar to the event that happened in Beslan is mostly based on adult populations who experienced the event as primary victims. A smaller number of studies investigated the prevalence of PTSD in children and adolescents who had been victims of similar disasters (Green et al., 1991; Pfefferbaum, et al., 2003; Vila, Porche, & Mouren-Simeoni, 1999). The assessment measures that have been used in studies of children are inconsistent, and many of the studies of children have documented PTSD symptoms only, limiting cross-study comparisons of the prevalence of PTSD. For example, a cross-sectional study of children conducted after a 1984 sniper attack on a school playground in Los Angeles, California, showed that 38.4% of the children had moderate or severe levels of PTSD symptoms one month after the incident (Pynoos et al., 1987). Following another school shooting in Winnetka, Illinois, in 1998, the prevalence of PTSD based on *DSM-III-R* (APA, 1987) criteria was assessed to be 8% among children eight to 14 months later (Schwarz & Kowalski, 1991).

Beslan elicits a further reflection on the nature of complex terrorist attacks. Children and adolescents who survive a terrorist attack like the Beslan massacre are likely to experience multiple traumatic exposures involving being a hostage, prolonged kidnapping, and liberation through the army's use of force. Some of these youths may also have been exposed to traumatic events prior to the attack. An online search on studies about Beslan retrieved 458,000 publications. When the keyword "children" was added to the search, only 1,100 publications were retrieved (June 4, 2008). These publications included studies on other traumatic events and applied their results to Beslan children. Only a few publications were specifically focused on children's outcomes of the Beslan traumatic experience.

The event at Beslan: background and description of the attack

Northern Caucasian republics are located to the west of the Republic of Ingushetia and they were considered relatively secure territories until the attack at Beslan (Northern Ossetia) occurred in School Number One. Contrary to Chechnya and Dagestan, the political perspective of Islam did not receive much support among the population; Ingushetian territories did not adhere to radical Islamic beliefs.

Beslan is a small town of 40,000 inhabitants in the Republic of North Ossetia, which is part of the Russian Federation. The Republic of North Ossetia has a population of 600,000 people, and the capital is Vladikavkaz. Although Ossetians are aware of their own culture, they adhere to the Russian Federation, which is considered as a protective wall against offenders due to the region's geographical location at the border of Chechnya and Ingushetia, two of the most dangerous regions in the world.

The aforementioned territories have gone through critical and traumatizing events across time. Because of suspected pro-Nazi sympathies, Stalin deported thousands of Chechen and Ingushetian families to Asia. Most of the men born during this deportation period became militant fighters in the Chechen war from 1994 to 1996 and again in 1999. At the 57th anniversary celebrations of the Great Patriotic War, more than 40 people died after a bomb attack by Chechen extremists. Likewise, the secession of Georgia from the Russian Federation caused family displacements and losses after the border was closed. Furthermore, the population suffered from the consequences of the lengthy war between the former USSR and Afghanistan.

This very difficult sector of the Russian population has not progressed, favoring a climate of silence and denial, which is at one with the atmosphere of the Soviet regime. Large proportions of the population are still influenced by this cultural view alongside other cultural beliefs, such as the importance of considering the family as a clan which welcomes numerous members. Trauma is deeply rooted in the Caucasian area. Williams and colleagues (2007) point out that a history of prolonged and multiple traumatic events is a key feature of a culture where violence begets violence in dealing with problems, and where violence is used as a dysfunctional defense mechanism. In their study on the situation in South Africa, Williams and colleagues (2007) highlighted the importance of shedding light on the cycle of traumatic events when attempting to understand the context in which a trauma has occurred. The same concepts could also be applied to an understanding of the situation in the Caucasian region.

The attack

On September 1, 2004 a new school term had started. In these territories, the first day of school is celebrated as a family day. Children are accompanied by parents and grandparents in order to commit to the "day of knowledge." School Number One was crowded with children, parents, and grandparents as the opening ceremony had just begun. At 9.30 a group of 33 terrorists, calling for an end to the Second Chechen War, entered the school yard and took 1,200 people hostage. Adults and children had to undress and remain in their underwear. They were all imprisoned in the smaller of the two gyms, which were also mined with bombs. It was a very warm day: hostages were not allowed to eat and drink. Just a few of them were able to escape in the early phase of the attack whereas the majority of hostages were forced to spend three days in the gym. On September 3, the Russian Army brought an end to the attack by force; of the 334 hostages who died, 186 were children.

One of the surviving terrorists was condemned to death in 2006. Jamil Basaev took responsibility for the attack, explaining that the Russian population should feel the pain of losing their children and describing the attack as an appropriate reaction to the cruelty of the war against the Chechen population. Until recently, there were rumors that the attack was in revenge for a violent act by Ossetians against Ingushetians.

Negotiations during the hostage phase attracted media attention worldwide. Jamil Basaev was executed in July 2006. The 33 terrorists were probably from a small village named Psedach in Ingushetia. A police officer, who attempted to stop them, became their first hostage. At the end of the attack 20 of the 33 terrorists had been identified.

Beslan families are left with many doubts and anger about the attack, its outcomes, the process of negotiation, liberation, and court proceedings. The event was surrounded by complaints about a fire in the gym which caused the deaths of many of the victims. Furthermore, numerous myths about heroic rescuers and accusations about those who escaped were circulated, which contributed to the tense atmosphere that developed within the Beslan population following the event.

Consequences of the terrorist attack

More than 700 children and adults were injured. Hundreds of children and adults spent more than 53 hours without food or water in an overcrowded, hot gym mined with explosives; 334 hostages were killed along with eight other civilians, two emergency workers, 11 Special Forces, and 31 terrorists. The majority of the children were treated for burns, gunshot and shrapnel wounds, and mutilation caused by explosions. Some had to have limbs amputated or eyes removed. Many children were left permanently disabled.

Investigation

Family members accused the security forces of incompetence and called for the authorities to be investigated. President Putin promised the mothers of Beslan an objective investigation. In December 2005, Russian prosecutors declared that the authorities had made no mistakes. In December 2006, the Russian parliamentary commission stated that security measures were not adequate and they questioned local authorities for not having reported the exact number of hostages who were victims of the terrorists. However, the authorities declared that there was no ban on the use of flamethrowers, which were reported to have done the most harm to the hostages. Victims of the massacre are still involved in court inquiries as some of them have appealed to the European Court of Human Rights.

Psychological sequelae

There are only a few studies and reports analyzing the psychological consequences of the school massacre. Parvitt (2004) described the procedure of psychological support in the aftermath of the event. Forty-eight psychiatrists and psychologists from the Serbsky Institute in Moscow arrived in Beslan on the first day of the siege, providing support to relatives. When the shootings began, they moved to the main hospital to assess all patients as they arrived at the hospital. There was no possibility of debriefing children separately from their parents because parents were not willing to leave their children alone. A 24-hour hotline was established. Furthermore, psychologists were located at morgues and accompanied ambulance teams at funerals. The Serbsky team experienced an initial reluctance by the population to accept psychological support, especially by the men, due to the Caucasian male-oriented cultural tradition.

In the acute phase immediately after the attack, most common symptoms were phobias, compulsive thoughts, intrusive memories, sleep disturbances, nightmares, emotional instability, irritability, anger, depression, feelings of guilt, and flashbacks. PTSD and other attack-related disorders were treated by neurolinguistic programming, Ericksonian hypnosis, trance techniques, and relaxation (Parvitt, 2004). A three-week rehabilitation program was provided in and around Moscow, including visits to the theater; furthermore, some patients were sent to the Black Sea to recover. Foreign psychological support was not accepted as the Serbsky Institute insisted that its team was able to deliver proper treatment to the victims. It was necessary to monitor professionals working with victims of trauma, and several religious groups offered help. Seminars were held for those local doctors and teachers who would have close contact with the affected children.

Three months after the attack Scrimin and colleagues (2006) found a high incidence of PTSD in a group of 22 children and their 20 caregivers. Children also showed difficulties in sustaining attention and in short-term memory. The study was undertaken during a recovery phase in Italy, where all the children spent at least one month in a pediatric hospital. Moscardino and colleagues (2007) recruited a convenience sample of 19 families from Beslan during their recuperation in Italy three months after the attack. They collected observational and interview data from the parents about everyday life events and experiences before and after the attack. Several general themes were found amongst the parents: concern about their children's physical health, psychological reactions to the trauma, rethinking the parenting role, coping with the loss of loved ones, searching for a meaning to the massacre, disruption of family/community ties, a sense of insecurity, uncertainty, and vulnerability as a citizen, the thread of cultural identity, reaffirmation of positive, culturally shared values.

Distress and resources

Children have different degrees of vulnerability. More resilient children may not develop psychopathological symptoms even when they have been exposed to severe traumatization and distress. Punamäki (1996) showed, in a group of Palestinian children, that resilience could be attributed to strong ideological and social commitment, high self-esteem, successful and active coping, and creative problem solving. Punamäki and Suleiman (1989) noted that living in chronically life-endangering conditions forces children to balance between distress and resilience, and to solve conflicts between fear and courage. Active and problem-solving strategies protect children's mental health status, whereas passive coping strategies undermine children's psychological well-being (Compas, Malcarne, & Fondacaro, 1988). Compas (1998) also pointed out that problem-focused coping may be effective when the victims perceive they are in control of the situation; conversely a problem-focused coping style may be not so effective when victims perceive they are not in control of the situation. In a longitudinal study (Qouta et al., 2007) with Palestinian children exposed to several phases of the Intifada, children were found to be more vulnerable to PTSD symptoms when they reached adolescence if they had experienced prolonged traumatic exposures and had poor cognitive capacities and high neuroticism during middle childhood. Prolonged exposure to military violence during childhood combined with other stressful life events predicted serious depression and low quality of life satisfaction in adolescence.

Social support as an environmental resource could be identified as a protective factor which promotes coping strategies directly and indirectly acting as a buffer. Directly, social support promotes self-esteem, self-efficacy, and self-worth. The buffer effect mediates the connection between stress and stress reaction and symptoms (Antonucci & Akiyama, 1994). The first and main source of children's social support is parents and their family (Hobfoll et al., 1991). Studies on the Gulf War (1991) highlighted the importance of support from families, friends, and teachers as capable of reducing children's fear reactions and stress (Greenbaum, Erlich, & Toubiana, 1993; Klingman, 2001). In another study, Rosenbaum and Ronen (1997) reported that children's fear resembled and was affected by parental fear reactions.

The aforementioned combination of factors is key to investigating PTSD reactions in children. Problem-focused coping and well-developed cognitive capacities protect from PTSD. Likewise, social support buffers stress symptoms and increases self-efficacy as well as performing a function of mediation and regulation of fear symptoms. For this reason, it would be appropriate to foster cognitive capacity within a traumatized population in a supportive environment. Specifically, those factors are at the scientific core of a comprehensive trauma center and can be used to provide guidelines and evaluation plans for such a service.

A model to provide a psychosocial comprehensive trauma center: the example of Beslan

Shortly after the liberation of the hostages, Austrian authorities wanted to provide support to the children who were victims of the attack. Because foreign professionals were not welcomed during the acute phase after the trauma, the support offered was transformed into a center for children and youth in Beslan. Initially, the center aimed to offer specific support to traumatized children; later, it was converted into a comprehensive day-care center providing school support and other activities for children and youths in Beslan.

This center was created by an established Austrian NGO, which delivers care and support in diverse regions of the world. The organization had already provided a support unit close to Beslan in Ingushetia; their staff was therefore knowledgeable about local culture, values, and the community structure.

Aims

The main objectives of the center were prevention and empowerment. A first aim was to complement and integrate clinical interventions. The second aim was to provide a generalized framework of intervention, easily adapted to the whole population of Beslan, establishing a place where both direct and indirect victims of the massacre could gather. A third aim was to promote conflict resolution and peace-building strategies.

Planning

In the planning phase, several basic assumptions were taken into consideration in order to identify the target groups: the specific needs of the population, the needs of local mental health professionals and authorities, and an understanding of how local culture could embrace psychological treatment and support, with reference to the specific role of the economy and politics in determining the level of acceptance of that support. There were other factors to consider, such as an analysis of whether the level of education of local professionals was appropriate to work at the center. This led to another issue regarding the selection and training of professionals. With regard to the victims, the goal of the planning phase was how to achieve and maintain long-lasting effects of empowerment and identify the criteria of success that could function as the benchmark for later evaluation.

In 2005, the World Health Organization recommended an integrated approach with the aim of creating a team of professionals made up of local mental health workers and foreign professionals. Furthermore, WHO recommends a multidimensional and transcultural approach to take into account the contextual economic background of the affected society. On the same lines, the International Society of Traumatic Stress Studies (ISTSS/RAND Draft Guidelines for International Trauma Training) attributed great importance to this approach in their recommendations.

Target groups

Target groups can be differentiated by the different levels of involvement in the traumatic experience and by the type of reactions to the traumatic event. Primary victims are directly involved in the event; secondary victims are close to the group of primary victims; tertiary victims are in contact with the survivors and their families, and the families of the dead. Each of the three identified groups has specific needs.

Generally, primary victims are vulnerable to post-traumatic symptoms, mainly those of PTSD and a strong need to understand what happened to them. In conflict areas there is also a strong desire for safety and security along with financial support and to be acknowledged in their suffering.

Secondary victims are affected by the uncertainty state and their effectiveness in providing support to their family members. They may also present grief-related symptoms if they lost family members. Furthermore, they also need safety and security, and desire to understand what happened. They sometimes feel guilty because they feel they were not able to protect their family members.

Tertiary victims may present compassion fatigue (Figley, 1995) and symptoms of extreme stress. They can become especially vulnerable when the event affected people close to them, triggered their personal traumas, or when the seriousness of injuries, traumatic symptoms, and reactions are beyond their capacity to provide support.

Key influential factors

Cultural factors and political and financial conditions play a significant role in determining how the population receives professional help. Collective-oriented societies do not usually welcome support from outside and they tend to feel ashamed if they are not able to cope within their family context. In patriarchal societies women rely on men when they are in need of help. Therefore, the men are limited by their role and may not seek help themselves because of the risk of not being considered as a strong human being capable of coping with everything. This cultural view of the male role is strongly connected with the risk of substance abuse, especially alcohol. Even boys have to adhere to these role criteria, an aspect that must also be taken into account in planning measures of support.

The financial status of the target population determines greatly the level of acceptance of support; when people suffer from a lack of basic provisions, the availability of food should be part of the intervention program.

Trust in the political authorities involved in foreign support is also an important factor. Trauma-exposed populations in conflict areas are generally mistrustful, particularly of the public authorities. Confidence-building strategies, such as transparent communication of goals, qualifications, work strategies, and respect, may help to foster a sense of trust.

Selection and further training of local staff

The qualifications of local experts and service providers can differ to a great extent from country to country. Nevertheless, the criteria of selection and evaluation of qualification should be done in a culturally sensitive manner, referring to the experience and criteria of local experts. A curriculum can compensate for limitations and empower local experts to provide adequate services. Their strength lies in the fact that they are part of the local culture and traditions, and therefore able to understand local values. This position helps to develop a relationship with the traumatized population. Specific skills on psychotraumatology could be developed in a series of workshops.

Creating long-lasting effects

Support from outside is highly dependent on the funding available to the external teams. In the planning phase long-term effects on mental health should be evaluated and integration into the basic provision of healthcare systems should be achieved. Trauma-exposed populations in conflict areas are vulnerable to chronic trauma reactions and therefore need a program of long-term stabilization.

Evaluation and possible criteria of success

Criteria of success depend on the recovery process of a society and not only on the reduction of PTSD symptoms. Criteria could be influenced by:

- the degree of conflict and violence in the community, in families, in classrooms or other settings
- school and vocational achievements
- coping with grief
- disclosure
- feelings of trust and safety
- resilience
- regaining control of everyday life.

Furthermore, criteria of success are closely related and depend on potential retraumatizing situations, such as ongoing lawsuits, financial claims or new traumatic events within the family or the community, and the level of traumatization before the event.

Establishing and managing a center

Along with the planning phase, there are other factors that contribute to the development and management of a comprehensive trauma center such as promotion, managing services, and assuring the quality of care provision. It is also crucial to promote the mental health of staff members, by preventing compassion fatigue and networking with other providers. The center should also develop an evaluation model to monitor the effects of intervention on the target groups.

Promotion of services

In traumatized populations mistrust, avoidance, feelings of guilt and shame, and increased levels of aggression are a common issue. Professionals should therefore envisage effective communication strategies to overcome avoidance, which might prevent the community from visiting the center as it could act as a reminder of the experience. Ignoring support is one of the possible coping mechanisms that maintain avoidance strategies, as does a sense of guilt and shame. Therefore, the services provided at the center should offer activities that are not just focused on trauma, and should aim to maintain a balance between ways to avoid (leisure, vocational training, sports) and ways to stabilize and deal with the traumatic exposure (counseling, social support, self-help groups). Nevertheless, the promotion of a specialized center inevitably results in a confrontation with the traumatic event.

Maintaining the quality of services

The support team is constantly confronted with victims during their professional activities. The traumatic impact on professionals requires further training.

Each member of staff should be able to give immediate support to children and parents and to handle a trauma-related crisis, which can be triggered by any stimulus. By offering diverse activities, staff members gain trust and establish relationships, which offer a basis for disclosure. Disclosure and confrontation necessitate more advanced training as the appropriate level of such disclosure and the processing of the trauma have to be monitored by staff and not by the clients. Further training empowers professionals, who are then more confident in promoting stability and a sense of safety in their clients through the various activities.

Monitoring the mental health of staff members

Professionals may be vulnerable to symptoms of extreme stress like intrusions, sleeping problems, anger, concentration problems, problems with transference and countertransference, exhaustion, lack of sense, controllability, and manageability of the task. For this reason, constant supervision and education should be provided along with team-building activities and acknowledgment of achievements. Safety-oriented guidance from a director, who is supporting the achievements and providing a vision to professionals and clients, may also promote mental health. Working on participation, transparency, and guidance are the core elements to be considered.

Networking with partners and other providers

In conflict areas, there may be instances of rivalry and mistrust among organizations as all forces involved have to report to their headquarters that they have succeeded in their mission. However, traumatized populations benefit from regular exchanges of information about cases and their development. This networking facilitates cooperation and promotes more effective interventions.

Evaluation of the effects on target groups

The evaluation process offers an insight into the progress of individuals and the community, and it may be useful when planning to envisage the project as a permanent center. Furthermore, the results obtained may help to monitor the services available and thus to respond better to the needs of the community. To enable the staff and clients to accept the evaluation process, stakeholders have to be involved and should be familiar with the methods, aims, and results of the project. Evaluation should not only be considered as a control mechanism, but also as a tool to monitor and challenge the quality of the services provided.

The reality of the Beslan project

Austrian experts were not allowed to enter the region because all psychological help from abroad was refused. However, the local organization, supported by Austrian experts and funding, opened a day-care center, with activities of school support and leisure. The team started to negotiate with local authorities and then succeeded in convincing them to allow Austrian professionals to enter the region. In August 2005, two Austrian experts, together with a representative from the Austrian NGO and an expert in local history and culture, who also served as interpreter, were allowed to visit Beslan. The results of this first visit were communicated and integrated into the center's activities. The staff at the center also received further training.

The experts held meetings with representatives of the victims, local mental health professionals, teachers from various schools, medical doctors from the local hospital, and local authorities. In each of the meetings the concept of the day-care center was presented and discussion encouraged in order to learn more about the needs of the population. The experts also visited School Number One, the new school, and the new cemetery, which had to be built after the massacre. Furthermore, other meetings were held with the international NGOs to introduce the project into the network of international support.

The experts were able to identify the following key aspects: complex traumatization within the Beslan population, dominating symptoms of denial, survivors' guilt, and aggressive behavior. The affected population had no experience of psychological services, and partly for this reason they refused most of the available help. When support was accepted, the victims usually had great expectations of healing that could not be met. There was mistrust of psychologists and psychology, and especially of local mental health professionals. This could be explained by the symptoms of denial; victims were more open to traveling abroad to obtain psychological help as this was also a way to escape from the Beslan reality.

The support offered by the outside world declined dramatically. In the mental health sector, there was good knowledge about mental health, but local professionals lacked practical experience.

There had been some bad experiences with foreign mental health professionals during the acute phase, as not all the help offered was of good professional quality. This enforced mistrust against all psychological help. Furthermore, most professionals from all sectors suffered from compassion fatigue and chronic exhaustion.

The population was divided into two groups: primary victims and secondary victims. Primary victims needed more help and tended to deny the needs of secondary victims. Social cohesion was shattered. And the investigation triggered PTSD symptoms and other post-trauma reactions.

As target groups for training, four groups were identified:

– staff for the day-care center in Beslan
– local mental health professionals
– local medical doctors and nurses who were in contact with the victims
– scientific staff from the nearby University of Vladikavkaz's Department of Education.

For each of the target groups a training curriculum was developed. The concept of the day-care center was enlarged to treat both groups of victims. Emphasis was put on languages and computing as well as on leisure activities (artwork and sports) for children and adolescents. Some offers were designed for mothers.

Back in Austria the expert team (three psychiatrists and two psychologists) designed a three-step training program (two in the region, and the third in Austria, which also served as an evaluation of the program). Center activities were accepted by the majority of the population; training days in Austria also worked on helplessness and fatigue and provided emotional distance from the situation at home. Establishing a center in combination with advanced training enhanced coping with post-traumatic stress symptomatology and improved self-efficacy and skills. All victims and professionals who had contact with the Austrian experts appreciated foreign efforts to overcome political borders, crossing countries, language barriers, and other frontiers. Nonetheless, establishing and managing the project was not an easy task because there were many factors to take into account regarding the victims and the authorities. To provide help to traumatized communities is always a venture into uncharted territory and unforeseen circumstances could not be fully planned for in advance. With a knowledge-based intervention, a caring attitude, and flexibility, it was possible to establish a comprehensive trauma center and to achieve long-term effects, which empowered a deeply traumatized society.

References

American Psychiatric Association (APA) (1987). *Diagnostic and Statistical Manual of Mental Disorders* (3rd ed., Rev.) (*DSM-III-R*). Washington, DC: Author

American Psychiatric Association (APA) (1994). *Diagnostic and Statistical Manual of Mental Disorders* (4th ed.) (*DSM-IV*). Washington, DC: Author.

Antonucci, T. C., & Akiyama, H. (1994). Convoys of attachment and social relations in children, adolescents, and adults. In F. Nestmann & K. Hurrelmann (Eds.), *Social networks and social support in childhood and adolescence* (pp. 37–52). New York: Walter de Gruyter.

Beigel, A., & Berren, M. (1985) Human-induced disasters. *Psychiatric Annals, 15*(3), 143.

Breslau, N., Wilcox, H. C., Storr, C. L., Lucia, V. C., & Anthony, J. C. (2004). Trauma exposure and posttraumatic stress disorder: A study of youths in urban America. *Journal of Urban Health: Bulletin of the New York Academy of Medicine, 81*, 530–44.

Compas, B. E. (1998). Agenda for coping research and theory. *International Journal of Behavioral Development, 22*, 231–7.

Compas, B. E., Malcarne, V. L., & Fondacaro, K. M. (1988). Coping with stressful events in older children and young adolescents. *Journal of Consulting and Clinical Psychology, 56*(3), 405–11.

Fairbank, J. A. (2008). The epidemiology of trauma and trauma-related disorders in children and youth. *PTSD Research Quarterly, 19*(1), 1–3.

Fairbrother, G., Stuber, J., Galea, S. et al. (2003). Posttraumatic stress reactions in New York City children after the September 11, 2001 terrorist attacks. *Ambulatory Pediatrics, 3*, 304–11.

Figley, C. R. (Ed.) (1995). *Compassion fatigue*. New York: Brunner/Mazel.

Finkelhor, D., Ormrod, R., Turner, H., & Hamby, S. L. (2005). The victimization of children and youth: A comprehensive, national survey. *Child Maltreatment, 10*, 5–25.

Frederick, C. (1980). Effects of natural versus human induced violence upon victims. *Evaluation and Change* (Special Issue), pp. 71–5.

Galea, S., Nandi A., & Vlahov, D. (2005). The epidemiology of Post-Traumatic Stress Disorder after disasters. *Epidemiologic Reviews, 27,* 78–91.

Green, B. L., Korol, M., Grace, M. C. et al. (1991). Children and disaster: age, gender, and parental effects on PTSD symptoms. *Journal of the American Academy of Child and Adolescent Psychiatry, 30,* 945–51.

Greenbaum, C. W., Erlich, C., & Toubiana, Y. H. (1993). Settler children and the Gulf War. In L. A. Leavitt & N. A. Fox (Eds.), *The psychological effect of war and violence on children* (pp. 109–30). Hillsdale, NJ: Erlbaum.

Hobfoll, S. E., Spielberger, C. D., Breznitz, S. et al. (1991). War-related stress: Addressing the stress of war and traumatic events. *American Psychologist, 46,* 848–55.

Hoven, C. W., Duarte, C. S., Lucas, C. P. et al. (2005). Psychopathology among New York City public school children 6 months after September 11. *Archives of General Psychiatry, 62,* 545–52.

ISTSS/Draft Guidelines for International Trauma Training. Retrieved from www.istss.org/resources/guidelines_for_trauma_training.cfm (accessed June, 2009).

Kessler, R. C., Sonnega, A., Bromet, E., Hughes, M., & Nelson, C. B. (1995). Posttraumatic Stress Disorder in the National Comorbidity Survey. *Archives of General Psychiatry, 52,* 1048–60.

Klingman, A. (2001). Stress responses and adaption of Israeli school-age children evacuated from homes during massive missile attacks. *Anxiety, Stress and Coping, 14,* 149–72.

Meichenbaum, D. (1994). *A clinical handbook/practical therapist manual for assessing and treating adults with post-traumatic stress disorder (PTSD).* Waterlook, Canada: Institute Press.

Moscardino, U., Axia, G., Scrimin, S., & Capello, F. (2007). Narratives from caregivers of children surviving the terrorist attack in Beslan: Issues of health, culture, and resilience. *Social Science & Medicine, 64,* 1776–87.

Parvitt, T. (2004). How Beslan's children learn to cope. *The Lancet, 364,* 2009–10.

Perkonigg, A., Kessler, R. C., Storz, S., & Wittchen, H. U. (2000). Traumatic events and posttraumatic stress disorder in the community: Prevalence, risk factors and comorbidity. *Acta Psychiatrica Scandinavica, 101,* 46–59.

Perkonigg, A., Pfister, H., Stein, M. B. et al. (2005). Longitudinal course of posttraumatic stress disorder and posttraumatic stress disorder symptoms in a community sample of adolescents and young adults. *The American Journal of Psychiatry, 161,* 1320–7.

Pfefferbaum, B., North, C. S., Doughty, D. E. et al. (2003). Posttraumatic stress and functional impairment in Kenyan children following the 1998 American Embassy bombing. *American Journal of Orthopsychiatry, 73,* 133–40.

Punamäki, R.-L. (1996). Can ideological commitment protect children's psychosocial well-being in political violence? *Child Development, 67,* 55–69.

Punamäki, R.-L., & Suleiman, R. (1989). Predictors and effectiveness of coping with political violence among Palestinian children. *International Journal of Social Psychology, 29,* 67–77.

Pynoos, R. S., Frederick, C., Nader, K. et al. (1987). Life threat and posttraumatic stress in school-age children. *Archives of General Psychiatry, 44,* 1057–63.

Qouta, S., Punamäki, R.-L., Montgomery, E., & El Sarraj, E. (2007). Predictors of psychological distress and positive resources among Palestinian adolescents: Trauma, child and mothering characteristics. *Child Abuse & Neglect, 31,* 699–717.

Rosenbaum, M., & Ronen, T. (1997). Parents' and children's appraisal of each other's anxiety while facing a common threat. *Journal of Clinical Child Psychology, 26,* 43–52.

Schwarz, E. D., & Kowalski, J. M. (1991). Malignant memories: PTSD in children and adults after a school shooting. *Journal of the American Academy of Child and Adolescent Psychiatry, 30,* 936–44.

Scrimin, S., Axia, G., Capello, F. et al. (2006). Posttraumatic reactions among injured children and their caregivers 3 months after the terrorist attack in Beslan. *Psychiatry Research, 141,* 333–6.

Vila, G., Porche, L. M., & Mouren-Simeoni, M. C. (1999). An 18-month longitudinal study of posttraumatic disorders in children who were taken hostage in their school. *Psychosomatics Medicine, 61,* 746–54.

Williams, S. L., Williams, D. R., Stein, D. J. et al. (2007). Multiple traumatic events and psychological distress: The South Africa Stress and Health Study. *Journal of Traumatic Stress, 20,* 845–55.

World Health Organization (WHO) (2005). Mental health and social health during and after acute emergencies: emerging consensus? *Bulletin of the World Health Organization, 83,* 71–6.

Part VI

Therapeutic Models

Chapter Fifteen

Use of Somatic Experiencing Principles as a PTSD Prevention Tool for Children and Teens during the Acute Stress Phase following an Overwhelming Event

Peter Levine and Maggie Kline

Introduction

Somatic experiencing (SE) is a method currently used successfully in both the prevention and healing of trauma (Leitch, 2007). This chapter will focus on a brief introduction to the theory of SE. The thrust will be on the practical application of its principles through skill-building. Ideally, professionals will be guided to bring children (and their parents) gently out of shock during the acute phase (first 30 days) following a traumatic episode in order to prevent secondary symptoms from developing. Information will include working with individuals as well as with groups of children in a crisis setting. Although the emphasis is on prevention, this approach can help build a preliminary capacity to heal PTSD symptoms as well.

The premise of SE is that trauma is a fact of life; but so is resilience. Trauma can result from events that are clearly extraordinary, such as violence and molestation, but it can also result from everyday, "ordinary" events. In fact, common occurrences such as accidents, falls, invasive medical procedures, and divorce can cause children to withdraw, lose confidence or develop anxiety and phobias. Traumatized children may also display behavioral problems, including aggression, hyperactivity, and, as they grow older, addictions of various sorts and dysfunctional relationships.

Despite a recent interest in trauma treatments, precious little has been written regarding the common causes or the prevention and the non-drug treatment

Post-Traumatic Syndromes in Childhood and Adolescence: A Handbook of Research and Practice, First Edition. Edited by Vittoria Ardino. © 2011 John Wiley & Sons, Ltd. Published 2011 by John Wiley & Sons, Ltd.

of trauma. Focus instead has been on the diagnosis and the medication of its various symptoms. Children are frequently exposed to *potentially* traumatic events. It is possible to minimize the effects of the ordinary situations mentioned above, as well as those from extraordinary events such as natural and man-made disasters, including violence, war, terrorism, and molestation, with a basic understanding of how trauma affects a youngster's equilibrium and how to assist him or her in the early stages to return the nervous system to homeostasis and balance.

Fortunately, professionals, especially those who are able to see children during the first month or so following the incident, are in a position to prevent, or at least mitigate, the damaging effects of overwhelming events. But in order to do the most good for the children, it is necessary to recognize the underlying roots of trauma, how the trauma response is held in the body as implicit memory, and how it disturbs the child's self-regulatory capacities. In other words, trauma is a physiological phenomenon, rather than purely a psychological one. As such psychologists, psychiatrists, and other helping professionals need to understand the core mechanisms of how to stabilize the body's reactions to an overwhelming incident at the physical level.

Trauma is not only in the event

Trauma happens when an intense experience stuns a child like a bolt out of the blue; it overwhelms the child, leaving him altered and disconnected from his body, mind, and spirit. Any coping mechanisms the child may have had are undermined, and he feels utterly helpless. It is as if his legs are knocked out from under him. Trauma can also be the result of ongoing fear and nervous tension. Long-term stress responses wear down a child, causing an erosion of health, vitality, and confidence.

Trauma is the antithesis of empowerment. Vulnerability to trauma differs from child to child depending on a variety of factors, especially age, quality of early bonding, trauma history, and genetic predisposition. The younger the child, the more likely she is to be overwhelmed by common occurrences that might not affect an older child or adult. Up until now, it has been commonly believed that the severity of traumatic symptoms is equivalent to the severity of the event. While the magnitude of the stressor is clearly an important factor, it does not define trauma. Here the child's capacity for resilience is paramount. In addition, "trauma resides not in the event itself; but rather [its effect] in the nervous system" (Levine, 1997). The basis of "single-event" trauma (as contrasted to ongoing neglect and abuse) is primarily *physiological* rather than psychological.

What we mean by *physiological* is that there is no time to think when facing threat; therefore, our primary responses are instinctual. Our brain's main function is survival! We are wired for it. At the root of a traumatic reaction is our 280 million-year heritage – a heritage that resides in the oldest and deepest structures of the brain. When these primitive parts of the brain perceive danger, they automatically activate an extraordinary amount of energy – like the adrenaline rush that allows a mother to lift an auto to pull her trapped child to safety. We personally know a woman whose arm was trapped under the tire of a truck as an eight-year-old girl. Rescue workers were unsuccessful in helping her until they were able to get her father to the scene. With his powerful, protective, bear-like surge of energy, he was able to lift the car enough to pull her out.

This fathomless "survival energy" that we all share elicits a pounding heart along with more than 20 other physiological responses designed to prepare us to defend and protect ourselves and our loved ones. These rapid involuntary shifts include the redirection of blood flow away from the digestive and skin organs and into the large motor muscles of flight, along with rapid respiration and a decrease in the normal output of saliva. Pupils dilate to increase the ability of the eyes to take in more information. Blood-clotting ability increases, while verbal ability decreases. Muscles become highly excited, stiffening in preparation for action with a vast expenditure of energy. Alternatively, when faced with mortal threat or prolonged stress, certain muscles may collapse in fear as the body shuts down in an overwhelmed state.

Fear of our own reactions

When a child or adolescent is uncomfortable with what is happening inside them (their inner sensations and feelings), the very responses that are meant to give a physical advantage can become downright frightening. This is especially true when, due to size, age or other vulnerabilities, one is either unable to move or it would be disadvantageous to do so. For example, an infant or young child doesn't have the option to run and escape from a source of danger or threat. However, an older child, teen or adult, who ordinarily could run, may also need to keep very still, such as in the case of surgery, rape, or molestation. There is no conscious choice. We are biologically programmed to freeze (or go limp, collapse) when flight or fight is either impossible or perceived to be impossible.

Freeze and collapse are the last-ditch, "default" responses to an inescapable threat, even if that threat is a microbe in our blood. Infants and children, because of their limited capacity to defend themselves, are particularly susceptible to freezing and therefore are vulnerable to being traumatized. This is why the adult's skill is so crucial in providing emotional first aid to a frightened youngster. Professional and parental support can slowly move a child out of acute stress to empowerment and even joy.

What must be understood about the freeze/collapse response is that although the body *looks* inert, those physiological mechanisms that prepare the body to escape may still be on "full charge." Muscles that were poised for action at the time of threat are thrown into a state of immobility or "shock." When in shock the skin is pale and the eyes vacant. Breathing is shallow and rapid, or just shallow. The sense of time is distorted. Underlying this situation of helplessness, however, there is an enormous vital energy. This potential energy lies in wait to finish whatever action had been initiated. In addition, very young children tend to bypass active responses, becoming motionless instead. Later, even though the danger is over, a simple reminder can send the exact same alarm signals racing once again through the body until it shuts down. When this happens we may see the child becoming sullen, depressed, whiney, clingy, and withdrawn. Whether a youngster is still fully charged or has shut down, the guidance of a healthcare worker, therapist, or parent is imperative to alleviate their traumatic stress response and to build up their resilience. Furthermore, younger children generally protect themselves not by running away, but by running toward the protective adult. Hence, to help the child resolve a trauma, there must be a safe adult to support them. The adult who has the skills of emotional first aid can help them literally "shake things off" and breathe freely again.

How does the outpouring of survival energy and multiple changes in physiology affect children and teens over time? The answer to this question is an important one in understanding the consequences of trauma. This depends on what happens during and after the threat. The catch is that to avoid being traumatized, the excess energy mobilized to defend oneself must be "used up." When the activation is not fully discharged, it does not simply go away; instead it remains as a kind of highly charged "body memory," creating the potential for repeated traumatic symptoms. This type of imprint is known as implicit procedural memory.

The recipe for trauma

The likelihood of developing traumatic symptoms is related to the level of shutdown as well as to the residual survival activation that was originally mobilized to fight or flee. This self-protective process has now gone haywire. Children need consistent, patient support to release this highly charged state and return to healthy, flexible functioning. The myth can be laid to rest that babies and toddlers "are too young to be affected" by adverse events or that "it won't matter because they won't remember." What was not so obvious becomes apparent as we learn that prenatal infants, newborns, and very young children are the most at risk to stress and trauma due to their undeveloped nervous, muscular, and perceptual systems. This vulnerability also applies to older children who have limited mobility because of permanent or temporary disabilities, such as having a splint, brace, or cast due to an orthopedic injury or correction. Included in this category are children less able-bodied due to cerebral palsy, congenital deformities or developmental delays.

The reason our bodies don't forget: What brain research has taught us

Why is it that once the threat is over we are not free of it? Why are we left with anxiety and vivid memories that alter us forever if we don't get the help that we need? The highly regarded neurologist Antonio Damasio, author of *Descartes' Error* and *The Feeling of What Happens* (Damasio, 1995, 1999), demonstrates that emotions literally have an anatomical mapping in the brain necessary for survival. That is to say, the emotion of fear has a very specific neural circuitry etched in the brain corresponding to specific physical sensations from various parts of the body. When something we see, hear, smell or taste arouses similar body sensations to a previous threat, the emotions of fear and helplessness are again evoked, mimicking what happened when the initial danger was present. Originally, the experience of fear served an important purpose. It helped the body to organize a "flee or freeze" plan to remove us from peril quickly. However, the trigger now produces a similar fear even though there is no conscious memory of its origin (just the identical physical response). The heart rate escalates rapidly or drops precipitously, sweat is produced, and the anguish occurs because the body is totally reengaged, mistaking the body's responses for the original threat as if it were actually happening in present time.

The recipe for resilience

Whether a child or teen remains distressed or bounces back with resilience depends on what happens during and/or after the threat. You have learned that to avoid being traumatized, the excess energy that had been mobilized in a failed attempt to protect or defend oneself *must* be accessed and then "metabolized." When this "emergency" energy is not fully engaged and discharged, it does not simply go away. Instead, it is capable of causing all sorts of troublesome symptoms, as you will see shortly with Henry. You will also see how Henry's aversion for and avoidance of certain foods and noises soon disappeared as he "used up" his anxious energy to joyfully rebound with a little adult support. After reading the case of Henry below, you will learn the step-by-step somatic approach to working with apprehensive, stressed or outright terrified children after a frightening challenge.

Henry

Four-year-old Henry's mother became concerned when he refused to eat his (previously) favorite foods: peanut butter and jelly with a glass of milk. When his mother placed them in front of Henry, he would get agitated, stiffen, and push them away. Even more disturbing was the fact that he would start shaking and crying whenever the family dog barked. It never occurred to her that this "pickiness" and fearfulness of the barking were directly related to an "ordinary" incident that had occurred almost a year before, when Henry was still using a high chair.

Sitting in his high chair, devouring his favorite foods – peanut butter, jelly and milk – he had proudly held out his half-empty glass for his mother to fill. As things like this happen, Henry lost his grip and the glass fell to the ground with a crash. This startled the dog, causing it to jump backward, knocking over the high chair. Henry hit his head on the floor and lay there, gasping, unable to catch his breath. Mother screamed and the dog started barking loudly. From his mother's perspective Henry's food aversion and apparent fear of the dog made no sense. However, from the vantage of trauma, the simple association of having milk and peanut butter right before the fall and the wild barking of his dog, in a Pavlovian response, conditioned his fear and aversion to his previously favorite foods.

So how can this symptomatic cycle be interrupted? By engaging Henry through playful, "practiced" controlled falling onto pillows, he learned to relax his previously stiffened muscles as he gradually surrendered to gravity. His protective reflexes were restored and his symptoms disappeared. Before this, he "simply" would not eat those foods and had trouble sleeping when dogs barked in the neighborhood. Fortunately, after a couple of play sessions this little boy was once again devouring his favorite foods and barking back at the dog in playful glee. In other words, Henry got to use up the energy that was bound up in his defenses against falling during these safe "tumbling sessions." As he gained mastery of his balance – with the help and safety of adult guidance – Henry's fear was transformed into delight.

Although this case example is a commonplace accident rather than an extraordinary event such as a sexual violation, a flood, auto accident or surgery, the same principles are involved in reworking the incident in terms of assisting the child or teen to complete the energetic cycle of the body's natural protective and defensive responses that were thwarted (or had not yet been established due to developmental stage) as he or she oriented to the original danger. In other words, establishing the sensory-motor sequence that satisfies the body's need to use up this excess energy stored somatically is what returns a youngster to equilibrium.

Building resilience by building sensory awareness skills

In order to build a child's or teen's capacity to rebound after overwhelming situations you will first need to learn and practice several skills. This chapter provides a variety of exercises that will enable you, and your child clients, to discover the rich sensory landscape that exists within the body. You will also be guided to acquire a *new* vocabulary for this *new* terrain. The language of sensation is communicated from the deep recesses of the brain – what we shall call the "body-brain." You will become adept at recognizing these spontaneous internal signals and promptings that arise from this instinctual part of you if you practice the exercises. Becoming proficient in these skills lessens the rift between conscious and unconscious bodily processes. This *experiential* knowledge of sensations will not only give you the tools to assist overwhelmed children; it has the side-benefit of helping the professional to become more intuitive, self-regulated, and attuned in order to provide more effective treatment for the child.

Giving appropriate support to an overwhelmed child

In order to prevent or minimize trauma and alleviate stress, it is important to make sure that as a therapist or parent, *you're* not overwrought by the traumatic event or by the child's reenactment of it. This may be difficult, especially if the episode was horrific. This is especially true for mental health professionals who work with children in disaster settings. It is also important for healing professionals to stabilize their own reactions first, then assist parents and children. It may be comforting for the practitioner to reassure the parents that children, by their nature, are both fragile *and* resilient. With proper support, they are usually able to rebound from stressful and traumatic events. In fact, as they begin to triumph over life's shocks and losses, kids grow into more competent, resilient, and vibrant beings. Because the capacity to heal is *innate,* the adult's role is simple: it is to help youngsters access this capacity. Your task is similar in many ways to the function of a Band-aid or a splint. The Band-aid or splint doesn't heal the wound, but protects and supports the body as it restores itself. The suggestions, exercises, and step-by-step guidelines provided here are meant to enable you to be a good "Band-aid" for the child.

Simple steps to build resilience

The experiential exercises provided will increase your ability to help a child or teen restore equilibrium, quickly and naturally. Once *your* body learns how to recognize cycles of nervous system activation, or arousal, and de-activation or deep settling after a discharge of energy, you will be in a position to give emotional first aid to a child in order to prevent or minimize post-traumatic stress symptoms from emerging with time. As you practice, your body will have an experiential understanding that "what goes up (charge/excitation/fear) *can* come down (discharge/relaxation/security)." As you develop a more resilient nervous system, you are in a position to help yourself and the parents and children you work with to weather both the stressful ups and downs of life, as well as, truly overwhelming events. When your body "gets it," you become contagious – in a good way. Through body language, facial expression, and tone of voice, your own nervous system communicates directly with the child's or teen's nervous system. This is how we *truly* connect with our clients! It's not our words that have the greatest impact; it's the nonverbal cues that create the feelings of safety and trust. Before you can attune to the child's sensations, rhythms, and emotions, you must first learn to attune to your own. Then your calm can become their calm.

The first step in this nonverbal attunement process is to understand the importance of experiencing both comfortable and uncomfortable sensations while learning to tolerate and, little by little, befriend them. It is essential in not only becoming a more resilient therapist, but also one that is able to resonate more deeply with what the child needs to feel supported. This deeper experience of ourselves, often neglected, shapes our core being. It is from our own breath and belly that we form our sense of self and help the children we serve to sense theirs.

If exploring physical sensations is new to you as you normally work with thoughts and feelings, it may be difficult to stay focused on them at first. But each time you practice, it becomes a bit easier. It is important to be able to tolerate displeasure long enough for the sensation to change, as it inevitably will. It is equally important to be able to experience increased pleasure and joy. As you practice, your body is able to hold (and "contain") more sensation and emotion without getting stressed or overwhelmed. Once you feel more "at home" with these new sensations, it becomes natural to assist our clients to become aware and tolerate their internal experience.

The body–brain connection

Humans have a complicated brain circuitry with distinctly different parts, which, while closely connected, have different functions. Paul MacLean in the 1980s posited the theory of the triune brain (three distinctive brains functioning together as one mind). With the advent of new brain research, we now know that the circuitry of the brain is far more complex and interrelated than once believed. However, for simplicity's sake, we know that various parts of the brain serve different functions, especially when there is a perception of danger or a life-threat as opposed to a perception of safety.

The neocortical or newest part of the brain, in the prefrontal cortex, is responsible for complex thinking skills such as problem solving, planning, and perception, as well as social functioning. The mammalian (midbrain) or limbic system is also referred to as the "emotional brain" (LeDoux, 1998) because it processes memories and feelings. The reptilian or "lower" brain is responsible for survival through the myriad functions that accompany the regulatory mechanisms of basic existence, such as heart rate and respiration. These include the workings of our nervous system that interact with our sensory and motor systems to move us quickly out of danger. The structures in the lower brain work overtime when the nervous system is overwhelmed. Each region of our triune brain has very specialized functions, and each speaks its own "language." The thinking brain speaks with words, while the emotional brain uses the language of feelings, such as anger, sorrow, joy, disgust, shame, and fear. Unlike the "newer" thinking and feeling brain segments, the primitive reptilian brain speaks the unfamiliar, but vastly important, language of *sensation*. The language of sensations is, to many, a foreign language. There is a world of sensation and sensation-based feeling inside of us that exists whether or not we are aware of it or not. Fortunately, it is a language that, with a little practice, is easy to learn. It's as essential to be familiar with sensations when traveling the road to recovery from being overwhelmed and stressed as learning basic survival phrases when traveling abroad. In order to help your clients, it makes sense to get acquainted with your own inner landscape first. All it takes is some unhurried time, set aside without distractions, to pay attention to how your body feels. Sensations can range from pressure or temperature changes on the skin to vibrations, "butterflies," muscular tension, constriction or spaciousness, trembling or tingling and heat. This is the language of the lower brain that acts on our behalf when in danger or when unexpected change occurs. It has a very different focus than most of us are accustomed to. Its signals may seem imperceptible, subtle or strange at first because of our customary reliance on feedback from language, thought, and emotion.

Getting acquainted with your own sensations

Although children may not be able to verbalize what they are feeling because they are too scared and/or too young to talk, they know *how* a shocking upset *feels* and so do you! It is the undeniable dread in the pit of the stomach, a racing heart, the tightness in the chest or the "lump in the throat." Turn on the news after a catastrophe or listen to a bystander who has just witnessed an accident describe his experience. "I don't have words for it." "It's such a cold feeling." "It was like getting the wind knocked out of me." "I just feel numb." "My heart wouldn't stop racing, but I couldn't move." "My legs were like lead."

Take a moment to think about your own experiences when something upsetting happened out of the blue. Can you recall some of the sensations you felt? Did your heart pound rapidly? Did you get dizzy? Did your throat or stomach tighten in a knot? And when the danger was over, how did the sensations gradually shift or change? Perhaps you noticed that you could breathe more easily or felt some tingling or vibration as your muscles began to relax.

Exercise: Noticing sensations

Let's try this brief experiment to get you started on deepening your awareness. Find a comfortable place to sit. Take some time to notice how you are feeling

physically. Pay attention to your breathing. Are you comfortable or uncomfortable? *Where* in your body do you register your comfort level? What do you
notice? Are you aware of your heart beating, or conscious of your breathing?
Perhaps you're more aware of muscle tension or relaxation or the temperature
of your skin; perhaps you notice sensations like "tingly." When you feel settled
enough to go on, try the simple exercise below.

Imagine it's a pleasant summer day and you're driving down a country road
through a beautiful natural landscape at the start of a well-deserved vacation.
You are playing your favorite music and singing along in delight. You're not in
any hurry because you have no deadlines, responsibilities or schedules today.
You love the countryside (or wherever it is you chose to go). You are free!
Take a minute to notice how you are feeling right now – before you read the
next paragraph. Note the sensations in various parts of your body, such as your
belly, limbs, breath, muscles, and skin. Also, notice any thoughts or mental
pictures you might have as you look around at the trees or meadow, orchards,
mountains or streams.

[Note: Pause here for a minute or two to give yourself enough time to notice
your bodily sensations. When ready, continue with the second part of the story.]

Suddenly, from out of nowhere, a hot-rod motorist cuts in front of you,
nearly causing a collision. Furthermore, he is rude and shouts profanities at you
as if *you* had done something to cause the mishap. What are you noticing in
your body and mind right now? Compare these feelings to the ones you had in
the first part of the exercise. Pay attention to changes. What feels different now?
Where does it feel different? Are you warm, hot or chilled? Do you feel tension
or constriction anywhere? Notice changes in your heartbeat and breath. Notice
if there is anything you feel like doing or saying. Or, do you just feel stunned?

There is no right or wrong way to answer. Each person has his or her own
individual experience. You may have been scared and felt your shoulders, arms,
and hands tightening to turn the steering wheel quickly to swerve. Or you
might have blanked out and gone numb. When you imagined the other driver
cursing at you, you might have felt irritated. If you did, where do you sense
the irritation and what does it feel like? You may have noticed the muscles in
your upper body tightening as your body prepared to fight. Or you might have
noticed a word forming in your vocal cords to shout back, but the sounds never
left your lips. When you check your body to feel your reactions and sensations
in the present moment, you are experiencing your *basic instincts* of survival.

Now take a little time to let any activation (charged-up feelings) settle down.
Think for a moment about the enclosed glass containers with a winter scene
inside that you shake up to make white flakes that look like it's snowing.
Remember that it takes a little time before all the flakes accumulate on the
ground so that the "snowing" stops. In order for you to settle, it certainly
doesn't help to get all shook up again. Instead, it takes a little quiet time of
stillness and calm, just like with the snow scene, for the settling to occur. It can

be very helpful to explore the room with your eyes, being aware that you are safe and that the visualization was only an exercise. As you continue to settle, place both feet flat on the floor to help you feel grounded. Next, direct your attention to something in the room that brings comfort, such as a flower, the color of the room, a tree or the sky outside the window, a photo or a favorite possession. Notice how you are feeling in your body at this moment *now*.

This brief exercise was intended to help you see that the language of sensation isn't really so foreign after all. Sitting around the dinner table, it's easy to feel a comfortable or overly stuffed stomach after a full meal or one that feels warm and cozy after sipping hot chocolate. But when people share their feelings, they typically express them as moods or emotions, such as happy, cranky, mad, excited or sad. Noticing sensations may seem odd at first, but the more you learn about the ups and downs of your own body's "moods," the more intuitive, instinctual, and confident you will become. You may not know this, but your basic sense of well-being is based on your body's ability to regulate itself – rather than to escalate out of control. To be in control this way means to be open to that which occurs spontaneously within you. This capacity for self-regulation is enhanced by your ability to be aware of your changing sensations and to know what to do if unpleasant sensations remain stuck over time, thereby causing distress.

Building a new vocabulary

When learning skills with any new language, it helps to develop and practice the new vocabulary. Since the vocabulary of resilience is sensation, building a "sensation vocabulary" is a central skill crucial in developing resilience. The box below is provided to get you started. To create a balance, be sure to notice and label sensations that are pleasurable or neutral, as well as those that may be uncomfortable.

Sensation vocabulary box

cold/warm/hot/chilly
twitchy/butterflies
sharp/dull/itchy
shaky/trembly/tingly
hard/soft/stuck
jittery/icy/weak
relaxed/calm/peaceful
empty/full/dry/moist
flowing/spreading
strong/tight/tense
dizzy/fuzzy/blurry
numb/prickly/jumpy
owie/tearful/goose-bumpy

light/heavy/open/icky
tickly/cool/silky
still/clammy/loose

*Note that sensations are different from emotions. They describe the *physical* way the body feels. A nonverbal child who seems frightened can be invited to point to where in their body they might feel shaky or numb, or where the owie is.

"Pendulating" between pleasant and unpleasant sensations, emotions, and images

The term "pendulation" refers to our body's natural rhythm of contraction and expansion. It is vital to know and *experience* this rhythm. Being familiar with it reminds us that no matter how bad we feel in the contraction phase, expansion *will inevitably* follow, bringing with it a sense of relief. One way to follow or "track" your body's own rhythm is as easy as paying attention to the pressure and flow of air in and out of your lungs and belly as you inhale and exhale. Notice if there is any tightness or whether the air seems to flow freely throughout your nostrils, throat, chest, and belly. You might also note if the inhale and exhale are even or if one is shorter than the other. Are there pauses before the inhale and the exhale? How do the pauses feel? Do your muscles tense and relax as you breathe? Rather than including only the expansion and contraction of the breath, however, pendulation is much more than that. It is the rhythm of our entire being as our internal state changes back and forth between uncomfortable sensations, emotions, and images to more comfortable ones. This allows for new experiences to freshly emerge at each moment. When uncomfortable feelings don't readily go away, they are usually associated with stress or trauma. If we were defeated and frozen in hopelessness, the ability to move out of that state through natural pendulation will be diminished. We may need a little help to get the pendulum moving again. When this natural resilience process has been shut down, it must be gradually restored. The mechanisms that regulate our mood, vitality, and health are dependent upon it. When this rhythm is reestablished there is, at least, a tolerable balance between the pleasant and unpleasant. And no matter how bad a particular feeling may be, knowing that it can change releases you from a sentence of helplessness and hopelessness. And, as you assist your child with their natural rhythms, you are giving them a stable foundation for self-confidence.

Exercise: Exploring sensations and the rhythm of pendulation

Take time to get comfortable in your chair. Notice where your body is touching the seat; notice how the chair supports your back and buttocks. Allow sufficient time to settle down into the chair. Notice your breathing and how you are feeling overall. As you slowly follow the story below, take the time to notice the sensations, thoughts, emotions, and images that come up. Some will be subtle and others obvious. The more attention and time you take, the more your awareness will grow. At the same time it is important not to overdo it; it is recommended that you take no more than 10 or 15 minutes with this exercise.

Now, imagine that today is your birthday. Even though it's a special day you feel lonely. You don't want to be alone so you decide to go see a movie. You start to get ready. As you reach for your wallet you have a dreadful feeling as you notice it is missing. What are you feeling? Take some time to notice feelings, sensations, and thoughts in your body and your mind.

If you feel dread, what does it feel like? Where do you feel it in your body? Common places to experience sensations are: gut, chest, throat, and the muscles in your neck and limbs. Do you feel a tightening or a sinking sensation – perhaps queasiness? Do you notice any temperature changes in your hands? Do they feel sweaty, hot or cold? Is there any place you feel unsteady or wobbly? And notice how these sensations change over time as you attend to them. Does the intensity increase or decrease? Does the tightening loosen or change to something else? Do the feelings spread or stay in one place?

As you settle, the thought comes to you that: "Oh, perhaps I left my wallet in the other room." Imagine that you go and look there. You check out other places you might have left it. You can't find it and you begin to get a bit frantic. Again, focus your attention inward and take time to notice your bodily sensations, your feelings, and your thoughts.

Now, you slow down a bit and your thoughts become a little clearer. You begin to hunt for your wallet more methodically. Is it in the drawer? Maybe when I came in I left it over there on the table . . . but then I went to the bathroom . . . (you wonder) . . . could I have left it in the bathroom; or was it at the supermarket? (Pause here to notice sensations.) However, while you're looking, you are interrupted by the ring of the telephone. You pick up the phone. It's your friend and she tells you that you left your wallet at her house. You take a big sigh of relief! Feel that and notice how you smile as you think about your previous frantic state of mind.

[Take plenty of time here, allowing your sensations to develop and be noticed before continuing with the story.]

Your friend tells you that she's leaving shortly, but she'll wait if you come right now. So you walk briskly to her house. Feel the strength in your legs as you walk fast. You arrive at her house and knock on her door, but there's no answer. You knock a second time and there's still no answer. You begin to think that you must have missed her. You feel a bit irritated. After all, she said that she would wait and you came as quickly as you could. Where do you feel the sensation of irritability? What does it feel like? Take your time and notice the range of sensations just as you did before. How do you experience the irritability? Where else do you feel it? What does it feel like?

From the back of the house, you hear your friend's muffled voice. She's telling you to come in. You open the door and it's really dark. You slowly find your way in the dark. You begin to make your way down the hallway. Notice how your body feels as you fumble through the darkness trying to get to the back of the house. You call again to your friend, but you're interrupted by a chorus of voices yelling, "Surprise!"

What are you feeling in your body now, *in this moment,* as you realize it's a surprise birthday party for you?! Again, take the time to notice your sensations, feelings, and thoughts.

This exercise was intended to acquaint you with a variety of sensations, such as frustration, expectancy, relief, conflict, and surprise. If you noticed different feeling states and were able to move smoothly from the pleasant to the unpleasant and back again, you now know what it feels like to pendulate.

The twists and turns of the visualization above were filled with many surprises. Surprise excites the nervous system. In the case of a good surprise, something gets registered in the body that makes you feel better. In the case of a horrifying surprise, distressing sensations may become stuck, resulting in a diminished sense of "OKness" and in feelings of helplessness. When you experience your sensations consciously, you can begin to move with fluidity out of one state and into another. Remember, whatever feels bad is never the final step. It is the movement from fixity to flow that frees us from the grip of trauma as we become more resilient and self-aware. Ideally, you were able to feel this fluidity within yourself. If you did, you are well on your way to learning the skills that will help you to help your child fluidly glide through their sensations. If, in any way, you felt "stuck" or frozen on an unpleasant sensation, emotion, thought or disturbing image while practicing, take the time now to look around, get up, move, and take notice of an object, movement, thought, person, pet or natural feature that makes you feel better. Take some time to sense how you know you are feeling better and where those sensations are located inside you. Then briefly "touch in" to the place in your body where you were previously stuck and notice what feelings you are having *now!*

Helping a child or teen focus on internal sensations

One way to help youngsters develop an awareness of their internal state is by helping them to "track" their sensations, noticing how they change moment by moment. To begin, you might ask a child to reflect on something that happened today or yesterday that made them feel either good or mildly upset. If they can't recall anything, have them notice how they are feeling as they are sitting with you in anticipation of working together. As images, thoughts, and emotions come and go, make a note of them and what impact they have on your client's fluctuating sensations. Help to develop more awareness of the details of his or her sensations. You can keep your client from getting stuck by moving forward in time by an occasional gentle question – keeping pace with your rhythm – such as, "And when you feel … what happens next?" Study the ideas that follow for more specific ideas on how to facilitate sensation-based therapy that leads to discharge and release of traumatic activation.

Language of sensation idea box

Your body-brain responds better to open-ended than closed-ended questions. An open-ended question invites curiosity. It suggests sensing rather than thinking. It defies a simple "yes" or "no" answer, which can be a communication dead-end. An example would be: "What do you notice in your body?" which summons a leisurely exploration and limitless answers. This is different from: "Are you feeling tense?" which forces a person to think rather than feel and then give a "yes" or "no" response.

Other examples of open-ended questions that you might consider when tracking sensations with your partner are listed below. These questions can be used judiciously from time to time to increase the ability to focus or to keep from getting stuck. For best results, use infrequently, allowing plenty of quiet time between each one. Allowing sufficient time is the key to developing sensory awareness. It's in the "quiet waiting" that our bodies begin to speak to us.

Open-ended
What do you notice in your body now?
> Where in your body do you feel that?
> What are you experiencing now?
> As you pay attention to that sensation, what happens next?
> How does it change?

Invitational
What else are you noticing?
> Would you be willing to explore how your body might want to move?
> Would you be willing to focus on that feeling with a sense of curiosity about what might happen next?

Explore sensation with details to increase focus
What are the qualities of that sensation?
> Does it have a size? Shape? Color? Weight?
> Does it spread? Notice the direction as it moves.
> Does the (pressure, pain, warmth, etc.) go from inward to outward, or vice versa?
> Do you notice a center point? An edge? (Where does the sensation begin and end?)

Broaden awareness of sensation

When you feel that, what happens in the rest of your body?
    When you feel that in your (area of the body), how does it affect you now?

Movement through time

What happens *next*? (even if the person reports feeling "stuck")
    As you follow that sensation, where does it go? How does it change?
    Where does it move to (or want to move to if it could)?

Savoring and deepening sensations

Allow yourself to enjoy that (warm, expansive, tingly, etc.) sensation as long as
you'd like.
    Is there anything else about that (sensation, feeling, etc.) that you are notic-
ing now?

First aid for trauma prevention: A step-by-step guide

Trauma prevention involves assisting a child to "unwind" the energy that was
stirred up during her upset. There are eight steps involved in this procedure.
The first seven steps teach you how to help your child's body rebound from fear,
shock, and shut-down. Step 8 helps you to help your child recover emotionally,
and to develop a coherent story of what happened. This final step helps your
child put the bad occurrence in the past, where it belongs. The eight simple
steps outlined below can be used as soon as your child is in a safe, quiet place.

1. *Check your own body's responses first*

Take time to notice your own level of fear or concern. Next, take a full deep
breath, and as you exhale s-l-o-w-l-y feel the sensations in your own body.
If you still feel upset, repeat until you feel settled. Feel your feet, ankles, and
legs, noticing how they make contact with the ground. Remember that any
excess energy you have will help you to stay focused to meet the challenge
at hand. The time it takes to establish a sense of calm is time well spent. It
will increase your capacity to attend fully to your child. If you take the time
to gather yourself, your own acceptance of whatever has happened will help
you to attend to your child's needs. Your composure will greatly reduce the
likelihood of frightening or confusing your child further. Remember, children
are very sensitive to the emotional states of adults, particularly their parents.

2. *Assess the situation*

If your child shows signs of shock (glazed eyes, pale skin, rapid or shallow pulse
and breathing, disorientation, appears overly emotional or overly tranquil, i.e.,
acting like nothing has happened), do not allow him to jump up and return
to play. You might say something like this: "Honey, you're safe now ... but
you're still in shock (or a bit shaken up). Mommy/Daddy will stay right here
with you until the shock wears off. It's important to stay still for a little while,

even though you might want to play." Remember, a calm, confident voice communicates to your child that you know what's best.

3. *As the shock wears off, guide your child's attention to his sensations*
Indications of coming out of shock that are easy to spot include some color returning to the skin, a slowing down and/or deepening of the breath, tears or some expression returning to the eyes (which may have seemed blank before). When you see one or more of these signs, softly ask your child how he or she feels "in their body." Next, repeat his or her answer as a question – "You feel OK in your body?" – and wait for a nod or other response. Be more specific with the next question: "How do you feel in your tummy (head, arm, leg, etc.)?" If he or she mentions a distinct sensation (such as "It feels tight or hurts"), gently ask about its location, size, shape, color or weight (e.g., heavy or light). Keep guiding your child to stay with the present moment with questions such as, "How does the rock (sharpness, lump, 'owie', sting) feel now?" If they are too young or too startled to talk, have them point to where it hurts. (Remember that children tend to describe sensations with metaphors such as "hard as a rock" or "butterflies".)

4. *Slow down and follow your child's pace by careful observation of changes*
Timing is everything! This may be the hardest part for the adult, but it's the most important part for the child. Providing a minute or two of silence between questions allows deeply restorative physiological cycles to engage. Too many questions asked too quickly disrupt the natural course that leads to resolution. Your calm presence and patience are sufficient to facilitate the movement and release of excess energy. This process cannot be rushed. Be alert for cues that let you know a cycle has finished. If uncertain whether a cycle has been completed, wait and watch for your child to give you clues. Examples of signs include a deep, relaxed, spontaneous breath, the cessation of crying or trembling, a stretch, a yawn, a smile or the making of eye contact. The completion of this cycle may not mean that the recovery process is over. Wait to see if another cycle begins or if there is a sense of enough for now. Keep your child focused on sensations for a few more minutes just to make sure the process is complete. If your child seems tired, stop. There will be other opportunities later to complete the process.

5. *Keep validating your child's physical responses*
Resist the impulse to stop your child's tears or trembling, while reminding him or her that whatever has happened is over and that she/he will be OK. Your child's reactions need to continue until they stop on their own. This part of the natural cycle usually takes from one to several minutes. Studies have shown that children who are able to cry and tremble after an accident have fewer problems recovering from it over the long term. Your task is to convey to your child through word and touch that crying and trembling are normal, healthy reactions! A reassuring hand on the back, shoulder or arm, along with a few gently spoken words as simple as "That's OK" or "That's right, just let the scary stuff shake right out of you" will help immensely.

6. *Trust in your child's innate ability to heal*

As you become increasingly comfortable with your own sensations, it will be easier to relax and follow your child's lead. Your primary function, once the process has begun, is to not disrupt it! Trust your child's innate ability to heal. Trust your own ability to allow this to happen. If it helps you in letting go, take a moment to reflect on and feel the presence of a higher power or the remarkable perfection of nature guiding you in the ordinary miracle of healing. Your job is to "stay with" your child. Your balanced presence makes a safe container for your child to release their tears, fears, and any strange new feelings. Use a calm voice and reassuring hand to let your child know that she/he is on the right track. To avoid unintentional disruption of the process, don't shift the child's position, distract their attention, hold them too tightly or position yourself too close or too far away for comfort. Notice when your child begins to look around to see what's happening with a sense of curiosity. This type of checking out the surroundings is called "orientation" and is a sign of resolution. It is a sign of completion, or letting go, of the stressful energy produced in response to the scary event. A natural orientation to what's happening in the environment may bring with it more sensory awareness, aliveness in the present moment and even feelings of joy.

7. *Encourage your child to rest even if she/he doesn't want to*

Deep discharge and processing of the event generally continue during rest and sleep. Do not stir up discussion about the mishap by asking questions about it during this stage. Later on, though, your child may want to tell a story about what happened, draw a picture or play it through. If a lot of energy was mobilized, the release will continue. The next cycle may be too subtle for you to notice, but this resting stage promotes a fuller recovery, allowing the body to gently vibrate, give off heat, and go through skin color changes, etc., as the nervous system returns to relaxation and equilibrium. In addition, dream activity can help move the body through the necessary physiological changes. These changes happen naturally. All you have to do is provide a calm, quiet environment. (**Caution:** Of course, if your child may have had a head injury (concussion), you will want him or her to rest but not sleep until your doctor tells you that it's safe.)

8. *The final step is to attend to your child's emotional responses and help them make sense of what happened*

Later, when your child is rested and calm – even the next day – set aside some time for them to talk about their feelings and what they experienced. Begin by asking them to tell you what happened. Children often feel anger, fear, sadness, worry, embarrassment, shame or guilt. Help your child to know that those feelings are OK and that you understand. Tell the child about a time when you or someone you know had a similar experience and/or felt the same way. This will encourage expression of what your child is feeling. It also helps them not to feel weird or defective in some way because of what happened or because of their reactions. Let your child know by your actions that whatever she/he is feeling is accepted by you and worthy of your time and attention. Set aside some time for storytelling or for relating the details of the incident to assess if there are any residual feelings. Drawing, painting, and working with clay can be very helpful in releasing strong emotions. If you notice your child becoming unduly upset at any point, again have them attend to their sensations in order to help the distress pass.

Crisis relief with groups

The somatic work can also be done with groups of children in a school or community setting. A psychotherapist or school counselor trained in working with the principles of tracking sensations, nervous system activation/deactivation, and sensory-motor defensive movements can lead the group with the assistance of other adults to provide safety and containment. As one child volunteers to process their symptoms and gets relief, the shyer youngsters gain confidence and ask for their turn. This is a very different approach from Critical Incidence Debriefing, which asks children to go over and tell the worst part of the trauma. Below are guidelines for working with groups of three to 12 students:

1. Invite as many parents (or other caregivers) as possible to participate.
2. Seat students in a circle so that everyone can see each other. Seat adults directly behind the children in a concentric circle for support.
3. It is very helpful, but not necessary, to have a child-size fitness ball for the student who is "working" to sit on. Sitting on the ball helps youngsters drop into and describe their sensations more easily. These balls are very comfortable and children love to sit on them. Using the balls motivates volunteers.
4. Educate the group on the trauma response and what they might expect to experience both during the shock phase of the event and as they begin to come out of shock to normalize their symptoms. Use the information that you have learned in this book. (For example, some may feel numb; others may have recurring images or troublesome thoughts, etc.) Explain what you will be doing to help them (i.e., that the group will be learning about their inner sensations and how they help to move stuck feelings, images, and worrisome thoughts out of their bodies and minds).
5. Do *not* probe the group to describe what happened during the event. Instead, explain to them that you will teach skills to relieve symptoms and help them to feel better.
6. Ask the group to share some of the trauma symptoms they may be having. (For example: difficulty sleeping, eating or concentrating, nightmares, feeling that it didn't really happen.)
7. Explain what a sensation is and have the group brainstorm various sensation words. You might even write these down for all to see, if convenient.

Explain what to expect: that they might feel trembling, shaking, tearful, jittery, warm, cool, numb, or they might feel like they want to run, fight, disappear or hide. Let them know that these are feelings that happen as they are moving out of the shock response.

8. Work with one volunteer at a time within the circle. Have that child notice the support of the adults and other students in the group. Invite them to make eye contact with a special friend or familiar adult for safety. At any time during the session, if the student needs extra support, invite them again to take a break and make contact with a special "buddy" in the group.

9. Ask the student to find a comfortable position in the chair or on the ball. Invite them to feel their feet touching the floor, the support of what they are sitting on, and their breath as they inhale and exhale. Make sure they feel grounded, centered, and safe.

10. Begin the sensation work as soon as they are ready. First have them describe a sensation of something that brings comfort or pleasure. If they haven't had any resourceful feelings since the event, have them choose a time before the event when they had good feelings and describe what they feel like *now* as they recall those good feelings.

11. The child might automatically describe symptoms or you may need to ask what kinds of difficulties she/he is struggling with since the event. Then ask them to describe what they are feeling. The following are sample questions to use as a guide for inviting awareness of sensations:

    a) And as you see the image of the man behind the tree, what do you notice in your body?

    b) And when you worry that he might come back, what do you notice in your body?

    c) And when you feel your tummy getting tight, what else do you notice? Tight like what? Can you show me?

    d) And when you look at the rock...or make the rock with your fist...What happens next?

    e) And when you feel your legs shaking, what do you suppose your legs want to do?

    f) When your legs feel like running, imagine you are running in your favorite place and your [insert name of a favorite safe person] will be waiting for you when you arrive.

    g) Or have the child imagine running like their favorite animal. Encourage them to feel the power in their legs as they move quickly with the wind on their face.

12. The idea is to follow the student's lead and help them to explore, with an attitude of curiosity, what happens next as they notice their internal responses.

Resolving a stress reaction does much more than eliminate the likelihood of developing trauma later in life. It also fosters an ability to move through any threatening situation with greater ease and flexibility. It creates, in essence, a natural resilience to stress. A nervous system accustomed to experiencing and releasing stress is healthier than a nervous system burdened with an ongoing, if not accumulating, level of stress. Children who are encouraged to attend to their instinctual responses are rewarded with a lifelong legacy of health and vigor!

References

Damasio, A. R. (1995). *Descartes' error: Emotion, reason, and the human brain.* New York: HarperPerennial.

Damasio, A. R. (1999). *The feeling of what happens: Body and emotion in the making of consciousness.* New York: Harcourt.

LeDoux, J. E. (1998). *The emotional brain: Mysterious underpinnings of emotional life.* New York: Simon & Schuster.

Leitch, M. L. (2007). Somatic experiencing treatment with Tsunami survivors in Thailand: Broadening the scope of early intervention. *Traumatology, 13,* 11.

Levine, P. (1997). *Waking the tiger: Healing trauma.* Berkeley, CA: North Atlantic Books.

Chapter Sixteen

EMDR and the Challenge of Treating Childhood Trauma: A Theoretical and Clinical Discussion with Case Examples

Barbara Wizansky

Introduction

Treating childhood trauma with EMDR (Eye Movement Desensitization Reprocessing) requires the practitioner to be aware of the challenge inherent in adapting a focused therapeutic model created for adults to young developing clients. Problems involved in exposing young children to disturbing, often terrifying memories loom large. How do we cope with parents' fear of damaging their son or daughter? How do we answer our own internal resistance to leading a young client into a difficult session and the dangers of retraumatizing a child? These are problems which demand solutions. Recent neurological research has defined the necessity of including the processing of traumatic material into the treatment plan as directly as possible. No part of the brain can change if it is not activated (Perry & Pollard, 1998; Schore, 2003; Stein & Kendall, 2004). The chapter aims to detail how EMDR meets this challenge.

The question of safety in the child's experience

A discussion of childhood trauma has been extensively addressed elsewhere in this book. But as we consider focused treatment with EMDR, we would like to keep in the forefront of our thinking the question of safety and its relation to several major elements of the child's experience. We will later consider the ways in which the EMDR approach addresses these issues.

Post-Traumatic Syndromes in Childhood and Adolescence: A Handbook of Research and Practice, First Edition. Edited by Vittoria Ardino. © 2011 John Wiley & Sons, Ltd. Published 2011 by John Wiley & Sons, Ltd.

Childhood trauma is defined in accordance with the child's experience and not in terms of the traumatic event (Scheeringa et al., 1995). The meaning which a child assigns to an event and the potential development of symptoms often depend on the presence and reactions of caretakers and the quality of the child's attachment relationships. In the same way, the presence of a caretaker in the therapy session can be a major safety factor during treatment (Schore, 2003; Siegel, 1999).

An appreciation of how a child experiences safety in relation to caretakers allows us to evaluate more effectively those events, seemingly banal to adult observers, which may have been experienced by the child as traumatic because of the caretakers' reactions. Often these past "small t" traumas (Shapiro, 2001) form the underpinnings of current symptoms and diagnoses. For the therapist and parent, a treatment model must include a cushion of assurance that the child will not be retraumatized or suffer after leaving the session. We must be able to reassure children that though they may experience unpleasant, scary feelings in the session, they will also find inside themselves feelings that are comfortable, feelings of strength and competence.

What is EMDR?

EMDR is an integrated therapeutic approach based upon Adaptive Information Processing (AIP), a model which describes varied disturbances as the result of unprocessed dysfunctional memories. EMDR incorporates many aspects of current psychological and neurological thinking into a focused, efficient treatment for a wide variety of emotional disturbances. In our discussion, we will relate to EMDR as it is used to treat symptoms associated with PTSD.

EMDR began modestly in 1989, when Dr Francine Shapiro began looking at the positive effects of mentally focusing on a traumatic memory while moving the eyes back and forth (Shapiro, 2001). Since then, Shapiro's thinking has developed, together with the accumulation of a rich body of clinical case material, creative theory, and research, into EMDR's present acceptance by the professional community as an approved treatment for PTSD (e.g., American Psychiatric Association (APA), 2004; US Dept of Veterans' Affairs & Department of Defense, 2004). There have been more independent controlled studies of EMDR than systematic desensitization, flooding or any other standardized method used in the treatment of PTSD (Van Etten & Taylor, 1998). For example, EMDR has been compared with Stress Inoculation and Prolonged Exposure (Rothbaum, Astin, & Marsteller, 2005), CBT (Jaberghaderi et al., 2004), and treatment with anti-depressant medication (Van der Kolk et al., 2007). For a summary of comparative research results, see Seidler and Wagner (2006).

The Adaptive Information Processing Model (AIP)

The Adaptive Information Processing model (AIP) on which EMDR is based was originally proposed to explain clinical observations. Although it does not pretend to detail neurological processes, current research has emphasized the fact that traumatic responses, as described by the model, have identifiable neurological underpinnings. (See Shapiro, 2001, pp. 29–54 for a comprehensive discussion.) In simple terms, when confronted with a potentially traumatic event the brain follows a natural pattern of processing toward balance and healing in the same way as does the healthy body. If we are cut, the body will naturally clot and heal. Only if there is a blockage, such as a foreign body in the wound, will the wound fester and cause pain. If the blockage is removed and the wound cleaned, the healthy body will resume the healing process. In the same way, the natural tendency of the brain's information-processing system is movement toward integration, balance, and mental health.

When a person retains symptoms of PTSD, the AIP model assumes that the brain's natural adaptive information process has been overwhelmed. Sensory, somatic, emotional, and cognitive modalities of information associated with the traumatic event have been stored in dysfunctional memory networks which enable little integration with present, reality-based information. Reactive patterns based on the unprocessed information have been set in motion so that sensory and body feelings, emotions, and cognitions connected to the initial event are constantly triggered.

Processing in this model involves accessing the traumatic event and using the focused protocol to encourage the natural associative movement of the traumatic material to more adaptive integration. EMDR therapists, indeed, report that their clients' chains of associations usually move rapidly toward more adaptive forms.

At its most successful, EMDR treatment leads to change not only relating to a single issue connected with the trauma and present functioning, but to a growth experience affecting basic self-esteem and the way the client organizes and views his or her life.

The Adaptive Information Processing Model and children

This model conforms to major elements of the child's development toward a positive ongoing sense of being. Healthy development requires continuous accommodation and assimilation of information from the outside world through the five senses, and from inner experience through the pro-perceptive sense, into a new schema (Piaget, 1954). This assimilation of information is accomplished as the brain moves from balance to excitation and back to a homeostatic balance (Perry & Pollard, 1998), usually with the aid of holding by a good-enough caretaker (Bowlby, 1980; Winnicott, 1965). A traumatic event causes a break in these processes. The information from a traumatic event does not undergo assimilation into a new, developmentally appropriate schema but is stored in a dysfunctional state and tends to resurface inappropriately. The brain's development of basic functions is impaired in multiple areas, expressed as hyper- or hypo-reactivity to stress-related triggers. Whereas in adults this process may cause trait changes, in children we may see changes in developmental states which lead to a personality organization around the traumatic material (Perry & Pollard, 1998). Whether we meet the child directly, following the traumatic experience or years after, the AIP model leads us to evaluate where in the child's development this ongoing sense of being has been interrupted. We must decide what new sensory, emotional or cognitive information about themselves, or their environment, they need, in order to integrate the traumatic event, or events, into their present level of development. Do they have sufficient ego strengths to undertake the process of integration? And most important, how do we best encourage the natural inter subjective process?

The EMDR protocol and children

The EMDR model is embodied within a detailed, eight-phase protocol (as described by Shapiro, 2001). On the surface, this focused adult protocol consists of a number of elements which seem difficult, if not impossible, to apply to young children. It relies on talking. It requires the naming of negative and positive beliefs about oneself, the identification and numerical scaling of emotion and sensation, the production of a chain of associations. And most important, it requires clients' active participation in exposing themselves to fearful emotions. How can a three-year-old cope with such demands? How can we enlist the cooperation of an unwilling 10-year-old? Child therapists know well their young clients' reluctance to face uncomfortable feelings. "I don't want to talk about that" is a common response to a therapist's questions.

As EMDR has developed and taken root, however, child therapists have, in fact, found that this protocol can not only be successfully adapted to the treatment of PTSD in children as young as two years, but often leads to a surprisingly swift alleviation of symptoms in youngsters of all ages (Adler-Tapia & Settle, 2008; Greenwald, 1999; Tinker & Wilson, 1999). Experienced EMDR child therapists throughout the world are providing clinical descriptions of their work in cases of both simple and complex traumas. They are conducting child workshops, demonstrating playful, safe approaches, while retaining the protocol's essential elements. The EMDR Europe Association now encompasses an active Child Section, whose members share clinical and research information and has qualified a pool of child trainers, who teach methods of adapting the protocol to children, in accordance with established standards. The protocol has also been adapted to group work in schools and in areas which have been exposed to natural and war-torn disasters (Birnbaum, 2005; Jarero, Artigas, & Hartug, 2006; Korkmazler & Pamuk, 2002; Laub & Bar-Sade 2009).

Research in the use of EMDR with children lags behind that of adults. To date, only 16 studies have documented the use of the EMDR protocol with children and adolescents. Eleven of these studies refer to individual EMDR treatment of children and adolescents, and only six were controlled studies (Ahmad, Larsson, & Sundelin-Wahlsten, 2007; Chemtob, Nakashima, & Carlson, 2002; Jaberghaderi et al., 2004; Muris et al., 1997; Puffer, Greenwald, & Elrod, 1997; Rubin et al., 2001). In addition, five studies have been published to date on the use of group EMDR protocols with children exposed to man made or natural disasters (Fernandez, Gallinari, & Lorenzetti, 2004; Jarero, Artigas, & Hartung, 2006; Korkmazlar-Oral, & Pamuk, 2002; Wilson et al., 2000; Zaghrout-Hodali, Alissa, & Dodson, 2008). The need for robust published studies, to establish EMDR as an evidence-based practice for the treatment of children, is recognized by the EMDR community. Hopefully, problems of both funding and adjusting a research protocol to the unique difficulties of working with children will be addressed and solved. (See Adler-Tapia & Settle, 2008, pp. 7–17 for a comprehensive discussion of research to date and new directions.)

The AIP Model and resource development – Finding the client's unique strengths

The client's resources, or positive memory networks, are considered most important in the AIP model and are essential to adaptive processing. The model assumes an intra-subjective movement between those neural networks containing emotional, cognitive, and sensory material resulting from the past traumatic event, and information, or desired beliefs, which apply to the reality-based present. Accessing and strengthening the client's own resources can greatly facilitate such movement. The more firmly clients are connected to their own resources, the richer and more confident will be the dialectical movement between past and present (Laub & Weiner, 2007). The EMDR literature is rich in auxiliary protocols for the identification and development of the client's resources (Kiessling, 2005; Korn & Leeds, 2002; Laub, 2001; Leeds & Shapiro, 2000).

Resources and children – The pathway to relationship and processing

The EMDR emphasis on resource identification and development serves well in treating children. It becomes crucial not only to the child's ability to process a traumatic event, but also as a road into relationship-building. As a child's self-esteem rises, barriers to cooperation with the therapist are lowered. Identification and strengthening of a child's own unique, personal resources take place during the preparation phase of the protocol. Safety is reinforced, as it is with adults, through the child's connection to his own "safe place," which is installed with the help of bilateral stimulation.

In addition, therapists have integrated procedures from other therapeutic models and created new developmentally appropriate techniques, geared specifically to EMDR. Children are helped to discover competencies connected with times they felt strong or had fun; memories of love, safety, nurturing, and comfort. They may hunt together for resources as they play. They may come upon an instance of the child's ability to move their body quickly as they jump with a basketball, to appreciate a joke as they laugh at a riddle, or to plan effectively as they win a game (Wizansky, 2007a). The therapist may search for unique outcomes (Selekman, 1997; White & Epson, 1990), or play games with the child, to show them the difference between comfortable feelings and scary feeling (Berg & Steiner, 2003). These positive qualities constitute the child's unique resources. In EMDR treatment, they are marked and strengthened with bilateral stimulation, as they appear in the therapy room. A child whose introduction to therapy stresses their strengths will more readily trust the therapist and cooperate with later exposure to unpleasant materials.

It is important to appreciate, however, that the bedrock of a child's resources is the original quality of attachment. Issues of inadequate attachment, or breaks in previous patterns of ongoing attachment, may disturb, or influence adversely, the timing of the processing and subsequent healing. Many EMDR child therapists have attempted to meet this challenge by stressing the need to evaluate attachment quality during the history-taking phase of the protocol and by using the protocol framework to repair and then install with bilateral stimulation a loving connection to parents or caretakers (Lovett, 1999; Wesselmann, 1998). Specialty protocols have been developed that help reinforce attachment cues and repair lacunae in attachment (Bar-Sade, 2005). In addition, many EMDR child therapists emphasize the importance of parents as principal sources of safety by including them actively in the sessions (Bar-Sade & Wizansky, 2007b).

Clinical examples

Each of the cases described here is a compilation of work with several patients, in order to protect privacy and to emphasize specific treatment issues.

The girl who disobeyed her mother: Treatment of simple trauma using the EMDR protocol

Simple trauma is defined as stemming from a single, overwhelming event, or a series of similar events, that took place in the past. There is a sudden break in the child's system of defenses and past coping mechanisms, which leads to overwhelming feelings of helplessness and fear (Terr, 1990). The event was experienced by a child, whose development, attachment patterns, and family functioning are adequate, with sufficient ego strengths to suit their developmental stage. EMDR treatments of such cases can usually be completed within several months.

Efrat is a seven-year-old girl, whose behavior changed drastically within a matter of months. She became anxious about leaving the house, fearful of separating from her mother, and was having trouble sleeping. She was described, before her symptoms developed, as a bright, cheerful second-grader, whose day-to-day life had seemed to be a reflection of very positive cognitions about herself and her world: "I'm safe"; "Life is fun"; "I'm a good girl"; "I can do many things".

The EMDR protocol, Phase 1: History taking

When taking the history of the trauma, one often discovers a time-lag between the traumatic event and the appearance of symptoms. Six months before the trauma, Efrat was involved in an automobile accident. Initially, her mother had refused permission for her daughter to go on a drive with her young aunt and uncle. Efrat, as seven-year-old girls do, begged until her mother angrily gave in. A truck rammed into the side of the car. The child had minor injuries, but her aunt was covered with blood. It took several hours for her mother to be located and to arrive at the hospital, where the little girl lay in an emergency room cubicle, alone, checked on from time to time by a busy nurse and worried that her mother would be angry with her. A careful intake revealed no other evidence of early trauma.

Only two months later did symptoms begin to appear. The fear, worry, and guilt that were hiding "behind the trauma wall" (Greenwald, 2005) began to pop out when her mother left for work or when a dog crossed her path. By the time she arrived at the therapy room, it was clear that her basic belief about herself had shifted. She was now operating from an internal place which believed: "I'm not safe"; "Bad things can happen"; "It's my fault" when she met new situations, such was the worldview to which they were accommodated.

Evaluation of resources   Efrat had an uncomplicated developmental and attachment history, sound ego strengths, and supportive parents. She learned well, had friends, and was successful at dancing. This was a child with many resources, to which she had good access. It was posited that these resources, as well as her good relations with adults, would allow her to be cooperative, able to trust that the therapist would help her to feel better. It was also determined that her present symptoms were rooted in the traumatic accident. The diagnosis was clearly PTSD. This might be a straight and relatively uncomplicated treatment with a child, who seemed to have enough resources to immediately face direct trauma processing. Efrat's mother was judged to be her main source of safety. The fact that she went on the drive against her mother's objections was a key influence in the formation of her symptoms. It was important that the mother be present during treatment to emphasize and repair their previously sturdy attachment. According to the initial evaluation, the outlook, as is common in EMDR treatment of simple trauma, was for two to four sessions to complete the trauma processing and see a reduction in symptoms.

The EMDR protocol, Phase 2: Preparation

This phase readies the child and her parents for the trauma processing, by establishing a relation of trust and control. Children's individual resources of safety are explored and installed with bilateral stimulation and they are given a special signal, which they can use to stop the process at any time. Both parents and children are given clear information of how trauma and symptoms are connected, how processing will take place, and where the protocol will lead. The knowledge that there is a clear, safe, and positive beginning and end to each session provides a Resource Connection Envelope (RCE) around the traumatic material (this term is used by Laub, 2001). It is important that the therapist encourage parents in their own familiar ways of calming and comforting their child if they are upset between sessions and help them to discover methods for doing this, should they have none.

Efrat's treatment   The therapist concretized the explanation to Efrat with drawings, as they sat side by side at the art table. The drawings showed how her fear of leaving Mommy and of visiting her friends was connected to her fear during the accident. She was told that the therapist would help her very good brain to find a way not to be afraid anymore. Efrat quickly found her own "safe place," which was installed with bilateral stimulation by tapping on alternate knees. She visualized lying on her bed in the evening, talking to her mother about the day's events. Efrat was instructed to notice the good feeling in her body. She also practiced with the therapist a stop signal to apply if she wanted to halt the process at any time.

The EMDR protocol, Phase 3: Assessment

This phase consists of the client establishing a target image that symbolizes the worst part of the event and a present negative and positive cognition (NC, PC) about themselves, relating to the past event. They then focus on a numerical scaled measure of the felt truth of the PC, the distress around the NC, and its body resonance. Developmentally appropriate adaptations are easily made when working with children. The target may be drawn or demonstrated with dolls. Scaling may be shown by building a block tower or asking the child to open her or his arms to the size of the distress. Most children, even those aged three or younger, can put their hands on the place in their body where they sense the bad feeling. Some therapists have found that the NC in children under eight or nine may be dispensed with, without weakening the process

(Tinker & Wilson, 1999). Others take pains to suit the negative statement to the developmental level of even the youngest children (Adler-Tapia & Settle, 2008). Defining a PC, however, is considered essential, and the therapist can help a young child to do this, often with the aid of the parent.

Efrat's treatment   Efrat targeted the worst part of the accident by drawing a picture of herself lying in the ambulance. When asked what bad words about herself came to her head as she looked at that picture, she thoughtfully answered: "I'm dead" (NC). She giggled and said, "but I know I'm alive." With help from her mother and the therapist she agreed that she would like to think: "I'm alive and I'm usually safe" (PC). When she looked at the picture she drew and thought about being dead, she rated her fear as 9, with 10 being the strongest on the 0–10 Subjective Unit of Disturbance (SUDS) scale (Wolpe, 1990). She located the fear in her stomach.

The EMDR protocol, Phase 4: Desensitization

Here children are asked to think about their target image, the level of disturbance it engenders, and where they feel it in their bodies. If they have drawn their target, they may look at it as they process. Parents can witness, together with the therapist, the work in process. Children are directed to focus on the fearful event for a very short time as bilateral stimulation is applied. They are then returned to the safe present with a deep breath to share as much as they want to about what they have just experienced. Again, they are asked to focus inward on whatever associations have arisen, again accompanied by the tapping on their knees or moving their eyes in time with the therapist's finger. This sequence is repeated until the SUDS scale reaches a 0 or 1 level of distress. This component of dual attention between past and present is another source of safety for children. It provides an in-and-out rhythm which strengthens feelings of security and control. Each time they go inward, they harvest new information, often resource-based, which they may then share with therapist and parent. Young children may process while sitting on a parent's knee.

Efrat's treatment   Efrat chose to follow the therapist's finger as it moved back and forth in front of her eyes, while she thought of the picture that she had drawn. After 10 to 15 passes the therapist stopped, instructed Efrat to take a deep breath and tell what she noticed/saw/ was happening. With each set of eye movements her associations changed:

Efrat: Now I'm in the ambulance.

Therapist moves fingers back and forth (BLS-Bilateral Stimulation)

Efrat: Now I'm lying on my bed in my room with my mom, talking.

BLS

Efrat: My aunt had blood all over her head. (E's body stiffened. She took her mother's hand.)

BLS

Efrat: It was a funny color. But she talked to me. She wasn't dead.

BLS

Efrat: Mommy told me not to go. I wish I didn't go. (She looks at her mother, who looks back at her and smiles.) It wasn't fun.

Therapist: Where do you feel that in your body?

Efrat: In my tummy.

BLS

Efrat: Now I'm in bed with Mommy.

Therapist moves fingers.

Efat: I thought that truck would hit me right in the stomach. Boom. I saw a guy on TV who was cut open. (Her face registers fear.)

BLS

Efrat: It didn't go through the door of the car. The car stopped it.

BLS

Efrat: My mom said I could drive a monkey crazy. (Laughter together with her mother.)

BLS

Efrat: I didn't used to come straight home from school. I went to Sivan's. You got mad at me, right? (Looking at her mother. Mother smiled: "I was worried because I love you.")

BLS

Efrat: I'm a better jump-roper than Sivan.

BLS

Efrat: When I was waiting for Mommy to come to the hospital the nurse gave me a balloon with ears.

BLS

Efrat: My dad lets me go to the store to buy rolls in the morning by myself.

BLS

Efrat: We have a school trip next week.

Therapist asks her to think about the accident again. What do you see now?

Efrat: I see the accident. (She mentions no details. Her affect is cheerful.)

Therapist: How about that bad feeling in your stomach? How much does it bother you now?

Efrat: Wrinkles her forehead. I can't feel it any more.

Therapist: So what number would you give it?

Efrat: No number.

Since her SUDS has decreased, the therapist goes to the next phase.

The EMDR protocol, Phase 5: Installation
When the SUDS level of disturbance is 0, the PC is installed and strengthened to the maximum with bilateral stimulation.

Efrat's treatment   She has now left behind the traumatic affect and is totally in contact with her mother, the therapist, and feelings of competence and fun; the school trip, going to buy rolls on her own. The therapist focuses on the PC and its felt sense.

Therapist: And when you think about the words that we said before: "I'm usually safe" does that feel like it's true? Can you show me with your hands how true it feels?

Efrat (spreads her two arms wide): I never was in an accident before. Dad said the guy in the van just lost control and that only happens once in a million times. So I guess it's all true. The most, I'm not allowed to go out in the dark by myself.

Therapist: Think about that and the words "I'm usually safe" and follow my fingers.

BLS

This is repeated until the positive feeling is maximally strengthened.

Therapist: Think of those words again, "I'm usually safe." Let's see if we make them feel any stronger.

BLS

Efrat: I fell yesterday playing jump-rope, but it stopped bleeding fast. The nurse put a Band-aid on the cut. After that I even jumped "hot peppers." Can we paint afterwards?

Therapist judged that the PC was adequately installed.

The EMDR protocol, Phase 6: Body scan
The client scans his body from head to toe to check for residues of distress while repeating the PC. If there are problem areas, they must be processed.

Efrat's treatment   The therapist asked Efrat's mother to pass her hand over her daughter's body from top to toe, without touching. Efrat was instructed to tell if she felt a bad feeling anywhere. Since she shook her head, meaning no, we went on to the final phase of this session.

The EMDR protocol, Phase 7: Closure

In order to ensure that the client leaves the session in a positive state, the therapist either returns the child to her safe place, leads her in another relaxation exercise or accesses any resource which came up during or before processing. The client or the client's parents are instructed to notice any changes, either good or bad, during the week to report at the next session.

Efrat's treatment   She was asked to think again about her safe place, lying on the bed chatting with her mother, while her mother sat close and hugged her. The therapist tapped on alternate knees to "let the good feeling go all through her body." The therapist was fulfilling the promise that she can make to every child beginning an EMDR session: "When we finish the session, you will feel much better."

The EMDR protocol, Phase 8: Reevaluation

In a case of simple trauma the change is often so dramatic that the therapist wonders if there has been a true shift or mere compliance. Only in the final stage of the protocol, when the parent and child return for the next session and report on the week, can we know. Parents are asked to take note of any changes, positive or negative, and report to the therapist.

Efrat's treatment   Her mother reported that she was almost back to normal behavior. She had been able to access her strong, age-appropriate resources and return to a life-view embodied in her more positive cognitions. In addition to safety, she was behaving as though she believed again that, "I can do things well." "It's not my fault." "I'm a good girl." Unprocessed, this accident could have led to a shifted personality organization based on fear and guilt.

The EMDR adult protocol is described as three-pronged. Treatment takes account of the first past traumatic event, the present events which trigger symptoms, and a future template to deal with feared situations which might cause distress. There were two more sessions to Efrat's treatment. In one, the target was a present trigger of the trauma – the scary feeling when she and her mother were driving to the clinic that morning. She rated this target at a SUD of 6 (0–10). It made her "not want to go places." Efrat cleared that picture and arrived at a PC of "I can feel safe in the car." In the last two sessions she worked on future templates: driving with relatives and a recently developed fear of dogs.

Discussion

Children over 9 or 10 years can usually relate to all of the protocol components although it is important to remember that associations are far fewer and processing is usually much faster, the younger the child. When working with children of all ages, however, it is desirable to stay as close as possible to the boundaries of the protocol, varying only in accordance with the individual child's developmental or temperamental needs (Tinker & Wilson, 1999). Efrat, an intelligent, well-developed seven-year-old, was able to work well within the framework. Her symptoms receded after processing only one image of the accident, lying alone in the ambulance. Other children may need to process, in separate sessions, a number of the disturbing images connected to the trauma before treatment is completed.

Efrat's process demonstrates nicely the associative movement between the traumatic material and positive information/resources: for example, the boom of the truck hitting the car and the sturdiness of the metal; the feeling of loneliness in the hospital and the nurse who brought her a balloon. Her processing demonstrates a quick integration of the traumatic material into a developmentally appropriate schema and a positive theme cluster (Shapiro, 2001; E. Shapiro & Laub, 2008).

Complex trauma and EMDR – An integrative approach

Complex trauma is defined as a series of ongoing or continuous events which massively and repeatedly overwhelm the child. In addition to suffering breaks in their ongoing sense of being and the fear at the time of each traumatic event, the child suffers the ongoing terror and anxiety in expectation of the next blow to come (Terr, 1990). These are cases which demand more comprehensive treatment planning and longer periods of time to address the child's difficulties. In addition to trauma processing, treating complex childhood trauma usually entails attention to primary functions which may have been delayed or damaged by exposure to events that were overwhelming to the developing organism. Some examples are stress response, impulse control, organizational skills, communication skills, and empathy. Children who have suffered cumulative trauma often have unsatisfactory attachment patterns and little or no access to personal resources (Schore, 2001). In these cases EMDR trauma processing and resource connection will be integrated into a comprehensive treatment plan to address varied issues as therapists make use of the methods with which they are most comfortable. EMDR has been integrated successfully with dynamic play therapy, behavioral therapies, solution-focused therapy, and narrative therapy. Treatments may take many months or even years, but clinicians have found that thinking in terms of the AIP model and the inclusion of the EMDR protocol as a significant part of the treatment can add to its depth and efficiency, not only in helping the child to clear trauma, but also in achieving developmental milestones.

The boy who no one understood: A case of complex trauma

Ron, a sturdy four-year-old, had been asked to leave three preschools because of his uncontrollable and sometimes even bizarre behavior. Without obvious triggers, he often sat whimpering in a corner, raced madly around the room sweeping toys off the shelves, bit and punched other children or approached other children to bang his own head against their foreheads. Sometimes his play was appropriate. At other times he gravitated only to rubber animals with flexible mouths into which he repetitively forced small objects. He could be loving, curious, and connected. At other times, he was unresponsive, unable to listen to a story or take part in a group activity. His teacher described him as a puzzle with no solution.

Phase I: History-taking

Ron had suffered ongoing trauma to his body from birth. He was born, after a normal pregnancy, with a heart defect. This defect was ultimately repaired at age 1 year, 10 months with major surgery. But in addition to spending his first three months in an incubator, he underwent four other serious operations in the first year and a half of his life. He was fed through tubes. His body was invaded, restricted, and hurt while the people who loved him stood by and watched.

Attachment history   Ron's parents were warm and loving caretakers, but his medical history seriously interfered with the development of secure, ongoing attachment. His parents had not only been unable to protect him from pain until he was almost two years, but had stood by watching him suffer. At four, Ron sometimes showed appropriate attachment behavior, but serious lacunae in his feelings of trust and love were also apparent.

Personal resources   Ron was an intelligent, curious, and now physically sound little boy. He loved and was interested in animals and, when communicative, demonstrated appropriate language skills. In addition to his parents, he had a warm and loving extended family.

Treatment planning   A careful evaluation of Ron's development, his history of cumulative trauma, and his present functioning led to a diagnosis of PTSD in a young child (Scheeringa et al., 1995). It was clear that Ron and his parents would need an extended period of treatment to develop trust, process trauma, as well as to better understand and advance the development of those neurological functions which were damaged. Some of his problems lay in his inability to maintain ongoing communication, to feel appropriate empathy, and to regulate hair-trigger impulse control.

Phase 2: Preparation

The preparation phase was aimed at building feelings of safety and comfort in the therapy room for both Ron and his parents. EMDR was helpful in strengthening and repairing lacunae in attachment patterns, as well as bolstering Ron's personal resources of competence in specific games and age-appropriate humor.

Resource work not only prepared Ron for the safe processing of past trauma with the EMDR protocol, but also helped to obtain his cooperation in the necessary work of stabilizing behavior and closing developmental gaps. Most important, EMDR became a vehicle for focusing and giving direction to the treatment. Because of questions about Ron's communication difficulties, the therapist chose to integrate EMDR resource installation and trauma processing with Floor Time, which works directly on improving communication skills (Greenspan, 1994).

One of Ron's parents was present at every session. Toys were offered and his parents were encouraged to allow Ron to lead the activity while they followed and expanded his productions. They were shown how to open and close circles of communication according to the Greenspan model. When his behavior became disorganized or disconnected, EMDR stabilization and resource connection were used. He was encouraged to cuddle into parent's lap and listen to him/her installing the PC of "You're safe now. Mommy/Daddy takes good care of you" while the therapist tapped on alternate knees with her "magic wand." Therapist and parents discovered "attachment cues" (Bar-Sade, unpublished attachment protocol), such as songs that his mother sang to him as an infant or a special way that she touched his cheek while he was in the incubator. These, too, were repeated as the therapist tapped his knees. Other personal resources were tracked during the play sessions and immediately emphasized and installed. When he successfully built a tower of blocks and shouted "hooray," when his father made him laugh or when he allowed his father to hold him after a temper tantrum, he was asked to feel the good feeling in his body and think, "I'm a good laugher," or "I am strong enough to calm myself," while parent or therapist tapped his knees or shoulders. Over a period of time Ron and his parents became comfortable with each other in the therapy room and outbursts of out-of-control behavior lessened.

Phases 3 and 4: Assessment and desensitization

Children of this age can usually find a target and identify a feeling and the body sensation that goes with the feeling. They can scale the feeling by opening their arms to the width of the fear or anger or by building a tower of blocks. Taller towers can represent stronger feelings. When the trauma is preverbal and the child is young, EMDR therapists often weave story-telling into the protocol to help access and organize the traumatic material into targets. The story should have a happy beginning and a happy end. The middle should be told simply and truthfully in language suited to the child, with an emphasis on emotions and body feelings. Usually the parents tell the story while making eye contact with the child. Either the parent or therapist administers bilateral stimulation. There are pauses from time to time to allow the child to associate and to connect with body feelings. In this way traumatic material can be processed according to the child's own rhythm. Often the story is processed bit by bit over many sessions.

Ron's treatment   The parents were helped to construct a story for Ron, framed by the happy beginning "when mommy was pregnant" and the happy end "when the doctor told them that Ron was again healthy with a good strong body." The middle was related, simply but honestly. The story gave an account of his birth and his illnesses. It told how he lay in an incubator and could be touched only on his fingers or his cheeks, how he had to be fed through tubes in his nose and his mouth, how his hands were often tied down so he wouldn't pull out the tubes, how the doctors and nurses had to prick his feet to test his blood. His parents imagined how much he must have wanted to kick his feet and hands. Maybe he had been frightened and angry that he couldn't. They talked about how sad they were and how much they had wanted to cuddle him but they had to let the doctors take care of him to make him well. The story continued with his final operation, the pain, the scary feelings, the anger, and finally his recovery. As Ron associated to the story, targets for direct processing gradually emerged. The therapist's gentle questioning helped him to access his feelings and body sensations.

At first, it was difficult for Ron to listen to his story. He wandered around the room, made sudden noises or manipulated small objects as one of his parents talked. Because he objected to being touched while he played or moved, the therapist chose to put small speakers on either side of the room and play tapes specially made for EMDR bilateral stimulation (Grand, 2001). Gradually, Ron began giving clues that his story was assuming form and meaning. He would now sit next to his parent to listen and allow tapping on his knees. Between sets he asked questions about which of his family came to see him, about presents that he had been given, about how small he had been. Two of the story's images on which he focused were the tying down of his hands and feet, and the tubes in his throat.

Therapist: What do you feel when Mommy tells you about having your hands tied?

Ron: Mad. I don't like it. I can punch that doctor.

Therapist: Can you show me with your hands how mad you feel? (She demonstrates opening them very wide for very mad and bringing them close together for "not mad at all.")

Ron opens his hands as wide as he can.

Therapist: Where do you feel that mad in your body?

Ron: Like this. He punches hard with his hands.

Therapist: Can you think about how your hands were tied while I tap your knees?

Ron: I didn't like to have my hands tied.

BLS

Ron: I don't like it.

Therapist: Can you show me how it felt to have your hands tied?

Ron lies flat and stiffens his body, his arms straight at his side.

BLS (shoulder tapping)

Ron stiffens even more and screws up his face.

BLS

Therapist: What's happening now?

Ron: I want to . . .

BLS

Ron: I want to move them.

Therapist: Think of how much you wanted to move them.

BLS

Ron screws up his face.

BLS

Therapist pauses: Your face tells me you wanted to move them very much. Where do you feel that wanting most?

Ron: In my fingers. (To his mother) Then what happened?

Mother: Then the doctor said that you were better and he could take the tubes out. So he undid your hands. We were all happy.

BLS

Ron: You were there, Mommy. And Grandpa was there too. Right?

Therapist: Think of Mommy and Daddy and Grandpa all there.

BLS

Ron shakes his hands and arms with great energy.

Therapist: Yes, now your arms are always free. Think of that.

BLS

Ron adds feet kicking and begins rolling back and forth.

BLS

Ron pounds his feet on the floor.

Therapist: How do you feel now that Ron's hands and feet are free, Mom? And he can move any way that he wants?

Mother: I feel so happy. So did Daddy and Grandpa.

Therapist: Can you feel that happy inside of you, Ron? And you, Mom?

Ron: Yes.

Mom: Yes.

Therapist: Where do you feel that happy feeling in your body?

Ron: All over. (He kicks and waves his hands.)

Mom: In my heart. (She puts her hand on her heart.)

Therapist: Can you show me with your hands how happy you feel?

Ron holds his arms wide.

BLS

Ron continues kicking and rolling back and forth.

BLS

He quietens down.

Therapist: Can you and Mom show how happy you are by giving a hug?

Ron climbs into Mom's lap and hugs her, then cuddles with a finger in his mouth.

Therapist: Feel that good feeling of hugging Mom and having hands and feet that can move as they like.

BLS

Therapist: Can you say, "I'm free to move whenever I want" and feel that good feeling in your body?

BLS

There were days when he objected to hearing the story, but instead continuously stuffed small marbles into the rubber dinosaur's mouth. This became an important target image and shed light on his repetitive play. Now he would allow his mother to tap his shoulders as he repeated the activity. The therapist directed her to pause from time to time and told Ron that now he could take a deep breath and tell us what he noticed. At the end of each set he returned to the play without speaking. After three sets he lifted his head and said:

Ron: They put a faucet in my mouth. (Angry affect). I'm gonna kill them. They turned on the water.

BLS

Therapist: Think about that.

Ron: I could punch him in the mouth. It was like a faucet.

Therapist: Can you show me with your hands how mad you are?

Ron punches the air hard with his fist.

Therapist: Wow. That sounds not just like mad. That sounds like very, very, very mad. Can you feel that mad in your body?

Ron punches the air again with his fist.

Ron: A million verys.

Therapist: Can you think about that faucet and the million verys?

BLS

Ron crawls into his mother's lap to feel the safety and softness that awaited him there. His brain was finding, within the pain and the anger, the resource of mother.

BLS

Mother: The doctors had to feed you special food. It was thick, like a milk shake. It had to go through a tube because you were sick.

BLS

Ron: I could throw it up – all over him.

BLS

Ron: I would pull it out. I'd make him eat like that too.

BLS

Therapist: Can you show us where you feel the tube.

Ron: hand on his throat.

BLS

Ron: Maybe it was a chocolate milkshake.

BLS

Ron: Now I can drink regular. Mom, can we get a chocolate milkshake after?

Therapist: Now you're healthy and can drink regular. Think of that.

BLS

Ron gets off of mother's lap and picks up the doctor kit.

Therapist: How much mad do you feel in your body now?

Ron: (pulling the instruments out of the doctor kit, thinking) There's no more "verys."

Ron finished the session by playing doctor. He examined and treated first the dinosaur and then his mother.

The processing of Ron's medical history continued in this fragmented manner over a matter of months, integrated with dyadic play therapy, Greenspan's Floor Time communication model, and work with his parents and teachers on limit-setting techniques. Ron was gradually able to hear and tell his story calmly. When he was asked about the anger or fear that he had expressed at various points of the telling, it was clear that the emotional impact of his experience had receded to a different place in his memory. There were either no "verys," or his arms stayed closed in front of his face to measure no fear. The cumulative medical trauma had left him with sensory anxiety and unanswered drives, which were constantly being triggered. As his body experiences were verbalized and integrated into present schemata, his behavior became more understandable and less reactive. By age five, communication with both adults and children had stabilized and showed the empathy suited to his developmental age. His play had normalized and he was able to both cooperate comfortably with a daily schedule and to cope more effectively with difficulties sustaining attention and conforming to limits.

Ron and small t trauma – Negative cognitions begin to develop

EMDR defines small t trauma as those incidents, seemingly banal to the on-looker, which may be experienced by a child as overwhelming. Small t trauma can involve such incidents as a bad school year with an unpleasant teacher, a period of being exposed to bullying, a family move which interferes with parents' functioning for a time. If the child has a history of trauma which has weakened him, or is surrounded by caretakers who react with anger, indifference or hysteria to his distress, even apparently minor life events may be experienced by the child as overwhelming and lead to the formation of negative cognitions and behavior patterns.

Ron's story illustrates the workings of small t trauma and the way that seemingly minor incidents can gradually eat away at a child's development of self-esteem and lay the groundwork for negative cognitions and symptom formation. The work with EMDR in the therapy room was helping Ron to process the sensory anxiety and drive to disorganized and reactive movement that had accompanied his traumatic experiences. Participating with him in the retelling of his story also helped his parents. There was, however, still work to be done. Both parents had functioned well during his illness. But his bizarre behaviors, and daily struggles over dressing, eating, and adjusting to preschool, continued to trigger anxiety about his development and anger that this had happened to them. Misbehavior of any kind was often met with either "walking-on-eggs" responses or anger and punishments followed by guilty over-compensation. All of these repeatedly sent Ron the message that something was wrong with him.

Ron was certainly not abused or neglected. He still received love and attention, but his parents had changed. They had been infinitely patient in his sickness but, as he grew, daily life was being turned into a series of small t traumas. By age four, when he began treatment, he was gradually storing up the anxious, over-careful responses or the harsh images and words that would attach to general sensory anxiety and form the cognitions around which his personality would be organized: "I'm a bad boy." "I can't do it." "There's something wrong with me."

Often child trauma and parent trauma go hand in hand. Understanding the importance of secure and confident attachment to the child's experience helps us to appreciate that part of a child's treatment involves the parents' processing of their own trauma. The mother's dominant cognitions about Ron's birth were: "Life brings catastrophe" and "I am inadequate." Each time Ron acted out, the feelings around these cognitions were triggered. Only after EMDR processing was she able to feel again the truth of her previously positive view of herself: "Good things happen in my life" and "I can be a good and competent mother." Only then was she able to wholly utilize the therapist's help in setting limits, the anchors to safe boundaries, so essential for a traumatized child like Ron.

The components of EMDR

The role of each of the elements of an EMDR treatment is not yet clear, but success seems to reside in the strength of the protocol as a whole. (For a comprehensive discussion of component research and clinical implications, see Shapiro, 2001, pp. 315–67.) For younger children we may eliminate some of the cognitive elements of the protocol and allow flexibility in the order and the manner of presentation to accommodate developmental demands, without weakening its effectiveness. The EMDR protocol seems to be a robust example of the whole being greater than the sum of its parts. The elements which seem, from clinical experience, to be essential to the process are:

- Dual attention – the process by which the client is directed to repeatedly move his focus of attention from the inner experience of the disturbing targeted image to the external reality of the safe therapy room. Bilateral stimulation is an important component of the phenomenon of dual attention.
- Associative chaining – the process of free association, which is stimulated by the bilateral stimulation, a minimum of therapist intervention and directions to "just notice what you are experiencing." It is important to remember that the child's free association process is much shorter than that of an adult. Even one or two associations are an indication that an internal process is occurring.
- Emphasis on physical sensations during all phases of the protocol.

EMDR and children – A unique experience

Our hope is that this discussion of the EMDR model and the clinical treatment examples make clear how this very effective treatment can be adapted to children. We have attempted to stress the contribution of the EMDR protocol to providing safety for child and parent without shying away from the traumatic event, as well as allowing flexibility to respond to attachment needs and the accessing and strengthening of personal resources. The protocol allows the child therapist room to integrate drawing, play, and methods of scaling which suit developmental needs. As the child shares his associative process, it is possible to observe the intra-subjective movement embodied in the AIP model between the negative/problem pole and the positive/resource pole which leads to the accessing of new information and a new balance (Laub & Weiner, 2007; Shapiro, 2001).

Beyond these, however, an EMDR treatment provides a unique experience for both child and therapist. As we follow the course of processing it becomes clear that we are dealing with more than the effects of exposure, desensitization or cognitive change. We have given the child the difficult task of being still, connecting to the traumatic experience, and plunging into his inner, subjective space. Usually he will do anything rather than allow that to happen, for he knows that he will there meet uncomfortable, scary feelings. But as he takes this plunge within the safety limits of the EMDR protocol he begins to find within his subjective being new information. He meets not only unpleasant feelings, but also his own resources, positive feelings of love, competence, fun or comfort. He experiences desensitization not only to traumatic memories and their accompanying emotions, but to the fear of being alone within himself. He copes with the fear of his fear as he is exposed to the unique and valuable experience of being rather than doing. Even the youngest of our clients engages in conscious subjective psychological work. Efrat, as she worked, found within herself a girl who disobeyed, integrated with the association to a laughing mother who fondly likened her to a monkey. Ron found a faucet choking his throat as well as the pleasant taste of a chocolate milkshake. As dual attention takes them in and out of this inner space, the child is led to understand that whatever they notice is fine. Their brain is doing just what is right for them so they can heal in whatever way is best for them. For the child as well as for the adult, EMDR treatment can provide a true growth experience as they discover within themselves their own unique psychological balance.

References

Adler-Tapia, R., & Settle, C. (2008). *The art of psychotherapy with children*. New York: Springer.

Ahmad, A., Larsson, B., & Sundelin-Wahlsten, V. (2007). EMDR treatment for children with PTSD: Results of a randomized controlled trial. *Nordic Journal of Psychiatry, 61*, 349–54.

American Psychiatric Association (APA) (2004). *Practice guidelines for the treatment of patients with acute stress disorder and post-traumatic stress disorder*. Arlington: Author.

Bar-Sade, E., (2005). Accessing attachment cues: An EMDR child protocol. Unpublished.

Bar-Sade, E., & Wizansky, B. (2007). *The challenge of using EMDR to treat children. Basic training manual*. Ra'anana: EMDR Israel Association.

Berg, I. K., & Steiner, T. (2003). *Children's solution work*. New York: Norton.

Birnbaum, A. (2005, October). Group EMDR with children and families following the Tsunami in Thailand. Conference of EMDR-Israel Humanitarian Assistance Program, Ra'anana.

Bowlby, J. (1980). *Child care and the growth of love.* New York: Penguin Books.

Chemtob, C. M., Nakashima, J., Hamada, R. S., & Carlson, J. G. (2002). Brief treatment for elementary school children with disaster-related posttraumatic stress disorder: A field study. *Journal of Clinical Psychology, 58,* 99–112.

Fernandez, I., Gallinari, E., & Lorenzetti, A. (2004). A school-based EMDR intervention for children who witnessed the Pirelli Building airplane crash in Milan, Italy. *Journal of Brief Therapy, 2,* 129–36.

Grand, D. (2001). *Beyond the inner mirror* (CD #5). Bellmore, NY: BioLateral Sound Recordings.

Greenspan, S. (1994). *Infancy and early childhood.* Madison, CT: International Universities Press.

Greenwald, R. (1999). *Eye movement desensitization and reprocessing (EMDR) in child and adolescent psychotherapy.* New York: Jason Aronson.

Greenwald, R. (2005). *The child trauma handbook.* Binghamtom, NY: Haworth Press.

Jaberghaderi, N., Greenwald, R., Rubin, A., Dolatabadim, S., & Zans, S. O. (2004). A comparison of CBT and EMDR for sexually abused Iranian girls. *Clinical Psychology and Psychotherapy, 11,* 358–68.

Jarero, I., Artigas, L., & Hartung, J. (2006). EMDR integrative group treatment protocol: A post-disaster trauma intervention for children and adults. *Traumatology, 12*(2), 121–9.

Kiessling, R. (2005). Integrating resource development strategies into your practice. In R. Shapiro (Ed.), *EMDR solutions* (pp. 57–88). New York: W. W. Norton & Co.

Korkmazler-Oral, U., & Pamuk, S. (2002). Group EMDR with child survivors of the earthquake in Turkey. *Association for Child Psychiatry and Psychology, Occasional Paper No. 19,* 47–50.

Korn, D. L., & Leeds, A. M. (2002). Preliminary evidence of efficacy for EMDR resource development and installation in the stabilization phase of treatment of complex posttraumatic stress disorder. *Journal of Clinical Psychology, 58*(12), 1465–87.

Laub, B. (2001). The healing power of resource connection in the EMDR protocol. *EMDRIA Newsletter, Special Edition,* 21–7.

Laub, B., & Bar Sade, E. (2009). The Imma EMDR Group Protocol. In M. Luber (Ed.), *Eye movement desensitization and reprocessing. EMDR scripted protocols: basic and special situations.* New York: Springer.

Laub, B., & Weiner, N. (2007). The pyramid model: Dialectical polarity in therapy. *Journal of Transpersonal Psychology, 39,* 2.

Leeds, A., & Shapiro, F. (2000). EMDR and resource installation: Principles and procedures for enhancing current functioning and resolving traumatic experiences. In J. Carlson & L. Sperry (Eds.), *Brief therapy strategies with individuals and couples.* Phoenix, AZ: Zeig/Tucker.

Lovett, J. (1999). *Small wonders.* New York: The Free Press.

Muris, P., Merckelbach, H., Van Haafren, H., & Mayer, B. (1997). Eye movement desensitization and reprocessing versus exposure in vivo: A single-session crossover study of spider-phobic children. *The British Journal of Psychiatry, 171,* 82–6.

Perry, B. D., & Pollard, R. (1998). Homeostasis, stress, trauma and adaptation. A neurodevelopmental view of childhood trauma. *Child and Adolescent Psychiatric Clinics of North America, 7*(1), 33–51.

Piaget, J. (1954). *The construction of reality in the child.* New York: Ballantine Books.

Puffer, M. K., Greenwald, R., & Elrod, D. E. (1998). A single session EMDR study with twenty traumatized children and adolescents. *Traumatology, 3*(2), Article 6.

Rothbaum, B. O., Astin, M. C., & Marsteller, F. (2005). Prolonged exposure versus eye movement desensitization (EMDR) for PTSD rape victims. *Journal of Traumatic Stress, 18,* 607–16.

Rubin, A., Bischofshausen, S., Conroy-Moore, K. et al. (2001). The effectiveness of EMDR in a child guidance center. *Research on Social Work Practice, 11*(4), 435–57.

Scheeringa M. S., Drell M. J., Larrieu J. A., & Zeanah, C. H. (1995). Two approaches to the diagnosis of Post-Traumatic Stress Disorder in infancy and early childhood. *Journal of the American Academy of Child and Adolescent Psychiatry, 34,* 191–200.

Schore, A. (2001). The effects of early relational trauma on right brain development, affect regulation, and infant mental health. *Infant Mental Health Journal, 22,* 201–69.

Schore, A. (2003). *Affect regulation and the repair of the self.* New York: W. W. Norton & Co.

Seidler, G. H., & Wagner, F. E. (2006). Comparing the efficacy of EMDR and exposure-focused cognitive behavioral therapy in the treatment of PTSD: A meta-analytic study. *Psychological Medicine, 36,* 1515–22.

Selekman, M. D. (1997). *Solution-focused therapy with children.* New York: Guilford Press.

Shapiro, E., & Laub, B. (2008). Early EMDR intervention (EEI): A summary, a theoretical model and the Recent Traumatic Episode Protocol (R-TEP). *Journal of EMDR Practice and Research, 2*(2), 79–96.

Shapiro, F. (2001). *Eye movement desensitization and reprocessing* (2nd ed.). New York: Guilford Press.

Siegel, D. J. (1999). *The developing mind: Toward a neurobiology of interpersonal experience.* New York: Guilford Press.

Stein, P., & Kendall, J. (2004). *Psychological trauma and the developing brain.* New York: Haworth Press.

Terr, L. (1990). *Too scared to cry.* New York: Basic Books.

Tinker, R., & Wilson, S. (1999). *Through the eyes of a child.* New York: W. W. Norton & Co.

US Department of Veterans' Affairs & Department of Defense (2004). *VA/DoD clinical practice guideline for the management of post-traumatic stress.* Washington, DC: Author.

Van Etten, M. L., & Taylor, S. (1998). Comparative efficacy of treatments for post-traumatic stress disorder: A meta-analysis. *Clinical Psychology and Psychotherapy, 5,* 126–44.

Van der Kolk, B., Spinazzola, J., Blaustein, M. D. et al. (2007). A randomized clinical trial of eye movement desensitization and reprocessing (EMDR), fluoxetine, and pill placebo in the treatment of posttraumatic stress disorder: Treatment effects and long-term maintenance. *Journal of Clinical Psychiatry, 68*(1), 37–46.

Wesselmann, D. (1998). *The whole parent: How to become a terrific parent even if you didn't have one.* New York: Plenum.

Wilson, S., Tinker, R., Hofmann, A., Becker, L., & Marshall, S. (2000, November). A field study of EMDR with Kosovar-Albanian refugee children using a group treatment protocol. Paper presented at the annual meeting of the International Society for the Study of Traumatic Stress, San Antonio, TX.

Winnicott, D. W. (1965). A clinical study of the effect of a failure of the average expectable environment on child's mental functioning, *International Journal of Psychoanalisis, 46*, 81–87.

Wizansky, B., (2007a). A clinical vignette: Resource connection in EMDR work with children. *Journal of EMDR Practice and Research, 1*, 1.

Wizansky, B. (2007b). Trauma-informed therapy. *Counseling Children and Young People, September.* Lutterworth: BACP.

White, M. & Epson, D. (1990). *Narrative means to therapeutic ends.* New York: Norton.

Wolpe, J. (1990). *The practice of behavior therapy* (4th ed.). New York: Pergamon Press.

Zaghrout-Hodali, M., Alissa, F., & Dodgson, P. (2008). Building resilience and dismantling fear: EMDR group protocol with children in an area of ongoing trauma. *Journal of EMDR Practice and Research, 2*(2), 106–113.

Chapter Seventeen

Recent Advances in Cognitive-Behavioral Therapy for Traumatized Children and Teenagers

Dirk Flower and Stefania Grbcic

Introduction

Cognitive-behavioral treatments have been the preferred choice for most PTSD cases; numerous studies have confirmed the effectiveness of this treatment for PTSD in children and young people (Cohen & Mannarino, 2008; Scheeringa et al., 2007; Smith et al., 2007). Cognitive Therapy (CT), developed in the 1960s, is a structured, short-term, present-oriented therapy, directed toward solving current difficulties and modifying dysfunctional thinking and behavior (Beck, 1995). The central principle is that cognitions, emotions, and behaviors are linked by an adaptive or maladaptive "schema" (Beck et al., 1979). Schemas are learned as a way of adapting to developmental demands and experiences and incorporate basic beliefs and attitudes (Beck, 1995). Core schemas are identified by looking at cognitions (the use of imagery and reawakening of past negative experiences can activate core schemas).

Various maladaptive schemas and their combinations contribute to the formation of particular problem behaviors. Within each problem situation, a consistent pattern of certain beliefs and strategies predominate and form maladaptive over- and underdeveloped strategies for interpreting the world.

For dealing with problem behaviors, schematic change is undertaken using reconstruction, modification or reinterpretation of the schema of the individual or family system. By changing schemas and behaviors, individuals can break away from self-defeating feelings and actions (Beck, 1970). This is based on

Post-Traumatic Syndromes in Childhood and Adolescence: A Handbook of Research and Practice, First Edition. Edited by Vittoria Ardino. © 2011 John Wiley & Sons, Ltd. Published 2011 by John Wiley & Sons, Ltd.

the assumption that how people think and act can lock them into unhelpful emotional states and patterns.

The main focus of CT is on: (1) relieving symptoms and helping individuals solve problems; (2) building on strengths and developing new ways of coping; and (3) preventing relapse. CT was further developed by including a focus on behavior, resulting in cognitive-behavioral therapy (CBT).

A variety of techniques are applied in order to help an individual access cognitions and emotions (Beck et al., 1979). Individuals are encouraged to recognize and own their emotions and assist them in identifying their automatic interpretations. They are further encouraged to search for evidence "for and against" the particular (reoccurring) views. Their thoughts and attitudes are reframed (Blackburn & Davidson, 1998).

The implementation of CBT usually relies on the structured implementation of: (1) data collection, hypothesis testing, and goal-setting; (2) joint problem solving using a collaborative alliance; (3) focus on learning and practicing new responses to life experiences; (4) focus on concrete or observable goals; (5) focus on changing current and future reactions; and (6) reduction of recidivism.

Behavioral techniques use direct and indirect therapeutic exposure and desensitization. Individuals reexperience and/or reexamine as many aspects of a problem as possible until the intense emotion surrounding the problem is relieved. Homework assignments play an integral part of therapy, as the time between the sessions is also deemed important and therapeutic (Blagys & Hilsenroth, 2002). A meta-analysis of 11 studies on the effects of homework use in CBT has provided positive results (Kazantzis, Deane, & Ronan, 2000).

CBT has been extensively researched and can be applied to a variety of problems, for example: depression (Beck, 1995), obsessive-compulsive disorder (Salkovskis & Kirk, 1989), irritable bowel syndrome (Boyce et al., 2000), hypochondriasis (Barsky & Ahern, 2004), PTSD (Nicholl & Thompson, 2004), phobias (Rosser et al., 2004), bipolar disorder (Patelis-Siotis, 2001), as well as childhood and adolescent anxiety disorders (Cartwright-Hatton et al., 2004). The effectiveness has been empirically supported and many trials report sustained improvements at follow-up periods (Cole & Vaughan 2005; Hagen et al., 2005).

Numerous trials have reported on the long-term benefits of CBT and that further gains are achieved even after therapy has ended (Rawson et al., 2006).

The approach applied with the case studies described in this chapter is usually conducted within the context of the client's present family situation, where the therapist balances empathic understanding with being active, directive, and takes a collaborative approach with the client and the family system to problem solve and achieve goals. The extension of individualized CBT to a family-based approach, including the child (the client), has been found to be more effective and inclusive of the family system, so that they contribute to the therapeutic process rather than at best be neutral or antagonistic. This approach also addresses family interactions that may be maladaptive to the therapeutic process, therefore engendering greater long-term therapeutic success.

The effectiveness of CBT for PTSD

Research supporting the use of CBT (consisting of some form of exposure and/or cognitive restructuring) for individuals with PTSD indicates that it is more effective than no treatment or supportive counseling (Cloitre et al., 2002; Ehlers et al., 2003; Foa et al., 1999; Olasov Rothbaum et al., 2000; Smith et al., 2007).

Although there is a number of competing CBT formulations for dealing with PTSD (Ehlers & Clark, 2000; Foa, Steketee, & Rothbaum, 1989; Resick & Schnicke, 1992), Zayfert and Black Becker (2007) consider that there is no clear evidence that any one particular formulation of CBT is consistently and markedly superior to another (Zayfert & Black Becker, 2007).

Nonetheless, the use of exposure has the most consistent evidential support across a number of trauma populations (Olasov Rothbaum et al., 2000; Smith et al., 2007; Zayfert & Black Becker, 2007). Exposure can be imaginal (i.e., exposure to the trauma memories), *in vivo* (i.e., exposure to real-life experiences and their stimuli), or systemic desensitization (i.e., progressive exposure to the feared stimulus paired with relaxation). It appears that the systematic desensitization procedure is not frequently applied as it is considered that the relaxing component does not enhance treatment effectiveness (Olasov Rothbaum et al., 2000). Various exposure procedures are often used in a variety of combinations as they address different aspects of the clients' PTSD; for example, the imaginal process often addresses fears of real-life situations and memories, while the *in vivo* process often addresses the contextual cues triggered by the real-life situations (Zayfert & Black Becker, 2007). The use of exposure may be particularly effective with individuals whose PTSD symptoms are characterized by feelings of anxiety and who have beliefs about danger (Zayfert & Black Becker, 2007).

Furthermore, with some individuals whose PTSD symptoms are characterized by feelings of intense guilt, shame, and anger, the cognitive restructuring technique is considered to be a more appropriate initial intervention strategy (Zayfert & Black Becker, 2007).

Procedures that have empirical support of treatment effectiveness, but not to the same level as exposure and cognitive restructuring, include: (1) Stress Inoculation Training (SIT) – found to be effective with particular populations, for example, with female sexual assault survivors (Olasov Rothbaum, et al., 2000; Zayfert & Black Becker 2007); and (2) Eye-Movement Desensitization Reprocessing (EMDR), which can also be used as a supportive intervention and/or in combination with other procedures, depending on the therapeutic formulation (Zayfert & Black Becker, 2007).

In addition, there are a number of more recent supportive procedures that are considered to be effective when implemented in conjunction with other approaches, particularly in the area of relapse prevention, for example, mindfulness (considered more effective for adolescents and adults; Segal, Williams, & Teasdale, 2002). Carol Dweck (2007) argues that a mindset influences one's perspective and behavior across a variety of settings. In her work, she has theorized that there is a learning mindset and a fixed achievement mindset. She considers that individuals who believe that they have innate fixed abilities like IQ, approach tasks as a way of confirming their ability, and individuals who have a learning mindset approach tasks as a way of exploring and learning about themselves. She advocates that a learning mindset is developmentally more appropriate and more effective over time. This approach is incorporated into case conceptualizations as it is a simple concept to convey to children and their parents in order for them to be able to use it as part of therapy procedure. Other mindsets have also been explored in case conceptualizations, for example, dependence versus independence, productive versus consumer and cooperative versus competitive.

Resilience enhancement (considered effective for children, adolescents, and adults; Shatté & Reivich, 2002; Werner, 1996) is a procedure that is considered to be effective when implemented in conjunction with other approaches. Christine Padesky and Kailen Mooney (2006) has used the concept of resilience as a way of enabling clients to access their strengths and build ways of dealing with adversity in the future. In her work, she considers various risk factors and protective factors that enable clients to be more successful in their future. Focusing on the characteristics of resilient individuals is helpful for children and their parents. Applying Padesky's four-step model for building resilience (searching, constructing, applying, and practicing) enables families to develop a new approach that allows them to grow and practice appropriate ways of dealing with future issues.

For effective intervention planning and reviewing of progress, it is particularly important, when dealing with more complex PTSD individuals, that therapeutic decision making and choice of procedures are driven by a hypothesis-testing formulation of the individual's particular symptoms and difficulties, also taking into account their relative strengths.

Defining PSTD in children

In children, as in adults, there is a great variety of symptoms (Hizli et al., 2009). In summary, they can be characterized by the following:

- Regulation of affect: negative emotional disturbance; depersonalization; anger; depression; anxiety
- Regulation of attention and arousal: zoning out; forgetfulness (e.g., selective amnesia)

– Regulation of cognitions: nightmares; flashbacks; persistent negative thoughts (including thoughts of death, killing self and others)
– Behaviors: anxious, challenging, and obsessional behaviors; victimizing self and others
– Physiological/psychosomatic responses: startle response; stomach and other health complaints; loss of memories
– Problems in functioning: communication difficulties, problems relating to others; school avoidance; inappropriate associates
– Changing self and worldviews: low self-esteem and the world is seen as more negative, more fearful; being misunderstood (i.e., nobody understands).

Assessment and case formulation

In a PTSD child assessment, it is necessary to gather basic information about the child's trauma history without exposing him/her to memories before it is therapeutic to do so. Assuming that the PTSD was not caused by the family member/s,[1] the assessment is initially conducted with other family members, in particular the parents, in order to gain a general overview of the likely problem areas before interviewing the child.

The core areas that are considered in an assessment include: the child's physical health status, such as: headaches, chronic pain, developmental growth rates, body mass index assessments, and listlessness, as well as post-viral conditions.

The level of PTSD can be determined by using measures, such as: *Children's PTSD Inventory: A Structured Interview for Diagnosing Posttraumatic Stress Disorder* (Saigh, 2004) and the *Childhood Trauma Questionnaire* (Bernstein & Fink, 1997).

The family culture and interactions are assessed informally by observation, self-report in the form of diaries, informal Likert-type scales measuring anger and anxiety, and parental relationship measures.

The level of behaviors and functioning, including comorbid conditions, is assessed by various measures, such as: The Child and Adolescent Functional Assessment Scale; The Adolescent Coping Scale; The Conner's Rating Scales; and The Devereux Rating Scales.

Furthermore, risk factors (e.g., parental separation, low socio-economic status) and protective factors (e.g., cognitive and academic ability, levels of optimism, problem-solving ability, and social/family support) are also considered.

---

[1] The case examples in this chapter and the approach outlined are not designed for abuse within the family system. For those situations, the effect of the family members on the child needs to be taken into account, and the effect of the involvement of various family members in the therapeutic process requires a risk analysis.

Hypothesis-driven decision-making regarding appropriate interventions

When considering therapeutic interventions with children, the usual process of adaptation to the traumatic situation, which also includes the family context that the child is within, are included in the case conceptualization.

Context factors within a family include the ways they view and address the traumatic event/s; for example, do they talk about it or do they avoid discussion? The family's tendency to accept, trivialize, discount or disconfirm the child's perception of the trauma is very important when deciding whom to include in the intervention.

Types of interventions depend on a variety of factors

CBT for PTSD can be implemented in a flexible manner in which the therapist is able to incorporate the various and complex needs of individuals. Various CBT models (e.g., model for anxiety, model for depression, etc.) can be combined using a hypothesis-testing approach for a particular child. In other words, the variety of models that provide research-based standardized procedures for addressing particular conditions (e.g., depression, anger) need to be integrated with the specific particular needs of the child. Decisions need to be made on whether the various interventions should be made sequentially or in parallel – depending on the presenting issues and effects on the child; for example, addressing anger versus addressing anxiety. For some children it is better to deal with anxiety, for others it is better to do both at the same time, before commencing specific PTSD treatment.

Furthermore, the age of the child, including their cognitive ability, needs to be considered before choosing the type and style of treatment, as well as the parental level of support.

As part of rapport-building and trust development, it is worthwhile developing a collaborative hypothesis formulation as this makes it more real for the child (client) and family. This is very important for later work when the therapist supports the client in addressing their symptoms. Often, the first form of intervention is meaningful to the client, but relatively easy to do so that a momentum of success can be established. Once this momentum has been developed it makes it easier to attempt the more difficult elements of the therapeutic process (e.g., exposure).

The level of stress that the child is currently experiencing within their environment is crucial when considering the intensity and frequency of intervention. For example, a child who is still going to school and experiencing bullying needs a high level of support and intervention at various levels, including at school level (ongoing chronic traumatization) versus a child who has had a car accident many months ago (acute trauma).

Age of child

The developmental level of the child influences the approach and intensity that is used. There varying age levels are:

- Level 1: basic level often carried out ideally with the parents as the therapists (age ranges:[2] 2 to 6).
- Level 2: the parents are co-therapists and/or in a support role (age ranges: 6 to 11).
- Level 3: the focus of the therapy with a therapist is on the young person (age ranges: 11 to adult); the parents are advised how to be supportive.

At the levels where the therapist is primarily working therapeutically with the child, the parents remain fully informed on the therapeutic procedures carried out. They are also given supportive homework tasks. In some situations where parents are unable to work in a supportive co-therapist role (e.g., the child does not trust the parent; parent lacks the emotional ability to relate well; parental issues interfere with their ability to be supportive, etc.), they are set clear guidelines on how to appropriately interact with their child, as part of the overall psychoeducation process.

In working within the family context, other significant family members have to be incorporated in the case formulation, including the intervention. For example, siblings and grandparents can have a significant impact on the effectiveness of the intervention, according to what and how they contribute to family dynamics.

The PTSD intervention

A modular approach when applying CBT intervention appears to be appropriate for dealing with the complex presentations of PTSD (Chorpita, 2007). Furthermore, using a variety of different techniques simultaneously also appears to be effective. Moreover, it is necessary to consider the various levels of interactions between the child and his/her environment. The three major levels of intervention are presented figuratively: child level of intervention (Figure 17.1); parent level of intervention (Figure 17.2); context level of intervention (Figure 17.3). Each level has three domains (e.g., physiological reactions; thoughts/assumptions; interactions/behaviors) which have appropriate interventions/techniques that are applied to them.

Further techniques that can be added to the interventions/techniques described in the figures include:

- Child: redefining the major story and creating a new narrative (form of imaginal exposure); development of coping skills and resilience. At each

---

[2] These age ranges are approximate and are for guidance only.

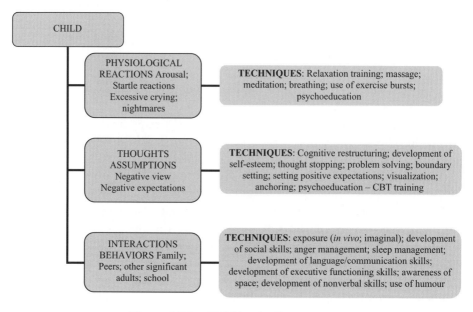

Figure 17.1   Child level of intervention

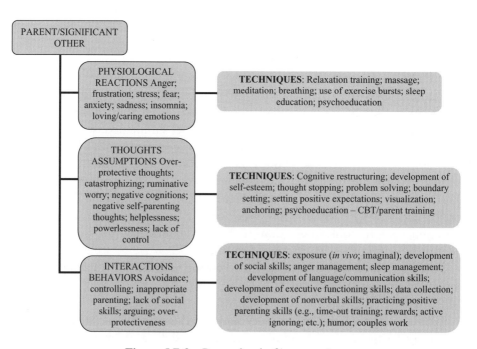

Figure 17.2   Parent level of intervention

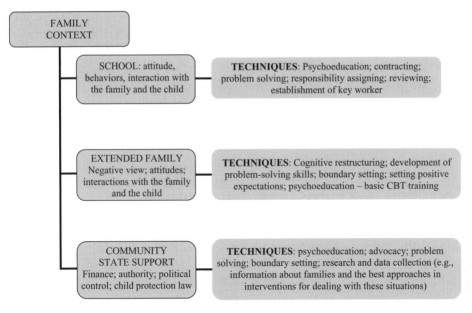

Figure 17.3   Context level of intervention

stage, a variety of worksheets are used, including a variety of homework tasks. During therapy, various forms of materials are also used (e.g., art materials – paints, sand, toys, books, games, and so on).

Further techniques can also be incorporated into the intervention (Table 17.1):

Table 17.1   Additional techniques for children

Dealing with attitudes	Dealing with the perpetrator's value/mindset; Going from victim to survivor; Development of self-esteem; Establishing values
Dealing with patterns of thinking	Thought stopping; Paired associations; Defining a safe place
Active problem solving	What to do when I don't know what to do What to do when I feel this way Situation/thoughts/feelings/behaviors assessments
Dealing with the feelings of hopelessness/depression	Setting things to look forward to on a daily basis; Setting things to look forward to on a weekly basis
Social skills	Setting up friendship groups; Developing trust
Dealing with self-victimizing and victimizing of others	Boundary setting; De-escalatory responses

– Involvement of parents: by including the parents as part of the therapeutic process, when problems occur at later development stages, there is a greater chance that the parents will be able to assist the child to the stage that the child does not require further extensive therapy. The parents' ability to be therapeutic needs to be taken into account, as well as their ability to be involved and the context that the initial situation occurred in. For example, the level the parents are responsible or feel for the situation that started the PTSD in the first place.

The following case examples are provided as they highlight elements of working with children within the system of a family. The examples do not include the full assessment process (i.e., the use of inventories, observations, and so on) or the full formulations, as the focus was placed on the interventions carried out.

Case example 1
Traumatic incident: Attempted kidnap of a three-year-old.

History

Kidnappers attempted to abduct a three-year-old girl, which the two family dogs foiled, but sustained serious injuries. As a consequence, whenever the door bell rang, the girl ran screaming to her mother, who understandably was extremely concerned and protective. The family dogs thereafter were further spoilt and were given pride of place within the family. The intervention was made at a number of levels.

Assessment and case formulation
Risk factors
The family had very little social support in the new environment; the personality of the mother, as she tended to overreact to situations (e.g., catastrophizing); the cultural context of the family (i.e., the father was away for periods of time due to work commitments).

Protective factors
There were no difficulties relating to financial resources; the relationship of the animals to the family (i.e., being protective of the family); the recent move to a new city, which allowed them to put the incident back in time; the initial event was unsuccessful which allowed them to see themselves as survivors.

Intervention

The intervention was at two major levels: (1) with the child, and (2) with the parents. There were overall 12 sessions.

Work with the child

The three-year-old was provided the reframe that her family was very protective, including the dogs. She was given cues as to when a visitor was likely to be threatening or nonthreatening, and strategies were provided for either assessment. These strategies were practiced *in vivo*, i.e., within the home situation.

Work with the mother

The mother was provided with psychoeducation including:

Strategies for dealing with her daughter, when she displayed distress, i.e., to listen and reassure until she was calm, including responding to the door bell after the appropriate security measures had been taken. It was explained that becoming emotional in response to her daughter's cries tended to exacerbate the situation. Implementing the agreed responses to her daughter's distress was practiced. Furthermore, the dogs were trained to react less aggressively toward strangers after they had been cued by the mother that the stranger was "a friend."

Case example 2

Traumatic incident: Unexpected shooting of a nine-year-old's mother.

History

A nine-year-old girl and her mother were crossing a pedestrian crossing when an unexpected assailant made repeated shots at another resulting in stray bullets hitting the mother. In the case formulation, focus was on the mindset of being a survivor rather than a victim. It was viewed that it was difficult to predict such a situation occurring and being prevented in the future.

Assessment and case formulation

Risk factors

The mother had a history of depression over a number of years; the incident occurred close to the family home, so it meant that they had to readjust their relationship with the surrounding environment (neighborhood); the father was frequently away on business.

Protective factors

Family wealth; the family culture was very supportive of each other; they held strong traditions of care within the family; the siblings, including the client, were all high achievers (i.e., they had strong intellectual ability allowing them to rationalize their experience with ease).

Intervention

The intervention was on the following levels:

Work with the child

Firstly, it was necessary to list the experiences that the child had had – this affirmed that her experiences were valid. Cognitive restructuring was conducted on how her siblings and mother responded to her experiences. She was provided the mindset of being a survivor and worked through levels of vigilance and the cues to monitor so she knew what level of vigilance to be at, i.e., within the home situation versus a public situation. She was then asked to imagine various scenarios and to assess levels of vigilance. This was then practiced within her local community. For relapse prevention, the child was exposed to the techniques used in developing mindfulness and in establishment of resilience.

Work with the siblings

The older siblings were taken through the situation, and similar scenarios to those above were discussed with them. This was done to reduce the tendency to trigger mutual over-reaction to imagined threats.

Work with the mother

The case formulation and subsequent therapeutic approaches were presented and discussed. Also the mother's responses to her daughter's reactions and imaginations were agreed and practiced. (As the mother was seriously injured, we also worked with her responses and reactions to the incident and dealt with her feelings of responsibility and PTSD reaction.)

Case example 3

Traumatic incident: Chronic reaction to "low-level" bullying

History

A 12-year-old female experienced a series of difficulties being accepted by her peer group; she was subjected to bullying by her classmates over a period of a year. This led to school-refusing to the stage where she could not attend school. Her symptoms further deteriorated and she developed social phobia, including a specific fear of dogs. This led her to become unwilling to leave the family home.

Assessment and case formulation

The girl had had a number of difficulties that initially stemmed from her bullying experiences at school. These negative experiences had led her to feel extremely fearful of social situations, where her self-image and self-concept were decreased. She became hypersensitive to the possibility of evaluation by others and regularly formed a vigilant cognitive set for rejection and abuse from others. She engaged in a constant negative-thinking spiral with set rigid rules she constructed about social behavior, including exaggerations about the consequences of failure (e.g., "I won't ever be able to cope").

Eventually, she started avoiding all social situations in order to minimize the likelihood of evaluation, rejection, and abuse, thus depriving herself of the opportunity to test the validity of her belief.

Risk factors

The girl's mother had generalized anxiety disorder, where she often maintained her daughter's anxiety by setting high expectations of her daughter and at the same time stating that she did not believe her daughter could cope. The girl's father had obsessive-compulsive tendencies, resulting in little tolerance for her perceived unacceptable behaviors. The girl had a prior tendency to experience anxiety and social phobia. She refused to cooperate with the parents and the therapist to start with. The family's previous experience with mental health professionals was strongly aversive.

Protective factors

The girl is highly intelligent; she was willing to do academic work by being home-educated; and at the time had one friend.

Intervention

Initially, the intervention was of low intensity with the parents only (once a month) as the child refused to attend the sessions. The parents were given homework tasks to provide acceptance of the girl, as they were not accepting her viewpoint and what she had been through. They were maintaining and exacerbating her PTSD symptoms by invalidating her reactions and experiences. The expectations placed on her by her parents were high.

The low-intensity contact enabled the parents to develop the mindset required for the child to be able to progress to the next stage of therapy. During this time, the therapist explained that early negative events/experiences can lead to strong emotional reactions; if these were not managed properly, i.e., the child being taught how to cope appropriately, they persist and lead to a pattern of extreme behaviors. Therefore, the parents had to follow a very specific program of acceptance and nonjudgmental affirmation of appropriate behavior. They also had to learn the strategies of not criticizing, complaining or talking in front of her about their emotional reactions to her behaviors. Once a more accepting environment was established, therapy with the child could begin.

Work with the child

Therapy with the child commenced a year after her parents started therapy. This was at a more intensive level (weekly sessions). The sessions focused on initially establishing a subjective units of distress (SUDs) scale in regard to her fears, which were then worked through during the subsequent sessions using imaginal exposure followed by graded situational exposure. Cognitive restructuring was conducted regarding her negative assumptions and perceptions about herself and others. Strategies were devised as to how to deal with perceived problem situations, e.g., dogs approaching her, meeting people unexpectedly, and unprovoked panic attacks. Her intelligence was utilized with the use of role-playing, record-keeping in regards to her keeping a thought record form, as well as joint problem formulation and problem solving. Goal-setting was also applied with her, including looking at future behaviors as this helped to establish a positive outlook as part of relapse prevention. As the child reported experiencing a number of physiological reactions (e.g., excessive crying, panic attacks, being over-aroused), work was conducted on reducing her overall arousal levels, which included progressive muscle relaxation technique, mindfulness of breathing, and set physical activities. Homework tasks included completing thought record forms, keeping a diary, completing various weekly projects, and continuing the various exposure procedures (e.g., going to the high street alone for a set period of time).

Work with the parents

In parallel with the therapy with the child, the parents worked on understanding PTSD symptoms as well as comorbid disorders (as in their daughter's case: social anxiety and specific phobias). Their contribution to the situation was sensitively discussed and target behaviors were identified. The parents developed a therapeutic interaction with her as well as learning appropriate parenting strategies for dealing with a young preadolescent. Their expectations were managed in regard to their daughter's ability to respond to the therapeutic process. For example, they wanted the therapeutic results to occur at an unrealistic pace.

Context

Firstly, a series of phone calls and letters were made to their local mental health team so that the team felt that a suitable intervention was occurring and that there was little need for their further involvement – in particular as the family had found their previous involvement detrimental. Secondly, documentation was provided for setting up a home-schooling situation. Thirdly, information was provided to the family's GP so that he was made aware of how to further support the family.

During the therapy, both the child and the parents received numerous letters from the therapist expressing encouragement and setting further tasks. This maintained the level of intensity so that the family felt supported and the tendency to revert to old behavior was minimized by constant reminders and by re-reading the material sent to them. An excerpt from a letter the therapist sent to the child:

> It was good to see you again today and to hear that going for walks down the road have pretty much become a routine and are not difficult anymore! That's great news!
>
> You have three challenges for the coming week: Tuesday is going for a walk taking a different route; Thursday is going to the newsagents to buy a magazine and some chewing gum; Friday is going for a walk again taking a different route to the one you are used to!
>
> Remember, it's really important to continue doing as you are and not give in to those feelings! Go through your notes from our sessions and remind yourself of all the techniques you can use: visualization (visualize yourself coping), write out the script with various scenarios, breathing (five to six deep breaths), complete the thought record form and really challenge those negative thoughts, breathe (again!), go for it, don't give in to the gremlin, use thought stopping (remember my previous letter), use distraction, and look up!

Case example 4

Traumatic incident: Chronic reaction to high-level bullying.

History

An eight-year-old middle child was regularly physically abused by older boys in his boarding school. Some examples of the bullying that occurred included: having his head put in the toilet to the stage where he felt he was drowning; simultaneous repeated punching by a number of boys. His school ineffectually attempted to address the situation resulting in a diminishing of the incidents. However, the parents who were separated eventually moved their son to a more supportive school. However, the child had difficulty trusting and establishing relationships with his new peer group. At times, he engaged in lesser but still unacceptable abusive behaviors that he was earlier subjected to.

Assessment and case formulation
Risk factors
His parents were separated, resulting in family discord regarding ways of addressing his difficulties. His father had attention deficit hyperactivity disorder, resulting in his having difficulty in controlling his impulsive behaviors (this was one of the reasons for the separation). The child suffered from a minimal processing disorder (often described as dyslexia). This interfered with his ability to process information, including new learning, leaving him susceptible to future bullying.

Protective factors
The child had a very caring mother and an older brother who "looked out for him." The family had moderate financial resources; his parents were overall highly educated professionals.

Intervention
Intervention with this child required working with him, working with his parents, together and separately, and working with the child's school.

Work with the child
The therapist focused on the child's arousal state and strong startle-response by implementing regular physical exercises, hypnotic inductions, and deep relaxation by listening to audiotapes. The child's understanding of boundaries was worked through, as well as de-escalatory responses to provocation. Managing his anger was implemented by teaching him self-regulatory skills, including awareness-building/monitoring, self-imposed time out, and use of exercise. Cognitive restructuring was used relating to friendships, appropriate peer interactions, violence, abusive behavior, and his responses to physical aggression. Imaginal exposure was conducted via drawing and telling stories regarding heroes. Role-plays were conducted regarding everyday experiences, for example, being a member of a football team by looking at acceptable/not acceptable behaviors, including how conflict can be resolved. These experiences were deepened by further problem solving on how the learnt skills can be applied in future situations.

Work with the parents
Mediating was carried out with both his mother and father on establishing the therapeutic input that was required for the child. Psychoeducation was carried out mainly with his mother, as she was the main carer at the time. The focus was on how to parent a child who had a tendency

to react violently to perceived injustice. The techniques included: time out, planned ignoring, moral discussions, talking through consequences, and rewarding appropriate behaviors. Numerous phone consultations were carried out with his father, which enabled him to enter into therapy for himself in dealing with his own behaviors.

Context
Working with the school in order to establish a specific caring discipline plan for the child. This involved the setting up of a key person who had direct responsibility for the child's behavior and the school's responses to that behavior. The key worker also coordinated the school's therapeutic input whilst the child was at school, enabling him to talk to her when feeling that his arousal levels were too difficult to deal with on his own. The school's therapeutic program also included controlled *in vivo* exposure to potential bullying situations.

Case example 5
Traumatic incident: Accident where the whole family was involved resulting in various serious injuries to all parties.

History

The parents were driving back from a family function with their sons, aged eight and 10 years, in the back of the car. As they were turning a corner, they were met by two trucks being overtaken by another. Various family members sustained multiple injuries, resulting in hospital stays and follow-up reconstructive surgery. Toward the end of the medical interventions the family went into assessment regarding their PSTD responses. The case formulation also included how the various family members responded to each other's distress and ways of thinking about the accident.

Assessment and case formulation
Risk factors
Low socio-economic status; numerous hospital interventions for three of the family members; loss of employment due to inability to perform the tasks following the accident by both parents.

Protective factors
Strong family cohesiveness; willingness to talk about what happened and to adopt new approaches and views.

Intervention

The therapy team focused on the following levels:

Work with the whole family

The accident was contextualized, i.e., the sequence of memories of each family member was put in a family story of what occurred. Various misunderstandings and concerns about other family members and what they were thinking were addressed. For example, the father who was driving and feeling responsibility for the injuries of the others, the child who had the fewest injuries feeling guilt for minimal medical intervention.

Work with the parents

The mindset was generated that this was a family experience that had been survived and nobody was killed; that there was potential for the family to become stronger from this experience. Work was also done on getting the parents to return to doing the things they used to do, i.e., cycling as a family, going on picnics as a family, and engaging various family members in walking the dog together.

Work with each of the siblings

Mindsets were generated for each child that enabled them to focus on surviving, engaging with their academic studies, and social activities with their peer group. Work was also done on addressing their feelings regarding the occurrence or nonoccurrence of injuries and how they can support their parents who were not as physically able as they used to be due to their respective injuries.

Engaging the local community support networks

As this family became isolated from the community due to the medical interventions (various members had to spend long stays in hospital for, e.g., skin grafts). The therapists had to access and set up strategies that allowed the family to engage and use the community support networks that were available.

Conclusions

As can be seen in the aforementioned examples, when carrying out a case formulation, it is generally easier to decide which technique to use once the therapist establishes the level of intervention. The case examples cover acute to chronic PTSD, and in each of these there are recurrent themes for intervention: (1) the focus is on psychoeducation; (2) establishing rapport; (3) developing ways of incorporating exposure; (4) the use of cognitive restructuring; and (5) addressing specific symptoms displayed by that particular child. If this is carried out in a collaborative fashion with the family, it has a high degree of relevance to the family and increases their willingness to complete the therapeutic process. In particular, PTSD can be actively addressed using CBT formulation. Due to the complexity of the various symptoms, it is clear that the most appropriate strategy is to use a concise case formulation that allows hypothesis-testing. When working with children, it is important to take into account their developmental level, developmental understanding, and ability to respond to the chosen interventions. When applying interventions that at times can be threatening to the child and to the family, it is extremely important to establish strong rapport and confidence in the therapist. This requires careful monitoring and recording of feedback to ensure that the child understands and is applying the procedures in a way that is helpful to them.

The use of parents when appropriate can be highly effective in addressing PTSD symptoms, especially when they are highly motivated and willing to change. Furthermore, the provision of homework including exercises for parents and children extends the therapeutic alliance and provides momentum for further engagement in dealing with difficult emotions and behaviors.

It is important to take into account the context that the family and child are in, in order to maximize the intervention. This is often carried out through meetings, correspondence, case notes, and clear communication with other professionals and community members. The communication includes explanation of the difficulties encountered when dealing with PTSD and the requirements of the family to provide a suitable intervention for the child.

Overall, it is clear when examining CBT for PTSD research studies, as well as observing the case examples above, that CBT is an effective treatment for different types and levels of PTSD.

Finally, there are some exciting new developments in the area of reducing relapse, for example, looking at mindfulness and resilience-building that are worth incorporating into complex case formulations to prevent recidivism.

References

Barsky, A. J., & Ahern, D. K. (2004). Cognitive behavior therapy for hypochondriasis: A randomized controlled trial. *Journal of the American Medical Association, 291*(12), 1464–70.

Beck, A. T. (1970). Role of fantasies in psychotherapy and psychopathology. *The Journal of Nervous and Mental Disease, 150,* 3–17.

Beck, A. T., Rush, A. J., Shaw, B. F., & Emery, G. (1979). *Cognitive therapy for depression: A treatment manual.* New York: Guilford Press.

Beck, J. S. (1995). *Cognitive therapy: Basics and beyond.* New York: Guilford Press.

Bernstein, D. P., & Fink, L. (1997). *The Childhood Trauma Questionnaire.* San Antonio, TX: PsychCorp, a brand of Harcourt Assessment, Inc.

Blackburn, I. M., & Davidson, K. (1998). *Cognitive therapy for depression and anxiety: A practitioner's guide.* Oxford: Blackwell Science.

Blagys, M. D., & Hilsenroth, M. J. (2002). Distinctive activities of cognitive-behavioral therapy: A review of the comparative psychotherapy process literature. *Clinical Psychology Review, 22*, 671–706.

Boyce, P., Gilchrist, J., Talley, N. J., & Rose, D. (2000). Cognitive-behavioral therapy as a treatment for irritable bowel syndrome: A pilot study. *Australian and New Zealand Journal of Psychiatry, 34*(2), 300–9.

Cartwright-Hatton, S., Roberts, C., Chitsabesan, P., Fothergill, C., & Harrington, R. (2004). Systematic review of the efficacy of cognitive behaviour therapies for childhood and adolescent anxiety disorders. *British Journal of Clinical Psychology, 43*(4), 421–36.

Chorpita, B. (2007). *Modular cognitive-behavioral therapy for childhood anxiety disorders.* New York: Guilford Press.

Cloitre, M., Koenen, K. C., Cohen, L. R., & Han, H. (2002). Skills training in affective and interpersonal regulation followed by exposure: A phase-based treatment for PTSD related to childhood abuse. *Journal of Consulting and Clinical Psychology, 70*(5), 1067–74.

Cohen, J., & Mannarino, A. P. (2008). Disseminating and implementing trauma-focused CBT in community settings. *Trauma, Violence & Abuse, 9*(4), 214–26.

Cole, K., & Vaughan, F. L. (2005). Brief cognitive behavioral therapy for depression associated with Parkinson's Disease: A single case series. *Behavioural and Cognitive Psychotherapy, 33*, 89–102.

Dweck, C. S. (2007). The secret to raising smart kids. *Scientific American: Mind.* December/January, 36–43.

Ehlers, A., & Clark, D. M. (2000). A cognitive model of posttraumatic stress disorder. *Behavioural Research and Therapy, 38*, 319–45.

Ehlers, A., Clark, D. M., Hackmann, A. et al., (2003). A randomised controlled trial of cognitive therapy, a self-help booklet, and repeated assessments as early interventions for posttraumatic stress disorder. *Archives of General Psychiatry, 60*, 1024–32.

Foa, E. B., Steketee, G., & Rothbaum, B. O. (1989). Behavioral/cognitive conceptualisations of post-traumatic stress disorder. *Behaviour Therapy, 20*, 155–76.

Foa, E. B., Dancu, C. V., Hembree, E. A. et al. (1999). The efficacy of exposure therapy, stress inoculation training and their combination in ameliorating PTSD for female victims of assault. *Journal of Consulting and Clinical Psychology, 67*, 194–200.

Hagen, R., Nordahl, H. M., Kristiansen, L., & Morken, G. (2005). A randomized trial of cognitive group therapy vs. waiting list for patients with co-morbid psychiatric disorders: Effect of cognitive group therapy after treatment and six and twelve months follow-up. *Behavioural and Cognitive Psychotherapy, 33*, 33–44.

Hizli, F. G., Taskintuna, N., Isikli, S., Kilic, C., & Zileli, L. (2009). Predictors of posttraumatic stress in children and adolescents. *Children & Youth Services Review, 31*(3), 349–54.

Kazantzis, N., Deane, F. P., & Ronan, K. R. (2000). Homework assignments in cognitive and behavioral therapy: A meta-analysis. *Clinical Psychology: Science and Practice, 7*, 189–202.

Nicholl, C., & Thompson, A. (2004). The psychological treatment of Post-Traumatic Stress Disorder (PTSD) in adult refugees: A review of the current state of psychological therapies. *Journal of Mental Health, 13*(4), 351–62.

Olasov Rothbaum, B., Meadows, E. A., Resick, P., & Foy, D. W. (2000). Cognitive-behavioral therapy. In E. B. Foa, T. M. Keane, & M. J. Friedman (Eds.), *Effective treatments for PTSD; Practise guidelines from the International Society for Traumatic Stress Studies*. New York: Guilford Press.

Padesky, C. A., & Mooney, K. A. (2006). *Uncover strengths and build resilience using CT*. Auckland, New Zealand: Workshop presented for the New Zealand College of Clinical Psychologists.

Patelis-Siotis, I. (2001). Cognitive-behavioral therapy: Applications for the management of bipolar disorder. *Bipolar Disorders*, *3*(1), 1–10.

Rawson, R. A., McCann, M. J., Flammino, F. et al. (2006). A comparison of contingency management and cognitive-behavioral approaches for stimulant-dependent individuals. *Addiction*, *101*(2), 267–74.

Resick, P.A., & Schnicke, M. K. (1992). Cognitive processing therapy for sexual assault victims. *Journal of Consulting and Clinical Psychology*, *60*, 748–56.

Rosser, S., Erskine, A., & Crino, R. (2004). Pre-existing antidepressants and the outcome of group cognitive-behavior therapy for social phobia. *Australian and New Zealand Journal of Psychiatry*, *38*(4), 233–9.

Saigh, P. A. (2004). *Children's PTSD Inventory: A structured interview for diagnosing posttraumatic stress disorder*. San Antonio, TX: PsychCorp, a brand of Harcourt Assessment, Inc.

Salkovskis, P. M., & Kirk, J. (1989). Obsessional disorders. In K. Hawton, P. M. Salkovskis, J. Kirk, & D. M. Clark (Eds.), *Cognitive-behavior therapy for psychiatric problems: A practical guide* (pp. 129–68). New York: Oxford University Press.

Scheeringa, M. S., Salloum, A., Arnberger, R. A. et al. (2007). Feasibility and effectiveness of cognitive-behavioral therapy for posttraumatic stress disorder in preschool children: Two case reports. *Journal of Traumatic Stress*, *20*(4), 631–6.

Segal, Z. V., Williams, J. M. G., & Teasdale, J. D. (2002). *Mindfulness-based cognitive therapy: A new approach to preventing relapse*. New York: Guilford Press.

Shatté, A., & Reivich, K. (2002). *The resilience factor: seven essential skills for overcoming life's inevitable obstacles*. New York: Broadway Books.

Smith, P., Yule, W., Perrin, S. et al. (2007). Cognitive-behavioral therapy for PTSD in children and adolescents: A preliminary randomized controlled trial. *Journal of the American Academy of Child & Adolescent Psychiatry*, *46*(8), 1051–61.

Werner, E. (1996). How children become resilient: Observations and cautions. *Resilience in Action*, Winter, 18–28.

Zayfert, C., & Black Becker, C. (2007). *Cognitive behavioural therapy for PTSD: A case formulation approach*. New York: Guilford Press.

Chapter Eighteen

A Constructivist Perspective on Post-Traumatic Stress in Children and Adolescents

Kenneth W. Sewell and Keith R. Cruise

Overview of trauma exposure and PTSD in youth

Trauma exposure and PTSD symptomatology are significant mental health concerns that affect children and adolescents in myriad and complex ways. In the United States, epidemiologic studies of children and adolescents have documented lifetime PTSD diagnoses between 2 and 9.2% (see Gabbay et al., 2004). Similarly, in a national representative sample of over 4,000 adolescent boys and girls, the estimated six-month prevalence of PTSD was 3.7% for boys and 6.3% for girls (Kilpatrick et al., 2003). Examination of prevalence data among specific subpopulations of youth suggests a much greater problem. For example, in a recent review, Ford and colleagues (2007) documented PTSD rates varying between a low of 3% and a high of 50% among youth in the juvenile justice system. Children from inner-city environments and lower-income families also appear to experience trauma exposure (see Youngstrom, Weist, & Albus, 2003) and PTSD symptoms at much higher rates than expected based on the general epidemiologic literature (see Silva et al., 2000). For example, Silva and colleagues reported that among 100 child and adolescent referrals to an inner-city psychiatric clinic, 32% had experienced a significant trauma, with 22% of this subgroup meeting full PTSD diagnostic criteria and 32% exhibiting significant symptoms. Research among clinical samples tends to identify high rates of trauma exposure and co-occurring PTSD. For example, Romero and colleagues (2009) documented that 20.6% of their sample of child and adolescent patients with Bipolar Disorder reported a lifetime history of physical or

Post-Traumatic Syndromes in Childhood and Adolescence: A Handbook of Research and Practice, First Edition. Edited by Vittoria Ardino. © 2011 John Wiley & Sons, Ltd. Published 2011 by John Wiley & Sons, Ltd.

sexual abuse. Child patients with histories of abuse were more likely to exhibit chronic and severe patterns of impaired clinical functioning and were over eight times more likely to be meet current diagnostic criteria for PTSD in addition to a host of other clinical diagnoses. Although clearly not an exhaustive review of the prevalence literature, this brief summary reinforces that PTSD is a significant clinical problem, adversely impacts male and female youth, and is found at alarmingly high rates among specific subgroups of children and adolescents.

A wide range of trauma exposures can lead to the development of PTSD symptoms (see Fairbank, 2008 for a review). For example, researchers calculated that approximately 25% of boys and girls interviewed as part of the Great Smokey Mountains Study had experienced one or more extreme lifetime stressors (Costello et al., 2002). Common stressors endorsed in the study included the death of a loved one, witnessing a traumatic event, learning about a traumatic event, and sexual abuse. Similar to the subgroup vulnerability identified above, recent reports from the United States Gulf Coast region continue to reinforce that significant trauma effects are found among children and adolescents exposed to natural disasters (Marsee, 2008; Scheeringa & Zeanah, 2008). Acts of domestic and international terrorism, including the Oklahoma City bombing and the 9/11 destruction of the World Trade Center, have also resulted in significant psychological trauma to children and adolescents (see Fairbanks, 2008; Guirwitch et al., 2002). In keeping with the literature that chronic exposure involving multiple traumas often results in greater overall impairment (see Youngstrom et al., 2003), researchers have documented that in addition to "high-dose exposure events," exposure pre- and post-event is associated with greater impairment and long-term symptom severity (Mullet-Hume et al., 2008). However, trauma sequelae in response to such disasters are not confined to those directly exposed. Otto and colleagues (2007) found that indirect exposure to 9/11 via extensive media coverage resulted in symptom expression among vulnerable children.

In addition to trauma exposures that primarily focus on event exposure per se, a wide body of literature examines stressors that are inextricably linked to the social network of the child victim. These stressors often involve traumatic event exposure that results in significant disruptions in social functioning. Acts of child maltreatment, witnessing and experiencing familial violence, and exposure to community violence, are primary examples of such events (Fairbanks, 2008). Finkelhor and colleagues recently updated past findings in documenting that a significant proportion of children and adolescents are victims of physical assault, child maltreatment, and sexual victimization. A particularly alarming result from this nationally representative sample of children and adolescents was that the average number of victimizations reported by youth was 3.0, with multiple victimizations often being reported within the same year (Finkelhor et al., 2005). Putman (2009) recently summarized findings regarding PTSD symptom development among child sexual abuse survivors. Although there is no uniform outcome associated with sexual abuse victimization, psychological impairment (including PTSD symptoms) varied from 46% to 90% across the reviewed studies. Finally, Wood and colleagues (2002) and Ariga and colleagues (2008) have documented that both adolescent boys and girls involved in delinquent activity report significant exposure to community violence, including witnessing a violent crime, witnessing the murder of someone close to them, and being the victim of a violent crime.

In response to such widespread need, clinicians and researchers alike have a range of clinical assessment tools (see Strand, Sarmiento, & Pasquale, 2005) and interventions (see Perrin, Smith, & Yule, 2004; Taylor, 2004) at their disposal in working with youth who have been exposed to traumatic stressors. Assessment tools range from brief self-report screening measures to comprehensive clinician-administered diagnostic interviews that focus on lifetime and current trauma exposures and PTSD symptoms. Interventions discussed in the literature range from applications of art and play therapy, group and individual therapy, to traditional cognitive-behavioral treatment. In the review of empirically supported treatments and promising practices, the National Child Trauma Stress Network website (2009) notes that cognitive-behavioral interventions predominate the list of treatments "that work." The goals of traditional cognitive-behavioral interventions typically are focused on reduction of presenting symptoms, enhancement of immediate coping skills and responses in the short term, and use of various forms of exposure therapy to promote broader processing of the trauma experience for long-term recovery. It is clear from the extant literature that different types of trauma exposure can differentially impact children at different stages of development, and that professionals must take into account the full range of internalizing and externalizing symptoms that so often co-occur with symptoms of PTSD. Although symptom management and reduction are often a critical component of treatment, we agree with the propositions by Wood and colleagues (2002) that (1) trauma exposure and subsequent responses are best understood via a social/ecological framework, and (2) it is critical to conceptualize the exposure, reaction, and response as primarily disruptions to a child's sense of self-efficacy (see Putman, 2009). Consistent with these propositions, we utilize a framework for approaching post-traumatic stress in children that allows the symptoms to be targeted while simultaneously addressing the child's disrupted identity and social embeddedness.

The constructivist perspective

In this chapter, we will present a constructivist framework for understanding and intervening with post-traumatic stress reactions in childhood and adolescence. Although we base much of our thinking on traditional personal construct psychology (Kelly, 1955/1991), the perspective has been extended and reformulated by other constructivist scholars, including ourselves. We will begin with a consideration of how personal constructs and personal identity develop in childhood. Next, we will consider adolescent development from a constructivist perspective. Then, we will turn attention to how traumatic experiences can serve to disrupt identity and personal functioning across these two developmental periods. Finally, we will present a constructivist approach to assisting children and adolescents in adapting to life after a traumatic disruption.

Development of personal constructs and identity in childhood

Personal construct theory begins with the philosophical assumption that there are always alternative constructions (interpretations, anticipations, etc.) to choose from in dealing with the world (known as *constructive alternativism*; Kelly, 1955/1991, p. 15, page numbers from the 1955 printing). Stated slightly differently, it is assumed that all current understandings of the world – no matter how useful they have been – are subject to revision or replacement. Within this framework, an individual is seen as an active agent, anticipating and categorizing lived experience in ways that are highly individualized. Thus, each person, beginning in infancy, starts to assertively build a system of constructs that can be considered analogous to a *theoretical system* for how the world operates. This *world*, of course, contains both happenings (events) as well as people (including the self). Development (psychologically speaking) thus involves the evolution of the construction system.

At the most rudimentary level, construction involves categorizing experiences in terms of similarities and differences, such that subsequent experiences can be anticipated and concurrently evaluated based on prior construction experiences. This process changes in complexity of organization across childhood, but begins during infancy. For example, newborns are able to discriminate certain visual patterns shortly after birth, indicating that some categorization is taking place (Pascalis et al., 1995). A *construct* has been defined as any way in which two elements of experience are alike, and yet different from a third element of experience (Kelly, 1955/1991, p. 61). Given that constructs involve discrimination, they are bipolar (i.e., both the similarity and the difference are part of the construction, such as happy/sad, kind/cruel, etc.). Constructs that infants develop very early include hungry/sated, comfort/discomfort, caretaker/other, and so forth. An infant's rudimentary construct system is viewed as reflecting interactions between the infant and caregiver.

Evolution (development) of the individual's construct system occurs in the context of repeated experimentation with the world, including encounters with novel experiences. As the child encounters experiences that differ – slightly or dramatically – from anticipations, they begin with the constructs previously developed and then either expand them to incorporate the novel experience (sometimes called *assimilation*), or else create new dimensions of anticipation to account for the novelty (sometimes called *accommodation*; Piaget, 1954).

As children develop language, they acquire an advanced tool for linking constructions together in creative ways, thus developing more and more complex constructions. These complex, interrelated construct groups can be understood as *anticipatory narratives* (Mancuso, 2003) that a person uses to anticipate sequential events.

As stated above, experience includes both events (happenings) and persons. Mancuso and Ceely (1980) theorized that complex construing on the part of a child gives rise to the construing of persons as possessing construct systems. This can (but does not necessarily) make the construing of persons (including the self) qualitatively distinct from the construing of other *objects* in the world. For example, consider the anticipation that a particular sharp object can cause discomfort. In construing the object, and devising a plan to interact with that object (and possibly avoid discomfort), there is no need to account for whether or not the object will *choose* to cause pain. Persons, on the other hand, can be attributed the capacity to choose, construe, anticipate, intend, and so forth. This is often referred to as the development of a *theory of mind* (cf., Baron-Cohen, 1989).

This development of a theory of mind has important implications for social and identity development. First of all, when a child accounts for the mind (or *construction processes*) of another person, the basis for a social interaction exists (termed *sociality* in personal construct theory). Stated differently, the child can now enact a *role* in relation to the other person. A role involves a set of anticipations about how others (usually important others) expect the person to be. As stated by Anderson (1990), the elaboration of role constructions is what we can otherwise call personality development.

The theory of mind is also applied to the self when the child evolves the self-awareness that her/his mental processes comprise intentions and expectations that translate into action. So, just as a child can construct a narrative framework for anticipating the role of a parent, the child can also construct a narrative that anticipates the self. Indeed, the child's self-narrative evolves in a close dialectic with sociality. In other words, constructions about the self (as a construer) are only relevant to the extent that the child is engaged in social interactions. Feedback from social interactions (validation or invalidation regarding expectations of the other person, finding that the other person is either similar to or different from the self in how she/he construes the world, etc.) comprises the experience out of which self-construction evolves.

Given that social interactions inherently involve power negotiations, social validation and invalidation are common avenues for the exercise (and understanding) of power. Mancuso and Lehrer (1986) noted that reprimands by authority figures comprise critical experiences that influence how a child orients toward, develops, and elaborates on socially agreed constructions (such as right/wrong, fair/unfair, etc.). Children who then apply such social conventions and align their own self-construals with the socially valued pole (e.g., right, fair, etc.) are then seen to be normal, competent, good, and so forth.

Earning the "good" or "normal" social labels then allows the child to weave these constructions into their anticipatory narratives.

Some aspects of construing appear to change (at least in degree) as children get older and approach adolescence. In early childhood, constructions of self and others tend to focus on concrete, observable characteristics based largely on physical attributes, activities, or personal preferences. Self/other comparisons tend to lack flexibility and are best described as "like me" or "not like me." In identifying attributes of others, younger children tend to focus on attributes (construct poles) they value in themselves (Adams-Webber, 2000). For example, a young child who sees him/herself as smart will tend to identify what he/she perceives to be intellectual talent in others and attract toward it, paying less attention to dullness in others. Continuing the example, an older self-attributed smart child would be more likely to be aggravated by the stupidity of others. As children age, they develop a greater number of constructs, more abstract constructs, more psychological constructs (applied to the self and to others), and more complex narratives of experience (Winter, 1992). The process of developing construct complexity can be attributed to the expanding interpersonal context of childhood which now includes same-age peers and the ability to consolidate aligned poles of related constructs into emerging abstract constructions.

Adolescent development from a personal construct perspective

Adolescence is marked by multiple transitions that ebb and flow at different rates of change across the maturational process. There are dramatic intra-individual changes in cognitive, physical, and emotional contexts that influence the developing adolescent's construct system. Further development in language and abstract thought facilitate greater elaboration of the adolescent's construct system, usually by extending the range, flexibility, and integration of constructs. Self-constructions undergo particularly dramatic shifts during adolescence. Dramatic expansion of the range and importance of extra-familial social contexts begin to impact the evolving construct system of adolescents in significant ways. Beginning early in this transitional developmental period, adolescents begin spending more time away from family and place a greater emphasis on interpersonal relationships within peer groups, school, and work settings. In earlier childhood, the family constituted the major influence on sociality and the concomitant balancing act of validation and invalidation of the developing construct system. The expanded social contexts of the typical adolescent's world become new sources of self/other construction, simultaneously expanding and testing the adolescent construct system. This combined intra-individual and social contextual change accelerates the experience cycle (Kelly, 1977,

p. 9), as the developing adolescent anticipates, integrates, and revises constructs to incorporate new internal and external experiences.

Empirical research has confirmed that a significant proportion of adolescents experience heightened vulnerabilities, emotional and behavioral problems, and increased experimentation with risky activities and behaviors (see Steinberg et al., 2006). Viewed through the lens of personal construct psychology, such problems likely result from significant changes in the anticipatory narrative of the adolescent based on radical alterations in core self-constructions and anticipation and negotiation of new self/other roles across the expanding social sphere.

The work of S. Harter and colleagues (see S. Harter 1999, 2006) provides excellent examples of normative changes in self-constructions and role adaptations that emerge across this developmental period. Although Harter's terminology is divergent from Personal Construct Theory, her concepts map easily onto the present conceptualization. For Harter, adolescence involves the rapid addition of new and more abstract constructions. As a rudimentary example, imagine a small child who has the social construct of good versus bad. People are thus understood as either good or bad. The developing adolescent may begin to add more abstract constructions such as friendly, talented, moral, brave (all poles that might be associated with the "good" pole of the rudimentary construct), as opposed to unfriendly, dull, immoral, and cowardly (poles that might be associated with "bad"). However, in early adolescence these higher-order constructions are likely still to be applied in a constellatory manner, such that it remains difficult to attribute one positive construct pole (e.g., friendly) to a person, while simultaneously attributing the negative pole of another (e.g., cowardly). Thus, when attempting to integrate such abstractions into a coherent self-construction, early adolescents are not likely to identify and resolve conflicts in their attributions about themselves. Thus, they often experience the self in a role-specific and rather fragmented manner.

A dramatic change occurs in middle adolescence, according to Harter. Adolescents now make finer discriminations using single attributes within and across roles. These adolescents develop more flexible self-construals across both positive and negative valences of a single construct and become aware of situations in which both poles can be applied to the self. Thus, the middle adolescent can now begin to form a more coherent self-construction system that allows integration of potentially opposite or contradictory aspects of the self across roles. However, the greater awareness of such contradictions may lead to uncertainty about defining features of self versus the true or "ideal" self. Grappling with the uncertainties is further complicated by heightened sensitivity to the awareness of the opinions and expectations of others. In other words, sociality takes on a paramount function in attempts at reconciling opposites across roles and construction of standards that represent the "ideal self." At the end of the adolescent period, there is a greater emphasis on balancing or reconciling the perceived opposites within and across roles which can lead to a more coherent self-narrative. Successful late-adolescents show increased capacity to anticipate and tolerate incongruities in the self across contexts, and no longer experience such incongruities as reflecting fragmented identities.

Traumatic disruptions to the evolving construction systems of children and adolescents

To understand traumatic experience from a constructivist perspective, a *planning* metaphor can be useful (cf. Sewell, 2005). Of course, a plan is a particular kind of anticipation. As described above, constructs are used for anticipation. When we plan, we construe in an overt and self-aware manner. Also, plans usually reflect anticipation over periods of time that can be measured at least in seconds, if not in hours, months or even years. Much of our moment-to-moment construing is not at such a cognitive level or over such protracted time frames, so we do not usually think of them as plans per se. For example, as you read the words on this page, you are rapidly anticipating the next word you will encounter (without being aware of planning for particular words). Nonetheless, each individual construal can be thought of as a *plan* of sorts.

As soon as children reach the point of sociality and self-awareness, such that they begin adopting and enacting social roles, there are two central questions that are addressed by virtually every plan: "What will happen in my life?" and "To whom am I personally/socially connected?" These two domains of planning can be referred to as *event* planning and *social* planning. Fine-grain plans, such as anticipating moment-to-moment phenomenal experience or evaluating the likeability of a new acquaintance, address these two overarching questions. Likewise, broader constructions about self-concept, life goals, and relationship maneuvering bear obvious relevance to these two central questions. At any instant, the sum total of personal plans relevant to the event or social domains could be said to comprise the *grand plan*. The initial development of the grand plan is linked to sociality and self-awareness; it appears in rudimentary forms in early childhood and is conceptually linked to the theory of mind which we view as marking the emergence of a child's capacity to choose, construe, anticipate, etc. Consistent with the description above, the depth and range of the grand plan is characterized by the qualitative changes in self-construction across development.

To continue the planning metaphor, let us give the grand plan another name: *Plan A*. When we develop Plan A, we anticipate experiences in the manner we believe/think/feel is the most likely to be validated. Plan A, at any one instant in the youngster's life, is thus composed of the poles of their event and social constructs that are applied to anticipating both happenings and people. Some are anticipated to be good, others bad. Some components of their plan involve anticipating success; others might involve struggle or challenge.

Implicit in using the term *Plan A* is the possibility that there is also a *Plan B*. Plan B is the way the world (events as well as social relationships) would need to be understood if Plan A had to be completely abandoned. Plan B might be thoroughly thought out, or else it might be left unelaborated (or implicit). We will return to this concept later; first, we will consider the fate of Plan A with traumatic experience.

No grand plan is perfect. In other words, unanticipated experiences will occur: friends will disappoint; potential dates will say "no"; cars will run out of gasoline; ankles will sprain. When unanticipated experiences occur, Plan A is adjusted and evolves through the process of assimilation or accommodation as discussed in the previous section. However, sometimes a youngster encounters experiences that so totally invalidate Plan A that they anticipate that Plan A may no longer be viable. This will be our metaphoric definition of a traumatic experience – an experience that renders Plan A apparently useless.

How does a youngster respond when Plan A seems annihilated by a traumatic experience? The individual response will depend upon many things. One contingency is the structure of the now-assaulted Plan A; the complexity and flexibility of both Plan A and Plan B will be related to the developmental level of the child or adolescent. Another contingency is the nature of the traumatic experience; some kinds of traumas are more likely to invalidate the event-planning portion of Plan A, whereas other traumas more seriously disrupt Plan A as it relates to social relationships. These contingencies will be addressed more fully below.

The younger (less psychologically developed) the child, the more likely that the child will react to the traumatic experience by abandoning Plan A altogether, without a viable or elaborate Plan B. This can be thought of as planning bankruptcy. Planning bankruptcy involves the complete inability of the child to assimilate the traumatic experience into Plan A or to accommodate the new experience by making changes in Plan A. Because plans are developed to cope with ongoing experience, the lack of viable anticipations will result in frantic anxiety and panic. In such situations, both event planning and social planning are rendered defunct. The planning bankrupt child will trust no one, be soothed by nothing, and will be unable to anticipate change and coping. Although such a state may persist long enough to cause much personal pain and social disruption, complete bankruptcy cannot endure when the child is out of the traumatic context (hence *post*-traumatic). Plan B, incomplete and ineffective as it might be at first, will begin to develop into a plan that at least eases the present panic. The development of Plan B follows the same basic principles referenced above; the child, as an active agent, once again engages the environment elaborating constructs via both assimilation and accommodation. Initially, the complexity of Plan B is low, making the child vulnerable to retraumatization and a repeat of the bankruptcy/panic experience. Additionally, Plan B is unlikely to resemble the defunct Plan A as formerly effective or efficient construction processes were abandoned due to the disrupting effects of the traumatic experience.

When a child or adolescent is traumatized, but has a complex enough Plan B to function as a stand-in Plan A, the nature of the trauma will often determine the type of emotional disruption and symptom responses. Traumas that introduce random dyscontrol into the youngster's world (things such as natural disasters, near-death experiences, and traumas that involve intense physical pain) are likely to trigger a dramatic constriction of event planning. This child will show intense anxiety when they cannot avoid contexts associated with the trauma, they will view themselves as ineffectual in relation to controlling their own outcomes and will find it difficult to construct overt plans for the future (perhaps even believing that they will not live long). Plan B is invoked, but the complexity of event planning remains constricted.

On the other hand, traumas that have dramatic social implications for the child are likely to prompt a different response, traumas that include the loss of peers or caretakers (cf. Meshot & Leitner, 1994) or the betrayal of trusted others (e.g., Collin-Vézina & Hébert, 2005). In this case, Plan B is more effective in the event domain, but remains constricted in social planning. As S. L. Harter (2004) noted, these sorts of trauma invalidate a child's emotional experiences in relation to self and others. This child would be less likely to appear anxious/panicked, and instead would present as nihilistically depressed, socially isolated, conduct disordered, and/or engaging social relationships at a chaotic level (what might be psychiatrically diagnosed as the precursors to adult personality disorders).

It is important to note that nearly all traumas involve at least some disruption in both event and social construing; however, one of these disruptions will likely predominate in the clinical presentation. Depending upon the age, gender, social context, and level of self-construction complexity of the youngster, these different presentations lead to differing intervention needs. These various intervention needs will be integrated into the next section, which focuses on treating traumatized children and adolescents.

Treating children and adolescents with trauma-disrupted construction systems

Given the understanding of traumatic experience outlined above, it should be clear that traumatized youth must be treated as whole individuals, embedded in their specific social contexts. Any attempt to isolate and "treat the PTSD" as a pathological entity would render this constructivist conceptualization impotent. Besides, as Ravenette (1996) says, when a child is brought to psychotherapy, "there is never just one problem" (p. 15). Rather, the youngster's complex situation, painful though it is, has been the result of their entire psychological system reacting to (and coping with) experiences that could not be incorporated without major psychological and social revision. Rowe (2001) stated that "as small children we need to develop confidence in the meanings we create"

(p. 74). Therefore, any useful constructivist treatment for traumatized children must have the goal and focus of restoring the child's confidence in their personal meanings. Similarly, Epting (1988) reminds us that, "the child has a complete world view" (p. 57) and should not be viewed as possessing a naive or sub-adult psychological position. Thus post-trauma intervention should not be considered as bringing the child to a more mature (adult-like) viewpoint, but rather as aiding the child in finding a more adaptive stance from the current developmental position. We offer treatment when traumatic disruption is so debilitating that the youngster's available coping resources continue over time to be outweighed by the magnitude of the needed revision, or when the revision itself causes ongoing distress.

The model of intervention we present below can be summarized with the following labels: joining, empowering, distancing, and collaborative bridge-building. These are not *stages* of therapy in the linear sense. For example, once joining is achieved and empowering efforts are undertaken, much of a therapist's attention may still be devoted to joining with the client. However, these aspects of therapy are sequential. In other words, focusing on distancing is not helpful (and would actually be counter-therapeutic) if it occurred prior to effective joining and empowerment work. With this sequential but nonlinear structure in mind, we will discuss each of these aspects of therapy separately.

Joining

A child or adolescent who has been faced with reconstructing their entire psy-chological world following a trauma almost always feels a sense of *difference* from others. The chaotic sense of dyscontrol that is associated with the disrup-tion of event construing leaves the youngster self-focused and circumspect – devoting so much attention to survival and tenuous control that little energy can be devoted to relationships. The disruption of social construing is a direct attack on the youngster's perceived sense of connection and belonging. Other persons – even if valued, loved, and available – are viewed by the traumatized child as separate and inaccessible. "I am the one without a viable plan; others have a Plan A that is working just fine for them." For the adolescent, there is often a more self-aware and overt belief that others simply cannot comprehend their subjective experiences, regardless of the others' intentions. This leads to the conclusions (whether tacit or acknowledged) that "I am alone," "I am different," "No one can know me," and "No one can help me." Joining with the traumatized youngster involves creating experiences that break into these conclusions based on the therapist's recognition that disruption in the grand plan, and forced shift to Plan B, has fostered the client's sense of isolation and aloneness.

A therapist's first aim in breaking down these isolative conclusions is to demonstrate presence and a willingness to help. The presence of the therapist is palpable when they patiently tolerate the youngster's expressions of aloneness without trying to get the client to change them for the sake of the therapist. For example, a traumatized child who is refusing to speak is accustomed to caretakers' attempts to cajole speech. To speak would be to take care of the desires/needs of the caretakers, thus reinforcing the perception that others cannot know the child's experience. The therapist tolerates this expression (or lack thereof) on the part of the child, and shows persistent willingness to understand the pain and coping strategies of the child, without demanding that the child change or give up on current (even if painful) coping tools. It is crucial that the child comes to believe that the therapists can "handle my silence," "cares for me – even in my silence," and even "understands my silence," before experiencing demands that the silence be abandoned. Thus, the therapist begins the process of joining by enacting a new social role that avoids further distancing and invalidation of the client's current experience.

Another example involves adolescent anger, a common, surface-level expression of traumatized adolescents. Joining with an angry adolescent need not involve the therapist agreeing with the client about the culpability of the anger targets. Rather, the therapist allows the client to be angry and attempts to understand the anger without demanding that the adolescent abandon it.

In addition to demonstrating a caring and unconditional presence, the therapist can often effectively join with a traumatized youngster by finding a way to relieve some current stressor impinging upon the client. Particularly when the youngster presents complaints (things they would like to have changed immediately), the therapist should be alert to any that are amenable to rapid intervention. When the complaints are psychological (such as problems sleeping, flashbacks, physical tension, etc.), then brief cognitive-behavioral or relaxation techniques can be employed to offer rapid relief (see Deblinger, Thakkar-Kolar, & Ryan, 2006). When the complaints are situational or social (such as someone bullying the client at school or difficulties interacting with a parent), the joining therapist should consider offering to intervene directly on behalf of the client (by calling the school principal, scheduling a meeting with the parent/s to suggest nonconfrontational parenting strategies, etc.). But even for problems that are medical (e.g., nausea, severe insomnia) or practical (e.g., unable to afford bus transportation to go to the movies), the joining therapist will show an eagerness to improve the youngster's situation by connecting the client to needed healthcare or social services. These interventions are not expected to prompt major breakthroughs in the functioning of the traumatized youngster, although relieving some immediate distress certainly can be helpful. The major impact of these interventions is to demonstrate behaviorally to the young client that this adult is willing (and perhaps even able) to make a positive difference in her/his life.

Another powerful joining maneuver involves the promotion of commonality. Kelly (1955/1991) asserted that when persons construe similarly, they are psychologically similar (termed *commonality*, p. 90). As described above, the traumatized youngster often perceives little or no commonality with others (the therapist included). So, in order to promote the joining process, the therapist must engineer interactions to convince the client that at least some of their constructions of experience are shared by other important persons. For the therapist conducting individual therapy, the target of such commonality is limited to therapists themselves. For therapists working with groups of traumatized youngsters, the commonality targets can include the other group members as well as the therapist. In either case, it is usually best to promote commonality by eliciting autobiographical disclosure (usually having little to do with the traumatic experience). In working with adults, this has been termed *life review* (e.g., Richert, 2006; Sewell, 2005). By disclosing autobiographical details to the therapist (and other group members, if available) and encountering the reactions of the other/, the client will be faced with validations of her/his construing – validation that can only be understood as the result of commonality (similarity between the self and other). Another benefit of eliciting such autobiographical details is that the therapist is offered a glimpse into the construction system prior to the disrupting experience of the trauma. In group settings, the autobiographical disclosure is usually overtly reciprocal, with each group member sharing personal details, any one of which then has the potential to reinforce a sense of commonality with other group members. In individual therapy, the therapist must decide upon specific truthful self-disclosures that will reinforce the development of commonality. For example, suppose an adolescent client struggles with a parent whose demands are based upon religious beliefs that the client either does not hold or is unsure of. A therapist who recalls a similar dynamic in their own family of origin might choose to disclose certain memories of that experience to foster commonality.

Once the seeds of commonality are planted, and the client begins to develop a sense of social belonging in the therapeutic setting, then the joining work can expand both within the therapeutic context and out into the youngster's social context. Within the therapeutic interaction, commonality based upon historical sharing can be bolstered by sharing views about ongoing interpersonal processes between the therapist and client (as well as between clients in therapy groups). For example, consider a therapist noticing that the client had an angry response to a question about what the client was planning to do for the upcoming weekend. To discuss the interaction and come to a common (joint) understanding of what transpired creates a demonstration of commonality in real time.

Outside the therapeutic setting, the client can be pointed to notice and cultivate commonality with other persons. Now that commonality seems possible for the traumatized youngster, the potential for garnering support from family members and friends expands dramatically. Clinicians working with traumatized youngsters will often find it useful to incorporate parents and other caretakers to extend the joining aspect of therapy. Particularly with young children, soliciting information from parents regarding the life review can greatly facilitate the therapist's development and expression of commonality. As another example, helping parents understand the sense of isolation or aloneness felt by the youngster, and assisting the parents in communicating that understanding to their troubled child, can be a powerful intervention. Likewise, instructing parents on carrying out short-term intervention efforts (e.g., relaxation, palliative distraction) can provide the youngster both with some immediate symptom relief and with a soothing connection with loved ones. Thus, via the joining process, the planning bankrupt youngster begins to experience a new social role via the therapist which can be expanded outward to incorporate others beyond the immediate therapeutic context. In the early stages of therapy, the new Plan A may still be tenuous, but they are at least connected with others whose plans are functioning.

Empowering

Foa and Riggs (1994) found that those persons most vulnerable to a post-traumatic stress response were not only those who believed themselves to be utterly powerless, but also those who viewed the world of events to be fully under their control. Traumatic experiences seem to crystallize the sense of powerlessness in those already possessing such a self-conception and explode invincibility in those whose construction systems were insufficiently flexible to accommodate the extreme experience. Regardless of the pre-traumatic self-conception, a youngster who has been debilitated by a traumatic experience does not view herself/himself as being an effective *agent* of action in the world. The typical self-conception can be translated into self-talk as follows: "Events in the world simply happen; I can do nothing to make good things happen or prevent bad things from happening. People in my world come and go; I can do nothing to bring the people I love nearer to me, prevent people I love from leaving, or insulate myself from people I hate." Therefore, empowering involves altering this self-conception, not to one of omnipotent agency, but to one of conditional, situational, and intentional agency.

Empowering involves the dual tasks of recognizing personal agency that is already being exercised (based on the renewed engagement and enhanced commonality within and beyond the therapeutic context) and becoming emboldened to exercise agency in arenas that are being avoided. Successes in the joining work described above provide the foundation for promoting empowerment within psychotherapy. At their most debilitated, traumatized youth see themselves as completely different from others, and (obviously, to them) lacking the ability to impact their worlds in the ways that others are able to do. As soon as commonality takes hold, the notion that agency is *possible* (even if not present) can enter the therapeutic conversation.

Therapists often can find fertile ground for identifying a client's unrecognized agency by jointly reliving the client's memories of the traumatic event(s). It is important to note that there is nothing inherently therapeutic about a straightforward recall of a traumatic experience for a person who has been de-bilitated by a post-traumatic stress response – particularly when the youngster is experiencing extreme disconnectedness and absence of agency discussed above. However, reliving the traumatic event with a now-trusted therapist can be a venue for the joint identification of how the youngster has exerted influence on their world, even in the midst of this most extreme and painful experience. Butler and Green (1998) remind us of the importance of "understanding the child's version" (p. 112), which must be the goal more so than historical va-lidity per se. Therapeutic reliving seeks this personal and subjective sharing of experience. As an example, imagine a 10-year-old boy recalling an automobile accident in which he was the sole survivor. He relates that when he saw his blood-stained shirt, he began to cry because the shirt had been a gift from his grandmother. But he questioned why he could not remember feeling bad when he saw his dead parents in the front seat. The boy and his therapist come to a joint recognition that the boy's initial emotional myopia was a way for him to pace himself and deal with his feelings a little bit at a time. The boy and his therapist thus construct a self-conception that has him acting on his internal world in a purposive and adaptive way, despite being unable to prevent an undesired outcome.

In empowering a youngster, the concept of *play* becomes crucial, regardless of the developmental level of the youngster. Play is the modality in which chil-dren experiment with agency in realms that lack the consequentiality of *reality*. For smaller children, this experimental agency can be invoked quite directly. For example, inviting a child to draw events and depict feelings associated with a traumatic memory can provide a powerful sense of agency as the child gives form and boundaries to what is otherwise a formless and boundless pain. En-acting a traumatic experience with toy figures can allow the child to introduce agency where none seemed available, even to the point of constructing alter-native outcomes. For example, a variation of Ravenette's (2003) "a drawing and its opposite technique" (p. 290) can involve asking the child to draw some aspect of the troubling experience, then draw its opposite. Of course, such play does not un-happen the event; rather it reintroduces agency and thus empow-ers the construction system of the child. These types of play activities allow the child to bring the therapist into and relive the trauma alongside the child. The therapist actively tracking and narrating important themes, depicted literally or figuratively through play, represents an active, in-the-moment acknowledge-ment of the child's efforts at enhancing agency.

Straightforward play activities can also be powerful and effective with ado-lescents to the extent that the adolescent can comfortably engage them. But the general concept of play should be maintained even when engaging the adolescent at a more verbal, cognitive level. For example, consider a 16-year-old female who was traumatized by a sexual assault when she was nine years old. The therapist can re-enter the memory of that traumatic experience with the client's 16-year-old self, and invite her to whisper into the ear of her nine-year-old self. The therapist can ask her to say all the things that she knows to be true now, despite what might have been going through her mind at the time of the assault. The client can be invited to comfort the nine-year-old girl and to reassure her that she will survive. Of course, this therapeutic exercise does not seem playful in the sense of enjoyment. But it has all the elements of imaginative play, albeit with verbal rather than physical devices.

When therapy with youngsters (particularly adolescents) is conducted in a group context, the potential of empowerment via imaginative play is greatly facilitated. Role enactments (either involving the traumatic memories themselves or involving later reactions and behavioral choices) make use of creative exploration in a peer-level context (cf. Truneckova & Viney, 2006; Viney & Henry, 2002).

Within the planning metaphor, the empowered youngster now sees that, although Plan A became unviable, bankruptcy was not as complete as might have been feared. The process of joining and reengaging others via commonality laid the groundwork for such recognition. Via reliving from a renewed sense of personal agency, the youngster begins to anticipate that workable plans are within reach.

Empowerment implies connection to others. Indeed, that is why joining must precede empowering. But for empowering to achieve its fullest form, it must be internalized and owned as agency that resides in the person – not *just* in the relationship with the empowering other. Thus, paradoxically there is a need for distancing.

Distancing

Whereas commonality refers to the principle that psychological similarity is produced by construing experiences similarly, *individuality* is the product of persons construing experiences differently (Kelly, 1955/1991, p. 55). For traumatized youngsters, treatment up to this point has involved a giant pendulum swing – from a sense of isolation and difference (at one extreme prior to treatment) to a sense of connectedness and similarity (at least with the therapist and/or others who have experienced similar traumas at the other extreme). Empowering experiences in the therapeutic context have dawned an awareness of the self as capable of impacting the world of events and the world of people, at least insofar as the connection is maintained with the empowering others. To continue with the pendulum metaphor, the next step is for the pendulum to gravitate back toward the center.

Often, traumatized persons who begin to feel empowered formulate their identity exclusively around their traumatic experience. This person sees herself as an empowered incest survivor; this person sees himself as an empowered gang violence survivor; and so on. This tendency may be, in part, explained by Erbes and Harter's (2002) suggestion that survivors often have self-constructions that are highly differentiated (some associated with the trauma and some not), but not well integrated within the totality of the construction system. The same self-constructions that are associated with the trauma can then be projected onto others who have endured the same trauma. The first step of evolving toward a fully empowered person who has transcended the trauma involves creating and acknowledging slight but real distance between self and others seen as connected with this narrow identity (e.g., other incest survivors, gang violence survivors, etc.). Thus the goal of distancing is elaborating non-trauma-based self-constructions and promoting integration with aspects of identity narrowly defined via the trauma.

For children and young adolescents, this aspect of intervention can be communicated most simply: distancing involves convincing the child that she/he is special, unique, and valuable. Convincing the child that these attributes apply to them is both straightforward and complex. At the most straightforward level, directly telling the child that you, the therapist, believe that they possess these qualities is powerful, especially given the status you now have after much joining and empowering work. The therapist can invite the child to describe themselves, then ask the child to consider contrasting persons (e.g., "How would you describe someone not like that," as per Ravenette, 1996, p. 16). If the child is in a group therapy setting, inviting the group to consider and evaluate differences among the members can create needed distance. At a more complex level, it is essential to point the child to evidence outside of the therapy room (accomplishments, social relationships, etc.) that confirms your claim that she/he is uniquely valuable. When possible, it can even be useful to recruit reinforcement of these values by consulting with parents, school teachers, and other authority figures in the child's life.

As adolescents mature toward adulthood, there often is an added stressor associated with distancing. To embrace one's uniqueness is to confront a certain amount of existential isolation (Yalom, 1980) that is a normal part of the adolescent's developmental striving for autonomy. Having finally found some relief from the intense anxiety associated with the post-traumatic response, the adolescent is reluctant to embrace a self-conception that inherently involves uncertainty and personal responsibility (and thus, anxiety). In order to avoid retreating from this developmental hurdle, the caring therapist must persist in the persuasion of the unique value of the adolescent, empathize with the discomfort provoked by confronting this isolation, and offer to be with the client as they cope with this anxiety without assuring them that it can be taken away. Ultimately, the only viable new Plan A must be the one constructed and adopted by the individual. In a final paradox of distancing, the therapist can reassure the adolescent client that they are not alone in confronting this anxiety of unique personhood (individuality), but rather the experience is shared by all who pursue authentic existence (yet another instance of commonality). Group work with adolescents can effectively promote the collective awareness of simultaneous individuality and commonality, and thereby achieve optimal distancing. When the adolescent realizes that identity need not exclusively be defined by the trauma, and that connectedness with others can be experienced on multiple levels (trauma and non-trauma-based), the foundation for collaborative bridge-building is firmly in place.

Collaborative bridge-building

The traumatic experience left the young person fragmented and frantic, with only disconnected islands of meaning scattered through the vast ocean of psychological space. At this point in the therapeutic process, the joined, empowered, and properly distanced survivor is now capable of viewing the self as unique yet connected with others. The survivor is beginning to feel powerfully agentic yet not in control of everything; thus, the survivor must be constantly adapting. Only from this position can the client engage therapy as a full collaborator in the building of a robust Plan A, along with multiple and flexible back-up plans (Plans B, C, and so forth). In constructing and adapting these plans (subsystems of the client's overall construction system) to the demands of the social and phenomenal world, vital connections can be forged between the past and present, the present and future, internal experience and external experience, the personal and the communal, and other disconnected psychological landscapes. We liken this intentional process of traversing back and forth across these pathways to the building of bridges.

Collaborative bridge-building begins with the identification of the client's important subjective *truths*. These psychological realities can include beliefs, memories, plans, attitudes, self-concept components, feelings, and habitual thoughts. By calling these construction levels *truths* is not to say that they are objectively correct or unchangeable. Rather, they are the psychological platforms (or areas of dry land, so to speak) upon which the construction system formulates plans. The therapist's role in the collaboration is to teach the client to identify disconnected truths and then consciously juxtapose them until a viable connection is built between them.

As an example of collaborative bridge-building, consider a 12-year-old girl who witnessed the violent assault of her mother by a street gang member. She recalls being a child who felt completely safe and trusting of strangers, as long as they appeared similar to her and her family members. For her, that memory of her existence is a psychological truth. However, now she is aware that she does not trust anyone who has not proven their benevolence, and that she is keenly aware of her physical vulnerability even in familiar environments (the second psychological truth). Her therapist asks her to script an argument between the two selves (the current self and the pre-trauma self) as a way to juxtapose the two levels of construction. In reviewing the script, the youngster notices the complex arguments presented by the older self and the relatively simple arguments of the small child. The trauma itself seemed relevant to the rift between the two points of view, but cannot seem to account for the dramatic difference. Instead, the girl begins to postulate that, in addition to witnessing the horrible attack, she was also "growing up" and realizing the complexity of life. As important as the traumatic experience remained, it did not make her untrusting and vulnerable. Instead, it had merely accelerated – and perhaps even exaggerated – a maturation process that was adaptive and desirable. She never really was as safe as she felt when she was very young, even though the naive belief was age-appropriate and adaptive. And now, she might not be as vulnerable as she feels (with her feelings being an understandable reaction to an extreme experience). Thus, the two psychological truths have been bridged, yielding an expanded and more flexible construction system involving how she construes personal safety in the past, currently, and in the future. Her anticipations of the trustworthiness of others and of her own safety (Plan A) are now more elaborate, both assimilating and accommodating past and present experiences via the more integrated yet flexible construction. In the future, her response in the face of inadvertently trusting an untrustworthy person will be more nuanced and less self-blaming than would have been the case without the newly constructed bridge (reflecting a more elaborate Plan B).

Similar examples could be offered for any number of disparate psychological truths. Feelings of intense anger toward a caretaker who failed to protect might be bridged with memories of the proud parent at a piano recital. An adolescent boy's firm belief that he is incapable of loving anyone might be bridged with intense affection that emerges toward the therapist. The peritraumatic belief that life was over might be bridged with the awareness of today's existence. A female child's view of herself as weak and ineffectual might be bridged with her knowledge that her parents see her as heroic.

A particular kind of psychological truth might need to be invented in the process of collaborative bridge-building: the truth of the future. Traumatized persons often feel a sense of foreshortened future. Viney and colleagues (1999) echo this by noting how youth can develop the anticipation that the "world is destroyable" (p. 178). Thus, these youngsters spend very little energy on the anticipation of the self extended into future years. An important part of collaborative bridge-building involves invoking the imagination to consider possible futures. Then, once possible futures are constructed, the therapist and client can build bridges between the present (and past) with these possible futures. As with empowerment, building bridges to possible futures benefits from play. This process works best when it does not have the quality of strategic planning (i.e., what the future *should* be), but rather it should have the quality of fantasy (i.e., what the future *could* be). Billy is invited by his therapist to draw three different pictures of himself doing three different jobs as an adult. He draws a figure on a horse with a rope, a physician giving a child an injection, and a firefighter rescuing a dog from a burning house. The therapist then draws a picture of a very small boy whom he calls Jonathan. He asks Billy to have each of his drawing characters explain to Jonathan how a boy who lost both his parents during childhood could grow up to be a cowboy ... a doctor ... a firefighter.

Stoker (1996) offers a useful technique for future building with youngsters. He invites the client to choose photos from magazines, newspapers, or from personal photos that communicate something about how the future might be. He offers several guidelines (p. 56) for the client to include corresponding photos (e.g., some event I would like to be involved in when I'm older), encouraging the client to draw pictures if suitable photos cannot be found for each guideline. Then he asks the client to view the photos from the perspective of a friend of the client (in the future) and comment on what sort of person the client is. Exercises such as these allow clients to utilize current self-construction as the platform from which to bridge back toward the disrupted self at the time of the trauma while simultaneously anticipating possible avenues toward future selves and further grand plan enhancement.

Thus, the two critical components of collaborative bridge-building are the identification/creation of the disparate truths and the active juxtaposition of the truths. The bridge-building is the natural response to the juxtaposition of disparate truths. The examples here involve the construction of verbal explanations (how to get from the first truth to the second); but these verbal tasks are merely devices to hold the two truths in juxtaposition. Often, the therapist must simply keep the two truths simultaneously before the client by repeated reminders; such disparate truths might be resistant to verbal connection. But if the therapist helps the client continue to juxtapose them, a psychological bridge will be built. Ecker and Hulley (1996) suggest that the juxtaposition transforms the truths into something completely new; the present metaphor suggests that two connected truths are fundamentally different from the original two dissociated constructions.

Additional case example

When a child or adolescent presents for treatment, the therapist will inevitably encounter a complex history and equally complex reactions. To further illustrate this point, and the constructivist perspective outlined here, we present an additional case example to show the complex and compounding trauma reactions that are common. We chose a youth who has experienced not just a single traumatic stressor, but multiple trauma exposures and disruptions across his development.

AJ, a 16-year-old male, was placed in a residential treatment center following allegations of inappropriate sexual behavior with his seven-year-old step-nephew. Information provided by the referral source indicated a difficult and chaotic childhood. AJ's mother was reported to have "abandoned" the family when AJ was approximately five years old. His father remarried two years later but this relationship was characterized as extremely volatile and violent, with law enforcement responding to multiple incidents of domestic violence between adult family members. Child protective services' records indicated multiple reports and investigations for physical violence toward AJ and his older siblings. Records also noted that AJ was himself a victim of sexual acts perpetrated by his older brothers (aged seven and 10) which were only disclosed by AJ within the past several months. Despite significant family difficulties and numerous experiences resulting in victimizations, AJ was described to the therapist as "somewhat resilient" by the placement caseworker. AJ was noted as being exceptionally bright, with a strong commitment to his educational goals/pursuits, and with the ability to maintain a positive peer network.

Within the first week of placement, AJ completed a number of self-report mental health screening instruments and was observed by residential staff. On self-report screening measures, AJ indicated spiraling mood symptoms, suicidal thoughts, frequent crying spells, and intrusive thoughts concerning the incident leading to his placement. On a self-report screening measure of trauma symptoms, AJ reported reexperiencing symptoms of intrusive thoughts and nightmares involving past sexual victimizations, as well as his own inappropriate sexual behavior involving his step-nephew. His primary avoidance symptoms centered around feelings of detachment and concerns about estrangement from his family. Arousal symptoms included transient feelings of irritability and difficulty concentrating. Residential staff confirmed that AJ often appeared "dazed" while in school and was isolating himself from unit activities. Despite clear report of PTSD symptoms on assessment measures, AJ insisted that he was "coping" and not letting the symptoms bother him much.

Therapy with AJ began with a very careful and deliberate process of joining. Instead of confronting or challenging AJ's construal of coping, the therapist (author KRC) supported this appraisal while also acknowledging his frustration at being in the residential treatment center. Knowing AJ's history of positive academic attainment, conversations promoting commonality occurred between the therapist and AJ through discussions of recent books AJ had read. The therapist listened attentively to AJ's descriptions of plots, characters, and storylines. He similarly discussed past academic successes and his desire to "put all this behind me" by excelling in school and "going to a good college." Ultimately, AJ's frustration with his placement at the facility became evident with daily problematic interactions with unit peers and frequent angry outbursts toward staff. These disruptions also began to interfere with AJ's "focus" in the classroom. In response, AJ brought these concerns into session and responded to the therapist's suggestions of distress tolerance skills and situational problem solving that involved direct verbal communication with unit staff to facilitate disengaging from group activities that he found "overwhelming."

Although clearly not yet a direct link into the trauma experiences per se, AJ responded well to the approach of "enhancing" his current coping via brief interventions. This allowed the therapist to begin to reflect that coping skills – although adaptive in some contexts/situations – have not always produced desired results.

To put it simply, "not coping" was not an option for AJ. To lapse in coping would be to fully experience the force of the psychological symptoms and responses to current and past events. The therapist joined with AJ to enhance his capacity to resolve the more immediate conflicts with peers. This was an initial step toward empowerment – the sense with AJ that he could exert, establish, and effectuate an influence on his immediate surroundings. The present coping focus allowed the therapist to introduce and then gently explore historical examples of coping to various degrees – times in which past coping "worked" and "didn't work." Drawing on AJ's fondness for fiction, he was encouraged to take the role of the narrator in providing a contemporary recounting of life stories as if they were chapters in a book. Through these narrations, AJ provided access to core constructions regarding families as cohesive and connected, and the importance of being stoic and showing strength (i.e., maintaining silence) in the face of adversity (i.e., past victimizations). His stoicism in the face of adversity was construed as a primary mechanism of maintaining family cohesion. Drawing further on the planning metaphor, these narrations allowed the therapist access to AJ's continued holding on to an increasingly unviable Plan A of his family as loving and connected. Silence in response to past victimizations was construed as a sign of strength and his primary mechanism to keep "the family together." However, with the breakdown of Plan A (keeping the family together via stoicism and strength), AJ reverts to a very cryptic Plan B that is little more than familial disintegration, personal weakness, and acting out. With his new realities confronting him (the disintegration of his nuclear family and the charges against him as a sex offender), AJ must either crystallize his cryptic Plan B as his new Plan A, or else develop some alternative constructions. Thankfully, AJ chose the latter.

Disentangling strength from the "cohesive family" versus "disintegrated family" construals became a priority of therapy sessions with AJ; these sessions illustrate the concept of distancing. This was a rather challenging task given that simultaneously with this work, AJ was confronted with incorporating the roles of "victim" (in relation to past acts of sexual victimization as discussed in therapy) and "offender" (in relation to legal charges he was facing for sexual assault). Continued intrusive thoughts and nightmares led to attempts by AJ at returning to silence as a primary way of coping (i.e., returning to a past coping skill as a source of strength). Renewed efforts at joining became a common occurrence. The therapist had to maintain an available presence to AJ during sessions as he often lapsed into silence after recounting interactions with family members during court appearances and visitations. These events served as unavoidable encounters with the unwanted "offender" (Plan B) role. Elaborating AJ's self-construal of strength to extend beyond silence in response to victimization became the starting point for a new Plan A. This entailed elaborating his past and current academic successes and efforts at engaging with peers on and off the treatment unit as sources of nontraumatic agentic movement. Recognition of his academic attainments by therapeutic unit staff and taking on the role of unit tutor were further elaborations on his self-construction of strength. Specific to the traumatic experiences, aspects of empowerment were also present in the therapeutic interventions. AJ was encouraged to give voice to past victimization experiences as well as full acknowledgment of his behaviors with his step-nephew, as these courageous acknowledgments were ways of elaborating his new construction of what it means to be strong. The ultimate challenge of distancing came with AJ beginning to acknowledge his physical and emotional separation from family members as part of his current reality. Maintaining connectedness with the therapist and continued elaboration of relationships with unit staff and peers, while also subsequently beginning the negotiation of a new role with a placement foster family, were all important steps in AJ's distancing process.

This therapist's treatment of AJ ended with his transition from the facility to placement with a foster family. The consolidation and elaboration of AJ's "strength" self-construction by incorporating overlooked and temporarily unavailable aspects of the self were viewed as key elements in his ability to begin negotiating and engaging with members of his placement family. While preparing for this transition, AJ came to examine and develop a new perspective on his past coping skill of silence. Silence came to be construed not as exhibiting strength, but more likely as an "adaptive" and "self-protective" response to avoid further victimization/harm. The ongoing legal process and the "offender" role remained an area of vulnerability for AJ as these realities were present and painful reminders of the collapsed original Plan A and his temporary invocation of an ineffective Plan B. Thus, even with a more elaborated strength construction, time periods of vulnerability and uncertainty emerged as he went through the juxtaposition of reminders of the old Plan A and his attempts at navigating and elaborating a new Plan A involving his foster family. Key to navigating this new Plan A was drawing on a broadened sense of strength that contained both nontraumatic components (i.e., strong student, smart, socially accepted) and current acknowledgment of both the victim and offender roles as occupying a manageable position within his overall construction system.

As can be gleaned from this case example, trauma exposures occur in numerous forms and lead to both event and social disruptions among affected youth. From the constructivist perspective, we have attempted to demonstrate that events, symptoms, and responses must be conceptualized as involving an unexpected and often chaotic disruption in the youth's overall construction system. As such, interventions are designed to capitalize on the youth's natural agentic tendency by the therapist enhancing a developmentally relevant and adaptive mode of relating within and outside the therapeutic relationship. Ultimately, the constructivist approach to intervention should lead to a restoration of the youth's self-construction process via newly elaborated personal meanings.

Lest constructivist therapy be viewed as constrained to a therapy room, it is important to note that the therapy with AJ occurred in a system with many layers (the unit, with peers, other treatment staff, custodial staff, and educational staff). Therapy extended into and utilized these contexts whenever possible to effect positive change in AJ. In this sense, it was multisystemic in nature – albeit taking place in an artificially small super-system in the form of the residential treatment center. We hope that AJ continued his development and constructive elaboration after joining his foster family in the community. Furthermore, we hope that if AJ seeks therapeutic assistance in the community, his therapist will likewise utilize the multilayered systems in which AJ functions (school, church, foster family, community, etc.) to extend the therapy beyond the consultation room.

Conclusions

Traumatized adults often yearn for a return to their identity and functioning prior to the trauma. This seems consistent with the prevailing disease model of mental illness, of which PTSD is an official diagnostic example. However, humans develop, and development – be it positive or negative – is never undone. When working with children and adolescents, the ever-flowing progression of their development keeps this truism so keenly in the awareness of the therapist that any sort of *cure* for PTSD likely seems absurd. To remove the trauma, like some surgical extraction procedure, appears nonsensical and counterproductive as a goal of constructivist treatment. Furthermore, interventions that are exclusively symptom-focused, while providing immediate relief and enhanced current coping, ignore the broader phenomenological disruption to the self and severe alteration or outright obliteration of the construction system that can occur from trauma experiences. Our constructivist approach outlined here begins with a developmentally informed perspective on the individual constructive capacities of the youngster and seeks to restart this natural process of construct system elaboration. This approach assists the youngster – whose life must now contain the trauma – to reengage and expand the horizons of her/his psychological sphere – to facilitate the growth and functioning that exists as potential energy in all human beings.

References

Adams-Webber, J. (2000). A further test of a model of self-reflection with children aged 10 and 11. *Journal of Constructivist Psychology, 13,* 289–301.

Anderson, R. (1990). Role relationships and personality development. *Early Child Development and Care, 55,* 81–8.

Ariga, M., Uehara, T., Takeuchi, K., et al. (2008). Trauma exposure and posttraumatic stress disorder in delinquent female adolescents. *Journal of Child Psychology and Psychiatry and Allied Disciplines, 49*(1), 79–87.

Baron-Cohen, S. (1989). The autistic child's theory of mind: A case of specific developmental delay. *Journal of Child Psychology and Psychiatry, 30,* 285–97.

Butler, R., & Green, D. (1998). *The child within.* Oxford: Butterworth-Heinemann.

Collin-Vézina, D., & Hébert, M. (2005). Comparing dissociation and PTSD in sexually abused school-aged girls. *Journal of Nervous and Mental Disease, 193,* 47–52.

Costello, E. J., Pine, D. S., Hammen, C., et al. (2002). Development and natural history of mood disorders. *Biol Psychiatry, 52,* 529–42.

Deblinger, E., Thakkar-Kolar, R., & Ryan, E. (2006). Trauma in childhood. In V. Follette & J. Ruzek (Eds.), *Cognitive-behavioral therapies for trauma* (2nd ed., pp. 405–532). New York: Guilford Press.

Ecker, B., & Hulley, L. (1996). *Depth-oriented brief therapy: How to be brief when you were trained to be deep – and vice versa.* San Francisco: Jossey-Bass.

Epting, F. R. (1988). Journeying into the personal constructs of children. *International Journal of Personal Construct Psychology, 1,* 53–61.

Erbes, C. R., & Harter, S. L. (2002). Constructions of abuse: Understanding the effects of childhood sexual abuse. In J. D. Raskin & S. K. Bridges (Eds.), *Studies in meaning: Exploring constructivist psychology* (pp. 27–48). New York: Pace University Press.

Fairbank, J. A., (2008, Winter). The epidemiology of trauma and trauma-related disorders in children and youth. *PTSD Research Quarterly, 19*(1). National Center for PTSD.

Finkelhor, D., Ormrod, R., Turner, H., & Hamby, S. L. (2005). The victimization of children and youth: a comprehensive national survey. *Child Maltreatment, 10*(1), 5–25.

Foa, E., & Riggs, D. (1994). Posttraumatic stress disorder and rape. In R. S. Pynoos (Ed.), *Posttraumatic stress disorder: A clinical review* (pp. 133–163). Baltimore, MD: Sidran Press.

Ford, J. D., Chapman, J. F., Hawke, J., & Albert, D. (2007, June). Trauma among youth in the juvenile justice system: Critical issues and new directions. *National Center for Mental Health and Juvenile Justice Research and Program Brief.* Retrieved from www.ncmhjj.com/publications/default.asp (accessed February 15, 2009).

Gabbay, V., Oatis, M. D., Silva, R. R., & Hirsch, G. S. (2004). Epidemiological aspects of PTSD in children and adolescents. In R. Silva (Ed.), *Posttraumatic stress disorders in children and adolescents: Handbook* (pp. 1–17). New York: W.W. Norton & Co.

Gurwitch, R. H., Kees, M., Becker, S. M., Schreiber, M., Pfefferbaum, B., & Diamond, D. (2004). When disaster strikes: Responding to the needs of children. *Prehosp Disaster Med, 19*(1), 21–28.

Harter, S. (2006). Self-processes and developmental psychopathology. In D. Cicchetti & D. Cohen (Eds.), *Developmental psychopathology, Vol. 1: Theory and method* (pp. 370–417). New York: John Wiley & Sons, Inc.

Harter, S. (1999). *The construction of the self: A developmental perspective.* New York: Guilford Press.

Harter, S. L. (2004). Making meaning of child abuse: Personal, social, and narrative processes. In J. D. Raskin & S. K. Bridges (Eds.), *Studies in meaning, 2: Bridging the personal and social in constructivist psychology* (pp. 115–135). New York: Pace University Press.

Kelly, G. A. (1955). *The psychology of personal constructs* (2 vols.). New York: Norton. Reprinted in 1991, London: Routledge.

Kelly, G. A. (1977). The psychology of the unknown. In D. Bannister (Ed.), *New perspectives in personal construct theory* (pp. 1–20). London: Academic Press.

Kilpatrick, D. G., Rugiero, K. J., Acierno, R. et al. (2003). Violence and risk of PTSD, major depression, substance abuse/dependence, and comorbidity: Results from the National Survey of Adolescents. *Journal of Consulting and Clinical Psychology, 71,* 692–700.

Mancuso, J. (2003). Children's development of personal constructs. In F. Fransella (Ed.), *International handbook of personal construct psychology* (pp. 275–82). London: John Wiley & Sons.

Mancuso, J., & Ceely, S. (1980). The self as memory processing. *Cognitive Therapy and Research, 4,* 1–25.

Mancuso, J. C., & Lehrer R. (1986). Cognitive processes in socializing reactions to rule violation. In R. D. Ashmore & D. M. Brodzinsky (Eds.), *Thinking about the family* (pp. 67–93). Englewood Cliffs, NJ: Lawrence Erlbaum Associates.

Marsee, M. A. (2008). Reactive aggression and posttraumatic stress in adolescents affected by Hurricane Katrina. *Journal of Clinical Child and Adolescent Psychology, 37,* 519–29.

Meshot, C. M., & Leitner, L. M. (1994). Death threat, parental loss, and interpersonal style: A personal construct investigation. In R. A. Neimeyer (Ed.), *Death anxiety handbook: Research, instrumentation, and application* (pp. 181–91). Washington, DC: Taylor & Francis.

Mullet, E., Neto, F., & da Conceincao Pinto M. (2008). What can reasonably be expected from a truth commission: a preliminary examination of East Timorese views. *Peace and Conflict: Journal of Peace Psychology, 14*(4), 369–93.

National Child Traumatic Stress Network (2009, April 1). Treatments that work. Retrieved from www.nctsnet.org/nccts/nav.do?pid=ctr_top_trmnt (accessed February 25, 2010).

Otto, R. K. & Martindale, D. A. (2007). The law, process and science of child custody evaluation. In M. Costanzo, D. A. Krauss, & K. Pezdek (Eds.), *Expert psychological testimony for the courts* (pp. 251–75). Mahwah, NJ: Erlbaum.

Pascalis, O. & de Schonen, S. (1995). Mother's face recognition by neonates: a replication and an extension. *Infant Behavior and Development, 18*(1), 79–85.

Perrin, S., Smith, P., & Yule, P. (2004). Treatment of PTSD in children and adolescents. In P. M. Barrett & T. H. Ollendick (Eds.), *Handbook of interventions that work with children and adolescents: Prevention and treatment.* John Wiley & Sons Ltd.

Piaget, J. (1954). *The construction of reality in the child* [transl. Margaret Cook]. London: Routledge & Kegan Paul.

Putman, S. E. (2009). The monsters in my head: Posttraumatic Stress Disorder and the child survivor of abuse. *Journal of Counseling and Development, 87,* 80–9.

Ravenette, T. (1996). What would happen if? Personal construct psychology and psychological intervention. *Education and Child Psychology, 13,* 13–20.

Ravenette, T. (2003). Constructive intervention when children are presented as problems. In F. Fransella (Ed.), *International handbook of personal construct psychology* (pp. 283–293). London: John Wiley & Sons.

Richert, A. J. (2006). Narrative psychology and psychotherapy integration. *Journal of Psychotherapy Integration, 16,* 84–110.

Romero, S., Birmaher, B., Axelson, D. et al. (2009). Prevalence and correlates of physical and sexual abuse in children and adolescents with bipolar disorder. *Journal of Affective Disorders, 112,* 144–50.

Rowe, D. (2001). An infant personal construct theorist (personal construct psychotherapy). In E. Spinelli & S. Marshall (Eds.), *Embodied theories* (pp. 65–80). London: Continuum.

Scheeringa, M. S., & Zeanah, C. H. (2008). Reconsideration of harm's way: Onsets and comorbidity patterns of disorders in preschool children and their caregivers following Hurricane Katrina. *Journal of Clinical Child and Adolescent Psychology, 37,* 508–18.

Sewell, K. W. (2005). Constructivist trauma psychotherapy: A framework for healing. In D. Winter & L. Viney (Eds.), *Personal construct psychotherapy: Advances in theory, practice, and research* (pp. 165–76). London: Whurr.

Silva, R. R., Alpert, M., Munoz, D. M. et al. (2000). Stress and vulnerability to posttraumatic stress disorder in children and adolescents. *The American Journal of Psychiatry, 157,* 1229–35.

Steinberg, L., Dahl, R. D., Keating, D. et al. (2006). The study of developmental psychopathology in adolescence: Integrating affective neuroscience with the study of context. In D. Cicchetti & D. Cohen, (Eds.), *Developmental psychopathology, Vol. 2: Developmental neuroscience* (pp. 710–41). New York: John Wiley & Sons, Inc.

Stoker, R. (1996). Enabling young people to become key actors in planning their future – A constructive perspective. *Education and Child Psychology, 13,* 49–59.

Strand, V. C., Sarmiento, T. L., & Pasquale, L. E. (2005). Assessment and screening tools for trauma in children and adolescents. A review. *Trauma, Violence & Abuse, 6*(1), 55–78.

Taylor, G. J. & Bagby, R. M. (2004). New trends in Alexithymia research. *Psychotherapy and Psychosomatics, 73*(2), 68–77.

Truneckova, D., & Viney, L. L. (2006). Personal construct group work with troubled adolescents. In P. Caputi, H. Foster, & L. Viney (Eds.), *Personal construct psychology: New ideas* (pp. 253–70). New York: John Wiley & Sons, Inc.

Viney, L. L., & Henry, R. M. (2002). Evaluating personal construct and psychodynamic group work with adolescent offenders and nonoffenders. In R. A. Neimeyer & G. J. Neimeyer (Eds.), *Advances in personal construct psychology: New directions and perspectives* (pp. 259–94). Westport, CT: Praeger.

Viney, L. L., Truneckova, D., Weekes, P., & Oades, L. (1999). Personal construct group work for adolescent offenders: Dealing with their problematic meanings. *Journal of Child and Adolescent Group Therapy, 9,* 169–85.

Winter, D. (1992). *Personal construct psychology in clinical practice: Theory, research and applications.* London: Taylor & Francis/Routledge.

Wood, J. J., Piacentini, J. C., Bergman, R. L., McCracken, J., & Barrios, V. (2002). Concurrent validity of the anxiety disorders section of the Anxiety Disorders Interview Schedule for DSM-IV: Child and parent versions. *Journal of Clinical Child and Adolescent Psychology, 31*(3), 335–42.

Yalom, I. D. (1980). *Existential psychotherapy.* New York: Basic Books.

Youngstrom, E., Weist, M. D., & Albus, K. E. (2003). Exploring violence exposure, stress, protective factors and behavioral problems among inner-city youth. *American Journal of Community Psychology, 32,* 115–29.

Chapter Nineteen

Trauma Systems Therapy: Intervening in the Interaction between the Social Environment and a Child's Emotional Regulation

B. Heidi Ellis, Glenn N. Saxe, and Jennifer Twiss

Introduction

Children's responses to trauma can be varied, and include dysphoria, anxiety, aggression, and self-injurious behavior. All of these diverse responses can be understood as manifestations of the central problem of child traumatic stress: emotional dysregulation. Traumatized children generally have great difficulty with self-regulatory functions (Cichetti & Lynch, 1993; Perry & Pollard, 1998; Perry et al., 1995; Putnam, 1997; Schore, 2001a, b; van der Kolk & Fisler, 1994; van der Kolk et al., 1996). Children who experience traumatic stress can find controlling emotion, behavior, and attention in the face of environmental threats, as well as reconstituting themselves to terminate their extreme responses, to be particularly challenging (Charney et al., 1993; De Bellis, 2001; Perry & Pollard, 1998; Perry et al., 1995; Schore, 2001a, b; van der Kolk, 1994). This cascade of events leading to dysregulation may be triggered by genuine environmental threats, perceived threats resulting from the child's misinterpretation of actual events, and/or the child's extreme response to seemingly innocuous stimuli. When confronted with threatening signals, children with traumatic stress respond immediately and extremely in ways that are not appropriate for the contemporaneous demands of the social environment.

Post-Traumatic Syndromes in Childhood and Adolescence: A Handbook of Research and Practice, First Edition.
Edited by Vittoria Ardino. © 2011 John Wiley & Sons, Ltd. Published 2011 by John Wiley & Sons, Ltd.

Child traumatic stress is, perhaps more than any other mental health issue, embedded in social context. Trauma itself frequently springs from a severe disruption in the environment, whether social or political in nature, or stemming from a natural disaster. Once the trauma has occurred the social environment is often a key determinant of how the path to healing will progress. In a world that continues to be fraught with stress, isolation or traumatic reminders, recovery can be greatly impeded. However, an environment that carefully contains and nurtures a traumatized child, fosters emotion-regulation skills, and decreases unnecessary stress, can help to move the child beyond the tragedy of the trauma. Consider the following case examples:

Case study 1

Lila is an 11-year-old girl who was repeatedly molested by her uncle from age eight to present. When she first disclosed the abuse to her mother, her mother became very upset and told Lila that she must be lying and should never say such things again. Later, when Lila told her teacher, her parents became very angry and changed Lila's school placement, despite the fact that Lila was doing very well at school. After an abuse report was filed by the teacher, social services became involved. The family agreed to not leave Lila alone with the uncle, but stated he was a member of the family and would still come for Sunday dinners. Lila became increasingly socially withdrawn and depressed, and began cutting her arms. Her teacher at the new school called the parents to inform them that Lila frequently played truant on Mondays and that she was in jeopardy of failing. The teacher noted that under-achievers such as Lila "brought down" the whole class.

Case study 2

Grace is an 11-year-old girl who was repeatedly molested by her uncle from age eight to the present. When she first disclosed the abuse to her mother, her mother became very upset and immediately made an appointment for a sexual abuse evaluation. In conversation with other family members, Grace's mother decided that the uncle could not have any contact with Grace and urged the uncle to enter treatment himself. Grace's parents met with her teacher at school to explain what they had learned and to request additional support should Grace have emotional or academic difficulties during this time. Because the teacher noted that Grace seemed to be having more trouble concentrating, she suggested that if she noticed a lack of focus, she could take Grace aside for some individual attention and also let Grace know she could request some time in the school nurse's office as needed. On Sundays, a day that her uncle had previously come to dinner, Grace would often become tearful. During these times her mother or father would make a point of being around and let her know they were there to talk with her if she wanted. Over time Grace's sadness diminished and her work at school returned to its previous high level. One day she told her parents that she was working on a special project at school: a family tree. "Uncle Leo is still in the family tree," she said, showing a picture she'd drawn of a tree, "but I've drawn my tree so that he's on a different branch than I am. My branch grows out this way into the sun. Sometimes people just go different ways."

What separates the experiences of Lila and Grace? Basically, their social environments are markedly different. Lila must contend not only with a history of abuse, but with an unsupportive mother, the loss of a positive school environment, and the ongoing stress of exposure to the perpetrator. Grace, on the other hand, benefits from nurturing and responsive parents, a continuation of a supportive school setting, and protection from ongoing exposure to the traumatic reminder of her uncle. It is not hard to see from these examples how central the social environment can be in promoting healing in traumatized children. But what is it exactly about the social environment that plays such a critical role in the healing process? Both children experienced emotional dysregulation, including sadness and difficulty concentrating, in the wake of the abuse and subsequent disclosures. This dysregulation occurred most specifically in response to the traumatic reminder of Sunday dinner. While Lila's family neither protects her from these reminders nor helps her to regulate in these moments of distress, Grace's family works to both diminish exposure to reminders and to help Grace cope with her difficult feelings. Particularly, it is this intersection of the social environment and the child's regulation that demarcates the experiences of the two children.

Trauma Systems Therapy (TST) (Hansen & Saxe, 2009; Saxe, Ellis, & Kaplow, 2007; Saxe et al., 2005) is an intervention that specifically targets a traumatized child's emotion regulation, the social environment, and the interface between these two elements. There are developing standards for effective social environmental interventions (England & Cole, 1998; Ghuman, Weist, & Sarles, 2002; Henggeler et al., 1998; Pumariega & Winters, 2003; Stroul & Friedman, 1994) as well as a growing amount of literature on effective interventions for both self-regulation and traumatic stress in children (Cohen & Mannarino, 1996; Cohen et al., 2000; Debler, McLeer, & Henry, 1990; Goenjian et al., 1997; March et al., 1998; Saltzman et al., 2001). TST incorporates these standards into an intervention program that specifically addresses the problems related to traumatic stress in children. TST is both a way of organizing services as well as a set of specific clinical interventions to address the core problems of child traumatic stress.

TST is designed to provide an integrated and highly coordinated system of services to support traumatized children that is guided by the specific knowledge of the nature of child traumatic stress. This model is based on the premise that development of traumatic stress in children results from two main elements: (1) a traumatized child who is not able to regulate emotional states, and (2) a social environment or system of care that is not sufficiently able to help the child contain this dysregulation. The essence of TST is to help the child to gain control over emotions and behavior by diminishing the ongoing stresses and threats in the social environment, and to build the child's emotional regulation skills, primarily by increasing the capacity of others in the child's environment to support him or her in developing appropriate emotional and behavioral regulation skills.

Details of TST are provided in our book *Collaborative Treatment of Traumatized Children and Teens: The Trauma Systems Therapy Approach*. The following sections are based on the standardization of TST as detailed in this treatment manual.

Overview of treatment structure (Saxe, Ellis, & Kaplow, 2007)

TST focuses interventions on the "trauma system." A trauma system is defined as the failure of the natural systemic balance between the developing child's ability to regulate emotional states and their social environment. Healthy development requires a regulatory balance or "goodness of fit" (Chess & Thomas, 1991) between the child and her or his social environment such that the social environment is properly equipped to meet the child's needs. When children enter service systems this goodness of fit also includes the balance between the child's development and the system of care, such as the social services department or the school system. A trauma system occurs when there is a failure of this regulatory balance between the traumatized child and the social environment and/or system of care.

TST offers an approach to assessing this "fit" between the child's emotional regulation capacities and adequacy of the social environment or system of care to support the child and suggests a variety of treatment modules based on the outcome of this assessment.

Assessment under Trauma Systems Therapy (Saxe, Ellis, & Kaplow, 2007)

TST assesses traumatized children along two dimensions: (1) a gradient of emotional regulation, and (2) a gradient of social environmental stability. Along the emotion regulation dimension, a child is assessed as regulated, emotionally dysregulated or behaviorally dysregulated. A child who is emotionally regulated has sufficient command over his or her emotional states and spends the majority of the time in this regulated emotional state. It is expected that a child who is emotionally regulated will at times exhibit negative emotions, such as anger, sadness, guilt, and fear; however, this child is capable of self-soothing and returning to a state of composure and connectedness with the environment. Changes may occur in this child's awareness (consciousness), affect (emotion) or action (behavior) in the face of traumatic stress, but an emotionally regulated child will only experience change in up to two of these elements when stressed. Furthermore, a child who is emotionally regulated will almost never engage in risky or dangerous behaviors when stressed.

A child who is emotionally dysregulated has a harder time controlling his or her emotional states. The transitions from a regulated state occur with changes in the three 'As': awareness, affect, and action. The changes in action, or behavior, however, do not involve risk (e.g., self-destructive behavior, aggressive behavior, dangerous eating or sexual behavior, or substance abusing). A child who is considered to be emotionally dysregulated experiences this state at least once a month and the episodes cause problems with school, home, personal relationships, or with the child him- or herself.

The child who is behaviorally dysregulated has great difficulty controlling his or her emotional states, and the emotional dysregulation at times spills over into potentially dangerous behaviors (e.g., self-destructive behavior, aggressive behavior, dangerous eating or sexual behaviors, or substance abusing). As with the emotionally dysregulated child, this child may spend most of his or her time in a regulated emotional state, at times experiencing changes in the three A's (affect, awareness, and action) that lead to dangerous behavior. Differences in the three categories of emotion regulation are noted below in Table 19.1. Importantly, although all children experience times of emotion regulation, the assessment of a child under TST is driven by the child's highest level of dysregulation over the past month. Thus, even if behavioral dysregulation does not occur on a regular basis, a single incidence that rises to a level of behavioral dysregulation – such as an episode of cutting – would be sufficient for the child to be designated as behaviorally dysregulated. This approach is not meant to pathologize the child, but to ensure that the services brought to bear are sufficient to help with the most acute levels of distress.

Along the social environment dimension, the child's system of care can be assessed as stable, distressed, or threatening. In order to clearly understand the differences between these levels of stability, it is necessary to frame the levels within the constructs of (1) help and (2) protect. *Help* refers to the capacity of the social environment or system of care to *help* the child regulate emotion. This capacity is defined by the caregiver's (including professional caregiver's) ability to be attuned to the child's emotional needs and to assist the child with these emotional needs, i.e., soothing the child when distressed and enhancing the child's developmental capacities to manage emotion.

Table 19.1 The three categories of emotion regulation

Emotionally regulated	Emotionally dysregulated	Behaviorally dysregulated
Child experiences full range of emotions, including negative emotions. Affect, awareness *or* actions may change with emotional states, but all three do not change simultaneously.	Child shows changes in affect, awareness, *and* action in response to certain stressors. Changes in affect may include numbing, or an absence of feeling, as well as heightened intensity of negative emotion. Child does not engage in dangerous behaviors as a result of the heightened emotions.	Child shows all of the changes present in emotional dysregulation (affect, awareness, and action) *and* this dysregulation results in dangerous behavior. Examples of dangerous behavior include self-injurious behavior, physical aggression, risk-taking, unsafe sexual behavior or eating disturbances.

Protect refers to the capacity of the social environment or system of care to *protect* the child from stresses that may lead to dysregulated emotional states. This capacity is defined by the caregiver's (including professional caregiver's) ability to be attuned to the child's history of trauma and reactions to it such that stimuli that remind the child of the trauma are identified and the environment is changed to diminish the stimuli.

Once the constructs of helping and protecting have been established, the level of stability of the child's social environment or system of care is easier to recognize. The child's social environment and system of care are considered stable when the child's family has the capacity to *help* the child manage emotion and to *protect* the child from stressors. Often, if the child's family is not able to *help and protect*, others in the social environment, such as the extended family, friends, and neighbors, might serve to *help and protect* the child. The capacity to help and protect expands even further to the child's system of care, such as school, social services or mental health systems. These are designed to support the child, his or her family, and extended social network in order to provide services that allow the child to achieve optimal functioning (in the case of child traumatic stress, optimal functioning usually means the regulation of emotion, as defined above).

The child's social environment and system of care are considered distressed when the child's family has difficulty *helping* him or her manage emotion or *protecting* him or her from stressors. In addition, others in the social environment, such as the extended family, friends, and neighbors, cannot adequately help and protect the child, and the system of care has not been accessed or services are not in place to adequately help the child regulate emotion or to protect him or her from stressors and traumatic reminders.

Table 19.2 The different layers of the social ecology

Stable	Distressed	Threatening
The child's caregivers within both the family and system of care are sufficiently able to help the child manage emotions in the face of normative stressors and protect the child from undue stress or danger. Typically, family has sufficient resources for child's basic needs, beneficial services are in place, and caregivers are well functioning and attuned to the child's emotions.	The child's caregivers within the family and system of care are not fully attuned to the child's emotional states and are unable to help the child to manage emotions and/or do not sufficiently protect the child from undue stressors in the social environment. Family may lack key resources for child's basic needs, services that might be indicated may not be in place or may not be effective, and/or caregivers may be low functioning or poorly attuned to child's emotions.	There is a frank threat to the child's safety within the social environment. This may include ongoing exposure to trauma (e.g., community or domestic violence) or risk of being retraumatized (e.g., continued exposure to a perpetrator). Services that should be protecting the child are not in place or are not functioning well enough to ensure the child's safety.

The child's social environment and system of care is considered *threatening* when not only do the child's immediate caregivers have difficulty *helping* him or her manage emotion and *protecting* him or her from stressors and traumatic reminders but there is a true threat of harm to the child in the social environment/system of care. Others in the social environment, such as the extended family, friends, and neighbors, either cannot adequately help and protect the child from this threat or are causing this threat. The system of care has either not been accessed to protect the child or (tragically) the system of care itself is threatening to the child.

Table 19.2 shows the gradient of assessing the social environment. All layers of the social ecology must be considered in assessing the stability of the social environment: the broader neighborhood and community context, the service system, the child's school, and the family. While strengths in the different layers of the social ecology should be noted, the assessment of a child's social environment is driven by the least stable aspect of the social environment. Thus, if there is considerable violence in the neighborhood, the environment would be deemed threatening, even if the family and school environments were quite safe and nurturing environments. Only once the violence was diminished – perhaps through a mobilization of the service system (the police), or through a family proactively protecting the child by moving out of the area – would the assessment change.

Determining the assessment of the social environment based on the least stable element of the social ecology is not meant to downplay the importance of the more stable layers of the social ecology – indeed, the strengths and positive aspects of other parts of the social ecology are often essential to leveraging change in the distressed area. Rather, the goal is to ensure that the treatment plan contains within it the intensity of services needed to address and make changes within the most stressed parts of the child's social ecology.

How would Lila and Grace be assessed? Along the emotion regulation gradient, Lila is socially isolated, truants, and cuts herself. Such self-injurious behavior, especially if it was assessed to be related to suicidal ideation, would suggest that she is experiencing *behavioral dysregulation* – her emotional dysregulation becomes so extreme that she is hurting herself. Along the social environment gradient, there are several pieces of information that point to deficiencies in both *helping* Lila to regulate and *protecting* her from unnecessary stress. Lila's mother is not attuned to Lila's distress, and indeed seems to be adding to her stress by conveying messages of disbelief. By removing Lila from what seemed to be a positive school placement, her mother also diminishes the support Lila might be receiving from other sources in her social environment. Finally, perhaps most egregiously, her mother fails to protect Lila from the traumatic reminder and stress of contact with her uncle. Although Lila is not faced with a frank threat, as might be the case if she was left unsupervised with her uncle, she clearly inhabits a highly *distressed* social environment.

Grace, on the other hand, demonstrates *emotional dysregulation* through her dysphoria. At present, however, there is no evidence that Grace's emotions spill into dangerous behavior. Her social environment is rife with examples of parents and teachers helping her to regulate emotions and protecting her from unnecessary stressors. Thus, Grace is an emotionally dysregulated child living in a stable social environment.

Why does this assessment matter? According to the TST model, the assessment of a child's emotional regulation and stability of the social environment drive a clinician's choice about what foci of treatment will be most useful for a given child. As can be seen from Table 19.3, the outcome of the assessment will place the interaction between the child and the social environment

Table 19.3 Assessment grid

		Social Environmental Stability		
		Stable	Distressed	Threatening
Emotion Regulation	Regulated	Phase 5 *Transcending*	Phase 4 *Understanding*	Phase 3 *Enduring*
	Emotionally dysregulated	Phase 4 *Understanding*	Phase 3 *Enduring*	Phase 2 *Stabilizing*
	Behaviorally dysregulated	Phase 3 *Enduring*	Phase 2 *Stabilizing*	Phase 1 *Surviving*

in one of five conditions of increasing dysregulation/instability. Intervention is then constructed around the particular condition (phase) the child and social environment are assessed to be in.

Each phase of treatment corresponds to a different theme of traumatic stress therapy and a different menu of services. For instance, as can be seen from Table 19.3, Lila would fall within the *stabilizing* stage of treatment and the focus would likely include working closely with the parents to help them understand the gravity of the allegations, the importance of supporting Lila by eliminating contact with the uncle, and working within the school setting to make it more accommodating. Simultaneously, psychopharmacology and emotion regulation skill-building might be implemented to help diminish Lila's suicidality and cutting. Grace, on the other hand, is in the *understanding* phase and would most likely benefit from cognitive processing of the trauma. The way in which this menu of services is used to help diminish identified clinical problems is detailed below in the section on "Services under TST."

The child, as well as those directly involved in the child's social environment, travel through the phases of therapy with a main goal to achieve regulation and stability. A child shifts from one phase to the next based on improvements in their emotion regulation and the social environmental stability, rather than based on a set number of sessions. These phases are defined by the results of the assessment reflected in Table 19.3.

Throughout, the approach to treatment is iterative, with additional information influencing the course and nature of interventions. Progress through treatment is rarely linear and families may move between stages as new challenges arise. Throughout the process, there is an ongoing effort to draw on the target family's strengths and to infuse culturally syntonic interventions into the clinical work.

How to identify the most important problem(s) to address in treatment (Saxe et al., 2007)

Children with traumatic stress usually have a great many problems that could be addressed in treatment. Think about Lila: Where would you start? Which of her problems is most important to treat? As we all know, if the clinician is trying to address too many problems with their limited time, they are unlikely to be successful. TST has a framework for using clinical information to hone in on the highest value problems to address in treatment. We call these problems *TST priority problems*.

TST priority problems are defined by identified patterns of links between emotional/behavioral dysregulation and the stimuli that provoke it. Priority is then assigned to a given problem based on the amount of dysfunction that the pattern causes. An example of a priority problem for Lila might be the pattern of "exposure to her uncle at Sunday dinner leads to cutting." Most children with traumatic stress have patterns to how they get dysregulated and under what conditions. TST clinicians are trained to identify these patterns via clearly assessing information about the social context in which dysregulation happens. When regularities are identified, the treatment plan documents a strategy to address these priority problems with a specified number of treatment modalities that are expected to occur within a given phase of treatment.

In Lila's case, the focus of the treatment would be to diminish the provocative social-environmental stimulus, her exposure to the perpetrating uncle. The clinician would help the parents to understand how ongoing contact with the uncle affects Lila and come up with a plan to eliminate Lila's contact with him. Simultaneously, services to address the dangerous cutting behavior, such as a combination of psychopharmacology and emotion regulation skills training, would be put in place.

An example of a priority problem for Grace might be the pattern of "family routines associated with Sunday dinners (at which the perpetrating uncle used to be present) results in Grace feeling sad and lonely." In this situation the provocative stimulus (Sunday dinner) is a potentially healthy and restorative time that should not be eliminated. Rather, the focus might be on helping Grace to manage her feelings through cognitive coping skills, and ultimately to process the trauma so that reminders of her uncle become more tolerable. In addition, the therapist might work with the family to find ways for Sunday dinner to incorporate new traditions that help Grace to feel particularly safe and loved.

Services under Trauma Systems Therapy (Saxe et al., 2007)

As described, the TST model is designed to address identified priority problems for traumatized children and families. These priority problems, by definition, focus on emotional/behavioral dysregulation in its social context. What tools does TST provide to help practitioners effectively address these priority problems?

TST recommends a series of specified treatment modules depending on the phase of treatment the child is assessed to be in. These treatment modules are used to remediate the priority problems. The treatment modules listed below are provided through four types of services: skill-based psychotherapy, home-based care, psychopharmacology, and legal advocacy. Not all children require all services; rather, a menu of services is compiled based on the phase of treatment the child is assessed to be in and the specific priority problems to be addressed. Table 19.4 shows the types of services most commonly engaged in the different phases of treatment.

An essential means of integrating these four services is through a weekly TST team meeting. All clinicians and providers from a TST program meet regularly to review new cases, conference ongoing cases, and provide consultation

Table 19.4 Phases of treatment and corresponding treatment modules

Phase		Surviving	Stabilizing	Enduring	Understanding	Transcending
Module	Stabilization on site	***	***	–	–	–
	Services advocacy	***	**	*	*	*
	Psychopharm	**	**	**	*	*
	Emotion regulation	*	**	***	–	–
	Cognitive processing	–	–	–	***	–
	Meaning making	–	–	–	–	***

***= essential, **= probably helpful, *= occasionally helpful, – = contraindicated

and perspective to one another. In this way the children being seen through a given program become held by the larger team rather than just the specific providers, and a culture of support and reinforcement for TST principles is developed. Fidelity to the treatment model is monitored during team presentations and discussions. An additional function of the TST team is to streamline communication and coordinate care. The team lends a degree of efficiency to communication; new or critical information is easily shared among providers who work with the same family. Finally, the team provides a place of support for the clinicians. Working with traumatized children and families is not easy; indeed, within the field burnout rates can be high. Within a TST program the burden of worrying about a child and family should never be left to a lone clinician. The team is a holder of the families and a holder of the clinicians, as well as a holder of the TST model.

Skill-based psychotherapy

This service is provided in an office-based setting. In earlier phases of treatment the focus is on emotion regulation skill-building. Sessions begin with updating the "Emotion Regulation Guide," a tool used to help children and families identify social-environmental triggers, the child's emotional and behavioral reactions, and appropriate interventions. The guide is based on four emotional states that a traumatized child moves through when triggered by a provocative stimulus: regulating (prior to being triggered), revving (following exposure to a provocative stimuli), reexperiencing (the child's coping skills have been overwhelmed and he/she becomes emotionally or behaviorally dysregulated), and reconstituting (a vulnerable period following regaining control). Therapists work with parents and child to help them to recognize when a child moves between these states and how to best prevent reexperiencing states and promote regulating states. The second half of the session focuses on specific coping skills and emotion identification/understanding skills.

In later phases of treatment, skill-based psychotherapy shifts to cognitive processing. This module of treatment is influenced by interventions such as Trauma-Focused Cognitive-Behavioral Therapy, as developed and described by Cohen and colleagues (2000). The primary objectives of these sessions are to help children acquire cognitive coping skills, increase their tolerance for discussions about the trauma, decrease the intensity of emotion associated with the trauma, and improve communication about the trauma among family members.

The final phase of skill-based psychotherapy is dedicated to "meaning making." The main goals of these sessions are to help the child identify lessons learned, articulate a positive self-image, enact meaningful experiences related to the trauma, and to terminate with the therapist.

Home and community-based care: Stabilization on site

Stabilization on site (SOS) involves clinicians working with a child and family in a community setting. Frequently, this involves home visits, but may also include intensive involvement on site at a school or other community setting if that is where the child is experiencing problems. In adaptations of TST for residential care, the milieu becomes the focus of the SOS work. Initially, SOS treatment is more intensive, occurring approximately two or three times a week. Over time, the frequency of visits decreases to once a week. Throughout this period, an emergency SOS clinician is always available by phone or pager, so that families can receive verbal assistance during crises. For safety reasons, an SOS team always involves two clinicians. Sessions should include these basic components: settling in, check-in about child functioning/recent events, problem solving/strength building, and closing ritual. The overall goal of SOS is to stabilize the family so that a child may stay safely in the home or community setting. The stability of the home placement may be threatened by the child's dysregulation, lack of environmental stability, or more commonly a combination of both. During the *surviving* phase of treatment, the primary goal of SOS is to assess the true risk of harm. If the child does not need to be assessed in an emergency room, the function of SOS is to provide the family with in-the-moment assistance in helping the child to regulate his or her emotions and to immediately remove triggers and stressors present in the home environment. In the *stabilizing* phase of treatment, the goal of SOS is to stabilize the family by either increasing the family's ability to support the child's emotion regulation, increasing the stability of the environment, or a combination of both. Specifically, SOS is about identifying elements of the day-to-day environment that may trigger a child's dysregulation and eliminating, or reducing, these triggers. SOS provides a critical service wherever the triggers occur, including at home, school or in the neighborhood, to help reduce the likelihood the child will encounter these traumatic reminders in the course of the day.

Psychopharmacology

Psychopharmacology fits closely with other treatment modalities of TST. In the earlier phases of treatment the main use of psychopharmacology is to avert crisis.

During these phases, when the social environment is unstable and the child is at high risk to engage in dangerous behavior, psychopharmacology can be used to help to prevent psychiatric emergencies, psychiatric hospitalizations, and out-of-home placements. Once the child transitions to the more advanced phases of treatment, the main goal of psychopharmacology is to enhance skill-building interventions. As can be seen from the TST Phase chart, psychopharmacology is not always indicated and is used in conjunction with other services to help maximize the chances that a child remains safe and is able to develop emotion regulation and coping skills.

Services advocacy

The fourth key service component within TST is a lawyer. Few mental health programs systematically involve lawyers in the clinical care and treatment planning for their clients. Yet sometimes the main drivers of a child's mental health problems are heavily impacted by systemic or structural problems that will not change without sophisticated advocacy. Within TST, legal advocacy is integrated to address these problems; when wishful thinking is not enough to make real change, advocacy comes into play.

TST delineates a four-step Advocacy Assessment and Plan process, oriented around the following four questions: (1) What are the identified social environmental issues that contribute to the child's difficulty regulating emotional states? (2) Are services or benefits to which the family is entitled currently in place to help with the problems? If no, (3) What barriers exist to putting appropriate services and benefits in place?, and (4) What advocacy steps should be employed to address these barriers? Advocacy steps may include providing parents with the skills and knowledge to advocate on their own behalf, or advocating on behalf of or in conjunction with a family. A consulting lawyer provides assistance to the clinical team in identifying best advocacy strategies.

Although at first glance the idea of involving a lawyer in a clinical team may seem cost-prohibitive, many TST teams have found creative ways to integrate legal expertise into their team. Typically, this is done through identifying a volunteer lawyer who will provide two hours of consultation per week. One hour is spent as a member of the TST team, listening to cases with an ear for areas where services or benefits might be put in place to change a social environmental stressor. The other hour is spent in consultation as needed with clinicians who are enacting an advocacy plan and may benefit from consultation about the most strategic way of framing a letter or argument.

Treatment duration (Saxe et al., 2007)

Because TST is phase-based, children who enter treatment in earlier phases of treatment (e.g., *surviving*) typically require longer treatment than children who enter in later phases (e.g., *understanding*). Each phase of treatment typically takes two to three months, but because the course of treatment is determined by the child's progress, rather than a set number of sessions completed, children may move through the phases at much faster or slower rates. TST has been shown to be effective at reducing symptoms and increasing environmental stability over a three-month period of time (Saxe et al., 2005).

Adaptations: TST in different settings and with different populations

TST was initially developed for children in an inner-city setting, who were living in complicated social environments in which ongoing violence and fractured systems of care were commonplace. At its core, TST is meant to serve children with a trauma history who face ongoing stressors and who are experiencing some degree of emotional dysregulation. Since its initial development this core has resonated with practitioners working with traumatized children in a variety of different settings. Refugee children, traumatized adolescents who are using substances, medically traumatized youth, and children in foster or residential care are all examples of youths with plausible trauma histories, problems with emotion regulation, and for whom TST may be appropriate. As developers of TST we have welcomed the adaptation of TST to best fit the needs of these different service settings and populations. Indeed, while the core goals, structures, and principles of TST remain unchanged, a great number of innovations have been made by practitioners working to implement TST in new settings. Several of the TST adaptations are described below.

TST for refugees (TST-R)

Refugee youths resettling in the United States frequently have been exposed to significant trauma during war, in a refugee camp or during migration. After resettling they often continue to confront significant stressors in their social environment, including acculturative stress, fractured systems of care, financial stress, inappropriate school placements, bullying or ongoing violence within their host communities. While many of these youths show great resilience, a subset experience significant emotional dysregulation. Despite significant need among this subset, very few ever access mental healthcare. Linguistic, cultural, and practical barriers render typical mental health services useless to much of this population.

TST-R is designed to enhance refugee youth engagement in services by offering services along a continuum of care. The first and broadest level of care involves community outreach to engage families and develop trust between communities and providers before a specific mental health need is identified;

mental health information is made available and efforts are made to destigmatize seeking care. Concrete assistance with family needs may be provided at this stage as a means of preventing stress within families and building rapport between the program and the community. Partnerships with religious and community agencies are key at this level.

The second level of care focuses on decreasing acculturative stress and increasing social support, factors known to be associated with better mental health among refugee youth. This is accomplished through acculturation peer groups held in the school setting. Working in a group format further helps to build rapport with families by providing non-stigmatizing, supportive services for the youth in a highly valued setting (school). Coming to know children in a group setting also allows clinicians to more effectively identify those children in need of more intensive services.

The final level of care is full TST and focuses on those children who are demonstrating problems with emotion regulation and for whom community-level and group-level care are not sufficient. TST services are provided for these youths in the school, with home-based care integrated for those in the *surviving* and *stabilizing* phases of treatment. Cultural provider (e.g., trained clinicians from a given community) and cultural broker (e.g., paraprofessionals partnering with clinicians who are not from the given community) models of care have both been used to help address cultural and linguistic barriers in the implementation of TST at this level of care. TST-R is currently being piloted in a school setting and has demonstrated excellent treatment engagement and improvements in child mental health and functioning.

TST for substance abuse (TST-SA)

TST has also been adapted to address issues related to substance abuse. In collaboration with Liza Suarez, Ph, this adaptation was developed to focus on helping those with traumatic stress identify ways of managing traumatic reminders present in their environment as an alternative to substance use. The foundation of this adaptation is based on the knowledge that those with a trauma history often become behaviorally dysregulated as a way to manage their traumatic stress. Therefore, this adaptation seeks to assist in fostering positive coping skills to manage negative emotional states while at the same time equipping the social environment or system of care with the tools necessary to decrease environmental threats and traumatic reminders.

TST for medically traumatized children (TST-M)

TST for medical settings is another adaption of TST that seeks to address symptoms of traumatic stress in children. Children who have endured life-threatening illness or injury often experience post-traumatic reactions when in recovery, as the medical setting is an environment that can be filled with an array of traumatic reminders. The goal of this adaptation is again to address issues related to emotional regulation and more specifically, to equip medical staff with the awareness to create a safe setting for these children depending on their specific trauma symptoms. In addition to providing psychopharmacology, skill-based psychotherapy, and advocacy as needed, TST-M focuses on the importance of providing home-based care for traumatized children and their families to help make a smooth transition from medical setting to home environment and to eliminate traumatic reminders in the home.

TST for residential care settings (TST-RES)

Another TST adaptation closely related to that of TST-M is TST for residential settings. The focus of this adaptation is again on creating and fostering the delicate balance between appropriate emotional regulation and stable social environment of a traumatized child. Traumatic triggers can be frequent in residential settings as children may be consistently coming in contact with reminders of past trauma. These children are often navigating two social environments, the residential milieu and their home and community. Therefore, the goal of TST-RES is to provide children with skills to cope effectively when faced with these traumatic reminders and to help those working in such settings to reduce triggers and provide a safe and stable social environment. Home-based care is also a critical intervention in TST-RES as it helps to address the often difficult transition from residential care to the home environment.

TST for child welfare (TST-CW)

TST has also been adapted for use in the child welfare system. TST-CW has been developed to focus on issues related to child protection concerns. More specifically, the aim of this adaptation is to equip the social environment of a traumatized child with important information related to the legalities of child protection, entitlements, and relevant processes of the legal and court system.

Conclusion

As we have described, TST is both an organizational model for bringing together key services, as well as a specific clinical model for intervening with the problems of child traumatic stress. TST is not something that can be done by an individual clinician, nor is it something an agency can mandate without putting in place partnerships and organizational support for the program. Perhaps what makes TST so powerful is that it is not only about effecting change at the level of the individual child, but it is also about effecting change at the level of the service system. Case management that used to be split off and seen as "separate" from clinical care becomes redefined as a powerful tool for clinical change. A chaotic or stressful home environment previously seen as an insurmountable barrier to progress in a child's therapy instead becomes the site and focus of treatment. A breakdown in the service system is no longer just another example of social injustice, but instead becomes the catalyst for advocacy and systemic change. Through TST the service system and providers can move out of the silos that have led to a fragmented system of care to a model of collaborative care for traumatized children.

References

Charney, D. C., Deutch, A. Y., Krystal, J. H., Southwick, S. M., & Davis, M. (1993). Psychobiologic mechanisms of posttraumatic stress disorder. *Archives of General Psychiatry, 50,* 294–305.

Chess, S., & Thomas, A. (1991). Temperament and the concept of goodness of fit. In J. Strelau & A. Angleitner (Eds.), *Explorations in temperament: International perspectives on theory and measurement* (pp. 15–28). New York: Plenum Press.

Cichetti, D., & Lynch, M. (1993). Toward an ecological/transactional model of community violence and child maltreatment: Consequences for children's development. *Psychiatry, 56*(1), 96–118.

Cohen, J. A., & Mannarino, A. P. (1996). A treatment outcome study for sexually abused preschool children: Initial findings. *Journal of the American Academy of Child and Adolescent Psychiatry, 35,* 42–50.

Cohen, J. A., Mannarino, A. P., Berliner, L., & Deblinger, E. (2000). Trauma focused cognitive behavior therapy: An empirical update. *Journal of Interpersonal Violence, 15,* 1203–23.

De Bellis, M. D. (2001). Developmental traumatology: The psychobiological development of maltreated children and its implications for research, treatment, and policy. *Development and Psychopathology, 13,* 539–64.

England, M. J., & Cole, R. F. (1998). Preparing for communities of care for child and family mental health for the twenty-first century. *Child and Adolescent Psychiatric Clinics of North America, 7,* 469–81.

Ghuman, H. S., Weist, M. D., & Sarles, R. M. (Eds.) (2002). *Providing mental health services to youth where they are: School- and community-based approaches.* New York: Brunner-Routledge.

Goenjian, A. K., Karayan, I., Pynoos, R. S. et al. (1997). Outcome of psychotherapy among early adolescents after trauma. *American Journal of Psychiatry, 154,* 536–42.

Hansen, S., & Saxe, G. N. (2009). Trauma Systems Therapy: A replication of the model. Integrating cognitive-behavioral play therapy into child and family treatment. In A. A. Drewes (Ed.), *Blending play therapy with cognitive-behavioral therapy: Evidence-based and other effective treatments and techniques* (pp. 139–64). Hoboken, NJ: John Wiley & Sons, Inc.

Henggeler, S. W., Schoenwald, S. K., Borduin, C. M., Rowland, M. D., & Cunningham, P. B. (1998). *Multisystemic treatment of antisocial behavior in children and adolescents.* New York: Guilford Press.

March, J. S., Amaya-Jackson, L., Murray, M. C., & Schulte, A. (1998). Cognitive-behavioral psychotherapy for children and adolescents with posttraumatic disorder after a single-incident stressor. *Journal of the American Academy of Child and Adolescent Psychiatry, 37,* 585–93.

Perry, B. D., & Pollard, R. (1998). Homeostasis, stress, trauma, and adaptation: A neurodevelopmental view of childhood trauma. *Child and Adolescent Psychiatric Clinics of North America, 7,* 33–51.

Perry, B. D., Pollard, R. A., Blakley, T. L., Baker, W. L., & Vigilante, D. (1995). Childhood trauma, the neurobiology of adaptation, and "use-dependent" development of the brain: How "states" become "traits". *Infant Mental Health Journal, 16,* 271–91.

Pumariega, A. J., & Winters, N. C. (Eds.) (2003). *The handbook of child and adolescent systems of care: The new community psychiatry.* San Francisco, CA: Jossey-Bass.

Putnam, F. W. (1997). *Dissociation in children and adolescents: A developmental perspective.* New York: Guilford Press.

Saltzman, W. R., Steinberg, A. M., Layne, C. M., Aisenberg, E., & Pynoos R. S. (2001). A developmental approach to school-based treatment of adolescents exposed to trauma and traumatic loss. *Journal of Child & Adolescent Group Therapy, 11,* 43–56.

Saxe, G. N., Ellis, B. H., Fogler, J., Hansen, S., & Sorkin, B. (2005). Comprehensive care for traumatized children: An open trial examines treatment using Trauma Systems Therapy. *Psychiatric Annals, 35*(5), 443–8.

Saxe, G. N., Ellis, B. H., & Kaplow, J. B. (2007). *Collaborative treatment of traumatized children and teens.* New York: Guilford Press.

Schore, A. N. (2001a). The effects of early relational trauma on right brain development, affect regulation, and infant mental health. *Infant Mental Health Journal, 22,* 201–69.

Schore, A. N. (2001b). The effects of a secure attachment relationship on right brain development, affect regulation, and infant mental health. *Infant Mental Health Journal, 22,* 7–66.

Stroul, B. A., & Friedman, R. M. (1994). *A system of care for children with severe emotional disturbances.* Washington DC: Georgetown University Child Development Center, National Technical Center for Children's Mental Health, Center for Child Health and Mental Health Policy.

van der Kolk, B. A. (1994). The body keeps the score: Memory and the evolving psychobiology of PTSD. *Harvard Review of Psychiatry, 1,* 253–65.

van der Kolk, B. A., & Fisler, R. E. (1994). Child abuse and neglect and loss of self-regulation. *Bull Menninger Clinic, 58,* 145–68.

van der Kolk, B. A., Pelcovitz, D., Roth, S. et al. (1996). Dissociation, somatization, and affect dysregulation: The complexity of adaptation to trauma. *The American Journal of Psychiatry, 153,* 83–93.

Chapter Twenty

PTSD in the Context of Childhood Endangerment: Implications for Assessment and Treatment

Patricia McKinsey Crittenden and Daniele Poggioli

Introduction

Our chapter explores the contribution of attachment theory to treatment of psychological disorder, in this case PTSD in childhood and adolescence. We use a specific case to consider the contribution of three theoretical orientations: (1) moral/religious, (2) medical/cognitive, and (3) attachment/systemic. Our interest is how theory can inform assessment, formulation, and treatment. Our case is an adolescent mother living with her husband and three-year-old daughter in a community for recovering drug addicts. The mother was given the Transition to Adulthood Attachment Interview (TAAI). The TAAI uses a dyadic exploration of past and current history to obtain a sample of discourse about response to danger. The transcribed text of the interview was submitted to formal discourse analysis to identify the mother's primary self-protective strategy as well as specific unresolved traumas and the psychological processing associated with them. Mother and daughter participated in a Strange Situation for preschool-aged children (PAA) to identify the daughter's pattern of attachment.

Our case is relevant to PTSD in childhood and adolescence because, after beginning recovery from drug and alcohol abuse, the mother was diagnosed with PTSD for repeated rape when she was 10–12 years old. Her mother was a prostitute and the perpetrators were her mother's clients. In addition, she had been physically abused and neglected by her mother to the point that she was removed from her mother's care. At that time, she displayed

Post-Traumatic Syndromes in Childhood and Adolescence: A Handbook of Research and Practice, First Edition.
Edited by Vittoria Ardino. © 2011 John Wiley & Sons, Ltd. Published 2011 by John Wiley & Sons, Ltd.

precocious sexual behavior, but the professionals were unaware of the sexual abuse. Retrospectively, it appears that her symptoms of PTSD began when she was being abused, were reduced when she was using alcohol or drugs, and became prominent again shortly after her daughter's birth. At that time, she experienced intense depression and attempted suicide, i.e., postpartum psychosis. This led to her seeking shelter and treatment in a community for recovering drug addicts.

We use this case to discuss how theoretical perspectives inform treatment, focusing on how the Dynamic-Maturational Model (DMM) of attachment and adaptation can add to current understandings and treatment approaches. In particular, we discuss how new approaches to understanding self-protection and sexuality might suggest which types of treatment might be most beneficial – and least harmful.

PTSD in childhood and adolescence: Implications for treatment of different theoretical approaches

The central question addressed in this chapter is whether attachment theory, in particular the Dynamic-Maturational Model of attachment and adaptation (DMM) (Crittenden, 2008), can inform treatment of PTSD in childhood and adolescence beyond current practice. The most commonly used treatments, drug treatment or cognitive-behavioral treatment (Carr, 2004), lack sound empirical data demonstrating their effectiveness (Green, 2003; Stallard, 2005). Moreover neither of these treatments is tied to the psychopathogenesis in childhood or information-processing in adulthood that precedes and under-lies PTSD; instead, both treatments focus on symptom reduction. We argue that they may be insufficient to resolve the array of problems facing children and adolescents with PTSD. Instead, we propose that assessing current psychological processes and their developmental roots can both explain patients' behavior in ways that are comprehensible to and respectful of the patients and also lead to treatment that can reduce suffering and increase adaptive behavior.

PTSD is defined by alternation of associative and dissociative processes around previous exposure to danger. DMM is concerned with individuals' strategies for coping with danger and protecting one's progeny. From the perspective of the DMM, many of the symptoms of PTSD could be viewed as part of a self-protective strategy and, therefore, as being adaptive under some conditions. Indeed, exposure to danger is conceptualized in the DMM as providing crucial information around which to organize self-protective strategies. "Unresolved trauma," on the other hand, is the failure to use this information productively. Trauma experienced early in life is the most likely to be irre-solvable, because children lack the ability to foresee or explain to themselves what has happened. Moreover, such trauma is widely thought to underlie adult PTSD (Cockburn & Pawson, 2007; Kessler et al., 1995; Mills, 2008; Roth et al., 1997; Stovall-McClough & Cloitre, 2006). Therefore, we think that assessment of possible PTSD in childhood and adolescence should address psychological processes by which children make sense of their experience and organize strategies to protect themselves.

A second issue concerns sexuality and sexual trauma. Sexual abuse and assault lead to more severe outcomes, including PTSD and mood disorders, than do physical abuse or accidents (Fergusson, Boden, & Horwood, 2007; Sullivan et al., 2006). Furthermore, mood disorders have been shown to have deleterious effects on the next generation (Downey & Coyne, 1990; Lovejoy et al., 2000). This is true even for the children of mothers who were sexually abused in childhood. We consider the possible reasons for this and how the presence of certain sorts of danger might affect sexual behavior. Throughout, we take a developmental perspective, considering what is threatening at different ages and how danger can be processed by the child's not-yet-mature brain (cf. Kozlowska & Williams, 2009).

Because the DMM is relatively new, we first provide a brief overview of DMM theory as it relates to danger, psychological trauma, and subsequent parental behavior. Then we present a case of PTSD in which sexual trauma occurred in early puberty, followed by a functional breakdown, with assessment and treatment offered during the transition from adolescence to adulthood. This case is used to highlight important issues in the intersection of moral/religious, disorder (symptom-based), and functional approaches to understanding PTSD and sexuality.

The Dynamic-Maturational Model of Attachment and Adaptation

The DMM is an expansion of the Bowlby–Ainsworth theory of attachment. The relevant points of this expansion for the issue of childhood PTSD are (1) reformulation of "patterns of attachment" as self-protective strategies, (2) use of information derived from exposure to danger to generate self-protective and progeny-protective "Type A" strategies, (3) the characteristics of the affect-inhibiting strategies, and (4) conditions that render strategies nonprotective.

Self-protective strategies
Bowlby (1969/1982, 1973, 1980) conceptualized attachment as children's way of protecting themselves from loss of, or separation from, attachment figures. Crittenden (1997b) expanded this to strategies for protection from any sort of danger and to include protection of progeny. Ainsworth (1989) described three basic strategies that infants employ to protect themselves. The "Type A" strategy consists of inhibiting display of negative affect and doing

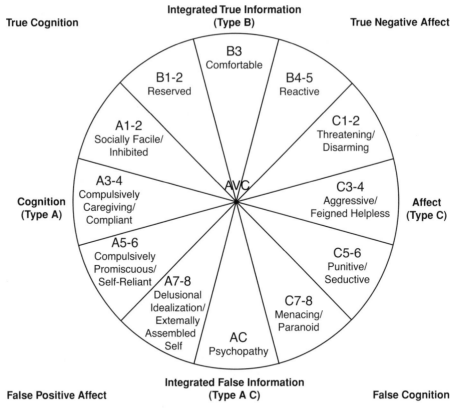

Figure 20.1 A dynamic-maturational model of patterns of attachment in adulthood. © Patricia M. Crittenden, 2001. Reprinted with permission from the author

what protective adults (attachment figures) want. The "Type B" strategy consists of accurately showing how one feels and signaling what one wants. The "Type C" strategy consists of showing exaggerated and mixed negative affects, thus giving confusing signals of what one wants. Crittenden (1997b) expanded Ainsworth's infant strategies to a lifespan developmental array of strategies that includes sexualized strategies (see Figure 20.1).

Danger and information processing

The propensity to form attachment relationships and use information from such relationships to organize self-protective strategies is universal among humans. The information used can be described as "cognition," i.e., temporal information about consequences, and "affect," information about arousal and feelings. Information about danger, threat, or discomfort is usually given priority.

Cognitive information consists of knowing what to do to achieve desired outcomes or to avoid undesired outcomes. It is sensorimotor *procedures* that function without language or consciousness. With language, cognitive information consists of semantic generalizations, both descriptive and prescriptive generalizations. Prescriptive generalizations tell children what they ought to do and, often, set such high standards that most children fail to meet them. If such failure is combined with parental or moral strictures, children may feel innately bad.

Arousal is important because high arousal prepares the individual to act whereas low arousal reduces the probability of action. High arousal is often experienced as negative feelings, i.e., desire for comfort (which motivates approach for protection and comfort), anger (which motivates approach with aggression) or fear (which motivates escape). In infancy, arousal is mediated by the mother who helps the baby to regulate by suckling, stroking the skin, rocking, etc. That is, arousal is regulated by chemical intake (e.g., milk) or rhythmic action (suckling, rocking). Both distress and comfort are experienced as somatic *images*. As they develop, children learn how to regulate their own arousal. Because the mouth and genitals are the most sensitive parts of the body, they often fulfill this function. Interpersonal genital stimulation is not usual until after puberty, but self-stimulation is common among children, especially those who are endangered and unprotected. In these cases, comfort and sexuality become associated even before there is the possibility of reproductive function. Affect is represented linguistically as connotative language, that is, the use of special words or effects to elicit feelings in the listener.

Preconscious, implicit processing is available at birth and consists of *cognitive procedures* of what to do and *affective images* that motivate approach, aggression or escape. Language creates the possibility of abstract and conscious representation of what is known implicitly. However, transformation of procedures and images to words takes additional time; if the danger is immediate, this time cannot be spared and implicitly motivated action with be taken. An adult (a protective attachment figure!) could assist the children to review what happened explicitly, but when the attachment figure is the source of danger (either through what they do or fail to do), it is unlikely that such review will occur. Moreover, if certain things are forbidden to say, they may not be represented linguistically at all. These forbidden-to-say things may both remain beyond conscious awareness and also feel prohibited to say or too dangerous to say even years later when there is no threat. If treatment were to be needed later, such an adult might follow the childhood prohibition, either talking about the trivial or not talking at all. To some therapists they might seem resistant. From a DMM information-processing perspective, they would be prudently self-protective, but in the wrong context.

Integrative processing develops between age seven and the mid-30s, occurs quite slowly, and must be learned. It consists of judiciously using the two basic cortical processes of associating information, i.e., putting ideas together (a posterior cortical process) and disassociating information, i.e., keeping ideas apart (a prefrontal cortical process). Learning to integrate occurs best when arousal is moderate and attachment figures help children to reflect about troubling experiences such that they keep and discard the right bits of information and identify accurately their own contribution to events. Endangered children rarely experience moderate arousal and rarely have protective adults who can help them to learn to integrate. One outcome is that they do not usually understand their own and others' contributions to events.

The compulsive Type A strategies

Children exposed to severe violence or neglect early in life tend to develop Type A strategies of inhibiting the display of negative affect, doing whatever reduces the probability of violence or abandonment, and, when it pleases adults, displaying false positive affect (Crittenden, 1981, 1985). Among the compulsive strategies are compulsive caregiving (of depressed or withdrawn caregivers) and compulsive compliance (to violent caregivers). When these strategies fail to protect children, children may seek other protectors using "indiscriminant" approaches to unfamiliar people. Sometimes these children attract adults who desire sexual contact. This may lead to a "promiscuous," self-protective strategy (Crittenden, 1997a). Children who use a compulsively promiscuous strategy have almost always been neglected and cared for by strangers; many have also been sexually abused.

Individuals using Type A strategies experience conflict between what they know intuitively that they *must* do to be safe and what they are told explicitly that they *should* do. For example, they may experience conflict between how they really feel and the feelings they display. In addition, they often (1) are afraid of both abandonment and also the strangers whom they approach, (2) inhibit evidence of fear and, instead (3) display false positive affect, often false sexualized affect. Because children do not have genuinely sexual feelings, the false sexual affect is often painted on with make-up or worn as sexy clothing. (See Figure 20.1.)

The coercive Type C strategies

Children exposed to unpredictable threats or violence early in life tend to develop Type C strategies of exaggerating displays of negative affect. Often this means using provocative or risk-taking behavior (Crittenden, 1995). The various coercive strategies can be described as threatening, disarming, aggressive, feigned helpless, punitive, and seductive. When these strategies fail to protect children, children may come to fear everyone and to consider anyone a potential target for their revenge, i.e., a menacing/paranoid strategy.

Children using Type C strategies experience conflict between desiring support and being very angry with the supportive figures who have failed them. Because these feelings are incompatible, they display one while inhibiting the other, then contingent with the response that they elicit, they maintain or reverse the display. (See Figure 20.1.)

Trauma

Experiencing danger provides individuals with information that can be used to reorganize their self-protective strategies to make them more adaptive. This "resolves" the danger. That is, the function of the mind after exposure to danger is to review the experience to (1) extract information that is relevant to future safety (and, therefore, self-relevant in the probable future), (2) discard information that is unique to the event (and, therefore, not self-relevant in the probable future), and (3) integrate the self-relevant information with the existing strategy to generate a reorganized, more effective protective strategy. A particularly important subset of information is that about the behavior of the self that might have elicited or precipitated the danger.

Unresolved trauma in childhood occurs before the child has the mental maturity to select and use the crucial information to develop a better strategy; sometimes the essential information is "forbidden." Cases of child sexual abuse very often lead to unresolved trauma because the child may be both unable to integrate the information adequately and also loath to acknowledge forbidden sexual feelings and behavior.

Unresolved trauma "punctuates" strategic behavior with moments of extremely high or low arousal when the implicit procedures or images associated with the past danger are elicited by something in the present. In this moment, strategic behavior breaks down – as though one was walking at ease, then stepped, without expecting anything, on a landmine. The procedures associated with the unresolved past trauma instigate protective routines (compulsions) whereas the images tied to the past event change the individuals' arousal (either lowering it in the direction of depression or raising it toward mania). In either case, the response suggests that the mind has access to information that needs more thorough evaluation.

Depression and intrusions

To fully understand the failure of strategies, depression and intrusions of forbidden negative affect must be considered. Depression can occur when the permissible information does not motivate an effective response. That is, one doesn't know what to do, thinks that failure is likely, and feels very little arousal. Pervasive tiredness and sadness are signifiers of depression. Alternatively, inhibited negative affect might suddenly be intruded intensively without being under regulatory control. In AAIs, these are seen as dramatic and forbidden changes in speech (e.g., shouting scatological or profane language); such intrusions in the discourse are associated with desperate acts in real life (e.g., cutting, violent aggression, suicide). Depression and intrusions reflect the opposite extremes of arousal and are equally dangerous.

A Case Example: Ali's history, symptoms of PTSD, and relationships

Ali's history

In her childhood, Ali lived with her parents, at first together and then separately, then with her grandmother, and later in a religious institution. Her alcoholic father cared tenderly for her, but when drunk, he sometimes beat her mother severely, frightening Ali very much. Ali's mother and grandmother were both prostitutes. When her mother was drunk or unavailable, Ali both cared for her younger sister and also turned to her for comfort. Both children were severely neglected and occasionally beaten.

When she was about 10 years old, Ali began dressing in sexualized ways and was sexually abused by several of her mother's clients. She also began consuming alcohol, possibly initially because the adults gave it to her and, later, to calm herself. Her sexy clothing and visible bruises attracted the attention of school authorities and she and her sister were placed in a religious institution run by nuns. Because she could not sleep, she was prescribed Valium.

When she was 14, Ali "escaped" from the institution and for two years she lived on the streets, surviving by selling – and using – heroin. During that time, she was occasionally protected by an older man who took her home to his family. This man died early, however, leaving Ali to fend for herself.

When she was 17, Ali married Robi, a man 15 years her senior. Their daughter Rachele was born soon after. After Rachele's birth, Ali became very depressed, tried to kill herself, and then entered a Community for recovering drug addicts. After a period in which she became somewhat stable in the Community, her daughter was brought to reside with her; this led to reactivation of many of her symptoms, such that she needed full-time assistance caring for Rachele. At age 20, Ali still lives in the Community near her husband and with their 30-month-old daughter and staff who assist her in caring for Rachele.

Ali's symptoms in the past and at present

When the sexual abuse began, Ali experienced moments of dissociation. These decreased while she was living in the religious institution and were again manifest after she ran away from the institution. During the period of drug addiction, Ali thought she had resolved her problems because the symptoms disappeared. Nevertheless, they reappeared at the birth of her daughter in ways that could easily fit a diagnosis of suicidal postpartum psychosis (Doucet et al., 2009).

When she arrived at the Community, Ali was deeply depressed. However, the symptoms subsided until her daughter arrived three months later. Then her PTSD symptoms returned strongly; she reported losing the thread of her thoughts, feeling "bewitched," and being unaware of time. Most distressing were nightmares during which she reexperienced the past violence. These both interrupted her sleep and, through repetitive flashbacks, haunted her days as well. Ali often felt tired and anxious. She actively tried to keep her mind away from thoughts of the trauma, speaking of sensations of distance and alienation toward other people. She wasn't able to imagine herself in the future and had confused and incomplete memories of the violence she suffered. Discussions of her past put her in a state of alert fearfulness such that she could not concentrate.

Ali's relationships

Ali's experience with women touched the extremes: her mother was herself victimized, was abusive and neglectful to Ali, and failed to protect Ali from sexual abuse. On the other hand, the nuns protected her, but also restricted her and disapproved of the moral conditions of her family.

Ali's experience with men is even more complex because it often combined positive and negative qualities in the same person. That is, her father was tender to her, but attacked her mother. Her mother's customers probably gave her money and attention, but also violated her sexually. Probably the most supportive man in Ali's childhood was the married man who gave her shelter and good advice. Finally, Robi, Ali's husband and Rachele's father, combined qualities of both Ali's father and the supportive man. That is, Robi was himself a drug abuser who, 10 years earlier, had been a resident of the same Community. From his perspective, Ali seemed childlike to the extent that, before they came to the Community, he cared for Rachele, their home, and even Ali – as a father would. From Ali's perspective, Robi was a bit superficial emotionally. These differences produced intense fighting between them, although there was no physical violence.

Ali's relationship with her daughter was also problematic. At times she was unable to care for her at all and she almost always felt out of synchrony with her. Their relationship was complicated by Ali's experience of having had to care for her younger sister and also turning to her sister as an attachment figure when their mother was unavailable.

Treatment of drug addiction and PTSD in the Community

The Community where Ali resides was established to promote recovery from drug addiction. In cases of dual diagnosis, psychotherapy may be offered. The treatment is cognitive therapy, within the context of the Community's moral/ethical belief system.

Treatment of addiction

As noted in materials distributed by the Community, the Community in which Ali resides seeks to introduce a lifestyle rooted in responsible personal behavior through social interaction, work, study, and athletic activity. The goal is to enable people to live realistically, with continuity, coherence, and a set of universally recognized human and social values that are completely opposed to those developed through addiction. These values are internalized through a process of recovery, usually taking three years or more.

The Community recognizes the family as central to a full and responsible life and, therefore, welcomes couples. To facilitate recovery, members of a couple initially have no direct contact with each other, but are reunited gradually, permitting the relationship to be rebuilt on a new and solid foundation.

The Community is organized as a microcosm of society (with staff representing desirable components of the outer world). Contact with outer society is used on an individual basis, when it is opportune to permit gradual and progressive return to the family and social context.

Ali and Robi currently live separately in single-gender residences in the Community. For three months, Rachele remained with her grandmother, but now lives with her mother and a rotating set of staff who help to care for her.

Treatment of PTSD

From the beginning, Ali refused pharmacological treatment, taking only melatonin for the night. She began individual psychotherapy for her PTSD after her daughter arrived because her symptoms increased and she had problems tolerating her daughter (e.g., she felt too exhausted to get up when Rachele cried in the night). Although treatment is individual, it is overseen by Community staff to ensure that it is consistent with the Community's program.

Cognitive therapy is being used to elaborate both Ali's family history and her mother's direct and indirect responsibility for the abuse that Ali suffered. The initial objective, establishing a trusting therapeutic relationship, has been slow and difficult to achieve and, after three years, is still in progress. Because Ali has a tendency to inhibit her feelings, she does not easily recognize them, even in simple daily events. In her treatment, therefore, integration of the cognitive and affective components of daily events proceeds in parallel with acknowledgment of past traumatic events. Because Ali has a very limited ability to reflect integratively, particular attention is given to (1) reconstructing the temporal order of the traumatic events and (2) reducing Ali's feelings of guilt.

After 18 months in the Community, Ali began to speak about her sexual abuse in early puberty. Until then, she had only spoken of physical violence from her mother. In order to re-elaborate this trauma, Ali, according to her therapist, needed to (a) recognize the traumatizing events and their repercussions, (b) relax and free previously unexpressed feelings associated with the sexual abuse,

(c) explore the range of her feelings from those of being victimized to those tied to her family, (d) carry out new cognitive appraisals of the abuse and, especially, (e) face the sense of guilt, inadequacy, and impotence that are frequent among victims of sexual abuse.

Six months later and in relation to a fight with another recovering addict, Ali fled from the Community, abandoning both her daughter and Robi. She was found a few hours later at the railway station in a dissociative state without a clear plan of what she would do next.

At present, Ali is again in the community, raising Rachele with assistance, suffering nightmares that have led her to use heroin again, complaining of numerous psychosomatic symptoms, and living apart from Robi who would prefer that they leave the community, but stays to maintain contact with Rachele.

The attachment perspective

Our interest was in what the DMM could add to the clinical understanding of Ali. Her primary diagnoses were chemical dependency and PTSD. We wondered whether knowing how she currently processed information, what threatened her, and what strategy she used to protect herself and how her childhood history connected (or didn't connect) with her current state would be useful. We were especially aware that DMM assessment methods often yield results that are not obvious and may be at odds with what symptom diagnoses and moral standards suggest is needed. We wondered if using these assessments would reveal any new perspectives on Ali that might be helpful to her.

DMM assessments for early childhood are nonverbal, observational procedures. In the case of 30-month-old Rachele, we used the Strange Situation, classified using the Preschool Assessment of Attachment (Crittenden, 1992). The PAA has been validated in more than 15 published studies, and in two studies (Crittenden, Claussen, & Kozlowska, 2007; Spieker & Crittenden, 2010) has been shown to be superior in precursor, concurrent, and subsequent validating measures and conditions to the alternative assessment, the MacArthur method for using the Strange Situation (Cassidy, Marvin, & the MacArthur Attachment Working Group, 1992). Moreover, the PAA is especially suited to children who are a risk – as Rachele was.

The DMM assessment for older adolescents is the TAAI, coded with the DMM discourse analysis that was developed for the Adult Attachment Interview (DMM-AAI). To date, there are no studies of the TAAI, but there are now quite a few using the DMM-AAI. Based on these studies, it appears that a number of serious disorders can be described as being typical of patients using a Type A compulsive strategy:

1. Most abusive and neglectful mothers of young children were classified as having dismissed unresolved trauma in an idealizing Type A strategy, sometimes in a depressed form (Seefeldt, 1997).

2. A subgroup of women with eating disorder used a compulsive compliant strategy (Ringer & Crittenden, 2007).
3. Most incestuous sexual offenders were classified as delusionally idealizing of their mothers (Wolsley, 2004).
4. Cases of diagnosed psychosis often displayed both compulsive compliance and delusional idealization (Crittenden, 2008).
5. A small subgroup of very serious cases of PTSD, usually those with serious comorbidity, showed disorganized unresolved trauma with compulsive caregiving, compliance, and sometimes promiscuity and delusional idealization (Crittenden & Heller, under review).

Diagnoses associated with Type C include:

1. Most cases of eating disorders have imagined unresolved trauma, together with obsession with revenge (Ringer & Crittenden, 2007).
2. Avoidant personality disorder is classified often as having unresolved trauma and triangulated obsession with revenge (Crittenden & Kulbotton, 2008; Rindal, 2000).
3. Most cases of PTSD have complex unresolved trauma and obsession with revenge (Crittenden & Heller, under review).
4. Borderline personality disorder appears to combine the characteristics of (1) the psychoses, (2) Type A PTSD, and (3) triangulated personality disorders.

Given Ali's presentation and diagnoses, we expect her to be classified as Type A with disorganized unresolved traumas, plus depression.

Attachment assessment of Ali and her daughter

In order to address Ali's self-protective strategy, we gave Ali the Transition to Adulthood Attachment Interview (TAAI). To better understand her relationship with her daughter, we asked them to participate in a Strange Situation.

TAAI   The TAAI is a semi-structured, audio-recorded interview that explores both childhood history and current issues in late adolescence. It does so by juxtaposing semantic probes with requests for episodic evidence. The speaker is then asked to synthesize information from related questions to articulate an integrated understanding. The TAAI is transcribed verbatim, retaining all dysfluence and mis-spoken words or phrases. The transcribed text is then coded for (1) dysfluence of speech and (2) incoherence of thought. The dysfluence and incoherence are then assigned to memory systems (i.e., cognitive procedures, affective images, semantic generalizations, connotative language, recalled episodes, and reflective integration). Based on (1) the severity of the errors of speech and thought, (2) the topics that produce dysfluence, and (3) the degree of transformation of meaning, the transcript is assigned to a subclassification (see Figure 20.1). In some cases, unresolved trauma and loss, depression, and/or intrusions are also assigned.

Ali's TAAI was given all three: (1) her subclassification was compulsive promiscuity with (2) unresolved trauma, in a dismissed form, for her parents' domestic violence, her physical abuse and neglect, and sexual abuse by her mother's clients as well as dismissed unresolved loss for a 45-year-old man who had treated her as a daughter. The whole of this was modified by strong markers of depression.

The TAAI suggests that Ali seriously distorts her understanding of her experience by (1) inhibiting true negative affect, (2) doing whatever other people require in order to elicit their caregiving, and (3) holding herself responsible for what happened to her. Specifically, Ali displays false sexual interest and engages in partner-pleasing sexual behavior. Sexuality and males feature strongly in Ali's experience – in contradictory ways. From her mother and grandmother, she experienced that having sexual access to males was essential to survival and more important than caring for one's children. From her mother's partners, she learned to display false sexual desire (e.g., dressing sexually) and tolerate sexual violation without protest; she may also have experienced more interpersonal synchrony and have been given more attention than with her mother or grandmother.

Two features of Ali's use of the compulsively promiscuous strategy stand out: its early onset with precocious sexuality prior to puberty and Ali's attraction to older men who are more like fathers than lovers. Functionally, sexual signals and behavior appear to substitute for the failed attachment to her parents and grandmother. Her inhibition of negative affect was probably adaptive when she was a child and could not change the dangerous conditions of her life. Now, however, this inhibition prevents her from establishing close and enduring attachments with her husband and daughter and, in addition, prevents her from using her feelings to avoid dangerous situations. To protect herself and her daughter, Ali needs to attend to the alerting and warning function of negative affect (i.e., anger, fear, desire for comfort, and pain). She also needs to recognize that sexual feelings sometimes indicate a desire for comfort.

PAA   Ali and Rachele's Strange Situation was classified with the PAA method (Crittenden, 1992). During the Strange Situation, Ali watched her daughter continuously, but her face showed no feelings. Her body was closed, i.e., there was no obvious way for Rachele to approach her. When the stranger came in, Rachele greeted her, then became competitive when her mother and the stranger began talking. Once the stranger turned her attention to Rachele, she settled, apparently "forgetting" about her mother. Ali slipped back into silence and stillness. Rachele seemed unconcerned when her mother left and failed to greet her upon her return. Ali just sat and silently watched. Rachele didn't protest at the second departure either. She became more relaxed when the stranger returned and played with her. When her mother entered, she was already facing the door and they shared a lovely, long mutual smile. It was completely unexpected. Her mother squatted down nearby and Rachele played, alone but facing her watching mother. When the stranger turned Rachele away from her mother, they both accepted this – and both seemed saddened by it. Rachele's lack of connection and initiation in a context of wanting her mother suggests a depressed Type A strategy.

The crucial points to extract from the PAA are that Ali does not initiate positive affect and Rachele, probably because she is not fully dependent upon her mother for her basic care and protection, has not acquired a potentially adaptive compulsive caregiving strategy. If she had, this might have provided a way for mother and daughter to find each other. Both appear to enjoy and want closeness, but only luck makes it possible and only in brief spurts.

Functional formulation of Ali's problems
A functional formulation takes the individual's history, current development, family constellation, diagnoses, and attachment assessments into account to understand which life functions are causing difficulties. In the case of Ali, the smallest of the three clusters of PTSD patients, those with co-morbidity, multiple confused unresolved traumas, and a pervasive and complex compulsive strategy, describes Ali's situation, symptoms, and behavior well (Crittenden & Heller, under review). In thinking about a formulation, we keep both the general picture of this cluster in mind and also the specific details of Ali's situation.

Strategy for coping with danger
Ali grew up in a context of observing her mother being beaten, pervasive and severe neglect, intermittent moderate physical abuse, repeated and promiscuous sexual abuse by strangers beginning in early puberty, institutionalization, and responsibility for herself from age 15. To cope with these situations, she turned to strangers for resources, protection, and comfort. The most recent instance is her turning to the Community when she could not manage in her own family. It is noteworthy that Robi did not want to come to the Community, but came because he was committed to her and their child; this bodes well. Ali needs skills (i.e., procedures) for resolving interpersonal problems without having to abandon her family. In addition, Ali both feels herself to be inherently "bad" and unworthy, and also has been told by religious and school authorities that she has not lived up to society's standards. That is, Ali knows what she *should do* in general, but not *how to do it* in ordinary social situations, especially those involving negative affect. In sum, Ali may have too many semantic and moral prescriptives and too few procedures for managing intimacy and conflict.

Life roles
Ali's situation can be formulated as having a history of disrupted family relationships that involved too many strangers fulfilling family functions, specifically,

the nuns (in the plural) functioning as a mother, the sexually abusive men functioning intimately, the 45-year-old man functioning like a father. Put another way, Ali has had too little experience with family members who were committed to loving and caring for her and too much experience with strangers (both benevolent and not) functioning in family roles. One functional problem is establishing boundaries around family roles and maintaining long-term, committed, and intimate relationships in ways that are different from relationships with friends and professionals.

Another may be the role of mother to a daughter, the role at which her own mother failed so badly, in part because her mother needed men too much – as does Ali. Ali's TAAI revealed the extent to which Ali overestimates her own responsibility for causing bad and dangerous events. This, combined with the brutality of her experiences as a child and her mother's rejection of her, may have generated in Ali a global and inexplicit dread of the harm she could cause as a mother, particularly as the mother of a daughter. *Because* Ali loves her daughter and wants to protect her from harm – as a good mother should – and in the context of believing herself to be inherently bad, even dangerous, Ali may have felt (not "thought") that the only way to protect Rachele from herself was to remove or even kill herself. Because her attribution of self-responsibility is highly distorted (i.e., irrational), because the full story of her childhood was not known, and because the illogical connection between Ali's mother and Ali as a mother was not explicit (even to Ali), her postpartum suicidal behavior and subsequent breakdown when Rachele came to the Community could not easily be understood as desperate attempts to protect her daughter from herself.

In other words, Ali may expect to fail as a mother and, knowing implicitly the cost to a daughter of such failure (but dismissing it explicitly as not causing her to suffer), she may both want and be unable to accept her own daughter. Explicit awareness of her own experience might enable her to differentiate it from her daughter's, enabling her not to act as her mother did and to recognize ways in which Robi is unlike her father and her mother's lovers. At a minimum, this explanation can reduce her feeling of shame and, possibly, enable her to respect herself for her good intentions.

Affect regulation

Ali's arousal vacillated between dangerously low (depressed) and dangerously high (agitated). She is prone to activating intrusions of intense negative affect. For example, she ran away from the institution, tried to kill herself, fought with another Community resident and, again, ran away. It appears that Ali flees when she can perceive no way to avoid failure if she stays. Since late childhood, Ali has also managed dangerously high arousal with chemical substances; she can sustain family life longer with drugs than without. Functionally, Ali needs to find ways to spend increasing amounts of time in a state of moderate arousal. Although trauma is known to change brain functioning (as does all experience, albeit not in such a dramatic response to a single event), the question is whether the brain is sufficiently plastic to respond to treatment (Diseth, 2005; Lester, Wong, & Hendren, 2003). The facts that the brain is the most plastic organ of the body and that Ali is in a naturally occurring period of maturational change should work to her advantage.

Precipitating conditions

Two conditions appear to account for variations in Ali's well-being. When she was being sexually abused, she had intrusive nightmares and turned to alcohol. Both symptoms were relieved when she was put in the religious institution in childhood, but even so she fled from it. On the street, drugs calmed her and she thought she was OK. But the birth of her daughter sent her into a suicidal "psychotic" depression. Coming to the Community relieved that – until her daughter arrived and then the nightmares returned. When her daughter was 21 months old, Ali first recalled and spoke about her sexual abuse.

A functional interpretation of this, using DMM notions of information about danger and self-protection and progeny protection, is that, when Ali is unsafe or feels her daughter to be unsafe, her mind keeps jarring her into wary alertness. Both drugs and structured, safe institutions calm her excessive, but self-protective, arousal. When her daughter was born, Ali felt overwhelmed by the impossibility of caring for her (i.e., protecting her progeny) and became depressed. Once in the Community, Ali felt better – and was actually safer and believed that her daughter was safe with her grandmother. When her daughter arrived in the Community, all the alarms went off again. How could she protect her daughter? When her daughter approached two years of age and began displaying coy/flirtatious behavior, did Ali suddenly fear that she could not protect her from sexual abuse? Was this progeny-protective fear behind her nightmares? If it was, it might be a powerful, strengths-oriented way to reframe her symptoms and to give her some of the human dignity that failing to fulfill religious and social prescriptives denied her.

If this is or approximates Ali's psychological and interpersonal situation, what sort of treatment does she need?

Treatment tied to the DMM functional formulation of depression, unresolved trauma and loss, and compulsive promiscuity   Here are several basic principles of a DMM approach to treatment. These include ensuring that the individual is safe before psychological treatment is undertaken. Ali's decision to enter the Community was a major step forward in making life safer for her and her family. The Community provides a predictable structure to daily life, freedom from drug use, and support for daily tasks that Community members cannot yet manage independently.

Concomitant with safety of the self is safety of one's attachment figures and attached children. In the Community, Ali feels safe and knows that Robi is safe. But when Rachele is brought to live with her, Ali perceives danger to Rachele. If the professionals do not understand this, they are likely to focus on Ali's mothering skills, seeking to bring her closer to Rachele. To Ali, this will be perceived as *increasing* the danger to her beloved daughter. To protect Rachele, Ali may feel that she needs to withdraw, maybe even to go away all together. However, Ali, not understanding her motivations as we conceive them through the DMM, would only see herself as having failed again. Moreover, these desperate attempts to protect her daughter would be seen by everyone, Rachele included, as Ali's rejection of her daughter. Reframing Ali's motivation positively could change how the Community managed her access to Rachele by, for example, having her reside longer with her grandmother and letting Ali visit her there in a protected way or by focusing first on Ali's negative self-attributions before asking her to assume parental functions. This would prevent psychological harm to both Ali and Rachele. Bringing Rachele in too soon may be an example of professionals' well-intentioned decisions that, in fact, caused harm. Furthermore, if our hypothesis that Ali feared harming her daughter and acted in a distorted understanding of loving and protecting Rachele was helpful to Ali, then she could eventually be guided to find the same sort of love from her mother – who let her be taken to an institution. Making the connection of love across three generations visible to Ali would be a gift of immeasurable value.

Another principle is that one must be free of dominating chemical influences, whether from prescribed or non-prescribed drugs, in order to change one's psychological processing and behavior. Ali has chosen to give up both illicit and prescribed drugs. As long as she can remain reasonably stable, this is likely to be beneficial.

Thirdly, the DMM approach to adaptation addresses the importance of information-processing for informing behavior. It presumes that thoughts and feelings are neither good nor bad; they are simply information whose meaning must be discerned and made self-relevant before appropriate action can be taken. From this perspective, Ali's depression would be seen as information about the futility of her current strategies and the need for reflective time in which to review her information, generate new strategies, and practice using them. Her intrusions of intense negative affect, tied to trauma, would be viewed as providing information that has previously been overlooked or misunderstood. The suggestion would be to attend to both sorts of information, to transform it into words, and to reconsider, in the present situation of early parenthood, what is meaningful now and what not. Only then can one decide what action to take. Residence in the Community might give Ali the chance to decouple thought and feeling from action by permitting her to express negative affect safely, promoting the transformation of feeling and intentions to words, and identifying the alternation of depression and agitation. Indeed, simply, recognizing these cycles might help Ali to know what to expect and thus modulate her arousal.

On the other hand, the Community's moral/evaluative approach could misfire for Ali by too quickly substituting prescriptive ideas for her own conclusions. Because she already organizes her thoughts semantically around prescriptive rules that she cannot meet behaviorally, she might conclude that she is a failure. Therefore, Ali may need to be encouraged to accept having negative feelings, to understand that they are meaningful and useful, and, slowly, to learn to regulate the feelings and select judiciously when and how to act on them. Too much attention to values and standards might interfere with this process.

It might be useful to outline with Ali some reasons why memories might be coming back now and the importance of extracting information from the flashbacks. Possibly she can reduce the need for the nightmares if she keeps a written diary of what she recalls. By having it safely kept in print, her mind may relax a bit. Once the traumatic memories exist on paper or in a listener's mind, Ali can begin considering what is relevant for her now. The timing of Rachele approaching two years old when Ali recalled her own sexual abuse should be explored.

A fourth DMM principle of treatment is that the work takes place in the individual's "zone of proximal development" (Vygotsky, 1987). For Ali, this is the establishment of family integrity, attachment to her daughter and husband, and, psychologically, management of her swings in arousal. Given her compulsively promiscuous strategy, Ali needs to focus on close, permanent family relationships, and to avoid relying on strangers to relieve her of problems tied to family members. By separating couples and arranging within-gender communal living, supported by Community staff, the treatment reflects Ali's existing strategy. It might be better if Ali were supported in living with her husband and daughter. Especially for Rachele, time is of the essence; to understand the meaning of family, Rachele needs to live with her family and without non-family. If Ali feels that she is the source of danger to Rachele, her need to be apart from Rachele (to protect her) conflicts with Rachele's need to identify her attachment figure. Possibly having Robi present in the family unit could reduce this conflict by enabling Ali to feel confident that Robi will protect their daughter. In addition, living with Robi with daytime staff support could give Ali the occasion to learn needed conflict resolution strategies. Robi has already demonstrated his willingness to support Ali and Rachele; with guidance on how to foster Ali's sense of safety, his assistance should be used in preference to that of professionals.

A service common in Scandinavia might suit Ali and her family well. There, families with severe problems (including especially drug addiction) are housed in single-family apartments within a therapeutic community building. The family is provided with necessary supplies, such as food, but they are responsible for preparing and serving it within their apartment. It is particularly worth noting that cooking, eating, dressing, bathing, and sleeping are carried out in the privacy of each family's apartment. This marks an important boundary between public and private life that has been violated far too often for Ali.

Because in the DMM every strategy is the right solution to some problem, but none is best for all problems, Ali needs to increase her repertoire of strategies. Some of this can be fairly simple and straightforward, like knowing what to do in daily interpersonal situations. Other issues will take longer. For example, discovering from review of her flashbacks ways that she contributed and contributes now to making herself a potential victim is essential, but risky. Care will need to be taken to ensure that Ali does not hold herself responsible for her childhood adaptations, while still understanding how continuing them in adulthood might be undesirable. The issue becomes differentiating making a causal contribution from bearing responsibility for that contribution. This distinction is not clear to all professionals and could be difficult for Ali to grasp without excessive self-blame.

Finally, a core idea of the DMM is that Types A and C are psychological opposites. Ali's TAAI suggests that she consistently uses a Type A strategy. Based on that, she would need to attend to affect more fully, reduce drawing conclusions based on temporal order alone, and rely less on semantic suggestions from others – no matter how helpful and appropriate these seem to be.

General conclusions

This case highlights issues tied to theory of treatment. Ali's actual treatment is influenced by two traditions: moral/religious and cognitive therapy. Although it is an overstatement in both cases, the moral/religious tradition reflects the belief that "craziness" is tied to good and evil, whereas cognitive therapy is tied to the more recent notion of craziness as a disease, i.e., mental illness. The DMM of attachment and adaptation reflects a third, more recent, notion: that maladaptive behavior reflects attempts to protect self and one's progeny. This notion, however, has roots going back at least to the 1960s (e.g., Szasz, 1960, 1961). Viewed functionally, each tradition offers something to Ali and individuals like her.

Moral/religious tradition

The Community first and foremost offers safety. In safety, one can begin to give up crutches, for example, substances. However, the function of these crutches in helping to regulate negative affect may have been insufficiently explored. In particular, the management of Ali's relationship with her daughter may have unintentionally harmed that relationship through lack of awareness of Ali's very deep and inexplicit dread that she could harm her daughter – as she herself was harmed by her mother. In addition, a community offers companionship and guided interpersonal experiences. Again, these are valuable, but in the Community in question, they come at the expense of family relationships and possibly misconstrue intimate and affiliative/professional relationships. For individuals using a Type A strategy, especially those using a compulsively promiscuous strategy, this could be detrimental. Finally, the emphasis on moral/religious precepts may reify Ali's existing self-blame. (On the contrary, saying Ali bears no responsibility for her behavior errs in the opposite direction and would give her no assistance in changing her behavior.)

Learning theory tradition

Cognitive therapy clearly has more sophisticated and powerful techniques and the Community acknowledges this by employing individual psychotherapy in cases of dual diagnoses, i.e., substance abuse and something else. Cognitive techniques take advantage of learning theory, but possibly are less explicit about affect. For Ali and other individuals using Type A strategies, affect, particularly negative affect, is central to their problems. Of course, cognitive techniques can effectively reduce the display of unwanted negative affect, but, possibly, in cases where the individual uses a Type A strategy, the meaning and function of the negative affect need to be explored before the display is regulated. Particularly in cases of PTSD, intrusive thoughts and deadened affect may contain important information for the individual in the present. Along the same line of thinking, reframing negative affect as information and symptoms as being part of strategies might allow troubled individuals to discover that they have competence and that their minds are working on their behalf. This is quite different from construing distress and maladaptive behavior as either moral laxity or a disorder with symptoms. Finally, using individual treatment for problems that were generated in past relationships and that affect current relationships also seems to miss the mark. A particular risk when couples and families are not treated together is that they may develop in incompatible ways such that their unshared experiences (e.g., Ali and Robi) or incompatible needs (e.g., Ali and Rachele) will stand in the way of marital or family unity.

Attachment/systemic

The DMM is a metatheory. That is, it integrates the best contributions of other theories (as opposed to competing with them). Central to the DMM are (1) the biological roots of behavior, both those that are unique to each individual and, even more importantly, those that are universal to humans; (2) empirical evidence regarding developmental processes; (3) information-processing; (4) general systems theory and all its derivatives; (5) learning theory; and (6) Gestalt theory. From this multifaceted perspective, the DMM treats behavior, even symptomatic or maladaptive behavior, as meaningful, dynamic, and interpersonal.

To use Ali and her family as an example, Ali's PSTD symptom of nightmares might be reframed in a meaningful ways as her mind's signal that danger to her daughter needs her attention, but that it isn't understood well enough to enable her to act consciously and protectively. Therefore, Ali should seek help in discovering what agitates her about her daughter's safety. This could lead both to her discovery of her fear regarding herself as a mother (foretold by the TAAI) and focus her on her daughter's coy behavior. Attending to the coy signals that develop in toddlerhood would help her to protect Rachele from eliciting sexual abuse. This is an attachment function, protecting the self and progeny. Ali's behavior, i.e., the timing of the onset of nightmares, suggests both that she feels herself to be a threat and also that she is developmentally aware that toddlerhood initiates new risks, including risks tied to sexuality. Of course, this information is known implicitly, i.e., outside of Ali's conscious awareness. Having a therapist engage with Ali around discovering meanings that can be derived from the timing of the nightmares and its possible protective function might (1) give Ali a basis in reality for feeling herself to be a responsible parent, (2) render the nightmares unnecessary, now that their possible meanings are being actively considered, and (3) enable Ali and her therapist to consider whether or not Rachele actually needs protection from her mother or sexually inappropriate men or both. Finally, this "technique" opens the door to thinking developmentally about Rachele and, for the past, about aspects of Ali's behavior that might have been (or even might still be) misinterpreted by men.

Along a similar line, addressing sexual signals might open discussions of the multiple possible meanings of any given behavior. That is, the behavior might appear sexual, but its function might be attachment and self-protection. Freeing Ali from believing that sexual body parts and behavior have only sexual meanings might enable her to feel less guilt about her contribution to her sexual abuse; instead she could reinterpret her precocious sexualized behavior as comfort-seeking. The same approach could be applied to thinking about maternal rejection: maybe her rejection of Rachele and her mother's rejection of her can both be understood as protection.

The DMM's careful attention to information-processing as a developmental process (Pivalizza, 2006) would guide the therapist to avoid using verbal and integrative approaches before implicit procedural and imaged information was made conscious. Further, the therapist would expect to need to assist Ali in learning how to verbalize implicitly known information and, later, to integrate it into episodes and, later yet, to reflect upon its meaning. Because the latter two processes are common in psychotherapy but probably beyond Ali's capacity early on, understanding the interaction of childhood history with the developmental processes underlying language and conscious thought would promote more successful treatment (Diseth, 2005).

Gestalt theory offers an especially important perspective. Once symptoms are viewed as information and as operating within psychological and interpersonal self-protective strategies, their import changes completely. This change has almost nothing to do with the accumulation of symptoms and, instead, is based on their functional organization. The whole is very different from the array of its components and eliminating any specific component would be seen as unimportant. Indeed, removal of one symptom would likely result in another behavior fulfilling its function, i.e., symptom substitution. Instead, focusing on the strategy would reduce the need for symptoms altogether.

Finally, a systemic approach is crucial to good treatment. The systems involved are Ali and her childhood family, Ali and her spouse, Rachele and both her parents, and Ali, her family, and the services. Other systems could be listed, but these are central. It is especially important that the "natural" systems of Ali and her family be protected from violation and supported in a harmonious process of change. The "artificial" inclusion of professionals in that process should be considered carefully to ensure both that the professionals form real relationships with Ali and her family and that these relationships respect, and do not usurp, her family relationship.

Conclusion

The three theory-based approaches offered each have the potential to help individuals suffering from PTSD. The first two have notable limits and possible undesirable effects. Specifically, the moral/religious approach lacks techniques for addressing PTSD symptoms and may have detrimental effects on family structure and stability and on self-respect. The cognitive therapy approach treats symptoms more effectively, but addresses the import of feeling and the centrality of interpersonal and familiar issues too little. These limitations could lead to symptom substitution and the weakening of family relationships.

The DMM approach being offered is more comprehensive. It is a strengths approach that reframes symptoms as mis-aimed attempts to solve important problems. It presumes that all humans are using the information made available by experience to improve their lives and those of their children. This perspective shifts someone like Ali, who could so easily appear as a damaged victim who was likely to transmit the effects of that damage to her child, to a coping adult with a particular developmental history that is functioning in the present to highlight risks and the need for support. It is a dynamic developmental approach that finds meaning in behavior based on the maturation and experience of the individual and finds the potential for change to be present in the discomfort experienced by troubled individuals. Finally, it is an interpersonal approach that seeks interpersonal meaning in each individual's behavior and works in an interpersonal context to strengthen protective and reproductive relationships. Framed this way, everyone has a basis for being understood, feeling good about themselves, and using difficult experiences to promote resiliency and family integrity.

References

Ainsworth, M. D. S. (1989). Attachments beyond infancy. *American Psychologist, 44,* 709–16.

Bowlby, J. (1969, 1982). *Attachment and loss. Vol. I: Attachment* (2nd ed.). New York: Basic Books. (Original work published 1969.)

Bowlby, J. (1973). *Attachment and loss. Vol. II: Separation.* New York: Basic Books.

Bowlby, J. (1980). *Attachment and loss. Vol. III: Loss, sadness and depression.* New York: Basic Books.

Carr, A. (2004). Interventions for post-traumatic stress disorder in children and adolescents. *Pediatric Rehabilitation, 7,* 231–44.

Cassidy, J., Marvin, R. S., & the MacArthur Attachment Working Group of the John D. and Catherine T. MacArthur Network on the Transition from Infancy to Early Childhood (1992). *Attachment organization in preschool children: Procedures and coding manual.* Unpublished coding manual, The Pennsylvania State University.

Cockburn, J., & Pawson, M. E. (2007). *Psychological challenges in obstetrics and gynecology: The clinical management* (pp. 193–208). New York: Springer.

Crittenden, P. M. (1981) Abusing, neglecting, problematic, and adequate dyads: Differentiating by pattern of interaction. *Merrill-Palmer Quarterly, 27,* 1–27.

Crittenden, P. M. (1985). Social networks, quality of parenting, and child development. *Child Development, 56,* 1299–313.

Crittenden, P. M. (1992). Children's strategies for coping with adverse home environments: an interpretation using attachment theory. *Child Abuse & Neglect, 16,* 329–43.

Crittenden, P. M. (1997a). Patterns of attachment and sexuality: Risk of dysfunction versus opportunity for creative integration. In L. Atkinson & K. J. Zuckerman (Eds.), *Attachment and psychopathology* (pp. 47–93). New York: Guilford Press.

Crittenden, P. M. (1997b). Toward an integrative theory of trauma: A dynamic-maturation approach. In D. Cicchetti & S. Toth (Eds.), *The Rochester Symposium on developmental psychopathology, Vol. 10: Risk, trauma, and mental processes* (pp. 34–84). Rochester, NY: University of Rochester Press.

Crittenden, P. M. (2008). *Raising parents: Attachment, parenting, and child safety.* Cullompton: Willan.

Crittenden, P. M., Claussen, A. H., & Kozlowska, K. (2007). Choosing a valid assessment of attachment for clinical use: A comparative study, *Australia New Zealand Journal of Family Therapy, 28,* 78–87.

Crittenden, P. M., & Heller, M. B. (under review). Validating the Dynamic-Maturational Model of attachment and adaptation: A comparison of patients with chronic PTSD, mixed-diagnosis patients, and non-patients.

Crittenden, P. M., & Kulbotton, G. R. (2007). Familial contributions to ADHD: An attachment perspective. *Tidsskrift for Norsk Psykologorening, 10,* 1220–9.

Diseth, T. H. (2005). Dissociation in children and adolescents as reaction to trauma: An overview of conceptual issues and neurobiological factors. *Nordic Journal of Psychiatry, 59,* 79–91.

Doucet, S., Dennis, C., Letourneau, N., & Blackmore, E. R. (2009). Differentiation and clinical implications of postpartum depression and postpartum psychosis. *Journal of Obstetric, Gynecologic, & Neonatal Nursing, 38,* 269–79.

Downey, G., & Coyne, J. C. (1990). Children of depressed parents: An integrative review. *Psychological Bulletin, 108,* 50–76.

Fergusson, D. M., Boden, J.M., & Horwood, L. J. (2007). Exposure to single parenthood in childhood and later mental health, educational, economic, and criminal behavior outcomes. *Archives of General Psychiatry, 64,* 1089–95.

Fergusson, D. M., Boden, J. M., & Horwood, J. (2010). Tests of causal links between alcohol abuse or dependence and major depression. *Archives of General Psychiatry, 66*(3), 260–6.

Green, M. R. (2003). Interventions with traumatized children. In L. T. Flaherty (Ed.), *Adolescent psychiatry: Developmental and clinical studies. Annals of the American Society for Adolescent Psychiatry* (Vol. 27, pp. 283–305). Hillsdale, NJ: Analytic Press.

Kessler, R. C., Sonnega, A., Bromet, E., Hughes, M., & Nelson, C. (1995). Post-traumatic stress disorder in the national comorbidity survey. *Archives of General Psychiatry, 52*, 1048–60.

Kozlowska, K., & Williams, L. (2009). Self-protective organization in children with conversion and somatoform disorders. *Journal of Psychosomatic Research, 67*(3), 223–33.

Lester, P., Wong, S. W., & Hendren, R. L. (2003). The neurobiological effects of trauma. In L. T. Flaherty (Ed.), *Adolescent psychiatry: Developmental and clinical studies. Annals of the American Society for Adolescent Psychiatry* (Vol. 27, pp. 259–82). Hillsdale, NJ: Analytic Press.

Lovejoy, M. C., Graczyk, P. A., O'Hare, E., & Neuman, G. (2000). Maternal depression and parenting behavior: A meta-analytic review. *Clinical Psychology Review, 20*, 561–92.

Mills, J. (2008). Attachment deficits, personality structure, and PTSD. *Psychoanalytic Psychology, 25*, 380–5.

Pivalizza, P. J. (2006). Review of post-traumatic stress disorders in children and adolescents. *Journal of Developmental & Behavioral Pediatrics, 27*, 279–80.

Rindal, G. (2000). Attachment patterns in patients diagnosed with avoidant personality disorder [Maskespill, Tilknytningsmxxnster Hos Pasienter med Unnvikende Personlighetsforstyrrelse] (Doctoral dissertation, Institute of Psychology, University of Oslo, Oslo, Norway). (ISBN 82-569-1568-4)

Ringer, F., & Crittenden, P. (2007). Eating disorders and attachment: The effects of hidden processes on eating disorders. *European Eating Disorders Review, 14*, 1–12.

Roth, S., Newman, E., Pelcovitz, D., van der Kolk, B., & Mandel, F. S. (1997). Complex PTSD in victims exposed to sexual and physical abuse: Results from the *DSM–IV* field trial for posttraumatic stress disorder. *Journal of Traumatic Stress, 10*, 539–55.

Seefeldt, L. (1997). Models of parenting in maltreating and non-maltreating mothers (Doctoral dissertation, Faculty of the School of Nursing, University of Wisconsin-Milwaukee, Milwaukee, USA).

Spieker, S., & Crittenden, P. M. (2010). Comparing two attachment classification methods applied to preschool strange situations. *Child Clinical Psychology and Psychiatry, 15*(1), 97–120.

Stallard, P. (2005). Comments on "Interventions for post-traumatic stress disorder in children and adolescents" by Alan Carr: Clinical implications. *Pediatric Rehabilitation, 8*, 29–31.

Stovall-McClough, K. C., & Cloitre, M. (2006). Unresolved attachment, PTSD, and dissociation in women with childhood abuse histories. *Journal of Consulting and Clinical Psychology, 74*, 219–28.

Sullivan, T. P., Fehon, D. C., Andres-Hyman, R. C., Lipschitz, D. S., & Grilo, C. M. (2006). Differential relationships of childhood abuse and neglect subtypes to PTSD symptom clusters among adolescent inpatients. *Journal of Traumatic Stress, 19*, 229–39.

Szasz, T. S. (1960). The myth of mental illness. *American Psychologist, 15*, 113–18.

Szasz, T. S. (1961). *The myth of mental illness: Foundations of a theory of personal conduct.* New York: Hoeber-Harper.

Vygotsky, L. S. (1987). Thought and word [transl. N. Minick]. In R. W. Rieber & A. S. Carlton (Eds.), *The collected works of L. S. Vygotsky.* New York: Plenum Press.

Wolsley, H. (2004). An exploratory study of defensive processes, motivational imagery, attributional style, attachment representations and perceptions of close relationships in Irish adult sexual offenders (submitted for a Doctoral degree in clinical psychology (D Psych Sc) to the School of Psychology, University College Dublin, Ireland).

Chapter Twenty-One

Compassion Fatigue, Vulnerability, and Resilience in Practitioners Working with Traumatized Children

Charles R. Figley, Cheri Lovre, and Kathleen Regan Figley

Introduction

In this penultimate chapter in a book on understanding and helping traumatized children, it is important to understand and help the practitioners who help traumatized children. So here we focus on the costs and benefits of working with traumatized children, day after day, and the ways in which practitioners can increase and maintain their resilience.

Reports of child trauma practitioners, excluding child protection workers, are rare and not reported in the literature because the practitioners love their jobs and know they are appreciated. Rather, they report symptoms similar to PTSD. These symptoms are now called secondary traumatic stress reactions (STS) or compassion fatigue. In addition to reviewing the compassion fatigue theory and research, this chapter suggests practical ways child trauma experts can enjoy their work and practice self-care to minimize their vulnerability and maximize their resilience.

We share in life's sadness and stressors with one of the most vulnerable beings, particularly children who survived abuse (Jenmorri, 2006). We must understand when no one else might. We often stand – literally and figuratively – between our clients and the cruelties they face daily. This comes at an emotional cost. The cost is worth it, of course. Most of us love our jobs and our life's work. But perhaps some perspective offered here may ensure that the cost is reduced. The price is too high when practitioners develop compassion fatigue STS reactions from their work with traumatized children.

Post-Traumatic Syndromes in Childhood and Adolescence: A Handbook of Research and Practice, First Edition. Edited by Vittoria Ardino. © 2011 John Wiley & Sons, Ltd. Published 2011 by John Wiley & Sons, Ltd.

Background

Lovre began in her field as an art and play therapist providing groups for students in schools. Unexpectedly, a principal brought a child who had witnessed his father's homicide to join her group. The father had been killed by an uncle, who used a shotgun at close range during a family gathering at the grandparents' home. Lovre asked the principal to find other students who had lost family members so the whole group could be grief-oriented. At that point, in the 1970s, there was little differentiation in the field between trauma and grief. This would be handled differently now.

Lovre expected to do one 10-week series on grief for these students. At the end of 10 weeks, she realized that children grieve so differently from adults that for some, the loss was just beginning to become "real" and the difficult work was just beginning. This coincided with the school identifying seven more students who needed a grief group. Lovre began a second group. Soon, the local funeral home offered to pay the therapist to do grief groups in the community so children who were not in the schools served by Lovre could also benefit.

Fastforward two years – Lovre is now doing several grief groups in schools and in the community, and is a grant-writer who offers to find funding for a program designed to serve youths dealing with issues related to death. She received two-year start-up funding which was continued a third year. Now she had between 30 and 57 youths per week with whom she was working in a variety of settings: hospital visits to terminally ill children and providing groups at the office for their siblings, grief groups for children who had lost a family member to a variety of kinds of deaths, and anticipatory grief groups for those youths who had a family member dying. The grant also afforded three hours per week with a mentor therapist who had 25 years' experience of working with adults and children, but not specifically with grief. This was early in the years of identifying these kinds of issues and the progression through which grieving children might move.

The rewards were immense. Lovre's love of the work was terrific and she experienced high levels of compassion satisfaction. Lovre always believed that she held a sacred contract to work with children, which was exemplified by a childhood experience. Lovre's best friend had cancer. Although Lovre was scared of losing her friend, she was not afraid of being fully present for her.

The first year Lovre was blessed with opportunities for her to bring the best of herself into her work and to learn by leaps and bounds what kids need in times of grief and loss. The work also raised deeper questions for which she was unprepared. Lovre's childhood religious experience taught her that God was angry and people would be punished for their wrongdoings. She could not reconcile this expression of God with the experiences of the children with whom she worked nor with her own question about the existence of a just and loving

God. Further, the meditation practice did nothing to sustain her spirit during the turbulent times when the weight of the work made her feel as if she would explode. Looking back, Lovre recognizes that she experienced a spiritual crisis which was a part of her compassion fatigue symptoms. The primary element of the spiritual crisis was questioning prior religious beliefs (Figley, 1995, 2002) in an effort to make meaning of both the children's grief and death experiences and Lovre's reactions to working with them. The spiritual crisis led to spiritual transformation. More will be said about Lovre's spiritual transformation later in the chapter.

The grant afforded generous funding for conferences as well, so Lovre began attending week-long workshops with Elisabeth Kübler-Ross (EKR). EKR was generous in her mentoring. Lovre was also invited to come to EKR's center and continue her learning.

As Lovre honed the process for the program, she was providing art and play therapy groups for siblings or children of terminally ill family members in schools, like groups in her office, individual sessions for high-need children, hospital visits for those in in-patient treatment, and home visits for the terminally ill. Her practice was to have children start each session by drawing a picture, either of something that she suggested or of anything they wished. These were used in her mentoring sessions to hone her ability to interpret children's artwork.

In an effort to manage the angst resulting from her work and her disconnect with a deeper spiritual life, Lovre became very active in silent retreats and in meditation. Having some sort of meditation as a part of her daily life was a goal – not always accomplished, but she was working at taking that time in her day. It was after about two years of this level of intensity that compassion fatigue set in.

Compassion fatigue stress

The work was intense. All children had deep issues that assaulted their sense of safety, of identity in the world, and circumstances that were tearing at the fabric of family. Every single family was in crisis or, at best, in the initial stages of recovery, which takes a long time following the death of a child or parent. Adding to the emotional burden was the sense that families with whom she worked over time embraced her as a family member. The nature and organization of her work included home and hospital visits, individual and group sessions for children, parents, and families, play therapy groups (which always started with art therapy), and groups in schools, sometimes working with a whole classroom.

There were numerous stressors, most of which she thought she was taking in her stride as she scurried through her day. She was wedging in as many family sessions as possible between groups, hospital and home visits. The grant didn't place any upper limit on her caseload, so no families were turned away.

One major stressor was the high numbers on her caseload (ranging into the 50s). Another stressor was paperwork and being forced to create a new filing system, case notes, and grant requirements in the midst of really wanting just to provide services to families. Another was the growing number of phone messages from those in need, which reflected the high level of crisis families felt. Yet another was addressing the spiritual questions around death for which Lovre had no answer. The void created by the absence of a spiritual practice was enhanced by the relentless reminders that God in Lovre's view was neither just nor loving.

Organizing a caseload with such diversity and such a diversity of settings was a continual challenge. The condition of patients sometimes changed quickly, so what was scheduled as a nearby home visit could overnight turn into a hospital visit some distance away. Working to meet with teachers of those on her caseload added to the time commitment for each child as well.

Processing these stressors and related emotions became more and more challenging: trying to accommodate to so many young patients dying was, at times, overwhelming. Yet she had to pick herself up and focus on the living.

After two years of these compassion stressors and so many deaths, her caseload included many of her clients' siblings. She'd attended numerous funerals, been at the bedsides of some children as they died, and taken many children to visit the body of a loved one when family members felt unable to do so.

By now many schools knew of her expertise and she was often called to help a classroom of students when a peer had died, particularly if it was a suicide. Because the grant was community-wide (not tied to a specific program or school or agency that would have defined a group to be served and others to refer on to someone else) it was difficult for her to know when to say "no" or whether it was really acceptable to say "no."

She became less and less motivated to do case notes and paperwork. It was just more than she could do, being that exhausted, and the paperwork and case notes gave the least positive reinforcement for her work.

This case is a good illustration of the kind of work that can bring about compassion fatigue. There are far-reaching effects of this work on the helper. Child trauma therapists absorb not only the distress of the children but also that of the parents.

Here we would like to first provide some definitions relevant to work-related compassion fatigue, then cite some definitive research that justifies our concern about the costs of caring. This introduction and overview is, by necessity, brief but we have included here some useful references and resources for readers who wish for more details.

Definitions

Perhaps a few definitions may be useful at this point and to contrast them with the focus of the chapter: secondary stress.

Burnout is defined in *Merriam-Webster's Collegiate Dictionary* as "exhaustion of physical or emotional strength or motivation usually as a result of prolonged stress or frustration." It is something that gradually builds to a breaking point and the stress and frustration comes from all types of work-related sources.

Secondary Traumatic Stress (Compassion Fatigue): a set of psychosocial and emotional factors caused by a specific event or series of events affecting helpers indirectly through another, such as a family member, friend or client. It sometimes takes just one case or situation to have a lasting effect.

Compassion Fatigue: "... state of exhaustion and dysfunction (biologically, psychologically and socially) as a result of prolonged exposure to compassion stress" (Figley, 1995). We become exhausted by exposure to experience after experience of emotionally draining clients who look to us for help.

Compassion Satisfaction: The perceived joys derived from experiencing the suffering of others and succeeding in helping to relieve their suffering in some way (Figley, 2002).

Case example of compassion fatigue effects

To continue with the case study, we might now examine the actual symptoms of compassion fatigue in this case. Initial signs were lower-level, free-floating anxiety, tightness in her chest, sometimes an inability to "catch her breath," which was characterized by continual yawning with no relief. Lovre felt lost and overwhelmed, but never hopeless. She believed if she showed up, it was better for the children and their families than if she did not.

At that same time, rather than only experiencing the overload of negative emotions (such as having feelings of being overwhelmed, of having less patience in her everyday life) she simultaneously felt a heightened sense of many positive emotions. Her relationships with her son and family members were the strongest they'd ever been and she experienced deep emotions in her connections in ways that were healthy, although with more tears of joy and depth than feeling "balanced." As the negative or overwhelming feelings became worse, simultaneously the positive aspects of her close relationships became higher and more joyful. She began to take nothing for granted. Seeing children die made her ever so filled with gratitude for her own son every day. She found herself tearing up more and more frequently and began to recognize that she had no "rest" from emotions. Even good emotions were almost overwhelming – everything was amplified.[1] As emotions were amplified, she began to experience difficulty falling asleep and also difficulty staying asleep. In the morning, with the poor quality of sleep, she was tired before she got into her day. She began to experience ambivalence about going to work, torn between how meaningful the exchanges were with children and families, but a beginning exhaustion from standing at the bedside of too many who were dying. It was equally difficult to be with children who were dying as it was to be with parents who were dying, helping a three- or four-year-old climb into the hospital bed, mindful of not pulling on any tubes or wires or equipment, to snuggle into mommy's breast for goodbye kisses – the goodbye that was forever.

She began to recognize, for the first time, that some of the losses of her childhood came to have new meaning. Therefore, another aspect of the time spent in therapy was to address those from this new vantage point.

Over the next few weeks, she verbalized a physical sensation in the chest, and described a sensation as if a whole army of tiny wind-up animals were beating on drums and crashing cymbals and marching around in her chest, and that if she truly relaxed, she would just explode, not emotionally, but almost a sense of exploding physically. She feared she would not survive if she took time to attend to herself and her spirit, yet needed immediate relief. Sleep continued to be a challenge, and she'd wake up at night both wondering about the children's welfare and her own ability (not skill-wise, but in terms of stamina for the emotional end) to work a full week.

Review of the relevant literature

What Lovre experienced is now referred to as compassion fatigue. The concept was coined by Carla Joinson (1992), a nurse and journalist who used it in a generic sense to describe the challenges of nurses constantly working with sad patients. Figley utilized the concept to represent secondary traumatic stress reactions first identified among the wives of Israeli solders with combat stress reactions reported by Zahava Solomon in the 1980s (cf. Solomon, 1994).

Today, compassion fatigue is now viewed by many as an occupational hazard of providing care to traumatized populations (Bride, 2007; Figley, 1999; Munroe et al., 1995; Pearlman, 1999). This view is supported by the many studies documenting compassion fatigue and STS symptoms in parents

---

[1] Lovre notes today: "I think back to Hans Selye's early research out of Canada on eustress and distress – I found references to that just a little after I went through this, and I really related his work to what had happened to me in some ways – that my new appreciation for life and gratitude for my loved ones was so amplified that it was almost like being in eustress when I wasn't in distress!"

(Barnes & Figley, 2005) and clinicians working not only with traumatized children (Bride, Jones, & MacMaster, 2007; Meyers & Cornille, 2002; Nelson-Gardell & Harris, 2003) but also practitioners working in mental health generally (Bride, 2004; Cunningham, 2003; Pearlman & Mac Ian, 1995); domestic violence (Bell, 2003); sexual assault (Ghahramanlou & Brodbeck, 2000; Schauben & Frazier, 1995); healthcare (Cunningham, 2003; Dane & Chachkes, 2001); substance abuse counselors (Bride & Hatcher, 2007); combat veterans; and social work (Adams, Boscarino, & Figley, 2006; Adams, Figley, & Boscarino, 2008; Boscarino, Figley, & Adams, 2004; Bride, 2007; Bride, Radey, & Figley, 2007; Bride et al., 2004).

This research clearly indicates that caregivers of the traumatized are at risk of experiencing symptoms of traumatic stress, disrupted cognitive schemas, and general psychological distress as a result of their work (Bride, 2004). What is less clear is the prevalence of compassion fatigue symptoms in caregivers. Although there has been a significant upturn in the amount of research on compassion fatigue symptoms in the past decade, much of it has focused on examining predictors rather than its prevalence. Those studies that do report such data are often not comparable due to measurement inconsistencies. To further complicate matters, some of the instruments being used have recognized psychometric limitations or unreported psychometric properties (Bride, Radey, & Figley, 2007).

Risk factors for compassion fatigue

Younger caregivers and those with less experience are at increased risk for STS (Arvay & Uhleman, 1996; Ghahramanlou & Brodbeck, 2000); however, this finding may be explained by the development of coping mechanisms that comes with increased experience in older workers. That is, younger professionals are likely to be newer to the field and less likely to have had the opportunity to develop protective strategies to deal with the difficulties of working with traumatized populations. The length of experience providing general psychosocial services seems to have less influence on risk for STS than the length of experience specifically providing trauma services. In addition, level of exposure to traumatized clients is more important than length of exposure in that higher proportions of traumatized clients on caseloads (Chrestman, 1999; Kassam-Adams, 1999; Schauben & Frazier, 1995) and a higher proportion of time spent in trauma-related clinical activities are more predictive of compassion fatigue symptoms (Brady et al., 1999). Results of several studies indicate that a caregiver's personal trauma history, particularly childhood trauma, is a significant risk factor (Ghahramanlou & Brodbeck, 2000; Kassam-Adams, 1999; Nelson-Gardell & Harris, 2003; Pearlman & Mac Ian, 1995), although two studies failed to find such a relationship (Follette et al., 1994; Ortlepp & Friedman, 2001). In Lovre's case the absence of a spiritual practice to sustain her was at the core of her compassion fatigue. The depth of the existential questions raised in her work environment plagued her. The work she was doing was what she was born to do, but she could not reconcile her view of God as just and loving in the presence of all the pain she witnessed.

Compassion fatigue or burnout?

Based on the above definitions, compassion fatigue is more about the emotional fallout from actually delivering the services to clients and why it is a "secondary" trauma. As psychologists we work with those who were in harm's way and we experience what they experienced secondarily. Certainly, the emotional wear-and-tear of this kind of stress can lead to burnout eventually. Most often, however, burnout takes longer and is a function of lots of things in addition to compassion fatigue: paperwork, the environment, colleagues, and the grind of work. The most important question to ask yourself is this: Do I love my work? If the answer is "no," it is most likely that you are suffering from burnout. If the answer is "YES!" you are more likely suffering from compassion fatigue.

Also, it is more likely that we experience compassion satisfaction when we experience compassion fatigue. In contrast with those who are burned out (Pines & Aronson, 1988), helpers experiencing compassion fatigue often love their job and the work they do. This was clear from a series of surveys among professionals and volunteers who work with animals (Figley & Roop, 2006). Indeed, the results of a survey of social workers working in the New York City region showed that working with traumatized people was unrelated to burnout but highly related to the development of compassion fatigue. Both burnout and compassion fatigue were associated with poor social support by colleagues (Boscarino, Figley, & Adams, 2004). Unlike burnout, compassion fatigue is accompanied by a rapid onset of symptoms and is likely to be more pervasive than burnout; it emerges suddenly with little warning; there is a sense of helplessness, shock, and confusion; there is a sense of isolation; and the symptoms seem disconnected from the real causes. Despite this, those who suffer from compassion fatigue often report an ongoing sense of responsibility for the care of the sufferer and their suffering. There is a near failure on the part of compassion fatigue sufferers for getting or even knowing how to get relief from burdens of responsibility to those they try to help.

One definitive way of determining burnout, compassion fatigue, and level of compassion satisfaction is to take a self-administered test that has been developed over the years (e.g., Figley, 1995, 2002).[2] Beth Stamm

---

[2] However, we now recommend the Professional Quality of Life Scale: Compassion Satisfaction and Fatigue Subscales – Revision IV (ProQOL) available at http://www.isu.edu/~bhstamm/ and http://www.isu.edu/~bhstamm/. The ProQOL is a free and handy tool for us to complete

(2008) has developed the latest version and it is available at her website (www.isu.edu/~bhstamm/tests.htm).

What should you do about compassion fatigue?

Again, turning to the example of the child trauma worker, Lovre's survival in the field was dependent on her finding new ways of integrating those experiences and giving them meaning, while still not "taking on" the deluge of emotion. Immediate relief was needed so that Lovre could continue her work. Once she and her mentor became clear about the need to address this issue (although it was not yet identified as compassion fatigue), the three-hour per week consulting sessions turned into three hours per week of therapy for her. It was absolutely clear that, if she were to continue this work, some kind of mechanism had to be in place that allowed her to process through the residual in a way that could leave her clean or cleared out of it enough to go home and be a joyful parent. At a deeper level, Lovre needed to find a way to address the mystery of emotional pain and death in a way that was consistent with her unfolding but yet undefined spiritual beliefs.

The first few weeks' sessions were predominantly simply putting words to what she'd watched, witnessed, and realized. It was like a major purging of thoughts, images, emotions, and visceral experiences. Coupled with that, many childhood losses again came up with new meaning and new insights, but nonetheless had to be processed in a therapeutic setting just to get through them in a timely manner and so have them impact work as little as possible. Because of her work as an art therapist and her appreciation of it as a tool, she and her mentor used art therapy as one way of accessing both her childhood and adult memories and issues. And ... all of this was exhausting!

As that was released, it seemed to create more room for distance, allowing her and the mentor, together, to look at the bigger picture. The mentor was clear that Lovre needed to (a) become clear about what sustained her and find a way to connect with that every day, (b) find ways to use that connection in "real time" when she was providing services in order to maintain equilibrium, (c) establish a means of "clearing" as she left each session, and (d) establish firm schedules for taking time away for both reflection (retreat kinds of times) and rejuvenation (just plain fun with no work-related reflection or goal planned). What was critical, however, was to change her perspective on life at the deepest levels; to take the costs of caring seriously enough to practice these new habits until they became a part of her being.

She changed her scheduling such that she was able to begin working a four-day work week, which was a great help, and it was determined that paperwork

---

in private, when we are ready, that can give us some unbiased feedback about how we are doing in our career. The results may motivate you to do something now about your self-care.

and other office-oriented details that could be handled from a distance would be done at home in order to shorten the work week to four eight-hour days, with eight hours of work to be done at home.

A series of visualizations and meditation focus options over several weeks yielded two specific meditations/visualizations that she began using, and ultimately continued to find remarkably useful for the next 25 years.

The first one is to visualize herself sitting cross-legged on a cushion, facing an open window with blue sky and leaves on trees in view. A gentle, warm breeze is blowing in the window. She then "pulls herself back" from herself so she is no longer "in" her body, but instead is watching herself on the cushion. Each "in-breath" is accompanied with imagining inhaling the warmth and inviting nature of the out-of-doors into her being, and each "out-breath" is accompanied with the imagining of her body exhaling through every cell, making her body increasingly porous with each cycle. Finally, she is able to "see" her body as so very porous that the sunshine actually passes through it and there is barely a faint shadow at all revealing where she is sitting. Then, as she inhales, she imagines that the lace curtain from the window blows up in the breeze and passes through her body, and with the exhale, the curtain passes back through her and rests once again on the windowsill.

From this porous place, she envisions the face of someone in pain, perhaps physical pain, perhaps emotional pain. As she sees this face, she imagines inhaling their pain and exhaling it through the top of her head to the Creator. On the next breath, she breathes in unconditional love and exhales that love out to the person in pain. The cycle begins again – breathe in the pain, give it up to the Creator, breathe in the love, send it out to the beloved.

Taking the time to establish this awareness each morning allowed her a great deal of freedom from having to protect herself from the pain of others. Instead, it was as if their crises could blow through her like wind through a screen door, and she could stand fully present with the person, with her feet to their fire, not flinching or feeling the need to protect herself. Also, as she left each encounter, she felt such freedom from fear of needing to protect herself that she was much more intuitive, much more able to "be with people where they were," much less need or desire to try to help people move more quickly to a place that was easier for them or for her, which meant giving them all of the time they needed to fully explore their experiences from exactly wherever they were. Now Lovre stays calm rather than experiencing an adrenaline rush when a crisis occurs. When a call comes in, she slows her breathing and her heart rate. Centered and grounded, she can open up to those who turn to her for help. Her process benefits her as a practitioner and the children and the families who reach out to her. Lovre can remind them that they have everything they need to repair themselves, and by being their best selves together, they can address their shattered lives.

That program with terminally ill and death-impacted children lasted four years until the grant ended. At that point she went to work for schools, creating crisis response teams in schools. The environment of grieving children went from a manageable number spread over time to intense days of hundreds of profoundly grieving and sometimes traumatized children and youths, coupled with great needs on the parts of staff and parents. At this point she began to see aspects of systems dynamics in the aftermath of crises, tragedies, and traumas. Having her daily ritual gave her the ability to be intimately involved yet clear and calm in the midst of sometimes overwhelming catastrophic events, including suicide clusters, several school shootings, spending two years working with schools in New York following 9/11, participating in a humanitarian effort to an orphanage in Sri Lanka following the tsunami, working with students displaced by Hurricane Katrina, and other such events.

Over time, many changes in her work became evident. One was that there was no stress in picking up the phone, even though the person at the other end might begin the conversation with, "I've been called in by my district to take the place of an injured principal and I'm standing at the entrance of a school where a shooting just happened and I'm not sure how to know whether it is safe for me to go inside . . . ." With her first inhale, being porous was possible and responding to their immediate needs continues to be smooth and at-the-ready without an adrenaline rush. In fact, for her to look at the stressors in her life now, they tend to be focused on a few specific aspects of her work that have nothing to do with the delivery of service, such as the immense amount of travel, the details of running a business (understanding enough about taxes, insurance, employee management), and dealing with the financial uncertainty of whether there is enough work on the books to support what has become a small work group of four.

In her work now, Lovre regularly trains teams who go into schools in the aftermath of tragedy, trauma, and crisis. The meditation techniques learned years ago remain a part of her spiritual practice. For Lovre, the resolution of compassion fatigue let to spiritual transformation. Over time Lovre resolved her question about God in a manner which allows her to relate to children and their families at the deepest levels during the most difficult times in their lives. For Lovre, the answer is simple yet complex: accept and embrace that which is in the moment, accept that there is a mystery in death greater than the human mind can comprehend, connect to something greater than oneself, and do no harm by silently bringing positive energy from the Creator to those who are in pain. Lovre has not had a relapse or reoccurrence of compassion fatigue as she continues to do the work that makes a difference in the lives of children and their families.

Implications

Working with suffering people is both rewarding and hard to take sometimes. Just as Lovre discovered, self-care and self-love are critical. In many ways it is unethical NOT to insure that you are OK before working with suffering clients.

Ethical responsibilities

Claudius Galen, born in 129 AD, was the chief physician to the gladiator school in Pergamum and went on to serve five Roman emperors. He was the first to use the adage *Primum non nocere* (first do no harm). This goal has guided all practitioners since then, including psychologists. However, it is time to recognize that our perception of doing harm may be altered by our own mental fitness; that exposure to the distress of others, day after day, can take an emotional toll. Recently it was found that there was a correlation between compassion fatigue and ethical violations. Therefore, we psychologists should consider an additional adage: First do no SELF-harm!

As practicing psychologists we are bound by the APA's *Code of Ethics* (see www.apa.org/ethics/code.html). One of the most relevant sections is as follows:

> 2.06 Personal Problems and Conflicts
> (a) Psychologists refrain from initiating an activity when they know or should know that there is a substantial likelihood that their personal problems will prevent them from performing their work-related activities in a competent manner.
> (b) When psychologists become aware of personal problems that may interfere with their performing work-related duties adequately, they take appropriate measures, such as obtaining professional consultation or assistance, and determine whether they should limit, suspend, or terminate their work-related duties. (See also Standard 10.10, Terminating Therapy.)

Professionals working with children are expected to be aware of personal problems such as STS reactions (compassion fatigue) that prevent – or significantly impair – our competence to practice. I view "taking appropriate measures" as reading articles like this one; taking a self-test as noted above; seeking supervision and consultation (including spiritual mentoring); and getting training. Later, I will note some useful resources for enabling psychologists to take such measures.

Go to the Green Cross Academy of Traumatology website (www.greencross.org) and begin with two basics: Standards of Practice and Standards of Self Care.

The *Standards of Practice, Section II.2. Responsible Caring* (www. traumatologyacademy.org/standards.htm) states:

> Traumatologists recognize that service to survivors of traumatic events can exact a toll in stress on providers. They maintain vigilance for signs in themselves and colleagues of such stress effects, and accept that dedication to the service of others imposes an obligation to sufficient self-care to prevent impaired functioning. (See Figley, 1995; Pearlman & Saakvitne, 1995.)

The *Standards of Self Care* (www.greencross.org/SelfCareStandards.htm) includes two sections of special value. *Section II. Ethical Principles of Self Care in Practice* establishes the ethics of self-care. It is unethical not to attend to your self-care as a practitioner because sufficient self-care prevents harming those we serve. Too often circumstances and employers require commitments to caseloads that are unmanageable. *Section V.A. Standards for Establishing and Maintaining Wellness* calls us to make a formal and tangible commitment to, in effect, having a life outside of work. This and other sections provide good guidance for doing so.

Resilience and compassion fatigue

How do practitioners working with children avoid compassion fatigue by becoming more resilient to it? There appear to be several factors that come into play in terms of resilience with practitioners.

- Taking good care of one's physical health through proper diet, exercise, routine sleep patterns, and regular medical/dental checkups.
- Seeking and sustaining contact and support from others inside and outside the work setting and thus avoiding isolation.
- Having a group that lives within high ethics of confidentiality with whom one can process one's work, reflect on successes, and identify lessons learned and similar kinds of shared support.
- Seeking out others who value what you do, understand what you do, and can empathize when you've had a particularly tough day.
- Maintaining a manageable schedule such that paperwork is handled during routine work hours and doesn't become one's at-home evening activity.
- Scheduling adequate true vacations – taking real breaks.
- Loving the work you do since it will sustain you through difficult days and periods.
- Finding success in the intrinsic reward of the work rather than depending on others in the world to give you "atta-boys."
- Maintaining an everyday connection with something greater than oneself in some way with what sustains you (e.g., yoga, faith, belief in the goodness of humankind). Seeking consultation as needed to address spiritual needs and issues.

Conclusion

We need more child trauma therapists like Lovre to break the conspiracy of silence about secondary traumatic stress reactions and the costs of compassion fatigue. We likewise need therapists like Lovre to help practitioners understand that the experience of compassion fatigue is one that can lead to growth professionally, personally, and spiritually. Most importantly, we need a concerted and systematic campaign to help transform the field toward positive psychology, as Marty Seligman and colleagues (Seligman et al., 2005) would urge us to do in viewing and helping our clients: focusing on increasing positive affect as well as decreasing unwanted symptoms and suffering, thus, focusing our efforts to enhancing positive affect, promoting self-care, resilience, and transformation among commiserators.

Life is short. The world will always need caring and passionate counselors. But to be really effective, compassionate psychologists must always abide by the motto of Hippocrates: First, do no harm. However, it is imperative that we first do no self-harm. We cannot rely on anyone else to do it for us. It is our responsibility.

References

Adams, R. E., Boscarino, J. A., & Figley, C. R. (2006). Compassion fatigue and psychological distress among social workers. *American Journal of Orthopsychiatry, 76*, 103–18.

Adams, R. E., Figley, C. R., & Boscarino, J. A. (2008). The compassion fatigue scale: Its use with social workers following urban disaster. *Research on Social Work Practice, 18*, 238–50.

Arvay, M. J., & Uhlemann, M. R. (1996). Counsellor stress in the field of trauma: A preliminary study. *Canadian Journal of Counselling, 30*, 193–210.

Barnes, M., & Figley, C. R. (2005). Family therapy: Working with traumatized families. In J. Lebow (Ed.), *Handbook of Clinical Family Therapy*. New York: John Wiley & Sons, Inc.

Bell, H. (2003). Strengths and secondary trauma in family violence work [electronic version]. *Social Work, 48*(4), 513–22.

Boscarino, J. A., Figley, C. R., & Adams, R. E. (2004). Evidence of compassion fatigue following the September 11 terrorist attacks: A study of secondary trauma among social workers in New York. *International Journal of Emergency Mental Health, 6*(2), 98–108.

Brady, J., Guy, J., Poelstra, P., & Brokaw, B. (1999). Vicarious traumatization, spirituality, and the treatment of sexual abuse survivors: A national survey of women psychotherapists. *Professional Psychology, 30*, 386–93.

Bride, B. E. (2004). The impact of providing psychosocial services to traumatized populations. *Stress, Trauma, and Crisis: An International Journal, 7*, 1–18.

Bride, B. E. (2007). Prevalence of secondary traumatic stress among social workers. *Social Work, 52*, 63–70.

Bride, B. E., & Hatcher, S. S. (2007, October). Secondary traumatic stress among substance abuse counselors. Poster presented at the Addiction Health Services Research Conference, Athens, GA.

Bride, B. E., Jones, J. L., & MacMaster, S. A. (2007). Correlates of secondary traumatic stress in child welfare workers. *Journal of Evidence-Based Social Work, 4*, 69–80.

Bride, B. E., Radey, M., & Figley, C. R. (2007). Measuring compassion fatigue. *Clinical Social Work Journal, 35,* 155–63.

Bride, B. E., Robinson, M. M., Yegidis, B, & Figley, C. R. (2004). Development and validation of the Secondary Traumatic Stress Scale. *Research on Social Work Practice, 14,* 27–35.

Chrestman, K. R. (1999). Secondary exposure to trauma and self-reported distress among therapists. In B. H. Stamm (Ed.), Secondary traumatic stress: Self-care issues for clinicians, researchers, and educators (2nd ed., pp. 29–36). Lutherville, MD: Sidran.

Cunningham, M. (2003). Impact of trauma work on social work clinicians: Empirical findings. *Social Work, 48*(4), 451–9.

Dane, B., & Chachkes, E. (2001). The cost of caring for patients with an illness: Contagion to the social worker. *Social Work in Health Care, 33,* 31–50.

Figley, C. R. (Ed.) (1995). *Compassion fatigue: Coping with Secondary Traumatic Stress Disorder in those who treat the traumatized. An overview* (pp. 1–20). New York: Brunner/Mazel.

Figley, C. R. (1999). Compassion fatigue: Toward a new understanding of the cost of caring. In B. H. Stamm (Ed.), *Secondary traumatic stress* (pp. 3–28). Towson, MD: Sidran Institute.

Figley, C. R. (Ed.). (2002). *Treating compassion fatigue.* New York: Brunner-Routledge.

Figley, C. R., & Roop, R. (2006). *Compassion fatigue in the animal care community.* Washington, DC: The Humane Society Press.

Follette, V. M., Polusny, M. M., & Milbeck, K. (1994). Mental health and law enforcement professionals: Trauma history, psychological symptoms, and impact of providing services to child sexual abuse survivors. *Professional Psychology, Research and Practice, 25,* 275–82.

Ghahramanlou, M., & Brodbeck, C. (2000). Predictors of secondary trauma in sexual assault trauma counselors. *International Journal of Emergency Mental Health, 2*(4), 229–40.

Jenmorri, K. (2006). Of rainbows and tears: Exploring hope and despair in trauma therapy. *Child and Youth Care Forum, 35*(1), 41–55.

Joinson, C. (1992). Coping with compassion fatigue. *Nursing, 92*(22), 116–21.

Kassam-Adams, N. (1999). The risks of treating sexual trauma: Stress and secondary trauma in psychotherapists. In B. H. Stamm (Ed.), *Secondary traumatic stress: Self-care issues for clinicians, researchers, and educators* (pp. 37–48). Towson. MD: Sidran Institute.

Meyers, T. W., & Cornille, T. A. (2002). The trauma of working with traumatized children. In C. R. Figley (Ed.), *Treating compassion fatigue* (pp. 39–55). New York: Brunner-Routledge.

Munroe, J. F., Shay, J., Fisher, L. et al. (1995). Preventing compassion fatigue: A treatment team model. In C. R. Figley (Ed.), *Compassion fatigue: Coping with secondary traumatic stress disorder in those who treat the traumatized* (pp. 209–31). New York: Brunner/Mazel.

Ortlepp, K., & Friedman, M. (2001). The relationship between sense of coherence and indicators of secondary traumatic stress in non-professional trauma counsellors. *South African Journal of Psychology, 31*(2), 38–44.

Pearlman, L. A. (1999). Self-care for trauma therapists: Ameliorating vicarious trauma-tization. In B. H. Stamm (Ed.), *Secondary traumatic stress: Self-care issues for clinicians, researchers, and educators* (2nd ed., pp. 51–64). Lutherville, MD: Sidran.

Pearlman, L. A., & Mac Ian, P. S. (1995). Vicarious traumatization: An empirical study of the effects of trauma work on trauma therapists. *Professional Psychology: Research and Practice, 26,* 558–63.

Pearlman, L. A., & Saakvitne, K. W. (1995). *Trauma and the therapist: Countertransference and vicarious traumatisation in psychotherapy with incest survivors.* London: W. W. Norton.

Pines, A., & Aronson, E. (1988). *Career burnout: Causes and cures.* New York: Free Press.

Schauben, L. J., & Frazier, P. A. (1995). Vicarious trauma: The effects on female counselors of working with sexual violence survivors. *Psychology of Women Quarterly, 19,* 49–64.

Seligman, M. E. P., Steen, T. A., Park, N., & Peterson, C. (2005). Positive psychology progress: Empirical validation of interventions. *American Psychologist, 60*(5), 410–21.

Solomon, Z. (1994). *Coping with war-induced stress: The Gulf War and the Israel response.* New York: Springer.

Stamm, B. H. (1993, 2008). *A review of reliability in mental tests.* Pocatello, ID: ProQOL.org. Retrieved from www.proqol.org/uploads/stamm-reliability.pdf (accessed February 10, 2009).

Chapter Twenty-Two

Future Directions in Conceptualizing Complex Post-Traumatic Stress Syndromes in Childhood and Adolescence: Toward a Developmental Trauma Disorder Diagnosis

Julian D. Ford

Introduction

The final chapter of the book is dedicated to the future directions of child trauma research and interventions with a focus upon an understanding of diagnosis of complex trauma toward a diagnosis of developmental trauma disorder.

Developmentally adverse interpersonal traumas (e.g., sexual, physical or emotional abuse, loss of or abandonment by caregiver(s), chronic and severe neglect, domestic violence, or death or gruesome injuries due to community violence, terrorism or war) derail psychological development in periods (e.g., infancy or adolescence) during which foundational self-regulatory capacities are being acquired or consolidated (Ford, 2005). Therefore, complex variants of Post-Traumatic Stress Disorder (PTSD) in childhood and adolescence involve not only problems with anxiety and arousal modulation, but also with the self-regulation of bodily processes, emotion, information-processing, impulse control and goal-directed behavior, and relational involvement. These are the capacities that shape and come to constitute the developing self and personality, and their disruption or distortion thus can lead to pervasive and persistent psychobiological impairments that may appear to be the symptoms of many severe disorders of childhood and adolescence (e.g., bipolar, conduct, addictive, dissociative, and psychotic disorders) as well as chronic forms of those disor-

Post-Traumatic Syndromes in Childhood and Adolescence: A Handbook of Research and Practice, First Edition. Edited by Vittoria Ardino. © 2011 John Wiley & Sons, Ltd. Published 2011 by John Wiley & Sons, Ltd.

ders and also personality disorders in adulthood. To the extent that exposure to psychological trauma during sensitive developmental periods contributes to these serious psychiatric problems, diagnosis and treatment will be enhanced by the formulation of a syndrome that extends PTSD to account for the impact of traumatic stress on development.

Psychological trauma and the developing child

A combination of traumatic victimization and disruption of attachment bonding with caregiver(s) has been hypothesized to constitute a form of traumatic stress that is particularly detrimental to psychosocial health and development in childhood and adolescence. Referred to as "complex trauma" (Cook et al., 2005) or "developmentally adverse interpersonal trauma" (Ford, 2005), these adversities are associated with a wide range of psychosocial impairments in childhood (Charney, 2004; Finkelhor, Ormrod, & Turner, 2007; Manly et al., 2001; Mazza & Reynolds, 1999; Scheeringa & Zeanah, 2001) and adulthood (McCauley et al., 1997; van der Kolk et al., 2005), including affect dysregulation (Ford, 2005), threat-biased perception (Pollak & Toley-Schell, 2005), dissociation (van der Kolk et al., 2005), and biological dysregulation (De Bellis, 2001) – placing the person at risk for not only psychological but also serious and chronic medical (cardiovascular, metabolic, immunologic) illness in adulthood (Felitti et al., 1998).

When psychological trauma alters normal psychobiological development in childhood and adolescence, there appears to be a shift from a brain (and body) focused on *learning* to a brain (and body) focused on *survival* (Ford, 2009). The *learning brain* is engaged in acquiring new knowledge that permits an expansion of the person's mental, emotional, and behavioral repertoire. By contrast, the *survival brain* is oriented to self-protection by identifying threats and establishing a limited set of mental, emotional, and behavioral reactions designed to maintain vigilance and defensively conserve bodily resources. The learning and survival brain are the same brain initially, but they evolve fundamentally different neural networks and self-capacities. The survival brain comes to rely upon rapid automatic processes in primitive areas of the brain that constitute the stress response system (e.g., brainstem, midbrain, parts of the limbic system such as the amygdala; Neumeister, Henry, & Krystal, 2007; Teicher et al., 2003) while largely bypassing or failing to fully develop areas of the brain and neural connections amongst them that are involved in more complex learning and adaptation (e.g., anterior cingulate, insula, prefrontal cortex, other parts of the limbic system, such as the hippocampus; Rauch, Shin, & Phelps, 2006).

The body's stress response system directly influences immune system activity, generally reducing its level of activity and potentially compromising its ability to detect and fight off pathogens and promote tissue and organ healing, as well as increasing autoimmune responses that can damage bodily integrity (Kendall-Tackett, 2007). The stress response system also tends to override and reduce the functionality of brain systems involved in seeking reward, recognizing emotions and managing distress, engaging in relationships, and making conscious judgments and plans (Rauch et al., 2006). A survival-focused brain appears to operate automatically to defend against external threats, but in so doing diverts crucial resources from brain/body systems that are essential to prevent exhaustion, injury or illness ("allostasis"; Friedman & McEwen, 2004), and to promote learning and relatedness (e.g., reward-seeking, distress tolerance, emotion modulation, problem solving, autobiographical memory). Fear and anxiety are adaptive foci for survival, but there is a substantial psychobiological tradeoff when threat is the focus, including potential serious problems with learning, healing, relatedness, and self-development.

The developing brain is a self-organizing set of neurons and interconnections amongst them in which "real-time processes" (i.e., new experiences, changes in the external and bodily environment, goal-directed thinking) "give rise to developmental trajectories, and developmental trajectories constrain the activities of [brain systems] in real time" (Lewis, 2005, p. 254). Developmental trajectories occur when neurons or the pathways interconnecting them become increasingly ("long-term potentiation") or decreasingly ("long-term depression") sensitized, and certain pathways and networks are selectively strengthened and become increasingly fixed as "structures" that define the individual's identity and way of approaching life experiences. The other way in which developmental trajectories (Andersen, 2003) are shaped occurs in periods of unusually rapid neuronal or neural network change evident in "developmental transitions" or critical periods (Lewis, 2005, p. 255), such as the burst of new neurons and connections between neurons that occurs with the emergence of verbal language and individuation in the second year of life, or the consolidation of neural pathways late in preadolescence and early in adolescence when more complex symbolic thought processes emerge. At the transitional periods of accelerated brain development, "behaviors become unmoored from their entrenched habits, a variety of new forms proliferate for a while ... then some subset of these forms stabilizes, providing new habits for the next stage of development" (Lewis, 2005, pp. 255–6).

When psychological trauma occurs during these transitional periods, the resultant brain structures and associated ways of perceiving, feeling, and thinking, and core beliefs behavior patterns, can be extremely difficult to alter – hence psychological trauma in those periods is likely to be *complex* in its effects precisely because it occurs in a one-time-only period of developmental growth (in childhood) or consolidation (in adolescence). Experience can shape the brain or alter neural networks at any time in life, but particularly so in early childhood and adolescence. These also are developmental periods when experiences with other human beings – as models, helpers, guides, comforters, competitors, and sources of validation and security – appear to be particularly catalytic for brain and self-development. Psychological trauma in these periods thus is likely to point a brain that is particularly malleable toward a focus on survival.

When exposure to traumatic stressors leads neural networks to be shaped to operate preferentially based on automatic processes organized by the stress response system, there is a corresponding consolidation of a fundamental personality orientation, *harm avoidance* (with traits such as anxiety, anger, introversion, guilt, shame, doubt, and dissociation) rather than the alternative orientation of *openness to experience* (e.g., interest, curiosity, pleasure, novelty-seeking, extraversion, trust, sociability, self-efficacy). Such a shift involves lasting – but not necessarily irreversible – changes in key brain systems involved in the self-regulation of the body, perception, emotions, information-processing, and relational involvement (Ford, 2005).

Regulation of self-states involves monitoring and maintaining the integrity of internal bodily states either automatically (e.g., visceral [bodily] thermoregulation – internal bodily adjustments to maintain body temperature) or self-reflectively (i.e., by cognitively identifying discrepancies between actual and ideal body states and environmental conditions, and purposefully interacting with the external sociophysical environment to reduce the discrepancy). Neural pathways from the medial and orbital areas of the prefrontal cortex reduce stress reactivity by inhibiting neural activation in the locus coeruleus (Southwick et al., 2007), amygdala (Amaral, 2002), and hippocampus (Bremner, 2008). The dorsolateral prefrontal cortex appears to exert "preemptive" control (that is, to rein in reactive responding; Matsumoto, Suzuki, & Tanaka, 2003), while the medial and orbital portions of the prefrontal cortex organize self-awareness of connections between emotions, goals, and behavioral options (Milad et al., 2007).

If a child has repeated success in coping with episodes of fear with the support of adults in regaining safety and a sense of mastery, emotion regulation is likely to be enhanced. However, if exposure to traumatic stressors prolongs, exacerbates, or prevents the learning of ways to behaviorally and biologically modulate fear of the unfamiliar, novelty may become a lasting source of unmanageable distress not because fear or novelty itself is toxic but *because of the failure to learn how to regulate the body when experiencing fear of the unfamiliar.* As a result, bodily feelings, emotions, and thoughts may become experienced as signals of danger, or in and of themselves as actual threats, leading to: (1) persistent affective states of anxiety, anger, sadness, and depression; (2) bodily (somatic) discomfort, pain, preoccupation, and loss of physical function (e.g., "hysterical" symptoms such as paralysis or pseudo-seizures); and (3) associated deficits in basic self-regulation (e.g., assertive problem solving, sleep waking cycles, self-soothing) and behavioral disinhibition (e.g., impulsivity, risk-taking, aggression, addictive behaviors) that can result in severe and persistent behavioral and physical health problems.

In early and middle childhood, inhibitory chemical messenger systems develop rapidly (Rogeness & McClure, 1996) while the brain's somatosensory cortices appear to shrink and become more efficient (Sowell et al., 2001), and prefrontal cortex areas activated by reward (May et al., 2004) appear to grow and become complex (Sowell et al., 2001). These brain changes are consistent with the shift away from impulsiveness and self-protectiveness toward "ego control" or "inhibition control" (Eisenberg et al., 1995). Emotions that emerge in this epoch involve learning to balance exploration with restraint and self-correction, and include guilt (e.g., regret following impulsive behavior), self-doubt and envy (e.g., evaluating oneself as falling short of an ideal), and vicarious pride or shame (Kagan, 2001).

Exposure to traumatic stressors in early or late childhood thus may reduce the brain's ability to create neural networks to support reflective self-awareness (the "learning brain") because the neural networks that enable the child to prepare for and survive danger become overdeveloped (the "survival brain"). Without the capacity to observe one's own thought processes, it is not possible to seek or create new knowledge (i.e., "experience-dependent" learning; Lewis, 2005), but only to react to experiences with relatively automatic, chaotic, and fixated perceptions, thoughts, and actions (i.e., "experience-expectant" reactivity; Lewis, 2005).

Complex traumatic stress syndromes as survival-based modes of self-regulation

Exposure to traumatic stressors in early childhood thus may lead to neural networks that operate outside conscious awareness to focus information-processing on anticipating and avoiding threat rather than seeking and utilizing self-awareness to regulate body state, emotion, thinking, and active involvement in goal-directed behavior and relationships (Koenen, 2006). In toddlerhood, these impairments take the form of stress reactivity, mood instability, difficulty delaying gratification, problems in maintaining attention and completing activities, irritability and oppositionality, and withdrawal from or overbearing relationships with peers and adults (Manly et al., 2001). In the school years and preadolescence, a survival orientation may result in behavioral problems consistent with internalizing (e.g., depression, agoraphobia and panic, social anxiety, phobias, dissociative), externalizing (e.g., oppositional defiant or conduct, attentional or impulse control, or mania/bipolar), and psychosomatic (e.g., eating, sexual and gender identity, or sleep) disorders (Cook et al., 2005). At the root of these complex traumatic stress-related impairments are survival-based neural patterns resulting in "emotional responses [that] lead to global stabilization, causing appraisals to become entrenched," without being able to shift to "some [other] activity (either physical or mental) [that] intervenes and reduces emotional activation" (Lewis, 2005, p. 262). Thus, what begin as neural and behavioral responses to traumatic experiences may become "stabilized" in the form of chronic biological, emotional, and mental hyperarousal and "entrenched" beliefs that survival is in jeopardy, from which the child is unable to disengage. Complex traumatic stress syndromes may be understood as oc-curring when a child (and subsequently, the adult) is trapped by and literally helpless to understand or change survival-based neural network patterns that result in extreme states of emotional emptiness or distress (emotion dysregula-tion), mental disorientation and confusion (dissociation), bodily hyperarousal and exhaustion (somatization), and fixed generalized beliefs and expectations of being betrayed, violated, permanently damaged, hopeless, and defeated. The adverse impact of such cross-systemic self-dysregulation on relationships can be profound, and prospective studies indicate that survival coping (often by the caregiver as well as the child) can fundamentally disorganize the child's capacity for relational involvement – which in turn adds to the severity and chronicity of self-dysregulation (Lyons-Ruth et al., 2006). "Disorganized attachment" is characterized by the chaotic mix of excessive help-seeking and dependency, so-cial isolation and disengagement, impulsiveness and inhibition, submissiveness and aggression (Lyons-Ruth et al., 2006) observed in complex traumatic stress syndromes.

Implications for assessment and treatment of traumatized children

Problems with self-regulation may be due to genetic and experiential factors associated with psychiatric disorders that are independent of exposure to trau-matic stressors. However, a first implication for assessment and treatment of a complex traumatic stress perspective is that the patient and clinician together need to identify if, and how, survival concerns have altered that patient's self-regulation of body state, emotion, and information-processing. This means that the significance of assessing memories of past traumatic experiences is *not primarily archeological* (i.e., unearthing the past; Ford, 2009), but instead to increase awareness of how survival-based dysregulation originated as an adap-tive but typically largely involuntary attempt to protect oneself from severe harm or to cope with the physical and emotional sequelae of being harmed.

For example, an adolescent girl in inpatient treatment had apparently unpre-dictable rage outbursts that were accompanied by apparently delusional beliefs and hallucinatory perceptual distortions. For the most part she was very placid and cooperative, but she was very detached in peer and adult relationships (causing concern that she was developing a schizoid or schizotypal personality disorder).The patient had been diagnosed and treated pharmacologically for bipolar disorder, psychotic disorder not otherwise specified, and intermittent explosive disorder, as well as psychotherapeutically for reactive attachment dis-order and dissociative disorder not otherwise specified, and with sensorimotor and behavioral therapy for pervasive developmental disorder. She made gradual progress in socialization and schoolwork over several years, but the problem behaviors did not abate. The girl was most content when alone exploring in the woods, and was fascinated with cataloguing and examining insects and animals – her career goal was to become an entomologist or comparative biologist. She had a history of being beaten so severely by her biological father as a six-month-old that she required a series of reconstructive facial surgeries for the next year while being cared for by her maternal grandparents. She had no memory of the assaults or surgeries, and had had no contact with her father who had been incarcerated for the crime and had made no efforts to contact her. When the treatment plan was reviewed with a DTD focus, her therapist began to work with her on recognizing changes in body state and emotion that she associated with feeling trapped in extended social interactions (which were precursors to the psychotic-like rage reactions) and finding ways to reduce the interpersonal stimulation while becoming absorbed in an interesting solitary activity ("like bringing the woods and the animals and insects with you, wherever you are"). With support from the milieu staff on the inpatient unit and educators in the school, the patient was assisted in generalizing this self-reflective awareness and engaging in the specific affect modulating activities on a regular basis in daily activities. The patient's rage and "psychotic" reactions became infrequent, occurring only when stressors and changes in routine (such as visits home with her mother and siblings) interrupted this routine.

The case example highlights the potential value of a complex traumatic stress syndrome diagnosis as a basis for focusing treatment on helping adult caregivers and mentors to organize the child's environment so as to enable her to anticipate and exert a meaningful degree of control over automatic survival reactions. Self-reflective awareness and self-regulation are a "work in progress" in childhood and adolescence, primarily learned not through didactic teaching but as a result of facilitative modeling, cues, rewards, and experiential activities that teach by example and experiential involvement. Reconfiguring the interactions in the case example patient's daily peer group, educational, recreational, and family activities to reduce exposure to triggers (especially those that appeared superficially to be benign, but which elicited substantial survival reactions in the form of symptomatic behavior, such as prolonged contact with friendly people) was of greater benefit than the educative and supportive psychotherapy the patient had been receiving on an intensive basis for months and years. This is not to diminish the potential value of traditional psychotherapy for a child with complex trauma history, but rather to highlight the importance of addressing the child's triggered stress reactivity as a means to reducing multisystem dysregulation and increasing her capacity for automatic and reflective self-regulation.

If the goal of therapy is to provide clients with carefully guided opportunities to experience the self-control and integrated self-awareness that is normal when in "learning" rather than "survival" mode, the therapeutic process must focus on enhancing self-reflection while also facilitating self-directed remembering, emotion-focused coping, and supportive relationships.

Treatment for complex traumatic stress disorders uses therapeutic activities to enhance self-reflective processing of bodily sensations, perceptions, emotions, hopes, intentions, plans, and appraisals, and parlays the resultant increases in self-regulation into reductions in avoidance of traumatic memories or reminders by increasing the capacity to make the self-directed choice to confront, recall fully, and reconstruct distressing current experiences and past memories.

Toward a Developmental Trauma Disorder diagnosis for childhood complex PTSD

The proposed new diagnosis of Developmental Trauma Disorder (DTD; van der Kolk, 2005; Table 22.1 below) provides a framework for delineating the goals of psychotherapy for children with complex traumatic stress disorders. DTD requires a history of exposure to early life developmentally adverse interpersonal trauma (Ford, 2005). DTD parallels PTSD's structure by including a trauma exposure criterion followed by symptom criteria and a functional impairment criterion. However, DTD differs from PTSD by requiring that trauma exposure involve prolonged exposure to developmentally adverse interpersonal traumas (Ford, 2005) in childhood such as abuse or violence (whereas PTSD involves any life-threatening event or violation of bodily integrity, of any chronicity), and subjective reactions of rage, betrayal, resignation or shame (in addition to or instead of PTSD's focus on reactions of fear, helplessness or horror).

Instead of PTSD's three symptom criteria (i.e., intrusive reexperiencing, avoidance and emotional numbing, hyperarousal and hypervigilance), DTD includes two symptom criteria which are defined as: (1) stressor-related dysregulation in several psychobiological domains (e.g., emotion, physiology, cognition), and (2) persistently altered beliefs and expectancies (e.g., distrust, mental defeat, self as permanently damaged). Thus, DTD is hypothesized to represent sequelae of chronic exposure to interpersonal trauma in childhood that parallel PTSD but involve dysregulation and altered beliefs that extend beyond pathological fear or anxiety. PTSD's anger, emotional numbing, flashback, and hypervigilance symptoms, as well as symptoms of depressive disorders, may, however, be sufficient to account for DTD symptoms. In adolescence, conduct disorder or substance use disorders (SUDs) may contribute to or account for DTD-like affective, somatic, and behavioral dysregulation and altered fundamental beliefs and expectancies.

Therefore, before a new diagnosis is contemplated, empirical research is needed to test the clinical utility (First et al., 2004) of existing diagnoses such as PTSD, major depressive episode (MDE) or SUDs to account for biopsychosocial problems associated with developmentally adverse interpersonal trauma. Two relevant recent studies were conducted to address several key questions related to the clinical utility of a diagnosis such as DTD: (1) can subgroups of

Table 22.1   Proposed criteria for developmental trauma disorder

A. Exposure. The child or adolescent has experienced or witnessed multiple or prolonged adverse events over a period of at least one year beginning in childhood or early adolescence, including:

A. 1. Direct experience or witnessing of repeated and severe episodes of interpersonal violence; and

A. 2. Significant disruptions of protective caregiving as the result of repeated changes in primary caregiver; repeated separation from the primary caregiver; or exposure to severe and persistent emotional abuse.

B. Affective and Physiological Dysregulation. The child exhibits impaired normative developmental competencies related to arousal regulation, including at least two of the following:

B. 1. Inability to modulate, tolerate or recover from extreme affect states (e.g., fear, anger, shame), including prolonged and extreme tantrums, or immobilization;

B. 2. Disturbances in regulation in bodily functions (e.g., persistent disturbances in sleeping, eating, and elimination; over-reactivity or under-reactivity to touch and sounds; disorganization during routine transitions);

B. 3. Diminished awareness/dissociation of sensations, emotions, and bodily states;

B. 4. Impaired capacity to describe emotions or bodily states.

C. Attentional and Behavioral Dysregulation: The child exhibits impaired normative developmental competencies related to sustained attention, learning or coping with stress, including at least three of the following:

C. 1. Preoccupation with threat, or impaired capacity to perceive threat, including misreading of safety and danger cues;

C. 2. Impaired capacity for self-protection, including extreme risk-taking or thrill-seeking;

C. 3. Maladaptive attempts at self-soothing (e.g., rocking and other rhythmical movements, compulsive masturbation);

C. 4. Habitual (intentional or automatic) or reactive self-harm;

C. 5. Inability to initiate or sustain goal-directed behavior.

D. Self and Relational Dysregulation. The child exhibits impaired normative developmental competencies in their sense of personal identity and involvement in relationships, including at least three of the following:

D. 1. Intense preoccupation with safety of the caregiver or other loved ones (including precocious caregiving) or difficulty tolerating reunion with them after separation;

D. 2. Persistent negative sense of self, including self-loathing, helplessness, worthlessness, ineffectiveness or defectiveness;

D. 3. Extreme and persistent distrust, defiance or lack of reciprocal behavior in close relationships with adults or peers;

D. 4. Reactive physical or verbal aggression toward peers, caregivers, or other adults;

(*Continued*)

Table 22.1 (*Continued*)

D. 5. Inappropriate (excessive or promiscuous) attempts to get intimate contact (including but not limited to sexual or physical intimacy) or excessive reliance on peers or adults for safety and reassurance;

D. 6. Impaired capacity to regulate empathic arousal as evidenced by lack of empathy for, or intolerance of, expressions of distress of others, or excessive responsiveness to the distress of others.

E. Post-Traumatic Spectrum Symptoms. The child exhibits at least one symptom in at least two of the three PTSD symptom clusters (B, C, D).

F. Duration of disturbance (symptoms in Criteria B, C, D, and E) at least six months.

G. Functional Impairment. The disturbance causes clinically significant distress or impairment in at least two of the following areas of functioning:

- Scholastic: underperformance, nonattendance, disciplinary problems, drop-out, failure to complete degree/credential(s), conflict with school personnel, learning disabilities or intellectual impairment that cannot be accounted for by neurological or other factors.
- Familial: conflict, avoidance/passivity, running away, detachment and surrogate replacements, attempts to physically or emotionally hurt family members, nonfulfillment of responsibilities within the family.
- Peer group: isolation, deviant affiliations, persistent physical or emotional conflict, avoidance/passivity, involvement in violence or unsafe acts, age-inappropriate affiliations or style of interaction.
- Legal: arrests/recidivism, detention, convictions, incarceration, violation of probation or other court orders, increasingly severe offences, crimes against other persons, disregard or contempt for the law or for conventional moral standards.
- Health: physical illness or problems that cannot be fully accounted for by physical injury or degeneration, involving the digestive, neurological (including conversion symptoms and analgesia), sexual, immune, cardiopulmonary, proprioceptive or sensory systems, or severe headaches (including migraine) or chronic pain or fatigue.
- Vocational (*for youth involved in, seeking or referred for employment, volunteer work or job training*): disinterest in work/vocation, inability to get or keep jobs, persistent conflict with co-workers or supervisors, under-employment in relation to abilities, failure to achieve expectable advancements.

Submitted to the American Psychiatric Association by the Developmental Trauma Disorder Work Group, January 2009: Bessel van der Kolk and Julian D. Ford, Co-Chairs; Robert Pynoos, Co-Director, National Center for Child Traumatic Stress; Wendy D'Andrea, Alicia Lieberman, Frank Putnam, Glenn Saxe, Joseph Spinazzola, Bradley Stolbach, Martin Teicher.

children or adolescents be identified based on distinctive trauma history profiles, some of which reflect complex trauma exposure? If so, (2) are there differences in the severity of psychosocial impairment associated with trauma history profiles, particularly profiles consistent with complex trauma? And (3) are existing psychiatric diagnoses differentially associated with trauma history profiles and able to account for differences in the type or severity of impairment associated with different trauma history profiles? To the extent that distinct trauma history profiles can be identified, the ability of PTSD or other psychiatric disorders to account for the psychosocial impairment associated with each trauma history profile can be tested. It is likely that PTSD and other psychiatric diagnoses are associated with different trauma histories, but to the extent that *the nature or complexity of trauma history makes an independent contribution to the severity of psychosocial impairment beyond that attributable to Axis I DSM-IV diagnoses*, a complex traumatic stress diagnosis for adolescents may warrant further delineation.

In the first study, latent class analysis procedures were used with data from a nationally representative sample of adolescents to determine if distinct subgroups could be identified with different trauma history profiles (Ford, Elhai, et al., 2010). Six trauma history profiles were identified, four of which (including approximately 33% of the sample) were characterized by a relatively high likelihood of sexual or physical assault/abuse (8%) or exposure to violence (25%). A history of sexual or physical abuse was associated with the greatest risk of PTSD, MDEs and SUDs, with a history of physical or sexual assault associated with intermediate risk levels, and witnessing violence or traumatic disaster/accidents least associated with each of the diagnoses. Abuse or violent victimization histories were associated with involvement in juvenile delinquency and in deviant peer group relationships independently of the PTSD, MDE, and SUD diagnoses and demographics. Therefore, the findings suggest that a substantial subgroup of adolescents have experienced complex profiles of traumatic stressors, and that those youths are at risk for psychosocial problems such as delinquency that cannot be fully accounted for by *DSM-IV* PTSD, MDE or SUD diagnoses.

In the second study (Ford, Connor, & Hawke, 2009), admissions data from a sample of 397 consecutive child psychiatry inpatients were cluster analyzed to identify distinct profiles with regard to their histories of documented physical or sexual abuse, parental impairment due to arrest, violence, or substance use), and disrupted caregiver attachment bonds (operationalized in the form of records of out-of-home placements). Four sub-groups were identified. Two ("low trauma") had infrequent histories of abuse and out-of-home placement, and were distinguished by low versus high levels of parental impairment. Two "complex trauma" subgroups were characterized by histories of either physical abuse or sexual abuse with multiple perpetrators, as well as extensive out-of-home placement and severe parental impairment. All subgroups had comparable profiles of psychiatric diagnoses, including internalizing (anxiety and affective) disorders, externalizing (conduct, oppositional-defiant, attention deficit hyper-activity) disorders, psychotic disorders (schizophrenia, psychosis not otherwise specified), developmental disorders (autism, pervasive developmental disorder not otherwise specified, learning disorders), and SUDs. Complex trauma status was associated with behavior problem severity (as rated on standardized scales by teachers) and lower body mass index, over and above the effects of gender, ethnicity, and psychiatric diagnosis. Child abuse history was a factor in subgroup membership, but multiple out-of-home placements were the most consistent correlate of externalizing and internalizing problems and psychosocial impair-ment. The findings of this study further suggest that childhood adversity that may constitute a source of complex traumatic stress is associated with psychobi-ological alterations among psychiatrically hospitalized children that cannot be accounted for fully by existing demographics or *DSM-IV* psychiatric diagnoses.

These two studies, while preliminary due to the use of cross-sectional (rather than prospective) data and not assessing DTD directly, suggest that in both community and clinical populations *DSM-IV* child diagnoses may fail to iden-tify particularly symptomatic and impaired subgroups of children who are dis-tinguished by histories of complex trauma exposure. Although the research on treatment of children with complex trauma histories is very limited (Ford & Cloitre, 2009), studies with adults suggest that treatment may require adapta-tion for these children in order to prevent suboptimal outcomes (Ford et al., 2005). With both adults and children, although evidence-based cognitive-behavior therapy approaches have been shown to have benefits across a range of severity and complexity of trauma histories, adaptations for patients with more complex trauma histories are commonly recommended to avoid iatrogenesis and enhance therapeutic alliance, engagement and retention. If the subtypes identified in the present studies can be replicated and shown to have symptoms consistent with DTD and also differential responses to standard therapeutic interventions (in terms of improvement and retention), they may constitute a syndrome warranting formal recognition as a diagnosis in order to guide future clinical treatment and research trials. Clinical decision making with treatment-refractory children with complex trauma histories may be enhanced if what clinicians see in these children that goes beyond extant diagnoses is systemati-cally articulated in diagnostic formulations and studied in treatment outcome research.

Studies exploring whether there are differential externalizing behavior prob-lem outcomes in randomized trials with evidence-based psychotherapies and pharmacotherapies for children with complex trauma histories and DTD-like symptoms and impairment also may be warranted, as well as systematic treat-ment adaptations to address DTD symptoms. Prospective studies also are needed to describe the trajectory(ies) of complex, trauma-related, symptomatic and impairment differentials over time, as are family studies of probands with complex trauma history and symptom/impairment profiles, in order to develop an understanding of the etiology and course of this potential syndrome that can be translated into treatment strategies.

The finding in the second study that multiple out-of-home placements contributed to the severity of behavior problems beyond the effects associated with abuse or parental impairment is consistent with views of childhood adversity and complex trauma that emphasize the importance of sustaining attachment relationships when children are exposed to abuse or impaired parenting. While the present data cannot specifically illuminate the role of caregiver–child attachment bonds, it appeared that neither early onset out-of-home placement (with one exception, attention problems) nor placement with nonfamily caregivers was as strongly associated with either externalizing or internalizing problems as the disruptions in security, safety, and continuity that occur with multiple placements. The findings also do *not* imply that physical or sexual abuse are unimportant in placing children at risk for behavior problems, because child abuse was a major distinguishing factor in the empirical identification of complex trauma subgroups in both studies. Research is needed on the pathways over time linking abuse and out-of-home placements, because abuse increases the risk of multiple out-of-home placements and children who are multiply placed are likely to be at risk for subsequent abuse.

Complex trauma also appears to be multifaceted rather than a single, monolithic adversity. Sexual abuse appears to have a distinct course and sequelae in comparison to physical abuse, but it commonly occurs along with physical and emotional abuse, and family violence or breakdown (Putnam, 2003). Physically abused children are reported by independent observers and caregivers to be more verbally and physically assaultive than other children and they are more likely to be described by peers as being mean and picking fights (Shields & Cicchetti, 1998). Thus, while psychotherapy for sexual abuse survivors requires specific adaptations in order to address survivors' unique experiences of betrayal, the present findings do not suggest that sexual abuse leads to or potentially warrants a differential approach to diagnostic classification.

Both nonclinical and psychiatrically impaired children thus appear to be heterogeneous with regard to psychological trauma history in ways that are not fully accounted for by *DSM-IV* psychiatric diagnoses. Children who have complex histories of potentially traumatic adversity characterized by multiple out-of-home placements, severe parental impairment, community or family violence, traumatic losses, or physical or sexual abuse, have more severe externalizing symptoms and psychosocial impairment and are more likely to be involved in delinquency and with deviant peer groups than comparable children or adolescents. Complex trauma history therefore warrants attention in clinical and research assessment, and the clinical utility of a focal diagnosis such as DTD for these children warrants empirical testing and consideration as a formal diagnosis within the next revision of the American Psychiatric Association's *DSM-V* as the next version of this diagnostic nosology heads toward anticipated finalization in 2012.

References

Amaral, D. (2002). The primate amygdala and the neurobiology of social behavior. *Biological Psychiatry, 51*, 11–17.

Andersen, S. (2003). Trajectories of brain development. *Neuroscience and Biobehavioral Reviews, 27*, 3–18.

Bremner, J. D. (2008). Hippocampus. In G. Reyes, J. D. Elhai, & J. D. Ford (Eds.), *Encyclopedia of psychological trauma*. Hoboken, NJ: John Wiley & Sons, Inc.

Charney, D. S. (2004). Psychobiological mechanisms of resilience and vulnerability. *The American Journal of Psychiatry, 161*, 195–216.

Cook, A., Spinazzola, J., Ford, J. D. et al. (2005). Complex trauma in children and adolescents. *Psychiatric Annals, 35*, 390–8.

De Bellis, M. (2001). Developmental traumatology. *Psychoneuroendocrinology, 27*, 155–70.

Eisenberg, N., Fabes, R. A., Murphy, B. et al. (1995). The role of emotionality and regulation in children's social functioning: A longitudinal study. *Child Development, 66*, 1360–84.

Felitti, V., Anda, R., Nordenberg, D. et al. (1998). Relationship of childhood abuse and household dysfunction to many of the leading causes of death in adults. *American Journal of Preventive Medicine, 14*, 245–58.

Finkelhor, D., Ormrod, R., & Turner, H. (2007). Poly-victimization: a neglected component in child victimization. *Child Abuse & Neglect, 31*, 7–26.

First, M., Pincus, H., Levine, J. et al. (2004). Clinical utility as a criterion for revising psychiatric diagnoses. *The American Journal of Psychiatry, 161*, 946–54.

Ford, J. D. (2005). Treatment implications of altered neurobiology, affect regulation and information processing following child maltreatment. *Psychiatric Annals, 35*, 410–19.

Ford, J. D. (2009). Translation of emerging neurobiological and developmental findings to the clinical conceptualization and treatment of complex psychological trauma. In C. Courtois & J. D. Ford (Eds.), *Treating complex traumatic stress disorders: An evidence-based guide* (ch. 2). New York: Guilford Press.

Ford, J. D., & Cloitre, M. (2009). Psychotherapy for children and adolescents with complex traumatic stress disorders: Overview and provisional practice principles. In C. Courtois & J. D. Ford (Eds.), *Treating complex traumatic stress disorders: An evidence-based guide* (ch. 3). New York: Guilford Press.

Ford, J. D., Connor, D. F., & Hawke, J. (2009). Complex trauma among psychiatrically impaired children: A cross-sectional, chart-review study. *Journal of Clinical Psychiatry, 70*(8), 1155–63.

Ford, J. D., Elhai, J. D., Connor, D. F., & Frueh, B. C. (2010). Poly-victimization and risk of posttraumatic, depressive, and substance use disorders and involvement in delinquency in a national sample of adolescents. *Journal of Adolescent Health*, 1–8. [Available online January 29, 2010.]

Friedman, M. J., & McEwen, B. (2004). Posttraumatic stress disorder, allostatic load, and medical illness. In P. Schnurr & B. L. Green (Ed.), *Physical health consequences of exposure to extreme stress* (pp. 157–88). Washington, DC: American Psychological Association.

Kagan, J. (2001). Emotional development and psychiatry. *Biological Psychiatry, 49,* 973–9.

Kendall-Tackett, K. (2007). Inflammation, cardiovascular disease, and metabolic syndrome as sequelae of violence against women. *Trauma, Violence, and Abuse, 8,* 117–26.

Koenen, K. (2006). Developmental epidemiology of PTSD: Self-regulation as a core mechanism. *Annals of the New York Academy of Sciences, 1071,* 255–66.

Lewis, M. D. (2005). Self-organizing individual differences in brain development. *Developmental Review, 25,* 252–77.

Lyons-Ruth, K., Dutra, L., Schuder, M., & Bianchi, I. (2006). From infant attachment disorganization to adult dissociation: Relational adaptations or traumatic experiences? *Psychiatric Clinics of North America, 29,* 63–86.

McCauley, J., Kern, D., Kolodner, K. et al. (1997). Clinical characteristics of women with a history of childhood abuse: Unhealed wounds. *Journal of the American Medical Association, 277,* 1362–8.

Manly, J., Kim, J., Rogosch, F., & Cicchetti, D. (2001). Dimensions of child maltreatment and children's adjustment. *Development and Psychopathology, 13,* 759–82.

Matsumoto, K., Suzuki, W., & Tanaka, K. (2003). Neuronal correlates of goal-based motor selection in the prefrontal cortex. *Science, 301,* 229–32.

May, J. C., Delgado, M., Dahl, R. et al. (2004). Event-related magnetic resonance imaging of reward-related brain circuitry in children and adolescents. *Biological Psychiatry, 55,* 359–66.

Mazza, J., & Reynolds, W. (1999). Exposure to violence in young inner-city adolescents. *Journal of Abnormal Child Psychology, 27,* 203–13.

Milad, M. R., Wright, C. I., Orr, S. P. et al. (2007). Recall of fear extinction in humans activates the ventromedial prefrontal cortex and hippocampus in concert. *Biological Psychiatry, 62,* 446–54.

Neumeister, A., Henry, S., & Krystal, J. (2007). Neurocircuitry and neuroplasticity in PTSD. In M. J. Friedman, T. M. Keane, & P. Resick (Eds.), *Handbook of PTSD* (pp. 151–65). New York: Guilford Press.

Pollak, S., & Toley-Schell, S. (2003). Selective attention to facial emotion in physically abused children. *Journal of Abnormal Psychology, 112,* 323–38.

Putnam, F. W. (2003). Ten-year research update review: Child sexual abuse. *Journal of the American Academy of Child and Adolescent Psychiatry, 42,* 269–78.

Rauch, S., Shin, L., & Phelps, E. (2006). Neurocircuitry models of posttraumatic stress disorder and extinction: Human neuroimaging research – past, present, and future. *Biological Psychiatry, 60,* 376–82.

Rogeness, G. A., & McClure, E. B. (1996). Development and neurotransmitter-environmental interactions. *Development and Psychopathology, 8,* 183–99.

Scheeringa, M., & Zeanah, C. (2001). A relational perspective on PTSD in early childhood. *Journal of Traumatic Stress, 14,* 799–816.

Shields, A, & Cicchetti, D. (1998). Reactive aggression among maltreated children: The contributions of attention and emotion dysregulation. *Journal of Clinical Child Psychology, 27,* 381–95.

Southwick, S. M., Davis, L., Aikins, D. et al. (2007). Neurobiological alterations associated with PTSD. In M. J. Friedman, T. M. Keane, & P. Resick (Eds.), *Handbook of PTSD* (pp. 166–89). New York: Guilford Press.

Sowell, E., Thompson, P., Tessner, K., & Toga, A. (2001). Mapping continued brain growth and gray matter density reduction in dorsal frontal cortex: Inverse relationships during post-adolescent brain maturation. *Journal of Neuroscience, 21,* 8819–29.

Teicher, M., Andersen, S., Polcari, A. et al. (2003). Neurobiological consequences of early stress and childhood maltreatment. *Neuroscience and Biobehavioral Reviews, 27,* 33–44.

van der Kolk, B. (2005). Developmental trauma disorder. *Psychiatric Annals, 35,* 439–448.

van der Kolk, B., Roth, S., Pelcovitz, D., Sunday, S., & Spinazzola, J. (2005). Disorders of extreme stress. *Journal of Traumatic Stress, 18,* 389–99.

Afterword

Giovanni Liotti

Older readers of this book – people like myself who, at the end of the 1970s, began to meet professionally with the tragic inner world of trauma survivors and victims of within-family abuse – have witnessed in a very gradual manner the growth of clinical knowledge in this domain of psychopathology and psychotherapy, from almost nothing in their professional youth to the wealth of solid research data, clinical theories, and treatment procedures now available. As the growth of a child is relatively imperceptible to the bystander, who only by summoning the memory of the newborn infant realizes how big the change has been, so the growth of our knowledge of trauma-related disorders has been relatively imperceptible to me while it was accumulating. My journeying through the chapters of this very well-organized book has been matched by memories of how little we knew only 30 years ago – yielding a vivid image of the enormous leap from the desert and arid intellectual shores where I wandered while treating my younger patients whose lives were filled with chaos and violence, to the fertile ground upon which it is now possible to purposefully proceed – an enthusiasm-arousing image indeed, which could stimulate endless comments on each chapter. To try to comment on each chapter, however, would amount to missing a major goal of the whole book, namely to be "[not] a comprehensive handbook of PTSD in children and adolescents, but rather a tool of reflection and a starting point to envision new areas of exploration after its reading" – as Vittoria Ardino writes in her Introduction.

Let me then put aside my enthusiasm and say just a few words about an area of exploration I kept constantly envisaging while reading this book – not to state that it will be the most important future development of the ideas and the inquiries collected in the book, but rather to invite readers to reflect on what future developments they may regard as more relevant.

Post-Traumatic Syndromes in Childhood and Adolescence: A Handbook of Research and Practice, First Edition.
Edited by Vittoria Ardino. © 2011 John Wiley & Sons, Ltd. Published 2011 by John Wiley & Sons, Ltd.

If dissociation is the kernel, throughout the lifespan, of the victim's reaction to psychological trauma – be it PTSD or any other mental disorder – as Eli Somer argues in Chapter 8, then we could expect that a major area of future exploration will coincide with the development of recent efforts to achieve wide consensus about what we should understand as "dissociation."[1] We badly lack a comprehensive and widely shared definition of dissociation. This problem should be explored and solved if we aim at inserting into a unitary conceptual framework the great wealth of empirical and research data about trauma-related psychopathology now available and widely represented in this book.

Is dissociation a particular class of psychopathological symptoms, a specific defense against mental pain, a type of mental process that normally interacts dialectically with the integrative processes of memory, consciousness, and identity, a pathological trauma-induced disruption of these integrative processes, or all of these and perhaps even more? Is there any relationship between dissociation and the now widely explored concept of metacognitive or mentalization deficit? Is dissociation a primarily intra-psychic process, or rather does it involve very basic intersubjective experiences? That dissociation may be primarily embedded in social exchanges involving powerful affects and meaning-making processes, rather than in purely intra-psychic defensive dynamics, is suggested by the implications of Freyd's shareability theory (Chapters 7) and attachment theory (Chapters 3 and 20), and possibly illustrated by the secondary traumatic stress reactions observed in those involved in affectional bonds or in compassionate relationships with survivors (Chapters 3 and 21). Cumulative child traumatic stress is, perhaps more than any other mental health issue, embedded in social context, as Vittoria Ardino aptly writes in her Introduction. Therefore, the study of cumulative traumas suffered by children of abusive families (Chapter 3), and the related topic of Developmental Trauma Disorder (child Complex PTSD: Chapter 22) may provide an ideal ground for understanding the relationships between trauma, dissociation as an intra-psychic defense, and dissociation as a primary disruption of the intersubjective processes that are constantly at work in the child's construction of a unitary sense of self.

We are going to live more and more in a professional world of randomized controlled trials (RCTs), however prosaic this may feel to old-fashioned, slightly romantic clinicians like me. This is why I feel it mandatory to close this Afterword with an auspice: may many RCTs soon tell us about the efficacy and effectiveness of the different healthcare, judicial, social, and educational

---

[1] A remarkable contribution to the search for a consensus on the definition of "dissociation" is the recent volume *Dissociation and the dissociative disorders; DSM-V and beyond*, edited by Paul Dell and John O'Neill (New York, Routledge, 2009). Just skimming through the more than 800 pages of this volume suggests how engaging an endeavor such a search is.

interventions the contributors to this book have masterfully summarized and illustrated. Every patient deserves it, but we owe the best possible treatment especially to the children whose hopes have been betrayed by the dark side of life, by the dark side of human nature. We owe it, I dare to say, not only to the individual children, but also to the future of the human spirit.

Index

Post-Traumatic Syndromes in Childhood and Adolescence: A Handbook of Research and Practice, First Edition.
Edited by Vittoria Ardino. © 2011 John Wiley & Sons, Ltd. Published 2011 by John Wiley & Sons, Ltd.